# Human Computer Interaction for Intelligent Systems

# Human Computer Interaction for Intelligent Systems

Editors

**Matúš Pleva**
**Yuan-Fu Liao**
**Patrick Bours**

MDPI • Basel • Beijing • Wuhan • Barcelona • Belgrade • Manchester • Tokyo • Cluj • Tianjin

*Editors*

Matúš Pleva
Department of Electronics
and Multimedia
Communications, Faculty of
Electrical Engineering and
Informatics,
Technical University of Košice
Košice
Slovakia

Yuan-Fu Liao
Artificial Intelligence
Innovation, Industry
Academia Innovation School
National Yang Ming Chiao
Tung University
HsinChu
Taiwan

Patrick Bours
Department of Information
Security and Communication
Technology, Faculty of
Information Technology and
Electrical Engineering,
Norwegian University of
Science and Technology
Gjøvik
Norway

*Editorial Office*
MDPI
St. Alban-Anlage 66
4052 Basel, Switzerland

This is a reprint of articles from the Special Issue published online in the open access journal *Electronics* (ISSN 2079-9292) (available at: www.mdpi.com/journal/electronics/special_issues/hci_systems).

For citation purposes, cite each article independently as indicated on the article page online and as indicated below:

LastName, A.A.; LastName, B.B.; LastName, C.C. Article Title. *Journal Name* **Year**, *Volume Number*, Page Range.

**ISBN 978-3-0365-6577-4 (Hbk)**
**ISBN 978-3-0365-6576-7 (PDF)**

© 2023 by the authors. Articles in this book are Open Access and distributed under the Creative Commons Attribution (CC BY) license, which allows users to download, copy and build upon published articles, as long as the author and publisher are properly credited, which ensures maximum dissemination and a wider impact of our publications.

The book as a whole is distributed by MDPI under the terms and conditions of the Creative Commons license CC BY-NC-ND.

# Contents

**About the Editors** . . . . . . . . . . . . . . . . . . . . . . . . . . . . . . . . . . . . . . . . . . . . . . . . . . . . . . . . vii

**Matúš Pleva, Yuan-Fu Liao and Patrick Bours**
Human–Computer Interaction for Intelligent Systems
Reprinted from: *Electronics* **2022**, *12*, 161, doi:10.3390/electronics12010161 . . . . . . . . . . . . . . . 1

**Eva Lieskovská, Maroš Jakubec, Roman Jarina and Michal Chmulík**
A Review on Speech Emotion Recognition Using Deep Learning and Attention Mechanism
Reprinted from: *Electronics* **2021**, *10*, 1163, doi:10.3390/electronics10101163 . . . . . . . . . . . . . . 5

**Daniel Hládek, Ján Staš and Matúš Pleva**
Survey of Automatic Spelling Correction
Reprinted from: *Electronics* **2020**, *9*, 1670, doi:10.3390/electronics9101670 . . . . . . . . . . . . . . . 35

**Audrey Aldridge and Cindy L. Bethel**
A Systematic Review of the Use of Art in Virtual Reality
Reprinted from: *Electronics* **2021**, *10*, 2314, doi:10.3390/electronics10182314 . . . . . . . . . . . . . . 65

**Erich Stark, Erik Kučera, Oto Haffner, Peter Drahoš and Roman Leskovský**
Using Augmented Reality and Internet of Things for Control and Monitoring of Mechatronic
Devices
Reprinted from: *Electronics* **2020**, *9*, 1272, doi:10.3390/electronics9081272 . . . . . . . . . . . . . . . 83

**Kristína Machová, Martin Mikula, Xiaoying Gao and Marian Mach**
Lexicon-based Sentiment Analysis Using the Particle Swarm Optimization
Reprinted from: *Electronics* **2020**, *9*, 1317, doi:10.3390/electronics9081317 . . . . . . . . . . . . . . . 105

**Martina Szabóová, Martin Sarnovský, Viera Maslej Krešňáková and Kristína Machová**
Emotion Analysis in Human–Robot Interaction
Reprinted from: *Electronics* **2020**, *9*, 1761, doi:10.3390/electronics9111761 . . . . . . . . . . . . . . . 127

**Shiliang Shao, Ting Wang, Yongliang Wang, Yun Su, Chunhe Song and Chen Yao**
Research of HRV as a Measure of Mental Workload in Human and Dual-Arm Robot Interaction
Reprinted from: *Electronics* **2020**, *9*, 2174, doi:10.3390/electronics9122174 . . . . . . . . . . . . . . . 159

**Stanislav Ondáš, Eva Kiktová, Matúš Pleva, Mária Oravcová, Lukáš Hudák and Jozef Juhár
et al.**
Pediatric Speech Audiometry Web Application for Hearing Detection in the Home Environment
Reprinted from: *Electronics* **2020**, *9*, 994, doi:10.3390/electronics9060994 . . . . . . . . . . . . . . . . 177

**Nancy Agarwal, Mudasir Ahmad Wani and Patrick Bours**
Lex-Pos Feature-Based Grammar Error Detection System for the English Language
Reprinted from: *Electronics* **2020**, *9*, 1686, doi:10.3390/electronics9101686 . . . . . . . . . . . . . . . 193

**Marián Trnka, Sakhia Darjaa, Marian Ritomský, Róbert Sabo, Milan Rusko and Meilin
Schaper et al.**
Mapping Discrete Emotions in the Dimensional Space: An Acoustic Approach
Reprinted from: *Electronics* **2021**, *10*, 2950, doi:10.3390/electronics10232950 . . . . . . . . . . . . . . 211

**Santosh Gondi and Vineel Pratap**
Performance Evaluation of Offline Speech Recognition on Edge Devices
Reprinted from: *Electronics* **2021**, *10*, 2697, doi:10.3390/electronics10212697 . . . . . . . . . . . . . . 227

**Soonshin Seo and Ji-Hwan Kim**
Self-Attentive Multi-Layer Aggregation with Feature Recalibration and Deep Length Normalization for Text-Independent Speaker Verification System
Reprinted from: *Electronics* **2020**, *9*, 1706, doi:10.3390/electronics9101706 . . . . . . . . . . . . . . **243**

**Michaela Bačíková, Jaroslav Porubän, Matúš Sulír, Sergej Chodarev, William Steingartner and Matej Madeja**
Domain Usability Evaluation
Reprinted from: *Electronics* **2021**, *10*, 1963, doi:10.3390/electronics10161963 . . . . . . . . . . . . . **257**

**Yi-Ling Lin, Shih-Yi Chien and Yi-Ju Chen**
Posting Recommendations in Healthcare Q&A Forums
Reprinted from: *Electronics* **2021**, *10*, 278, doi:10.3390/electronics10030278 . . . . . . . . . . . . . **285**

**Natinai Jinsakul, Cheng-Fa Tsai and Paohsi Wang**
Sentiment Level Evaluation of 3D Handicraft Products Application for Smartphones Usage
Reprinted from: *Electronics* **2021**, *10*, 199, doi:10.3390/electronics10020199 . . . . . . . . . . . . . **305**

# About the Editors

**Matúš Pleva**

Matúš Pleva (Matus Pleva) graduated Ph.D. in telecommunications from the Department of Electronics and Multimedia Communications of the Faculty of Electrical Engineering and Informatics at the Technical University of Kosice (2010). He works as an associate professor in the field of informatics and is Head of the Department. His research interests are acoustic modeling, acoustic event detection, speaker recognition, speech processing, human–machine interaction, embedded systems and parallel computing, security and biometrics, computer networking, IoT, etc. He is now leading the Slovak part of the project NITRO Clubs EU. He just successfully finished "Deep Learning for Advanced Speech Enabled Applications" bilateral project with the National Taipei University of Technology and "Content innovation and lecture textbooks for Biometric Safety Systems" project as principal investigator. He also participated in more than 50 national and international projects and COST actions. He is a member of ACM (Association for Computing Machinery) and HiPEAC (High Performance Embedded Architecture and Compilation). He is a member of Multi-modal Imaging of Forensic Science Evidence tools for Forensic Science and Wearable Robots for Augmentation, Assistance, or Substitution of Human Motor Functions COST actions. He was an MC member of the IC1106 COST action "Integrating Biometrics and Forensics for the Digital Age". He recently started a bilateral collaboration between TUKE and CAVS, MSU, US—the first demo output of the cooperation in the field of robotics and HCI. This collaboration resulted in bilateral Erasmus, MoU, and MoA agreements. He also participated in more than 50 national and international projects and COST actions. He has published over 150 technical papers in journals and conference proceedings with over 1000 citations to date.

**Yuan-Fu Liao**

Yuan-Fu Liao received B.S., M.S., and Ph.D. degrees from the Department of Communication Engineering, National Chiao Tung University (NCTU), Hsinchu, Taiwan, in 1991, 1993, and 1998, respectively. From January 1999 to June 1999, he was a Postdoctoral Researcher at the Department of Communication Engineering, National Chiao-Tung University. From September 1999 to February 2002, he became a Research Engineer at Philips Research East Asia, Taiwan. From February 2002 to July 2022, he was with the Department of Electronic Engineering, National Taipei University of Technology, Taipei, Taiwan. Since August 2022, he has joined the Institute of Artificial Intelligence Innovation, Industry Academia Innovation School, National Yang Ming Chiao Tung University, HsinChu, Taiwan, where he is currently a full Professor. His major research interests are Speech Signal Processing (Speech, Speaker, Language and Emotion Recognition, Speech Synthesis), Audio Signal Processing (Speech Enhancement, Microphone Array), Natural Language Processing (Machine Translation), and Machine Learning (Deep Learning, Deep Neural Networks).

**Patrick Bours**

Patrick Bours studied Discrete Mathematics at Eindhoven University of Technology in the Netherlands (M.Sc. 1990, Ph.D. 1994). Worked 10 years at the Netherlands National Communication Security Agency (NLNCSA) as a senior policy member in the area of crypto with a focus on public key crypto and random number generation. He started in 7/2005 as a PostDoc at the Norwegian Information Security Laboratory (NISlab) at Gjøvik University College in a project "Authentication in a Health Service Environment". As of 7/2008 he was appointed as Associate Professor at NISlab and specialized in authentication and more specifically biometrics. His main research interest is in behavioural biometrics with many papers on Gait Recognition (recognizing a person by his/her walking style), Keystroke Dynamics (recognizing a person by his/her typing style), and Continuous Authentication (making sure that the person that is using a device is the same as the person that logged on to that device, so detecting a change of user). Since 9/2012 he have a full professor position at NISlab. He was also head of NISlab in the period from 7/2009 to 6/2012. He is currently working on the "Chatroom Security" project where the goal is to detect people with fake profiles and child predators based on their typing and stylometric behaviour. Additionally, he is working on the detection of contract cheating to detect the academic dishonesty of students.

*Editorial*

# Human–Computer Interaction for Intelligent Systems

Matúš Pleva [1,*], Yuan-Fu Liao [2] and Patrick Bours [3]

[1] Department of Electronics and Multimedia Communications, Faculty of Electrical Engineering and Informatics, Technical University of Košice, Němcovej 32, 040 01 Košice, Slovakia
[2] Artificial Intelligence Innovation, Industry Academia Innovation School, National Yang Ming Chiao Tung University, No.1001, University Road, Hsinchu 30010, Taiwan
[3] Department of Information Security and Communication Technology, Faculty of Information Technology and Electrical Engineering, Norwegian University of Science and Technology, Teknologivegen 22, NO-2815 Gjøvik, Oppland, Norway
* Correspondence: matus.pleva@tuke.sk; Tel.: +421-055-602-2294

## 1. Introduction

The further development of human–computer interaction applications is still in great demand as users expect more natural interactions. For example, speech communication in many languages is expected as a basic feature for intelligent systems, such as robotic systems, autonomous vehicles, or virtual assistants. For this Special Issue, we invited submissions from researchers addressing the unique opportunities and challenges associated with human–computer interaction with intelligent systems. We encouraged authors to submit reports describing systems built for different languages and multilingual systems. We also invited submissions from researchers studying the linguistic, emotional, prosodic, and dialogue aspects of speech communication. We proposed to have a dialogue about other input and output modalities, including multimodal systems, fusion/fission algorithms, and deep learning methods. We encouraged the authors to report in detail the state-of-art results, and provide useful reviews and data used to build such systems to support development in those areas. The rapidly growing domain of virtual reality applications is of interest both as an application domain in which new interfaces and interaction methods are needed and as a potential testbed for evaluating speech and other interface modalities.

## 2. Short Presentation of the Papers

Every high-quality research started using a deep state-of-the-art review. We are proud to present great reviews in our collection about speech emotions [1], automatic spelling correction [2] and the usage of art in virtual reality [3].

### 2.1. Review Papers

Lieskovská et al. [1] presented a review of the recent development in speech emotion recognition and also examines the impact of various attention mechanisms on speech emotion recognition performance. Overall comparison of the systems was performed on a widely used IEMOCAP [4] benchmark database.

Hládek et al. [2] created a survey of automatic spelling correction algorithms. It follows from the previous work by Kukich [5] from 1992. It covers almost 20 years of research conducted since this paper. The article proposes a theoretical framework, overview of the approaches, benchmarks, and evaluation methods. It gives great insight for researchers after the last comprehensive survey because it is the first comprehensive survey paper about this topic after a long period.

Aldridge and Bethel [3] conducted an assessment of how art is being used in virtual reality (VR), and the feasibility of brain injury patients to participate in virtual art therapy was investigated. Studies included in this review highlight the importance of the artistic

Citation: Pleva, M.; Liao, Y.-F.; Bours, P. Human–Computer Interaction for Intelligent Systems. *Electronics* **2023**, *12*, 161. https://doi.org/10.3390/electronics12010161

Received: 26 December 2022
Accepted: 27 December 2022
Published: 29 December 2022

Copyright: © 2022 by the authors. Licensee MDPI, Basel, Switzerland. This article is an open access article distributed under the terms and conditions of the Creative Commons Attribution (CC BY) license (https://creativecommons.org/licenses/by/4.0/).

subject matter, sensory stimulation, and measurable performance outcomes for assessing the effect art therapy has on motor impairment in VR.

## 2.2. Research Papers

Stark et al. [6] described design and implementation of a new method for control and monitoring of mechatronic systems connected to the IoT network using a selected segment of extended reality to create an innovative form of the human–machine interaction. In the proposed solution, modern detection and recognition methods of 3D objects in augmented reality are used instead of conventional methods of control and monitoring of mechatronic IoT systems based on scanning QR codes.

Machová et al. [7] focus on increasing the effectiveness of the lexicon-based sentiment analysis. Within the research, two lexicons were built: the first was a big, domain-dependent lexicon created by translating and merging several existing dictionaries, and the second was a small, domain-dependent lexicon since it contained only words with the same meaning in different domains. These lexicons were labeled by assigning a degree of polarity to each word in the lexicon using Particle Swarm Optimization methods. The article also contains the results of experiments with the distribution of polarity values for different labeling techniques. The created lexicons were used in a new approach to sentiment analysis and evaluated. Sometimes, when the lexicon does not contain the words used in an analyzed text, the lexicon-based sentiment analysis itself fails. For such cases, it was supplemented with a machine learning model for sentiment analysis. This hybrid approach achieved very good results.

Szabóová et al. [8] paper is from the field of the analysis of emotions from a text that was obtained from a dialogue between a human and a robot and thus combines the field of sentiment analysis with HRI (human–robot interaction). Information about the emotional state of the person the robot is interacting with can help the robot choose the most appropriate response. Both a lexicon-based approach and machine learning were used for the emotion recognition (Naïve Bayes (multi-nomial, Bernoulli, and Gaussian), Support Vector Machine, and feed-forward neural network using various data representations, such as Bag-of-Words, TF-IDF, and sentence embeddings (ConceptNet Numberbatch)). The result of the experiments was an ensemble classifier consisting of the nine best models for each emotion. The model was demonstrated in four different scenarios with the humanoid robot NAO. Results concluded, that the best scenario for human acceptance is the one with emotional classification accompanied by emotional movements of the robot.

Shao et al. [9] presented the classification of dual-arm robot operator's mental workload by using the heart rate variability (HRV) signal. Average classification accuracy of 98.77% was obtained using the K-Nearest Neighbor (KNN) method.

Ondáš et al. [10] introduced a novel pediatric audiometry application for hearing detection in the home environment. Conditioned play audiometry principles were adopted to create a speech audiometry application, where children help the virtual robot Thomas assign words to pictures. Several game scenarios together with the setting condition issues were created, tested, and discussed.

Agarwal et al. [11] focuses on designing a grammar detection system that understands both structural and contextual information of sentences for validating whether the English sentences are grammatically correct. The paper proposes a new Lex-Pos sequencing approach that contains both information, linguistic, as well as syntactic, of a sentence. Long Short-Term Memory (LSTM) neural network architecture has been employed to build the grammar classifier. The study conducts nine experiments to validate the strength of the Lex-Pos sequences. The results showed that the Lex-Pos-based models are observed as superior in giving more accurate predictions and they are more stable.

Trnka et al. [12] depicted a system for predicting the values of Activation and Valence (AV) directly from the sound of emotional speech utterances without the use of its semantic content or any other additional information. The system uses X-vectors to represent sound characteristics of the utterance and a Support Vector Regressor for the estimation of the

AV values. The aim of the work was to test whether in each unseen database the predicted values of Valence and Activation will place emotion-tagged utterances in the AV space in accordance with expectations based on Russell's circumplex model of affective space.

Gondi and Pratap [13] from Facebook AI Research presented an innovative performance evaluation of offline speech recognition on Raspberry Pi CPU compared to Jetson Nano GPU. It was shown that after PyTorch mobile optimization and quantization, the models can achieve real-time inference on the Raspberry Pi CPU with a small degradation to word error rate. On the other hand, the Jetson Nano GPU has inference latency three to five times better, compared to Raspberry Pi.

Seo and Kim [14] presented a self-attentive multi-layer aggregation with feature recalibration and deep length normalization for a text-independent speaker verification system. The ResNet with the scaled channel width and layer depth was used to reduce the number of model parameters as a baseline. A self-attention mechanism was applied to perform multi-layer aggregation with dropout regularizations and batch normalizations. Further, deep-length normalization was used on a recalibrated feature in the training process. Experimental results using the VoxCeleb1 [15] evaluation dataset showed that the performance of the proposed methods was comparable to that of state-of-the-art models.

Bačíková et al. [16] used the term domain usability (DU) to describe the aspects of the user interface related to the terminology and domain. A new method called ADUE (Automatic Domain Usability Evaluation) for the automated evaluation of selected DU properties on existing user interfaces was introduced. The authors executed ADUE on several real-world Java applications and report their findings.

Lin et al. [17] developed posting recommendation systems (RSs) to support users in composing reasonable posts and receiving effective answers. The posting RSs were evaluated by a user study containing 27 participants and three tasks to examine if users engaged more in the question-generation process. The results show that the proposed mechanism enables the production of question posts with better understanding, which leads experts to devote more attention to answering their questions.

Jinsakul et al. [18] presented an innovative approach to improve Thailand's government's systems to include handicraft products with a 3D display option for smartphones. The 1775 participants' evaluation results in this study proved that the proposed 3D handicraft product application affected users by attracting their attention towards them.

**Author Contributions:** Conceptualization, M.P.; methodology, M.P. and Y.-F.L.; writing—original draft preparation, M.P.; writing—review and editing, M.P. and P.B.; supervision, Y.-F.L.; funding acquisition, M.P. All authors have read and agreed to the published version of the manuscript.

**Funding:** This paper was supported by the Slovak Research and Development Agency (Agentúra na podporu výskumu a vývoja) under projects APVV-SK-TW-21-0002 and APVV-SK-TW-17-0005; the Scientific Grant Agency (Vedecká grantová agentúra MŠVVaŠ SR a SAV), project numbers VEGA 1/0753/20 & VEGA 2/0165/21; and the Cultural and Educational Grant Agency (Kultúrna a edukačná grantová agentúra MŠVVaŠ SR), project number KEGA 009TUKE-4-2019, both funded by the Ministry of Education, Science, Research, and Sport of the Slovak Republic.

**Acknowledgments:** We would like to thank all the authors for the papers they submitted to this Special Issue. We would also like to acknowledge all the reviewers for their careful and timely reviews to help improve the quality of this Special Issue.

**Conflicts of Interest:** The authors declare no conflict of interest.

# References

1. Lieskovská, E.; Jakubec, M.; Jarina, R.; Chmulík, M. A Review on Speech Emotion Recognition Using Deep Learning and Attention Mechanism. *Electronics* **2021**, *10*, 1163. [CrossRef]
2. Hládek, D.; Staš, J.; Pleva, M. Survey of Automatic Spelling Correction. *Electronics* **2020**, *9*, 1670. [CrossRef]
3. Aldridge, A.; Bethel, C.L. A Systematic Review of the Use of Art in Virtual Reality. *Electronics* **2021**, *10*, 2314. [CrossRef]
4. Busso, C.; Bulut, M.; Lee, C.C.; Kazemzadeh, A.; Mower, E.; Kim, S.; Chang, J.N.; Lee, S.; Narayanan, S.S. IEMOCAP: Interactive emotional dyadic motion capture database. *Lang. Resour. Eval.* **2008**, *42*, 335–359. [CrossRef]

5. Kukich, K. Techniques for automatically correcting words in text. *Acm Comput. Surv. (CSUR)* **1992**, *24*, 377–439. [CrossRef]
6. Stark, E.; Kučera, E.; Haffner, O.; Drahoš, P.; Leskovský, R. Using Augmented Reality and Internet of Things for Control and Monitoring of Mechatronic Devices. *Electronics* **2020**, *9*, 1272. [CrossRef]
7. Machová, K.; Mikula, M.; Gao, X.; Mach, M. Lexicon-based Sentiment Analysis Using the Particle Swarm Optimization. *Electronics* **2020**, *9*, 1317. [CrossRef]
8. Szabóová, M.; Sarnovský, M.; Maslej Krešňáková, V.; Machová, K. Emotion Analysis in Human–Robot Interaction. *Electronics* **2020**, *9*, 1761. [CrossRef]
9. Shao, S.; Wang, T.; Wang, Y.; Su, Y.; Song, C.; Yao, C. Research of HRV as a Measure of Mental Workload in Human and Dual-Arm Robot Interaction. *Electronics* **2020**, *9*, 2174. [CrossRef]
10. Ondáš, S.; Kiktová, E.; Pleva, M.; Oravcová, M.; Hudák, L.; Juhár, J.; Zimmermann, J. Pediatric Speech Audiometry Web Application for Hearing Detection in the Home Environment. *Electronics* **2020**, *9*, 994. [CrossRef]
11. Agarwal, N.; Wani, M.A.; Bours, P. Lex-Pos Feature-Based Grammar Error Detection System for the English Language. *Electronics* **2020**, *9*, 1686. [CrossRef]
12. Trnka, M.; Darjaa, S.; Ritomský, M.; Sabo, R.; Rusko, M.; Schaper, M.; Stelkens-Kobsch, T.H. Mapping Discrete Emotions in the Dimensional Space: An Acoustic Approach. *Electronics* **2021**, *10*, 2950. [CrossRef]
13. Gondi, S.; Pratap, V. Performance Evaluation of Offline Speech Recognition on Edge Devices. *Electronics* **2021**, *10*, 2697. [CrossRef]
14. Seo, S.; Kim, J.H. Self-Attentive Multi-Layer Aggregation with Feature Recalibration and Deep Length Normalization for Text-Independent Speaker Verification System. *Electronics* **2020**, *9*, 1706. [CrossRef]
15. Nagrani, A.; Chung, J.S.; Zisserman, A. Voxceleb: a large-scale speaker identification dataset. *arXiv* **2017**, arXiv:1706.08612.
16. Bačíková, M.; Porubän, J.; Sulír, M.; Chodarev, S.; Steingartner, W.; Madeja, M. Domain Usability Evaluation. *Electronics* **2021**, *10*, 1963. [CrossRef]
17. Lin, Y.L.; Chien, S.Y.; Chen, Y.J. Posting Recommendations in Healthcare Q&A Forums. *Electronics* **2021**, *10*, 278. [CrossRef]
18. Jinsakul, N.; Tsai, C.F.; Wang, P. Sentiment Level Evaluation of 3D Handicraft Products Application for Smartphones Usage. *Electronics* **2021**, *10*, 199. [CrossRef]

**Disclaimer/Publisher's Note:** The statements, opinions and data contained in all publications are solely those of the individual author(s) and contributor(s) and not of MDPI and/or the editor(s). MDPI and/or the editor(s) disclaim responsibility for any injury to people or property resulting from any ideas, methods, instructions or products referred to in the content.

*Review*

# A Review on Speech Emotion Recognition Using Deep Learning and Attention Mechanism

Eva Lieskovská *, Maroš Jakubec, Roman Jarina and Michal Chmulík

Faculty of Electrical Engineering and Information Technology, University of Žilina, Univerzitná 8215/1, 010 26 Žilina, Slovakia; maros.jakubec@feit.uniza.sk (M.J.); roman.jarina@uniza.sk (R.J.); michal.chmulik@uniza.sk (M.C.)
* Correspondence: eva.lieskovska@feit.uniza.sk

**Abstract:** Emotions are an integral part of human interactions and are significant factors in determining user satisfaction or customer opinion. speech emotion recognition (SER) modules also play an important role in the development of human–computer interaction (HCI) applications. A tremendous number of SER systems have been developed over the last decades. Attention-based deep neural networks (DNNs) have been shown as suitable tools for mining information that is unevenly time distributed in multimedia content. The attention mechanism has been recently incorporated in DNN architectures to emphasise also emotional salient information. This paper provides a review of the recent development in SER and also examines the impact of various attention mechanisms on SER performance. Overall comparison of the system accuracies is performed on a widely used IEMOCAP benchmark database.

**Keywords:** speech emotion recognition; deep learning; attention mechanism; recurrent neural network; long short-term memory

## 1. Introduction

The aim of human–computer interaction (HCI) is not only to create a more effective and natural communication interface between people and computers, but its focus also lies on creating the aesthetic design, pleasant user experience, help in human development, online learning improvement, etc. Since emotions form an integral part of human interactions, they have naturally become an important aspect of the development of HCI-based applications. Emotions can be technologically captured and assessed in a variety of ways, such as facial expressions, physiological signals, or speech. With the intention of creating more natural and intuitive communication between humans and computers, emotions conveyed through signals should be correctly detected and appropriately processed. Throughout the last two decades of research focused on automatic emotion recognition, many machine learning techniques have been developed and constantly improved.

Emotion recognition is used in a wide variety of applications. Anger detection can serve as a quality measurement for voice portals [1] or call centres. It allows adapting provided services to the emotional state of customers accordingly. In civil aviation, monitoring the stress of aircraft pilots can help reduce the rate of a possible aircraft accident. Many researchers, who seek to enhance players' experiences with video games and to keep them motivated, have been incorporating the emotion recognition module into their products. Hossain et al. [2] used multimodal emotion recognition for quality improvement of a cloud-based gaming experience through emotion-aware screen effects. The aim is to increase players' engagement by adjusting the game in accordance with their emotions. In the area of mental health care, a psychiatric counselling service with a chatbot is suggested in [3]. The basic concept consists of the analysis of input text, voice, and visual clues in order to assess the subject's psychiatric disorder and inform about diagnosis and treatment. Another suggestion for emotion recognition application is a conversational chatbot, where speech emotion identification can play a role in better conversation [4]. A real-time SER application should find an optimal trade-off between less computing power, fast processing times, and a high degree of accuracy.

In this review, we focus on works dealing with the processing of acoustic clues from speech to recognise the speaker's emotions. The task of speech emotion recognition (SER) is traditionally divided into two main parts: feature extraction and classification, as depicted in Figure 1. During the feature extraction stage, a speech signal is converted to numerical values using various front-end signal processing techniques. Extracted feature vectors have a compact form and ideally should capture essential information from the signal. In the back-end, an appropriate classifier is selected according to the task to be performed.

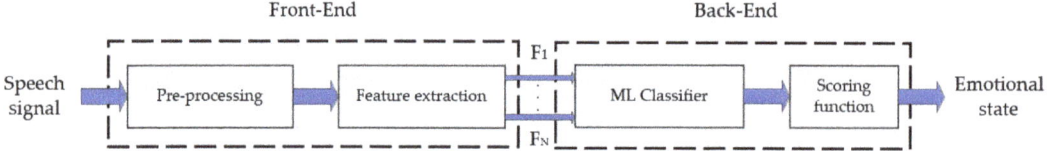

**Figure 1.** Block scheme of general speech emotion recognition system.

Examples of widely used acoustic features are mel-frequency cepstral coefficients (MFCCs), linear prediction cepstral coefficients (LPCC), short-time energy, fundamental frequency (F0), formants [5,6], etc. Traditional classification techniques include probabilistic models such as the Gaussian mixture model (GMM) [6–8], hidden Markov model (HMM) [9], and support vector machine (SVM [10–12]. Over the years of research, also various artificial neural network architectures have been utilised, from the simplest multilayer perceptron (MLP) [8] through extreme learning machine (ELM) [13], convolutional neural networks (CNNs) [14,15], to deep architectures of residual neural networks (ResNets) [16] and recurrent neural networks (RNNs) [17,18]. In particular, long short-term memory (LSTM) and gated recurrent units (GRU)-based neural networks (NNs), as state-of-the-art solutions in time-sequence modelling, have been widely utilised in speech signal modelling. In addition, various end-to-end architectures have been proposed to learn jointly both extraction of features and classification [15,19,20].

Besides LSTM and GRU networks, the introduction of an attention mechanism (AM) in deep learning may be considered as another milestone in sequential data processing. The purpose of AM is, as with human visual attention, to select relevant information and filter out irrelevant ones. The attention mechanism, first introduced for a machine translation task [21], has become an essential component of neural architectures. Incorporating AM into encoder–decoder-based neural architectures significantly boosted the performance of machine translation even for long sequences [21,22]. Motivated by the success of attention on machine translation, many researchers have considered it as an essential component of neural architectures for a remarkably large number of applications including natural language processing (NLP) and speech processing. Since emotional salient information is unevenly distributed across speech utterances, an integration of AM into NN architecture is also of interest among the SER research community.

Although several review articles have been devoted to automatic speech emotion recognition [23–29], to the best of the authors' knowledge, a comprehensive overview of SER solutions containing attention mechanisms is lacking. Motivated by this finding, in this article, we provide a review of the recent development in the speech emotion recognition field with a focus on the impact of AM in deep learning-based solutions on SER performance.

The paper is organised as follows: Firstly, the scope and methodology of the survey are discussed in Section 2. In Section 3, we address some of the key issues in deep learning-based SER development. Section 4 provides a theoretical background of the most commonly used neural architectures incorporating AM. Then, we review recently proposed

SER systems incorporating different types of AM. Finally, we compare the accuracy of the selected systems on the IEMOCAP benchmark database in Section 5. The section is concluded by a short discussion on the impact of AM on SER system performance.

## 2. Scope and Methodology

The paper is divided into two main parts: the first part discusses a general concept of SER and related works, including a description of the novel and deep features, and transfer learning and generalisation techniques, and the focus of the second part is on DNN models incorporating attention mechanism. We used Scopus and Web of Science (WoS) citation databases to search for relevant publications. A number of published papers by year of publication is given in Table 1. This is a general amount of works when searching by the keywords: speech, emotion, recognition, attention. Due to the excessive amount of research work dealing with this topic, only selected papers from the last 4 to 5 years of intensive research are reported in our study. In this review, the speech-related works were mainly taken into consideration; papers dealing with other physiological signals such as EEG, heart rate variability, as well as a fusion of multiple modalities were excluded.

Table 1. Number of publications during the initial search for speech emotion recognition and attention speech emotion recognition.

| Year | Scopus | | WoS | |
| --- | --- | --- | --- | --- |
| | General SER | Attention SER | General SER | Attention SER |
| 2016 | 519 | 34 | 344 | 30 |
| 2017 | 631 | 42 | 348 | 24 |
| 2018 | 829 | 82 | 446 | 54 |
| 2019 | 979 | 125 | 415 | 63 |
| 2020 | 886 | 133 | 325 | 59 |

For an additional overview of research work dealing with SER from previous and latest years, we refer a reader to reviews and surveys listed in Table 2. Note, our review does not cover all the topics related to SER such as detailed descriptions of speech features, classifiers, and emotional models, which are addressed more closely in other survey papers. We assume a reader's knowledge in probabilistic and machine learning-based approaches in data classifiers as well as in the basic DNN architectures. To the best of the authors' knowledge, none of the other reviews or surveys (listed in Table 2) deal with attention mechanism in more detail; hence, we consider it to be our main contribution.

Table 2. A brief summary of reviews and surveys related to SER.

| References | Description of the Content |
| --- | --- |
| [23]; 2011 | A comprehensive survey discusses acoustic features, classification methods (both traditional and artificial neural networks (ANNs)), and multimodal approaches. The authors pointed out that some of the existing databases were not sufficient for automatic SER and the development of benchmark emotional speech databases is necessary. |
| [24]; 2015 | Survey from 2000 to 2011 describing various features (considering non-linguistic and linguistic information) and feature selection methods, and providing a comparison of classification performance of traditional classifiers, ANNs, and their combinations. The major shortcoming for direct comparison of SER systems is considered to be a lack of uniformity in the way the methods are evaluated and assessed. |

Table 2. Cont.

| References | Description of the Content |
|---|---|
| [25]; 2018 | The review provides a thorough description of emotion datasets and speech features (excitation source, prosodic and vocal tract features) from 2000 to 2017. It also discusses the classification of emotions in general. |
| [26]; 2018 | A review article, which traces 20 years of progress in SER. The author discusses the techniques of representation of emotional speech (considering audio and textual features) and the ongoing trends. Benchmark results of the SER challenges are also provided. |
| [27]; 2018 | The survey covers existing emotion detection research efforts, emotion models, datasets, detection techniques, their features, limitations, and some possible future directions. Emotion analysis from text is also thoroughly described. |
| [28]; 2019 | Review of the deep learning techniques for SER: RNN, recursive neural network, deep belief network (DBN), CNN, and auto encoder (AE). |
| [29]; 2020 | A review discusses current methodologies in SER. It covers a wide area of SER topics such as emotional models, databases, features, pre-processing methods, supporting modalities, and classifiers. The authors address challenges in SER: the need for natural datasets with a sufficient amount of data; they also pointed out that unsatisfactory results are still being achieved with cross-language scenarios. |

*Evaluation Metrics*

In this section, common metrics of accuracy evaluation are listed. For a multiclass classification task, accuracy is assessed per class firstly and then the average accuracy is determined. This is denoted as unweighted accuracy hereafter. If the class accuracies are weighted according to the number of per-class instances, then the evaluation metric may not reflect the unbalanced nature of data (which is very common with databases of emotional speech). Therefore, the unweighted accuracy is often a better indicator of the system's accuracy. The common evaluation metrics for the SER tasks are as follows:

- Precision is the ratio of all correctly positively classified samples (true positive—TP) to all positive classified samples (TP and false positive—FP). For K-class evaluation, the precision is computed as follows:

$$\text{precision} = \frac{\sum_{k=1}^{K} \frac{TP_k}{TP_k + FP_k}}{K}. \tag{1}$$

- Recall is the ratio of all correctly positively classified samples (TP) to the number of all samples in a tested subgroup (TP and false negative FN). Recall indicates a class-specific recognition accuracy. Similarly, as in the case of precision, the recall for a multiclass classification problem is computed as the average of recalls for individual classes.

$$\text{recall} = \frac{\sum_{k=1}^{K} \frac{TP_k}{TP_k + FN_k}}{K}. \tag{2}$$

- In the literature, the multiclass recall is referred to as unweighted average recall (UAR), which is recommended metric for SER. UAR corresponds to unweighted accuracy (UA), computed similarly as the average over individual class accuracies.
- Weighted accuracy is often given as weighted average recall (WAR), which is computed as the class-specific recalls weighted by the number of per-class instances $s_k$ according to (3). This metric is also interchangeable with weighted accuracy (WA; or accuracy), which is defined as correct predictions over a total number of predictions. Note that evaluation metrics were not clearly defined in previous works. Thus, we unified them as described above.

$$\text{WAR} = \frac{\sum_{k=1}^{K} |s_k| \cdot \text{recall}_k}{\sum_{k=1}^{K} |s_k|} \qquad (3)$$

- F1 score is defined as the harmonic mean of the precision and recall.

$$F1 = 2 \frac{\text{precision} \cdot \text{recall}}{\text{precision} + \text{recall}} \qquad (4)$$

Note, all of the above-mentioned classification metrics are in the range of [0, 1] ($\times 100$ %).

A regression problem is often encountered when dealing with a continuous emotional scale. The appropriate metric for the regression is the correlation coefficient determined in two ways:

- Pearson's correlation coefficient (PCC; $\rho$) measures the correlation between the true and predicted values (x and y, respectively). Given the pairs of values $\{(x_n, y_n)\}$, n = 1, 2, ..., N, Pearson's correlation coefficient is computed as follows:

$$\rho = \frac{\sum_{n=1}^{N}(x_n - \mu_x)(y_n - \mu_y)}{\sqrt{\sum_{n=1}^{N}(x_n - \mu_x)^2 \sum_{n=1}^{N}(y_n - \mu_y)^2}}, \qquad (5)$$

where n denotes the index of the current pair, and $\mu_x$ and $\mu_y$ are mean values of $x_n$ and $y_n$, respectively.

- Concordance Correlation Coefficient (CCC; $\rho_c$) examines the relationship between the true and predicted values from a machine learning model. CCC lies in the range of [−1, 1], where 0 indicates no correlation and 1 is perfect agreement or concordance.

$$\rho_c = \frac{2\rho \sigma_x \sigma_y}{\sigma_x^2 + \sigma_y^2 + (\mu_x - \mu_y)^2}, \qquad (6)$$

where $\mu$ is the mean value and $\sigma$ is standard deviation, and $\rho$ is Pearson's correlation coefficient.

A comparison of published SER solutions is difficult due to the different experimental conditions used. Thus, we tried to do at least an intuitive comparative analysis of the published DNN-based SER systems performance. We grouped the systems according to the emotional datasets used for the conduction of experiments. Since the settings of the datasets differ significantly, we also group the compared works according to emotional labelling (discrete/continuous SER) and/or the number of classes being recognised and common cross-validation scenario. For the evaluation, we use the most widely used IEMOCAP database, on which most of the state-of-the-art systems have been tested. For comparison, we also listed the performance of the systems tested on EmoDB and RECOLA datasets.

## 3. Speech Emotion Recognition and Deep Learning

In this section, we review the most relevant issues in today's SER system development in general: (1) emotional speech database development, (2) speech features extraction and DL based emotion modelling, and (3) selected techniques for SER performance improvement, such as data augmentation, transfer learning, and cross-domain recognition (the attention mechanism is addressed in Sections 4 and 5). A comparison of the state-of-the-art works (excluding AM) based on common criteria is provided at the end of this Section.

### 3.1. Databases of Emotional Speech

Since the state-of-the-art SER solutions are exclusively based on data-driven machine learning techniques, the selection of a suitable speech database is naturally a key task in building such SER systems. Several criteria have to be taken into account when selecting a proper dataset, such as the degree of naturalness of emotions, the size of the database, and the number of available emotions. The databases can be divided into three basic categories:

- Simulated (acted): Professional actors express emotions through scripted scenarios.
- Elicited (induced): Emotions are created via artificially induced situations. With this approach, it is possible to achieve more natural recordings and simultaneously to have control over the emotional and lexical content of recordings.
- Spontaneous (natural): Spontaneous audio recordings are being extracted from various reality shows. The disadvantage of real-world audio samples is that they may be distorted by background noise and reverberation [30]. Another drawback is that the natural or spontaneous databases often contain unbalanced emotional categories.

Naturally, speech databases are created in various languages, and they may consist of a variety of emotional states. However, emotion labelling is not unified. Recognised emotion can be labelled into several discrete emotional classes, as shown in Table 3. The common way is labelling to six basic (known as the big six) emotional categories—anger, disgust, fear, happiness, sadness, surprise, and neutral. If SER is considered a regression problem, the emotions are mapped to continuous values representing the degree of emotional arousal, valence, and dominance. Valence is a continuum ranging from unhappiness to happiness, arousal ranges from sleepiness to excitement, dominance is in a range from submissiveness to dominance (e.g., control, influence) [31]. In Table 3, the most widely used databases of emotional speech are listed.

We would like also to draw attention to the following issue related to speech emotion rating and annotation. It has to be distinguished between emotion perceived (or observed) and emotion elicited (induced). Unlike in music emotion recognition, or affective analysis of movies where attention is paid to the listener's or spectator's experience, in the case of speech emotion recognition, the focus is on the speaker and his emotional state. The way the data is annotated is of much importance, especially in the case of annotation of spontaneous and induced emotions of the speaker. The emotion in speech is usually annotated by a listener. Another option is to use the rating provided by the speaker himself (felt or induced emotions) or obtained by analysis of the speaker's physiological signals. Since the experimental studies have shown a considerable discrepancy between emotion ratings by speaker and observer, correct and unambiguous emotion rating is still an open issue [32].

Table 3. Comparison of databases of emotional speech.

| Database | Language | Num. of Subjects | Num. of Utterances | Discrete Labels | Dim. Labels | Modality |
|---|---|---|---|---|---|---|
| AESDD [33] | Greek | 3 F/2 M | 500 | A, D, F, H, S | – | A |
| EmoDB [34] | German | 5 F/5 M | 500 | A, B, D, F, H, N, S | – | A |
| eNTERFACE'05 [35] | English | 42 | 5 utt./emotion | A, D, F, H, N, S, $S_r$ | – | A, V |
| FAU-AIBO [36] | German | 30 F/21 M (children) | 18 216 | A, B, $E_m$, $H_e$, I, J, M, N, O, R, $S_r$ | – | A |
| IEMOCAP [37] | English | 5 F/5 M | 10,039 | A, D, E, F, $F_r$, H, N, s, $S_r$ | √ | A, V, T, MCF |
| MSP-PODCAST [38] | English | – | 62,140 | A, D, F, H, S, $S_r$, N, C, O | √ | A |
| Polish DB [39] | Polish | 4 F/4 M | 240 | A, B, F, J, N, S | – | A |
| RAVDESS [40] | English | 12 F/12 M | 104 | A, D, F, H, N, S, $S_r$ | √ | A, V |
| RECOLA [41] | French | 46 (27) [1] | – | – | √ | A, V, ECG, EDA |
| SAVEE [42] | English | 4 M | 480 | A, D, F, H, S, $S_r$, N | – | A, V |

Meaning of acronyms are as follows: Num. of subjects: F—female, M—male; Discrete labels: A—anger, B—boredom, C—contempt, D—disgust, E—excitement, $E_m$—emphatic, F—fear, H—happiness, $H_e$—helplessness, I—irritation, J—joy, M—motherese, N—neutral, O—other, R—reprimanding, S—sadness, $S_r$—surprise; Dim. Labels: dimensional labels (arousal, valence, dominance); Modality: A—audio, V—video, T—text, MCF—motion capture of face, ECG—electrocardiogram, EDA—electrodermal activity. [1] Overall, 46 subjects participated in samples recording; however, only 27 subjects were available for audio–visual emotion recognition challenge (AVEC) [43].

### 3.2. Acoustic Features

The purpose of SER is to automatically determine the emotional state of the speaker via a speech signal. Changes in the waveform's frequency and intensity may be observed when comparing different emotionally coloured speech signals [9]. The aim of SER is to capture these variations using different discriminative acoustic features. Acoustic features (referred to as low-level descriptors (LLDs) are often aggregated by temporal feature integration methods (e.g., statistical and spectral moments) in order to obtain features at a global level [44]. High-dimensional feature vectors can be transformed into a compact representation using feature selection (FS) techniques. The aim is to find substantial information from the feature set and discard redundant values simultaneously. In this way, it is possible to optimise the time complexity of the system while maintaining similar accuracy.

Over the many years of research, the focus has been placed on the selection of the ideal set of descriptors for emotional speech. MFCCs originally proposed for speech/speaker recognition are well established also for the derivation of emotional clues. Prosodic descriptors (such as pitch, intensity, rhythm, and duration), as well as voice quality features (jitter and shimmer), are common indicators of human emotions as well [8]. In addition, numerous novel features and feature selection techniques have been developed and successfully applied to SER [7,44–50]. For instance, Gammatone frequency cepstral coefficients proposed by Liu [45] yielded a 3.6% average increase in accuracy compared to MFCCs. Epoch-based features extracted by the zero time windowing also provided emotion-specific and complementary information to MFCCs [46]. Ntalampiras et al. [44] proposed a multiresolution feature called perceptual wavelet packet based on critical-band analysis. It takes into account that not all parts of the spectrum affect human perception in the same way. In [7], the nonlinear Teager–Kaiser energy operator (TEO) was used in combination with MFCC for the detection of stressed emotions. Kerkeni et al. [47] proposed modulation spectral features and modulation frequency features—based on empirical mode decomposition of the input signal and TEO extraction of the instantaneous amplitude and instantaneous frequency of the AM–FM components. Yogesh et al. [48] extracted nonlinear bispectral features and bicoherence features from speech and glottal waveforms.

However, despite great research efforts, there is still no single solution for the most appropriate features. For better comparability of SER systems and their obtained results, attempts to unify feature extraction have been made. When selecting appropriate audio features for SER, it is a common practice to use the openSMILE open-source audio feature extraction toolkit. It contains several feature sets intended for automatic emotion recognition, some of which were proposed in several emotion-related challenges and benchmark initiatives.

- The INTERSPEECH 2009 (IS09) [51] feature set consists of fundamental frequency, voicing probability, frame energy, zero-crossing rate, and 12 MFCCs and their first-order derivatives. With statistical functionals applied to LLDs, 384-dimensional feature vectors can be obtained.
- The feature set of the INTERSPEECH 2010 (IS10) paralinguistic challenge [52] contains 1582 features, which are obtained in three steps: (1) a total of 38 LLDs are smoothed by low-pass filtration, (2) their first order regression coefficients are added, and (3) 21 functionals are applied.
- The extended Geneva minimalistic acoustic parameter set (eGeMAPS) [53] contains LLD features, which paralinguistic studies have suggested as most related to emotions. The eGeMAPS consists of 88 features: the arithmetic mean and variation of 18 LLDs, 8 functionals applied to pitch and loudness, 4 statistics over the unvoiced segments, 6 temporal features, and 26 additional cepstral parameters and dynamic parameters.
- The INTERSPEECH 2013 computational paralinguistic challenge (ComParE) [54] is another feature set from the openSMILE extractor, which is mostly used to recognise emotions. ComParE consists of 6373 features based on extraction of 64 LLDs (prosodic, cepstral, spectral, sound quality), adding their time derivates (delta features), and applying statistical functions.

*3.3. Data-Driven Features*

Apart from speech parameterisation from handcrafted features, another popular approach is to let a neural network (NN) to perform feature extraction. A typical example is the utilisation of CNN to learn from 2D speech spectrograms, log-mel spectrograms, or even from the raw speech signals [19,55]. CNN is usually supplemented by fully connected (FC) layers and softmax for classification [56]. Architecture, which consists of multiple convolutional layers, is often referred to in literature as deep CNN (DCNN). Huang and Narayanan [55] examined the ability of CNN to perform task-specific spectral decorrelation using log-mel filter-bank (MFB, or log-mel spectrogram) as input features. Since MFCCs are log-mels decorrelated by discrete cosine transform (DCT), the authors demonstrated that the CNN module was a more effective task-specific decorrelation technique under both clean and noisy conditions (experiments were conducted on eNTERFACE'05 [35] database). Aldeneh and Provost [14] experimentally proved that a system based on the minimum set of 40 MFB features and CNN architecture can achieve similar results as SVM trained on a large feature set (1560). Compared to a complex system based on deep feature extraction derived from 1582-dimensional features and an SVM classifier [10], the proposed 40 MFB-CNN provides a more effective and end-to-end solution. Fayek et al. [15] proposed various end-to-end NN architectures to model intra-utterance dynamics. CNN had better discriminative performance than DNN and LSTM architectures, all trained with MFB input features. Vrysis et al. [57] conducted a thorough comparison between standard features, temporal feature integration tactics, and 1D and 2D DCNN architectures. The designed convolutional algorithms delivered excellent performance, surpassing the traditional feature-based approaches. The best 2D DCNN architecture achieved higher accuracy than 1D DCNN with the comparable number of parameters. Moreover, 1D DCNN was four times slower on execution. Hajarolasvadi and Demirel [58] proposed 3D CNN model for speech emotion recognition. The utterances in form of overlapping frames were processed in two ways—88 dimensional features and spectrogram were extracted for each frame. The representation of 3D spectrogram was based on the selection of $k$ most discriminant frames with $k$-means clustering algorithm applied to the extracted features. Using this approach, it is possible to capture both spectral and temporal information. The proposed architecture was able to outperformed pretrained 2D CNN model transferred to SER task. Mustaqeem and Kwon [59] proposed plain CNN architecture called deep stride CNN, which used strides for downsampling of input feature maps instead of the pooling layer. The authors dealt with proper pre-processing in form of noise reduction through novel adaptive thresholding and decreasing of computational complexity by utilising simplified CNN structure. This stride CNN improved accuracy by 7.85% and 4.5% on IEMOCAP and RAVDESS datasets, respectively and significantly outperformed state-of-the-art systems.

*3.4. Temporal Variations Modelling*

Emotional content in speech varies through time; therefore, it is appropriate to leverage the techniques which are effective for temporal modelling, such as stochastic HMM or neural networks with recurrent units (e.g., LSTM or GRU).

Tzinis and Potamianos [17] studied the effects of variable sequence lengths for LSTM-based recognition (see Section 4 for RNN–LSTM description). Recognition on sequences concatenated at frame-level yielded better results on phoneme length (90 ms). The best results were achieved over statistically aggregated segments at the word level (3 s)—64.16% WA and 60.02% UA (IEMOCAP). In this case, extraction of higher-level statistical functions from multiple LLDs over speech segments led to a more salient representation of underlying emotional dynamics. The proposed solution yielded comparable results to a more complex system based on deep feature extraction and SVM classifiers [10,60].

Recurrent layers are often used in combination with CNN (referred to as CRNN) for the exploitation of temporal information from emotional speech [61]. In this way, both local and global characteristics are modelled. Zhao et al. [62] compared the performance of 1D and 2D-CNN LSTM architectures with raw speech and log-mel spectrograms as input, respectively. Moreover, 2D-CNN LSTM performed better in the modelling of local and global representations than its 1D counterpart. The 2D-CNN LSTM outperformed traditional approaches such as DBN and CNN. Luo et al. [63] proposed a two-channel system with joint learning of handcrafted HSFs/DNN and log-mel spectrogram/CRNN learned features. In this way, it is possible to obtain different kinds of information from emotional speech. The authors also designed another jointly learned architecture—multi-CRNN with one CRNN channel learning from a longer time scale of spectrogram segment and a second CRNN channel for deeper layer-based feature extraction. Their CRNN baseline consisted of CNN–LSTM with a concatenation of three pooling layers (average, minimum, and maximum). Jointly learned SER systems extracted more robust features than the plain CRNN system and HSF–CRNN outperformed multi-CRNN. Satt et al. [64] proposed CNN–BiLSTM architecture with spectrogram as input and worked with two different frequency resolutions. The results indicated that lower resolution yields lower accuracy by 1–3%. The combination of CNN and BiLSTM achieved better results in comparison with the stand-alone CNN model. Moreover, unweighted accuracy was improved by the proposed two-step classification, where special emphasis was put on a neutral class. Ma et al. [65] dealt with the accuracy loss introduced by the speech segmentation process, i.e., division of longer utterances into segments of the same length. They proposed a similar approach to Satt et al. [64] (a combination of CNN and BiGRU), except that spectrogram of the whole sentence, was used as input. They introduced padding values and dealt with the appropriate processing of valid and padded sequences. Moreover, different weights were assigned to the loss so that the length of the sentence does not affect the bias of the model. There was a significant performance improvement over segmentation methods with fixed-length inputs. Compared to [64], the proposed model using variable-length input spectrograms achieved absolute improvements of 2.65% and 4.82%, in WA and UA.

A significant part of the works on SER prefers to model emotions on continuous scale (usually in the activation–valence emotional plane). Several works on continuous SER have also proven that CNN-based data-driven features outperform traditional hand-engineered features [19,66,67]. For example, authors of [19,67] proposed end-to-end continuous SER systems, in which 1D CNN was applied on the raw waveform and temporal dependencies were then modelled by the Bi-LSTM layers. Khorram et al. [66] proposed two architectures for continuous emotions recognition—dilated CNN with a varying dilation factor for different layers and downsampling/upsampling CNN—with different ways of modelling long-term dependencies. AlBadawy and Kim [68] further improved the accuracy of valence with joint modelling of the discrete and continuous emotion labels. Table 4 summarises the top performances of the continuous SER systems tested on the RECOLA dataset.

**Table 4.** Comparison of continuous SER on RECOLA datasets: A–V = activation–valence, $\rho_c$—concordance correlation coefficient.

| References | Audio Parametrization | Classification Method | Reported Accuracy ($\rho_c$) | |
|---|---|---|---|---|
| Trigeorgis et al. [19]; 2016 | Raw signal (6 s long sequences) | end-to-end CNN–BiLSTM | 0.686 A | 0.261 V |
| Khorram et al. [66]; 2018 | MFB | Down/Up CNN | 0.681 A | 0.502 V |
| Tzirakis et al. [67]; 2018 | Raw signal (20 s long sequences) | end-to-end CNN–LSTM | 0.787 A | 0.440 V |
| AlBadawy and Kim [68]; 2018 | MFB | Deep BLSTM | 0.697 A | 0.555 V |

*3.5. Transfer Learning*

The methods based on leveraging pretrained neural networks can often obtain better results than traditional techniques [11,12]. As a result of some studies, pretrained neural networks also outperform randomly initialised networks [69]. The use of transfer learning is especially appropriate for SER, due to the lack of large speech emotion corpora. The deep spectrum features proposed in [12], which were derived from feeding spectrograms through the pretrained network designed for the image classification task, AlexNet [70], is reported to match and even outperform some of the conventional feature extraction techniques. Zhang et al. [11] proposed the use of the AlexNet DCNN pretrained model to learn from three-channel log-mel spectrograms extracted from emotional speech (the additional two channels contained first and second-time derivates of the spectra, known as delta features). The authors also proposed discriminant temporal pyramid matching (DTPM) pooling strategy to aggregate segment-level features (obtained from the DCNN block) to the discriminative utterance-level representations. According to the results obtained with four different databases, AlexNet fine-tuned on emotional speech performed better in comparison with the simplified DCNN model and at the same time, DTPM based pooling outperformed the conventional average pooling method. Xi et al. [16] conducted several experiments with the utilisation of a pretrained model for speaker verification tasks. The authors proposed a residual adapter which is the residual CNN ResNet20 trained on the VoxCeleb2 speaker dataset with adapter modules trained on IEMOCAP emotion data. The residual adapter outperformed ResNet20 trained on emotional data only. This proved the inadequacy of using a small dataset for training with the ResNet architecture.

*3.6. Generalisation Techniques*

The lack of sufficient size of datasets and their imbalanced nature are problems often encountered in SER. With the increase in complexity and size of DNNs, the need for a large dataset is essential for their good performance. One of the solutions is to extend the dataset by various deformation techniques. This approach is limited by the possibility of losing the emotional content by inappropriate deformation of speech samples. The insufficient amount of data can also be addressed by utilising data from other emotional databases. However, there arises a problem of mismatched conditions between training and testing data or in other words problem of mismatched domains.

3.6.1. Data Augmentation

Audio datasets can be effectively expanded (or augmented) using various deformation techniques such as pitch and/or time shifting, the addition of background noise, and volume control [71]. The addition of various noise levels can expand the dataset up to several times [72]. In this subsection, data augmentation techniques applied specifically for the SER task are briefly listed.

In [14], the augmentation based on speed perturbation resulted in an improvement of 2.3% and 2.8% on IEMOCAP and MSP–IMPROV datasets, respectively. Etienne et al. [73] applied several augmentation techniques on highly unbalanced samples from the IEMO-CAP database: vocal tract length perturbation based on rescaling of the spectrograms along the frequency axis, oversampling of classes (happiness and anger), and the use of a higher frequency range. Compared to baseline, the application of all three techniques increased the UA by about 4% (absolute improvement). Vryzas et al. [74] pointed out the fact that changes in the timing and tempo characteristics could result in an undesired loss of emotional clues. They used pitch alterations with constant tempo based on sub-band sinusoidal modelling synthesis for augmentation of data. Although augmentation has not increased the accuracy of the proposed CNN system (for the AESDD dataset [33]), it can improve its robustness and generalisation.

The popular approach of data augmentation is the use of generative adversarial networks (GANs) for generating new in-distribution samples. GAN consists of two networks, which are trained together: generator for generating new samples and discriminator for deciding the authenticity of samples (generated vs. true sample) [75]. Sahu et al. [76] employed vanilla and conditional GAN networks (trained on the IEMOCAP dataset) for generating synthetic feature vectors. The proposed augmentation made slight improvements in SVM's performance when real data were appended with synthetic data. The authors pointed out that a larger amount of data is needed to have a successful GAN framework. Chatziagapi et al. [77] leveraged GAN for spectrogram generation to address the data imbalance. Compared to standard augmentation techniques, authors achieved 10% and 5% relative performance improvement on IEMOCAP and FEEL-25k, respectively.

Fu et al. [78] designed an adversarial autoencoder (AAEC) emotional classifier, through which the dataset was expanded in order to improve the robustness and generalisation of the classifier. The proposed model generated most of the new samples almost within the real distribution.

### 3.6.2. Cross-Domain Recognition

In the domain adaptation approach, there is an effort to generalise the model for effective emotion recognition across different domains. The performance of a speech emotion recognition system tuned for one emotional speech database can deteriorate significantly for different databases, even if the same language is considered. One may encounter mismatched domain conditions such as different environments, speakers, languages, or various phonation modes. All these conditions worsen the accuracy of the SER system in a cross-domain scenario. Therefore, a tremendous effort has been made to improve the generalisation of the classifier.

Deng et al. [79] proposed unsupervised domain adaptation based on autoencoder. The idea was to train the model on a whispered speech from the GeWEC emotion corpus, while normal speech data were used for testing. Inspired by Universum learning, the authors enhanced the model by integration of the margin-based loss, which adds information from unlabelled data (from another database) to the training process. The results showed that the proposed method outperformed other domain adaptation methods. Abdelwahab and Busso [80] discussed the negative impact of mismatched data distributions between training and testing dataset (target and source domain) on the emotion recognition task. To compensate for the differences between the two domains, the authors used domain adversarial neural network (DANN) [81], which is an adversarial multitask training technique for performing emotion classification tasks and the domain classification. DANN effectively reduced the gap in the feature space between the source and target domains. Zheng et al. [82] presented a novel multiscale discrepancy adversarial (MSDA) network for conducting multiple timescales domain adaptation for cross-corpus SER. The MSDA is characterised by three levels of discriminators, which are fed with global, local, and hybrid levels of features from the labelled source domain and unlabelled target domain. MSDA integrates multiple timescales of deep speech features to train a set of hierarchical domain discriminators and an emotion classifier simultaneously in an adversarial training network. The proposed method achieved the best performance over all other baseline methods. Noh et al. [83] proposed a multipath and group-loss-based network (MPGLN), which supports supervised domain adaptation from multiple environments. It is an ensemble learning model based on a temporal feature generator using BiLSTM, a transferred feature extractor from the pretrained VGG-like audio classification model, and simultaneous minimisation of multiple losses. The proposed MPGLN was evaluated over five multidomain SER datasets and efficiently supported multidomain adaptation and reinforced model generalisation.

Language dependency and emotion recognition with consideration of different languages are common issues that may be encountered in SER. One of the solutions would be to identify language firstly and then to perform language-dependent emotion recognition [5]. Another solution would be to share different language databases and to process them jointly. This is denoted as a multilingual scenario. In the case of a cross-lingual scenario, one dataset is used for training and the other one for testing. Tamulevičius et al. [72] put together a cross-linguistic speech emotion dataset with the size of more than 10.000 emotional utterances. It consists of six emotion datasets of different languages. Moreover, augmentation of data was performed with the addition of white noise and application of Wiener filtering (expansion of dataset up to nine times). For the representations of speech emotion, authors chose several two-dimensional acoustic feature spaces (cochleagrams, spectrograms, mel-cepstrograms, and fractal dimension-based features), and they used CNN for classification. The results showed the superiority of cochleagrams over the other utilised feature spaces and confirmed that emotions are language dependent. With the increase of different language datasets in the training partition, the results obtained by testing with remaining datasets slightly increased.

*3.7. DNN Systems Comparison*

In this subsection, we tried to do at least a coarse comparison of the performance of related works discussed above (remark, it is not possible to make an exact comparison due to different test conditions, even if the same dataset was used). Note this summary does not contain works incorporating attention mechanisms. The attention mechanism is discussed in Section 4.

We focused on finding common criteria and the selection of datasets for comparative analysis. From literature review, we selected the two most widely used databases—EmoDB and IEMOCAP—and sorted out the related works in terms of the number of emotions used for classification and cross-validation scheme. The resulted comparison of the SER systems on EmoDB and IEMOCAP is in Tables 5 and 6 respectively.

For the EmoDB dataset, we considered research works that used all emotion classes and the leave-one speaker-out (LOSO) method of cross-validation—speaker-independent scenario. The human evaluation of emotions from EmoDB showing the average recognition rate of 84.3% was surpassed by most of the works under comparison.

As seen in Table 5, the system incorporating handcrafted features with proper temporal feature integration method yielded state-of-the-art results (>90% WA) in [44]. Thus, the aggregation of different descriptors carries significant emotional information. However, the disadvantage is that the high dimensional feature sets often cause an increase in computational complexity. The low accuracy of pretrained AlexNet in [84] was caused by the reduction of bandwidth and μ-law companding for the purpose of the development of a real-time SER system (7% reduction in accuracy). Table 5 shows that end-to-end CRNN architecture [62], outperformed other works under comparison.

**Table 5.** Comparison of SER systems based on classification using a complete EmoDB dataset.

| References | Audio Parametrisation | Applied Techniques | Reported Accuracy |
|---|---|---|---|
| Ntalampiras et al. [44]; 2012 | Log-likelihood fusion level with optimally integrated feature sets | Simple logistic recognition | 93.4% WA |
| Huang et al. [85]; 2014 | Spectrogram | semi-CNN with SVM | 85.2% WA |
| Yogesh et al. [48]; 2017 | BSFs, BCFs, IS10 (1632 features) FS: PSOBBO | ELM | 90.31% WA |
| Zhang et al. [11]; 2018 | 3D Log-mels (static, Δ, ΔΔ) DCNN–DTPM | linear SVM | 87.31% WA |
| Zhao et al. [62]; 2019 | Log-mel spectrograms | 2D CNN LSTM | 95.89% WA |
| Lech et al. [84]; 2020 | Spectrograms converted into RGB | AlexNet (real-time SER) | 82% WA |

In the case of IEMOCAP, the expansion of highly underrepresented class Happiness, by merging it together with Excitement, naturally yields better results, especially in UA measure. This effect can be seen in the first part of Table 6. (Emotions: A, E + H, N, S). The common procedure for dataset partition is to employ a leave-one session-out cross-validation (fivefold). A common approach is to use data from one speaker for validation and data from the remaining speakers for testing. IEMOCAP contains both scripted and improvised scenarios. Scripted recordings are often not incorporated into SER systems, due to possible correlation with lingual content (systems working with improvised data are marked with an asterisk in Table 6). Note that the SER system trained on the improvised dataset outperformed the system applied on the scripted dataset [86,87]. The degree of naturalness of emotional speech has a significant impact on recognition accuracy. Learning on improvised data only can result in better performance than the combination of improvised and scripted data. This means that better accuracies can often be achieved with smaller data set.

**Table 6.** Comparison of SER systems for IEMOCAP dataset. Meaning of acronyms: A—anger, E—excitement, H—happiness, N—neutral, S—sadness.

| References | Audio Parametrisation | Applied Techniques | Weighted Accuracy | Unweighted Accuracy |
|---|---|---|---|---|
| | Emotions: A, E + H, N, S | | | |
| Fayek et al. [15]; 2017 | MFB | LSTM–RNN<br>DNN<br>CNN | 61.71% WA<br>62.55% WA<br>64.78% WA | 58.05% UA<br>58.78% UA<br>60.89% UA |
| Aldeneh and Provost [14]; 2017 | 40 MFB<br>Speed data augment. | CNN | – | 61.8% UA |
| Xia and Liu [10]; 2017 | 1582 features from IS10 | DBN with MTL<br>SVM | 60.9% WA | 62.4% UA |
| Kurpukdee et al. [60]; 2017 | ConvLSTM–RNN<br>phoneme-based feature extractor | SVM | 65.13% WA | – |
| Sahu et al. [76]; 2018 | 1582-dimensional openSMILE<br>feature space<br>Augment. with GAN | SVM | – | 60.29% UA |
| Luo et al. [63]; 2018 | 6373 HSFs features<br>Log-mel spec. | DNN/CRNN | 60.35% WA | 63.98% UA |
| Chatziagapi et al. [77]; 2019 | Mel-scaled<br>Spectrograms<br>Augment. with GAN | CNN(VGG19) | – | 53.6% UA |
| | Emotions: A, H, N, S | | | |
| Lee and Tashev [13]; 2015 | Segment-level features + DNN | ELM | 52.13% WA * | 57.91% UA * |
| Tzinis and Potamianos [17]; 2017 | Statistical features over 3 s segments | LSTM | 64.16% WA | 60.02% UA |
| Satt et al. [64]; 2017 | STFT spectrograms | CNN–BiLSTM | 68.8% WA * | 59.4% UA * |
| Ma et al. [65]; 2018 | Variable length spectrograms | CNN–BiGRU | 71.45% WA * | 64.22% UA * |
| Yenigalla et al. [4]; 2018 | Phoneme embedding and spectrogram | 2 CNN channels | 73.9% WA * | 68.5% UA * |
| Wu et al. [88]; 2019 | Spectrograms | CNN–GRU–SeqCap | 72.73% WA | 59.71% UA |
| Xi et al. [16]; 2019 | Magnitude spectrograms | Residual Adapter on VoxCeleb2 | 72.73% WA * | 67.58% UA * |
| Mustaqeem and Kwon [59]; 2019 | Noise reduction Spectrograms | DSCNN | 84% WA | 82% UA |

* Improvised data only.

For the IEMOCAP database, with the fivefold cross-validation technique and four emotions for classification (anger, sadness, happiness, and neutral), DNN–ELM [13], based on deep feature extraction and ELM classifier, yielded an accuracy of about 52.13% in WA and 57.91% in UA. These results were considered as a baseline for further evaluation. These results were surpassed by the RNN architecture with the proper extraction of higher-level statistical functionals from multiple LLDs over speech segments. The results of 64.16% WA and 60.02% UA were obtained even on a full dataset (improvised and scripted).

Deep features extracted by CNN often surpass the traditional feature-based approaches [57,89]. A combination of CNN and BiLSTM (CRNN) is effective in the derivation of both local and global characteristics. CRNN often achieves better results in comparison with the stand-alone CNN models [62,64]. Ma et al. [65] emphasised the importance of using the whole sentences for classification because the segmentation of utterances caused the degradation of accuracy. The proposed CRNN architecture with variable-length spectrograms as input features increased the baseline results by 19% and 6% in WA and UA, respectively. Compared to hybrid models, the CRNN end-to-end approach is more effective for implementation.

There is also discussion about the performance of 1D and 2D convolutions. In our study, 2D DCNN outperformed 1D DCNN with a similar number of parameters [57]. Moreover, 1D DCNN was four times slower on execution. In the case of CRNN, 2D-CNN–LSTM outperformed its 1D counterpart in [62]. Yenigalla et al. [4] used phoneme embeddings in addition to spectrograms as input to a model consisting of two separate CNN channels. This two-channel solution further improved results obtained by CRNN proposed by Ma et al. [65] (from 71.45% WA* to 73.9% WA* and from 64.22% UA* to 68.5% UA*). The approach based on transfer learning utilising a pretrained model from a speaker verification task yielded similarly high-performance [16]. The authors further proved the benefits of applying domain-agnostic parameters for SER and the inadequacy of using a small dataset for training with the ResNet architecture. According to Table 6, the deep stride CNN architecture [59] achieved the highest accuracy for both WA and UA. The proposed stride CNN increases the accuracy by using salient features extraction from raw spectrograms and reducing computational complexity. However, the experiments were conducted with an 80/20% split of the dataset, which differs from the LOSO model with an additional validation data partition.

## 4. Speech Emotion Recognition with Attention Mechanism

Before discussing the attention mechanism, we provide the theoretical background of the LSTM recurrent networks, which were first used as the base architecture for AM.

### 4.1. LSTM–RNN

Let the input sequence $\mathbf{X} = (\mathbf{x}_1, \mathbf{x}_2, \ldots, \mathbf{x}_T)$, $\mathbf{X} \in R^{T \times d}$, be transformed by RNN into hidden state vectors representation $\mathbf{H} = (\mathbf{h}_1, \mathbf{h}_2, \ldots, \mathbf{h}_T)$, $\mathbf{H} \in R^{T \times n}$. Here, d and n denote the dimension of input vectors and the number of hidden units, respectively. A basic principle of RNN lies in the fact that the previous information from sequence $\mathbf{h}_{t-1}$ contributes to shaping the current outcome $\mathbf{h}_t$. Output vector $\mathbf{y}_t$ of the simple RNN is obtained as follows:

$$\mathbf{h}_t = f(\mathbf{W}\mathbf{x}_t + \mathbf{U}\mathbf{h}_{t-1}), \tag{7}$$

$$\mathbf{y}_t = g(\mathbf{V}\mathbf{h}_t), \tag{8}$$

where $\mathbf{W} \in R^{n \times d}$, $\mathbf{U} \in R^{n \times n}$, $\mathbf{V} \in R^{n \times n}$ are learnable weights, and $f, g$ are activation functions.

Note that long-term dependencies in a sequence cannot be captured by a simple RNN unit due to the gradient vanishing problem [90]. Various recurrent units (such as Long short-term memory (LSTM), gated recurrent unit (GRU)) with different internal infrastructure were developed to enable capture dependencies over a longer period.

LSTM [91] uses internal gates to overcome the above-mentioned constraints of the simple recurrent units. The input sequence flows through three types of gates—forget gate $\mathbf{f}_t$ (9), input gate $\mathbf{i}_t$ (10), and output gate $\mathbf{o}_t$ (13). Another component of LSTM is a memory cell $\mathbf{c}_t$ (12), whose state is updated at each time step. The process of cell state update depends on the previous hidden state vector $\mathbf{h}_{t-1}$, current input vector $\mathbf{x}_t$, and the previous cell state $\mathbf{c}_{t-1}$ (previous cell state can be also included into gates, and this is called peephole connection). The inner structure of LSTM is shown in Figure 2. Here, $\mathbf{X} = (\mathbf{x}_1, \mathbf{x}_2, \ldots, \mathbf{x}_T)$ denotes input sequence, where T is the length of the sequence. The individual operations in LSTM are formalised as follows:

$$\mathbf{f}_t = \sigma(\mathbf{W}_f \mathbf{x}_t + \mathbf{U}_f \mathbf{h}_{t-1} + \mathbf{V}_f \mathbf{c}_{t-1} + \mathbf{b}_f), \tag{9}$$

$$\mathbf{i}_t = \sigma(\mathbf{W}_i \mathbf{x}_t + \mathbf{U}_i \mathbf{h}_{t-1} + \mathbf{V}_i \mathbf{c}_{t-1} + \mathbf{b}_i), \tag{10}$$

$$\mathbf{z}_t = \tanh(\mathbf{W}_z \mathbf{x}_t + \mathbf{U}_z \mathbf{h}_{t-1} + \mathbf{b}_z), \tag{11}$$

$$\mathbf{c}_t = \mathbf{f}_t \circ \mathbf{c}_{t-1} + \mathbf{i}_t \circ \mathbf{z}_t, \tag{12}$$

$$\mathbf{o}_t = \sigma(\mathbf{W}_o \mathbf{x}_t + \mathbf{U}_o \mathbf{h}_{t-1} + \mathbf{V}_o \mathbf{c}_t + \mathbf{b}_o), \tag{13}$$

$$\mathbf{h}_t = \mathbf{o}_t \circ \tanh(\mathbf{c}_t). \tag{14}$$

Here, $\mathbf{W}_l \in R^{n \times d}$, $\mathbf{U}_l \in R^{n \times n}$, $\mathbf{V}_l \in R^{n \times n}$, and $\mathbf{b}_l \in R^n$, $l \in \{f, i, z, o\}$ are weight matrixes and bias terms. Tanh and $\sigma$ are the hyperbolic tangent function and sigmoid function. Sign ○ denotes the Hadamard product.

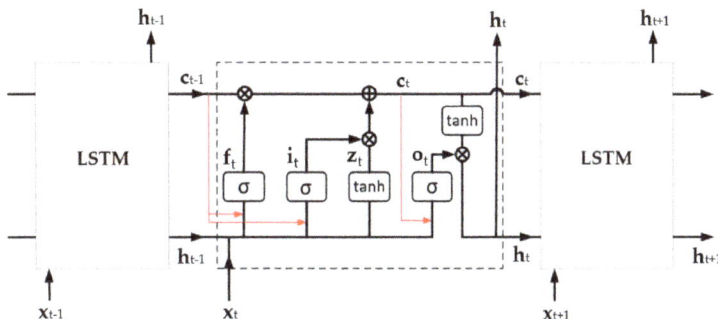

**Figure 2.** Detail of inner structure of LSTM. The peephole connections are depicted with red lines.

In contrast to LSTM, which incorporates past information into DNN, the ability to look into the future is added in bidirectional LSTM architecture (BiLSTM). As the name implies, BiLSTM is composed of forward and backward LSTM layers. The calculation process of layers depends on the way from which direction the input sequence is read.

*4.2. Attention Mechanism*

Incorporation of the attention mechanism (AM) into DNN-based SER systems was often motivated by research in the NLP field [18,91,92] and computer vision [92]. We give a brief explanation of the attention mechanism from the NLP's point of view due to the similarity of the tasks. "Language" attention can be traced back to work related to neural machine translation [21]. Here, the typical encoder–decoder approach was supplemented by the network's ability to soft-search for salient information from a sentence to be translated. The authors used BiRNN/RNN as encoder/decoder, both with the GRU inner structure [93]. The machine translation decoding process can be described as the prediction of the new target word $\mathbf{y}_t$, which is dependent on context vector $\mathbf{c}$ obtained from a current sentence and previously predicted words [93].

$$P(\mathbf{y}_t \mid \mathbf{y}_{<t}, \mathbf{c}) = g(\mathbf{h}_t, \mathbf{y}_{t-1}, \mathbf{c}) \tag{15}$$

Fixed encoding of sentences, which was considered to be a drawback in performance, was substituted by a novel attention mechanism. The main idea behind the attention is to obtain a context vector created as a weighted sum of encoded annotations (18), while attention weights $\mathbf{a}$ are learned by the so-called alignment model (16)—i.e., jointly trained feedforward neural network.

$$e_{kj} = \mathbf{v}_a^T \tanh(\mathbf{W}_a \mathbf{h}_{k-1} + \mathbf{U}_a \mathbf{h}_j) \tag{16}$$

$$\mathbf{a}_{kj} = \frac{\exp(e_{kj})}{\sum_{\tau=1}^{T} \exp(e_{k\tau})} \tag{17}$$

$$\mathbf{c}_k = \sum_{j=1}^{T} \mathbf{a}_{kj} \mathbf{h}_j \tag{18}$$

where $\mathbf{v}_a \in \mathbb{R}^n$, $\mathbf{W}_a \in \mathbb{R}^{n \times n}$, and $\mathbf{U}_a \in \mathbb{R}^{n \times 2n}$ are weight matrices. Assuming two RNNs as the encoder and decoder, the attention weights are obtained by considering hidden states of the encoder $\mathbf{h}_j$ and hidden states of the decoder $\mathbf{h}_{k-1}$ of the last predicted word. A context vector is computed at each time step and the proposed network architecture is trained jointly. Figure 3 shows a general scheme of the described process incorporating AM.

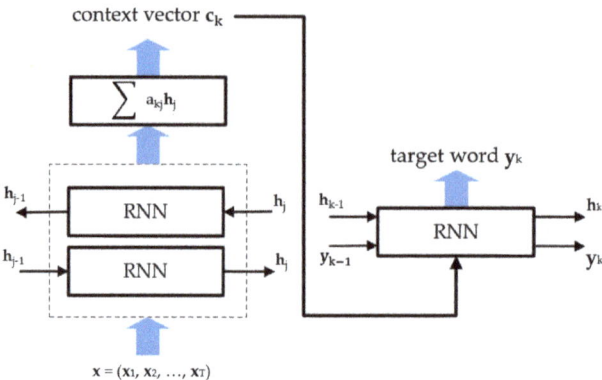

**Figure 3.** Encoder–decoder framework with an attention mechanism.

AM Modifications

As during the last years, numerous AM concepts and variations have been proposed and implemented, several different taxonomies of AM already exist. Different strategies of classification of AM can a reader find e.g., in [94,95]. Here, we point out some of the key works addressing different implementations of AM.

Luong et al. [22] proposed implementing AM globally and locally. Global attention uses whole information from a source sentence. In this case, the context vector was computed as the weighted average of all source hidden states, while attention weights were obtained from the current target hidden state $h_k$ and each source hidden state $h_j$. This approach works on a principle similar to Bahdanau et al. [21], but it differs in simplified computation. Moreover, various alignment functions were examined (see Table 7). As the name implies, *local attention* focuses only on the subset from the source sentence. It is a computationally more efficient method. Context vector takes into account a preselected range of source hidden states with an aligned position corresponding to each target word. Thus, this type of context vector has a fixed length. The aligned position is either at the current target word at time $t$ or can be learned to be predicted. According to results, dot alignment worked well for the global attention and general was better for the local attention. The best performance achieved local attention model with predictive alignments. The machine translation model with the attention mechanism outperformed conventional non-attentional models.

**Table 7.** Computation of different alignment scores.

| | |
|---|---|
| Dot | $h_k^T h_j$ |
| General | $h_k^T W_a h_j$ |
| Concatenation | $v_a^T \tanh(W_a [h_k, h_j])$ |

Lin et al. [96] applied AM on sentiment analysis tasks. This approach allowed the system to perform a standalone search for significant parts of a sentence and thus reducing redundant information. Firstly, BiLSTM encoded words from source sentences into individual hidden states **H** and then the attention weights are computed as an alignment model from **H**. Sentence embedding vector was created as a weighted sum of hidden states. It was not enough to focus only on a certain component of the sentence. Therefore, a concept of multiple hops of attention was proposed, where more such embeddings for different parts of the sentence were created. The sentence embeddings in a form of 2D matrices were then used for sentiment recognition. Moreover, the authors proposed a penalisation technique to ensure that the summation weights cannot be similar.

AM is also a powerful tool for fine-grained aspect-level sentiment classification. Based on the aspect information, the sentiment of the sentence can take on different meanings. Wang et al. [97] firstly proposed an embedding representation of each aspect. Then attention-based LSTM learns the sentiment of a given sentence and is able to focus on important parts by considering a given aspect. Aspect embeddings were incorporated as concatenation to hidden states vectors and attention weights were obtained subsequently. Embeddings could be additionally appended to word vectors as well. In this way, the information from the aspect is preserved in a hidden vector. This novel approach for aspect-level sentiment classification outperformed baseline systems. In [98], the aspect expression from sentences was formed as a weighted summation of aspect embeddings. The number of aspects was preselected and the weights were computed so that context information, as well as aspect expression, were included. An unsupervised objective was applied to improve the training procedure. Another way how to improve the attention model was the inclusion of words, which are in vicinity to the target aspect expression. This method takes advantage of the fact that that context words closer to the target offer complementary clues in sentiment classification. The application of both methods improved results in comparison with various LSTM attention systems.

Chorowski et al. [99] divided encoder–decoder-based attention mechanism into three different categories according to parameters used during the alignment process. Here, the computation of attention weights vector $\mathbf{a}_k$ can be based on location in form of previous attention vector $\mathbf{a}_{k-1}$, current content $\mathbf{H}$, or a combination of both in hybrid AM. Table 8 shows different implementations of AM. Even though hybrid AM seeming to be the best solution for encoder–decoder based speech recognition [99], the decoder part is omitted in SER, and therefore, the AM for SER task is simplified.

**Table 8.** The implementations of the attention mechanisms.

| | |
|---|---|
| Location-based AM | $\mathbf{a}_k = Attend(\mathbf{h}_{k-1}, \mathbf{a}_{k-1})$ |
| Content-based AM | $\mathbf{a}_k = Attend(\mathbf{h}_{k-1}, \mathbf{H})$ |
| Hybrid AM | $\mathbf{a}_k = Attend(\mathbf{h}_{k-1}, \mathbf{a}_{k-1}, \mathbf{H})$ |

*4.3. Attention Mechanism in Speech Emotion Recognition*

This section provides a description of various implementations of AM for speech emotion recognition. As for emotional speech, one label is often used to characterise the whole utterance, although it is clear that the sentence may contain unemotional and silent intervals as well. Therefore, the searching techniques for important parts of emotional speech have been developed.

The first attempts to make the model focus on emotionally salient clues were proposed before the invention of the attention weights. Han et al. considered the speech segments with the highest energy to contain the most prominent emotional information [100]. Lee and Tashev [13] proposed the BiLSTM–ELM system for SER and the importance of each frame is decided using the expectation maximisation algorithm. Moreover, to represent the uncertainty of emotional labels, a speech sample is able to acquire one of two possible states—given emotion and "zero" emotion. The benefit of this system was leveraging RNN's ability to model long contextual information from emotional speech and addressing the uncertainty of emotional labels. The BiLSTM–ELM outperformed the DNN–ELM system, implemented according to [100], with 12% and 5% absolute improvement in UA and WA, respectively.

Most of the attention mechanisms in the SER field are based on the previously described method of attention weights computation using Equations (16) and (17). However, various modifications of AM were proposed, e.g., different input features can be used (feature maps) and simplified computations were developed (the decoder part is omitted for SER systems).

4.3.1. Attentive Deep Recurrent Neural Networks

Huang and Narayanan [101] implemented two types of attention weights: content-based AM (19) inspired by [21,99] and its simplified version (20).

$$a_j = \text{softmax}\left(\mathbf{v}_a^T \sigma_a(\mathbf{W}_a \mathbf{h}_j)\right) \qquad (19)$$

$$a_j = \text{softmax}\left(\mathbf{v}_a^T \mathbf{h}_j\right) \qquad (20)$$

In order to avoid overfitting, the authors proposed separate training of BiLSTM and AM components as well as application of dropout before the summation of hidden vectors. According to the results, the simplified implementation of the attention weights defined by (20) yielded better results. The AM-based system outperforms the non-AM system—an improvement from 57.87% to 59.33% in WA and from 48.54% to 49.96% in UA was observed. Moreover, the authors experimentally proved that the attention selection distribution was not just correlated to the frame energy curve.

In [18], Mirsamadi et al. pointed out the fact that only a few words in the labelled utterance were emotional. They highlighted the importance of considering silence intervals and emotionless parts of the utterance as well. Here, the attention weights were computed using the softmax function on the inner product between trainable attention vector $\mathbf{u}$ and RNN output $\mathbf{y}_t$ at each time step, similarly as (20). In the subsequent step, the weighted average in time was performed, and the softmax layer was applied for final emotion classification. This deep RNN architecture with AM is able to focus on emotionally significant cues and on their temporal variations at the utterance level. The proposed combination of BiLSTM and the novel mean-pooling approach with local attention revealed improved performance over many-to-one training and slightly increased results over the mean-pooling method. With only 32 LLDs, the absolute improvement of 5.7% and 3.1% (in WA and UA) was achieved over the traditional SVM model, which needed additional statistical functions for satisfactory results. Tao and Liu [102] discussed the limitation of the time-dependent RNN model and the proposed advanced LSTM (A–LSTM) for better temporal context modelling. Unlike LSTM, which uses the previous state to compute a new one, A–LSTM makes use of multiple states by combining information from preselected time steps. The weights were learned and applied to the inner states of LSTM. The authors proposed the DNN–BiLSTM model with the learning of multiple tasks—emotion, speaker, and gender classification. Moreover, BiLSTM was followed by an attention-based weighted pooling layer. A relative improvement of 5.5% was achieved with A–LSTM, compared to conventional LSTM. Thus, the time dependency modelling capability of LSTM was improved. The proposed solution did not outperform Mirsamadi attentive RNN [18].

AM was also introduced into the forgetting gate $f_t$ of LSTM cell in [103]. Here, the updating of the cell state (21) is viewed as a weighted sum of the previous cell state $c_{t-1}$ and the current value for update $z_t$.

$$c_t = f_t \circ c_{t-1} + (1 - f_t) \circ z_t \qquad (21)$$

$$f_t = \sigma(\mathbf{W}_f \tanh(\mathbf{V}_f c_{t-1})) \qquad (22)$$

The weights for the cell state updating were obtained by training of the self-attention model (20), with $\mathbf{W}_f \in \mathbb{R}^{n \times n}$ and $\mathbf{V}_f \in \mathbb{R}^{n \times n}$ as trainable parameters. Calculation complexity of the proposed attention gate was reduced by taking into account only the cell state at the previous moment $c_{t-1}$. The ComParE frame-level features were used for classification, while the proposed network had the ability to learn high-level dependencies. The second AM was utilised in the output gate. It was in form of weights applied in both time and feature dimensions. Compared to the traditional LSTM, the obtained results showed an absolute improvement of 2.8%, 13.8%, and 8.5% in UAR for CASIA, eNTERFACE, and GEMEP, respectively. Xie et al. [104] proposed a dense LSTM with attention-based skip connections between the layers. In order to address the variable distribution of significant emotional information in speech, attention weights were incorporated into the LSTMs output in the time dimension. This approach was inspired by the global attention described in [22]. Assuming that different speech features have different abilities to distinguish emotion categories, weighting on feature dimension was also implemented. Results showed that attention applied to the output of each layer improved unweighted average recall and accelerated convergence speed in comparison with the general LSTM approach.

### 4.3.2. Attentive Deep Convolutional Neural Network

Neumann and Vu [86] performed a comparison of different speech features with an attentive CNN architecture. It contains an attention layer based on a linear scoring function. Additionally, the authors applied MTL for both categorical and continuous labels (activation and valence). The results indicated a small difference in performance between MFB, MFCC, and eGeMAP features and a slight improvement of accuracy with the MTL approach. The best results were reported with a combination of MFB features, attentive CNN with MTL learning. Li et al. [92] used two types of convolution filters for extraction of time-specific and frequency-specific features from the spectrograms. Feature extraction was followed by CNN architecture for modelling high-level representation. Inspired by attention-based low-rank second-order pooling proposed for the task of action classification from single RGB images [105], the authors applied this novel pooling method after the last convolutional layer. It was based on a combination of two attention maps—the class-specific top-down and class-agnostic bottom-up attention. The authors reported on the strong emotional representation ability of the proposed architecture. In order to preserve the information from variable length utterance as a whole without the need for segmentation, Zhang et al. [69] designed fully convolutional network (FCN) architecture—adapted AlexNet with removed fully connected layers. The proposed pretrained FCN architecture takes spectrograms of variable length as input without the need for division of utterances or padding to the required length [64,65]. Furthermore, the attention mechanism identifies important parts of spectrograms and ignores nonspeech parts. FCN architecture outperformed the nonattentive CNN–LSTM method proposed in [64] and achieved comparable results with attention-based convolutional RNN [106]. Thus, the proposed FCN architecture is able to capture the temporary context without the need for additional recurrent layers.

### 4.3.3. Attentive Convolutional–Recurrent Deep Neural Network

In many cases, the extraction of large feature sets is replaced by direct learning of emotional speech characteristics by deep CNN architectures. Satt et al. [64] segmented utterances into 3 s intervals firstly. Then, the spectrograms were extracted and were directly fed to the CNN–LSTM architecture. Harmonic modelling was applied on spectrogram to eliminate nonspeech parts of the emotional utterance. This step was particularly useful for the classification of emotion in noisy conditions. Lastly, the attention mechanism was added to the LSTM layer, which did not improve the achieved results. Zhao et al. [107] used two streams for feature extraction—fully convolutional network (FCN) with temporal convolutions and Attention–BiLSTM layers—and concatenated the outputs for further DNN based classification. The results indicated improvements over attention–BiLSTM and Att–CNN [86] architectures. Sarma et al. [20] proposed a raw speech waveform-based end-to-end time delay neural network (TDNN) with LSTM–attention architecture. Accuracy improvement on the IEMOCAP database, as well as reduction of confusion among individual categories, was observed with the use of AM. Huang and Narayanan [55] proposed CLDNN architecture with the convolutional AM. System leveraged task-specific spectral decorrelation of CNN applied on log-mel features and temporal modelling by BiLSTM layers. Main modules were frozen during the training of attention weights. Improved results were achieved with the use of AM under the clean test-set conditions. Chen et al. [106] discussed the negative impact that the personalised features (containing speaker's characteristics, content, etc.) have on the ability of the SER system to generalise well. Assuming that the time derivates of the coefficients (delta features) reduce these undesirable effects, a 3D log-mel spectrogram (consisted of log-mels including delta and delta–delta features) was proposed for the compensation of the personalised features. The authors proposed an attention-based convolutional RNN system (ACRNN) for emotion recognition. When compared with DNN–ELM-based system [100], 3D-ACRNN achieved significant improvement in recognition accuracy on IEMOCAP and EmoDB databases. 3D-ACRNN also outperformed 2D-ACRN based on standalone log-mels. Li et al. [108] proposed an end-to-end self-attentional CNN–BiLSTM model. The attention mechanism based on the same procedure as in [96] concentrates on salient parts of speech. Additionally, the gender recognition task was added to improve emotion recognition in a multitask learning manner. As the gender of the speaker affects the emotional speech, these variations can be taken advantage of. The state-of-the-art results were reported with increased overall accuracy on the IEMOCAP database. Dangol et al. [109] proposed an emotion recognition system based on 3D CNN–LSTM with a relation-aware AM that integrates pairwise relationships between input elements. The 3D spectrogram representations provided both spectral and temporal information from the speech samples. In order to increase the accuracy of emotion recognition, the computation process of attention weights was modified and the synthetic individual evaluation oversampling technique was used to update the feature maps.

In [110], the authors used prosodic characteristics with a fusion of three classifiers working at the syllable, utterance, and frame levels. They used a combination of methods such as the mechanism of attention and the feature selection based on RFE. System performance was improved by identification of relevant features, incorporating attention and score-level fusion. Zheng et al. [111] performed ensemble learning by the integration of three models/experts, each focusing on different feature extraction and classification tactics. Expert 1 is a two-channel CNN model that effectively learns time- and frequency-domain features. Expert 2 is GRU with AM that learns short-term speech characteristics from the principal component analysis (PCA) processed spectrograms with a further fusion of mean value features of the spectrograms. Expert 3 performs end-to-end multilevel emotion recognition using BiLSMT with attention mechanism with a combination of local (CRNN model learning from speech spectrum) and global features (HSFs). Each expert accessed emotional speech in a different way and their combination reduced the negative effects of data imbalance and results in better generalization ability.

For better clarity, the AM-based SER systems are also summarised in Table 9.

**Table 9.** Comparison of SER systems with an attention mechanism. Meaning of acronyms: A—anger, E—excitement, $F_r$—frustration, H—happiness, N—neutral, S—sadness; A/V—activation/valence.

| References | Techniques of Audio Parametrisation | Proposed Machine Learning Method | Database (Emotions) |
|---|---|---|---|
| IEMOCAP | | | |
| Huang and Narayanan [101]; 2016 | 28 LLDs: 13 MFCC, F0, Δ | BiLSTM | A, H, N, S |
| Mirsamadi et al. [18]; 2017 | F0, voice probab., frame energy, ZCR, 12 MFCC, Δ | BiLSTM—weighted-pooling with local attention | A, H, N, S |
| Neumann and Vu [86]; 2017 | Max. length of the utterance: 7.5 s MFB (26) | Attentive CNN with MTL | A, E + H, N, S A–V |
| Tao and Liu [102]; 2018 | 13 MFCC, ZCR, energy, entropy of energy, spectral characteristics, 12 D chroma, chroma dev., HR, pitch | DNN–BiLSTM–MTL with Advanced LSTM | A, H, N, S |
| Zhao et al. [107]; 2018 | 743 features + PCA | Att–BiLSTM–FCN | A, E + H, N, S |

Table 9. Cont.

| References | Techniques of Audio Parametrisation | Proposed Machine Learning Method | Database (Emotions) |
|---|---|---|---|
| Sarma et al. [20]; 2018 | Raw waveform front end | TDNN–LSTM–attention | A, H, N, S |
| Chen et al. [106]; 2018 | 3D Log-mel spectrograms | Attention-based convolutional RNN (ACRNN) | A, H, N, S |
| Li et al. [92]; 2018 | Spectrogram (2 s segments with 1 s overlap) | CNN–TF–Att.pooling | A, H, N, S |
| Xie et al. [104]; 2019 | The ComParE frame-level features | LSTM with skipped connections | A, E, $F_r$, N, S |
| Zhang et al. [69]; 2019 | Spectrogram (variable utterance length) | Fully convolutional network + attention layer | A, H, N, S |
| Li et al. [108]; 2019 | Mel spectrogram + Δ, ΔΔ (max. length of the utterances: 7.5 s) | CNN–BiLSTM–MTL: + Attention mechanism | A, E + H, N, S |
| Alex et al. [110]; 2020 | Prosodic and spectral features extracted at various levels + RFE | Fusion of three separate DNNs + Attention at the syllable-level | A, E + H, N, S |
| Zheng et al. [111]; 2020 | (1) Spectrogram (2) Spectrogram + PCA (3) LLDs and their HSFs; spectrogram and CRNN with attention m. | Ensemble model: (1) two-channel CNN (2) GRU with attention m. (3) BiLSTM with attention m. | A, E + H, N, S |
| Dangol et al. [109]; 2020 | Silence/noise removal 3D Log-mel spectrograms | Relation-aware attention-based 3D CNN–LSTM | A, H, N, S |
| Other databases | | | |
| Huang and Narayanan [55]; 2017 | MFB | CLDNN with convolutional attention mechanism | eNTERFACE'05 |
| Chen et al. [106]; 2018 | 3D Log-mel spectrograms | Attention-based convolutional RNN (ACRNN) | EmoDB full data set |
| Xie et al. [103]; 2019 | The ComParE frame-level features (openSMILE) | LSTM with attention gate and time/frequency attention | CASIA, (6) eNTERFACE (6) GEMEP (12) |
| Xie et al. [104]; 2019 | The ComParE frame-level features (openSMILE) | LSTM with skipped connections | eNTERFACE (6) |
| Dangol et al. [109]; 2020 | Silence/noise removal 3D Log-mel spectrograms | Relation-aware attention-based 3D CNN and LSTM | EmoDB SAVEE |

## 5. Impact of Attention Mechanism on SER

We performed a comparison of related works based on the most common settings to study the impact of AM on speech emotion recognition. We applied the same methodology as in Section 3.7. Since IEMOCAP is the most commonly used database in the published works, we chose it for further analysis.

Tables 10 and 11 show the comparison of SER systems on IEMOCAP for two kinds of classes of emotions: (1) anger, happiness, neutral and sad and (2) an extension of the 'excitement' class. As previously explained, it is not possible to make an exact comparison of the systems due to different test conditions, even if the same dataset was used. Thus, the reported accuracies listed in Tables 10 and 11 provide only coarse information in terms of their performance comparison.

Table 10. Comparison of system accuracies on IEMOCAP database for four emotions. Meaning of acronyms: AM—attention mechanism, A—anger, H—happiness, N—neutral, S—sadness.

| References | AM | Description of System | Emotions | WA | UA |
|---|---|---|---|---|---|
| | | Recurrent architectures | | | |
| [101]; 2016 | √ | 28 LLDs<br>BiLSTM | A, H, N, S | 59.33% | 49.96% |
| [18]; 2017 | √ | 32 LLDs<br>BiLSTM—with local AM | A, H, N, S | 63.5% | 58.8% |
| [17]; 2017 | × | Statistical features over 3 s segments and LSTM | A, H, N, S | 64.16% | 60.02% |
| [102]; 2018 | √ | LLDs<br>Advanced LSTM | A, H, N, S | 55.3% | – |
| | | Convolutional architectures | | | |
| [92]; 2018 | √ | Spectrograms<br>CNN–TF–Att.pooling | A, H, N, S (improvised) | 71.75% | 68.06% |
| [4]; 2018 | × | Phoneme embedding and spectrogram<br>Two CNN channels | A, H, N, S (improvised) | 73.9% | 68.5% |
| [69]; 2019 | √ | Spectrogram and FCN<br>+ attention layer | A, H, N, S (improvised) | 70.4% | 63.9% |
| [16]; 2019 | × | Magnitude spectrograms<br>Residual Adapter on VoxCeleb2 | A, H, N, S (improvised) | 72.73% | 67.58% |
| | | Combination of CNN and RNN | | | |
| [64]; 2017 | × | Spectrograms<br>CNN–BiLSTM | A, H, N, S (improvised) | 68.8% | 59.4% |
| [20]; 2018 | √ | Raw waveform front end<br>TDNN–LSTM–attention | A, H, N, S | 70.1% | 60.7% |
| [65]; 2018 | × | Spectrograms<br>CNN–BiGRU | A, H, N, S (improvised) | 71.45% | 64.22% |
| [106]; 2018 | √ | 3Dlog-mel spec.;<br>Att.–CRNN | A, H, S, N (improvised) | – | 64.74% |
| [88]; 2019 | × | Spectrograms<br>CNN–GRU–SeqCap | A, H, N, S | 72.73% | 59.71% |
| | | Hybrid systems | | | |
| [13]; 2015 | × | Segment-level features<br>DNN–ELM | A, H, N, S (improvised) | 52.13% | 57.91% |
| [13]; 2015 | × | 32 LLDs<br>BiLSTM–ELM | A, H, N, S (improvised) | 62.85% | 63.89% |
| [10]; 2017 | × | DBN–MTL feat. Extract.<br>SVM classifier | A, H, N, S | 60.9% | 62.4% |

Table 11. Comparison of system accuracies on IEMOCAP database for additional combination of excitement and happiness. Meaning of acronyms: AM—attention mechanism, A—anger, E—excitement, H—happiness, N—neutral, S—sadness.

| References | AM | Description of System | Emotions | WA | UA |
|---|---|---|---|---|---|
| | | Convolutional architectures | | | |
| [86]; 2017 | √ | MFB; Attentive CNN with MTL | A, E + H, N, S<br>A–V | 56.10% | – |
| [14]; 2017 | × | MFB and CNN | A, E + H, N, S | – | 61.8% |

Table 11. *Cont.*

| References | AM | Description of System | Emotions | WA | UA |
|---|---|---|---|---|---|
| [15]; 2017 | × | Log-mel spectrogram ConvNet | A, E + H, N, S | 64.78% | 60.89% |
| [77]; 2019 | × | Mel-scaled spectrograms Augment. With GAN CNN(VGG19) | A, E + H, N, S | – | 53.6% |
| Combination of CNN and RNN | | | | | |
| [107]; 2018 | √ | 743 features + PCA Att–BiLSTM–FCN | A, E + H, N, S | 59.7% | 60.1% |
| [108]; 2019 | √ | Log-mel spectrograms, Δ, ΔΔ; CNN–BiLSTM with MTL | A, E + H, N, S | 81.6% | 82.8% |
| Hybrid systems and ensemble models | | | | | |
| [60]; 2017 | × | ConvLSTM feature extractor | SVM | 65.13% | – |
| [63]; 2018 | × | HSFs–DNN Log-mel spec.-CRNN | A, E + H, N, S | 60.35% | 63.98% |
| [76]; 2018 | × | 1582-dimensional openSMILE feature space Augment. With GAN | SVM | – | 60.29% |
| [111]; 2020 | √ | Ensemble model | A, E + H, N, S | 75% | 75% |

The following conclusions, in particular, can be drawn from the works under study:

- AM has improved over the last years and a growing trend of AM use can be observed. Certainly, the performance improvement when using AM is evidenced by many research studies on SER [18,20,69,92,102–104,107,108,111]. On the other hand, two works [63,68] did not report improvements when using AM. Learning the attention weights for emotional representations of speech seems to be a reasonable way to address the variability of emotional clues across utterance; however, we have to note that the resulting benefit in terms of accuracy increment is not always so obvious. As seen from Tables 10 and 11, the properly configured systems without AM may outperform the systems with AM (although one may argue about the correctness of such judgment due to different testing conditions among published works). The reason for ambiguity might be that AM-based SER system performance is subject to implementation issues as follows:
  - The implementation of appropriate AM can be linked to various factors such as the derivation of accurate context information from speech utterances. As in NLP, the better the contextual information obtained from the sequence, the better the performance of the system. The duration of divided segments significantly influences the accuracy of emotion recognition [20,63,86]. Therefore, appropriate input sequence lengths must be determined in order to effectively capture the emotional context.
  - Proper representation of emotional speech is also an important part of deriving contextual information. RNN is suitable for modelling long sequences. Extraction of higher-level statistical functions from multiple LLDs over speech segments with a combination of LSTM [18] can be compared to 32 LLDs with BiLSTM and local AM [18]. Transfer learning is a suitable solution particularly for small emotional datasets [16]. However, more works should be considered to make conclusions. End-to-end systems that combined CNN as feature extractor and RNN for modelling of the long-term contextual dependencies achieved high performance on IEMOCAP data and on EmoDB [62,106]. Various combinations of RNN and CNN are able to outperform separate systems [62,107]. The two-channel CNN taking phoneme embeddings and spectrograms on input seem to further improve the accuracy [4]. Thus, it can be beneficial to allow the model

to learn different kinds of features. Moreover, leveraging multitask Learning for both the discrete and continuous recognition tasks improves the accuracy of SER systems [10,112]. CRNN architecture together with multitask learning was a part of the state-of-the-art solution on IEMOCAP proposed in [108]. Here, AM clearly improved system performance.

- Recurrent networks provide temporal representation for the whole utterance and better results are obtained with its aggregation by pooling for further recognition [18,20]. Several works compare different pooling strategies. The attention pooling is able to outperform global max pooling and global average pooling (GAP) [18,102,107]. The same was true for the attention pooling strategy for convolutional feature maps in [92] (attention-based pooling outperformed GAP). It can be concluded that learning of the attention weights indeed allows the model to adapt itself to changes in emotional speech.

## 6. Conclusions

This study provides a survey on speech emotion recognition systems from very recent years. The aim of the SER research can be summarised as the search for innovative ways how to appropriately extract emotional context from speech. We can observe a trend in the use of deep convolutional architectures that can learn from spectrogram representations of utterances. Together with recurrent networks, they are considered as a strong base for SER systems. Throughout the years, more complex SER architectures were developed with an emphasis on deriving emotionally salient local and global contexts. As can be inferred from our study, the attention mechanism can improve the performance of the SER systems; however, its benefit is not always evident. Although AM modules have become a natural part of today's SER systems, AM is not an indispensable element for the achievement of high accuracies or even state-of-the-art results.

**Author Contributions:** Conceptualisation, E.L., R.J. and M.J.; methodology, E.L. and M.J.; writing—original draft preparation, E.L. and M.J.; writing—review and editing, R.J. and M.C.; supervision, R.J. All authors have read and agreed to the published version of the manuscript.

**Funding:** This research received no external funding.

**Conflicts of Interest:** The authors declare no conflict of interest.

**Abbreviations and Acronyms**

| Abbreviation | Meaning |
| --- | --- |
| AM | Attention Mechanism |
| BiGRU | Bidirectional Gated Recurrent Unit |
| BiLSTM | Bidirectional Long Short-Term Memory |
| CCC | Concordance Correlation Coefficient |
| CLDNN | Convolutional Long Short-Term Memory Deep Neural Network |
| CNN | Convolutional Neural Network |
| DANN | Domain Adversarial Neural Network |
| DBN | Deep Belief Network |
| DCNN | Deep Convolutional Neural Network |
| DNN | Deep Neural Networks |
| DSCNN | Deep Stride Convolutional Neural Network |
| DTPM | Discriminant Temporal Pyramid Matching |
| ECG | Electro-Cardiogram |
| EDA | Electro-Dermal Activity |
| ELM | Extreme Learning Machine |
| FC | Fully Connected layer |
| FCN | Fully Convolutional Network |
| FS | Feature Selection |

| | |
|---|---|
| GAN | Generative Adversarial Network |
| GeWEC | Geneva Whispered Emotion Corpus |
| GRU | Gated Recurrent Unit |
| HMM | Hidden Markov Model |
| HSF | High-Level Statistical Functions |
| LSTM | Long Short-Term Memory |
| MFB | Log-Mel Filter-Bank |
| MFCCs | Mel-Frequency Cepstral Coefficients |
| MTL | Multitask Learning |
| NLP | Natural Language Processing |
| NN | Neural Network |
| PCA | Principal Component Analysis |
| ResNet | Residual Neural Network |
| RFE | Recursive Feature Elimination |
| RNN | Recurrent Neural Network |
| SER | Speech Emotion Recognition |
| STFT | Short Time Fourier Transform |
| SVM | Support Vector Machine |
| WoS | Web of Science |

## References

1. Burkhardt, F.; Ajmera, J.; Englert, R.; Stegmann, J.; Burleson, W. Detecting anger in automated voice portal dialogs. In Proceedings of the Ninth International Conference on Spoken Language Processing, Pittsburgh, PA, USA, 17–21 September 2006.
2. Hossain, M.S.; Muhammad, G.; Song, B.; Hassan, M.M.; Alelaiwi, A.; Alamri, A. Audio–Visual Emotion-Aware Cloud Gaming Framework. *IEEE Trans. Circuits Syst. Video Technol.* **2015**, *25*, 2105–2118. [CrossRef]
3. Oh, K.; Lee, D.; Ko, B.; Choi, H. A Chatbot for Psychiatric Counseling in Mental Healthcare Service Based on Emotional Dialogue Analysis and Sentence Generation. In Proceedings of the 2017 18th IEEE International Conference on Mobile Data Management (MDM), Daejeon, Korea, 29 May–1 June 2017; pp. 371–375.
4. Yenigalla, P.; Kumar, A.; Tripathi, S.; Singh, C.; Kar, S.; Vepa, J. Speech Emotion Recognition Using Spectrogram & Phoneme Embedding. In Proceedings of the INTERSPEECH, Hyderabad, India, 2–6 September 2018.
5. Deriche, M.; Abo absa, A.H. A Two-Stage Hierarchical Bilingual Emotion Recognition System Using a Hidden Markov Model and Neural Networks. *Arab. J. Sci. Eng.* **2017**, *42*, 5231–5249. [CrossRef]
6. Pravena, D.; Govind, D. Significance of incorporating excitation source parameters for improved emotion recognition from speech and electroglottographic signals. *Int. J. Speech Technol.* **2017**, *20*, 787–797. [CrossRef]
7. Bandela, S.R.; Kumar, T.K. Stressed speech emotion recognition using feature fusion of teager energy operator and MFCC. In Proceedings of the 2017 8th International Conference on Computing, Communication and Networking Technologies (ICCCNT), Delhi, India, 3–5 July 2017; pp. 1–5.
8. Koolagudi, S.G.; Murthy, Y.V.S.; Bhaskar, S.P. Choice of a classifier, based on properties of a dataset: Case study-speech emotion recognition. *Int. J. Speech Technol.* **2018**, *21*, 167–183. [CrossRef]
9. New, T.L.; Foo, S.W.; Silva, L.C.D. Classification of stress in speech using linear and nonlinear features. In Proceedings of the 2003 IEEE International Conference on Acoustics, Speech, and Signal Processing, 2003 Proceedings (ICASSP '03), Hong Kong, China, 6–10 April 2003; Volume 2, p. II-9.
10. Xia, R.; Liu, Y. A Multi-Task Learning Framework for Emotion Recognition Using 2D Continuous Space. *IEEE Trans. Affect. Comput.* **2017**, *8*, 3–14. [CrossRef]
11. Zhang, S.; Zhang, S.; Huang, T.; Gao, W. Speech Emotion Recognition Using Deep Convolutional Neural Network and Discriminant Temporal Pyramid Matching. *IEEE Trans. Multimed.* **2018**, *20*, 1576–1590. [CrossRef]
12. Cummins, N.; Amiriparian, S.; Hagerer, G.; Batliner, A.; Steidl, S.; Schuller, B.W. An Image-based Deep Spectrum Feature Representation for the Recognition of Emotional Speech. In *Proceedings of the 25th ACM International Conference on Multimedia*; Association for Computing Machinery: New York, NY, USA, 2017; pp. 478–484.
13. Lee, J.; Tashev, I. High-level feature representation using recurrent neural network for speech emotion recognition. In Proceedings of the INTERSPEECH, Dresden, Germany, 6–10 September 2015.
14. Aldeneh, Z.; Provost, E.M. Using regional saliency for speech emotion recognition. In Proceedings of the 2017 IEEE International Conference on Acoustics, Speech and Signal Processing (ICASSP), New Orleans, LA, USA, 5–9 March 2017; pp. 2741–2745.
15. Fayek, H.M.; Lech, M.; Cavedon, L. Evaluating deep learning architectures for Speech Emotion Recognition. *Neural Netw.* **2017**, *92*, 60–68. [CrossRef]
16. Xi, Y.; Li, P.; Song, Y.; Jiang, Y.; Dai, L. Speaker to Emotion: Domain Adaptation for Speech Emotion Recognition with Residual Adapters. In Proceedings of the 2019 Asia-Pacific Signal and Information Processing Association Annual Summit and Conference (APSIPA ASC), Lanzhou, China, 18–21 November 2019; pp. 513–518.

17. Tzinis, E.; Potamianos, A. Segment-based speech emotion recognition using recurrent neural networks. In Proceedings of the 2017 Seventh International Conference on Affective Computing and Intelligent Interaction (ACII), San Antonio, TX, USA, 23–26 October 2017; pp. 190–195.
18. Mirsamadi, S.; Barsoum, E.; Zhang, C. Automatic speech emotion recognition using recurrent neural networks with local attention. In Proceedings of the 2017 IEEE International Conference on Acoustics, Speech and Signal Processing (ICASSP), New Orleans, LA, USA, 5–9 March 2017; pp. 2227–2231.
19. Trigeorgis, G.; Ringeval, F.; Brueckner, R.; Marchi, E.; Nicolaou, M.A.; Schuller, B.; Zafeiriou, S. Adieu features? End-to-end speech emotion recognition using a deep convolutional recurrent network. In Proceedings of the 2016 IEEE International Conference on Acoustics, Speech and Signal Processing (ICASSP), Shanghai, China, 20–25 March 2016; pp. 5200–5204.
20. Sarma, M.; Ghahremani, P.; Povey, D.; Goel, N.K.; Sarma, K.K.; Dehak, N. Emotion Identification from Raw Speech Signals Using DNNs. In Proceedings of the Interspeech 2018, Hyderabad, India, 2–6 September 2018; pp. 3097–3101.
21. Bahdanau, D.; Cho, K.; Bengio, Y. Neural Machine Translation by Jointly Learning to Align and Translate. *arXiv* **2014**, arXiv:1409.0473.
22. Luong, T.; Pham, H.; Manning, C.D. Effective Approaches to Attention-based Neural Machine Translation. In Proceedings of the 2015 Conference on Empirical Methods in Natural Language Processing, Lisbon, Portugal, 17–21 September 2015; Association for Computational Linguistics: Lisbon, Portugal, 2015; pp. 1412–1421.
23. El Ayadi, M.; Kamel, M.S.; Karray, F. Survey on speech emotion recognition: Features, classification schemes, and databases. *Pattern Recognit.* **2011**, *44*, 572–587. [CrossRef]
24. Anagnostopoulos, C.-N.; Iliou, T.; Giannoukos, I. Features and classifiers for emotion recognition from speech: A survey from 2000 to 2011. *Artif. Intell. Rev.* **2015**, *43*, 155–177. [CrossRef]
25. Swain, M.; Routray, A.; Kabisatpathy, P. Databases, features and classifiers for speech emotion recognition: A review. *Int. J. Speech Technol.* **2018**, *21*, 93–120. [CrossRef]
26. Schuller, B.W. Speech emotion recognition: Two decades in a nutshell, benchmarks, and ongoing trends. *Commun. ACM* **2018**, *61*, 90–99. [CrossRef]
27. Sailunaz, K.; Dhaliwal, M.; Rokne, J.; Alhajj, R. Emotion detection from text and speech: A survey. *Soc. Netw. Anal. Min.* **2018**, *8*, 28. [CrossRef]
28. Khalil, R.A.; Jones, E.; Babar, M.I.; Jan, T.; Zafar, M.H.; Alhussain, T. Speech Emotion Recognition Using Deep Learning Techniques: A Review. *IEEE Access* **2019**, *7*, 117327–117345. [CrossRef]
29. Akçay, M.B.; Oğuz, K. Speech emotion recognition: Emotional models, databases, features, preprocessing methods, supporting modalities, and classifiers. *Speech Commun.* **2020**, *116*, 56–76. [CrossRef]
30. Kamińska, D.; Sapiński, T.; Anbarjafari, G. Efficiency of chosen speech descriptors in relation to emotion recognition. *EURASIP J. Audio Speech Music Process.* **2017**, *2017*, 3. [CrossRef]
31. Bakker, I.; van der Voordt, T.; Vink, P.; de Boon, J. Pleasure, Arousal, Dominance: Mehrabian and Russell revisited. *Curr. Psychol.* **2014**, *33*, 405–421. [CrossRef]
32. Truong, K.P.; Van Leeuwen, D.A.; De Jong, F.M. Speech-based recognition of self-reported and observed emotion in a dimensional space. *Speech Commun.* **2012**, *54*, 1049–1063. [CrossRef]
33. Vryzas, N.; Kotsakis, R.; Liatsou, A.; Dimoulas, C.A.; Kalliris, G. Speech Emotion Recognition for Performance Interaction. *J. Audio Eng. Soc.* **2018**, *66*, 457–467. [CrossRef]
34. Burkhardt, F.; Paeschke, A.; Rolfes, M.; Sendlmeier, W.; Weiss, B. A database of German emotional speech. In Proceedings of the Ninth European Conference on Speech Communication and Technology, Lisbon, Portugal, 4–8 September 2005; Volumn 5, pp. 1517–1520.
35. Martin, O.; Kotsia, I.; Macq, B.; Pitas, I. The eNTERFACE' 05 Audio-Visual Emotion Database. In Proceedings of the 22nd International Conference on Data Engineering Workshops (ICDEW'06), Atlanta, GA, USA, 3–7 April 2006; p. 8.
36. Steidl, S. *Automatic Classification of Emotion Related User States in Spontaneous Children's Speech*; Logos-Verlag: Berlin, Germany, 2009.
37. Busso, C.; Bulut, M.; Lee, C.-C.; Kazemzadeh, A.; Mower, E.; Kim, S.; Chang, J.N.; Lee, S.; Narayanan, S.S. IEMOCAP: Interactive emotional dyadic motion capture database. *Lang. Resour. Eval.* **2008**, *42*, 335. [CrossRef]
38. Lotfian, R.; Busso, C. Building Naturalistic Emotionally Balanced Speech Corpus by Retrieving Emotional Speech from Existing Podcast Recordings. *IEEE Trans. Affect. Comput.* **2019**, *10*, 471–483. [CrossRef]
39. Kamińska, D.; Sapiński, T. Polish Emotional Speech Recognition Based on the Committee of Classifiers. *Przegląd Elektrotechniczny* **2017**, *2016*, 101–106. [CrossRef]
40. Livingstone, S.R.; Russo, F.A. The Ryerson Audio-Visual Database of Emotional Speech and Song (RAVDESS): A dynamic, multimodal set of facial and vocal expressions in North American English. *PLoS ONE* **2018**, *13*, e0196391. [CrossRef]
41. Ringeval, F.; Sonderegger, A.; Sauer, J.S.; Lalanne, D. Introducing the RECOLA multimodal corpus of remote collaborative and affective interactions. In Proceedings of the 2013 10th IEEE International Conference and Workshops on Automatic Face and Gesture Recognition (FG), Shanghai, China, 22–26 April 2013. [CrossRef]
42. Haq, S.; Jackson, P. Speaker-dependent audio-visual emotion recognition. In Proceedings of the AVSP, Norwich, UK, 10–13 September 2009.

43. Ringeval, F.; Schuller, B.; Valstar, M.; Jaiswal, S.; Marchi, E.; Lalanne, D.; Cowie, R.; Pantic, M. AV + EC 2015—the first affect recognition challenge bridging across audio, video, and physiological data. In Proceedings of the 5th International Workshop on Audio/Visual Emotion Challenge, Brisbane, Australia, 26–30 October 2015.
44. Ntalampiras, S.; Fakotakis, N. Modeling the Temporal Evolution of Acoustic Parameters for Speech Emotion Recognition. *IEEE Trans. Affect. Comput.* **2012**, *3*, 116–125. [CrossRef]
45. Liu, G.K. Evaluating Gammatone Frequency Cepstral Coefficients with Neural Networks for Emotion Recognition from Speech. *arXiv* **2018**, arXiv:1806.09010.
46. Fahad, M.S.; Deepak, A.; Pradhan, G.; Yadav, J. DNN-HMM-Based Speaker-Adaptive Emotion Recognition Using MFCC and Epoch-Based Features. *Circuits Syst. Signal Process.* **2021**, *40*, 466–489. [CrossRef]
47. Kerkeni, L.; Serrestou, Y.; Raoof, K.; Mbarki, M.; Mahjoub, M.A.; Cleder, C. Automatic speech emotion recognition using an optimal combination of features based on EMD-TKEO. *Speech Commun.* **2019**, *114*, 22–35. [CrossRef]
48. YogeshC, K.; Hariharan, M.; Ngadiran, R.; Adom, A.H.; Yaacob, S.; Berkai, C.; Polat, K. A new hybrid PSO assisted biogeography-based optimization for emotion and stress recognition from speech signal. *Expert Syst. Appl.* **2017**, *69*, 149–158. [CrossRef]
49. Liu, Z.-T.; Wu, M.; Cao, W.-H.; Mao, J.-W.; Xu, J.-P.; Tan, G.-Z. Speech emotion recognition based on feature selection and extreme learning machine decision tree. *Neurocomputing* **2018**, *273*, 271–280. [CrossRef]
50. Chen, L.; Mao, X.; Xue, Y.; Cheng, L.L. Speech emotion recognition: Features and classification models. *Digit. Signal Process.* **2012**, *22*, 1154–1160. [CrossRef]
51. Schuller, B.; Steidl, S.; Batliner, A. The Interspeech 2009 Emotion Challenge. In Proceedings of the 10th Annual Conference of the International Speech Communication Association, Brighton, UK, 6–10 September 2009; pp. 312–315.
52. Schuller, B.; Steidl, S.; Batliner, A.; Burkhardt, F.; Devillers, L.; Müller, C.; Narayanan, S. The INTERSPEECH 2010 paralinguistic challenge. In Proceedings of the 11th Annual Conference of the International Speech Communication Association, Makuhari, Chiba, Japan, 26–30 September 2010; pp. 2794–2797.
53. Eyben, F.; Scherer, K.R.; Schuller, B.W.; Sundberg, J.; André, E.; Busso, C.; Devillers, L.Y.; Epps, J.; Laukka, P.; Narayanan, S.S.; et al. The Geneva Minimalistic Acoustic Parameter Set (GeMAPS) for Voice Research and Affective Computing. *IEEE Trans. Affect. Comput.* **2016**, *7*, 190–202. [CrossRef]
54. Weninger, F.; Eyben, F.; Schuller, B.W.; Mortillaro, M.; Scherer, K.R. On the Acoustics of Emotion in Audio: What Speech, Music, and Sound have in Common. *Front. Psychol.* **2013**, *4*, 292. [CrossRef] [PubMed]
55. Huang, C.; Narayanan, S.S. Deep convolutional recurrent neural network with attention mechanism for robust speech emotion recognition. In Proceedings of the 2017 IEEE International Conference on Multimedia and Expo (ICME), Hong Kong, China, 10–14 July 2017; pp. 583–588.
56. Badshah, A.M.; Ahmad, J.; Rahim, N.; Baik, S.W. Speech Emotion Recognition from Spectrograms with Deep Convolutional Neural Network. In Proceedings of the 2017 International Conference on Platform Technology and Service (PlatCon), Busan, Korea, 13–15 February 2017; pp. 1–5.
57. Vrysis, L.; Tsipas, N.; Thoidis, I.; Dimoulas, C. 1D/2D Deep CNNs vs. Temporal Feature Integration for General Audio Classification. *J. Audio Eng. Soc.* **2020**, *68*, 66–77. [CrossRef]
58. Hajarolasvadi, N.; Demirel, H. 3D CNN-Based Speech Emotion Recognition Using K-Means Clustering and Spectrograms. *Entropy* **2019**, *21*, 479. [CrossRef]
59. Mustaqeem; Kwon, S. A CNN-assisted enhanced audio signal processing for speech emotion recognition. *Sensors* **2020**, *20*, 183. [CrossRef]
60. Kurpukdee, N.; Koriyama, T.; Kobayashi, T.; Kasuriya, S.; Wutiwiwatchai, C.; Lamsrichan, P. Speech emotion recognition using convolutional long short-term memory neural network and support vector machines. In Proceedings of the 2017 Asia-Pacific Signal and Information Processing Association Annual Summit and Conference (APSIPA ASC), Kuala Lumpur, Malaysia, 12–15 December 2017; pp. 1744–1749.
61. Lim, W.; Jang, D.; Lee, T. Speech emotion recognition using convolutional and Recurrent Neural Networks. In Proceedings of the 2016 Asia-Pacific Signal and Information Processing Association Annual Summit and Conference (APSIPA), Jeju, Korea, 13–16 December 2016; pp. 1–4.
62. Zhao, J.; Mao, X.; Chen, L. Speech emotion recognition using deep 1D & 2D CNN LSTM networks. *Biomed. Signal Process. Control* **2019**, *47*, 312–323. [CrossRef]
63. Luo, D.; Zou, Y.; Huang, D. Investigation on Joint Representation Learning for Robust Feature Extraction in Speech Emotion Recognition. In Proceedings of the Interspeech 2018, Hyderabad, India, 2–6 September 2018; pp. 152–156.
64. Satt, A.; Rozenberg, S.; Hoory, R. Efficient Emotion Recognition from Speech Using Deep Learning on Spectrograms. In Proceedings of the INTERSPEECH, Stockholm, Sweden, 20–24 August 2017.
65. Ma, X.; Wu, Z.; Jia, J.; Xu, M.; Meng, H.; Cai, L. Emotion Recognition from Variable-Length Speech Segments Using Deep Learning on Spectrograms. In Proceedings of the Interspeech 2018, Hyderabad, India, 2–6 September 2018; pp. 3683–3687.
66. Khorram, S.; Aldeneh, Z.; Dimitriadis, D.; McInnis, M.; Provost, E.M. Capturing Long-term Temporal Dependencies with Convolutional Networks for Continuous Emotion Recognition. *arXiv* **2017**, arXiv:1708.07050. Cs.
67. Tzirakis, P.; Zhang, J.; Schuller, B.W. End-to-End Speech Emotion Recognition Using Deep Neural Networks. In Proceedings of the 2018 IEEE International Conference on Acoustics, Speech and Signal Processing (ICASSP), Calgary, AB, Canada, 15–20 April 2018; pp. 5089–5093.

68. AlBadawy, E.A.; Kim, Y. Joint Discrete and Continuous Emotion Prediction Using Ensemble and End-to-End Approaches. In Proceedings of the 20th ACM International Conference on Multimodal Interaction, Boulder, CO, USA, 16–20 October 2018; Association for Computing Machinery: New York, NY, USA, 2018; pp. 366–375.
69. Zhang, Y.; Du, J.; Wang, Z.; Zhang, J.; Tu, Y. Attention Based Fully Convolutional Network for Speech Emotion Recognition. In Proceedings of the 2018 Asia-Pacific Signal and Information Processing Association Annual Summit and Conference (APSIPA ASC), Honolulu, HI, USA, 12–15 November 2018; pp. 1771–1775.
70. Krizhevsky, A.; Sutskever, I.; Hinton, G.E. ImageNet Classification with Deep Convolutional Neural Networks. *Adv. Neural Inf. Process. Syst.* **2012**, *25*, 1097–1105. [CrossRef]
71. Salamon, J.; Bello, J.P. Deep Convolutional Neural Networks and Data Augmentation for Environmental Sound Classification. *IEEE Signal Process. Lett.* **2017**, *24*, 279–283. [CrossRef]
72. Tamulevičius, G.; Korvel, G.; Yayak, A.B.; Treigys, P.; Bernatavičienė, J.; Kostek, B. A Study of Cross-Linguistic Speech Emotion Recognition Based on 2D Feature Spaces. *Electronics* **2020**, *9*, 1725. [CrossRef]
73. Etienne, C.; Fidanza, G.; Petrovskii, A.; Devillers, L.; Schmauch, B. CNN+LSTM Architecture for Speech Emotion Recognition with Data Augmentation. *arXiv* **2018**, arXiv:1802.05630, 21–25.
74. Vryzas, N.; Vrysis, L.; Matsiola, M.; Kotsakis, R.; Dimoulas, C.; Kalliris, G. Continuous Speech Emotion Recognition with Convolutional Neural Networks. *J. Audio Eng. Soc.* **2020**, *68*, 14–24. [CrossRef]
75. Goodfellow, I.J.; Pouget-Abadie, J.; Mirza, M.; Xu, B.; Warde-Farley, D.; Ozair, S.; Courville, A.; Bengio, Y. Generative adversarial nets. In Proceedings of the 27th International Conference on Neural Information Processing Systems (NIPS 2014), Montréal, QC, Canada, 18–22 November 2014; MIT Press: Cambridge, MA, USA, 2014; Volume 2, pp. 2672–2680.
76. Sahu, S.; Gupta, R.; Espy-Wilson, C. On Enhancing Speech Emotion Recognition using Generative Adversarial Networks. *arXiv* **2018**, arXiv:1806.06626. Cs.
77. Chatziagapi, A.; Paraskevopoulos, G.; Sgouropoulos, D.; Pantazopoulos, G.; Nikandrou, M.; Giannakopoulos, T.; Katsamanis, A.; Potamianos, A.; Narayanan, S. Data Augmentation Using GANs for Speech Emotion Recognition. In Proceedings of the INTERSPEECH 2019, Graz, Austria, 15–19 September 2019; pp. 171–175.
78. Fu, C.; Shi, J.; Liu, C.; Ishi, C.T.; Ishiguro, H. AAEC: An Adversarial Autoencoder-based Classifier for Audio Emotion Recognition. In Proceedings of the 1st International on Multimodal Sentiment Analysis in Real-life Media Challenge and Workshop (MuSe'20), Seattle, WA, USA, 16 October 2020; Association for Computing Machinery: New York, NY, USA, 2020; pp. 45–51.
79. Deng, J.; Xu, X.; Zhang, Z.; Frühholz, S.; Schuller, B. Universum Autoencoder-Based Domain Adaptation for Speech Emotion Recognition. *IEEE Signal Process. Lett.* **2017**, *24*, 500–504. [CrossRef]
80. Abdelwahab, M.; Busso, C. Domain Adversarial for Acoustic Emotion Recognition. *arXiv* **2018**, arXiv:1804.07690. Cs Eess. [CrossRef]
81. Ganin, Y.; Ustinova, E.; Ajakan, H.; Germain, P.; Larochelle, H.; Laviolette, F.; Marchand, M.; Lempitsky, V. Domain-Adversarial Training of Neural Networks. *arXiv* **2016**, arXiv:1505.07818. Cs Stat.
82. Zheng, W.; Zheng, W.; Zong, Y. Multi-scale discrepancy adversarial network for crosscorpus speech emotion recognition. *Virtual Real. Intell. Hardw.* **2021**, *3*, 65–75. [CrossRef]
83. Noh, K.J.; Jeong, C.Y.; Lim, J.; Chung, S.; Kim, G.; Lim, J.M.; Jeong, H. Multi-Path and Group-Loss-Based Network for Speech Emotion Recognition in Multi-Domain Datasets. *Sensors* **2021**, *21*, 1579. [CrossRef]
84. Lech, M.; Stolar, M.; Best, C.; Bolia, R. Real-Time Speech Emotion Recognition Using a Pre-trained Image Classification Network: Effects of Bandwidth Reduction and Companding. *Front. Comput. Sci.* **2020**, *2*, 14. [CrossRef]
85. Huang, Z.; Dong, M.; Mao, Q.; Zhan, Y. Speech Emotion Recognition Using CNN. In Proceedings of the 22nd ACM international conference on Multimedia, Orlando, FL, USA, 3–7 November 2014; Association for Computing Machinery: New York, NY, USA, 2014; pp. 801–804.
86. Neumann, M.; Vu, N.T. Attentive Convolutional Neural Network Based Speech Emotion Recognition: A Study on the Impact of Input Features, Signal Length, and Acted Speech. *arXiv* **2017**, arXiv:1706.00612. [CrossRef]
87. Latif, S.; Rana, R.; Qadir, J.; Epps, J. Variational Autoencoders for Learning Latent Representations of Speech Emotion: A Preliminary Study. *arXiv* **2020**, arXiv:1712.08708.
88. Wu, X.; Liu, S.; Cao, Y.; Li, X.; Yu, J.; Dai, D.; Ma, X.; Hu, S.; Wu, Z.; Liu, X.; et al. Speech Emotion Recognition Using Capsule Networks. In Proceedings of the ICASSP 2019—2019 IEEE International Conference on Acoustics, Speech and Signal Processing (ICASSP), Brighton, UK, 12–17 May 2019; pp. 6695–6699.
89. Papakostas, M.; Spyrou, E.; Giannakopoulos, T.; Siantikos, G.; Sgouropoulos, D.; Mylonas, P.; Makedon, F. Deep Visual Attributes vs. Hand-Crafted Audio Features on Multidomain Speech Emotion Recognition. *Computation* **2017**, *5*, 26. [CrossRef]
90. Goodfellow, I.; Bengio, Y.; Courville, A. *Deep Learning*; MIT Press: Cambridge, MA, USA, 2016; ISBN 978-0-262-03561-3.
91. Hochreiter, S.; Schmidhuber, J. Long Short-Term Memory. *Neural Comput.* **1997**, *9*, 1735–1780. [CrossRef] [PubMed]
92. Li, P.; Song, Y.; McLoughlin, I.V.; Guo, W.; Dai, L.-R. An Attention Pooling based Representation Learning Method for Speech Emotion Recognition. In Proceedings of the Interspeech 2018, Hyderabad, India, 2–6 September 2018; International Speech Communication Association: Hyderabad, India, 2018.

93. Cho, K.; van Merriënboer, B.; Gulcehre, C.; Bahdanau, D.; Bougares, F.; Schwenk, H.; Bengio, Y. Learning Phrase Representations using RNN Encoder–Decoder for Statistical Machine Translation. In Proceedings of the 2014 Conference on Empirical Methods in Natural Language Processing (EMNLP), Doha, Qata, 25–29 October 2014; Association for Computational Linguistics: Doha, Qatar, 2014; pp. 1724–1734.
94. Karmakar, P.; Teng, S.W.; Lu, G. Thank you for Attention: A survey on Attention-based Artificial Neural Networks for Automatic Speech Recognition. *arXiv* **2021**, arXiv:2102.07259.
95. Chaudhari, S.; Mithal, V.; Polatkan, G.; Ramanath, R. An attentive survey of attention models. *arXiv* **2019**, arXiv:1904.02874.
96. Lin, Z.; Feng, M.; dos Santos, C.N.; Yu, M.; Xiang, B.; Zhou, B.; Bengio, Y. A Structured Self-attentive Sentence Embedding. *arXiv* **2017**, arXiv:1703.03130.
97. Wang, Y.; Huang, M.; Zhu, X.; Zhao, L. Attention-based LSTM for Aspect-level Sentiment Classification. In Proceedings of the 2016 Conference on Empirical Methods in Natural Language Processing, Austin, TX, USA, 1–5 November 2016; Association for Computational Linguistics: Austin, TX, USA, 2016; pp. 606–615.
98. He, R.; Lee, W.S.; Ng, H.T.; Dahlmeier, D. Effective Attention Modeling for Aspect-Level Sentiment Classification. In Proceedings of the 27th International Conference on Computational Linguistics, Santa Fe, NM, USA, 20–26 August 2018; Association for Computational Linguistics: Santa Fe, NM, USA, 2018; pp. 1121–1131.
99. Chorowski, J.; Bahdanau, D.; Serdyuk, D.; Cho, K.; Bengio, Y. Attention-based models for speech recognition. In Proceedings of the 28th International Conference on Neural Information Processing Systems (NIPS 2015), Montréal, QC, Canada, 7–12 December 2015; MIT Press: Cambridge, MA, USA, 2015; Volume 1, pp. 577–585.
100. Han, K.; Yu, D.; Tashev, I. Speech Emotion Recognition Using Deep Neural Network and Extreme Learning Machine. In Proceedings of the 15th Annual Conference of the International Speech Communication Association, Singapore, 14–18 September 2014.
101. Huang, C.-W.; Narayanan, S.S. Attention Assisted Discovery of Sub-Utterance Structure in Speech Emotion Recognition. In Proceedings of the INTERSPEECH 2016, San Francisco, CA, USA, 8–12 September 2016; pp. 1387–1391.
102. Tao, F.; Liu, G. Advanced LSTM: A Study about Better Time Dependency Modeling in Emotion Recognition. In Proceedings of the 2018 IEEE International Conference on Acoustics, Speech and Signal Processing (ICASSP), Calgary, AB, Canada, 15–20 April 2018; pp. 2906–2910.
103. Xie, Y.; Liang, R.; Liang, Z.; Huang, C.; Zou, C.; Schuller, B. Speech Emotion Classification Using Attention-Based LSTM. *IEEEACM Trans. Audio Speech Lang. Process.* **2019**, *27*, 1675–1685. [CrossRef]
104. Xie, Y.; Liang, R.; Liang, Z.; Zhao, L. Attention-Based Dense LSTM for Speech Emotion Recognition. *IEICE Trans. Inf. Syst.* **2019**, *E102.D*, 1426–1429. [CrossRef]
105. Girdhar, R.; Ramanan, D. Attentional Pooling for Action Recognition. *arXiv* **2017**, arXiv:1711.01467. CsCV.
106. Chen, M.; He, X.; Yang, J.; Zhang, H. 3-D Convolutional Recurrent Neural Networks with Attention Model for Speech Emotion Recognition. *IEEE Signal Process. Lett.* **2018**, *25*, 1440–1444. [CrossRef]
107. Zhao, Z.; Zheng, Y.; Zhang, Z.; Wang, H.; Zhao, Y.; Li, C. Exploring Spatio-Temporal Representations by Integrating Attention-based Bidirectional-LSTM-RNNs and FCNs for Speech Emotion Recognition. In Proceedings of the Interspeech 2018, Hyderabad, India, 2–6 September 2018; pp. 272–276.
108. Li, Y.; Zhao, T.; Kawahara, T. Improved End-to-End Speech Emotion Recognition Using Self Attention Mechanism and Multitask Learning. In Proceedings of the INTERSPEECH, Graz, Austria, 15–19 September 2019.
109. Dangol, R.; Alsadoon, A.; Prasad, P.W.C.; Seher, I.; Alsadoon, O.H. Speech Emotion Recognition UsingConvolutional Neural Network and Long-Short TermMemory. *Multimed. Tools Appl.* **2020**, *79*, 32917–32934. [CrossRef]
110. Alex, S.B.; Mary, L.; Babu, B.P. Attention and Feature Selection for Automatic Speech Emotion Recognition Using Utterance and Syllable-Level Prosodic Features. *Circuits Syst. Signal Process.* **2020**, *39*, 5681–5709. [CrossRef]
111. Zheng, C.; Wang, C.; Jia, N. An Ensemble Model for Multi-Level Speech Emotion Recognition. *Appl. Sci.* **2020**, *10*, 205. [CrossRef]
112. Parthasarathy, S.; Busso, C. Jointly Predicting Arousal, Valence and Dominance with Multi-Task Learning. In Proceedings of the Interspeech 2017, Stockholm, Sweden, 20–24 August 2017; pp. 1103–1107.

*Review*

# Survey of Automatic Spelling Correction

Daniel Hládek *, Ján Staš and Matúš Pleva

Department of Electronics and Multimedia Communications, Faculty of Electrical Engineering and Informatics, Technical University of Košice, Němcovej 32, 040 01 Košice, Slovakia; jan.stas@tuke.sk (J.S.); matus.pleva@tuke.sk (M.P.)
* Correspondence: daniel.hladek@tuke.sk; Tel.: +421-055-602-2298

Received: 13 August 2020; Accepted: 6 October 2020; Published: 13 October 2020

**Abstract:** Automatic spelling correction has been receiving sustained research attention. Although each article contains a brief introduction to the topic, there is a lack of work that would summarize the theoretical framework and provide an overview of the approaches developed so far. Our survey selected papers about spelling correction indexed in Scopus and Web of Science from 1991 to 2019. The first group uses a set of rules designed in advance. The second group uses an additional model of context. The third group of automatic spelling correction systems in the survey can adapt its model to the given problem. The summary tables show the application area, language, string metrics, and context model for each system. The survey describes selected approaches in a common theoretical framework based on Shannon's noisy channel. A separate section describes evaluation methods and benchmarks.

**Keywords:** spelling correction; natural language processing; diacritization; error model; context model

## 1. Introduction

There are many possible ways to write the same thing. Written text sometimes looks different from what the reader or the author expects. Creating apprehensive and clear text is not a matter of course, especially for people with a different mother language. An unusually written word in a sentence makes a spelling error.

A spelling error makes the text harder to read and, worse, harder to process. Natural language processing requires normalized forms of a word because incorrect spelling or digitization of text decreases informational value. A spelling error, for example, in a database of medical records, diminishes efficiency of the diagnosis process, and incorrectly digitized archive documents can influence research or organizational processes.

A writer might not have enough time or ability to correct spelling errors. Automatic spelling correction (ASC) systems help to find the intended form of a word. They identify problematic words and propose a set of replacement candidates. The candidates are usually sorted according to their expected fitness with the spelling error and the surrounding context. The best correction can be selected interactively or automatically.

Interactive spelling correction systems underline incorrectly written words and suggest corrections. A user of the system selects the most suitable correction. This scenario is common in computer-assisted proofreading that helps with the identification and correction of spelling errors. Interactive spelling correction systems improve the productivity of professionals working with texts, increase convenience when using mobile devices, or correct Internet search queries. They support learning a language, text input in mobile devices, and web search engines. Also, interactive spelling correction systems are a component of text editors and office systems, optical character recognition (OCR) systems, and databases of scanned texts.

Most current search engines can detect misspelled search queries. The suggestion is shown interactively for each given string prefix. A recent work by Cai and de Rijke [1] reviewed approaches for correcting search queries.

A large quantity of text in databases brought new challenges. An automatic spelling correction system can be a part of a natural language processing system. Text in the database has to be automatically corrected because interactive correction would be too expensive. The spelling correction system automatically selects a correction candidate according to the previous and following texts. Noninteractive text normalization can improve the performance of information retrieval or semantic analysis of a text.

Figure 1 displays the process of correction-candidate generation and correction. The error and context models contribute to ranking of the candidate words. The result of automatic correction is a sequence of correction candidates with the best ranking.

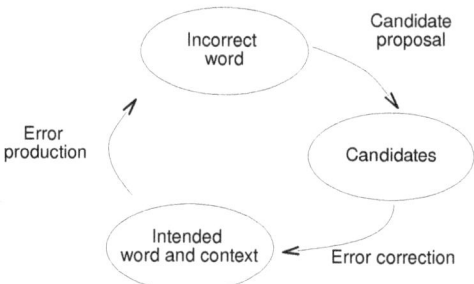

**Figure 1.** Interactive processes of error production and correction.

In the next section, you'll find an explanation of the method we used to select and sort the articles in this report. Subsequently, in Section 3, we describe the characteristic spelling errors and divide them into groups according to how they originated. Section 4 defines the task of correcting spelling errors and describes the ASC system. This survey divides the ASC systems into three groups, each with its section: a priori spelling correction (Section 5), spelling correction in the context (Section 6), and spelling correction with a learning error model (Section 7). Section 8 introduces the methods of evaluation and benchmarking. The concluding Section 9 summarizes the survey and outlines trends in the research.

## 2. Methodology

The survey selected papers about spelling correction indexed in Scopus (http://scopus.com) and Web of Science (https://apps.webofknowledge.com) (WoS) from 1991 to 2019. It reviews the state-of-the-art and maps the history from the previous comprehensive survey provided by Kukich [2] in 1992.

First, we searched the indices with a search query "spelling correction" for the years 1991–2019. Scopus returned 1315 results, WoS returned 794 results. We excluded 149 errata, 779 corrections, 7 editorials, 45 reviews, and around 140 papers without any citations from both collections. We removed 250 duplicates, and we received 740 results (440 journal articles and 300 conference papers). We read the titles and abstracts of the remaining papers and removed 386 works that are not relevant to the topic of automatic spelling correction.

We examined the remaining 354 documents. Then, we removed articles without clear scientific contribution to spelling correction, without proper evaluation, or that just repeated already known things. We examined, sorted, and put the remaining 119 items into tables. We included additional references that explain essential theoretical concepts and survey papers about particular topics in the surrounding text.

First, we defined the spelling correction problem and established a common theoretical framework. We described the three main components of a spelling correction system.

This work divides the selected papers into three groups. The first group uses a set of expert rules to correct a spelling error. The second group adds a context model to rearrange the correction candidates with the context. The third group learns error patterns from a training corpus.

Each group of methods has its own section with a summarizing table. The main part of the survey is the summary tables. The tables briefly describe the application area, language, error model, and context model of the spelling correction systems. The tables are accompanied by a description of the selected approaches.

The rows in the tables are sorted chronologically and according to author. We selected chronological order because it shows the general scientific progress in spelling correction in the particular components of the spelling correction system. An additional reference in the table indicates if one approach enhances the previous one.

Special attention is paid to the evaluation methods. This section identifies the most frequent evaluation methods, benchmarks and corpora.

## 3. Spelling Errors

The design of an automatic spelling correction system requires knowledge of the creation process of a spelling error [3]. There are several works about spelling errors. A book by Mitton [4] analyzed spelling-error types and described approaches to construct an automatic spelling correction system. The authors in Yannakoudakis and Fawthrop [5] demonstrated that the clear majority of spelling errors follow specific rules on the basis of phonological and sequential considerations. The paper [5] introduced and described three categories of spelling errors (consonantal, vowel, and sequential) and presented the analysis results of 1377 spelling error forms.

Moreover, the authors in Kukich [2], Toutanova and Moore [6], and Pirinen and Lindén [7] divided spelling errors into two categories according to their cause:

1. Cognitive errors (also called orthographic or consistent): They are caused by the disabilities of the person that writes the text. The correct way of writing may be unknown to the writer. The writer could have dyslexia, dysgraphia, or other cognitive problems. The person writing the text could just be learning the language and not know the correct spelling. This set of errors is language- and user-specific because it is more dependent on using the rules of the language [7].
2. Typographic errors (also called conventional): They are usually related to technical restrictions of the input device (physical or virtual keyboard, or OCR system) or depend on the conditions of the environment. Typing in haste often causes substitution of two close keys. Typographic errors caused by hasty typing are usually language-agnostic (unrelated to the language of the writer), although they can depend on local keyboard mapping or a localized OCR system [7].

Examples of typographic and cognitive spelling errors are in Table 1.

Table 1. Examples of cognitive and typographic errors.

| Error Type | Example |
|---|---|
| Cognitive error: | I don't know the correct spelling of Levenstain distance. |
| Typographic: | THis sentence was typed in haser. |
| Typographic (OCR): | SUppLEMENTAhy INFOhMATlON. |
| Typographic (Diacritic): | The authors of this article are Daniel Hladek, Matus Pleva and Jan Stas. |

Note: The spelling errors are underlined.

OCR errors are a particular type of typographic error caused by software. The process of document digitization and optical character recognition often omits or replaces some letters in a typical way. Spelling correction is part of postprocessing of the digitized document because OCR systems are usually proprietary and difficult to adapt. Typical error patterns appear in OCR texts [8]. The standard set for evaluation of an OCR spelling correction system is the TREC-5 Confusion Track [9].

Some writing systems (such as Arabic, Vietnamese, or Slovak) use different character variants that change the meaning of the word. The authors in [10] confirmed that the omission of diacritics is a common type of spelling error in Brazilian Portuguese. Texts in Modern Standard Arabic are typically written without diacritical markings [11]. This is a typographic error when the author omits additional character markings and expects the reader to guess the original meaning. The missing marks usually present short vowels or modification of the letter. They are placed either above or below the graphemes. The process of adding vowels and other diacritic marks to Arabic text can be called diacritization or vowelization [11]. Azmi and Almajed [12] focused on the problem of Arabic diacritization (adding missing diacritical markings to Arabic letters) and proposed an evaluation metric, and Asahiah et al. [13] published a survey of Arabic diacritization techniques.

## 4. Automatic Spelling Correction

An automatic spelling correction system detects a spelling error and proposes a set of candidates for correction (see Figure 2). Kukich [2] and Pirinen and Lindén [7] divide the whole process into three steps:

1. detection of an error;
2. generation of correction candidates;
3. ranking of candidate corrections.

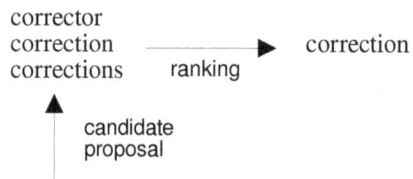

The spelling correciton systems.

**Figure 2.** Process of automatic spelling correction.

*4.1. Error Detection*

A word could either be new or just uncommon, could be a less-known proper name, or could belong to another language. However, a correctly spelled word could be semantically incorrect in a sentence. Kukich [2] divided spelling errors according to the dictionary of correct words:

- real-word errors, where the word is spelled incorrectly but its form is in the dictionary of correct words, and
- non-word errors, where the incorrect word form is not in the dictionary of correct words.

Most spelling correction systems detect a non-word error by searching for it in a dictionary of correct words. This step requires a fast-lookup method such as hash table [14] or search tree [15,16].

Many non-word error spelling correction systems use open-source a priori spelling systems, such as Aspell or Hunspell for error detection, correction-candidate generation, and preliminary candidate ranking.

An automatic spelling correction system identifies real-word errors by semantic analysis of the surrounding context. More complex error-detection systems may be used to detect words that are correctly spelled but do not fit into the syntactic or semantic context. Pirinen and Lindén [7] called it real-word error detection in context.

Real-word errors are hard to detect because detection requires semantic analysis of the context. The authors in [17] used a language model to detect and correct a homophonic real-word error in the Bangla language. The language model identifies words that are improbable with the current context.

Boytsov [18] examined methods for indexing a dictionary with approximate matching. Deorowicz and Ciura [19] claim that a lexicon of all correct words could be too large. Too large a lexicon can lead to many real-word errors or misdetection of obscure spellings.

The situation is different for languages where words are not separated by spaces (for example, Chinese). The authors in [20] transformed characters into a fixed-dimensional word-vector space and detected spelling errors by conditional random field classification.

*4.2. Candidate Generation*

ASC systems usually select correction candidates from a dictionary of correct words after detection of a spelling error. Although it is possible to select all correct words as correction candidates, it is reasonable to restrict the search space and to inspect only words that are similar to the identified spelling error.

Zhang and Zhang [21] stated that the task of similarity joining is to find all pairs of strings for which similarities are above a predetermined threshold, where the similarity of two strings is measured by a specific distance function. Kernighan et al. [22] proposed a simplification to restrict the candidate list to words that differ with just one edit operation of the Damerau–Levenshtein edit distance—substitution, insertion, deletion, or replacement of succeeding letters [23].

The spelling dictionary generates correction candidates for the incorrect word by approximately searching for similar words. The authors in [24] used a character-level language model trained on a dictionary of correct words to generate a candidate list. Reffle [25] used a Levenshtein automaton to propose the correction candidates. Methods of approximate searching were outlined in a survey published by Yu et al. [26].

An index often speeds up an approximate search in the dictionary. The authors in [19,27] converted the lexicon into a finite-state automaton to speed up searching for a similar string.

*4.3. Ranking Correction Candidates*

A noisy-channel model proposed by Shannon [28] described the probabilistic process of producing an error. The noisy channel transfers and distorts words (Figure 3).

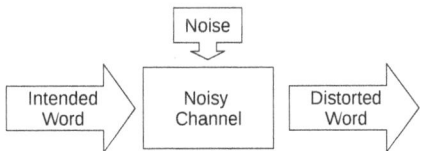

**Figure 3.** Word distorted by noisy channel.

The noisy-channel model expresses similarity between two strings as a probability of transforming one string into another. Probability $P(s|w)$ that a string $s$ is produced instead of word $w$ describes how similar the two strings are. The similarity between two strings is defined by an expert or depends on a training corpus with error patterns.

A more formal definition of automatic spelling correction uses the maximum-likelihood principle. Brill and Moore [29] defined the automatic spelling correction of a possibly incorrect word $s$ as finding the best correction candidate $w_b$ from a list of possible correction candidates $w_i \in W$ with the highest un-normalized probability:

$$w_b = \arg\max_{w_i \in C(s)} P(s|w_i)P(w_i), \tag{1}$$

where $P(s|w_i)$ is the probability of producing string $s$ instead of word $w_i$ and $P(w_i)$ is the probability of producing word $w_i$. $C(s)$ is a function that returns valid words from dictionary $W$ that serve as correction candidates for erroneous string $s$.

*4.4. Components of Automatic Spelling Correction Systems*

Equation (1) by Brill and Moore [29] identified three components of an automatic spelling correction system. The components are depicted in Figure 4:

1. Dictionary: It detects spelling errors and proposes correction candidates $w_i \in C$ for each input token. $C(s)$ is a list of correction candidates $w_i$ for a given token $s$. The list of correction candidates belongs to the set of all correct words ($C(s) \in W$). If the dictionary does not propose any candidate, the word is considered correct.
2. Error model (channel model) $P(s|w_i)$: It is an essential component of the automatic spelling correction system. It measures the "fitness" of the correction candidate with the corrected string. The model expresses the similarity of strings $w_i$ and $s$ or the probability of producing string $s$ instead string $w_i$. This measure does not have to be purely probabilistic but can be similar to a distance between the two strings. The non-probabilistic string distance can always be converted into probabilistic string similarity (see Equation (3) in Section 6). An error model allows for identification of the most probable errors and consequently the most probable original forms.
3. Context model (source model $P(w_i)$, the prior model of word probabilities): This expresses the probability of correct word occurrence and often takes the context of the word into account. Candidates that best fit into the current context have a higher probability of being the intended word. The context model focuses on finding the best correction candidate by using the context of the incorrect word and statistical methods of classification. The model observes features that are outside the inspected word and improves the evaluation of candidate words. It can detect an unusual sequence of features and identify real-word errors.

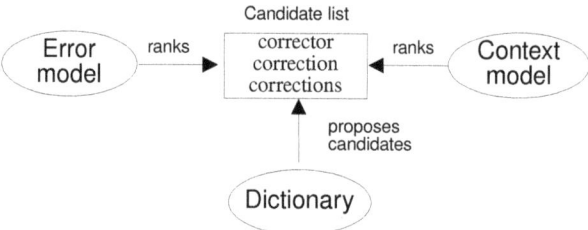

**Figure 4.** Components of an automatic spelling correction system.

## 5. Spelling Correction with a Priori Error Model

A combination of error and context models is often not necessary. In some scenarios, a set of predefined transcription rules can correct a spelling error. An expert identifies characteristic string transcriptions. These rules are given in advance (a priori) by someone who understands the problem.

Approaches in this group detect non-word errors and propose a list of correction candidates that are similar to the original word (presented in Table 2). The a priori error model works as a guide in the search for the best-matching original word; best-matching words are proposed first, and it is easy to select the correction.

A schematic diagram for an ASC system with a priori error model is in Figure 5. The input of the a priori error model is an erroneous word. The spelling system applies one or several transcription operations to the spelling error to create a correction candidate. The rank of the correction candidate depends on the weights of the transcription rules. The output of the a priori error model is a sorted list with correction candidates.

**Table 2.** Summary of a priori spelling correction systems.

| Reference | Application | Language | Error Model |
|---|---|---|---|
| Khairul Islam et al. [30], 2019 | General | Bangla | LD |
| Hawezi et al. [31], 2019 | General | Kurdish | LD, DLD, LCS |
| Thaiprayoon et al. [32], 2018 | Search query | Thai | LD, Soundex |
| Christanti et al. [33], 2018 | General | Indonesian | DLD |
| Hagen et al. [34], 2017 | Search query | English | DLD |
| Sakuntharaj and Mahesan [35], 2016 | General | Tamil | LD, common $n$-grams |
| Vobl et al. [36], 2014 | OCR, historical | Old German | Interactive |
| Rees [37], 2014 | Animal taxonomy | Latin | Soundex |
| Mühlberger et al. [38], 2014 | OCR, historical | German | Interactive |
| Patrick and Nguyen [39], 2014 | General, medical | English | Interactive |
| Kashefi et al. [40], 2013 | Diacritization | Farsi | Modified DLD |
| Andrade et al. [41], 2012 | General | Portuguese | DLD |
| Sha et al. [42], 2011 | General | Chinese | Keyboard-based edit distance |
| Reffle [25], 2011 | OCR, historical | Old German | LD, FSA |
| Naji and Savoy [43], 2011 | General, historical | Middle High German | Stemmer |
| Bustamante et al. [44], 2006 | General | Spanish | Interactive + generalized LD |
| Deorowicz and Ciura [19], 2005 | General | English | FSA |
| UzZaman and Khan [45], 2005 | General | Bangla | Bangla double metaphone |
| Vilares et al. [27], 2004 | General | Galician | FSA |
| van Delden et al. [46], 2004 | General | English | LD, stemming |
| Schulz and Mihov [47], 2002 | General | Bulgarian, German | FSA |
| Taghva and Stofsky [48], 2001 | OCR | English | Interactive + LCS subsequence |
| Vagelatos et al. [49], 1995 | General | Greek | Interactive |

Note: DLD, Damerau–Levenshtein distance; FSA, finite-state automaton; LCS, longest common subsequence; LD, Levenshtein distance; OCR, optical character recognition.

**Figure 5.** A priori spelling correction.

The most commonly used open-source spelling systems are Aspell (http://aspell.net) and Hunspell (http://hunspell.github.io/). Hunspell is a variant of Aspell with a less restrictive license, used in LibreOffice word processor, Firefox web browser, and other programs. They are available as a standalone text filter or as a compiled component in other spelling systems or programs. The basic component of the Aspell system is a dictionary of correct words, available for many languages. The dictionary file contains valid morphological units for the given language (prefixes, suffixes, or stems). The dictionary is compiled into a state machine to speed up searching for correction candidate words.

Aspell searches for sounds-like equivalents (computed for English words by using the Metaphone algorithm) up to a given edit distance (the Damerau–Levenshtein distance) [50]. The detailed operation of the spelling correction of Aspell is described in the manual (http://aspell.net/man-html/Aspell-Suggestion-Strategy.html#Aspell-Suggestion-Strategy).

*5.1. Edit Distance*

Edit distance expresses the difference between two strings as a nonnegative real number by counting edit operations that are required to transform one string into another. The two most commonly used edit distances are the Levenshtein edit distance [51] and the Damerau–Levenshtein distance [52]. Levenshtein identifies atomic edit operations such as

- Substitution: replaces one symbol into another;
- Deletion: removes a symbol (or replaces it with an empty string $\epsilon$); and
- Insertion: adds a symbol or replaces an empty string $\epsilon$ with a symbol.

In addition, the Damerau–Levenshtein distance adds the operation of

- Transposition, which exchanges two subsequent symbols.

The significant difference between the Levenshtein distance (LD) and the Damerau–Levenshtein distance (DLD) is that the Levenshtein distance does not consider letter transposition. The edit operation set proposed by Levenshtein [51] did not consider transposition as an edit operation because the transposition of two subsequent letters can be substituted by deletion and insertion or by two substitutions. The Levenshtein distance allows for representation of the weights of edit operations by a single letter-confusion matrix, which is not possible for DLD distance.

Another variation of edit distance is longest common subsequence (LCS) [53]. It considers only insertion and deletion edit operations. The authors in [54] proposed an algorithm for searching for the longest common sub-string with the given number of permitted mismatches. More information about longest-common-subsequence algorithms can be found in a survey [55].

*5.2. Phonetic Algorithms*

Many languages have difficult rules for pronunciation and writing, and it is very easy to make a spelling mistake if rules for writing a certain word are not familiar to the writer. A word is often replaced with a similarly sounding equivalent with a different spelling.

An edit operation in the phonetic algorithm describes how words are pronounced. They recursively replace phonetically important parts of a string into a special representation. If the phonetic representation of two strings is equal, the strings are considered equal. In other words, a phonetic algorithm is a binary relation of two strings that tells whether two strings are pronounced in a similar way:

$$D(s_s, s_t) \to 0 \text{ or } 1 . \tag{2}$$

The phonetic algorithm is able to identify a group of phonetically similar words to some given string (e.g., to some unknown proper noun). It helps to identify names that are pronounced in a similar way or to discover the original spelling of an incorrectly spelled word. Two strings are phonetically similar only if their phonetic forms are equal.

Phonetic algorithms for spelling corrections and record linkage are different from phonetic algorithms used for speech recognition because they return just an approximation of the true phonetic representation.

One of the first phonetic algorithms is Soundex (U.S. Patent US1435663). Its original purpose was the identification of similar names for the U.S. Census. The algorithm transforms a surname or name so that names with a similar pronunciation have the same representation. It allows for the identification of similar or possibly the same names. The most phonetically important letters are consonants. Most vowels are dropped (except for in the beginning), and similar consonants are transformed into the same representation. Other phonetic algorithms are Shapex [56] and Metaphone [57]. Evaluation of several phonetic-similarity algorithms on the task of cognate identification was done by Kondrak and Sherif [58].

## 6. Spelling Correction in Context

An a priori model is often not sufficient to find out the best correction because it takes only incorrect word into account. The spelling system would perform better if it could distinguish whether the proposed word fits with its context. It is hard to decide which correction is more useful if we do not know the surrounding sentence. For example, if a correction for string "smilly" is "smelly", the correction "smiley" can be more suitable for some contexts.

Approaches in this group are summarized in Tables 3 and 4. The components and their functions are displayed in Figure 4. The authors in [59] described multiple methods of correction with context. This group of automatic spelling correction systems use a probabilistic framework by Brill and Moore [29] defined in the Equation (1). The error models in this group usually use the a priori rules (edit distance and phonetic algorithms). The context model is usually an $n$-gram language model. Some approaches noted below use a combination of multiple statistical models.

Table 3. Spelling correction systems with learning of context model—part I.

| Reference | Application | Language | Context Model | Error Model |
|---|---|---|---|---|
| Azmi et al. [60], 2019 | General, OCR | Arabic | LM | LD, DLD |
| Dong et al. [61], 2019 | MT | Uygur, Chinese | LM, BLEU score | LD |
| Yazdani et al. [62], 2019 | Medical | Farsi | LM | DLD |
| Damnati et al. [63], 2018 | POS | French | Word embedding | DLD |
| Dashti [64], 2018 | General | English | LM | CFG |
| Fahda and Purwarianti [65], 2018 | General | Indonesian | LM, POS, Viterbi | DLD |
| Heyman et al. [66], 2018 | General | Dutch | Suffix probability | BiLSTM |
| Mashod Rana et al. [17], 2018 | General | Bangla | Golding and Schabes [67] | WCS |
| Dziadek et al. [68], 2017 | Medical ontology | Swedish | LM, POS | LD |
| Sorokin [69], 2017 | General | Russian | LM, LR | LD, Metaphone |
| Zhao et al. [70], 2017 | General | Chinese | CRF, decoder | Graph |
| de Mendonça Almeida et al. [71], 2016 | General | Brazilian Portuguese | Decision tree | Modified Soundex |
| Lv et al. [72], 2016 | OCR, Medical | Chinese | LM, ME | WCS |
| Melero et al. [73], 2016 | General | Spanish | LM | WCS |
| Mirzababaei and Faili [74], 2016 | General | Farsi, English | LM, SVM, PMI | DLD |
| Sorokin and Shavrina [75], 2016 | General | Russian | LM, LR | LD |
| Vilares et al. [76], 2016 | IR | Cross-language | POS | Character $n$-grams, DLD |
| Lhoussain et al. [77], 2015 | General | Arabic | LM | LD |
| Ferrero et al. [78], 2014 | General, proofreading | Spanish | Bayes | Interactive |
| Miangah [14], 2014 | General | Farsi | Word frequency | Letter $n$-grams, DLD |
| Pirinen and Lindén [7], 2014 | General | Finish, Greenlandic | WFST, LM | WFST |
| Sagiadinos et al. [79], 2014 | General | Greek | Id3, C4.5, k-NN, naïve Bayes, RF | Suffix |

Note: BLEU, bilingual evaluation understudy; BiLSTM, bidirectional long short-term memory; CFG, context-free grammar; CRF, conditional random fields; IR, information retrieval; k-NN, k-nearest neighbors; LM, language model; LR, linear regression; ME, maximum entropy; POS, part-of-speech tagging; PMI, pointwise mutual information; RF, random forests; SVM, support vector machine; WCS, word-confusion set; WFST, weighted finite-state transducer.

Table 4. spelling correction systems with learning of context model—part II.

| Reference | Application | Language | Context Model | Error Model |
|---|---|---|---|---|
| Ehsan and Faili [80], 2013 | General | Farsi, English | SMT, ME | DLD |
| Hladek et al. [81], 2013 | General | Slovak | LM, HMM | Aspell |
| Flor [59], 2012 | General, proofreading | English | LM, Bouma [82] | Custom |
| Alkanhal et al. [83], 2012 | General | Arabic | A-star, LM | DLD |
| Grozea [84], 2012 | Diacritic | Romanian | LM, HMM | Trivial WCS |
| Stüker et al. [85], 2011 | General, diagnosis | German | HMM, LM | Phonetic algorithm |
| Wong and Glance [86], 2011 | General, medical | English | Bayes | Aspell |
| Abdulkader and Casey [87], 2009 | OCR | English | ANN | Interactive |
| Ahmed et al. [50], 2009 | Search query | English | Ternary search trees, letter $n$-grams | Trivial WCS |
| Farooq et al. [88], 2009 | Handwritten OCR | English | Topic LM, ME | Aspell |
| Carlson and Fette [89], 2007 | General | English | Banko and Brill [90] | Modified LD |
| Mykowiecka and Marciniak [91], 2006 | General, medical | Polish | LM | Interactive |
| Héja and Surján [92], 2003 | General, medical | Hungarian | $n$-gram tree | WCS |
| Jin et al. [93], 2003 | OCR | English | ME | Interactive |
| Ruch et al. [94], 2003 | General, medical | English, French | POS, ME, WSD | Interactive |
| Li and Wang [95], 2002 | General | Chinese | Golding and Roth [96] | LD |
| Banko and Brill [90], 2001 | General | English | Bayes classifier ensemble | WCS |
| Carlson et al. [97], 2001 | General | English | Golding and Roth [96] | WCS |
| Ruch et al. [98], 2001 | General, medical | French | POS, WSD | Interactive |
| Golding and Roth [96], 1999 | General | English | Winnow algorithm | WCS |
| Jones and Martin [99], 1997 | General | English | LSA | WCS |
| Golding and Schabes [67], 1996 | General | English | Naïve Bayes | WCS |

Note: ANN, artificial neural network; HMM, hidden Markov model; LM, language model; LSA, latent semantic analysis; ME, maximum entropy; OCR, optical character recognition; POS, part-of-speech; SMT, statistical machine translation; WCS, word-confusion set; WSD, word-sense disambiguation.

The edit distance $D(s|w)$ of the incorrect word $s$ and a correction candidate $w$ in the a priori error model is a positive real number. In order to fit the probabilistic framework, it can be converted into the probabilistic framework by taking a negative logarithm [100]:

$$P(s|w_i) = -\log D(s,w). \tag{3}$$

Methods of spelling correction in context are similar to morphological analysis, and it is possible to use similar methods of disambiguation from part-of-speech taggers in a context model of automatic spelling correction systems.

*6.1. Language Model*

The most common form of a language model is $n$-gram language model, calculated from the frequency of word sequences of size $n$. It gives the probability $P(w_i|w_{i-1,i-(n-1)})$ of a candidate word given its history of $(n-1)$ words. If the given $n$-gram sequence is not presented in the training corpus, the probability is calculated by a back-off that considers shorter contexts. The $n$-gram language model only depends on previous words, but other classifiers can make use of arbitrary features in any part of the context. The language model is usually trained on a training corpus that represents language with correct spelling.

Neural language modeling brought new possibilities, as it can predict a word given arbitrary surrounding context. A neural network maps a word into a fixed-size embedding vector. Embedding vectors form a semantic space of words. Words that are close in the embedding space usually occur in the same context and are thus semantically close. This feature can be used in a spelling correction system to propose and rank a list of correction candidates [63,101,102].

*6.2. Combination of Multiple Context Models*

Context modeling often benefits from a combination of multiple statistical models. A spelling system proposed by Melero et al. [73] used a linear combination of language models, each with a certain weight. Each language model can focus on a different feature: lowercase words, uppercase words, part-of-speech tags, and lemmas.

The authors in [67] proposed a context model with multiple Bayesian classifiers. The first component of the context model is called "trigrams". This system uses parts of speech as a feature for classification. The first part of the model assigns the highest probability to a candidate word and its context containing the most probable part-of-speech tags. The second part of the context model is a naïve Bayes classifier that takes the surrounding words and collocations (preceding word and current tag).

Another form of a statistical classifier for the context modeling with multiple models is the Winnow algorithm [96,103]. This approach uses several Winnow classifiers trained with different parameters. The final rank is their weighted sum.

The model uses the same features (occurrence of a word in context and collocation of tags and surrounding word) as those in the previous approach [67]. The paper by Golding and Roth [96] was followed by Carlson et al. [97], which used a large-scale training corpus. Also, Li and Wang [95] proposed a similar system for Chinese spelling correction.

An approach published by Banko and Brill [90] proposed a voting scheme that utilized four classifiers. This approach focused on learning by using a large amount of data—over 100 million words. It uses a Winnow classifier, naïve Bayes classifier, perceptron, and a simple memory-based learner. Each classifier has a complementarity score defined by Brill et al. [104] and is separately trained. The complementarity score indicates how accurate the classifier is.

*6.3. Weighted Finite-State Transducers*

If components of an ASC system (dictionary, error model, or context model) can be converted into a state machine, it is possible to create a single state machine by composing individual components. The idea of finite-state spelling was formalized by Pirinen and Lindén [7]. They compared finite-state automatic spelling correction systems with other conventional systems (Aspell and Hunspell) for English, Finnish, and Icelandic on the corpus of Wikipedia edits. They showed that this approach had comparable performance to that of others.

A weighted state transducer (WFST) is a generalization of a finite-state automaton, where each transcription rule has an input string, output string, and weight. One rule of the WFST system represents a single piece of knowledge about spelling correction—an edit operation of the error model or a probability of succeeding words in the context model.

Multiple WFSTs (dictionary, error model, and context model) can be composed into a single WFST by joining their state spaces and by removing useless states and transcription rules. After these three components are composed, the resulting transducer can be searched for the best path, which is the sequence of best-matching letters.

For example, the approach by Perez-Cortes et al. [105] took a set of hypotheses from the OCR. The output from OCR is an identity transducer (an automaton that transcribes the set of strings to the same set of strings) with weights on each transition that represents the probability of a character in the hypothesis. The character-level $n$-gram model represents a list of valid strings from the lexicon. The third component of the error model is a letter-confusion matrix calculated from the training corpus. The authors in [106,107] used handcrafted Arabic morphological rules to construct a WFST for automatic spelling correction.

A significant portion of text errors involves running together two or more words (e.g., ofthe) or splitting a single word (sp ent, th ebook) [2]. Weighted finite-state transducer (WFST) systems can identify word boundaries if the spacing is incorrect (http://openfst.org/twiki/bin/view/FST/FstExamples). However, inserting or deleting a space is still considered problematic because spaces have the annoying characteristic of not being handled by edit-distance operations [106].

## 7. Spelling Correction with Learning Error Model

The previous sections presented spelling correction systems with a fixed set of rules, prepared in advance by an expert. This section introduces approaches where the error model learns from a training corpus. The optimization algorithm iteratively updates the parameters of the error model (e.g., weights of the edit operations) to improve the quality of the ASC system.

A diagram in Figure 6 displays a structure of a learning error model. The algorithm for learning the error model uses the expectation-maximization procedure. A complete automatic spelling correction system contains a context model that is usually learned separately. The authors in [108] proposed to utilize the context model in the learning of the error model. Context probability is taken into account during the expectation step. Some approaches do not consider context at all. A comparison of approaches with the learning error model is shown in Tables 5 and 6.

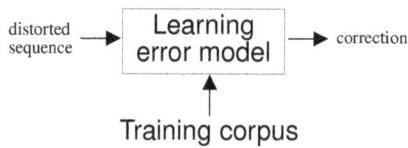

**Figure 6.** Spelling correction with learning error model

**Table 5.** Spelling correction systems with learning of context model and error model—part I.

| Reference | Application | Language | Context Model | Error Model |
|---|---|---|---|---|
| Han et al. [109], 2019 | General | Chinese | N/a | BiLSTM seq2seq [110] |
| Jain et al. [111], 2019 | General | Hindi | LM | LD, LCM |
| Kinaci [24], 2019 | General | Turkish | N/a | LSTM character LM |
| Lu et al. [112], 2019 | Diacritic | Mongolian | N/a | Evolved transformer seq2seq |
| Mammadov [113], 2019 | General | Azerbaijani | N/a | Seq2seq [110] |
| Roy [114], 2019 | General | English | N/a | Seq2seq transformer |
| Yang et al. [115], 2019 | Speech postprocessing | Chinese | N/a | CRF, seq2seq [110], BERT, character embeddings |
| Zaky and Romadhony [102], 2019 | General | Indonesian | N/a | POS, word embeddings, BiLSTM seq2seq [110] |
| Zhang et al. [116], 2019 | Speech postprocessing | Chinese | N/a | Transformer seq2seq |
| Zhou et al. [117], 2019 | General | English | N/a | BiLSTM seq2seq [110] |
| Barteld et al. [118], 2018 | Historical POS | Middle High German | N/a | Character LM |
| Sooraj et al. [119], 2018 | General | Malayan | N/a | LSTM character LM |
| Sbattella and Tedesco [120], 2018 | General | Italian | N/a | seq2seq LSTM |
| Fivez et al. [101], 2017 | Medical | English, Dutch | Word embedding | DLD, double-Metaphone, character embeddings |
| Hládek et al. [8], 2016 | OCR | English | HMM, LM | Ristad and Yianilos [100] |
| Silfverberg et al. [121], 2016 | OCR | Finnish | N/a | WFST, Eger et al. [122], Lindén [123] |
| Abandah et al. [124], 2015 | Diacritization | Arabic | N/a | Recurrent ANN |
| Hasan and Heger [125], 2015 | Search query | English | LM | DLD, SMT |
| Lai et al. [126], 2015 | General, medical | English | CRF for NER | Kernighan et al. [22] |
| Ramasamy et al. [127], 2015 | General | Czech | Golding and Roth [96] | Church and Gale [128] |
| Evershed and Fitch [129], 2014 | OCR | English | LM | LCM |
| Makazhanov et al. [130], 2014 | General | Kazakh | N/a | Church and Gale [128] |

Note: ANN, artificial neural network; BERT, bidirectional encoder representations from transformers; BiLSTM, bidirectional long short-term memory; CRF, conditional random fields; HMM, hidden Markov model; LCM, letter-confusion matrix; LSTM, long short-term memory; NER, named entity recognition; OCR, optical character recognition; POS, part-of-speech; seq2seq, sequence-to-sequence; WFST, weighted finite-state transducer.

**Table 6.** spelling correction systems with learning of context model and error model—part II.

| Reference | Application | Language | Context Model | Error Model |
|---|---|---|---|---|
| Mitankin et al. [131], 2014 | OCR, historical | Old English | ME, LM | SMT |
| Sariev et al. [132], 2014 | Historical text, OCR | Early Modern English, Bulgarian | SMT, LM, ME | LD, SMT |
| Wang et al. [133], 2014 | Search query | English | N/a | ME |
| Huang et al. [134], 2013 | General, automotive | English | N/a | Maximum of common characters, LD, ANN |
| Reffle and Ringlstetter [135], 2013 | OCR, historical | Old German | LM | Bayes |
| Duan et al. [136], 2012 | Search query | English | LM | SVM |
| Rashwan et al. [137], 2011 | Diacritization | Arabic | LM | FSA, A star, ME |
| Perez-Cortes et al. [105], 2010 | OCR, record linkage | Spanish | N/a | WFST, generalized LD, letter $n$-grams |
| Takasu [138], 2009 | OCR | Japanese | N/a | Ristad and Yianilos [100], Takasu and Aihara [139] |
| Magdy and Darwish [140], 2008 | OCR | Arabic | LM | LCM |
| Beaufort and Mancas-Thillou [141], 2007 | OCR | English | WFST | LCM |
| Byun et al. [142], 2007 | General | Korean | N/a | Learning general edit operations |
| Magdy and Darwish [143], 2006 | OCR | Arabic | LM | Brill and Moore [29] |
| Oncina and Sebban [144], 2006 | OCR | None | N/a | Ristad and Yianilos [100] |
| Ahmad and Kondrak [108], 2005 | Search query | English | LM | Ristad and Yianilos [100] |
| Toutanova and Moore [6], 2002 | General | English | N/a | Brill and Moore [29] |
| Brill and Moore [29], 2000 | General | English | LM | DLD, extended Church and Gale [128] |
| Ristad and Yianilos [100], 1998 | General | English | N/a | LCM |
| Church and Gale [128], 1991 | General | English | N/a | Four LCMs |
| Kernighan et al. [22], 1990 | General | English | N/a | Four LCMs |

Note: ANN, artificial neural network; FSA, finite-state automaton; LCM, letter-confusion matrix; LM, language model; LSTM, long short-term memory; ME, maximum entropy; OCR, optical character recognition; seq2seq, sequence-to-sequence; SMT, statistical machine translation; SVM, support vector machine; WFST, weighted finite state transducer.

ASC systems with a learning error model often complement optical character recognition systems (OCR). The digitized document contains spelling errors characteristic of the quality of the paper, scanner, and OCR algorithm. If the training database (original and corrected documents) is large enough, the spelling system is adapted to the data. A training sample from the TREC-5 confusion track corpus [9] is displayed in Figure 7.

```
Correct:    bulletin
Incorrect:  bM.etin  ,bWetin  bMetinh  bUletin
Cunt:          2        2        4       23
```

**Figure 7.** Example misspellings of word the "bulletin" from optical character recognition (OCR).

*7.1. Word-Confusion Set*

The simplest method of estimating the learning error model is a word-confusion set that counts the cooccurrences of correct and incorrect words in the training corpus. It considers a pair of correct and incorrect words as one big edit operation. The word-confusion set remembers possible corrections for each frequently misspelled form (See Figure 7). This method was used by Gong et al. [145] to improve the precision of e-mail spam detection.

Its advantages are that it can be easily created and manually checked. The disadvantage of this simple approach is that it is not possible to obtain a corpus that has every possible misspelling for every possible word. The second problem of the word-confusion set is that error probabilities are far from "real" probabilities because training data are always sparse. Shannon's theorem states that it is not possible to be 100% accurate in spelling correction.

*7.2. Learning String Metrics*

The sparseness problems of the word-confusion set are solved by observing smaller subword units (such as letters or morphemes). For example, Makazhanov et al. [130] utilized information about morphemes in the Kazakh language to improve automatic spelling correction. The smallest possible subword units are letters. Estimating parameters of edit operations partially mitigates the sparseness problem because smaller sequences appear in the training corpus more frequently. The authors in [29] presented an error model that learned general edit operations. The antecedent and consequent parts of the edit operations can be arbitrary strings called partitions. The partition of the strings defines the edit operations.

Generalized edit distance is another form of a learning error model. The antecedent and consequent part of an edit operation is a single symbol that can be a letter or a special deletion mark. Edit distance is generalized by considering the arbitrary weight of an operation. Weights of each possible edit operation of the Levenshtein distance (LD) can be stored in a single letter-confusion matrix (LCM). $\Delta$ weights for generalized edit distance are stored in four matrices [128]. The generalized edit distance is not always a metric in the strict mathematical sense because the distance in the opposite direction can be different. More theory about learning string metrics can be found in a book [146] or in a survey ([147], Section 5.1).

Weights $\Delta$ in an LCM express the weight of error types (Figure 8). If the LCM is a matrix of ones with zeros on the main diagonal, it expresses the Levenshtein edit distance. Each edit operation has a value of 1, and the sum of edit operations is the Levenshtein edit distance. The edit distance with weights is calculated by a dynamic algorithm [53,148].

The LCM for a Levenshtein-like edit distance can be estimated with an expectation-maximization algorithm [100]. The learning algorithm calculates weights of operations for each training sample that are summed and normalized to form an updated letter confusion matrix.

If the training corpus is sparse (which it almost always is), the learning process brings the problem of overfitting. Hládek et al. [8] proposed a method for smoothing parameters in a letter-confusion matrix. Bilenko and Mooney [149] extended string-distance learning with an affine gap penalty (allowing for random sequences of characters to be skipped). Also, Kim and Park [150] presented an algorithm for learning a letter-confusion matrix and for calculating generalized edit distance. This algorithm was further extended by Hyyrö et al. [151].

```
        a b c d              a    b    c~d
    a   1 0 0 0        a    0.2  0.1  0.2  0.3
    b   0 1 0 0        b    0.2  0.5  0.2  0.3
    c   0 0 1 0        c    0.2  0.1  0.6  0.3
    d   0 0 0 1        d    0.2  0.1  0.2  0.8
```

**Figure 8.** Example of a letter-confusion matrix for the alphabet of symbols a, b, c, and d for Levenshtein distance (left) and arbitrary letter confusion matrix (right): the matrix gives a weight of transcription of the letter in the vertical axis to the letter in the horizontal axis.

### 7.3. Spelling Correction as Machine Translation of Letters

Spelling correction can be formulated as a problem of searching for the best transcription of an arbitrary sequence of symbols into another sequence. This type of problem can be solved with methods typical for machine translation. General string-to-string translation models are not restricted to the spelling error correction task but can also be applied to many problems, such as grapheme-to-phoneme conversion, transliteration, or lemmatization [122]. The machine-translation representation of the ASC overcomes the problem of joined and split words but requires a large corpus to properly learn the error model.

Zhou et al. [117] defined the machine-translation approach to spelling correction by the following equation:

$$s' = \arg\max_s P(s|S), \qquad (4)$$

where $S$ is the given incorrect sequence, $s$ is the possibly correct sequence, and $s'$ is the best correction.

Characters are "words" of "correct" and "incorrect" language. Words in the training database are converted into sequences of lowercase characters, and white spaces are converted into special characters. The machine-translation system is trained on a parallel corpus of examples of spelling errors and corrections. Sariev et al. [132] and Koehn et al. [152] proposed an ASC system that utilizes a statistical machine-translation system called Moses (http://www.statmt.org/moses/).

The authors in [125] cast spelling correction into the machine translation of character bigrams. The spelling system is trained on logs of search queries. It was assumed that the corrections of queries by the user follow misspelled queries. This heuristics creates a training database. To improve precision, character bigrams are used instead of single characters.

Statistical machine-translation models based on string alignment, translation phrases, and $n$-gram language models are replaced by neural machine-translation systems. The basic neural-translation architecture, based on a neural encoder and decoder, was proposed by Sutskever et al. [110]. The translation model learns $P(y_1..y_T|x_1...x_T)$ by encoding the given sequence into a fixed-size vector [117]:

$$s = f_e(x_1, ..., x_T) = h_T. \qquad (5)$$

The sequence-embedding vector is decoded into another sequence by a neural decoder [117]:

$$y_t = f_d(s, y_1, ..., y_{t-1}) = h_T. \qquad (6)$$

The decoder takes the encoded vector language model and generates the output. Zhou et al. [117] showed that, by using $k$-best decoding in the string-to-string translation models, they achieved much better results on the spelling correction task than those of the three baselines, namely edit distance, weighted edit distance, and the Brill and Moore model [104].

## 8. Evaluation Methods

The development of automatic spelling correction systems requires a way to objectively assess the results. It is clear though that it is impossible to propose a "general" spelling benchmark because the problem is language- and application-dependent.

Three possible groups of methods exist for evaluating automatic spelling correction:

- accuracy, precision, and recall (classification);
- bilingual-evaluation-understudy (BLEU) score (machine translation); and
- mean reciprocal rank and mean average precision (information retrieval).

The most common evaluation metrics is classification accuracy. The disadvantage of this method is that only the best candidate from the suggestion list is considered, and order and count of the other proposed correction candidates are insignificant. Therefore, it is not suitable for evaluating an interactive system.

Automatic spelling correction is similar to machine translation. A source text containing errors is translated to its most probable correct form. The approach takes the whole resulting sentence, and it is also convenient for evaluating the correction of a poor writing style and non-word errors. It was used by Sariev et al. [132], Gerdjikov et al. [153] and Mitankin et al. [131].

Machine-translation systems are evaluated using the BLEU score, which was first proposed by Papineni et al. [154]:

"The task of a BLEU implementation is to compare $n$-grams of the candidate with the $n$-grams of the reference translation and to count the number of matches. These matches are position-independent. The more matches, the better the candidate translation."

The process of automatic spelling correction is also similar to information retrieval. An incorrect word is a query, and the sorted list of the correction candidates is the response. This approach evaluates the whole list of suggestions and favors small lists of good (highly ranked) candidates for correction. The two following evaluation methodologies are used to evaluate spelling:

- Mean reciprocal rank: A statistical measure for evaluating any process that produces a list of possible responses to a sample of queries ordered by the probability of correctness. The reciprocal rank of a query response is the multiplicative inverse of the rank of the first correct answer. The mean reciprocal rank is the average of the reciprocal ranks of results for a sample of queries [155].
- Mean average precision: Average precision observes how many times a correct suggestion is on the $n$-th place or better in a candidate list [40]. It is calculated from average precision for $n$ in the range from 1 to $k$ ($k$ is a constant, e.g., 10).

Machine translation and information retrieval are well-suited for evaluating interactive systems because they consider the whole candidate list. A smaller candidate list is more natural to comprehend. The best correction can be selected faster from fewer words. On the other hand, the candidate list must be large enough to contain the correct answer.

*8.1. Evaluation Corpora and Benchmarks*

Several authors proposed corpora for specific tasks and languages, but no approach was broadly accepted. The authors in [12] proposed the Koran as a benchmark for the evaluation of Arabic diacritizations. Reynaert [156] presented an XML format and OCR-processed historical document set in Dutch for the evaluation of automatic spelling correction systems.

The most used evaluation set for automatic spelling correction of OCR is TREC-5 Confusion Track [9]. It was created by scanning a set of paper documents. The database consists of original and recognized documents, so it is possible to identify correct–incorrect pairs for system training and evaluation. The other common evaluation set is Microsoft Speller Challenge (https://www.microsoft.com/en-us/download/details.aspx?id=52351).

Also, Hagen et al. [34] proposed a corpus of corrected search queries in English (https://www.uni-weimar.de/en/media/chairs/computer-science-and-media/webis/corpora), and provided an evaluation metric. They re-implemented the best-performing approach [157] from the Microsoft Speller Challenge (https://github.com/webis-de/SIGIR-17).

Tseng et al. [158] presented a complete publicly available spelling benchmark for the Chinese language, preceded by Wu et al. [159]. Similarly, the first competition on automatic spelling correction for Russian was published by Sorokin et al. [160].

*8.2. Performance Comparison*

Table 7 gives a general overview of the performance of automatic spelling correction systems. It lists approaches with well-defined evaluation experiments performed by the authors. The table displays the best value reached in the evaluation and summarizes the evaluation corpora. Only a few corpora were available that are suitable for evaluating an ASC system (such as TREC-5).

It is virtually impossible to compare the performance of state-of-the-art spelling correction systems. Each author solves a different task and uses their methodology, custom testing set, and various evaluation corpora with different languages. The displayed values cannot be used for mutual comparison but are instead a guide for selecting an evaluation method. A solution would be a spelling correction toolkit that implements state-of-the-art methods for error modeling and context classification. A standard set of tools would allow for comparison of individual components, such as error models.

**Table 7.** Reported evaluation results.

| Approach | Evaluation (%) | Test Corpus |
|---|---|---|
| Azmi et al. [60], 2019 | A 98, F 90.7, P 83.5, R 99.2 | Arabic Newspaper Corpora |
| Han et al. [109], 2019 | A 62.67, F 49.33, P 81.12, R 36.33 | Tseng et al. [158], Wu et al. [159] |
| Lv et al. [72], 2016 | A 95.72, F 95.78 | Chinese OCR Medical Records |
| Melero et al. [73], 2016 | P 82.56 | Twitter texts (baseline 56.88%) |
| Attia et al. [107], 2015 | A 93.64 | Arabic Gigaword Corpus 5th Edition |
| Lai et al. [126], 2015 | A 88.2, F 94.4, P 96.2, R 92.7 | Clinical Notes of Patients |
| Ramasamy et al. [127], 2015 | F 95.4, P 95.0, R 95.9 | WebColl, CzeSL-MAN, Czech National Corpus: SYN2005 and SYN2010 |
| Evershed and Fitch [129], 2014 | W 6.4 | Sydney Morning Herald, 1842-1954 |
| Mitankin et al. [131], 2014 | A 93.96 | 1641 Depositions Old English |
| Sariev et al. [132], 2014 | W 16.84/4.98/4.25/3.27 | ICAMET/IMPACT BG/1641 Deposition/TREC-5 |
| Sagiadinos et al. [79], 2014 | F 97.4, P 97.8, R 97.0 | Eleftherotypia—The Modern Greek Text Corpus |
| Wang et al. [133], 2014 | F 85.89 | Microsoft Speller Challenge |
| Ehsan and Faili [80], 2013 | F 36, P 56, R 31 | Persian Corpus Peykareh |
| Duan et al. [136], 2012 | F 94.9/92.8, P 96.3/90.3, R 94.4/95.3 | TREC-5/Microsoft Speller Challenge |
| Flor [59], 2012 | F 85.87, P 85.50, R 86.25 | ETS Spelling Corpus |
| Sha et al. [42], 2011 | A 93.3 | User Behavior Records in Real Online Study Website Chinese |
| Stüker et al. [85], 2011 | W 9.7 | The Fay Database—Children's Free Writing German |
| Wong and Glance [86], 2011 | A 88.73 | Clinical Progress Notes (http://physionet.org) |
| Takasu [138], 2009 | A 94.2 | 1000 Japanese Articles |
| Beaufort and Mancas-Thillou [141], 2007 | A 65.4 | English ICDAR 2003 Corpus |
| Byun et al. [142], 2007 | A 92.75 | SMS messages in Korean |
| Carlson and Fette [89], 2007 | A 95.2/95.8 | Brown Corpus/Wall Street Journal Corpus |
| Magdy and Darwish [143], 2006 | W 11.7 | Arabic Book "The Provisions of the Return" (2000 words) |
| van Delden et al. [46], 2004 | A 93.3 | Misspellings from two NASA databases, Structural and Fuel Cells |
| Héja and Surján [92], 2003 | P 37.2, R 82.6 | Corpus of 92 Clinical Diagnoses in Hungarian |

Note: A, accuracy; F, F-measure/F1-score; P, precision; R, recall; W, word error rate.

## 9. Conclusions

The chronological sorting and grouping of the summary tables with references in this work reveal several findings. The research since the last comprehensive survey [2] brought new methods for spelling correction. On the other hand, we can say that the progress of spelling correction in all areas was slow until the introduction of deep neural networks.

New, a priori spelling correction systems are often presented for low-resource languages. Authors propose rules for a priori error model that extend the existing phonetic algorithm or adjust the edit distance for the specifics of the given language.

Spelling correction systems in context are mostly proposed for languages with sufficient language resources for language modeling. Most of them use $n$-gram language models, but some approaches use neural networks or other classifiers. Scientific contributions for spelling in context explore various context features with statistical classifiers.

Spelling correction with the learning error model shows the biggest progress. The attention of the researchers moves from statistical estimation of the letter confusion matrices to utilization of the statistical machine translation.

This trend is visible mainly in Tables 5 and 6, where we can observe the growing popularity of the use of encoder–decoder architecture and deep neural networks since 2018. New approaches move from word-level correction to arbitrary character sequence correction because new methods based on deep neural networks bring better possibilities. Methods based on machine translation and deep learning solve the weakest points of the ASC systems, such as language-specific rules, real-word errors, and spelling errors with spaces. The neural networks can be trained on already available large textual corpora.

The definition of the spelling correction stated in the Equation (1) begins to be outdated because of the new methods. Classical statistical models of context-based (n-gram, log-linear regression, and naïve Bayes classifier) on the presence of word-level features in the context are no longer important. Instead, feature extraction is left to the hidden layers of the deep neural network. The correction of spelling errors becomes the task of transcribing a sequence of characters to another sequence of characters using a neural network, as it is stated in Equation (4). Research in the field of spelling error correction thus approaches other solutions to other tasks of speech and language processing, such as machine translation or fluent speech recognition.

On the other hand, the scientific progress of learning error models is restricted by the lack of training corpora and evaluation benchmarks. Our examination of the literature shows that there is no consensus on how to evaluate and compare spelling correction systems. Instead, almost every paper uses its own evaluation set and evaluation methodology. In our opinion, the reason is that most of the spelling approaches strongly depend on the specifics of the language and are hard to adapt to another language or a different application. Recent algorithms based on deep neural networks are not language dependent, but their weak point is that they require a large training set, often with expensive manual annotation. These open issues call for new research in automatic spelling correction.

**Author Contributions:** Conceptualization, D.H.; methodology, D.H.; formal analysis, J.S.; investigation, D.H.; resources, D.H.; writing—original draft preparation, D.H.; writing—review and editing, M.P. and J.S.; supervision, M.P.; project administration, J.S.; funding acquisition, M.P. All authors have read and agreed to the published version of the manuscript.

**Funding:** Research in this paper was supported by the Slovak Research and Development Agency (Agentúra na podporu výskumu a vývoja) under projects APVV-15-0517 and APVV-15-0731; the Scientific Grant Agency (Vedecká grantová agentúra MŠVVaŠ SR a SAV), project number VEGA 1/0753/20; and the Cultural and Educational Grant Agency (Kultúrna a edukačná grantová agentúra MŠVVaŠ SR), project number KEGA 009TUKE-4-2019, both funded by the Ministry of Education, Science, Research, and Sport of the Slovak Republic.

**Acknowledgments:** The authors want to thank Jozef Juhár for the team leadership, and personal and financial support.

**Conflicts of Interest:** The authors declare no conflict of interest.

## Abbreviations

The following abbreviations were used in this manuscript:

| | |
|---|---|
| ANN | Artificial neural network |
| ASC | Automatic spelling correction |
| CFG | Context-free grammar |
| CRF | Conditional random fields |
| DLD | Damerau–Levenshtein distance |
| EM | Expectation maximization |
| FSA | Finite-state automaton |
| HMM | Hidden Markov model |
| IR | Information retrieval |
| k-NN | k-nearest neighbors |
| LCS | Longest common subsequence |
| LD | Levenshtein distance |
| LCM | Learning letter-confusion matrix |
| LM | Language model |
| LR | Linear regression |
| LSA | Latent semantic analysis |
| LSTM | Long short-term memory |
| seq2seq | Sequence-to-sequence |
| ME | Maximum entropy |
| OCR | Optical character recognition |
| PMI | Pointwise mutual information |
| POS | Part-of-speech tagging |
| RF | Random forests |
| SMT | Statistical machine translation |
| SVM | Support vector machine |
| WFST | Weighted finite-state transducer |
| WSD | Word-sense disambiguation |
| WCS | Word-confusion set |

## References

1. Cai, F.; de Rijke, M. A Survey of Query Auto Completion in Information Retrieval. *Found. Trends Inf. Retr.* **2016**, *10*, 273–363. [CrossRef]
2. Kukich, K. Techniques for automatically correcting words in text. *Acm Comput. Surv.* **1992**, *24*, 377–439.
3. Baba, Y.; Suzuki, H. How are spelling errors generated and corrected? A study of corrected and uncorrected spelling errors using keystroke logs. In Proceedings of the 50th Annual Meeting of the Association for Computational Linguistics, Jeju Island, Korea, 8–14 July 2020; pp. 373–377.
4. Mitton, R. *English Spelling and the Computer*; Longman Group: Harlow, Essex, UK, 1996; p. 214.
5. Yannakoudakis, E.J.; Fawthrop, D. The rules of spelling errors. *Inf. Process. Manag.* **1983**, *19*, 87–99. [CrossRef]
6. Toutanova, K.; Moore, R.C. Pronunciation Modeling for Improved Spelling Correction. In Proceedings of the 40th Annual Meeting of the Association for Computational Linguistics (ACL), Philadelphia, PA, USA, 7–12 July 2002; pp. 144–151. [CrossRef]
7. Pirinen, T.A.; Lindén, K. State-of-the-art in weighted finite-state spell-checking. In *Computational Linguistics and Intelligent Text Processing, Proceedings of the CICLing 2014, Kathmandu, Nepal, 6–12 April 2014*; Lecture Notes in Computer Science; Springer: Berlin/Heidelberg, Germany, 2014; Volume 8404, Part 2, pp. 519–532. [CrossRef]
8. Hládek, D.; Staš, J.; Ondáš, S.; Juhár, J.; Kovács, L. Learning string distance with smoothing for OCR spelling correction. *Multimed. Tools Appl.* **2017**, *76*, 24549–24567. [CrossRef]
9. Kantor, P.B.; Voorhees, E.M. The TREC-5 Confusion Track: Comparing Retrieval Methods for Scanned Text. *Inf. Retr.* **2000**, *2*, 165–176. [CrossRef]

10. Gimenes, P.A.; Roman, N.T. Spelling error patterns in Brazilian Portuguese. *Comput. Linguist.* **2015**, *41*, 175–184. [CrossRef]
11. Zitouni, I.; Sarikaya, R. Arabic diacritic restoration approach based on maximum entropy models. *Comput. Speech Lang.* **2009**, *23*, 257–276. [CrossRef]
12. Azmi, A.M.; Almajed, R.S. A survey of automatic Arabic diacritization techniques. *Nat. Lang. Eng.* **2015**, *21*, 477–495. [CrossRef]
13. Asahiah, F.O.; Odéjobi, O.A.; Adagunodo, E.R. A survey of diacritic restoration in abjad and alphabet writing systems. *Nat. Lang. Eng.* **2018**, *24*, 123–154. [CrossRef]
14. Miangah, T.M. FarsiSpell: A spell-checking system for Persian using a large monolingual corpus. *Lit. Linguist. Comput.* **2014**, *29*, 56–73. [CrossRef]
15. Shang, H.; Merrettal, T. Tries for approximate string matching. *IEEE Trans. Knowl. Data Eng.* **1996**, *8*, 540–547. [CrossRef]
16. Pal, U.; Kundu, P.K.; Chaudhuri, B.B. OCR error correction of an inflectional Indian language using morphological parsing. *J. Inf. Sci. Eng.* **2000**, *16*, 903–922.
17. Mashod Rana, M.; Tipu Sultan, M.; Mridha, M.F.; Eyaseen Arafat Khan, M.; Masud Ahmed, M.; Abdul Hamid, M. Detection and Correction of Real-Word Errors in Bangla Language. In Proceedings of the 2018 International Conference on Bangla Speech and Language Processing, ICBSLP 2018, Sylhet, Bangladesh, 21–22 September 2018; pp. 1–4. [CrossRef]
18. Boytsov, L. Indexing methods for approximate dictionary searching. *J. Exp. Algorithmics* **2011**, *16*, 11–91. [CrossRef]
19. Deorowicz, S.; Ciura, M.G. Correcting spelling errors by modelling their causes. *Int. J. Appl. Math. Comput. Sci.* **2005**, *15*, 275–285.
20. Wang, Y.R.; Liao, Y.F. Word vector/conditional random field-based Chinese spelling error detection for SIGHAN-2015 evaluation. In Proceedings of the Eighth SIGHAN Workshop on Chinese Language Processing, Beijing, China, 30–31 July 2015; pp. 46–49. [CrossRef]
21. Zhang, H.; Zhang, Q. EmbedJoin: Efficient edit similarity joins via embeddings. In Proceedings of the ACM SIGKDD International Conference on Knowledge Discovery and lData Mining, Halifax, NS, Canada, 13–17 August 2017; pp. 585–594. [CrossRef]
22. Kernighan, M.D.; Church, K.W.; Gale, W.A. A spelling correction program based on a noisy channel model. In Proceedings of the 13th Conference on Computational Linguistics, Helsinki, Finland, 20–25 August 1990; pp. 205–210. [CrossRef]
23. Jurafsky, D.; Martin, J.H. *Speech and Language Processing*; Prentice Hall: Upper Saddle River, NJ, USA, 2014.
24. Kinaci, A.C. Spelling Correction Using Recurrent Neural Networks and Character Level N-gram. In Proceedings of the 2018 International Conference on Artificial Intelligence and Data Processing, IDAP 2018, Malatya, Turkey, 28–30 September 2018. [CrossRef]
25. Reffle, U. Efficiently generating correction suggestions for garbled tokens of historical language. *Nat. Lang. Eng.* **2011**, *17*, 265–282. [CrossRef]
26. Yu, M.; Li, G.; Deng, D.; Feng, J. String similarity search and join: A survey. *Front. Comput. Sci.* **2016**, *10*, 399–417. [CrossRef]
27. Vilares, M.; Otero, J.; Barcala, F.M.; Domínguez, E.; Dominguez, E. Automatic spelling correction in Galician. In *Advances in Natural Language Processing*; Lecture Notes in Computer Science; Springer: Berlin/Heidelberg, Germany, 2004; Volume 3230, pp. 45–57.
28. Shannon, C.E. A mathematical theory of communication. *Bell Syst. Tech. J.* **1948**, *27*, 623–656. [CrossRef]
29. Brill, E.; Moore, R.C. An improved error model for noisy channel spelling correction. In Proceedings of the 38th Annual Meeting on Association for Computational Linguistics ACL 00, Hong Kong, China, 7 October 2000; pp. 286–293. [CrossRef]
30. Khairul Islam, M.I.; Meem, R.I.; Abul Kasem, F.B.; Rakshit, A.; Habib, M.T. Bangla Spell Checking and Correction Using Edit Distance. In Proceedings of the 1st International Conference on Advances in Science, Engineering and Robotics Technology 2019, ICASERT 2019, Dhaka, Bangladesh, 3–5 May 2019. [CrossRef]
31. Hawezi, R.S.; Azeez, M.Y.; Qadir, A.A. Spell checking algorithm for agglutinative languages 'Central Kurdish as an example'. In Proceedings of the 5th International Engineering Conference, IEC 2019, Erbil, Iraq, 23–25 June 2019; pp. 142–146. [CrossRef]

32. Thaiprayoon, S.; Kongthon, A.; Haruechaiyasak, C. ThaiQCor 2.0: Thai Query Correction via Soundex and Word Approximation. In Proceedings of the ICAICTA 2018—5th International Conference on Advanced Informatics: Concepts Theory and Applications, Krabi, Thailand, 14–17 August 2018; pp. 113–117. [CrossRef]
33. Christanti, M.V.; Naga, D.S. Fast and accurate spelling correction using trie and Damerau-levenshtein distance bigram. *Telkomnika (Telecommun. Comput. Electron. Control.)* **2018**, *16*, 827–833. [CrossRef]
34. Hagen, M.; Potthast, M.; Gohsen, M.; Rathgeber, A.; Stein, B. A large-scale query spelling correction corpus. In Proceedings of the 40th International ACM SIGIR Conference on Research and Development in Information Retrieval, Tokyo, Japan, 7–11 August 2017. [CrossRef]
35. Sakuntharaj, R.; Mahesan, S. A novel hybrid approach to detect and correct spelling in Tamil text. In Proceedings of the 2016 IEEE International Conference on Information and Automation for Sustainability: Interoperable Sustainable Smart Systems for Next Generation, ICIAfS 2016, Galle, Sri Lanka, 16–19 December 2016. [CrossRef]
36. Vobl, T.; Gotscharek, A.; Reffle, U.; Ringlstetter, C.; Schulz, K.U. PoCoTo—an open source system for efficient interactive postcorrection of OCRed historical texts. In Proceedings of the First International Conference on Digital Access to Textual Cultural Heritage—DATeCH '14, Brussels, Belgium, 8–10 May 2019. [CrossRef]
37. Rees, T. Taxamatch, an algorithm for near ('Fuzzy') matching of scientific names in taxonomic databases. *PLoS ONE* **2014**, *9*, e107510. [CrossRef]
38. Mühlberger, G.; Zelger, J.; Sagmeister, D. User-driven correction of OCR errors: combing crowdsourcing and information retrieval technology. In Proceedings of the First International Conference on Digital Access to Textual Cultural Heritage—DATeCH '14, Brussels, Belgium, 8–10 May 2019. [CrossRef]
39. Patrick, J.; Nguyen, D. Automated Proof Reading of Clinical Notes. In Proceedings of the 25th Pacific Asia Conference on Language, Information and Computation (PACLIC 25), Singapore, 16–18 December 2011; pp. 303–312.
40. Kashefi, O.; Sharifi, M.; Minaie, B. A novel string distance metric for ranking Persian respelling suggestions. *Nat. Lang. Eng.* **2013**, *19*, 259–284.
41. Andrade, G.; Teixeira, F.; Xavier, C.R.; Oliveira, R.S.; Rocha, L.C.; Evsukoff, A.G. HASCH: High performance automatic spell checker for portuguese texts from the web. *Procedia Comput. Sci.* **2012**, *9*, 403–411. [CrossRef]
42. Sha, S.; Jun, L.; Qinghua, Z.; Wei, Z. Automatic Chinese Topic Term Spelling Correction in Online Pinyin Input. In Proceedings of the International Conference on Human-centric Computing 2011 and Embedded and Multimedia Computing 2011, Enshi, China, 11–13 August 2011; pp. 23–36. [CrossRef]
43. Naji, N.; Savoy, J. Information retrieval strategies for digitized handwritten medieval documents. In *Asia Information Retrieval Symposium—AIRS 2011: Information Retrieval Technology*; Lecture Notes in Computer Science; Springer: Berlin/Heidelberg, Germany, 2011; Volume 7097, pp. 103–114. [CrossRef]
44. Bustamante, F.R.; Arnaiz, A.; Ginés, M. A spell checker for a world language: The new Microsoft's Spanish spell checker. In Proceedings of the 5th International Conference on Language Resources and Evaluation (LREC 2006), Genoa, Italy, 22–28 May 2006; pp. 83–86.
45. UzZaman, N.; Khan, M. A Double Metaphone encoding for Bangla and its application in spelling checker. In Proceedings of the 2005 IEEE International Conference on Natural Language Processing and Knowledge Engineering, IEEE NLP-KE'05, Wuhan, China, 30 October–1 November 2005; Volume 2005, pp. 705–710. [CrossRef]
46. van Delden, S.; Bracewell, D.; Gomez, F. Supervised and unsupervised automatic spelling correction algorithms. In Proceedings of the 2004 IEEE International Conference on Information Reuse and Integration, IRI 2004, Las Vegas, NV, USA, 8–10 November 2004; pp. 530–535. [CrossRef]
47. Schulz, K.U.; Mihov, S. Fast string correction with Levenshtein automata. *Int. J. Doc. Anal. Recognit.* **2003**, *5*, 67–85. [CrossRef]
48. Taghva, K.; Stofsky, E. OCRSpell: An interactive spelling correction system for OCR errors in text. *Int. J. Doc. Anal. Recognit.* **2001**, *3*, 125–137. [CrossRef]
49. Vagelatos, A.; Triantopoulou, T.; Tsalidis, C.; Christodoulakis, D. Utilization of a lexicon for spelling correction in modern Greek. In Proceedings of the 1995 ACM symposium on Applied computing—SAC '95, Nashville, TN, USA, 26–28 February 1995; pp. 267–271. [CrossRef]

50. Ahmed, F.; de Luca, E.W.; Nürnberger, A. Revised N-Gram based Automatic Spelling Correction Tool to Improve Retrieval Effectiveness. *Polibits* **2009**, *40*, 39–48. [CrossRef]
51. Levenshtein, V.I. Binary Codes Capable of Correcting Deletions, Insertions and Reversals. *Sov. Phys. Dokl.* **1966**, *10*, 707–710.
52. Damerau, F.J. A Technique for Computer Detection and Correction of Spelling Errors. *Commun. ACM* **1964**, *7*, 171–176. [CrossRef]
53. Wagner, R.a.; Fischer, M.J. The String-to-String Correction Problem. *J. ACM* **1974**, *21*, 168–173. [CrossRef]
54. Flouri, T.; Giaquinta, E.; Kobert, K.; Ukkonen, E. Longest common substrings with k mismatches. *Inf. Process. Lett.* **2015**, *115*, 643–647. [CrossRef]
55. Bergroth, L.; Hakonen, H.; Raita, T. A survey of longest common subsequence algorithms. In Proceedings of the 7th International Symposium on String Processing and Information Retrieval, SPIRE 2000, A Coruña, Spain, 27–29 September 2000; pp. 39–48. [CrossRef]
56. Naseem, T.; Hussain, S. A novel approach for ranking spelling error corrections for Urdu. *Lang. Resour. Eval.* **2007**, *41*, 117–128. [CrossRef]
57. Philips, L. Hanging on the metaphore. *Comput. Lang.* **1990**, *7*, 38–44.
58. Kondrak, G.; Sherif, T. Evaluation of several phonetic similarity algorithms on the task of cognate identification. In Proceedings of the Workshop on Linguistic Distances—LD '06, Sydney, Australia, 23 July 2006; pp. 43–50. [CrossRef]
59. Flor, M. Four types of context for automatic spelling correction. *TAL Trait. Autom. Des Langues* **2012**, *53*, 61–99.
60. Azmi, A.M.; Almutery, M.N.; Aboalsamh, H.A. Real-Word Errors in Arabic Texts: A Better Algorithm for Detection and Correction. *IEEE/ACM Trans. Audio Speech Lang. Process.* **2019**, *27*, 1308–1320. [CrossRef]
61. Dong, R.; Yang, Y.; Jiang, T. Spelling correction of non-word errors in Uyghur-Chinese machine translation. *Information* **2019**, *10*, 202. [CrossRef]
62. Yazdani, A.; Ghazisaeedi, M.; Ahmadinejad, N.; Giti, M.; Amjadi, H.; Nahvijou, A. Automated Misspelling Detection and Correction in Persian Clinical Text. *J. Digit. Imaging* **2019**, *33*, 555–562. [CrossRef]
63. Damnati, G.; Auguste, J.; Nasr, A.; Charlet, D.; Heinecke, J.; Béchet, F. Handling normalization issues for part-of-speech tagging of online conversational text. In Proceedings of the 11th International Conference on Language Resources and Evaluation (LREC 2018), Miyazaki, Japan, 7–12 May 2018; pp. 88–92.
64. Dashti, S.M.S. Real-word error correction with trigrams: correcting multiple errors in a sentence. *Lang. Resour. Eval.* **2018**, *52*, 485–502. [CrossRef]
65. Fahda, A.; Purwarianti, A. A statistical and rule-based spelling and grammar checker for Indonesian text. In Proceedings of the 2017 International Conference on Data and Software Engineering, ICoDSE 2017, Palembang, Indonesia, 1–2 November 2017; pp. 1–6. [CrossRef]
66. Heyman, G.; Vulić, I.; Laevaert, Y.; Moens, M.F. Automatic detection and correction of context-dependent dt-mistakes using neural networks. *Comput. Linguist. Neth. J.* **2018**, *8*, 49–65.
67. Golding, A.R.; Schabes, Y. Combining Trigram-based and feature-based methods for context-sensitive spelling correction. In Proceedings of the 34th annual meeting on Association for Computational Linguistics, Santa Cruz, CA, USA, 23–28 June 1996; pp. 71–78. [CrossRef]
68. Dziadek, J.; Henriksson, A.; Duneld, M. Improving Terminology Mapping in Clinical Text with Context-Sensitive Spelling Correction. *Stud. Health Technol. Inform.* **2017**, *235*, 241–245. [CrossRef]
69. Sorokin, A. Spelling Correction for Morphologically Rich Language: A Case Study of Russian. In Proceedings of the 6th Workshop on Balto-Slavic Natural Language Processing, Valencia, Spain, 4 April 2017; pp. 45–53. [CrossRef]
70. Zhao, H.; Cai, D.; Xin, Y.; Wang, Y.; Jia, Z. A Hybrid Model for Chinese Spelling Check. *ACM Trans. Asian -Low-Resour. Lang. Inf. Process.* **2017**, *16*, 1–22. [CrossRef]
71. de Mendonça Almeida, G.A.; Avanço, L.; Duran, M.S.; Fonseca, E.R.; Volpe Nunes, M.d.G.; Aluísio, S.M. Evaluating phonetic spellers for user-generated content in Brazilian Portuguese. In Proceedings of the PROPOR 2016: Computational Processing of the Portuguese Language, Tomar, Portugal, 13–15 July 2016; pp. 361–373. [CrossRef]
72. Lv, Y.Y.; Deng, Y.I.; Liu, M.L.; Lu, Q.Y. Automatic error checking and correction of electronic medical records. *Front. Artif. Intell. Appl.* **2016**, *281*, 32–40. [CrossRef]

73. Melero, M.; Costa-Jussà, M.; Lambert, P.; Quixal, M. Selection of correction candidates for the normalization of Spanish user-generated content. *Nat. Lang. Eng.* **2016**, *22*, 135–161. [CrossRef]
74. Mirzababaei, B.; Faili, H. Discriminative reranking for context-sensitive spell-checker. *Digit. Scholarsh. Humanit.* **2016**, *31*, 411–427. [CrossRef]
75. Sorokin, A.; Shavrina, T. Automatic spelling correction for Russian social media texts. In Proceedings of the International Conference "Dialogue 2016", Moscow, Russia, 1–4 June 2016; pp. 688–701.
76. Vilares, J.; Alonso, M.A.; Doval, Y.; Vilares, M. Studying the effect and treatment of misspelled queries in Cross-Language Information Retrieval. *Inf. Process. Manag.* **2016**, *52*, 646–657. [CrossRef]
77. Lhoussain, A.S.; Hicham, G.; Abdellah, Y. Adapting the levenshtein distance to contextual spelling correction. *Int. J. Comput. Sci. Appl.* **2015**, *12*, 127–133.
78. Ferrero, C.L.; Renau, I.; Nazar, R.; Torner, S. Computer-assisted Revision in Spanish Academic Texts: Peer-assessment. *Procedia-Soc. Behav. Sci.* **2014**, *141*, 470–483. [CrossRef]
79. Sagiadinos, S.; Gasteratos, P.; Dragonas, V.; Kalamara, A.; Spyridonidou, A.; Kermanidis, K. Knowledge-Poor Context-Sensitive Spelling Correction for Modern Greek. In *Artificial Intelligence: Methods and Applications*; Springer International Publishing: Cham, Switzerland, 2014; Volume 8445, pp. 360–369. [CrossRef]
80. Ehsan, N.; Faili, H. Grammatical and context-sensitive error correction using a statistical machine translation framework: Grammar and Context-Sensitive Error Checker. *Softw. Pract. Exp.* **2013**, *43*, 187–206. [CrossRef]
81. Hladek, D.; Stas, J.; Juhar, J.; Hládek, D.; Staš, J.; Juhar, J.; Hladek, D. Unsupervised spelling correction for Slovak. *Adv. Electr. Electron. Eng.* **2013**, *11*, 392–397. [CrossRef]
82. Bouma, G. Normalized (Pointwise) Mutual Information in Collocation Extraction. In Proceedings of the German Society for Computational Linguistics (GSCL 2009), Darmstadt, Germany, 25–27 September 2009; pp. 31–40.
83. Alkanhal, M.I.; Al-Badrashiny, M.A.; Alghamdi, M.M.; Al-Qabbany, A.O. Automatic stochastic arabic spelling correction with emphasis on space insertions and deletions. *IEEE Trans. Audio, Speech Lang. Process.* **2012**, *20*, 2111–2122. [CrossRef]
84. Grozea, C. Experiments and Results with Diacritics Restoration in Romanian. In Proceedings of the 15th International Conference on Text, Speech and Dialogue, TSD 2012, Brno, Czech Republic, 3–7 September 2012; Springer: Berlin/Heidelberg, Germany, 2012; Volume 7499 LNAI, pp. 199–206. [CrossRef]
85. Stüker, S.; Fay, J.; Berkling, K. Towards Context-Dependent Phonetic Spelling Error Correction in Children's Freely Composed Text for Diagnostic and Pedagogical Purposes. In Proceedings of the Annual Conference of the International Speech Communication Association, INTERSPEECH 2011, Florence, Italy, 27–31 August 2011; pp. 1601–1604.
86. Wong, W.; Glance, D. Statistical semantic and clinician confidence analysis for correcting abbreviations and spelling errors in clinical progress notes. *Artif. Intell. Med.* **2011**, *53*, 171–180. [CrossRef]
87. Abdulkader, A.; Casey, M.R. Low cost correction of OCR errors using learning in a multi-engine environment. In Proceedings of the International Conference on Document Analysis and Recognition, ICDAR, Barcelona, Spain, 26–29 July 2009; pp. 576–580. [CrossRef]
88. Farooq, F.; Bhardwaj, A.; Govindaraju, V. Using topic models for OCR correction. *Int. J. Doc. Anal. Recognit.* **2009**, *12*, 153–164. [CrossRef]
89. Carlson, A.; Fette, I. Memory-based context-sensitive spelling correction at web scale. In Proceedings of the 6th International Conference on Machine Learning and Applications, ICMLA 2007, Cincinnati, OH, USA, 13–15 December 2007; pp. 166–171. [CrossRef]
90. Banko, M.; Brill, E. Scaling to Very Very Large Corpora for Natural Language Disambiguation. In Proceedings of the 39th Annual Meeting on Association for Computational Linguistics, Toulouse, France, 5–10 July 2011; Association for Computational Linguistics: Stroudsburg, PA, USA, 2001; pp. 26–33. [CrossRef]
91. Mykowiecka, A.; Marciniak, M. Domain-driven automatic spelling correction for mammography reports. *Adv. Soft Comput.* **2006**, *35*, 521–530.
92. Héja, G.; Surján, G. Using N-gram method in the decomposition of compound medical diagnoses. *Stud. Health Technol. Inform.* **2002**, *90*, 455–459. [CrossRef]

93. Jin, R.; Zhai, C.; Hauptmann, A.G. Information retrieval for OCR documents: A content-based probabilistic correction model. *Proc. SPIE— Int. Soc. Opt. Eng.* **2003**, *5010*, 128–135. [CrossRef]
94. Ruch, P.; Baud, R.; Geissbühler, A. Using lexical disambiguation and named-entity recognition to improve spelling correction in the electronic patient record. *Artif. Intell. Med.* **2003**, *29*, 169–184. [CrossRef]
95. Li, J.; Wang, X. Combining trigram and automatic weight distribution in Chinese spelling error correction. *J. Comput. Sci. Technol.* **2002**, *17*, 915–923. [CrossRef]
96. Golding, A.R.; Roth, D. A Winnow-Based Approach to Context-Sensitive Spelling Correction. *Mach. Learn.* **1999**, *34*, 107–130. [CrossRef]
97. Carlson, A.J.; Rosen, J.; Roth, D. Scaling Up Context-Sensitive Text Correction. In Proceedings of the Thirteenth Conference on Innovative Applications of Artificial Intelligence Conference, Seattle, WA, USA, 7–9 August 2001; AAAI Press: Palo Alto, CA, USA, 2001; Volume 51, pp. 45–50. [CrossRef]
98. Ruch, P.; Baud, R.; Geissbuhler, A. Toward filling the gap between interactive and fully-automatic spelling correction using the linguistic context. In Proceedings of the IEEE International Conference on Systems, Man and Cybernetics, Tucson, AZ, USA, 7–10 October 2001; Volume 1, pp. 199–204. [CrossRef]
99. Jones, M.P.; Martin, J.H. Contextual spelling correction using latent semantic analysis. In Proceedings of the Fifth Conference on Applied Natural Language Processing—ANLC '97, Washington, DC, USA, 31 March– 3 April 1997; Association for Computational Linguistics: Stroudsburg, PA, USA, 1997; pp. 166–173. [CrossRef]
100. Ristad, E.S.; Yianilos, P.N. Learning string-edit distance. *IEEE Trans. Pattern Anal. Mach. Intell.* **1998**, *20*, 522–532. [CrossRef]
101. Fivez, P.; Šuster, S.; Daelemans, W. Unsupervised context-sensitive spelling correction of English and Dutch clinical free-text with word and character N-Gram embeddings. *Comput. Linguist. Neth. J.* **2017**, *7*, 39–52.
102. Zaky, D.; Romadhony, A. An LSTM-based Spell Checker for Indonesian Text. In Proceedings of the 2019 International Conference on Advanced Informatics: Concepts, Theory, and Applications, ICAICTA 2019, Yogyakarta, Indonesia, 20–21 September 2019. [CrossRef]
103. Littlestone, N. Learning Quickly When Irrelevant Attributes Abound: A New Linear-Threshold Algorithm. *Mach. Learn.* **1988**, *2*, 285–318. [CrossRef]
104. Brill, E.; Brill, E.; Wu, J.; Wu, J. Classifier Combination for Improved Lexical Disambiguation. In Proceedings of the 17th International Conference on Computational Linguistics, Montreal, QC, Canada, 10–14 August 1998; Association for Computational Linguistics: Stroudsburg, PA, USA, 1998; Volume 1, pp. 191–195. [CrossRef]
105. Perez-Cortes, J.C.; Llobet, R.; Navarro-Cerdan, J.R.; Arlandis, J. Using field interdependence to improve correction performance in a transducer-based OCR post-processing system. In Proceedings of the 12th International Conference on Frontiers in Handwriting Recognition, ICFHR 2010, Kolkata, India, 16–18 November 2010; pp. 605–610. [CrossRef]
106. Attia, M.; Pecina, P.; Toral, A.; Tounsi, L.; van Genabith, J. An open-source finite state morphological transducer for modern standard Arabic. In Proceedings of the 9th International Workshop on Finite State Methods and Natural Language Processing, Blois, France, 12–15 July 2011; Association for Computational Linguistics: Stroudsburg, PA, USA, 2011; pp. 125–133.
107. Attia, M.; Pecina, P.; Samih, Y.; Shaalan, K.; Van Genabith, J.; Genabith, J.V. Arabic spelling error detection and correction. *Nat. Lang. Eng.* **2015**, *22*, 1–23. [CrossRef]
108. Ahmad, F.; Kondrak, G. Learning a spelling error model from search query logs. In Proceedings of the Conference on Human Language Technology and Empirical Methods in Natural Language Processing HLT 05, Vancouver, BC, Canada, 6–8 October2005; Association for Computational Linguistics: Stroudsburg, PA, USA, 2005; pp. 955–962. [CrossRef]
109. Han, Z.; Lv, C.; Wang, Q.; Fu, G. Chinese Spelling Check based on Sequence Labeling. In Proceedings of the 2019 International Conference on Asian Language Processing, IALP 2019, Shanghai, China, 15–17 November 2019; pp. 373–378. [CrossRef]
110. Sutskever, I.; Vinyals, O.; Le, Q.V. Sequence to Sequence Learning with Neural Networks. In *Advances in Neural Information Processing Systems 27 (NIPS 2014)*; MIT Press: Cambridge, MA, USA, 2014; pp. 3104–3112. [CrossRef]

111. Jain, A.; Jain, M.; Jain, G.; Tayal, D.K. "UTTAM": An efficient spelling correction system for Hindi language based on supervised learning. *ACM Trans. Asian -Low-Resour. Lang. Inf. Process.* **2019**, *18*, 1–26. [CrossRef]
112. Lu, C.J.; Aronson, A.R.; Shooshan, S.E.; Demner-Fushman, D. Spell checker for consumer language (CSpell). *J. Am. Med Informatics Assoc. JAMIA* **2019**, *26*, 211–218. [CrossRef] [PubMed]
113. Mammadov, S. Neural Spelling Correction for Azerbaijani Language. In Proceedings of the 13th IEEE International Conference on Application of Information and Communication Technologies, AICT 2019, Baku, Azerbaijan, 23–25 October 2019. [CrossRef]
114. Roy, S. Denoising Sequence-to-Sequence Modeling for Removing Spelling Mistakes. In Proceedings of the 1st International Conference on Advances in Science, Engineering and Robotics Technology 2019, ICASERT 2019, Dhaka, Bangladesh, 3–5 May 2019. [CrossRef]
115. Yang, L.; Li, Y.; Wang, J.; Tang, Z. Post text processing of chinese speech recognition based on bidirectional LSTM networks and CRF. *Electronics* **2019**, *8*, 1249. [CrossRef]
116. Zhang, S.; Lei, M.; Yan, Z. Investigation of transformer based spelling correction model for CTC-based end-to-end Mandarin speech recognition. In Proceedings of the Annual Conference of the International Speech Communication Association, INTERSPEECH, Graz, Austria, 15–19 September 2019; pp. 2180–2184. [CrossRef]
117. Zhou, Y.; Porwal, U.; Konow, R. Spelling correction as a foreign language. In *2019 SIGIR Workshop on eCommerce, eCOM 2019*; CEUR-WS: Aachen, Germany, 2019; Volume 2410.
118. Barteld, F.; Biemann, C.; Zinsmeister, H. Variations on the theme of variation: Dealing with spelling variation for fine-grained POS tagging of historical texts. In Proceedings of the 14th Conference on Natural Language Processing (KONVENS 2018), Vienna, Austria, 19–21 September 2018; Austrian Academy of Sciences: Wien, Austria; Institut für Germanistik, Universität Hamburg: Hamburg, Germany, 2018; pp. 202–212.
119. Sooraj, S.; Manjusha, K.; Anand Kumar, M.; Soman, K. Deep learning based spell checker for Malayalam language. *J. Intell. Fuzzy Syst.* **2018**, *34*, 1427–1434. [CrossRef]
120. Sbattella, L.; Tedesco, R. How to simplify human-machine interaction: A text complexity calculator and a smart spelling corrector. In Proceedings of the 4th EAI International Conference on Smart Objects and Technologies for Social Good, GOODTECHS, Bologna, Italy, 28–30 November 2018; pp. 304–305. [CrossRef]
121. Silfverberg, M.; Kauppinen, P.; Lindén, K. Data-Driven Spelling Correction using Weighted Finite-State Methods. In Proceedings of the SIGFSM Workshop on Statistical NLP and Weighted Automata, Berlin, Germany, 12 August 2016; pp. 51–59. [CrossRef]
122. Eger, S.; vor der Brück, T.; Mehler, A. A Comparison of Four Character-Level String-to-String Translation Models for (OCR) Spelling Error Correction. *Prague Bull. Math. Linguist.* **2016**. [CrossRef]
123. Lindén, K. Multilingual modeling of cross-lingual spelling variants. *Inf. Retr.* **2006**. [CrossRef]
124. Abandah, G.A.; Graves, A.; Al-Shagoor, B.; Arabiyat, A.; Jamour, F.; Al-Taee, M. Automatic diacritization of Arabic text using recurrent neural networks. *Int. J. Doc. Anal. Recognit. (IJDAR)* **2015**, *18*, 183–197. [CrossRef]
125. Hasan, S.; Heger, C. Spelling Correction of User Search Queries through Statistical Machine Translation. In Proceedings of the 2015 Conference on Empirical Methods in Natural Language Processing (EMNLP 2015), Lisbon, Portugal, 17–21 September 2015; pp. 451–460.
126. Lai, K.K.H.; Topaz, M.; Goss, F.R.F.; Zhou, L.L. Automated misspelling detection and correction in clinical free-text records. *J. Biomed. Informatics* **2015**, *55*, 188–195. [CrossRef]
127. Ramasamy, L.; Rosen, A.; Stranák, P. Improvements to Korektor: A Case Study with Native and Non-Native Czech. In *ITAT (Information technologies–Applications and Theory)*; CEUR-WS: Aachen, Germany, 2015; pp. 73–80.
128. Church, K.W.; Gale, W.A. Probability scoring for spelling correction. *Stat. Comput.* **1991**, *1*, 93–103. [CrossRef]
129. Evershed, J.; Fitch, K. Correcting noisy OCR: context beats confusion. In Proceedings of the First International Conference on Digital Access to Textual Cultural Heritage—DATeCH '14, Madrid, Spain, 19–20 May 2014; ACM: New York, NY, USA, 2014; pp. 45–51. [CrossRef]

130. Makazhanov, A.; Makhambetov, O.; Sabyrgaliyev, I.; Yessenbayev, Z. Spelling correction for Kazakh. In *Computational Linguistics and Intelligent Text Processing, Proceedings of the International Conference on Intelligent Text Processing and Computational Linguistics, CICLing 2014, Kathmandu, Nepal, 6–12 April2014*; Lecture Notes in Computer Science; Gelbukh, A., Ed.; Springer: Berlin/Heidelberg, Germany, 2014; Volume 8404, pp. 533–541. [CrossRef]
131. Mitankin, P.; Gerdjikov, S.; Mihov, S. An Approach to Unsupervised Historical Text Normalisation. In Proceedings of the First International Conference on Digital Access to Textual Cultural Heritage—DATeCH '14, Madrid, Spain, 19–20 May 2014; ACM: New York, NY, USA, 2014; pp. 29–34. [CrossRef]
132. Sariev, A.; Nenchev, V.; Gerdjikov, S.; Mitankin, P.; Ganchev, H.; Mihov, S.; Tinchev, T. Flexible Noisy Text Correction. In Proceedings of the 11th IAPR International Workshop on Document Analysis Systems, DAS 2014, Tours-Loire Valley, France, 7–10 April 2014; pp. 31–35. [CrossRef]
133. Wang, Z.; Xu, G.; Li, H.; Zhang, M. A Probabilistic Approach to String Transformation. *IEEE Trans. Knowl. Data Eng.* **2014**, *26*, 1063–1075. [CrossRef]
134. Huang, Y.; Murphey, Y.L.; Ge, Y. Automotive diagnosis typo correction using domain knowledge and machine learning. In Proceedings of the 2013 IEEE Symposium on Computational Intelligence and Data Mining, CIDM 2013, Singapore, 16–19 April 2013; pp. 267–274. [CrossRef]
135. Reffle, U.; Ringlstetter, C. Unsupervised profiling of OCRed historical documents. *Pattern Recognit.* **2013**, *46*, 1346–1357. [CrossRef]
136. Duan, H.; Li, Y.; Zhai, C.; Roth, D.; Ave, N.G. A discriminative model for query spelling correction with latent structural SVM. In Proceedings of the 2012 Joint Conference on Empirical Methods in Natural Language Processing and Computational Natural Language Learning, Jeju Island, Korea, 12–14 July 2012; Association for Computational Linguistics (ACL): Stroudsburg, PA, USA, 2012; pp. 1511–1521.
137. Rashwan, M.A.A.; Al-Badrashiny, M.A.S.A.A.; Attia, M.; Abdou, S.M.; Rafea, A. A stochastic Arabic diacritizer based on a hybrid of factorized and unfactorized textual features. *IEEE Trans. Audio Speech Lang. Process.* **2011**, *19*, 166–175. [CrossRef]
138. Takasu, A. Bayesian similarity model estimation for approximate recognized text search. In Proceedings of the International Conference on Document Analysis and Recognition, ICDAR 2009, Barcelona, Spain, 26–29 July 2009; pp. 611–615. [CrossRef]
139. Takasu, A.; Aihara, K. DVHMM: Variable length text recognition error model. In Proceedings of the 16th International Conference on Pattern Recognition, Quebec City, QC, Canada, 11–15 August 2002; pp. 110–114. [CrossRef]
140. Magdy, W.; Darwish, K. Effect of OCR error correction on Arabic retrieval. *Inf. Retr.* **2008**, *11*, 405–425. [CrossRef]
141. Beaufort, R.; Mancas-Thillou, C. A weighted finite-state framework for correcting errors in natural scene OCR. In Proceedings of the 9th International Conference on Document Analysis and Recognition, Curitiba, Brazil, 23–26 September 2007; pp. 889–893. [CrossRef]
142. Byun, J.; Rim, H.C.; Park, S.Y. Automatic spelling correction rule extraction and application for spoken-style Korean text. In Proceedings of the ALPIT 2007 6th International Conference on Advanced Language Processing and Web Information Technology, Luoyang, China, 22–24 August 2007; IEEE Computer Society: Washington, DC, USA, 2007; pp. 195–199. [CrossRef]
143. Magdy, W.; Darwish, K. Arabic OCR error correction using character segment correction, language modeling, and shallow morphology. In Proceedings of the 2006 Conference on Empirical Methods in Natural Language Processing—EMNLP '06, Sydney, Australia, 22–23 July 2006; Association for Computational Linguistics: Morristown, NJ, USA, 2006; pp. 408–414. [CrossRef]
144. Oncina, J.; Sebban, M. Learning stochastic edit distance: Application in handwritten character recognition. *Pattern Recognit.* **2006**, *39*, 1575–1587. [CrossRef]
145. Gong, H.; Li, Y.; Bhat, S.; Viswanath, P. Context-sensitive malicious spelling error correction. In Proceedings of the World Wide Web Conference, WWW 2019, San Francisco, CA, USA, 13–17 May 2019; pp. 2771–2777. [CrossRef]
146. Kulis, B. Metric learning: A survey. *Found. Trends Mach. Learn.* **2012**, *5*, 287–364. [CrossRef]
147. Bellet, A.; Habrard, A.; Sebban, M. A Survey on Metric Learning for Feature Vectors and Structured Data. *arXiv* **2013**, arXiv:1306.6709, 1–59.

148. Needleman, S.B.; Wunsch, C.D. A general method applicable to the search for similarities in the amino acid sequence of two proteins. *J. Mol. Biol.* **1970**, *48*, 443–453. [CrossRef]
149. Bilenko, M.; Mooney, R.J. Adaptive duplicate detection using learnable string similarity measures. In Proceedings of the Ninth ACM SIGKDD International Conference on Knowledge Discovery and Data Mining, Washington, DC, USA, 24–27 August 2003; pp. 39–48. [CrossRef]
150. Kim, S.R.; Park, K. A dynamic edit distance table. *J. Discret. Algorithms* **2004**, *2*, 303–312. [CrossRef]
151. Hyyrö, H.; Narisawa, K.; Inenaga, S. Dynamic edit distance table under a general weighted cost function. In *SOFSEM 2010: Theory and Practice of Computer Science, Proceedings of the International Conference on Current Trends in Theory and Practice of Computer Science, Špindleruv Mlýn, Czech Republic, 23–29 January 2010*; Lecture Notes in Computer Science; Springer: Berlin/Heidelberg, Germany, 2010; Volume 5901 LNCS, pp. 515–527. [CrossRef]
152. Koehn, P.; Hoang, H.; Birch, A.; Callison-Burch, C.; Federico, M.; Bertoldi, N.; Cowan, B. Moses: Open source toolkit for statistical machine translation. In Proceedings of the 45th Annual Meeting of the Association for Computational Linguistics Companion Volume Proceedings of the Demo and Poster Sessions, Prague, Czech Republic, 23–30 June 2007; Association for Computational Linguistics: Stroudsburg, PA, USA, 2007; pp. 177–180.
153. Gerdjikov, S.; Mitankin, P.; Nenchev, V. Realization of common statistical methods in computational linguistics with functional automata. In Proceedings of the International Conference Recent Advances in Natural Language Processing RANLP 2013, Hissar, Bulgaria, 9–11 September 2013; INCOMA Ltd. Shoumen, BULGARIA and Association for Computational Linguistics: Stroudsburg, PA, USA, 2013; pp. 294–301.
154. Papineni, K.; Roukos, S.; Ward, T.; Zhu, W.J. BLEU: a method for automatic evaluation of machine translation. In Proceedings of the 40th Annual Meeting on Association for Computational Linguistics—ACL '02, Philadelphia, PA, USA, 7–12 July 2002; pp. 311–318. [CrossRef]
155. Voorhees, E.M. The TREC-8 Question Answering Track Report. *Nat. Lang. Eng.* **1999**, *7*, 77–82. [CrossRef]
156. Reynaert, M. On OCR ground truths and OCR post-correction gold standards, tools and formats. In *DATeCH 2014: Digital Access to Textual Cultural Heritage 2014, Madrid, Spain, 19–20 May 2014*; ACM: New York, NY, USA, 2014; pp. 159–166. [CrossRef]
157. Lueck, G. A data-driven approach for correcting search queries. In Proceedings of the Spelling Alteration for Web Search Workshop, Bellevue, WA, USA, 19 July 2011; p. 6.
158. Tseng, Y.H.; Lee, L.H.; Chang, L.P.; Chen, H.H. Introduction to SIGHAN 2015 Bake-off for Chinese Spelling Check. In Proceedings of the Eighth SIGHAN Workshop on Chinese Language Processing, Beijing, China, 30–31 July 2015; Association for Computational Linguistics: Stroudsburg, PA, USA; pp. 32–37. [CrossRef]
159. Wu, S.H.; Liu, C.L.; Lee, L.H. Chinese Spelling Check Evaluation at SIGHAN Bake-off 2013. In Proceedings of the Seventh SIGHAN Workshop on Chinese Language Processing, Nagoya, Japan, 14–18 October 2013; Asian Federation of Natural Language Processing: Nagoya, Japan, 2013; pp. 35–42.
160. Sorokin, A.; Baytin, A.; Galinskaya, I.; Rykunova, E.; Shavrina, T. SpellRuEval: The first competition on automatic spelling correction for Russian. In Proceedings of the International Conference "Dialogue 2016", Moscow, Russia, 1–4 June 2016.

© 2020 by the authors. Licensee MDPI, Basel, Switzerland. This article is an open access article distributed under the terms and conditions of the Creative Commons Attribution (CC BY) license (http://creativecommons.org/licenses/by/4.0/).

*Review*

# A Systematic Review of the Use of Art in Virtual Reality

Audrey Aldridge *[ ] and Cindy L. Bethel [ ]

Department of Computer Science and Engineering, Mississippi State University, Starkville, MS 39762, USA; cbethel@cse.msstate.edu
* Correspondence: ala214@msstate.edu

**Abstract:** Brain injuries can create life-altering challenges and have the potential to leave people with permanent disabilities. Art therapy is a popular method used for treating many of the disabilities that can accompany a brain injury. In a systematic review, an assessment of how art is being used in virtual reality (VR) was conducted, and the feasibility of brain injury patients to participate in virtual art therapy was investigated. Studies included in this review highlight the importance of artistic subject matter, sensory stimulation, and measurable performance outcomes for assessing the effect art therapy has on motor impairment in VR. Although there are limitations to using art therapy in a virtual environment, studies show that it can feasibly be used in virtual reality for neurorehabilitation purposes.

**Keywords:** virtual reality; art therapy; rehabilitation; neurorehabilitation; neuroplasticity; brain injury

## 1. Introduction

Art has been used as part of the healing process for a variety of therapeutic practices, including: mental health treatment, social problems, language and communication difficulties, medical problems, physical disabilities, and learning difficulties [1]. Art therapy involves interacting with a form of art to help patients through recovery. It works by using personal artwork from therapy, third-party artwork, or the creative process to help people explore their emotions or improve social skills. The creative process refers to the stages involved in transforming an idea into its final form. In art therapy the process is more important than the final masterpiece. The act of making art encourages creative expression without placing constraints on experience level. It provides an outlet where there are no right or wrong answers, and one is free to release any internal struggles and frustration that can form in the beginning stages of recovery [2].

As with most aspects of life, one size does not fit all and this holds true for therapy and rehabilitation. Researchers agree that the individualized treatment capability offered by the creative aspect of art therapy is essential for accommodating specific needs of patients [3–5]. By not requiring an end goal in art therapy, people have the ability to make their own choices and express themselves at their own pace and skill level. The individualization aspect of creative art therapy permits a wider range of patients to be treated and unleashes the potential for more therapeutic applications, including neurorehabilitation. Neurorehabilitation is the process of restoring the functions of the brain, usually for people who suffer from a neurological disease or brain injury. One main focus in neurorehabilitation is the plasticity of the brain, or its ability to make adaptive changes or form new connections in place of damage when exposed to environmental stimuli. Although plasticity occurs more in younger ages (developmental years) [6], it has also been found to occur in older ages at reduced levels [7].

One way to ensure the promotion of neural plasticity, regardless of age, is to have participants enter a creative state of flow [8]. Flow, one of the psychometric measures of creativity highlighted in Jung et al.'s (2010) study, has implications for promoting neuroplasticity [9]. Entering the state of flow is said to feel like being in autopilot mode—all focus is on one activity, and everything else seems to fade away [8]. In art therapy, reaching the state of flow not only means achieving the optimal experience but also performing the activity successfully [4,8,9]. Jung et al. (2010) also found that creativity involves the activation within and between multiple brain areas, which has implications for use-dependent plasticity, healing individual parts of the brain [9]. Similarly, Makuuchi et al. (2003) found in their fMRI study that the following brain areas, shown in Figure 1, are activated during creative behavior: the parietal lobe, the premotor cortex, and the sensorimotor area (primary motor cortex and somatosensory cortex), among others [10]. These areas are considered to be involved in motor cognition [11], suggesting that art therapy can be used for restoring damaged motor areas of the brain and for inducing use-dependent neuroplasticity.

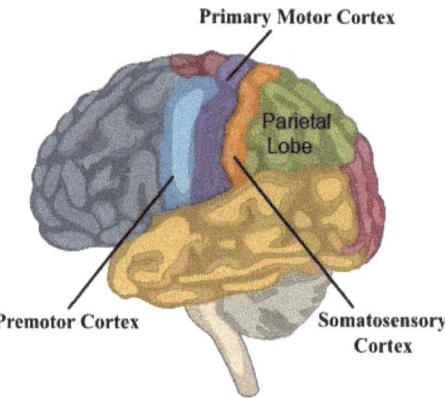

**Figure 1.** Some of the brain areas activated during creative behavior [12].

Promoting plasticity is vital for rehabilitating brain injuries. There are two types of brain injuries, traumatic, and acquired. An acquired brain injury (ABI) refers to any brain damage or alteration of brain function, i.e., stroke, tumor, or meningitis, that occurs after birth and is not hereditary or caused by a degenerative disease. A traumatic brain injury (TBI) refers to any brain damage or alteration of brain function caused by an external impact to the head, such as from a military blast. In 2016, roughly 27 million people suffered TBIs around the world [13]. In the United States, approximately 5.3 million people are currently living with a permanent disability caused by brain injury [14]. Typically after suffering from a TBI, patients are unable to recognize the injury's impact and cannot shift into a new sense of self [4]. Because they suffer from poor self awareness, brain injury patients can potentially benefit from the creativity component of art therapy, which allows for the rehabilitation of self awareness, helping patients adapt to their new disabilities [15]. Of the disabilities that can form after brain injury, including problems with behavioral and mental health, sensory processing, and communication, motor impairment will be the focus of this investigation.

Traditional methods of art therapy often requires a hands-on approach that excludes many people suffering from cognitive and motor impairments. With the technological advancements happening in the realm of human–computer interaction, new and innovative systems are being created to provide treatment to those excluded from the traditional methods of art therapy. Virtual reality (VR) systems are being used as an alternative modality to the traditional methods of therapy. Because VR is a real-time simulation of an environment, it has the capacity to accommodate the specific needs of elderly and impaired populations. In an effort to rehabilitate impaired motor functioning, researchers have studied the effect of VR on motor rehabilitation and have found it to aid in the rehabilitation of physical impairment [16–23]. With evidence supporting the use of VR in rehabilitative practices for motor impairment, an investigation into the efficacy of using art therapy in VR for neurorehabilitation needs to be conducted.

## 2. Objectives

This systematic review consists of an exploratory analysis of how art therapy is being used in VR for neurorehabilitation in non-adolescent people. To formulate the research questions guiding this review, the PICO (Population, Intervention, Comparison, Outcome) format was used [24]. The following research questions will be investigated and answered:
1. What is the feasibility for non-adolescent brain injury patients to experience art therapy for motor neurorehabilitation in a virtual environment?
2. What are the limitations of performing art therapy in VR?

To adequately assess the limitations presented by VR, studies involving art therapy for neurorehabilitation in a non-VR setting are also included in this review.

## 3. Methods

A systematic review conducted according to the Preferred Reporting Items for Systematic Reviews and Meta-Analyses (PRISMA) was performed using Google Scholar, ScienceDirect, and PubMed. The following keywords were used to find relevant studies: "art", "art therapy", "brain injury", "virtual reality", "neurorehabilitation", and "motor rehabilitation". If an article's title related to the objectives of this systematic review, the abstract was read to determine further relevance. If the abstract contained helpful information for answering this review's objectives, then the article was added to a list for further review. Additionally, any relevant-sounding references found in previously reviewed articles were added to the list.

### 3.1. Inclusion Criteria

To be selected as relevant or helpful in reaching the objectives of this review, an article must meet the inclusion criteria. Studies were considered eligible for inclusion if they were written in English and used art or art therapy in non-VR or in VR applications, particularly for neurorehabilitation purposes or with implications toward rehabilitating motor impairment. The desired population for inclusion was healthy adults and brain injury patients. Brain injury must refer to an ABI or a TBI for inclusion.

### 3.2. Exclusion Criteria

Articles with no access to full text were excluded along with review articles. Populations that included patients suffering from disorders, such as cerebral palsy that can be congenital or acquired were excluded as the condition of its occurrence is not always specified. Studies that only measured emotional and mental states were also excluded.

### 3.3. Study Selection

All articles that matched with the keyword "art" specifically because of the phrases "state of the art" or "state of art" were excluded from the initial search results. Studies published in English were eligible if they used art in a therapy setting, set the intervention in a non-VR or VR environment, used a non-adolescent population of healthy people or brain injury patients, and either focused on neurorehabilitation or had implications for use in neurorehabilitation. Once the list of potentially relevant articles was compiled, each article was read in full and evaluated for relevance by two researchers.

## 4. Search Results

Using art neurorehabilitation motor virtual "art therapy", "state of the art", "state of art"" in Google Scholar, 138 results were returned. Of the 138, only 1 article was deemed relevant. To increase search specificity, the following phrase was used in Google Scholar: "allintitle: art neurorehabilitation "state of the art", "state of art"". From this search, 6 results were returned, and 1 article was used in this review. The phrase "allintitle: art therapy "virtual reality", "state of the art", "state of art"" in Google Scholar returned 12 articles, 2 of which are reviewed below. Using the phrase, "(art or "art therapy") and (neurorehabilitation or "neurological rehabilitation" or "motor rehabilitation") and "virtual reality" not "state of the art"" in ScienceDirect returned 36 results. Zero of the results were relevant for this review. To reduce the specificity and yield more results, the phrase ""art therapy" and ("neurorehabilitation" or "motor rehabilitation")" was used to match with words in the title, abstract, or keywords category. One result was returned but was a duplicate of an article found in the Google Scholar search. Using the phrase "art in neurorehabilitation" and filtering to full text available and non-review article types yielded 13 results from PubMed. Of the 13 results, 0 articles were used. Various other combinations of keywords were used to search the databases, especially Google Scholar as it always returned the largest number of results. The combinations of phrases used in Google Scholar that returned the most relevant articles were as follows: "art in neurorehabilitation", "art and brain injury", "art in virtual reality", and "art therapy and neuroplasticity". The phrase "state of the art" was used to eliminate many of the results from these searches. Along with the articles collected from the these database searches, relevant articles found within reference lists of the approved articles were used in this systematic review.

*4.1. Article Exclusion*

Several studies were included in the initial potentially relevant article list but then later removed after reading the abstract or full paper. One example of this is the study conducted by Jones et al. (2019) [25]. The authors conducted a study using art therapy to treat military service members suffering from post-traumatic stress disorder and TBI. The reason for excluding the study is that the focus was on helping the participants understand lingering trauma symptoms and improve communication and quality of life [25]. Another example of an article excluded from the final list of relevant sources is one by Kline (2016) [4]. Kline's (2016) article, titled *"Art Therapy for Individuals With Traumatic Brain Injury: A Comprehensive Neurorehabilitation-Informed Approach to Treatment"* [4], was excluded for being a literature review-based approach that did not provide experimental data.

*4.2. Data Extraction*

Nine articles were found to be relevant for evaluating the feasibility of using art therapy for non-adolescent and brain injury patients. Table 1 shows the diversity of the research conducted in the nine studies being reviewed. Once the list of relevant articles was finalized, studies were briefly analyzed to compare similarities and differences for grouping. To more easily display characteristics of the studies, data including population features, art practice used, intervention setting, and results of the studies performed were collected and compiled into three tables: non-VR (Table 2), VR brain injury patients (Table 3), and VR healthy participants (Table 4).

**Table 1.** Diversity of the reviewed studies.

| Author (Year) | Pop Size (Avg Age) | Condition | Setting | Art Medium |
|---|---|---|---|---|
| Worthen-Chaudhari et al. (2013) [26] | 21 (57 ± 18) | motor impaired | non-VR | digital drawing |
| Bolwerk et al. (2014) [27] | 28 (64 ± 4) | healthy | non-VR | mixed media |
| Paczynski et al. (2017) [28] | 5 (84 ± 8) | stroke | VR | 3D painting (Splashboard) |
| Cucca et al. (2018) [29] | 20 (45–80) * 20 (45–80) * | Parkinson's Disease, age-matched healthy | non-VR | mixed media |
| Kaimal et al. (2019) [30] | 17 (18–65) * | healthy | VR | 3D painting (GTB) |
| McDonald (2020) [31] | 1 (64–65) * | stroke | non-VR | mixed media |
| Alex et al. (2021) [32] | 14 (55–84) * | stroke | non-VR VR | mixed media, 3D painting (GTB) |

Table 1. *Cont.*

| Author (Year) | Pop Size (Avg Age) | Condition | Setting | Art Medium |
|---|---|---|---|---|
| Iosa et al. (2021) [33] | 4 (60 ± 13) | stroke | VR | 2D painting |
| Hacmun et al. (2021) [34] | 7 (42–75) * | expert art therapists | VR | 3D painting (GTB) |

* denotes age range because average age statistics missing from article. (GTB) is the Google Tilt Brush program built for VR.

Table 2. Summary of studies in non-VR environment.

| Author (Year) | Pop Size (Avg Age) | Condition | Art Medium | Results |
|---|---|---|---|---|
| Worthen-Chaudhari et al. (2013) [26] | 21 (57 ± 18) | motor impaired | digital drawing | Interactive art applications are appropriate and helpful in neurorehabilitation |
| Bolwerk et al. (2014) [27] | 28 (64 ± 4) | healthy | mixed media | Art-making promotes improved connectivity in sensorimotor cortex |
| Cucca et al. (2018) [29] | 20 (45–80) * 20 (45–80) * | Parkinson's Disease, age-matched healthy | mixed media | Improvement in impaired visuospatial functions |
| McDonald (2020) [31] | 1 (64–65) * | stroke | mixed media | Art medium and artistic subject matter influenced motor improvement |
| Alex et al. (2021) [32] (non-VR) | 14 (55–84) * | stroke | mixed media | Participants were socially interactive, situated, and reflective |

* denotes age range because average age statistics missing from article.

Table 3. Summary of studies using brain injury patients in VR environment.

| Author (Year) | Pop Size (Avg Age) | Condition | Art Medium | Results |
|---|---|---|---|---|
| Alex et al. (2021) [32] (VR) | 14 (55–84) * | stroke | 3D painting (GTB) | Patients were immersed, physical, and lacked control |
| Iosa et al. (2021) [33] | 4 (60 ± 13) | stroke | 2D painting | Significant improvements in art masterpiece group compared to control |
| Paczynski et al. (2017) [28] | 5 (84 ± 8) | stroke | 3D painting (Splashboard) | Patients enjoyed art program and showed above average velocities in upper body movement |

* denotes age range because average age statistics missing from article. (GTB) is the Google Tilt Brush program built for VR.

Table 4. Summary of studies using healthy participants in VR environment.

| Author (Year) | Pop Size (Avg Age) | Condition | Art Medium | Results |
|---|---|---|---|---|
| Kaimal et al. (2019) [30] | 17 (18–65) * | healthy | 3D painting (GTB) | Felt in control and free; enjoyed sense of alternate world |
| Hacmun et al. (2021) [34] | 7 (42–75) * | expert art therapists | 3D painting (GTB) | Enjoyed experience; user-friendly; felt empowered |

* denotes age range because average age statistics missing from article. (GTB) is the Google Tilt Brush program built for VR.

## 5. Traditional Art Therapy

Transitioning art therapy to neurorehabilitation therapy does not seem like a far stretch. Researchers are already using art therapy to address visuospatial dysfunction and related symptoms of Parkinson's disease [29], analyzing art to detect perspective and preferences of those with limited verbal capabilities [35], and using an interactive art application to provide movement feedback in therapy [26]. With the success of art therapy in treating mental illness and assisting in physical therapy, implications that art therapy may promote treatment progress and recovery in neurorehabilitation are apparent.

Table 2 shows the extracted data from each of the studies using art therapy in a non-VR setting. A brief summary as well as discussion of results and limitations are included for each study.

*5.1. Digital Art Application*

Worthen-Chaudhari et al. (2013) conducted a study assessing the feasibility of using an interactive art application in neurorehabilitation therapy [26]. Ranging from 19 to 86 years of age (average 57 ± 18 years), 21 patients suffering from motor impairment and requiring at least 75% assistance on cognitive and motor-related tasks participated in the study. Over 1–7 sessions of their assigned therapy (physical, occupational, or recreational), participants performed movements in the form of drawing in an interactive art application and were able to see their movements in real-time in the form of visual art feedback. The researchers concluded from user feedback and therapists' responses that interactive art applications are appropriate and helpful for use in neurorehabilitation [26].

The results of the feasibility study conducted by Worthen-Chaudhari et al. (2013) have implications on enhancing neurorehabilitation therapy [26]. The interactive art application kept the participants engaged and showed their movements from a different perspective. By seeing visual feedback in the form of art, participants were able to understand their movements. Another implication found from using the interactive art application was that the quality of engagement may allow participants to experience a longer period of flow [26], hence a higher chance of neuroplastic changes. A limitation with this study was the lack of measurable outcomes on performance or improvements. The participants and therapists reported the interactive art application having a positive effect on motor functioning. From this and other feedback provided by the participants and therapists, one can conclude that it is feasible for this type of art application to be used in the neurorehabilitation setting [26]. Any continuing or future work from this study should include an investigation into whether or not this type of interactive art application improves any measurable outcomes of performance or motor impairment.

*5.2. Art-Making Changes Brain Connectivity*

To investigate how visual art production affects functional connectivity in the brain, Bolwerk et al. (2014) recruited 28 healthy adults, 64 ± 4 years of age, to participate in one of two art interventions: art production or art evaluation [27]. With age, certain areas of the brain begin to lose specialized functioning and turn to alternative brain regions for compensation [36]. Although Bolwerk et al.'s (2014) study investigates several areas of the brain, the focus for this review will be on the sensorimotor cortex because it is involved in motor functioning [10,11,27]. From the results, Bolwerk et al. (2014) found a significant improvement in the intraregional connectivity strength of the sensorimotor cortex with less connectivity in surrounding regions for both groups of participants. However, the art production group yielded stronger changes and stronger connectivity, suggesting a reversal in the loss of specialization and a better improvement in the distinctiveness of the sensorimotor cortex. These results show that art-making promotes improved, efficient interaction between brain regions [27] and holds implications for using art therapy for neurorehabilitating motor impairment.

*5.3. Art Therapy for Parkinson's Disease*

In Cucca et al.'s (2018) study, 20 patients with Parkinson's Disease (Group 1) and 20 age-matched healthy people (Group 2) underwent 20 sessions of art therapy [29]. The researchers' main goals were to identify general characteristics of visuospatial dysfunction and the impact art therapy has on motor and non-motor symptoms of Parkinson's disease. Using various art mediums, including oils, pastels, clay, watercolor, and paint, participants in both groups completed 9 art therapy projects designed to build in complexity and focus on different processes of visuospatial functioning [29]. For example, projects 2, 3, 4, and 6 were all created for the purpose of assessing an aspect of motor functioning: physical control, physical and cognitive capacity, fine motor coordination, and perceptions of physical limitations and strengths.

Cucca et al. (2018) found art therapy to be a safe and reproducible rehabilitation practice for Parkinson's disease patients [29]. Due to their results, the researchers theorized that art therapy rehabilitates by either recruiting underlying neural networks of impaired visuospatial functions, similar to action-observation and motor imagery methodologies, or by recruiting compensatory networks associated with targeted visuospatial functions [29]. Both theories have implications for promoting neuroplasticity [9] and neurorehabilitating motor areas of the brain [11]. The results from the study conducted by Bolwerk et al. (2014) seem to follow Cucca et al.'s (2018) first theory of recruiting underlying neural networks and contradict the second theory because the connectivity strength of the compensatory networks in Bolwerk et al. (2014) was reduced after the art-making intervention [27,29]. If Cucca et al's (2018) first theory is correct, research on a combined art therapy and motor imagery intervention might yield significantly stronger motor improvement results.

*5.4. Personal Journey Back to Mobility*

Not many articles exist that discuss measurable outcomes of using art therapy for neurorehabilitation. Most of the studies on art therapy for neurorehabilitation or art therapy in VR are testing for feasibility and usability. McDonald's (2020) own personal experience with art therapy involves using various art forms to rehabilitate her mind and body after suffering a stroke [31]. In her journey back to almost full mobility, McDonald (2020) used a variety of art mediums including paint, charcoal, colored pencils, and water colors. As her mobility improved, she moved on to a harder movement in art-making. Each medium had its own special movement required for proper use, i.e., charcoal on paper required full arm movement and was good for practicing control; colored pencils and brush strokes worked whole hand and wrist extension; and dabbing paint with a paint brush worked the fine motor movements of the fingers and wrist [31]. Along with changing art mediums, the subject matter of the art changed. Art compositions moved from familiar nature scenes to self-portrait style brain-to-muscle pieces. She also began to incorporate visualization of movement or motor imagery into her drawing process. Prior to one of her brain-muscle drawings, an electromyography reading of her deltoid (shoulder) muscle revealed a lack of muscle activation (loss of muscle control). Within days of drawing the brain-to-deltoid muscle connection, McDonald (2020) was able to raise her arm thirty degrees higher. Similar results were seen after incorporating combined brain-muscle and physical activity, such as swimming, running, and smiling, into her artwork [31].

Although it is not a typical experimental study, the results of McDonald's (2020) efforts to perform art therapy on herself further verify how important participation and engagement are in the art activity. Having completed more than thirty types of therapy post-stroke with little to no improvement, McDonald (2020) underwent art therapy and acquired the confidence, enjoyment, and physical goals she desired [31]. One limitation in this self-styled art therapy treatment was that no specific protocol was followed. McDonald (2020) moved through art projects of varying media at her leisure and based her next move off of feelings and observations. Another limitation in her personal journey article was the lack of measurable outcomes from her art therapy. There were, however, several implications to future research and practice involving the subject matter that she used in her art. Once she incorporated visualization or motor imagery and began drawing movements and brain–muscle connections, she started seeing significant improvements in her physical mobility. By the end of her journey in the article, she noted being able to lightly jog and freestyle swim [31]. Motor imagery has already successfully been used for neurorehabilitating motor functioning in brain injury patients [22,37–44]. More research needs to be done to see whether McDonald's (2020) improvements in physical mobility stem from the subject matter change to brain-muscle connection-based art or from the addition of motor imagery and mental practice to the new subject matter.

Because the article written by Alex et al. (2021) contains one experiment in a non-VR setting and a second experiment in VR, the article was split between Tables 2 and 3, the summary and results will be discussed following Tin the next section.

## 6. Art Therapy in Virtual Reality: Brain Injury

This section includes a brief summary of studies consisting of brain injury patients interacting with a virtual art program. Each of the studies contained in Table 3 used stroke patients to observe different aspects of art-making in VR. Some of those include user experience, art content, and range of motion. Investigating these areas of virtual art therapy produced important points that should be considered in future research. Table 3 shows the extracted data from each of the studies using art therapy in a VR setting for brain injury patients, followed by a discussion of results and limitations for each study.

### 6.1. Traditional Art-Making vs. Virtual Reality Art-Making

Although this article does not focus on neurorehabilitation, it uses brain injury patients to directly compare art therapy interventions in VR to non-VR, and it highlights several important aspects and limitations of performing art therapy in both environments. The main goals of the study conducted by Alex et al. (2021) were to gain a better understanding of the art-making process in a therapeutic setting for stroke patients and to identify potential design opportunities for stroke rehabilitation using art therapy in VR [32]. The researchers observed 14 stroke patients, 55–84 years old, make art traditionally (non-VR) then make it in VR. From their notes and observations, the researchers established the following three themes for comparing traditional (non-virtual) art-making to virtual art-making: artistic subject matter, aesthetics of materials, and art-making process. Figure 2 shows an example of virtual art created by one of the authors of this review using Google's Tilt Brush [45].

**Figure 2.** Artwork from virtual art setting.

In the traditional art-making setting, the subject matter mostly consisted of landscapes, portraits, and animals while in the VR setting, the subject matter was described as abstract (random shapes and lines), intentional (specific objects), or emergent (inspired by characteristics of the VR paint) [32]. The artistic subject matter in the traditional setting seemed very intentional with most participants using the familiar as inspiration for their art pieces. The subject matter in the VR setting, however, seemed very fluid and less precise, even with the participants who painted specific objects. The participants' inexperience with VR and lack of control of the VR controllers could explain why the virtual subject matter came across as more abstract and whimsical.

The aesthetic nature of materials in both settings differed in the art mediums available, the color selection process, and the malleability of the medium. Although the VR system was designed specifically for painting, the traditional setting offered a variety of different mediums, including graphite pencils, paint, watercolor, crayons, colored pencils, rollers, sponges, etc. Another difference was seen in color availability. The traditional setting allowed participants to create their own colors, if not already provided, by mixing paints together. The colors in the VR system were luminescent, seen in Figure 2, and restricted to the participants' abilities to successfully select a desired color from the color wheel or from predetermined color choices displayed in small circles below the color wheel [32]. It was observed that in the VR environment some participants had to ask for assistance in navigating the color picker menu or for help with gauging the depth of an object they wanted to erase [32].

Regarding the final theme, art-making process, used for comparing the two interventions, the participants had opposite approaches for the traditional and VR environments [32]. The participants were very socially interactive with other participants and facilitators in the traditional art setting, but when immersed into the virtual environment, they were more focused on creating art. This is likely due to the group setting of the non-VR environment and the virtual intervention being done individually. Another way that the art-making processes appear to be opposites is in the pace that was used to create the art. In the traditional art environment, the participants were situated and reflective. They made careful decisions before committing something to their artwork by taking the time to identify all their options, reflect upon previous choices, view their artwork from different perspectives, practice with the tools, and use different techniques to apply or shape their chosen medium. In the VR setting, however, the participants were more physical and lacked control. Because the virtual environment provided more space for creating, participants used more of their body in the process and were able to create art all around them instead of just right in front of them. The participants seemed out of control because they were very quick to fill the available space and reported that the controller was not doing what they wanted it to do. It was speculated that the participants did not have comparable control of the VR controllers as they had with the traditional tools and that their lack of control might have been from the mid-air movements draining their physical capabilities [32].

In the traditional setting, the participants worked at tables or desks and were able to rest their arms while they created art [32]. In the virtual environment, the participants engaged more of their upper body in the art-making process. The researchers noticed the wider range of motion used in virtual art-making and hinted towards this increase in physical activity having implications for improving motor impairments in stroke patients. They believe VR offers the unique benefit of allowing for adaptability in the scale of movement translation [32]. Changing the movement scale to translate large movements to smaller brush strokes could encourage more physical movement and lead to greater improvements in physical ability. Alternatively, changing the scale in the opposite direction would allow individuals with smaller or shorter ranges of motion to see their brush strokes covering larger areas, potentially helping to overcome the feeling of being physically impaired. This switch in focus from disability to ability is important in promoting progress and recovery [3,4,46].

There were limitations in the speed at which art was made in the VR environment and in the virtual art program that was used. Participants spent only minutes creating artwork in VR but spent hours creating art in the traditional setting. In the short amount of time the participants were in the virtual environment, they would not have been able to experience the benefits of art therapy, such as Csikszentmihalyi and Csikszentmihalyi's (1992) state of flow [8], or even the same benefits experienced in the traditional setting [32]. Using the same virtual art program, participants from Kaimal et al. (2020) made comments about how navigating the virtual art environment was easier after they adjusted to the controllers [30]. The groups from both studies were taken through an exploratory session to familiarize themselves with the art software, VR controllers, and virtual environment [30,32]. It is unclear whether the participants from Alex et al.'s (2021) [32] study were finding difficulty in the art program itself or in using the VR controllers. It is clear, however, that they did not use the same careful approach to creating art in the virtual environment as they did in the traditional setting.

From the responses made by the participants and their favoritism towards traditional art-making, it is likely that the participants were overwhelmed by their virtual art-making experience [32]. The VR intervention always took place after the traditional non-VR intervention, and some patients participated in more than one session of the traditional art therapy. It would be interesting to see results from a similar study that compares the same number of sessions and counterbalances the art therapy environments. Another limitation, being in the virtual art program, is present in the interaction between the participants and the art mediums. In the traditional (non-VR) art setting, participants gained a sort of physical connection from being able to touch the art mediums and tools and mix the paints. Part of the art therapy experience is the sensory stimulation that physical materials provide. It is especially important for brain injury patients to experience that sensory stimulation as it is known to enhance awareness and focus [47]. Having one controller in place of various art tools takes away that physical connection that was seen in other studies [29,31]. The resulting gap in feeling connected to virtual art-making caused by this limitation has implications to introducing haptic feedback to virtual art therapy. Iosa et al. (2021) tried to rectify the missing tactile information that comes with virtual environments by adding visual feedback of color and shadow to the virtual tool used in their VR program [33].

*6.2. Art Improves Performance in Virtual Reality*

Iosa et al. (2021) conducted two experiments, but the first was excluded due to the population used. In the second experiment, four (4) stroke patients with an average age of 60 ± 13 years performed four (4) sessions of virtually interacting with either an art-masterpiece or a piece of control art [33]. The virtual art system consisted of a 2D canvas covered in a white film. Using the VR controller, participants were to "paint" over the canvas, revealing either an art masterpiece or the control art. The illusion of painting was provided by the white film disappearing when the virtual art tool came into contact with the canvas. To add visual feedback to the system, the virtual art tool (a sphere) would turn green when in contact with the canvas but would turn red when the participant moved beyond the canvas. The movement of the virtual sphere and participant's hand were tracked and recorded for performance measures during the sessions. The two participants who interacted with the art masterpiece had significant improvements for all computed parameters compared to the two participants who were assigned the control artwork. The participants also reported high scores of usability for the virtual reality task, hinting at implications of future use for VR-based rehabilitation. Limitations include small sample size and differences in details of the art masterpieces used [33]. Some of the art masterpieces contained humans while others consisted of fluid nature scenes. Artistic subject matter used in art therapy needs to be further studied, as it seems to have made an impact in three of the five studies reviewed so far [31–33]. There are implications that if art therapy can be performed while the brain is monitored using an electroencephalogram (EEG), then certain details and aspects of artwork, such as landscapes versus people in motion, can be used to target specific areas of the brain for rehabilitation [33].

*6.3. Digital Art Program in Virtual Reality*

Paczynski et al. (2017) studied the interaction between elderly people and an art program designed for creating digital artwork in VR [28]. Fifteen older adults, ranging from 69 to 96 years of age (average 84 ± 8 years), living in an aged-care facility took turns using the digital art system for six weeks. On average, the participants engaged in four 11.6 min sessions where they were free to create art without trying to reach a specific goal. Right and left hand movement was tracked along with lower body movement to show changes in performance. To analyze how their digital art program impacted movement, cognitive stimulation, and creativity, Paczynksi et al. (2017) separated the participants into the following categories of impairment: stroke, dementia or memory impairment, and depression [28]. For the purpose of this systematic review, only the stroke and dementia groups' results will be discussed. For the five participants affected by stroke, all showed above average velocities and upper body movements. The majority of the stroke participants enjoyed interacting with the digital art program and felt a positive impact on their physical and cognitive states. The art program allowed for the stroke participants to express themselves creatively, despite their mental or physical impairments. For the group of participants suffering from dementia or memory impairment, four of the nine felt a positive impact on their cognitive health, and five of the nine felt a positive impact on their physical health. Data results for movement and creativity were not provided for this group [28].

Paczynski et al.'s (2017) results revealed that art in VR can be enticing and flexible for many types of users if they can stay engaged long enough to reap the benefits. A trend of growing indifference toward the art program can be seen from the recorded distances of the hands and lower body traveled in the first sessions compared to those traveled in the final sessions. Having seven participants who traveled furthest in their first session implies that the novelty of the art system and the initial excitement and engagement provided a strong motivation for interaction that appears to have slowly faded [28]. If an aspect of sensory stimulation were added to the digital art program, attention might have been more easily sustained [47]. Adding a goal or theme of subject matter to create also might entice participants to stay motivated over several sessions of use. Having only six participants complete four or more sessions raises the question of whether those six were able to reach the state of flow easier than the other participants or if they were the only six to reach the state of flow. The virtual art program presented in Paczynski et al. (2017) afforded accessibility to a creative outlet for multiple disabilities that otherwise might not be able to express themselves [28]. There are implications to cognitive motor repair in the results of the participants who saw an increase in average velocity of one or more body parts. Because this study was for learning about interaction between participants and technology, any future work should investigate if the increased velocity was due to improved motor functioning or due to the excitement created by the new art program.

### 7. Art Therapy in Virtual Reality: Healthy

A summary and discussion of results and limitations are included for each study. The two studies being reviewed in this section used healthy participants in virtual art making to examine user experience and interaction with the same virtual art program. Based on the reports from both groups of participants, it is noticeable that the healthy participants had an easier time navigating the virtual art program than the brain injury participants. Table 4 summarizes the data extracted from each study of the studies that used art therapy in a VR setting for healthy people. ¶

*7.1. Experiencing Art Therapy in Virtual Reality*

The study performed by Kaimal et al. (2020) was included because of its implications toward using the specified art therapy system on individuals with motor impairment. Kaimal et al. (2020) studied 17 individuals, aged 18–65 years old, to gain an understanding of their experiences with art therapy in VR from one free-form art-making session [30]. From the feedback provided by the participants, the researchers identified key aspects art therapy in VR offers that traditional art-making does not. Creating art in the virtual environment engaged full body movements, which the participants found to be enjoyable. Being able to erase part of the artwork eased the sense of permanence typically associated with traditional art mediums. Participants did not have to worry about making mistakes and instead were able to focus on exploration and creative expression [30]. Many participants noted that once they familiarized themselves with the controllers, they felt in control and were able to feel the art flow from them without any distractions. They also expressed their enjoyment in the feeling of being transported to an alternative or imagined space away from the constraints, pressure, and stress of the real world [30].

A practical implication that can be drawn from Kaimal et al.'s (2020) study includes using virtual art therapy on individuals lacking fine motor skills [30]. Experimental limitations are seen more from the system used rather than the virtual environment. The art program does not allow for changing colors of the environment or background, and the art tools sometimes came across as the clunky version of traditional tools [30]. Similar comments were made by the participants in Alex et al.'s (2021) study [32]. Although Kaimal et al. (2020) and Alex et al. (2021) used the same art software in VR, they yielded conflicting results. The population in Kaimal et al.'s (2020) study consisted of younger healthy people [30] while Alex et al.'s (2021) study consisted of elderly stroke patients [32]. The younger population reported more enjoyment in regards to art therapy in VR and did not seem to have as much trouble navigating the menus or using the controller(s) [30]. Another difference is the approach to art-making in the virtual environment. The elderly stroke population seemed overwhelmed by their lack of control of the controller and rushed through creating an art piece [32]. The younger, healthy population seemed to take the time to master the controller and move through the space during the creating process to view their artwork from different perspectives [30]. It is unclear if the participants from Alex et al.'s (2021) [32] study underwent the VR intervention on the same day as their last non-VR art therapy session, but, if so, that could have influenced the quick pace seen from those participants in the VR session.

*7.2. Expert Art Therapists on Art Therapy in Virtual Reality*

To examine the potential for art therapy in VR, Hacmun et al. (2021) had seven expert art therapists, 42–75 years old, observe art-making and create their own art in a virtual environment [34]. Each participant was introduced to the VR medium prior to the creation and observation sessions. In the creation session, participants were allowed to make 3D art in a 360-degree space. In the observation session, participants simultaneously watched the creator in the real-world environment and viewed the virtual art on a computer screen. In the results from the study, the researchers found that most of the participants were surprised by how much they enjoyed creating art in VR and how user-friendly they found the medium. Participants reported missing the physical contact that traditional art-making provides but described the ability to freely move through the art as fun and unique. Some participants noted that they felt their body's physical movement to be a sort of tactile feedback even though there was a lack of physical substrate in the art created. All of the participants reported that VR was suitable for art therapy, but some stated that it should be used along with other creative media. Most of the participants agreed that the ideal population for using art therapy in VR is adolescents who are already familiar with and attached to technology and screens. They reported that they were unsure whether VR could be beneficial to the elderly or physically disabled [34].

Hacmun et al. (2021) point out that a big limitation in their study is that the participants mainly consisted of digital immigrants who do not consider themselves to be technologically savvy [34]. Another limitation that the authors mention is the participants only performed one session of creating art in VR. They acknowledge that feedback from the art therapy experts might change with more practice and familiarization with the VR medium. In terms of movement during virtual art-making, the participants spoke a lot about the freeing feeling of using their whole body to create art but did not connect this feeling of embodied expression with implications toward motor neurorehabilitation or even physical rehabilitation. However, the researchers associate the participants' reporting on movement with results from other studies that have shown movement enhances the feeling of being present in VR due to the increase in connection between the real and virtual worlds [34]. Having the connection between reality and VR can provide an alternative point of view for patients to establish a new sense of self or self-awareness [4,15].

## 8. Discussion

Brain injuries remain a serious public health concern and leave many individuals with long-lasting disabilities. Attempts to create new, innovative ways of using art therapy to treat and repair disabilities caused by brain injury have been made and show promising results in multiple areas of therapy [15,25,35,46,48] with implications toward using art therapy in neurorehabilitation practices [1,10,49–51]. When using art therapy for motor neurorehabilitation, especially for brain injuries, promoting brain plasticity needs to be considered. Neuroplastic changes of motor areas in the brain are thought to happen from a variety of stimuli, including: creative state of flow [9], subject matter [8], motor imagery, action observation, and action execution [22].

In answering the first research question, consider the results from the studies that were reviewed, see Figure 3. Bolwerk et al. (2014) showed that the process of art-making significantly improves intraregional connectivity strength in the sensorimotor cortex [27], which holds implications for using art therapy for motor neurorehabilitation. With the positive improvements in motor functioning seen from Worthen-Chaudhari et al. (2003) and Paczynski et al. (2017), it seems feasible that art therapy can be used for neurorehabilitation purposes outside VR [26,29] and inside VR [28] for patients suffering from brain injury. Hacmun et al. (2021) revealed that the freedom of movement offered in VR can help establish the connection between the real and virtual worlds [34], which can provide an alternative point of view for patients to establish a new sense of self or self-awareness [4,15].

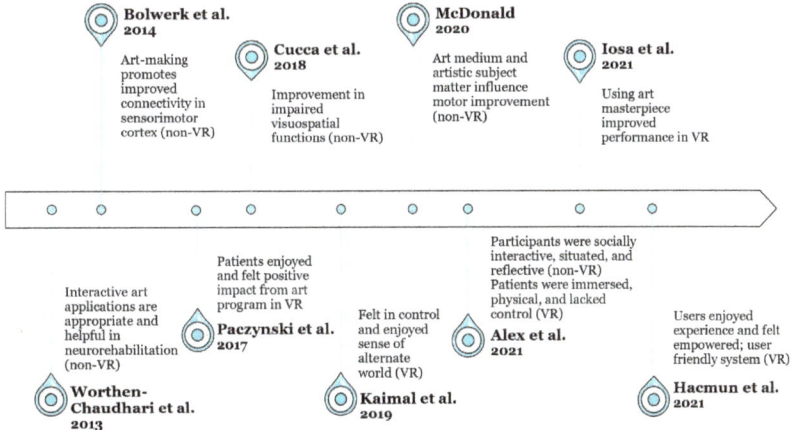

**Figure 3.** Timeline of study contributions.

McDonald (2020) performed art therapy in a traditional (non-VR) setting and began seeing significant improvements in her physical mobility once the artistic subject matter changed to brain-muscle connections and movement visualization was added [31]. From these results, though, the question is raised of whether it was the physical art-making or the combination of subject matter and movement visualization (motor imagery) that improved her motor functioning. If the answer is the latter, then those aspects of art therapy can easily be transferred to a virtual environment. Many researchers are already successfully using motor imagery for neurorehabilitation in VR [22,37,39,42,44]. If the answer is the former (physical art-making), such as that seen in the results from Cucca et al. (2018) [29], then the physical contact and skill required of specific art mediums might play a more significant role in rehabilitation and should be incorporated into virtual art therapy programs in the form of haptic feedback [20,34]. If it turns out to be due to a combination of art-making and subject matter or motor imagery, then the results from Iosa et al. (2021) show that it is possible to yield motor improvements, based on subject matter, in a virtual setting [33]. Although further research into artistic subject matter and combining art therapy with motor imagery needs to be conducted, it is evident that using art therapy in VR for rehabilitating motor functioning is feasible.

Looking at the studies performed by Alex et al. (2021), Kaimal et al. (2020), and Hacmun et al. (2021), they all used the same VR art program on different populations but yielded varying results and limitations [30,32,34]. The elderly stroke population, though seated in a swivel chair, were quick and chaotic in filling the available space [32] while the younger, healthy population was slow and deliberate with their actions and placements [30]. It can be inferred that the physical limitations of the stroke patients affected their control when having to hold the VR controller in mid-air to paint [32]. Additionally, there likely is a limitation in the older, stroke group being confined to a swivel chair [32] while the two healthy groups were free to walk around the space [30,34]. To attain the freedom to create art in VR using full body movements, like those seen in healthy participants, the available population of brain injury patients would have to be reduced to the physically impaired of a certain degree. Unless a mobility support system is used in conjunction with VR or an alternative way of making art in VR is created, it is unsafe to allow patients, specifically with lower limb impairments, to physically move freely around the virtual environment.

A recurring theme appears in several of the studies that were reviewed. Patients seem to quickly lose engagement when art therapy is performed outside of the traditional setting [26,28,32]. It can be deduced that the participants in Iosa et al.'s (2021) study did not lose interest in the VR art task because of the added visual feedback on the virtual art tool [33]. Adding visual feedback follows the idea that sensory stimulation is engaging and draws focus to the task at hand [47]. Following the same principle, switching from traditional art mediums and tools to a VR controller causes a disconnect between the user and the art-making process. Haptic feedback has the potential to recreate a physical connection between user and art medium or tool in a virtual environment. The participant groups from Alex et al. (2021) and Hacmun et al. (2021) agreed on the missing physical connection to art mediums in VR. However, the group from Hacmun et al.'s (2021) study reported the virtual art program to be user-friendly [34] while the group from Alex et al.'s (2021) study seemed to struggle using the program [32]. Because the two healthy populations had an easier time using the virtual art program than the stroke population, future studies should allow brain injury patients extra time or practice sessions to familiarize themselves with navigating virtual art applications and VR controllers. In addition to balancing the learning curve, implementing alternative modalities of controlling virtual art programs has the potential to establish the missing connection between user and virtual art mediums. Adding that kind of sensory stimulation to virtual art programs might also be effective in helping brain injury patients gain control inside the virtual environment. Comparing the reviewed studies, most of the limitations and differences appear to stem from the experimental design(s) or the virtual art system used rather than from the virtual environment [26,28,30,32,34]. If adjustments can be made to the virtual art software, interactivity of materials, and experimental design to ensure a more usable, accessible, and stimulating VR experience, then there is a high probability that brain injury patients can enter the state of flow and induce neuroplasticity, making it feasible to use art therapy in VR for neurorehabilitation. Future work in virtual art therapy will need to assess the correlation between performance and artistic subject matter, as well as overcome the lack of measurable outcomes for showing performance and motor improvements. Utilizing mobility tests for pre and post study measurements, such as the Functional Independence Measure$^{TM}$ [26] and the Fugl–Meyer assessment [52] conducted to assess patients for inclusion criteria, is a way of reducing heterogeneity and allowing for comparable results between studies. Another way of producing measurable outcomes is by combining EEG and art therapy. Using EEG during art therapy could reveal how artistic subject matter influences activation in certain brain areas and promotes use-dependent plasticity [9,33] by studying power levels in different brain regions. It also presents a way for measuring neuroplastic changes [51]. In their study of surveying cortical activation patterns after making art and after performing a physical task, King et al. (2017) revealed a statistically significant difference in cortical activation after art-making compared to baseline data. Their findings have implications toward being able to produce measurable outcomes from art therapy used in neurorehabilitation [51].

## 9. Conclusions

The systematic review conducted in this paper defined the terms of feasibly using art therapy in VR for the motor neurorehabilitation of brain injury patients and outlined the need for future research to use post-study assessments to reduce the heterogeneity of results. Although limitations exist, researchers are continually finding ways to advance the use of art therapy in VR. More research involving multiple sessions of art therapy in VR needs to be conducted to study the learnability and usability of virtual art programs. With further research into artistic subject matter and sensory stimulation in virtual art applications, approaches to art therapy in VR can be fine-tuned for targeting and rehabilitating motor areas of the brain to achieve results similar to those observed in more traditional art therapies.

**Author Contributions:** Conceptualization, A.A. and C.L.B.; methodology, A.A. and C.L.B.; validation, A.A. and C.L.B.; formal analysis, A.A.; investigation, A.A. and C.L.B.; resources, A.A.; data curation, A.A.; writing—original draft preparation, A.A.; writing—review and editing, C.L.B.; supervision, C.L.B.; project administration, A.A. and C.L.B. All authors have read and agreed to the published version of the manuscript.

**Funding:** This research received no external funding.

**Acknowledgments:** The authors acknowledge Kasee Gadke-Stratton for her assistance and information regarding the use of VR for art therapy that formed the basis for this research.

**Conflicts of Interest:** The authors declare no conflict of interest.

## References

1. Van Lith, T.; Fenner, P.; Schofield, M.J. Art Therapy in Rehabilitation. In *International Encyclopaedia of Rehabilitation*; Stone, J.H., Blouin, M., Eds.; Center for International Rehabilitation Research Information and Exchange (CIRRIE): Buffalo, NY, USA, 2009.
2. The Daily Californian. Available online: https://www.dailycal.org/2019/02/28/art-therapy-rehab/ (accessed on 4 August 2021).
3. Perrin, T. Don't Despise the Fluffy Bunny: A Reflection from Practice. *Br. J. Occup. Ther.* **2001**, *64*, 129–134. [CrossRef]
4. Kline, T. Art Therapy for Individuals With Traumatic Brain Injury: A Comprehensive Neurorehabilitation-Informed Approach to Treatment. *J. Abbr.* **2016**, *33*, 67–73. [CrossRef]
5. McGraw, M.K. Art therapy with brain-injured patients. *Am. J. Art Ther.* **1989**, *28*, 37–44.
6. Kolb, B. Synaptic plasticity and the organization of behaviour after early and late brain injury. *Can. J. Exp. Psychol.* **1999**, *10*, 62–76. [CrossRef] [PubMed]
7. Stepankova, H.; Lukavsky, J.; Buschkuehl, M.; Kopecek, M.; Ripova, D.; Jaeggi, S.M. The malleability of working memory and visuospatial skills: A randomized controlled study in older adults. *Dev. Psychol.* **2014**, *50*, 1049–1059. [CrossRef]
8. Csikszentmihalyi, M.; Csikszentmihalyi, I.S. *Optimal Experience: Psychological Studies of Flow in Consciousness*, 1st ed.; Cambridge University Press: New York, NY, USA, 1992; pp. 1–31.
9. Jung, R.E.; Segall, J.M.; Bockholt, H.J.; Flores, R.A.; Smith, S.M.; Chavez, R.S.; Haier, R.J. Neuroanatomy of creativity. *Hum. Brain Mapp.* **2010**, *31*, 398–409. [CrossRef] [PubMed]
10. Makuuchi, M.; Kaminaga, T.; Sugishita, M. Both parietal lobes are involved in drawing: A functional MRI study and implications for constructional apraxia. *Cogn. Brain Res.* **2003**, *16*, 338–347. [CrossRef]
11. Hoshi, E.; Tanji, J. Distinctions between dorsal and ventral premotor areas: Anatomical connectivity and functional properties. *Curr. Opin. Neurobiol.* **2007**, *17*, 234–242. [CrossRef]
12. Chegg. Diagram of Premotor Cortex. Available online: https://www.chegg.com/learn/biology/anatomy-physiology-in-biology/diagram-of-premotor-cortex (accessed on 5 September 2021).
13. James, S.L.; Theadom, A. Global, regional, and national burden of traumatic brain injury and spinal cord injury, 1990–2016: A systematic analysis for the Global Burden of Disease Study 2016. *Lancet Neurol.* **2019**, *18*, 56–87. [CrossRef]
14. Brain Injury Association of America. Brain Injury Facts & Statistics. Available online: https://www.biausa.org/public-affairs/public-awareness/brain-injury-awareness (accessed on 4 August 2021).

15. Smith, C. Innovative rehabilitation after head injury: Examining the use of a creative intervention. *J. Soc. Work Pract.* **2007**, *21*, 297–309. [CrossRef]
16. Adamovich, S.V.; Merians, A.S.; Boian, R.; Tremaine, M.; Burdea, G.S.; Recce, M.; Poizner, H. A virtual reality based exercise system for hand rehabilitation post-stroke: Transfer to function. In Proceedings of the 26th Annual International Conference of the IEEE Engineering in Medicine and Biology Society, San Francisco, CA, USA, 1–5 September 2004; pp. 4936–4939. [CrossRef]
17. Jang, S.H.; You, S.H.; Hallett, M.; Cho, Y.W.; Park, C.M.; Cho, S.H.; Lee, H.Y.; Kim, T.H. Cortical reorganization and associated functional motor recovery after virtual reality in patients with chronic stroke: An experimenter-blind preliminary study. *Arch. Phys. Med. Rehabil.* **2005**, *86*, 2218–2223. [CrossRef]
18. Holden, M.K.; Dyar, T. Virtual Environment Training: A New Tool for Neurorehabilitation. *Neurol. Rep.* **2002**, *26*, 62–71. [CrossRef]
19. Merians, A.S.; Jack, D.; Boian, R.; Tremaine, M.; Burdea, G.C.; Adamovich, S.V.; Recce, M.; Poizner, H. Virtual Reality–Augmented Rehabilitation for Patients Following Stroke. *Phys. Ther.* **2002**, *82*, 898–915. [CrossRef]
20. Broeren, J.; Rydmark, M.; Sunnerhagen, K.S. Virtual reality and haptics as a training device for movement rehabilitation after stroke: A single-case study. *Arch. Phys. Med. Rehabil.* **2004**, *85*, 1247–1250. [CrossRef] [PubMed]
21. Bermudez i Badia, S.; Fluet, G.G.; Llorens, R.; Deutsch, J.E. Virtual Reality for Sensorimotor Rehabilitation Post Stroke: Design Principles and Evidence. In *Neurorehabilitation Technology*; Reinkensmeyer, D., Dietz, V., Eds.; Springer: Cham, Switzerland, 2016; pp. 573–603. [CrossRef]
22. Vourvopoulos, A.; Jorge, C.; Abreu, R.; Figueiredo, P.; Fernandes, J.C.; Bermudez i Badia, S. Efficacy and Brain Imaging Correlates of an Immersive Motor Imagery BCI-Driven VR System for Upper Limb Motor Rehabilitation: A Clinical Case Report. *Front. Hum. Neurosci.* **2019**, *13*, 244. [CrossRef] [PubMed]
23. Piron, L.; Tonin, P.; Piccione, F.; Iaia, V.; Trivello, E.; Dam, M. Virtual Environment Training Therapy for Arm Motor Rehabilitation. *Presence* **2005**, *14*, 732–740. [CrossRef]
24. Tawfik, G.M.; Dila, K.A.S.; Mohamed, M.Y.F.; Tam, D.N.H.; Kien, N.D.; Ahmed, A.M.; Huy, N.T. A step by step guide for conducting a systematic review and meta-analysis with simulation data. *Trop. Med. Health* **2019**, *47*, 46. [CrossRef]
25. Jones, J.P.; Drass, J.M.; Kaimal, G. Art therapy for military service members with post-traumatic stress and traumatic brain injury: Three case reports highlighting trajectories of treatment and recovery. *Arts Psychother.* **2019**, *63*, 18–30. [CrossRef]
26. Worthen-Chaudhari, L.; Whalen, C.N.; Swendal, C.; Bockbrader, M.; Haserodt, S.; Smith, R.; Bruce, M.K.; Mysiw, W.J. A feasibility study using interactive graphic art feedback to augment acute neurorehabilitation therapy. *NeuroRehabilitation* **2013**, *33*, 481–490. [CrossRef]
27. Bolwerk, A.; Mack-Andrick, J.; Lang, F.R.; Dorfler, A.; Maihofner, C. How Art Changes Your Brain: Differential Effects of Visual Art Production and Cognitive Art Evaluation on Functional Brain Connectivity. *PLoS ONE* **2014**, *9*, e116548. [CrossRef]
28. Paczynski, A.; Diment, L.; Hobbs, D.; Reynolds, K. Using Technology to Increase Activity, Creativity and Engagement for Older Adults Through Visual Art. In *Mobile e-Health. Human-Computer Interaction Series*; Marston, H., Freeman, S., Musselwhite, C., Eds.; Springer: Cham, Switzerland, 2017; pp. 97–114. [CrossRef]
29. Cucca, A.; Acosta, I.; Berberian, M.; Lemen, A.C.; Rizzo, J.R.; Ghilardi, M.F.; Quartarone, A.; Feigin, A.S.; Di Rocco, A.; Biagioni, M.C. Visuospatial exploration and art therapy intervention in patients with Parkinson's disease: An exploratory therapeutic protocol. *Complement. Ther. Med.* **2018**, *40*, 70–76. [CrossRef] [PubMed]
30. Kaimal, G.; Carroll-Haskins, K.; Berberian, M.; Dougherty, A.; Carlton, N.; Ramakrishnan, A. Virtual Reality in Art Therapy: A Pilot Qualitative Study of the Novel Medium and Implications for Practice. *J. Am. Art Ther. Assoc.* **2019**, *37*, 16–24. [CrossRef]
31. McDonald, B. My Journey Using Art as Physical Therapy. *J. Humanit. Rehabil.* **2020**. Available online: https://www.jhrehab.org/2020/05/08/my-journey-using-art-as-physical-therapy/ (accessed on 1 May 2020).
32. Alex, M.; Wunsche, B.C.; Lottridge, D. Virtual reality art-making for stroke rehabilitation: Field study and technology probe. *Int. J. Hum.-Comput. Stud.* **2021**, *145*, 102481. [CrossRef]
33. Iosa, M.; Aydin, M.; Candelise, C.; Coda, N.; Morone, G.; Antonucci, G.; Marinozzi, F.; Bini, F.; Paolucci, S.; Gaetano, T. The Michelangelo Effect: Art Improves the Performance in a Virtual Reality Task Developed for Upper Limb Neurorehabilitation. *Front. Psychol.* **2021**, *11*, 1–8. [CrossRef]
34. Hacmun, I.; Regev, D.; Salomon, R. Artistic creation in virtual reality for art therapy: A qualitative study with expert art therapists. *Arts Psychother.* **2021**, *72*, 101745. [CrossRef]
35. Smith, D.; Wright, C.J.; Lakhani, A.; Zeeman, H. Art processes: A research tool for acquired brain injury and residential design. *Arts Health* **2017**, *9*, 251–268. [CrossRef]
36. Park, D.C.; Reuter-Lorenz, P. The Adaptive Brain: Aging and Neurocognitive Scaffolding. *Annu. Rev. Psychol.* **2009**, *60*, 173–196. [CrossRef]
37. Dickstein, R.; Dunsky, A.; Marcovitz, E. Motor Imagery for Gait Rehabilitation in Post-Stroke Hemiparesis. *Phys. Ther.* **2004**, *84*, 1167–1177. [CrossRef] [PubMed]
38. Jackson, P.L; Doyon, J.; Richards, C.L.; Malouin, F. The Efficacy of Combined Physical and Mental Practice in the Learning of a Foot-Sequence Task after Stroke: A Case Report. *Neurorehabil. Neural Repair* **2004**, *18*, 106–111. [CrossRef] [PubMed]
39. Page, S.J. Imagery Improves Upper Extremity Motor Function in Chronic Stroke Patients: A Pilot Study. *Occup. Ther. J. Res.* **2000**, *20*, 200–215. [CrossRef]
40. Page, S.J.; Levine, P.; Sisto, S.A.; Johnston, M.V. Mental Practice Combined with Physical Practice in Upper-Limb Motor Deficit in Subacute Stroke. *Phys. Ther.* **2001**, *81*, 1455–1462. [CrossRef]

41. Yoo, E.; Park, E.; Chung, B. Mental practice effect on line-tracing accuracy in persons with hemiparetic stroke: A preliminary study. *Arch. Phys. Med. Rehabil.* **2001**, *82*, 1213–1218. [CrossRef]
42. Crosbie, J.H.; McDonough, S.M.; Gilmore, D.H.; Wiggman, M.I. The adjunctive role of mental practice in the rehabilitation of the upper limb after hemiplegic stroke: A pilot study. *Clin. Rehabil.* **2004**, *18*, 60–68. [CrossRef]
43. Stevens, J.A.; Stoykov, M.E.P. Using Motor Imagery in the Rehabilitation of Hemiparesis. *Arch. Phys. Med. Rehabil.* **2003**, *84*, 1090–1092. [CrossRef]
44. Dijkerman, H.C.; Ietswaart, M.; Johnston, M.; MacWalter, R.S. Does motor imagery training improve hand function in chronic stroke patients? A pilot study. *Clin. Rehabil.* **2004**, *18*, 538–549. [CrossRef]
45. Tilt Brush by Google. 2018. Available online: https://www.tiltbrush.com (accessed on 16 September 2021).
46. Symons, J.; Clark, H.; Williams, K.; Hansen, E.; Orpin, P. Visual Art in Physical Rehabilitation: Experiences of People with Neurological Conditions. *Br. J. Occup. Ther.* **2011**, *74*, 44–52. [CrossRef]
47. Chantios, E. Art Therapy. In *Proceedings of the Frontiers of Clinical Practice—Environments for Recovery (3rd VBIRA Workshop)*; Victorian Brain Injury Recovery Association: Melbourne, Australia, 2005; pp. 56–61.
48. Agnihotri, S.; Gray, J.; Colantonio, A.; Polatajko, H.; Cameron, D.; Wiseman-Hakes, C.; Rumney, P.; Keightley, M. Arts-based social skills interventions for adolescents with acquired brain injuries: Five case reports. *Dev. Neurorehabil.* **2014**, *17*, 44–63. [CrossRef] [PubMed]
49. Zeki, S. Neural Concept Formation & Art: Dante, Michelangelo, Wagner. *J. Conscious. Stud.* **2002**, *9*, 53–76. [CrossRef]
50. Lusebrink, V.B. Art Therapy and the Brain: An Attempt to Understand the Underlying Processes of Art Expression in Therapy. *J. Am. Art Ther. Assoc.* **2014**, *21*, 125–135. [CrossRef]
51. King, J.L.; Knapp, K.E.; Shaikh, A.; Li, F.; Sabau, D.; Pascuzzi, R.M.; Osburn, L.L. Cortical Activity Changes after Art Making and Rote Motor Movement as Measured by EEG: A Preliminary Study. *Biomed. J. Sci. Tech. Res.* **2017**, *1*, 1062–1075. [CrossRef]
52. Fugl-Meyer, A.R.; Laasko, L.; Leyman, I.; Olsson, S.; Steglind, S. The post-stroke hemiplegic patient. 1. A method for evaluation of physical performance. *Scand. J. Rehabil. Med.* **1975**, *7*, 13–31. [PubMed]

Article

# Using Augmented Reality and Internet of Things for Control and Monitoring of Mechatronic Devices

Erich Stark [1], Erik Kučera [2,*], Oto Haffner [2], Peter Drahoš [2] and Roman Leskovský [2]

1. Faculty of Informatics, Pan-European University, 851 05 Bratislava, Slovakia; erich.stark@paneurouni.com
2. Faculty of Electrical Engineering and Information Technology, Slovak University of Technology in Bratislava, 812 19 Bratislava, Slovakia; oto.haffner@stuba.sk (O.H.); peter.drahos@stuba.sk (P.D.); roman.leskovsky@stuba.sk (R.L.)
* Correspondence: erik.kucera@stuba.sk

Received: 19 July 2020; Accepted: 6 August 2020; Published: 7 August 2020

**Abstract:** At present, computer networks are no longer used to connect just personal computers. Smaller devices can connect to them even at the level of individual sensors and actuators. This trend is due to the development of modern microcontrollers and singleboard computers which can be easily connected to the global Internet. The result is a new paradigm—the Internet of Things (IoT) as an integral part of the Industry 4.0; without it, the vision of the fourth industrial revolution would not be possible. In the field of digital factories it is a natural successor of the machine-to-machine (M2M) communication. Presently, mechatronic systems in IoT networks are controlled and monitored via industrial HMI (human-machine interface) panels, console, web or mobile applications. Using these conventional control and monitoring methods of mechatronic systems within IoT networks, this method may be fully satisfactory for smaller rooms. Since the list of devices fits on one screen, we can monitor the status and control these devices almost immediately. However, in the case of several rooms or buildings, which is the case of digital factories, ordinary ways of interacting with mechatronic systems become cumbersome. In such case, there is the possibility to apply advanced digital technologies such as extended (computer-generated) reality. Using these technologies, digital (computer-generated) objects can be inserted into the real world. The aim of this article is to describe design and implementation of a new method for control and monitoring of mechatronic systems connected to the IoT network using a selected segment of extended reality to create an innovative form of HMI.

**Keywords:** mechatronic devices; Internet of Things; cyber-physical systems; system control; augmented reality; mixed reality; Azure cloud

## 1. Introduction

Extended reality, as a modern technology, is used in Industry 4.0 to virtualize the efficient design of optimal production structures and work operations with their effective ergonomic evaluation and design [1,2]. New forms of process monitoring, control, diagnostics and visualization are currently being sought in digital factories [3]. It is the extended reality that brings such forms [4].

Under extended reality we understand virtual, augmented and mixed reality [5]. At present, there is no general consensus on the distinction between augmented and mixed reality. There are several definitions.

The first definition is the definition from The Foundry, which develops software for 3D modeling and texturing [6]. This definition is often used in industrial practice.

Virtual reality (VR) replicates an environment that simulates a physical presence in places in the real world or an imagined world, allowing the user to interact in that world [6]. Devices for virtual reality are Oculus Rift, Oculus Quest, HTC Vive, and so forth [7].

Augmented reality (AR) is a live, direct or indirect view of a physical, real-world environment whose elements are augmented (or supplemented) by computer-generated sensory input such as sound, video, graphics or GPS data [6]. Augmented reality is an overlay of content on the real world, but that content is not anchored to or part of it. The real-world content and the CG content are not able to respond to each other [8].

Mixed reality (MR) is the merging of real and virtual worlds to produce new environments and visualisations where physical and digital objects co-exist and interact in real time. MR is an overlay of synthetic content on the real world that is anchored to and interacts with the real world. The key characteristic of MR is that the synthetic content and the real-world content can react to each other in real time [6]. Technologies for mixed reality are Microsoft HoloLens (Windows Mixed Reality platform), Apple ARKit and Android ARCore [8].

Another definition is often used in scientific teams rather than in industrial practice. In 1994, the authors Milgram and Kishiho [9] introduced the spectrum between real and virtual environment—reality-virtuality continuum (Figure 1). This continuum defines a mix of real and virtual world. They understand mixed reality as anything between real environment and full virtual reality. Between reality and virtual reality, they distinguish between augmented reality, which is practically identical to augmented reality according to The Foundry definition, and augmented virtuality. It can be stated that augmented virtuality corresponds to mixed reality according to The Foundry definition.

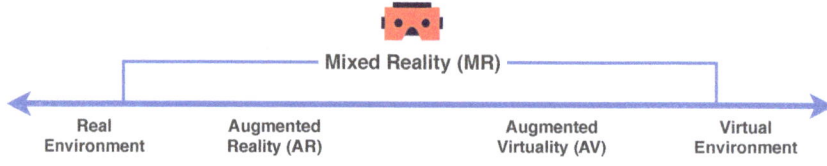

**Figure 1.** Reality-virtuality continuum.

*1.1. Motivation*

The current emerging trend in the Internet of Things has an impact not only in applications for households [10], smart buildings and services, but also on industries and manufacturing [11,12]. The application of IoT principles in industries is called the Industrial Internet of Things (IIoT). In this case, individual machine parts, sensors and actuators act as interconnected devices [13]. In particular, the interconnection of devices should be wireless and bring about new possibilities for their mutual interaction as well as for their diagnostics, control and provision of advanced services.

The research included several meetings and discussions with industry partners who demanded the Internet of Things to be connected to the augmented or mixed reality. It has shown that it is an obvious fact that integration of augmented and mixed reality technologies into production processes in digital factories is inevitable.

1. **British company dealing with the implementation of Industry 4.0 principles**

    One of the modern trends in the industrial field is the use of increasingly powerful, more durable and more affordable mobile devices, such as a smartphone or tablet. Such devices allow the use of modern technologies that have not been widely used in industry so far. We mean augmented and mixed reality and its applications for control and monitoring of devices. The use of augmented or mixed reality creates a qualitatively new and better way of solving HMI. In conventional approaches, it is necessary to select a specific device (sensor, actuator ...) on the display device so we need to know its specific location in the production hall or its ID. After selecting the device, the required data (for example in the form of a graph or a table) is displayed on the display unit. When using the augmented or mixed reality application, it is possible to operatively search for individual sensors within the production hall environment and interactively display the required values or change the settings and parameters of the given device via the display unit. An interesting feature would be the advanced functionality that would allow you to see in the environment which device the selected device is connected to or is forwarding data. It is the localization and identification of individual sensors and actuators that is currently an open problem that can be solved by several approaches.

2. **Slovak company dealing with tire diagnostics**

   The use of augmented or mixed reality in the diagnosis of different devices is also an open question that is being addressed by several companies. During the meeting, one of the industrial partners formulated a request for a tire fault diagnosis system via a headset or mobile device for mixed reality. At the same time, this system should make it possible to display diagnostic information from various devices in the factory, which is a similar requirement as in the previous point.

3. **Slovak manufacturer of advanced cutting machines**

   The use of augmented or mixed reality for the maintenance and operation of complex machines, the area of which reaches several tens of meters, is currently also an open topic, which requires a comprehensive multidisciplinary approach. International leaders in cutting technologies have already begun to implement such solutions. Therefore, a discussion about the possibilities of implementing maintenance and diagnostic systems using extended reality also took place with a Slovak company in this area (Figure 2).

4. **Control of sophisticated industrial devices with limited access**

   Another of the industrial partners demanded the use of augmented or mixed reality in the control and diagnostics of various sophisticated devices, to which only a limited group of employees have access. This eliminates the need to implement physical control panels, to which even a regular employee can have access. The requirement is that the device can be controlled only by an employee who has access to a mobile device (smartphone/tablet) with an augmented or mixed reality application. In addition to security, such an application also brings the advantages described in the previous points.

**Figure 2.** Testing of augmented and mixed reality for cutting machine maintenance.

*1.2. Related Research*

In the analysis of the state-of-the-art of the solved problem, we focused on searching scientific works and existing solutions in the subject field. The found projects showed the possibilities of using augmented or mixed reality for control and monitoring of mechatronic systems within the IoT networks. Another important aspect considered was whether a project was developed using open source code, and whether it was put into practice.

References [14,15] refer about the use of standard communication protocols, which should be used in the design of an IoT system with the implementation of web standards. This creates the so-called Web of Things. Web of Things is designed for easy integration of systems into the current web. It is therefore an idea to create a common application level for IoT based on web technologies and protocols. Subsequently, this idea was extended in Reference [16] by the term Augmented Worlds. The Augmented World concept can be defined as a software application that adds digital objects to the surrounding physical environment (e.g., city, building, room) that users or software agents can interact with. The combination of Web of Things and Augmented World created the concept of Web of Augmented Things.

The concept of Augmented Things was presented in Reference [17]. The idea is to create a database of digital copies of real objects (typically it can be consumer electronics) and assign various information to them. This can be, for example, maintenance information, instructions for use, and so forth. After capturing a real object (its digital copy is in the database of Augmented Things), information about this real object will be displayed on mobile device's screen in the augmented reality.

Close to the focus of the research is the concept of the author Phillipe Lewicki [18]. He created a demonstration application that could be used to control a Phillips Hue smart light bulb using a Microsoft HoloLens headset. With the help of HoloLens, it was possible to select the color of the light of a given bulb with a simple gesture in augmented/mixed reality. The author realized that today's solutions allow you to control light bulbs through a mobile application. In them, it is then necessary to find a specific room and a light bulb that he wants to control. This may not always be practical, and control with a headset provides greater convenience. However, the described concept has not been further developed.

There is a concept by designer Ian Sterling and engineer Swaroop Pala [19]. This concept demonstrates the control of smart devices using gestures. Microsoft HoloLens is used. The task was to provide a user interface for Android Music Player and an Arduino microcontroller with a connected fan with light. As in the previous case, it is not a complete system, but a single-purpose demonstration application.

The better solution is presented in Reference [20]. The presented AR/MR-IoT framework uses standard and open-source protocols and tools like MQTT (Message Queuing Telemetry Transport), HTTPS (Hypertext Transfer Protocol Secure) or Node-RED. The solution relies on QR codes. The article focuses mainly on the time aspects of communication in the presented framework.

A comprehensive commercial software system for diagnosing and controlling mechatronic systems is Vuforia Studio [21], which was formerly called ThingsWorx Studio. The rebranding took place after the purchase of the library for augmented and mixed reality Vuforia by the technology company PTC. Such an acquisition was a logical step, as PTC reacted very flexibly to the emergence of the Industry 4.0 and Industrial IoT concept. Vuforia Studio uses its closed-source tool, where it is possible to insert 3D and 2D objects, which will be displayed in augmented reality after capturing and recognizing the mechatronic device. This technology does not recognize devices directly, but using its own 2D tags ThingMark, which are actually a conventional technology similar to a QR code. The content is then visualized using Vuforia View.

ŠKODA AUTO has introduced the Smart Maintenance project, which uses augmented reality for maintenance tasks [22]. The Microsoft HoloLens headset is used. It is a relatively simple software application that uses HoloLens cameras to recognize a metal tube with handles. The goal is to diagnose the distances of the handles, which are likely to deviate over time. In the case of a tube detection, the real object is covered by a digital tube with the handles in the right place. Based on the visual information, it is possible to easily identify any displacement and then fix the handle so then it sits with the position of the virtual counterpart. This method of maintenance simplifies and speeds up the work of technicians, as they are relieved of the need to constantly measure the distance. A custom 3D engine was developed for the application. However, after a real test of the application within the solution of Reference [23], it is possible to state that the application reacted badly to the lighting conditions and also suffered from the limitations of the HoloLens headset. The holograms were too pale and did not copy objects correctly. Field of view was limited. The real use of the presented solution is therefore questionable.

Development of methods for control and monitoring of mechatronic systems using new information and communication technologies belongs to modern directions in cybernetics, automation and mechatronics. Based on the analysis of available literature sources and recent research projects it was found out that control and monitoring methods of mechatronic systems connected to IoT using extended reality are implemented in the form of various prototype solutions for selected device types or as closed-source single-purpose application systems. These systems are dedicated and are not easy-to-extend to control and monitor different mechatronic devices without a modification of the client software application. Such systems cannot be considered as generalized and modular solutions. Excursions and discussions with industrial partners have shown that there is interest in such comprehensive solutions. In the context of the ongoing Industry 4.0 industrial revolution, small and medium-sized enterprises are already interested in implementing modern digital technologies such as the Internet of Things, cloud and extended reality, into their manufacturing processes.

## 2. Materials & Methods

Control and monitoring of mechatronic systems connected in IoT networks using a selected segment of extended reality brings new challenges, as this concept combines hardware and its mechanical parts, microcontrollers and electronic systems, 3D engine for extended reality, mobile devices and communication protocols within the IoT and the cloud. With the proper design of the methodology of control and monitoring of mechatronic IoT systems and the supporting software module, it is possible to synergistically combine the above digital technologies bringing about a functional, original and modular system applicable for a selected class of mechatronic systems.

Nowadays, mechatronic systems in IoT networks are controlled and monitored mainly via industrial panels or console, mobile or web applications. In the case of using such conventional methods of control and monitoring mechatronic systems in a smaller room, this process can be simple and efficient. The list of devices being on one screen, we can set, monitor and control them almost immediately. However, if there are several rooms, buildings or a large digital factory, sorting these items can already be confusing and cumbersome. In these cases, the developed methodology of control and monitoring of mechatronic IoT systems based on augmented reality can yield effective solutions.

Once the system was developed it was important to determine how to recognize and identify the individual mechatronic devices. These devices are subsequently used to anchor computer-generated elements in augmented reality. There are more alternatives [8]:

- *Using a QR Code*—The name of the QR code comes from Quick Response, as this code has been developed for quick decoding. It is a two-dimensional bar code printed either on paper or in digital form. Using a mobile device camera we can decode the encoded information. The QR code is a square matrix consisting of square modules. The color of the QR code is black and white. The advantages of using QR codes include the rapid generating of a new QR code for application system build and extension. Next advantage is that each device or sensor can have a unique QR code, so using a QR code we can distinguish the objects with the same shape. The drawback is that we need to keep the mobile device parallel to the code when the recognition process is running, and close enough to the device.

- *Using an image*—It is possible to generate augmented or mixed reality using the two-dimensional image. The benefit of this approach is that one image is enough for a single object and it is easy to make images so we do not need any complicated or advanced tools or devices. Only a mobile device is needed for development and use of the application. It is also easy to extend the system. However, there are drawbacks while using the images. Also, as in the case of QR code, we must keep the mobile device close enough to the object when recognizing it, and the mobile device must be parallel to the image, or at the same angle as when making the images. The problem may also be with the same-looking objects not to be distinguished by the application based on the image. It is easier to use QR code for those situations. After researching the creation of an appropriate image, we find that the image has to satisfy certain properties. The image size (width and height) should range from 500 to 1000 pixels. The image can not include patterns of repetition, low texture and low contrast. The image color can be tricky because the computer sees the image in shades of gray. With this technology, colors which can be differentiated very well by the human eye, can be almost the same for computer. The textured portion layout must be uniform, contain only little text, and the white portion must be kept as small as possible.
- *Using a three-dimensional (3D) model*—An interesting option is a creation of 3D map based on 3D objects. This approach is very similar to that used above. An application based on the device's live camera stream is seeking conformity with the model that was created. This approach has the advantage of being able to locate the target object from a greater distance and from any angle. In addition, the mobile application does not lose as easily found an object as in the case of the previous two approaches. The drawback is that creating of 3D map is a complicated and lengthy task, which may also reduce the ease of scalability of the application system. In practice, image recognition is usually done using convolutional neural networks [24]. At present, convolutional neural networks are also used in natural language processing research and other areas of computational intelligence [25].

After considering the advantages and disadvantages of the above alternatives, we decided to use a 3D model. Although creating and extending the system is more time-consuming, smooth running and more intuitive application design was more important to our case. The use of a three-dimensional model and a three-dimensional map is original in the issue of monitoring and control of mechatronic systems using augmented reality and is one of the benefits of the proposed solution.

Based on the analysis, a concept of the application system is proposed, which is shown in Figure 3.

1. **The software application analyzes the image from the camera of the mobile device and recognizes the mechatronic system**

    The augmented reality mobile app recognizes a real mechatronic device using a camera and a 3D map created in the Wikitude Studio [26]. The 3D map of the mechatronic device is created using photographs of the device taken from several angles. Subsequently, the Wikitude SDK (software development kit) augmented and mixed reality library can interpret this 3D map from a database. The database is stored in a software application on an Apple iPad tablet. The advantage of this method is the ability to recognize the object from any angle. Consequently, even with less visibility tracking does not have to be interrupted as Wikitude can also store also close surroundings of the object. Thus, the implementation of the proposed solution can do without conventional methods of recognizing objects relying on QR codes.

2. **The mobile device connects to the server and the mechatronic system's device twin in the cloud**

    The mobile device is connected to the cloud where the recognized mechatronic system has its digital copy (*device twin*).

3. **The data from sensors of the mechatronic device is sent to the server, and the device twin in the cloud is synchronized**

The mechatronic device automatically sends data under its identifier from sensors to the server where the data is also stored. For this purpose, the InfluxDB database is used [27], designed for time-dependent data which can then be visualized in the Grafana environment [28]. At the same time, the digital copy of the mechatronic device is synchronized at the level of the Microsoft Azure Device Twin, which ensures the visibility of current data even in the cloud environment [29].

4. **The application obtains information about the type of the mechatronic device, downloads the definition of the user interface and draws a graphical interface for control and monitoring of the system**

The proposed system works in such a way that the mobile application recognizes the mechatronic device and—according to its identifier- obtains a unique definition scheme of the user interface for the needs of its monitoring and control. The concept of definition schemes for a dynamic generation of a graphical user interface in augmented reality is one of the pillars of modularity of the implemented solution and at the same time one of the application benefits. The mobile application has access to these definition schemes due to the connection to the database. The connection is realized by means of visual flow-based programming in the Node-RED environment [30], where a suitable scheme is obtained based on the parameter.

5. **The user interacts with the mechatronic device through a graphical interface in the augmented reality—a new form of HMI**

Based on a unique definition scheme, the mobile application displays a graphical user interface in augmented reality consisting of two parts. The first part is diagnostics and displays current data from available sensors. The second part is control and shows the control elements directly designed for the mechatronic device. Subsequently, the user is allowed to interact with the mechatronic device through a graphical interface in augmented reality, which is one of the new modern forms of human-machine interface (HMI).

6. **Control commands are sent to the server which sends them to the connected mechatronic device**

Control commands are sent from the mobile device to the server using the MQTT communication protocol. On the server, they are processed and executed. The software application on the mechatronic device listens on the MQTT topic and subsequently sends these requests to sensors and actuators via serial communication.

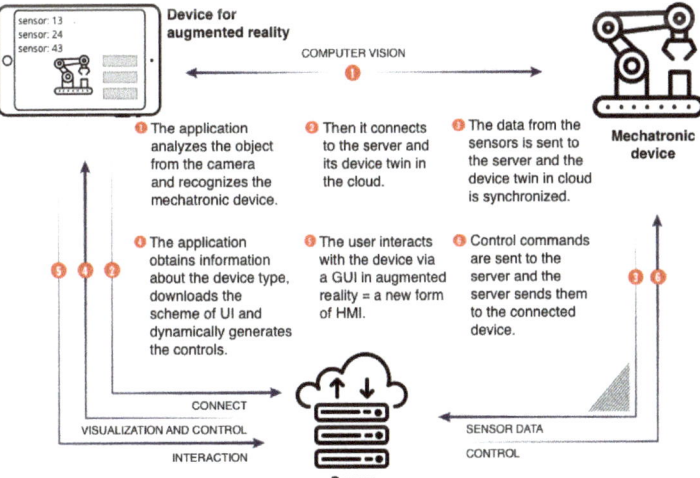

**Figure 3.** Proposal of mechatronic device monitoring and control using augmented reality.

To achieve the set objectives, it is necessary to design and implement a comprehensive hardware-software system for control and monitoring of mechatronic IoT systems based on the augmented reality and the concept of definition schemes for dynamic generation of graphical user interface. The developed system will be tested on a laboratory mechatronic system connected to the IoT.

## 3. Results

The development of such a complex system had to be done in cooperation with other workers and in several parallel lines to cover all four component parts of mechatronics (mechanics, electronics, automation and information-communication technologies). In what follows, the the whole system will be described using the description of its individual parts: server, augmented reality mobile device (Apple iPad), laboratory mechatronic device and cloud Microsoft Azure.

*3.1. Server*

The tools, which are implemented on the server side (Figure 4) in the described project, can be run on practically any Linux-based operating system. In the developed solution, Raspberry Pi 3 microcomputer and Raspbian operating system were used as a server. It is based on the Debian distribution with an emphasis on optimization for this type of microcomputer.

The MQTT broker (mosquitto) runs on the server and serves as the main central point through which all communication between the mobile device and the currently recognized mechatronic system takes place. Messages are sent to the broker using publish-subscribe communication on undefined topics. It is therefore not necessary to define them in advance, but the application that wants to obtain data from the address must be subscribed to receive this type of message.

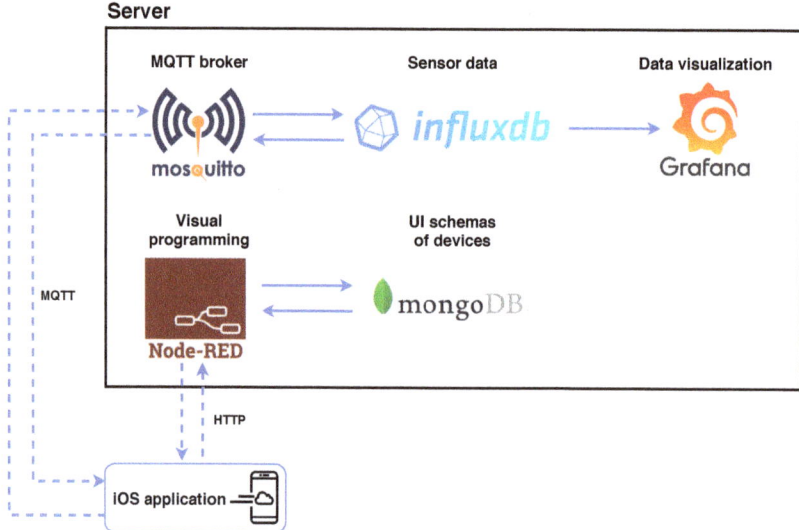

**Figure 4.** Server part of the solution for monitoring and control of mechatronic systems.

3.1.1. Flow-Based Programming of Communication Interface Using Node-RED

Node-RED consists of a runtime based on Node.js and a visual editor. The program is created in the browser by dragging functional nodes from the palette into the workspace. Then it is necessary to interconnect these nodes. The application is then deployed to production automatically using the *deploy* button. Additional nodes can be easily added by installing new nodes created by the programming community. Flows that are created in the workspace can be exported and shared as JSON (JavaScript Object Notation) files.

First, connection to a local MQTT broker is required. Additional settings, such as login details or additional messages for connections, can also be filled in within the settings. In this case, however, we can do with the IP address 127.0.0.1 and the port 1883.

When we have the connection to the MQTT broker implemented, we can use this broker as an I/O (input/output) node. In Figure 5, there is an input MQTT node connected to a local MQTT broker and subscribed to incoming messages from **makeblock-tank/sensor/ultrasonic** topic. This is followed by the transformation function **ultrasonicTransformDB** (Figure 6), which ensures the transformation of the incoming message into the required format. When editing a block of this type, it is possible to insert classic JavaScript code. This transformation function is performed whenever a message arrives at a given topic. First, the body of the message that came from the mechatronic system is obtained, and then a new object is prepared in the already required format, which is suitable for storage in the database. Said type of coupling is created for all available sensors within one mechatronic system.

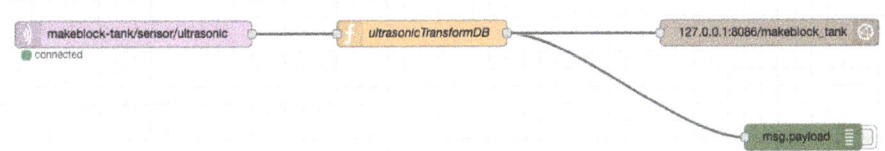

**Figure 5.** Connection of the input MQTT node to the output node of the InfluxDB database.

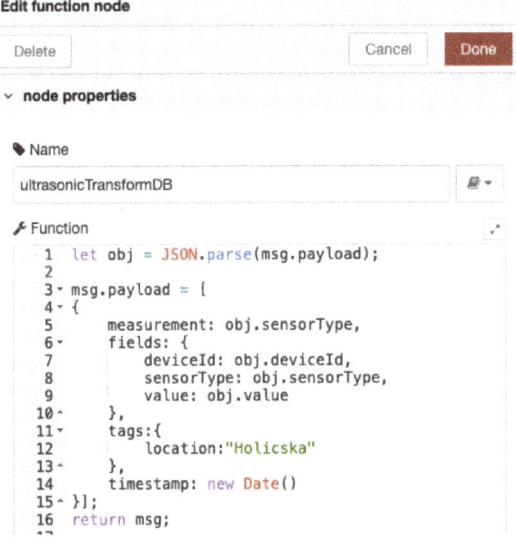

**Figure 6.** MQTT message transformation function.

In Figure 7 it is possible to see the flow in Node-RED (scheme of all interconnected I/O nodes) for mechatronic device Makeblock Tank. Due to the fact that the system is designed with emphasis on modularity, it is possible to add another mechatronic device to the new tab, where the flow for this new device will be located.

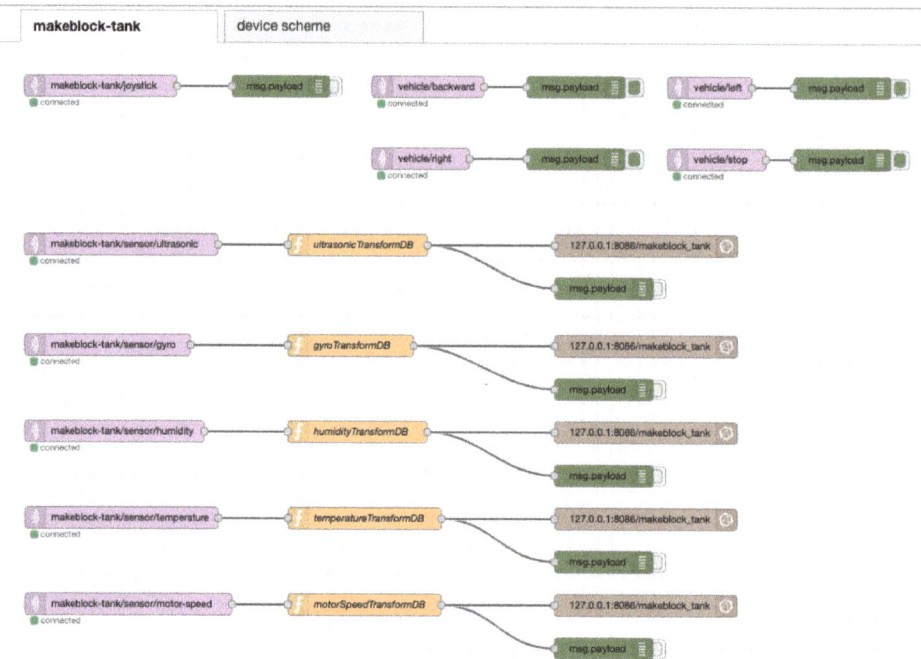

**Figure 7.** Node-RED flow for mechatronic device Makeblock Tank.

In case we would like to add another mechatronic device to the system, then it is necessary to add another flow here. It determines which data should be transformed and in what way, and also, if necessary, in which specific database it should be stored. The stream can also be exported and dynamically loaded into Node-RED using the available API (https://nodered.org/docs/api/) (application programming interface).

3.1.2. Definition Scheme for Generating a Graphical User Interface

To generate a customizable graphical interface for control and monitoring a mechatronic device in an augmented reality mobile application, it was necessary to design a way for this interface generation to be implemented. The concept of definition schemes for a dynamic generation of the graphical user interface is one of the pillars of modularity of the proposed system for control and monitoring of mechatronic systems using IoT and augmented reality. This is an original concept developed by the authors of the article. The scheme had to be designed with the emphasis on the solution versatility so that it would be applicable also in case of using other display technology than the augmented reality. The format selected was the JSON document as the JSON data format is supported in every relevant programming language. This means that it can be parsed in software applications and it is easy to work with its objects and attributes. In the first part of the scheme, there are the network settings of the master node (MQTT broker), that is, what IP address and port it is located on. These properties are defined at the top of the JSON document as **url** and **port**. This is followed by the **topic** property, which corresponds to the MQTT topic. This unambiguously determines the path of the mechatronic IoT device within the MQTT channel.

In the next part, there are two types of element labels (**sensors** and **controls**) in terms of their functionality. **Sensors** is used for reading elements—for example for data from sensors. **Controls** is for control elements. Both elements may contain multiple nested GUI (graphical user interface) elements according to the needs of the recognized mechatronic device.

In the current version of the definition scheme, three different GUI elements are available—**joystick**, **button** and **text**. **Joystick** and **button** belong to the control elements. They contain these *properties*):

- **element**—element name (joystick, button)
- **label**—is optional, as in the case of a joystick it is not necessary and represents the description of the element on the screen
- **posX** and **posY**—determine the generation of the element to the given position, while the elements for control we try to place to the right side of the mechatronic device
- **subTopic**—specifies the path for a specific control within the MQTT channel, or the path for the sensor from which the data will be read

The last element is **text**, which contains the same properties as controls. However, it can also have the **unit** property, which adds a unit to the read values.

When this JSON document is parsed, it creates a GUI element and then creates a connection to the MQTT broker. The path will then look like this: **url:port/topic/subTopic**.

In Table 1, there is an overview of elements and their data types for the correct operation of parsing and subsequent generation of a graphical user interface. A question mark for a specific element property indicates that it is optional.

**Table 1.** Overview of elements and their data types in the definition scheme.

| GUI Element | Element Property | Use in a Functional Element |
|---|---|---|
| text | element: *string*<br>label: *string*<br>unit?: *string*<br>posX: *float*<br>posY: *float*<br>subTopic *string* | sensors |
| joystick | element: *string*<br>posX: *float*<br>posY: *float*<br>subTopic *string* | controls |
| button | element: *string*<br>label: *string*<br>posX: *float*<br>posY: *float*<br>subTopic *string* | controls |

Figure 8 shows the definition scheme for the mechatronic device Makeblock Tank. The scheme is written in JSON format. In the first part, the access data (**url**, **port** and **topic**) are defined, which defines the network access for the given device.

Subsequently, depending on the configuration, the mechatronic device may contain two types of elements on the screen: for read (**sensors**) and control (**controls**). The first type is intended only for reading and displaying data from sensors. The controls are those that actively interfere with the device—so they access its actuators.

The specific types of controls and information elements that appear on the screen of a mobile device in augmented reality may be diverse in terms of functionality, so that the system can be expanded in the future. Three types were created for the selected device: **joystick**, **button** and **text**. The first two elements are used to perform the action. The text element is read-only. In the case of this element, there is also the **label** attribute. With this one, it is possible to add a description—for example the type of a specific sensor.

The displaying control elements also depends on the set position (**posX** and **posY**), while the controls are generated from the lower right corner upwards. For reading elements, this is for clarity from the top left corner.

```json
{
    "url": "192.168.100.72",
    "port": "1880",
    "topic": "makeblock-tank",
    "controls": [
        {
            "element": "joystick",
            "posX": -160,
            "posY": 160,
            "subTopic": "/motor"
        }
    ],
    "sensors": [
        {
            "element": "text",
            "label": "Ultrasonic",
            "posX": 50,
            "posY": -100,
            "subTopic": "/sensor/ultrasonic"
        },
        {
            "element": "text",
            "label": "Humidity",
            "unit": "%",
            "posX": 50,
            "posY": -200,
            "subTopic": "/sensor/humidity"
        },
        {
            "element": "text",
            "label": "Temperature",
            "unit": "°C",
            "posX": 50,
            "posY": -300,
            "subTopic": "/sensor/temperature"
        }
    ]
}
```

**Figure 8.** JSON definition scheme for mechatronic device Makeblock Tank.

The common attribute for both types is **subTopic**. It determines the network path where the actuator or sensor is located. If you create the entire path from the **url**, **port**, **topic**, **subTopic** attributes (e.g., for a joystick), it would look like this: **192.168.100.72:1880/makeblock-tank/motor**.

Definition schemes with user interfaces for all available mechatronic devices have their own flow in the Node-RED, where they are connected to the communication. At the top of Figure 9, you can see the *inject* nodes, which store the current version of the definition schema. When the scheme is changed, it is necessary to activate the node *inject*, which ensures the sending of the saved definition scheme to the next block. The schema is inserted into the MongoDB database. also shows two different collections—**raspberry-pi** and **makeblock-tank**. In each of these collections, there is a diagram for a given device, but its element layout may be different. For example, there could be two mechatronic devices of the type Makeblock Tank, but each has a different identifier and different equipment with sensors and actuators.

The blocks at the bottom of Figure 9 are used to obtain a definition scheme for an application on a mobile device that provides augmented reality. The input is an HTTP GET node that allows to create an HTTP server for requests without having to program it. This node has *url* set to **/schema/:device**. The IP address and port of the local server must be specified before this entry. The address also contains the HTTP parameter **:device**, which represents the name of the mechatronic device (which we want to obtain the definition scheme for). Then the *switch* node evaluates which device it is and sends requests to the MongoDB database. When using an HTTP node, it is necessary to have an output node of this type. The HTTP output node provides a response for the called service, where the output will be data and HTTP status code. The green nodes are only used to list and check the values in the Node-RED.

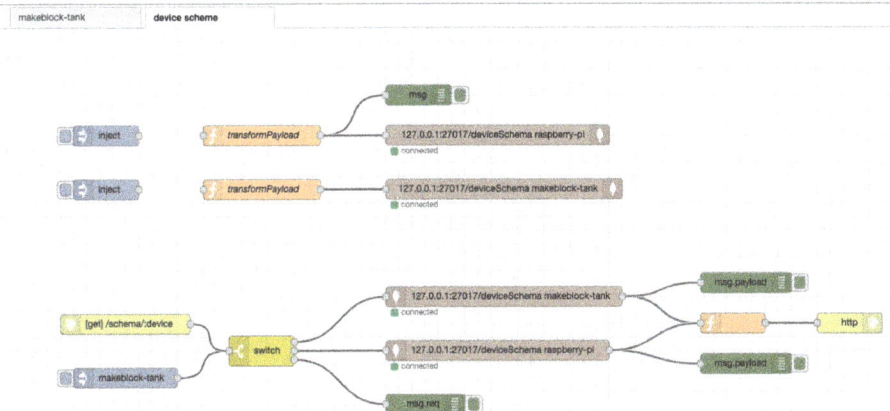

**Figure 9.** The flow in Node-RED for JSON definition schemes of mechatronic devices.

*3.2. Mobile Device and Augmented Reality Application*

The mobile application includes the Wikitude SDK, which provides methods and algorithms for recognizing 3D objects in a real environment using a mobile device camera. A software package in Unity engine format (*.unitypackage*) is available on the official website of this tool.

Real-world 3D objects are detected by Wikitude by trying to match pre-created references in video streams from mobile device's camera. Such a prepared reference is called *Object Target*. It can also be understood as a SLAM map. *Object Target* is created using input images of a real model (mechatronic device). These are then converted into so-called *Wikitude Object Target Collection*, which is saved as a **.wto** file. The procedure for creating a collection is as follows:

1. Creating photos of an object from different angles (up to 30 photos can be inserted)
2. Convert photos to *Wikitude Object Target Collection* (.wto)
3. Use of the .wto file in the project in the Unity 3D engine

In Figure 10 we can see a list of created Object Targets. Each of the objects contains the *Point Cloud*, which can be seen in Figure 11. It represents a 3D map which Wikitude uses for recognition of a 3D object. If the user finds Point Cloud insufficient at some angles, it can be expanded with additional photos.

**Figure 10.** List of objects in the collection.

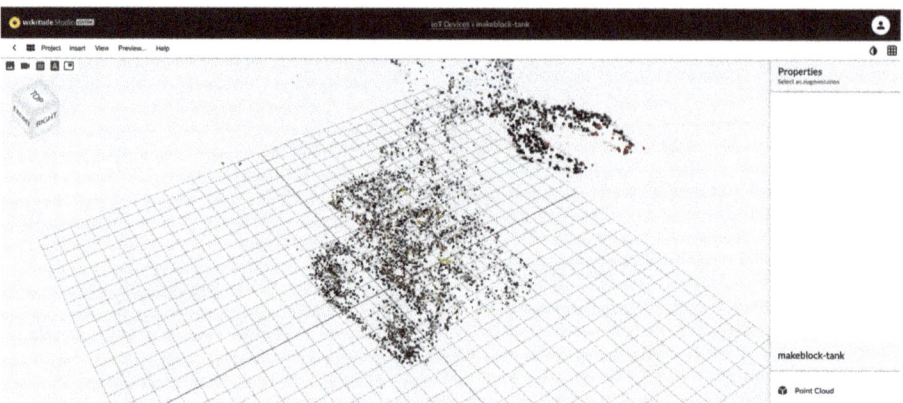

**Figure 11.** Point Cloud (map of significant points) of the processed 3D object—mechatronic device Makeblock Tank.

Generating of User Interface Using Definition Scheme

The generation of a dynamic graphical user interface takes place at the Unity engine level via a definition scheme. Its format has been described in the previous text. A sequence diagram describing the method of generating a GUI in the Unity engine is shown in Figure 12.

After launching the mobile application, all necessary libraries are initialized. Each application created in Unity contains `void Start ()` method containing initialization code. First, an asynchronous connection to the MQTT broker is made using the `Connect ()` method. Now the Unity mobile application is ready to recognize mechatronic devices. If the device is recognized, we get its name in the method named `OnObjectrecognized (ObjectTarget)`. This name is sent as an HTTP GET request to the Node-RED using the `GetDeviceSchema (deviceType)` method, where a connection is established in a separate thread of the mobile application and a schema is obtained. Subsequently, Node-RED starts the programmed flow (Figure 9). The obtained definition scheme with GUI elements is processed in the mobile application using the JSON data format parser and then the methods `InitUIDeviceControls(DeviceSchema)` and `InitUIDeviceSensors (DeviceSchema)` are called.

These methods initialize prefabs of native UI elements in the Unity engine. UI element prefab is created in the hierarchy of game objects and all required visual properties are added to it. When this *GameObject* is set up as needed in the hierarchy, it is necessary to move it to the project structure in the *Prefabs* folder. This saves the prefab and can then be initialized at any time in the Unity application.

The generation itself works in such a way that the parsed definition schema (parsed JSON) is sent to the `InitUIDeviceControls` method. It determines which elements are available according to the attributes of the object. Depending on the element, it is possible to initialize a prefab named **button** or **joystick**.

During initialization, it is necessary to insert the generated object also on the canvas, which renders the UI objects. Otherwise, they would not appear in the mobile application.

According to the sequence diagram (Figure 12) it is clear how the whole process works in the mobile application. The mobile device is aimed by the user at a mechatronic device/object that the application can recognize. After the whole process of device recognition, obtaining the necessary definition schemes and data, the GUI is displayed, as can be seen in Figure 13. The control part of UI was in terms of *user experience* situated to the right part of the generated GUI on the mechatronic device. In the lower right part, we can use the thumb in a simple way. In the described case of the Makeblock Tank device, only the **joystick** is needed, which is used to control the belts and thus the movement of the device. Elements such as sensor data that does not need to be clicked are visualized in augmented reality at the top of the device.

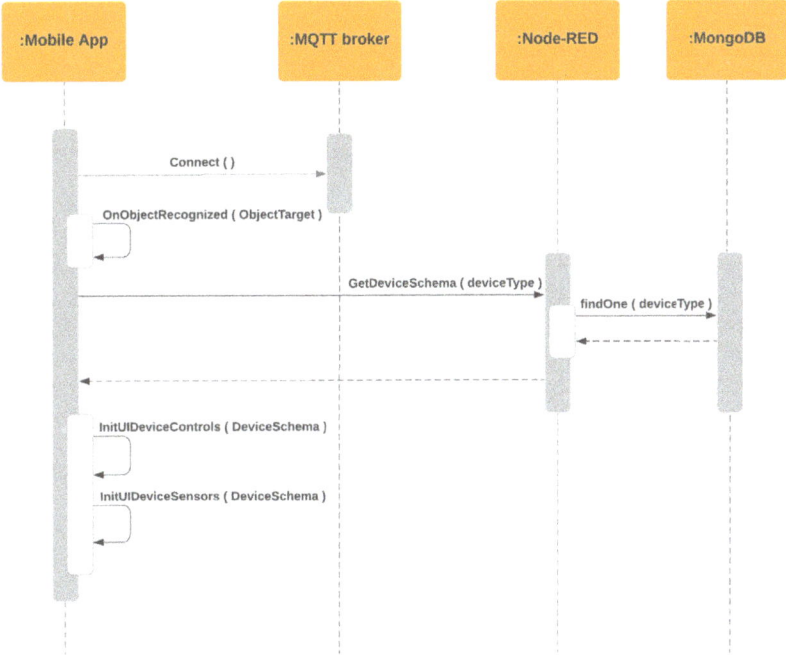

**Figure 12.** Sequence diagram: How a user interface is generated in Unity engine.

**Figure 13.** Recognized mechatronic device with dynamically generated GUI in augmented reality.

### 3.3. Laboratory Mechatronic Device

To implement and verify the method of monitoring and control of mechatronic systems using IoT and augmented reality, it was necessary to build a suitable laboratory physical model. For this purpose, the mechatronic kit Makeblock Ultimate 2 was selected. The Robotic Arm Tank model was built, which best met the requirements for testing and demonstration of the developed software system. A diagram of the laboratory model showing the connected electronic systems, sensors and actuators can be seen in Figure 14.

The main electronic element of the laboratory model is the Makeblock MegaPi development board, which is built on the Arduino MEGA 2560 platform, while supporting programming using the Arduino IDE. The development board contains three ports for connecting motors with an encoder. Sensors for measuring the distance of the vehicle from the obstacle (ultrasonic sensor) and a humidity/temperature sensor were connected. RGB LED (Light-Emitting Diode) was connected as another actuator.

A key element of the laboratory mechatronic system is its wireless control. The package contained a bluetooth communication module, which was not suitable as it was designed to control a device with a ready-made application from Makeblock. So another alternative was chosen—the connection of MegaPi with a Raspberry Pi 3 microcomputer, which has a built-in WiFi module. The MegaPi is ready for connection to the Raspberry Pi, as it has three screw holes in the same places as the Raspberry Pi 3. It also allows serial communication with this microcomputer.

Laboratory mechatronic device Makeblock Robotic Arm Tank can be seen in Figure 15.

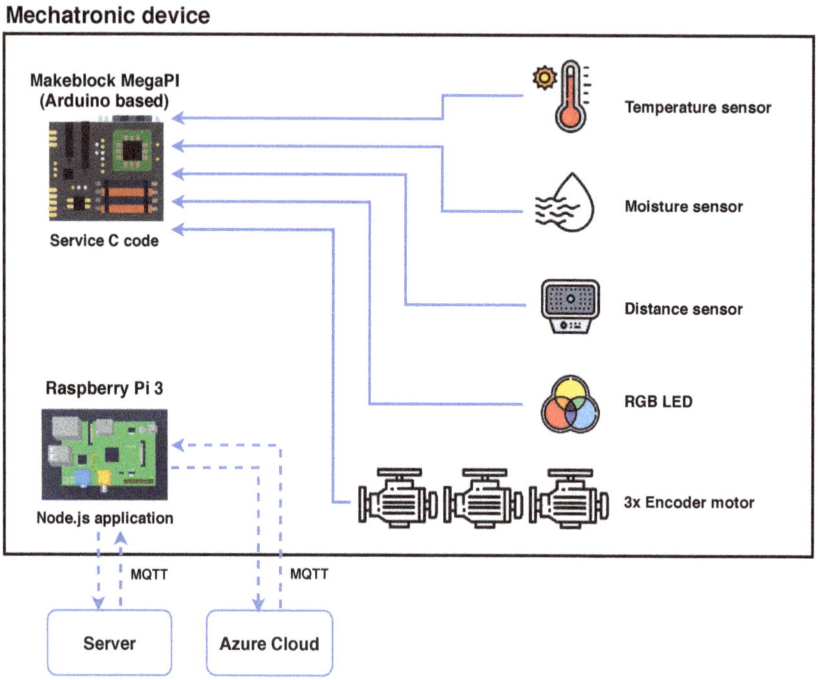

**Figure 14.** Illustrative diagram of mechanical and electronic elements of mechatronic device.

**Figure 15.** Laboratory mechatronic device Makeblock Robotic Arm Tank.

After assembling the laboratory mechatronic system, MegaPi had to be programmed. The mBlock tool is available for teaching programming. However, in the described solution, it is necessary to have the complete MegaPi functionality available and to access the device control using the API interface. This is suitable to implement via the Arduino IDE, where the complete service code is loaded to access all sensors and actuators that Makeblock can work with. It is then possible to access the sensors and actuators by calling the API interface, specifically in our case by sending parameters from the Raspberry Pi via a serial line. These parameters can be sent, for example, using a library in JavaScript or Python. In our case we use JavaScript.

Before using the library, it is necessary to upload the service code to the MegaPi microcontroller via the Arduino IDE. This means that it is no longer necessary to program all the functionalities for actuators and sensors manually, but we are making available an interface for higher programming languages, as it was mentioned.

MegaPi is physically connected to the Raspberry Pi 3 and the service code is loaded at the same time, the next step is to install the MegaPi control library. It can be done using the *Node Package Manager* (NPM) and the **npm install megapi** command. During development, it was found that this interface is not sufficiently maintained and some methods are no longer functional. It was therefore necessary to study how the communication works from publicly available source code. Subsequently, it was necessary to make adjustments to the service source code as well as the JavaScript library code.

At the beginning of the JavaScript program, the MegaPi constructor is called, where two parameters are required:

- serial communication access path
- the body of the function to be executed after initialization

Subsequently, it is possible to call functions for access to ports and sensors. All functions are described on GitHub (https://github.com/Makeblock-official/NodeForMegaPi).

*3.4. Device Twin in Azure Cloud*

The system design assumes the synchronization (Figure 16) of current data from the sensors of the mechatronic system to the cloud using *device twin*. This technology is available as part of the Microsoft Azure IoT Hub and is created for each added mechatronic device.

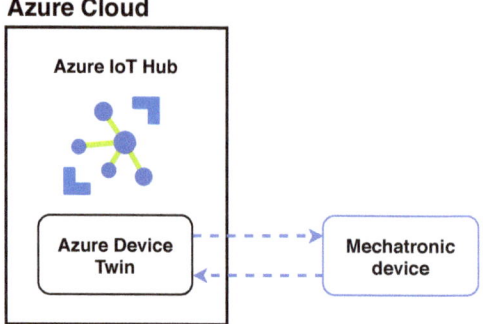

**Figure 16.** Device twin in Azure cloud.

Azure IoT Hub is a managed service that runs in the Microsoft Azure cloud. It serves as a central point for two-way communication between IoT applications and IoT devices. Azure IoT Hub can be used to create Internet of Things solutions with reliable and secure communication between the cloud-based backend and millions of IoT devices. It is possible to connect virtually any device to it.

Device twins are JSON documents that store information about the state of an IoT device, including configurations, metadata, and conditions. The Azure IoT Hub maintains such a device twin for each IoT device that is connected to the IoT Hub [31].

## 4. Conclusions

The article deals with a modern form of control and monitoring of mechatronic systems connected within the Internet of Things networks using augmented reality.

Based on the analysis of available literature sources and recent research projects, it was found that methods for control and monitoring of mechatronic systems connected within IoT using extended reality are implemented in the form of various prototype solutions for dedicated devices or as closed-source single-purpose application systems; such systems are not complete and without a modification of the client software application it is not feasible to easily extend the control and monitoring also for different mechatronic devices. Such solutions cannot be considered as generalized and modular ones. Excursions and discussions with industrial partners have shown that there is a growing interest in such comprehensive solutions. In the context of the ongoing Industry 4.0 industrial revolution, small and medium-sized enterprises are already interested in the implementation of modern digital technologies such as the Internet of Things, cloud and extended reality, into their manufacturing processes.

The result of the proposed research is a modular program system with a new form of human-machine interface (HMI) implemented in augmented reality. The graphical user interface uses a new concept of definition schemes for its dynamic generation. In the proposed solution, modern detection and recognition methods of 3D objects in the augmented reality are used instead of conventional methods of control and monitoring of mechatronic IoT systems based on scanning QR codes.

The scientific and application contributions can be summarized in the following points:

- Design of a modern form of control and monitoring of mechatronic systems using the Internet of Things and augmented reality.

- Implementation of an application system for control and monitoring of mechatronic systems connected to the Internet of Things with a new form of human-machine interface based on detection and recognition of 3D objects.
- Design and implementation of the concept of definition schemes for dynamic generation of a graphical user interface for control and monitoring of mechatronic systems.
- Verification of the designed and implemented application system on a laboratory mechatronic system.

An important result of this part of the presented work is the design and development of an application platform of a modular solution with a modern HMI form in augmented reality. The proposed solution complements and improves conventional augmented reality-based methods of control and monitoring of mechatronic IoT systems (relying on QR code scanning). The new application platform represents an original approach based on modern software for detecting and recognizing 3D objects. The generalizability and modularity of the developed solution is supported by the original concept of definition schemes for dynamic generation of a graphical user interface in augmented reality.

It turned out that the Wikitude SDK is sufficiently robust and advanced to scan the mechatronic device even in different lighting conditions though this was not the primary aim of this research.

In the discussion [32], a situation is addressed when it was necessary to recognize marks and objects under very low light conditions (less than 10 LUX). The Wikitude SDK can handle this situation as well. Wikitude is able to recognize objects with a high success [33] even if there are low light, shades, reflections or noisy surroundings in the environment.

If the lighting conditions are very low, it is possible to use the Input Plugins API [34] as suggested in the discussion in Reference [32]. It works so that the input image is preprocessed using for example, the OpenCV library. The resulting image is further processed by Wikitude and evaluated in the real time. In such a case, it is possible to obtain a very acceptable recognition of marks and objects as can be seen in the video in Reference [35].

Possible limitations of the presented system result from the fact that in a digital factory there can be several devices with a similar shape or devices with large dimensions. In this case, it would be possible to use own 3D identifiers, unique for each machine. However, such identifiers are difficult to copy with sufficient accuracy only using a set of photographs. The 3D identifiers open up new ways and opportunities for future research and development of optimal shapes, dimensions and algorithms for generating them using generative modeling. It is expected that 3D identifiers will be produced using the 3D printing technology which allows to create and test identifiers of different shapes and dimensions without the need to manufacture expensive conventional molds for plastic castings.

Scientific and application contribution to the field of Internet of Things and extended reality as declared in the four above points consists in the developed original solution generalizable and modifiable for further research and technical practice in Industry 4.0.

## 5. Patents

Proposed "Method for monitoring and control of mechatronic systems using augmented reality" is patent pending under application number 158-2019 in Industrial Property Office of the Slovak Republic [https://wbr.indprop.gov.sk/WebRegistre/Patent/Detail/158-2019].

**Author Contributions:** E.S. and E.K. proposed the idea in this paper and prepared the software application; O.H., P.D. and R.L. designed the experiments; E.S. and E.K. performed the experiments; O.H., and R.K. analyzed the data; E.K. wrote the paper; E.S., O.H., P.D. and R.L. edited and reviewed the paper. All authors have read and agreed to the published version of the manuscript.

**Funding:** This work has been supported by the Cultural and Educational Grant Agency of the Ministry of Education, Science, Research and Sport of the Slovak Republic, KEGA 038STU-4/2018 and KEGA 016STU-4/2020, by the Slovak Research and Development Agency APVV-17-0190, and by the Tatra banka Foundation within the grant programme Quality of Education, project No. 2019vs056 (Virtual Training of Production Operators in Industry 4.0).

**Conflicts of Interest:** The authors declare no conflict of interest.

## References

1. Kozák, Š.; Ružický, E.; Štefanovič, J.; Schindler, F. Research and education for industry 4.0: Present development. In Proceedings of the 2018 Cybernetics & Informatics (K & I), Lazy pod Makytou, Slovakia, 31 January–3 February 2018; pp. 1–8. [CrossRef]
2. Wolniak, R.; Saniuk, S.; Grabowska, S.; Gajdzik, B. Identification of Energy Efficiency Trends in the Context of the Development of Industry 4.0 Using the Polish Steel Sector as an Example. *Energies* **2020**, *13*, 2867. [CrossRef]
3. Lin, Y.-C.; Yeh, C.-C.; Chen, W.-H.; Hsu, K.-Y. Implementation Criteria for Intelligent Systems in Motor Production Line Process Management. *Processes* **2020**, *8*, 537. [CrossRef]
4. Dobrowolska, M.; Knop, L. Fit to Work in the Business Models of the Industry 4.0 Age. *Sustainability* **2020**, *12*, 4854. [CrossRef]
5. Kościelniak, H.; Łęgowik-Małolepsza, M.; Łęgowik-Świącik, S. The Application of Information Technologies in Consideration of Augmented Reality and Lean Management of Enterprises in the Light of Sustainable Development. *Sustainability* **2019**, *11*, 2157. [CrossRef]
6. The Foundry. VR? AR? MR? Sorry, I'M Confused. Available online: https://www.foundry.com/insights/vr-ar-mr/vr-mr-ar-confused (accessed on 16 June 2020).
7. Sánchez-Herrera-Baeza, P.; Cano-de-la-Cuerda, R.; Oña-Simbaña, E.D.; Palacios-Ceña, D.; Pérez-Corrales, J.; Cuenca-Zaldivar, J.N.; Gueita-Rodriguez, J.; Balaguer-Bernaldo de Quirós, C.; Jardón-Huete, A.; Cuesta-Gomez, A. The Impact of a Novel Immersive Virtual Reality Technology Associated with Serious Games in Parkinson's Disease Patients on Upper Limb Rehabilitation: A Mixed Methods Intervention Study. *Sensors* **2020**, *20*, 2168. [CrossRef] [PubMed]
8. Bucsai, S.; Kučera, E.; Haffner, O.; Drahoš, P. Control and Monitoring of IoT Devices Using Mixed Reality Developed by Unity Engine. In Proceedings of the 2020 Cybernetics & Informatics (K & I), Velke Karlovice, Czech Republic, 29 January–1 February 2020; pp. 1–8. [CrossRef]
9. Milgram, P.; Kishino, F. A taxonomy of mixed reality visual displays. *IEICE Trans. Inf. Syst.* **1994**, *77*, 1321–1329.
10. Salamone, F.; Belussi, L.; Danza, L.; Galanos, T.; Ghellere, M.; Meroni, I. Design and Development of a Nearable Wireless System to Control Indoor Air Quality and Indoor Lighting Quality. *Sensors* **2017**, *17*, 1021. [CrossRef] [PubMed]
11. Geng, Z.; Chen, N.; Han, Y.; Ma, B. An improved intelligent earlywarning method based on MWSPCA and itsapplication in complex chemical processes. *Can. J. Chem. Eng.* **2020**, *98*, 1307–1318 [CrossRef]
12. Minchala, L.I.; Peralta, J.; Mata-Quevedo, P.; Rojas, J. An Approach to Industrial Automation Based on Low-Cost Embedded Platforms and Open Software. *Appl. Sci.* **2020**, *10*, 4696. [CrossRef]
13. Erasmus, J.; Vanderfeesten, I.; Traganos, K.; Keulen, R.; Grefen, P. The HORSE Project: The Application of Business Process Management for Flexibility in Smart Manufacturing. *Appl. Sci.* **2020**, *10*, 4145. [CrossRef]
14. Trifa, V.; Guinard, D.; Carrera, D. Web Thing Model. Available online: http://model.webofthings.io/ (accessed on 16 June 2020).
15. Guinard, D.; Trifa, V.; Pham, T.; Liechti, O. Towards physical mashups in the web of things. In Proceedings of the 2009 Sixth International Conference on Networked Sensing Systems (INSS), Pittsburgh, PA, USA, 17–19 June 2009; pp. 1–4.
16. Croatti, A.; Ricci, A. Towards the web of augmented things. In Proceedings of the 2017 IEEE International Conference on Software Architecture Workshops (ICSAW), Gothenburg, Sweden, 5–7 April 2017; pp. 80–87.
17. Rambach, J.; Pagani, A.; Stricker, D.; Aleksy, M.; Schmitt, J.; Langfinger, M.; Schneider, M.; Schotten, H.; Malignaggi, A.; Ko, M. Augmented things: Enhancing AR applications leveraging the Internet of Things and universal 3d object tracking. In Proceedings of the IEEE International Conference on Industrial Technology (ICIT), Nantes, France, 9–13 October 2017; Volume 22, p. 25.
18. Lewicki, P. Controlling Lights with the Hololens and Internet of Things. Available online: http://blog.htmlfusion.com/controlling-lights-with-the-hololens-and-internet-of-thingsatch-one-of-philippes-appearances-in-june/ (accessed on 1 June 2020).

19. Sterlink, I.; Swaroop, P. Control with Your Smart Devices by Staring and Gesturing. Available online: https://blog.arduino.cc/2016/07/26/control-with-your-smart-devices-by-staring-and-gesturing/ (accessed on 16 June 2020).
20. Blanco-Novoa, Ó.; Fraga-Lamas, P.; A Vilar-Montesinos, M.; Fernández-Caramés, T.M. Creating the Internet of Augmented Things: An Open-Source Framework to Make IoT Devices and Augmented and Mixed Reality Systems Talk to Each Other. *Sensors* **2020**, *20*, 3328. [CrossRef] [PubMed]
21. Gallash, A. Thingworx–plattform zur integration herausfordernder anforderungen auf dem shopfloor. In *Produktions-und Verfügbarkeits-Optimierung Mit Smart Data Ansätzen*; sierke VERLAG-Internationaler Wissenschaftsverlag: Goettingen, Germany, 2018; pp. 83–92.
22. FOXON Automation. What Is the Smart Maintenance Project in ŠKODA AUTO a.s. Available online: https://www.youtube.com/watch?v=v48vZt7aNw4 (accessed on 17 June 2020).
23. Leskovský, R. Modern Methods of Control and Diagnostics of Mechatronic Devices Using IoT and Mixed Reality. Ph.D. Thesis, Slovak University of Technology in Bratislava, Bratislava, Slovakia, 2020. (In Slovak)
24. Han, Y.; Zhang, S.; Geng, Z.; Wei, Q.; Ouyang, Z. Level set based shape prior and deep learning for image segmentation. *IET Image Process.* **2020**, *14*, 183–191. [CrossRef]
25. Han, Y.; Ding, N.; Geng, Z.; Wang, Z.; Chu, C. An optimized long short-term memory network based fault diagnosis model for chemical processes. *J. Process. Control* **2020**, *92*, 161–168. [CrossRef]
26. Fierro, F.A.S.; Manosalvas, C.A.P.; Hidrobo, S.R.A.; Rodríguez, N.N.C. Comparativa técnica de herramientas para realidad aumentada: Wikitude, Vuforia y ARtoolkit. *Revista Científica Axioma* **2019**, *19*, 86–96.
27. Ganz, J.; Beyer, M.; Plotzky, C. Time-Series Based Solution Using InfluxDB. Available online: https://beyermatthias.de/papers/2017/Time-series_based_solution_using_influxdb.pdf (accessed on 17 June 2020).
28. Betke, E.; Kunkel, J. Real-time I/O-monitoring of HPC applications with SIOX, elasticsearch, Grafana and FUSE. In *International Conference on High Performance Computing*; Springer: Cham, Switzerland, 2017; pp. 174–186.
29. Stackowiak, R. Azure IoT Hub. In *Azure Internet of Things Revealed*; Apress: Berkeley, CA, USA, 2019; pp. 73–85.
30. Blanco-Novoa, Ó.; Fraga-Lamas, P.; Vilar-Montesinos, M.A.; Fernández-Caramés, T.M. Towards the Internet of Augmented Things: An Open-source Framework to Interconnect IoT Devices and Augmented Reality Systems. *Proceedings* **2020**, *42*, 50. [CrossRef]
31. Contributors of Azure IoT Hub. Understand and Use Device Twins in IoT Hub. Available online: https://docs.microsoft.com/en-us/azure/iot-hub/iot-hubdevguide-device-twins/ (accessed on 17 June 2020).
32. Low light SLAM & Marker Triggering. Available online: https://support.wikitude.com/support/discussions/topics/5000082906 (accessed on 1 August 2020).
33. Wikitude. SDK 5 vs. SDK 6 Comparison. Available online: https://www.youtube.com/watch?v=zeu8XIJyxKE (accessed on 1 August 2020).
34. Wikitude. Input Plugins API. Available online: https://www.wikitude.com/external/doc/documentation/latest/unity/inputpluginsapiunity.html#input-plugins-api (accessed on 1 August 2020).
35. Dykier, M. IMG 0135. Available online: https://www.youtube.com/watch?v=1vBxK-9HQ8c (accessed on 1 August 2020).

© 2020 by the authors. Licensee MDPI, Basel, Switzerland. This article is an open access article distributed under the terms and conditions of the Creative Commons Attribution (CC BY) license (http://creativecommons.org/licenses/by/4.0/).

Article

# Lexicon-based Sentiment Analysis Using the Particle Swarm Optimization

Kristína Machová [1], Martin Mikula [1], Xiaoying Gao [2] and Marian Mach [1,*]

[1] Department of Cybernetics and Artificial Intelligence, Faculty of Electrical Engineering and Informatics, Technical University of Košice, Letna 9, 04200 Košice, Slovakia; kristina.machova@tuke.sk (K.M.); martin.mikula@tuke.sk (M.M.)

[2] School of Engineering and Computer Science, Victoria University of Wellington, P.O. Box 600, Wellington 6140, New Zealand; xiaoying.gao@ecs.vuw.ac.nz

* Correspondence: marian.mach@tuke.sk; Tel.: +421-902-683736

Received: 26 May 2020; Accepted: 13 August 2020; Published: 15 August 2020

**Abstract:** This work belongs to the field of sentiment analysis; in particular, to opinion and emotion classification using a lexicon-based approach. It solves several problems related to increasing the effectiveness of opinion classification. The first problem is related to lexicon labelling. Human labelling in the field of emotions is often too subjective and ambiguous, and so the possibility of replacement by automatic labelling is examined. This paper offers experimental results using a nature-inspired algorithm—particle swarm optimization—for labelling. This optimization method repeatedly labels all words in a lexicon and evaluates the effectiveness of opinion classification using the lexicon until the optimal labels for words in the lexicon are found. The second problem is that the opinion classification of texts which do not contain words from the lexicon cannot be successfully done using the lexicon-based approach. Therefore, an auxiliary approach, based on a machine learning method, is integrated into the method. This hybrid approach is able to classify more than 99% of texts and achieves better results than the original lexicon-based approach. The final hybrid model can be used for emotion analysis in human–robot interactions.

**Keywords:** sentiment analysis; opinion classification; lexicon-based approach; hybrid approach; lexicon generation; lexicon labelling; particle swarm optimization

## 1. Introduction

Online discussions generate a huge amount of data every day, which are hard to process manually by a human. The processing of this discourse content of social networks can bring useful information about the opinions of the crowd on some web trend, political event, person, or product. Approaches to sentiment analysis, particularly to opinion classification, can be used in recognition of antisocial behavior in online discussions, which is a hot topic at present. Negative opinions are often connected with antisocial behavior; for example, "trolling" posting behaviors. This approach can also be used in HRIs (Human–Robot Interactions), where a robot can use information about the polarity of an opinion or mood of the human, in order to communicate appropriately. When a robot communicates with a human (e.g., an elder), it must choose one from many answers which are suitable to the situation. For example, it can choose an answer which can cheer up the person, if it has information that the current emotional situation/mood of the person is sad. It can also adapt its movements and choose a movement from all possible movements, in order to cheer up the human. Therefore, understanding of the emotional moods of humans can lead to better acceptance of communication with robots by humans.

Opinion analysis can be achieved using either a lexicon-based approach or a machine learning approach. These approaches are used, in opinion analysis, to distinguish between positive or negative (sometimes also neutral [1]) opinions with respect to a certain subject. Machine learning approaches are most often based on the Naive Bayes classifier, Support Vector Machines, Maximum Entropy, k-Nearest Neighbors [2–4], or Deep Learning (i.e., based on neural network training) [5,6]. The study [5] presented an approach based on a new deep convolutional neural network which exploits character- to sentence-level information to perform sentiment analysis of short texts. This approach was tested on movie reviews (SSTb, Stanford Sentiment Treebank) and Twitter messages (STS, Stanford Twitter Sentiment). For the SSTb corpus, they achieved 85.7% accuracy in binary positive/negative sentiment classification, while for the STS corpus, they achieved a sentiment prediction accuracy of 86.4%. The study [6] proved that deep learning approaches have emerged as effective computational models which can discover semantic representations of texts automatically from data without feature engineering. This work presented deep learning approaches as a successful tool for sentiment analysis tasks. They described methods to learn a continuous word representation: the word embedding. As a sentiment lexicon is an important resource for many sentiment analysis systems, the work also presented neural methods to build large-scale sentiment lexicons.

The study [7] presented an approach for classifying a textual dialogue into four emotion classes: happy, sad, angry, and others. In this work, sentiment analysis is represented by emotional classification. The approach ensembled four different models: bi-directional contextual LSTM (BC-LSTM), categorical Bi-LSTM (CAT-LSTM), binary convolutional Bi-LSTM (BIN-LSTM), and Gated Recurrent Unit (GRU). In this approach, two systems achieved Micro F1 = 0.711 and 0.712. The two systems were merged by assembling, the result of which achieved Micro F1 = 0.7324.

However, machine learning methods have a disadvantage: they require a labelled training data set to learn models for opinion analysis. An interesting fact is that the lexicon approach can be used for the creation of labelled training data for machine learning algorithms.

On the other hand, the lexicon-based approach requires a source of external knowledge, in the form of a labelled lexicon which contains sentiment words with an assigned polarity of opinion expressed in the word. The polarity of opinion has the form of a number that indicates how strong the word is correlated with positive or negative polarity, which is assigned to each word in the lexicon. However, this information is very unbalanced across different languages. In this paper, we focus on adapting and modifying existing approaches to the Slovak language.

This work focuses on an opinion analysis based on a lexicon. In the process of lexicon creation, the lexicon must be labelled to find optimal values for the polarity of words in the lexicon. To assign correct polarity values to words, a human annotator is needed for manual labelling. The manual labelling is time-consuming and expensive. Thus, we tried to replace a human annotator by the Particle Swarm Optimization (PSO) algorithm, as lexicon labelling can be considered an optimization problem. The goal of labelling is to find an optimal set of polarity values; that is, labels for all words in the generated lexicon. These labels are optimized recursively until the opinion classification of texts in data sets using this lexicon with the new labels gives the best results. Therefore, the resulting values of the Macro F1 measure of the opinion classification represent the values of the fitness function in the optimization process. We compare the effectiveness of opinion classification using the lexicon labelled by PSO and using the lexicon annotated by a human.

On the other hand, even when we use the best lexicon, it may still not cover all sentiment words. For this reason, some analyzed posts could not be classified as having positive or negative opinion. To solve this problem, we extend the lexicon approach with a machine learning module, in order to classify unclassified posts using the lexicon-based approach. This module was trained on training data labelled using a lexicon approach for opinion classification. We applied the Naive Bayes classifier to build the module.

The contributions of the paper are as follows:

- A new approach to lexicon labelling using the PSO algorithm is presented. PSO optimizes the values of opinion polarity for all words in a labelled lexicon, where the fitness function is represented by the effectiveness measure of sentiment analysis using the labelled lexicon. This automatic labelling avoids the subjectivity of human labelling.
- We generated 60 lexicons using PSO (30 small and 30 big lexicons) for an analysis of the distributions of value polarities in lexicons and an analysis of the values preferred by PSO, in comparison with those preferred by a human.
- We present a hybrid approach which integrates a machine learning model into the sentiment analysis method, in order to classify texts not containing words in the lexicons.
- Extending the new sentiment analysis approach by topic identification in the texts and providing a new means for the interactive combination of switch and shift negation processing.
- The creation of two lexicons—Small and Big—in the Slovak language and the creation of a new General data set of short texts. The lexicons (Small and Big, labelled by human) and the General data set are available at (http://people.tuke.sk/kristina.machova/useful/).

The proposed approach is focused on lexicon-based sentiment analysis. The effectivity of a lexicon approach to sentiment analysis depends on the quality of the used lexicon. The quality of the lexicon is influenced by selection of words in the lexicon, as well as by a measure of precision of the estimated polarity values of words in the lexicon. Our approach uses PSO and BBPSO for the optimal estimation of polarity values. The deep learning method cannot satisfactorily generate the polarity values of words in the lexicon, as clear information about these weight values is lost in the large number of inner layers involved. On the other hand, deep learning can be successfully used in the auxiliary model for the hybrid approach trained by machine learning methods. It is generally assumed that deep learning can achieve better results than the Naive Bayes method in the field of text processing.

## 2. Related Works

Lexicon-based approaches to opinion analysis require a sentiment lexicon to classify posts as having positive or negative opinion. The lexicon can be generated in three ways: manual, automatic, and semi-automatic. Manually generated lexicons are more accurate and usually involve only single words. They can be translated from another language or collected from a corpus of texts. The value of polarity can then be copied from the original lexicon or calculated from the corpus, based on some metrics. However, this approach is time-consuming. A majority of lexicons separate words into positive and negative groups [8] or provide additional types of words, such as intensifiers (words that can shift polarity) [9,10]. On the other hand, lexicons such as the Warriner lexicon [11] or the Crowdsourcing, a word–emotion association Lexicon [12] provide some additional information about the value of polarity for each word. Polarity values allow us to compare the polarities of words and to find more positive and negative words.

Automatically generated lexicons require less human effort. They assign polarity values based on relationships between words in existing lexicons (e.g., SentiWordNet) [13]. These lexicons contain automatically annotated WordNet synsets, according to their degrees of positivity, negativity, and neutrality. In the WordNet-Affect [14], emotional values were added to each WordNet synset. SenticNet [15] includes common-sense knowledge, which provides background information about words. The main weakness of automatically generated lexicons is that they might contain words without polarity or incorrectly assigned polarities. For this reason, the semi-automatic generation of lexicons was introduced. These lexicons are created automatically and are then manually corrected by a human.

Various optimization methods can be used for lexicon labelling. For example, the study [16] presented a global optimization framework which provides a unified way to combine several human-annotated resources for learning the 10-dimensional sentiment lexicon SentiRuc. By minimizing the error function, an optimal labelling of the lexicon can be found. The work also presented a sentiment disambiguation algorithm, in order to increase the flexibility of this lexicon. The experiments of sentiment disambiguation achieved nice results (Accuracy up to 0.987), but the experiments of sentiment classification based on different lexicons achieved an F1 rate value between 0.383 and 0.726.

Several studies have also used nature-inspired algorithms for text classification. In the study [17], Particle Swarm Optimization was applied to find the most useful attributes, which were added as an input for a framework based on Conditional Random Field. PSO has also been used to select attributes and combined with Support Vector Machines to classify reviews [18]. In this paper, PSO is used to generate numbers which represent the polarity values of specific words in the lexicon.

Escalante et al. proposed an approach for increasing the effectiveness of learning term-weighting schemes using a genetic program [19]. The schemes were used to improve classification performance. Standard term-weighting schemes were combined with the new term-weighting schemes, which were more discriminative due to the use of the genetic algorithm. They reported an experimental study comprising a data set for thematic and non-thematic text classification, as well as for image classification. Unlike their approach, we use a genetic program to find not only the weights of words, but values of their opinion polarity as well, which is a different problem and cannot be computed only based on the frequency of words in the text. Nevertheless, the average result of their best-performing approaches for all data sets was F1 = 0.775. Our average result for all data sets was Macro F1 = 0.759, which is comparable with the results in [19].

The study [20] proposed an approach to simultaneously train a vanilla sentiment classifier and adapt word polarities to the target domain. The adaptation was based on tracking wrongly predicted sentences and using them for supervision. On the other hand, our approach builds a domain-independent lexicon of labelled words. In this paper, the best results of testing on the Movie data set was Accuracy = 0.779. Our best results on the Movie data set (MacroF1 = 0.743, see Table 11) were comparable with the results in [20]. It is easier to achieve higher results in Accuracy than in F1 rate, even though both measures of classification effectiveness consider both false positive and false negative classifications.

## 2.1. Nature-Inspired Optimization

Nature-inspired algorithms are motivated by biological systems such as beehives, anthills, and swarms of fish, birds, and so on. They investigate the behaviors of individuals in a population, their mutual interactions, and their interactions with an environment. For example, PSO was inspired by a flock of birds searching for food. We suppose that only some birds know about food and where it is situated. Therefore, the best strategy is to follow the individual nearest to the food. Every individual in a population represents a bird and has a fitness value in the search space.

Particle Swarm Optimization is an optimization algorithm which is inspired by a flock of birds. PSO converges to the final solution; in this case, it has the form of the best-labelled lexicon. The possible solutions are called particles, which are parts of the population. Each particle keeps its best solution (evaluated by the fitness function) called *pbest*, while the best value chosen from the whole swarm is called *gbest*. The standard PSO consists of two steps: change velocity and update positions. In the first step, each particle changes its velocity towards its *pbest* and *gbest* [21]. In the second step, the particle updates its position. A new position is calculated, based on previous position and a new velocity. Each particle is represented as a vector in a D-dimensional space. The i[th] particle can be represented as $X_i = (x_{i1}, x_{i2}, \ldots, x_{iD})$. The velocity of the i[th] particle is represented as $V_i = (v_{i1}, v_{i2}, \ldots, v_{iD})$ and the best previous position of the particle is represented as $P_i = (p_{i1}, p_{i2}, \ldots, p_{iD})$. The best particle in the swarm is represented by $g$ and $w$ is the inertia weight, which balances the exploration and exploitation abilities of the particles. The velocity and position are updated using Equations (1) and (2):

$$v_{id}^{n+1} = w v_{id}^n + c_1 r_1^n \left( p_{id}^n - x_{id}^n \right) + c_2 r_2^n \left( p_{gd}^n - x_{id}^n \right) \tag{1}$$

$$x_{id}^{n+1} = x_{id}^n + v_{id}^{n+1} \tag{2}$$

where

- $d = 1, 2, \ldots, D$ (in our system, $D$ represents the number of words in the dictionary);
- $i = 1, 2, \ldots, N$, where $N$ is the number of particles in the swarm;
- $n = 1, 2, \ldots$, max denotes the iteration number;
- $r_1$ and $r_2$ are uniformly distributed random values which avoid the particles falling into local optima; and
- $c_1$ and $c_2$ are important parameters, known as the self-confidence factor and the swarm confidence factor, respectively. They define the type of trajectory the particle travels on, so they control the searching behavior of the particle [22].

The stopping criteria of the algorithm often depends on the type of the problem. In practice, PSO is run until a fixed number of function evaluations is carried out or an error bound is reached.

PSO uses *pbest* and *gbest* to update the position of a particle. The impacts of these values were studied in [23]. In this work, *pbest* and *gbest* were set as constants and the trajectories of the particles were investigated. These results show that the trajectory can be determined by the difference between *pbest* and *gbest*. These positions can determine the particle's movement. Based on this knowledge, a new PSO method was designed; the so-called Bare-bones PSO (BBPSO). BBPSO uses a Gaussian distribution $N(\mu,\sigma)$ with the mean $\mu$ and standard deviation $\sigma$, as shown in Equation (3):

$$x_{id}^{t+1} = \begin{cases} N(\mu, \sigma), & \text{rand}() < 0.5 \\ p_{id'}^{t} & \text{othetwise} \end{cases} \tag{3}$$

where $\mu$ is the center of *pbest* and *gbest*, and $\sigma$ is the absolute difference between *pbest* and *gbest*. The rand() function is used to speed up convergence by retaining the previous best position, *pbest*.

### 2.2. Naive Bayes Learning Method

Naive Bayes is a probabilistic classifier based on Bayes' theorem and the independence assumption between attributes.

For n observations or attributes (respectively, words) $x_1, \ldots, x_n$, the conditional probability for any class $y_j$ can be expressed as Equation (4):

$$P(y_j/x_1,\ldots,x_n) = \beta P(y_j) \prod_{i=1}^{n} P(x_i/y_j) \tag{4}$$

This model is called the Naive Bayes classifier. Naive Bayes is often applied as a baseline for text classification [2]. We used the Naïve Bayes learning method in two ways:

1. For the labelling of words in a lexicon.
2. For learning a model for opinion classification of posts when the lexicon approach fails. This approach to opinion classification is called the hybrid approach and is discussed below.

When we used Naive Bayes for labelling words in a lexicon, all labelled words in the lexicon played the role of attributes in the Bayes learning method. We had to calculate the numerical value representing the measure of polarity of each word in the lexicon. This value is based on probability of the word to belong to a class (positive or negative). We needed a training data set to calculate these values (probabilities). A training data set was used to calculate the probability $P$ that a word $w$ from the post text relates to each class $c$ (positive or negative). Labels assigned using this probability were used to build a lexicon. The probability can be calculated by the simple probability method described by Equation (5):

$$P(w_c) = \frac{\sum w_c}{\sum w} \tag{5}$$

where

- $P(w_c)$—the probability that the word (from class $c$) is the polarity value of the word.
- $\sum w_c$—the number of occurrences of word w in class $c$.
- $\sum w$—the number of occurrences of word $w$ in the whole data set.

In case that the word is not assigned to a specific class, the probability would be zero; therefore, a method which returns a very low number, instead of zero, was implemented.

## 3. Lexicon Generation

There are many approaches for the generation of a lexicon. A lexicon can be generated for a given domain. This lexicon is obviously very precise in this domain, but usually has a weak performance in different domains. Another way is to generate a general lexicon. This lexicon usually has the same effectiveness in all domains, which is mostly not very high.

We generated two lexicons to analyze opinion in Slovak posts using a lexicon approach. We used two different methods of generation: translation and composition from many relevant lexicons. The first (Big) lexicon was translated from English and then extended by a human. It was enlarged by domain-dependent words, in order to increase its effectiveness. The domain-dependent words were words which may be common, but which have different meanings in different domains. For example, the word "long" has a different opinion polarity in the electrical domain (i.e., "long battery life") than in the movie domain (i.e., "too long movie"). Thus, the Big lexicon was domain-dependent, which is its disadvantage. For this reason, we decided to generate another new (Small) lexicon. This lexicon was expected to be domain-independent, as it was extracted from six English lexicons in which only domain-independent words were included. Domain-independent words are words which have the same meaning in different domains. They were analyzed and only overlapping words from all lexicons were picked up. The advantage of the Small lexicon is its smaller size, in comparison with the Big lexicon. This is an important feature, as each particle in our PSO implementation represents the whole labelled lexicon; more precisely, a set of polarity values for all words in the lexicon. A smaller lexicon, thus, means that a smaller set of labels must be optimized. So, the size of the lexicon influences the time needed to find the optimal solution. The words in the lexicon were selected once, but the labels of those words (i.e., polarity values) were found by optimization using PSO and BBPSO in 60 iterations. During optimization, the labels of the words were recursively changed many times, until the fitness function gave satisfactory results.

For both lexicons, three versions were generated: The first version was labelled manually by a human annotator, the second version was labelled by PSO, and the third one using BBSPO. Then, all versions were used for opinion analysis of post texts in the Slovak language and tested. We could engage more annotators in the process of human labelling, but the subjectivity of labels would remain, and averaging the values of labels may obscure the accurate estimation of the word polarities by one expert human.

The Big lexicon was generated by manual human translation from an original English lexicon [10], which consists of 6789 words including 13 negations. The generated lexicon in Slovak was smaller than original lexicon, as some words have in Slovak less synonyms than in English. We translated only positive and negative words to Slovak. Synonyms and antonyms of original words were found in a Slovak thesaurus. The thesaurus was also used to determine intensifiers and negations. The final Big lexicon consisted of 1430 words: 598 positive words, 772 negative words, 41 intensifiers, and 19 negations. The first version of this lexicon was labelled by a human. The range of polarity from −3 (the most negative word) to +3 (the most positive word) was chosen to assign the polarity value to each word. For each word in the lexicon, the English form was searched in a double translation. "Double translation" means that each word from the lexicon was translated into English and then was translated back to Slovak, in the case that the word had the same meaning before and after translation, the final form of the word was added to the lexicon.

The Small *lexicon* was derived from six different English lexicons, as used in the works [10,15,24–27]. The English lexicons were analyzed and only overlapping words were chosen to form the new lexicon.

To translate these words to Slovak, the English translations from the Big lexicon were used. Overlapping words were found, and their Slovak forms were added to the lexicon. This new lexicon contained 220 words, including 85 positive words and 135 negative words. Intensifiers and negations were not added, as they were not included in all original lexicons. The first version of the lexicon was labelled manually, with a range of polarity from −3 to 3. The details of the lexicons used for the creation of the Small lexicon are as follows:

- Hu and Liu lexicon [10] (4783 positives, 2006 negatives, and 13 opposites)
- SenticNet 4.0 [15] (27,405 positives and 22,595 negatives)
- Sentiment140 [24] (38,312 positives and 24,156 negatives)
- AFINN [25] (878 positives and 1598 negatives)
- Taboada lexicon [26] (2535 positives, 4039 negatives, and 219 intensifiers)
- SentiStrength [27] (399 positives, 524 negatives, 28 intensifiers, and 17 opposites).

## 4. Lexicon Labelling Using Particle Swarm Optimization

Particle Swarm Optimization (PSO) was chosen as a method for the lexicon labelling, as labelling is an optimization problem where a combination of values of labels for all words in a lexicon has to create the best overall evaluation of the polarity of a given text. PSO is an efficient and robust optimization method, which has been successfully applied to solve various optimization problems. In the optimization process of lexicon labelling using PSO, each particle represents one version of the lexicon for labelling. A lexicon can be encoded as a vector $X_i = (x_{i1}, x_{i2}, \ldots, x_{iD})$. Each word of the lexicon is labelled by a number, representing the measure of polarity from negative to positive $x_{ij} \in \{-3,3\}$, $i = 1, 2, \ldots, N$, where $N$ is the number of particles and $j = 1,2, \ldots, D$, where $D$ denotes the number of words in the lexicon. Thus, the particle size depends on the size of the lexicon.

From the Big lexicon, only positive and negative words were used. Therefore, the particle size was decreased from 1470 to 1370 polarity values. The particle representing the Small lexicon had 220 polarity values. The designed approach is described in the following Algorithm 1:

---
**Algorithm 1:** PSO algorithm
---
*generate the initial population*
*for number of iterations do*
    *for particle_i do*
        $\phi_i$ *evaluate particle_i using fitness function*
        $\zeta_i$ *compute value of fitness function for pbest of particle_i*
        *if $\phi_i > \zeta_i$ then update pbest*
        *end if*
        *if pbest > gbest then update gbest*
        *end if*
    *end for*
    *for each particle_i do*
        *for each dimension d do*
            *compute new velocity according (1)*
            *compute new position according (2)*
        *end for*
    *end for*
*end for*
*return the value of gbest particle*

---

The goal of labelling a lexicon using PSO is to find an optimal set of polarity values for all words in this lexicon. One position of the particle represents one potential solution (one set of labels of words), which is recursively changed during the process of optimization. Each potential solution can be represented as a vector in D-dimensional space, where D is the number of words in the lexicon. In our approach, the initial population was generated randomly and then, the PSO method was applied. In PSO optimization, each particle was evaluated based on the fitness function (values of MacroF1). For each actual particle, *pbest* (particle best) was set and *gbest* for the whole swarm (global best) was searched. For the next iteration, a velocity of each particle was calculated (1) based on its *pbest* and *gbest*, and then the position of the particle was updated using Formula (2). Then, the particle was evaluated again and *pbest* and *gbest* were updated again. This process was run recursively until a fixed number of iterations was met. For experiments with standard PSO, the following parameters were used:

- inertia weight = 0.729844
- number of particles = 15,000
- number of iterations = 100
- $c_1 = 1.49618$
- $c_2 = 1.49618$
- max velocity = 2

*4.1. Labelling by Bare-Bones Particle Swarm Optimization*

Bare-Bones PSO uses a different approach to find an optimal polarity value for each word in a lexicon. BBPSO works with a mean and standard deviation of a Gaussian distribution. The mean and deviation are calculated from *pbest* and *gbest*. The process of labelling is shown in the following Algorithm 2:

---
**Algorithm 2:** BBPSO algorithm
---
*generate the initial population*
*for number of iterations do*
    *for particle_i do*
        $\phi_i$ *evaluate particle_i using fitness function*
        $\zeta_i$ *compute value of fitness function for pbest of particle_i*
        *if* $\phi_i > \zeta_i$ *then update pbest*
        *end if*
        *if pbest > gbest then update gbest*
        *end if*
    *end for*
    *for each particle_i do*
        *for each dimension d do*
            *compute new position using Gaussian distribution*
        *end for*
    *end for*
*end for*
*return the value of gbest particle*
---

BBPSO uses a Gaussian distribution $N(\mu_{id}, \sigma_{id})$ with mean $\mu_{id}$ and standard deviation $\sigma_{id}$. These values are calculated using Equations (6) and (7):

$$\mu_{id} = \frac{gbest_d + pbespbest_{id}}{2} \qquad (6)$$

$$\sigma_{id} = |gbest_d - pbest_{id}| \qquad (7)$$

where

- $d = 1, 2, \ldots, D$, with $D$ representing the number of words in the lexicon, and
- $i = 1, 2, \ldots, N$, where $N$ is the number of particles in the swarm.

## 4.2. Fitness Function for Optimization

The fitness function was based on the lexicon approach used to classify the opinion of post texts in data sets. This classification was provided repetitively with all lexicons generated by PSO (or BBPSO). Every opinion classification using all particular lexicons was evaluated by the F1 rate, which is a harmonic mean between Precision and Recall, calculated by Equation (8). The F1 rate played the role of the fitness function.

$$F1 = \frac{2 \times Precision \times Recall}{Precision + Recall} \tag{8}$$

The opinion classification was implemented in the following way: Each input post text was tokenized. Each word was compared with words in the temporary test lexicon. If the word was found in the dictionary, the polarity value of the post was updated. If the word was positive, the polarity of the post was increased and if the word was negative, the post polarity was decreased, according to Equation (9):

$$P_p = \sum p_{vw} \tag{9}$$

where

- $P_p$ is the post's polarity and
- $p_{vw}$ is the word's polarity.

Precision and Recall were calculated based on the comparison of the automatically assigned labels with the gold-standard class labels. These were applied to calculate the F1 rate. However, the final values of the fitness function were not derived from F1 rate, but instead from the MacroF1 rate (10), which better evaluates the performance on an unbalanced data set. The MacroF1 rate (10) shows the effectiveness in each class, independent of the size of the class:

$$MacroF1 = \frac{F1_p + F1_n}{2}, \tag{10}$$

where

- $F1_p$ is the F1 *rate* for positive posts and
- $F1_n$ is the F1 *rate* for negative posts.

The use of this fitness function was based on the defined measure of classification effectivity (MacroF1). All words in the lexicon were repeatedly labelled and the effectivity of opinion classification of texts from the data set using this lexicon (with new labels) was evaluated, until the labels were found to be optimal. In this way, the labelled polarity of words in the lexicon could be domain-dependent, if the data set of texts was domain-dependent. Therefore, we used two data sets: one being domain-dependent (Movie), while the other was domain-independent (Slovak-General). The labelling of a lexicon is an optimization problem and, in this case, supervised learning was used only for computing the values of the fitness function. However, supervised learning was also used for model training in the hybrid approach for opinion classification (see Section 7.2). This model was then used for classification of texts with a difficult dictionary.

## 5. Experiments with Various Labelling

### 5.1. Data Sets

Experiments with different labelling methods were tested on two data sets. The General data set contained 4720 reviews from different websites in the Slovak language. It consisted of 2455 positive and 2265 negative comments. Neutral comments were removed. The reviews referred to different domains such as electronics reviews, books reviews, movie reviews, and politics. The data set included 155,522 words. The Slovak-General data set is available at (http://people.tuke.sk/kristina.machova/useful/).

The Movie data set [2] contained 1000 positive and 1000 negative posts collected from rottentomatos.com. The data set was pre-processed and translated to Slovak. All data sets were labelled as positive or negative by human annotators. Each data set was randomly split with a ratio of 90:10—90% for training and 10% unseen posts for validation. All results were obtained on the testing set. The same subsets were applied in all experiments, including the human-labelled lexicon.

## 5.2. Experiments with PSO and BBPSO Labelling

In the process of optimizing the labelling of the Big and Small lexicons, the initial labelling, a set of polarity values for all words in the lexicon was first found (1370 values for Big and 220 values for Small lexicon; the Big lexicon originally had 1430 words, but only positive and negative words were included in the experiments). This set of values (1370 or 220) represented one particle for PSO optimization. Then, this set of values was changed with the aid of *pbest* and *gbest*, until the effectiveness of using the particle (set of labelling values for each word in the lexicon) in the lexicon-based opinion classification was the highest. Within the labelling optimization, not only one but 30 labels for the Small lexicon and 30 labels for the Big lexicon were generated, in order to achieve statistically significant results.

A set of experiments were carried out, where both data sets (General and Movie) were used for testing of labelling for both lexicons (Big and Small). Two methods for labelling these lexicons were tested: using PSO and BBPSO.

Each experiment was repeated 30 times, in order to achieve statistically significant results. The following tables show only the results for the best experiment and the average results of all 30 repeats. The achieved results of these experiments were obtained on the respective validation sets. The results are presented in Tables 1–8. The results of these experiments are measured by Precision in the positive class (Precision Pos.), Precision in the negative class (Precision Neg.), Recall in the positive class (Recall Pos.), Recall in the negative class (Recall Neg.), F1 Positive, F1 Negative, and Macro F1.

Tables 1 and 2 represent experiments on the Movie data set using the Big lexicon. Table 1 shows that using the lexicon labelled by BBPSO was more precise for opinion classification than PSO in all cases, with only one exception. Another observation was that, in all experiments, Precision in classification of positive posts was better than Precision in classification of negative posts; however, for Recall, the observation was opposite. The Macro F1 rate in Table 2 gives us more results. There were no significant differences between classification of positive and negative posts. The important result is that labelling by BBPSO led to a more precise lexicon than labelling by PSO.

Table 1. The results of Precision and Recall in positive and negative class on **Movie** data set using **Big** lexicon labelled by Particle Swarm Optimization (PSO) and Bare-bones Particle Swarm Optimization (BBPSO).

| Labelling | Precision Pos. | Precision Neg. | Recall Pos. | Recall Neg. |
|---|---|---|---|---|
| PSO best | 0.795 | 0.734 | 0.780 | 0.822 |
| PSO average | 0.702 | 0.691 | 0.687 | 0.703 |
| BBPSO best | 0.814 | 0.779 | 0.769 | 0.822 |
| BBPSO average | 0.758 | 0.730 | 0.719 | 0.767 |

Table 2. Results of F1 rate in positive and negative classes and Macro F1 rate on **Movie** data set using **Big** lexicon labelled by PSO and BBPSO.

| Labelling | F1 Positive | F1 Negative | Macro F1 |
|---|---|---|---|
| PSO best | 0.742 | 0.767 | 0.750 |
| PSO average | 0.694 | 0.696 | 0.695 |
| BBPSO best | 0.791 | 0.787 | 0.795 |
| BBPSO average | 0.738 | 0.748 | 0.743 |

Tables 3 and 4 represent experiments on the Movie data set using the Small lexicon. Comparison of Table 1 with Tables 2 and 3 with Table 4 shows that using the Small and Big lexicons gave very similar results, in terms of Precision, Recall, and Macro F1 rate, on the Movie data set.

**Table 3.** The results of Precision and Recall in positive and negative classes on **Movie** data set using **Small** lexicon labelled by PSO and BBPSO.

| Labelling | Precision Pos. | Precision Neg. | Recall Pos. | Recall Neg. |
|---|---|---|---|---|
| PSO best | 0.769 | 0.767 | 0.791 | 0.811 |
| PSO average | 0.740 | 0.718 | 0.707 | 0.749 |
| BBPSO best | 0.789 | 0.761 | 0.769 | 0.822 |
| BBPSO average | 0.752 | 0.727 | 0.718 | 0.760 |

**Table 4.** Results of F1 rate in positive and negative classes and Macro F1 rate on **Movie** data set using **Small** lexicon labelled by PSO and BBPSO.

| Labelling | F1 Positive | F1 Negative | Macro F1 |
|---|---|---|---|
| PSO best | 0.769 | 0.785 | 0.768 |
| PSO average | 0.722 | 0.732 | 0.727 |
| BBPSO best | 0.764 | 0.776 | 0.773 |
| BBPSO average | 0.734 | 0.742 | 0.738 |

We also provide results for four similar experiments on the General data set, which are presented in Tables 5–8. The results in Table 5 show that experiments on the General data set led to similar results to the experiments on the Movie data set. Precision in classification of positive posts was better than classification of negative posts; however, the observation was opposite in Recall.

The results in Tables 5 and 6 show that using the lexicon labelled by BBPSO was more precise for opinion classification than PSO, in most cases. Table 7 demonstrates that using the Small lexicon on the General data set led to very poor results; only Recall in positive posts gave good results.

**Table 5.** The results of Precision and Recall in positive and negative classes on **General** data set using **Big** lexicon labelled by PSO and BBPSO.

| Labelling | Precision Pos. | Precision Neg. | Recall Pos. | Recall Neg. |
|---|---|---|---|---|
| PSO best | 0.708 | 0.829 | 0.889 | 0.620 |
| PSO average | 0.670 | 0.754 | 0.808 | 0.595 |
| BBPSO best | 0.775 | 0.860 | 0.889 | 0.746 |
| BBPSO average | 0.773 | 0.775 | 0.775 | 0.775 |

**Table 6.** The results of F1 rate in positive and negative classes and Macro F1 rate on **General** data set using **Big** lexicon labelled by PSO and BBPSO.

| Labelling | F1 Positive | F1 Negative | Macro F1 |
|---|---|---|---|
| PSO best | 0.760 | 0.717 | 0.745 |
| PSO average | 0.732 | 0.664 | 0.698 |
| BBPSO best | 0.811 | 0.787 | 0.799 |
| BBPSO average | 0.775 | 0.775 | 0.775 |

**Table 7.** The results of Precision and Recall in positive and negative classes on **General** data set using **Small** lexicon labelled by PSO and BBPSO.

| Labelling | Precision Pos. | Precision Neg. | Recall Pos. | Recall Neg. |
|---|---|---|---|---|
| PSO best | 0.537 | 0.563 | 0.713 | 0.376 |
| PSO average | 0.519 | 0.528 | 0.683 | 0.359 |
| BBPSO best | 0.542 | 0.572 | 0.713 | 0.404 |
| BBPSO average | 0.533 | 0.552 | 0.693 | 0.384 |

The Macro F1 rate, presented in Table 8, confirms this finding. The reason for this failure could be that the Small lexicon was generated from six English lexicons and only overlapping words from all lexicons were chosen. So, the Small lexicon may have not contained specific words which were important for polarity identification in a given text; that is, it did not contain all necessary words with sentiment polarities needed for the successful sentiment classification of general texts.

**Table 8.** Results of F1 rate in positive and negative classes and Macro F1 rate on **General** data set using **Small** lexicon labelled by PSO and BBPSO.

| Labelling | F1 Positive | F1 Negative | Macro F1 |
|---|---|---|---|
| PSO best | 0.612 | 0.451 | 0.532 |
| PSO average | 0.590 | 0.427 | 0.509 |
| BBPSO best | 0.613 | 0.469 | 0.540 |
| BBPSO average | 0.603 | 0.453 | 0.528 |

The significance test is also provided. Paired sample $t$-test was used to prove the statistically significant improvement between PSO and BBPSO. A 95% confidence interval and 29 degrees of freedom were applied. We tested the Macro F1 measure, and the results (see Table 9) showed that BBPSO was significantly better than PSO.

**Table 9.** Results of significance test of Macro F1 rate in experiments on **Movie** and **General** data sets using **Big** and **Small** lexicons.

| | t-Statistics | $p$-Value |
|---|---|---|
| Movie data set using Big lexicon | 06.304 | $8.116 \times e^{-7}$ |
| Movie data set using Small lexicon | 02.425 | 0.022 |
| General data set using Big lexicon | 16.707 | $2.018 \times e^{-16}$ |
| General data set using Small lexicon | 09.357 | $2.916 \times e^{-10}$ |

The $p$-value represents the probability that there is no statistically significant difference between the results. The $p$-values were small in all cases. This means that the probability that there was no statistically significant difference between the results presented in Tables 1–8 is small. Thus, we can say that the difference between the results was statistically significant. This statement is valid with 95% confidence.

The complexity of the automatic labelling of lexicons using the optimization methods PSO and BBPSO is $O(I_{MAX} \cdot N \cdot D)$, where $I_{MAX}$ is the maximum number of iterations, N is the total number of words in the training set, and D is the number of words in the lexicon. This means that the complexity is linear in the size of the training set and the lexicon. In our case, the General data set contained 155,522 words and the Big lexicon contained 1370 words. The complexity of the lexicon approach for opinion classification, which was used for computing the values of the fitness function, was linear in the size of posts in the training set M and the number of words in the lexicon D, such that its complexity is $O(M \cdot D)$.

### 5.3. Comparison of PSO and BBPSO Labelling with Human Labelling

In the previous section, it was shown that BBPSO was better than simple PSO. We wanted to also compare this approach to human labelling. Within this experiment, we decided to evaluate results of the opinion classification only in terms of Macro F1 rate. The results are illustrated in Table 10. It was shown that automatic labelling using nature-inspired optimization algorithms, especially BBPSO, was better than human labelling of lexicons for the lexicon approach to opinion classification.

**Table 10.** The comparison of labelling by human, PSO, and BBPSO in Macro F1 rate on **Movie** and **General** (Slovak) data sets using **Big** and **Small** lexicons labelled by PSO and BBPSO.

| Macro F1 | Labelling | Movie | General |
|---|---|---|---|
| BIG | human | 0.629 | 0.767 |
| | PSO | 0.694 | 0.698 |
| | BBPSO | 0.743 | 0.775 |
| SMALL | human | 0.679 | 0.501 |
| | PSO | 0.727 | 0.509 |
| | BBPSO | 0.738 | 0.528 |

The results in Table 10 confirm the findings in Tables 7 and 8: that using the Small lexicon on the General (Slovak) data set led to very poor results, not only when using PSO and BBPSO labelling but also for human labelling. The most important fact is that BBPSO was able to find the best polarity values for the words in the lexicon, independently of the used lexicon (Big or Small) and data set (Movie or General—Slovak). These results are illustrated also in Figure 1a,b for the Big and Small lexicons, respectively.

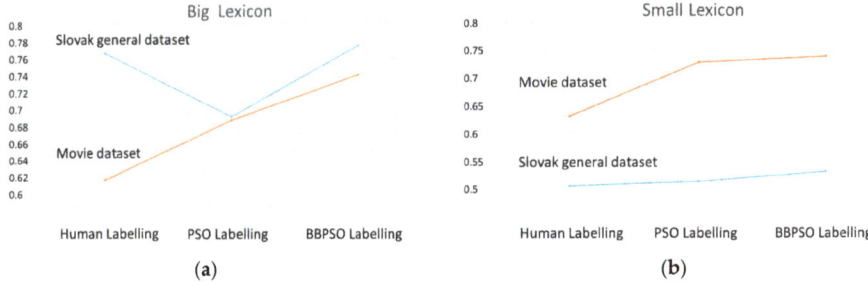

**Figure 1.** The comparison of the **Big** lexicon in part (**a**) and **Small** lexicon in part (**b**) labelling by a human, Particle Swarm Optimization (PSO), and Bare-bones Particle Swarm Optimization (BBPSO) in Macro F1 rate.

We found seven other approaches which used the Movie data set. Table 11 contains a comparison of our approach to those other related works with experiments on the Movie data set. For our needs, the data set was automatically translated into Slovak language, which had an impact on the overall results of our tests. The last row of the Table 11 contains results of our hybrid approach (Section 7.2) on Movie data set, but the results of the same approach on General dataset were better (Accuracy = 0.865).

**Table 11.** The comparison of effectiveness of our approaches with seven other related approaches tested on **Movie** data set. The last row contains results of our hybrid approach (Section 7.2), which uses the lexicon approach composed with a machine learning approach (Naive Bayes).

| Used Methods | Representation | Accuracy | Reference |
|---|---|---|---|
| Naive Bayes, SVM | min. cuts in graphs | 0.872 | [28] |
| Contextual Valence Shifters, SVM | n-grams | 0.862 | [29] |
| FT-IDF, SVM | n-grams, bag-of-words | 0.881 | [30] |
| ML (un)supervised | word vectors | 0.889 | [31] |
| Tree-based Word Dependency | word embedding | 0.885 | [32] |
| Naive Bayes, SVM | bag-of-words, LDA | 0.879 | [33] |
| LSTM, ConvLSTMConv | word embedding | 0.890 | [34] |
| Lexicon approach | BBPSO labelling | 0.743 | our approach |
| Lexicon app. & Naive Bayes | BBPSO labelling | 0.807 | our approach |

## 6. Distribution of Values of Polarities in Generated Lexicons

The main purpose of this section is the comparison of human labelling and automatic labelling, in order to answer the following questions: Which integer labels are preferred in PSO and BBPSO labelling, in comparison with human labelling? Can the subjectivity of human labelling cause a decrease of effectiveness of lexicon-based opinion classification?

We worked under the assumption that automatic labelling is not subjective, like human labelling. This is because, in the process of PSO labelling, the effectivity of lexicon use in lexicon-based opinion classification is a decisive factor. Many human annotators can easily agree on whether an opinion is positive or negative, but when determining the intensity degrees of the polarity of opinions, it is difficult to reach an agreement. So, labelling using PSO optimization seemed to be a good solution. This assumption was supported by our results, which are shown in Figures 2–5.

We also examined the distribution of polarity values, which were assigned by the automatic labelling in the interval of integers <−3, +3> in labelled lexicons. We wanted to know if there were some differences between labelling by human and automatic labelling (PSO, BBPSO); in other words, we wanted to find some integer values in the interval <−3, +3> which are preferred by a human or an automatic annotator, respectively. Our findings are illustrated in Figures 2–5.

The models of PSO and BBPSO labelling were generated using both General and Movie data sets. Of course, human labelling is independent of any data set. In Figures 2 and 3, the result distributions of the intensity of polarity values in the Big lexicon are shown. Figure 2 illustrates the results of comparison of PSO and human labelling, while Figure 3 illustrates the comparison of BBPSO and human labelling. We can see, in these two figures, that the human annotator avoided labelling words with zero. They expected only positive or negative words in the lexicon and no neutral ones. On the other hand, PSO frequently used a zero-polarity label. BBPSO also used zero polarity values, but they were not applied as often.

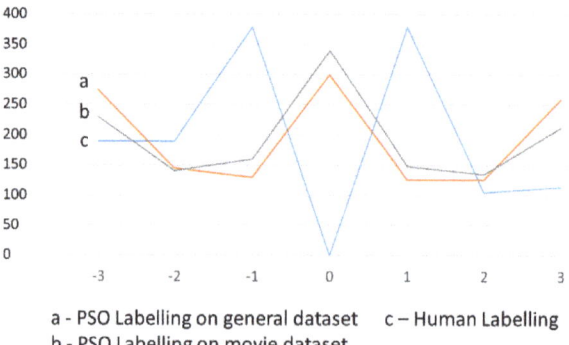

a - PSO Labelling on general dataset    c – Human Labelling
b - PSO Labelling on movie dataset

**Figure 2.** Distribution of values of the intensity of polarities acquired in the process of the **Big** lexicon labelling (1370 words) using PSO, in comparison to human labelling. Axis X represents the intensity of a word polarity and axis Y represents the number of words with the given intensity of polarity.

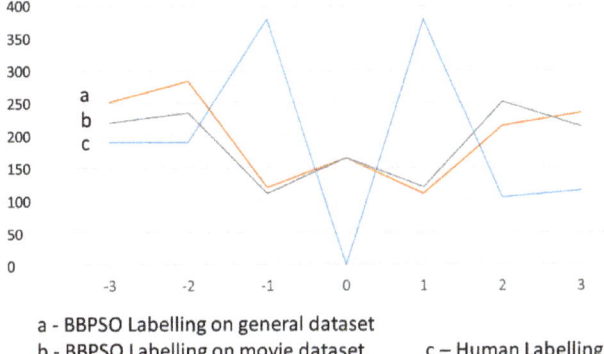

a - BBPSO Labelling on general dataset
b - BBPSO Labelling on movie dataset     c – Human Labelling

**Figure 3.** Distribution of values of the intensity of polarities acquired in the process of **Big** lexicon labelling (1370 words) using BBPSO, in comparison to human labelling. Axis X represents the intensity of a word polarity and axis Y represents the number of words with the given intensity of polarity.

We ran similar experiments with the Small lexicon. Figures 4 and 5 illustrate the resulting distributions of the intensity of polarity values in the Small lexicon. These results confirm similar findings as for the Big lexicon; in that PSO labelling most often used intensity polarity labels equal to zero. BBPSO labelling of the Small lexicon often used extreme (−3 and 3) polarity values.

We must point out that labelling some words with a zero value means rejecting this word from the lexicon, as the word is not helpful in the process of opinion classification. An interesting discovery is the fact that labelling by nature-inspired algorithms (PSO, BBPSO) achieved very good results, despite the fact that they rejected some words in the process of the opinion classification. PSO labelling rejected from 21% to 25% of all words from the Big lexicon and from 25% to 28% of all words from the Small lexicon. BBPSO labelling rejected approximately 12% of words from the Big lexicon and from 12% to 16% of words from the Small lexicon.

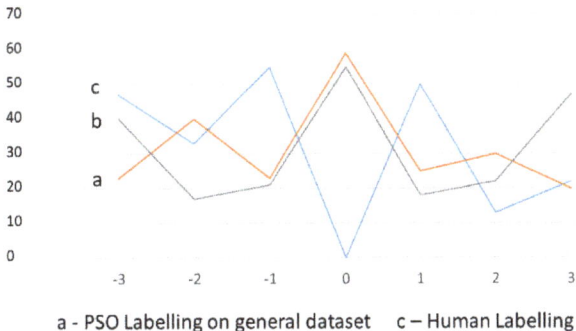

a - PSO Labelling on general dataset    c – Human Labelling
b - PSO Labelling on movie dataset

**Figure 4.** Distribution of values of the intensity of polarities acquired in the process of the **Small** lexicon labelling (220 words) using PSO, in comparison to human labelling. Axis X represents the intensity of a word polarity and axis Y represents the number of words with the given intensity of polarity.

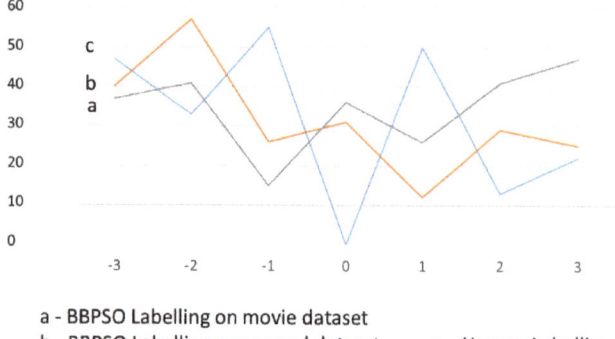

a - BBPSO Labelling on movie dataset
b - BBPSO Labelling on general dataset    c – Human Labelling

**Figure 5.** Distribution of values of the intensity of polarities acquired in the process of the **Small** lexicon labelling (220 words) using BBPSO, in comparison to human labelling. Axis X represents the intensity of a word polarity and axis Y represents the number of words with the given intensity of polarity.

## 7. New Lexicon Approach to Opinion Analysis

The new approach proposes a new means for negation processing, by combining switch and shift negation. It also incorporates a new means for intensifier processing, which is dependent on the type of negation.

Besides summing polarities of words in analyzing the opinion of posts, according to (9), intensifiers and negations should be processed in the opinion classification. Intensifiers are special words which can increase or decrease the intensity of polarity of connected words. In our approach to opinion analysis, the intensifiers are processed using a special part of the lexicon. In this part of the lexicon, words are accompanied by numbers, which represent a measure of increasing or decreasing the polarity of connected words. This means that words with strong polarity (positive or negative) are intensified more than words with weak polarity. The value of the intensification is set with the value "1" from the beginning. After that, a connected word's polarity is multiplied by the actual value of the intensifier; for example, in the sentence "It is very good solution", the polarity $P = 1$ of the word "good" is increased by the word "very" to the final polarity of $P = 2*[1] = 2$.

In our approach, negations are processed in a new way, using the interactivity of switch and shift negation [26]. Switch negation only turns polarity to its opposite (e.g., from +2 to −2), as illustrated in Figure 6a. Shift negation is more precise than switch negation, only shifting the polarity of a connected word towards the direction to opposite polarity, as illustrated in Figure 6b.

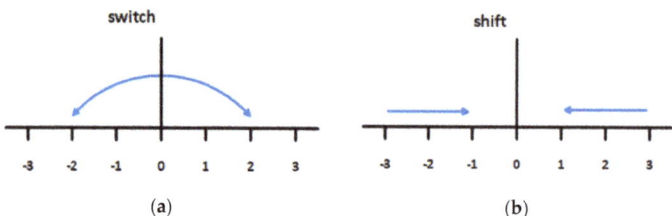

**Figure 6.** Illustration of switch negation (**a**) and shift negation (**b**) of polarity intensity of connected words in analyzed posts.

We designed the interactive so-called 'combined negation processing', where shift negation is applied to extreme values of polarity of connected words (+/−3) and switch negation is used for processing most obvious polarities (with absolute value 1 or 2). The combined approach significantly increases the effectivity of opinion classification, as illustrated in Table 12.

Table 12. The effectivity of composite approach to negation processing of words in analyzed posts, in terms of Macro F1 rate.

| Type of Negation Processing | Macro F1 |
|---|---|
| Without negation | 0.591 |
| Switch negation | 0.593 |
| Shift negation | 0.590 |
| Combined negation | 0.605 |

After involving intensifiers and negations, the polarity of the whole post is not calculated using the simple approach (9) but, instead, using the new approach (11):

$$P_p = \sum P_w (\prod P_i)(\prod P_n) \quad (11)$$

where

- $P_p$ is the post's polarity,
- $P_w$ is the word's polarity,
- $\prod P_i$ is the multiplication of polarity of words by intensifiers in a post, and
- $\prod P_n$ is the multiplication of polarity of words by negations in a post.

*7.1. Topic Identification in Opinion Classification*

Another method that we used to increase the effectiveness of the opinion classification was involving topic identification. Topic identification can be helpful in increasing the influence of a text of post concentrated on the topic of an online discussion. Polarity of these posts was increased using greater weights. We tested two methods for topic identification: Latent Dirichlet Allocation (LDA) and Term Frequency (TF). LDA is a standard probabilistic method, based on the Dirichlet distribution of probability of topic for each post. In the output of the LDA, there is a list of words accompanied with their relevancy to all texts in the data set (so called topics). An experiment was carried out, with all texts in the data set processed using LDA. The output was a list of 50 words relevant to topics present in the texts. As there were too many "topics", the list was reduced to 15 words with the highest relevancy to the topics of the processed texts.

The second method was topic identification based on the term frequencies of words in posts. We assumed that the words in posts relevant to the topic of online discussion should have higher occurrence in these texts. A disadvantage of this method is the highest occurrence of stop words in texts. For this reason, stop words must be excluded in pre-processing. We did not create this list, instead using a known list of stop words.

First, the opinion polarity of posts was estimated. In the second step, words relevant to the identified topic of discussion were searched for in the post. If such words were found in the post, then the opinion polarity of the post was increased (by multiplication with value 1.5). The value of 1.5 was set experimentally, after experiments with three values: 1.5, 2, and 3. The double and triple changes of polarity led to slight decreases in the quality of the results obtained. Results of experiments with topic identification in the opinion analysis are illustrated in Table 13.

The results of the experiments, as presented in Table 13, show that the implementation of topic identification increased the Precision and Recall of the opinion classification of posts in online discussions. Topic identification using LDA achieved better results than using the term frequency method. People often express negative opinions while talking about the main topic. This negative opinion is usually compensated for by more positive posts related to less important aspects of the discussed problem. In this case, topic identification can significantly increase the precision of opinion classification.

**Table 13.** Results of Precision Recall in positive and negative classes and Macro F1 without Topic Identification (TI) and with TI using Term Frequency (TF) and Latent Dirichlet Allocation (LDA) methods.

| TI      | Precision Pos. | Precision Neg. | Recall Pos. | Recall Neg. | Macro F1 |
|---------|----------------|----------------|-------------|-------------|----------|
| without | 0.600          | 0.780          | 0.870       | 0.442       | 0.637    |
| TF      | 0.605          | 0.792          | 0.878       | 0.448       | 0.644    |
| LDA     | 0.690          | 0.780          | 0.910       | 0.430       | 0.670    |

*7.2. A Hybrid Approach to Opinion Classification*

The proposed hybrid approach to opinion classification combines the advantages of two different techniques for an opinion classification model creation. The first technique is the lexicon-based approach, which is simple and intuitive; however, it can fail when the lexicon is not sufficiently expressive. The second technique—The machine learning approach—Does not depend on the quality of the lexicon, but requires a labelled training set as an input for training an opinion classification model. Therefore, we designed the hybrid approach to increase the effectiveness of the opinion analysis of posts when the lexicon approach fails (see Figure 7). The posts which were successfully classified as having positive or negative opinion using the lexicon (and, in this way, were labelled) were put into the training data set, in order to train a probability model based on the Naive Bayes machine learning method. This model was then able to classify posts that did not contain words from the lexicon and could not be classified using the lexicon approach.

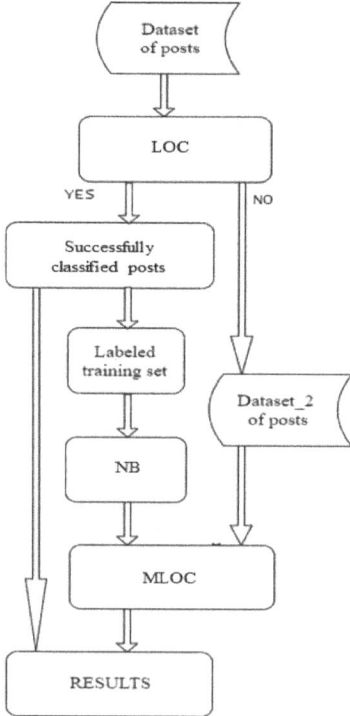

**Figure 7.** Illustration of new hybrid approach for opinion classification. In this approach, there is co-operation between the lexicon approach for opinion classification (LOC) and the machine learning approach for opinion classification (MLOC), represented by the Naïve Bayes model (NB).

At first, Lexicon-based Opinion Classification (the "LOC" block) is applied to classify all posts in the data set. Once all posts are classified either successfully (YES) or unsuccessfully (NO), the dataset is split into two groups: labelled and unlabelled posts (Dataset_2). Labelled posts represent the training set, which is used for Naïve Bayes model training (the "NB" block). The trained Naïve Bayes model is then applied to classify posts in Dataset_2 which were not classified by Lexicon-based Opinion Classification; this is the "MLOC" (Machine Learning Opinion Classification) block. All classified posts, as classified by LOC and MLOC, are then saved (the "RESULTS" block).

The hybrid approach for opinion classification was tested and compared with the original lexicon approach. The results of testing are presented in Table 14, in the form of F1 rate—particularly, F1 Positive (F1 rate on positive posts), F1 Negative (F1 rate on negative posts), and Macro F1 rates—on the General data set. The results in Table 14 show a strong increase of efficiency, as measured by F1 rate, when the hybrid approach for opinion classification was used. The reason for this increase of efficiency can be explained by decreasing of the number of unclassified posts. The unclassified posts decreased the precision of classification, as positive and negative posts were classified to neutral ones due to absence of positive or negative words in the lexicon. Using the hybrid approach, the number of unclassified posts was reduced from 18% to 0.03%. In future research, we would like to use deep learning [35] for the machine learning-based opinion analysis method in the hybrid approach.

**Table 14.** Effectivity of hybrid approach, in comparison to simple lexicon approach, for labelling by human, PSO, and BBPSO in F1 Positive, F1 Negative, and Macro F1 rates.

| Approach | Labelling | F1 Positive | F1 Negative | Macro F1 |
|---|---|---|---|---|
| LEXICON | human | 0.740 | 0.645 | 0.694 |
|  | PSO | 0.717 | 0.608 | 0.663 |
|  | BBPSO | 0.743 | 0.667 | 0.705 |
| HYBRID | human | 0.852 | 0.826 | 0.839 |
|  | PSO | 0.847 | 0.821 | 0.834 |
|  | BBPSO | 0.869 | 0.860 | 0.865 |

The complexity of the lexicon approach for opinion classification is $O(M \cdot D)$, thus being linear in the size of posts in the training set M and the size of lexicon D. The complexity of the machine learning approach for opinion classification using the Naive Bayes algorithm is $O(M \cdot N)$, thus linearly depending on the total number of posts in the training set M and the number of attributes (words) in the training set N. It follows that the complexity of the hybrid approach is $O(M \cdot N \cdot D)$.

## 8. Discussion

The main purpose of this paper is to find the best method for labelling a lexicon for a lexicon-based approach to opinion classification. Therefore, it is natural that our baseline was the lexicon-based approach, not a machine learning approach. This is the reason for comparison of the effectiveness of the hybrid approach with the lexicon approach as a baseline. This basic lexicon approach was extended by a machine learning approach, in order to achieve better results in the case when the lexicon could not overlay texts using another dictionary.

It was not our goal to test all machine learning methods but, instead, to discover whether a supplementary model trained by machine learning can decrease the number of failures in the opinion classification of problematic texts. The use of Naïve Bayes was a natural choice, as this method also gives weights to words (i.e., labels) in the form of a conditional probability of the word belonging to a given class in the data. Deep learning also trains the weights of attributes (words, in this case), but clear information about these weights is lost due to the large number of inner layers used. In the field of text processing, we also often use Random Forest or kernel SVM methods. However, these machine learning methods do not provide intuitive and explainable solutions with clear information about the measure of sensitivity of words in a model either.

The findings of the presented work are useful for our research in the field of antisocial behavior recognition in online communities and in the field of human–robot interaction. Our approach can provide the results of opinion and mood analysis of texts for use in these fields. The presented work is focused on opinion classification using a lexicon approach and, so, we needed to generate a high-quality lexicon using effective labeling.

In this paper, an automated method for lexicon labelling was proposed. It used nature-inspired optimization algorithms—Particle Swarm Optimization (PSO) and Bare-bones Particle Swarm Optimization (BBPSO)—to find optimal polarity values for words in the lexicon. The results of numerous tests on two data sets (Movie and General) were provided and presented in the paper. These tests showed that BBPSO labelling is better than PSO labelling, and that both are better than human labelling. Two lexicons (Big and Small) were created, in order to achieve good performance, which were labelled by both PSO and BBPSO. The experiments showed another finding: the human annotator avoided labelling words with a number close to zero, whereas PSO or BBPSO assigned zero values to some words.

We tested the labelling of lexicons using our new lexicon approach. The novelty of this approach comprised a new approach for intensifier processing and an interactive approach for negation processing. This new approach also involved topic identification and a hybrid approach for opinion classification, using not only lexicon-based, but also machine learning-based opinion classification methods. The hybrid approach was applied to classify the posts which were not classified by the lexicon approach.

For the future, we would like to extend our automatic lexicon labelling to learn polarity values representing the concept-domain pair. In some cases, the polarity of the word can be different in different domains. In that case, the polarity value represents the polarity of the word in the given domain. Furthermore, we would like to focus on the statistical analysis of words labelled by PSO and BBPSO, respectively. On one hand, the optimized labels will be compared with human labelling. On the other hand, removed words (i.e., the words labelled with zero) will be analyzed deeper, in order to answer the following questions: Which words were removed from the lexicons? How often are they removed?

The final hybrid model for sentiment analysis can be used in our research in the field of emotion analysis in human–robot interactions, where understanding of human mood by a robot can increase the acceptance of a robot as an assistant.

We are also using our work in sentiment analysis in the field of recognition of antisocial behavior in online communities. We would like to model the sentiment and mood of society in connection with the phenomenon of CoViD-19 [36].

**Author Contributions:** Conceptualization, K.M. and M.M. (Martin Mikula); methodology, K.M.; software, M.M. (Martin Mikula); validation, M.M. (Martin Mikula); formal analysis, X.G.; investigation, X.G.; resources, M.M. (Martin Mikula); data curation, M.M. (Martin Mikula); writing—original draft preparation, K.M.; writing—review and editing, K.M., M.M. (Marian Mach) and X.G.; visualization, M.M. (Marian Mach); supervision, K.M.; project administration, K.M.; funding acquisition, K.M. All authors have read and agreed to the published version of the manuscript.

**Funding:** This work was supported by the Slovak Research and Development Agency under the contract No. APVV-17-0267 "Automated Recognition of Antisocial Behavior in Online Communities" and the contract No. APVV-16-0213 "Knowledge-based Approaches for Intelligent Analysis of Big Data".

**Conflicts of Interest:** The authors declare no conflict of interest. The funders had no role in the design of the study; in the collection, analyses, or interpretation of data; in the writing of the manuscript, or in the decision to publish the results.

## References

1. Chaturvedi, I.; Ragusa, E.; Gastaldo, P.; Zunino, R.; Cambria, E. Bayesian network based extreme learning machine for subjectivity detection. *J. Frankl. Inst.* **2018**, *355*, 1780–1797. [CrossRef]
2. Pang, B.; Lee, L.; Vaithyanathan, S. Thumbs up? Sentiment classification using machine learning technique. In Proceedings of the EMNLP, Philadelphia, PA, USA, 6–7 July 2002; pp. 79–86.
3. Ahmad, M.; Aftab, S.; Muhamad, S.S.; Ahmad, S. Machine learning methods for sentiment analysis: A Review. *Int. J. Multidiscip. Sci. Eng.* **2013**, *8*, 27–32.
4. Tan, S.; Zhang, J. An empirical study of sentiment analysis for Chinese documents. *Expert Syst. Appl.* **2008**, *34*, 2622–2629. [CrossRef]
5. Dos Santos, C.N.; Gatti, M. Deep Convolutional Neural Networks for Sentiment Analysis of Short Texts. In Proceedings of the COLING 2014—25th International Conference on Computational Linguistics, Dublin, Ireland, 23–29 August 2014; pp. 69–78.
6. Tang, D.; Wei, F.; Qin, B.; Liu, T.; Zhou, M. Coooolll: A Deep Learning System for Twitter Sentiment Classification. In Proceedings of the SemEval 2014—8th International Workshop on Semantic Evaluation, Dublin, Ireland, 23–24 August 2014; pp. 208–212.
7. Rebiai, Z.; Andersen, S.; Debrenne, A.; Lafargue, V. SCIA at SemEval-2019 Task 3: Sentiment analysis in textualconversations using deep learning. In Proceedings of the SemEval-2019—13th International Workshop on SemanticEvaluation, Minneapolis, MN, USA, 6–7 June 2019; pp. 297–301.
8. Mikula, M.; Gao, X.; Machová, K. Adapting sentiment analysis system from English to Slovak. In Proceedings of the 2017 IEEE Symposium Series on Computational Intelligence (SSCI), Honolulu, HI, USA, 27 November–1 December 2017.
9. Stone, P.J.; Dunphy, D.C.; Smith, M.S.; Ogilvie, D.M. *The General Inquirer: A Computer Approach to Content Analysis*; The MIT Press: Cambridge, MA, USA, 1966; 704p.
10. Hu, M.; Liu, B. Mining and Summarizing Customer Reviews. In Proceedings of the KDD 04—10th International Conference on Knowledge Discovery and Data Mining, Seattle, WA, USA, 22–25 August 2004; pp. 168–177.
11. Warriner, A.B.; Kuperman, V.; Brysbaert, M. Norms of valence, arousal, and dominance for 13,915 English lemmas. *Behav. Res. Methods* **2013**, *45*, 1191–1207. [CrossRef] [PubMed]
12. Mohammad, S.M.; Turney, P.D. Crowdsourcing a word-emotion association Lexicon. *Comput. Intell.* **2012**, *29*, 436–465. [CrossRef]
13. Baccianella, S.; Esuli, A.; Sebastiani, F. SentiWordNet 3.0: An Enhanced Lexical Resource for Sentiment Analysis and Opinion Mining. In Proceedings of the LREC, Valletta, Malta, 17–18 May 2010; pp. 2200–2204.
14. Strapparava, C.; Valittutii, A. WordNetAffect: An Affective Extension of WordNet. In Proceedings of the LREC 2004—4th International Conference on Language Resources and Evaluation, Lisbon, Portugal, 26–28 May 2004; pp. 39–46.
15. Bajpai, R.; Cambria, E.; Poria, S.; Schuller, B.W. SenticNet 4: A semantic resource for sentiment analysis based on conceptual primitives. In Proceedings of the COLING, Osaka, Japan, 11–16 December 2016; pp. 2666–2677.
16. Yang, X.; Zhang, Z.; Zhang, Z.; Mo, Y.; Li, L.; Yu, L.; Zhu, P. Automatic construction and global optimization of a multi-sentiment lexicon. *Comput. Intell. Neurosci.* **2016**, *2016*, 2093406. [CrossRef] [PubMed]
17. Gupta, D.K.; Reddy, K.S.; Sôhweta, A.; Ekbal, A. PSO-ASent: Feature Selection Using Particle Swarm Optimization for Aspect Based Sentiment Analysis. In Proceedings of the NLDB, Passau, Germany, 13–15 June 2002; Volume 9103, pp. 79–86.
18. Basari, S.; Hussin, B.; Anantaa, L.G.P.; Zeniarja, J. Opinion mining of movie review using hybrid method of support vector machine and particle swarm optimization. *Procedia Eng.* **2013**, *53*, 453–462. [CrossRef]
19. Escalante, H.J.; Garcia-Limon, M.A.; Morales-Reyes, A.; Graff, M.; Montes-y-Gomez, M.; Morales, E.F.; Martinez-Carranza, J. Term-weighting learning via genetic programming for text classification. *Knowl.-Based Syst.* **2015**, *83*, 176–189.
20. Xing, F.Z.; Pallucchini, F.; Cambria, E. Cognitive-inspired domain adaptation of sentiment lexicons. *Inf. Process. Manag.* **2019**, *56*, 554–564. [CrossRef]
21. Kacprzyk, J.; Pedrycz, J. *Handbook of Computational Intelligence*; Springer: Berlin/Heidelberg, Germany, 2015; 1663p, ISBN 978-3-662-43504-5.

22. Van den Bergh, F.; Engelbrecht, A.P. A study of particle swarm optimization particle trajectories. *Inf. Sci. Inform. Comput. Sci. Intell. Syst. Appl. Int. J.* **2006**, *176*, 937–971.
23. Kennedy, K. Bare bones particle swarms. In Proceedings of the SIS 03—IEEE Swarm Intelligence Symposium, Indianapolis, IN, USA, 8–10 June 2003; pp. 80–87.
24. Mohammad, S.M.; Kiritchenko, S.; Zhu, X. NRC-Canada: Building the State-of-the-Art in Sentiment Analysis of Tweets. In Proceedings of the SemEval 13—7th International Workshop on Semantic Evaluation Exercises, Atlanta, GA, USA, 14–15 June 2013; pp. 321–327.
25. Nielsen, F.A. A new ANEW: Evaluation of a word list for sentiment analysis in microblogs. In Proceedings of the ESWC2011 Workshop on 'Making Sense of Microposts': Big Things Come in Small Packages, Heraklion, Crete, Greece, 30 May 2011; pp. 93–98.
26. Taboada, M.; Brooke, J.; Tofiloski, M.; Voli, K.; Stede, M. Lexicon-based Methods for Sentiment Analysis. *Comput. Linguist.* **2011**, *38*, 267–307. [CrossRef]
27. Thelwall, M.; Buckley, K.; Paltoglou, G.; Cai, D. Sentiment strength detection in short informal text. *J. Am. Soc. Inf. Sci. Technol.* **2010**, *61*, 2544–2558. [CrossRef]
28. Pang, B.; Lee, L. A sentimental education: Sentiment analysis using subjectivity summarization based on minimum cuts. In Proceedings of the 42nd Annual Meeting on Association for Computational Linguistics, Barcelona, Spain, 21–26 July 2004; pp. 271–278.
29. Kennedy, A.; Inkpen, D. Sentiment classification of movie reviewsusing contextual valence shifters. *Comput. Intell.* **2006**, *22*, 110. [CrossRef]
30. Martineau, J.; Finin, T.; Joshi, A.; Patel, S. Improving binary classificationon text problems using differential word features. In Proceedings of the 18th ACM Conference on Information and Knowledge Management, Hong Kong, China, 2–6 November 2009; pp. 2019–2024.
31. Maas, A.L.; Daly, R.E.; Pham, P.T.; Huang, D.; Ng, A.Y.; Potts, C. Learning wordvectors for sentiment analysis. In Proceedings of the 49th Annual Meetingof the Association for Computational Linguistics: Human Language Technologies, Portland, OR, USA, 19–24 June 2011; Volume 1, pp. 142–150.
32. Tu, Z.; He, Y.; Foster, J.; Van Genabith, J.; Liu, Q.; Lin, S. Identifyinghigh-impact sub-structures for convolution kernels in document-levelsentiment classification. In Proceedings of the 50th Annual Meeting of the Association for Computational Linguistics, Jeju Island, Korea, 8–14 July 2012; Volume 2, pp. 338–343.
33. Nguyen, D.Q.; Nguyen, D.Q.; Pham, S.B. A two-stage classifier forsentiment analysis. In Proceedings of the Sixth International Joint Conference on Natural Language Processing, Asian Federation of Natural Language Processing, Nagoya, Japan, 14–18 October 2013; pp. 897–901.
34. Ghorbani, M.; Bahaghighad, M.; Xin, Q.; Ozen, F. ConvLSTMConv network: A deep learning approach for sentiment analysis in cloud computing. *J. Cloud Comput. Adv. Syst. Appl.* **2020**, *9*, 16. [CrossRef]
35. Dang, N.C.; Moreno-Garcia, M.N.; De la Prieta, F. Sentiment Analysis Based on Deep Learning: A Comparative Study. *Electronics* **2020**, *9*, 483. [CrossRef]
36. Alamo, T.; Reina, D.G.; Mammarella, M.; Abella, A. Covid-19: Open-data Resources for Monitoring, Modeling, and Forecasting the Epidemic. *Electronics* **2020**, *9*, 827. [CrossRef]

© 2020 by the authors. Licensee MDPI, Basel, Switzerland. This article is an open access article distributed under the terms and conditions of the Creative Commons Attribution (CC BY) license (http://creativecommons.org/licenses/by/4.0/).

*Article*

# Emotion Analysis in Human–Robot Interaction

Martina Szabóová, Martin Sarnovský, Viera Maslej Krešňáková and Kristína Machová *

Department of Cybernetics and Artificial Intelligence, Technical University of Košice,
Letná 9, 040 01 Košice, Slovakia; martina.szaboova@tuke.sk (M.S.); martin.sarnovsky@tuke.sk (M.S.); viera.maslej.kresnakova@tuke.sk (V.M.K.)
* Correspondence: kristina.machova@tuke.sk

Received: 25 September 2020; Accepted: 20 October 2020; Published: 23 October 2020

**Abstract:** This paper connects two large research areas, namely sentiment analysis and human–robot interaction. Emotion analysis, as a subfield of sentiment analysis, explores text data and, based on the characteristics of the text and generally known emotional models, evaluates what emotion is presented in it. The analysis of emotions in the human–robot interaction aims to evaluate the emotional state of the human being and on this basis to decide how the robot should adapt its behavior to the human being. There are several approaches and algorithms to detect emotions in the text data. We decided to apply a combined method of dictionary approach with machine learning algorithms. As a result of the ambiguity and subjectivity of labeling emotions, it was possible to assign more than one emotion to a sentence; thus, we were dealing with a multi-label problem. Based on the overview of the problem, we performed experiments with the Naive Bayes, Support Vector Machine and Neural Network classifiers. Results obtained from classification were subsequently used in human–robot experiments. Despise the lower accuracy of emotion classification, we proved the importance of expressing emotion gestures based on the words we speak.

**Keywords:** sentiment analysis; human–robot interaction; dictionary approach; machine learning approach; social robotics

## 1. Introduction

The population is getting older. According to the World Health Organization (WHO), it is estimated that by the year 2050, the elderly will account for 25% of the world population (35% of the population in Europe) (https://www.un.org/en/development/desa/population/publications/pdf/ageing/WPA2017_Highlights.pdf). Caring for these seniors—physically, emotionally and mentally—will be an enormous undertaking, and experts say there will be a shortage of trained professionals and those willing to take on the job. Robots may fill the gap, taking care of older people. The shortage of trained professionals and desire to age-in-place can be solved by social assistive robotics. While there exist assistive robotics [1] (e.g., intelligent walkers, wheelchair robots, manipulator arms and exoskeletons), they lack the social aspect as well as the affective component.

In this situation, it is essential to devote research that goes beyond the concept of assistive robotics, and which will focus on the development of a robot that would also be a companion of an elderly. In this type of robot, the key factor is its acceptance by humans. We need to equip the robot with abilities that would make it a pleasant companion and thus a companion who can at least partially understand the emotional mood of the elderly. This means that based on what the person says, looks like and how the person behaves, the robot will be able to choose the right answers and movements or gestures. We focused on estimating the emotional state of the elderly, mainly from what the person says. We also focused on the analysis of speech, specifically in its written form, as today numerous the speech to text systems able to reliably transform speech into text. We used the text as the input and analyzed it in terms of emotions, which falls into a very current area of research—analysis of sentiment.

Wada et al. [2] studied the psychological effects of a seal robot, PARO, used to engage seniors at a day service center. Results show moods of elderly people were improved by interaction with the robots over the course of a 6-week period. Šabanovic et al. [3] used PARO in a study with older adults with dementia. They showed that PARO provides indirect benefits for users by increasing their activity in particular modalities of social interaction, including visual, verbal and physical interaction. PARO also has positive effects on older adults' activity levels over the duration of study, suggesting they are not due to short-term 'novelty effects'. Huang and Huang [4] conveyed a study to explore the elderly's acceptance of companion robots from the perspective of user factors. They found that the elderly living with parents, with master's (or doctor's) education, medical professional background and experience in the use of scientific and technological products expressed more positive attitudes in the responses to the items on the constructs of attitude and perceived usefulness, while the attitude of those with primary school education and humanities professional background, with no experience in scientific and technological products, was relatively negative.

The presented studies indicate that the communication of older adults with a robot can be beneficial, it can improve their emotional mood, increase their activity in particular modalities of various kinds of interactions. On the other hand, there is a big obstacle in their negative approach to communication with the robot, especially in the group of people with only primary education and with no experience with scientific and technological products. We focused on this problem and tried to help break down these people's prejudices about robots, for example, by equipping the robot with the ability to be sensitive to the emotions that an older adult expresses in some way. The scenario in which we wanted to verify the achieved results was as follows. A robot can use information about the polarity of a mood of the elderly to communicate with him/her friendly, sensitive and appropriately. When a robot communicates with a human (e.g., an elder), it must choose one from many answers which are suitable for the situation. For example, it can choose an answer which can cheer up the person, if it has information that the current emotional mood of the person is sad. It can also adapt its movements and choose a movement from all possible ones to cheer up this elderly. The robot should have prepared answers and movements for all possible basic emotions of an elderly. Finally, the understanding of the emotional moods of humans can lead to better acceptance of a communication with robots.

The main contributions of the paper can be summarized as follows:

- The development of the new approach to emotions analysis from texts. Whereas the field of sentiment analysis is quite well-researched, emotions analysis faces a problem of insufficient accuracy because it represents the multi-class classification problem, where the classes correspond to the emotions. We trained machine learning methods, particularly for each emotion and then the ensemble of binary classifiers was used for emotions classification in a human–robot interaction scenario.
- We used lexicon-based and machine learning approaches to the emotion analysis. Models for emotion classification were trained using various machine learning methods, e.g., Naive Bayes (Multi-nomial, Bernoulli and Gaussian), Support Vector Machine and feed-forward neural network using various data representations such as Bag-of-Words, TF-IDF and sentence embeddings (ConceptNet Numberbatch).
- The ensemble classifier consisted of nine best models for each emotion. The model was demonstrated in four different scenarios with the humanoid robot NAO.
- Results of the experiments, which conclude that the best scenario for human acceptance is the one with emotions classification accompanied by emotional movements of the robot. Experiments with communication between human and robot NAO showed that human acceptance of a robot could be increased using an analysis of the emotional mood of the human.

## 2. Background

*2.1. Sentiment Analysis*

Sentiment analysis is an interdisciplinary field connecting natural language processing (NLP), computational linguistic and text mining. As we can see from the number of papers published by reputable conferences and journal papers in NLP and computational linguistics, it is an admittedly hot topic. The vital role is to deal with opinion, sentiment and subjectivity in text. It attempts to analyze and take advantage of extensive quantities of user-generated content and enables the computer to 'understand' text.

2.1.1. Research Tasks in Sentiment Analysis

Sentiment analysis involves various research tasks [5], such as:

- **subjectivity detection** aiming to discover subjective or neutral terms, phrases or sentences and is frequently used as an initial step in polarity and intensity classifications, to separate subjective information from the objective. Adjectives (beautiful) and adverbs (perfectly) are remarkably capable of expressing subjectivity. On the other hand, also to achieve a high degree of accuracy, we must include the verb (destroy). These subjective words are embedded into dictionaries along with their polarity;
- **polarity classification** attempts to classify texts into positive, negative or neutral terms. It forms the basis for determining the polarity of the text as a whole. There are three degrees of polarity: positive (excellent), neutral (average) and negative (poor). Determining the polarity of words is closely connected with switching polarity problems. Switching polarity [6] can be done by negation, which is the reason for extending the polarity of words to determine the polarity of combinations of words (taking into account entire sentences or parts of the sentence);
- **intensity classification** goes a step further and attempts to identify the different degrees of positivity and negativity; e.g., strongly-negative, negative, fair, positive and strongly positive. It can be best described by numbers or words. A numerical description is helpful when processing on computers. The intensity of polarity significantly changes the polarity of collocation; e.g., surprisingly good, highly qualitative;
- **opinion spam** is another problem inhibiting accurate sentiment analysis. In recent years we noticed an increased demand for opinion classification, but almost no attention has been paid to examining the credibility of opinions in reviews. Since there is no such quality control, anybody has an opportunity to write whatever they like on the web, lowering the quality of reviews. The largest problem is the chaos of deceptive public opinion. These days, users usually come to the web to check products they have an intention to buy. Spam distorts product quality evaluation. We distinguish three types of opinion spam: the first is a misguided opinion, the second an opinion that does not relate directly to the subject and the last is distortion, as in text not relevant to opinion analysis [7];
- **emotion detection** seeks to identify if a text conveys any type of emotion or not. It is similar to subjectivity detection. Within the scope of emotion detection we discriminate *emotion classification*—fine-grained classification of existing emotion in a text into one (or more) of a set of specific emotions (e.g., anger, fear, etc.), *emotion intensity*—degree or amount of an emotion (such as anger—very angry or sadness—slightly sad, etc.) [8] and finally *emotion cause detection*—extracting potential causes that lead to emotion expressions in text [9].

*2.2. Emotion Analysis*

Emotion analysis can be viewed as a natural evolution of sentiment analysis and its more fine-grained model. Digging deeper into psychology, we have to differentiate between terms *emotion, mood, feeling*. *Emotion* is an instantaneous perception of a feeling. They can be over in a matter of seconds to minutes, at most [10]. *Mood* is considered as a group of persisting feelings associated with evaluative and cognitive states which influence all the future evaluations, feelings and actions [11]. Unlike emotions, moods are non-intentional, though they may be elicited by a particular event or things. It is challenging to identify triggers causing mood; however, while in the state of a certain mood, the threshold is lowered for arousing related emotion. *Feeling* is mental associations and reactions to an emotion that are personal and acquired through experience.

How can we determine emotions? To be able to identify emotions in text, firstly, we need emotion models to estimate them.

2.2.1. Emotion's Models

According to Grandjean et al. [12], three major directions in affect computing are recognized: categorical/discrete, dimensional and appraisals-based approaches.

- **Basic emotion model**—The categorical approach claims there are a small number of basic emotions that are hard-wired in our brain, and recognized across the world. Each affective state is classified into a single category, Table 1. However, a couple of researchers proved that people show non-basic, subtle and rather complex affective states that could be impossible to handle, such as thinking, embarrassment or depression. Assigning text to a specific category can be done either manually or using learning-based techniques.
- **Dimensional feeling model**—The dimensional approach is based on Wundt's proposal that feelings (which he distinguishes from emotions) can be described as pleasantness–unpleasantness, excitement–inhibition and tension–relaxation, as well as Osgood's work on the dimensions of affective meaning (arousal, valence and potency). Most recent models concentrate on only two dimensions, valence and arousal. Valence (pleasure/displeasure) depicts how positive or negative an emotion may be. Arousal (activation/deactivation) depicts how excited or apathetic an emotion is.
- **Componential appraisal models**—This proposes that emotions are extracted from our "appraisals" (i.e., our evaluations, interpretations and explanations) of events. These appraisals lead to different specific reactions in different people. OCC model is presumably the most widely accepted cognitive appraisal model for emotions [13] and it proposes three aspects of the environment to which humans react emotionally: events of concern to oneself, agents that one considers responsible for such events and objects of concern. It defines emotions as a valenced reaction to events, agents and objects, and considers valenced reactions as a means to differentiate between emotions and non-emotions. This approach is very suitable for affect sensing from the text.

**Table 1.** Listing emotion models and their appertaining emotions.

| Authors | Emotions | Approach |
| --- | --- | --- |
| Ekman [10] | Anger, disgust, fear, joy, sadness, surprise | Categorical |
| Izard (1977) | fear, anger, distress, disgust, contempt, shame, guilt, surprise, joy, interest | Categorical |
| Plutchik (1980) | fear, anger, sadness, disgust, surprise, joy, acceptance, anticipation | Dimensional Wheel (Figure 1) |
| Russell [14] | frustrated, distressed, annoyed, afraid, angry, tense, alarmed, aroused, astonished, excited, delighted, happy pleased, glad, serene, content, at ease, satisfied, relaxed, calm, sleepy, tired, droopy, bored, depressed, gloomy, sad, miserable | Dimensional Circumplex (valence, arousal) |
| Tomkins (1984) | fear/terror, anger/rage, distress/anguish, disgust, contempt/disgust, shame/humiliation, surprise, enjoyment/joy, Interest/excitement | Categorical |
| Shaver et al. (1987) | fear, anger, sadness, surprise, joy, love | Categorical |
| Oatley and Johnson-Laird (1987) | fear, anger, sadness, disgust, joy/happiness | Categorical |
| Ortony et al. [13] | joy, distress, happy-for, sorry-for, resentment, gloating, hope, fear, satisfaction, fears-confirmed, relief, disappointment, shock, surprise, pride, shame, admiration, reproach, gratification, remorse, gratitude, anger, love, hate | Appraisal Tree |
| Lövheim [15] | fear/terror, anger/rage, distress/anguish, disgust, contempt/disgust, shame/humiliation, surprise, enjoyment/joy, Interest/excitement | Dimensional Cube |
| Shuman et al. [16] | disappointment, regret, envy, jealousy, disgust, repulsion, contempt, scorn, irritation, anger, involvement, interest, amusement laughter, pride, elation, happiness, joy, enjoyment, pleasure, tenderness, love, wonderment, feeling awe, feeling disburdened, astonishment, surprise, longing, nostalgia, pity, compassion, sadness, despair, worry, fear, embarrassment, shame, no emotion left, other emotion felt | Dimensional Wheel (valence, control) |

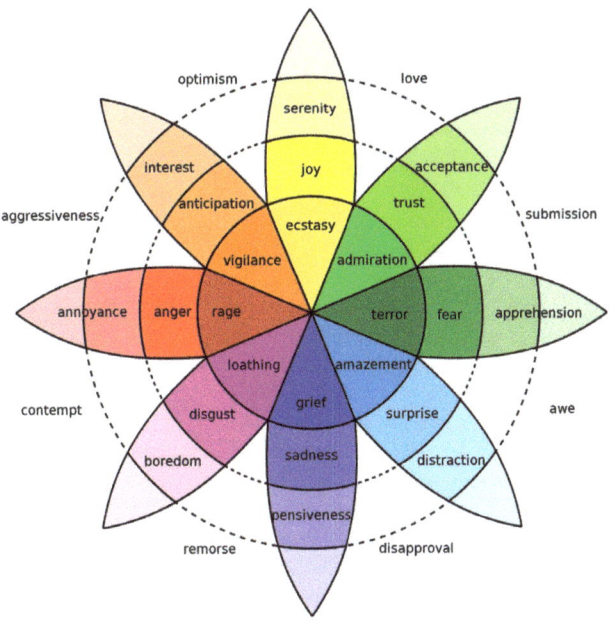

**Figure 1.** Plutchik's wheel of emotion.

Despite the existence of various other models, the categorical and dimensional approaches are the most commonly used models for automatic analysis and prediction of affect in continuous input.

It is worth mentioning the survey made by Ekman [17]. The authors surveyed 248 scientists working in the field of emotion. Authors looked for the answer if/how the nature of emotion has changed over time. Which proposal—either Darwin's Darwin [18] (emotions are discrete) or Wundt's Wundt [19] (emotions differentiate into dimensions of pleasant–unpleasant and low–high intensity)—is most used nowadays? Findings from this survey indicate that scientists agreed upon five emotions (all of which were described by both Darwin and Wundt): anger (91%), fear (90%), disgust (86%), sadness (80%) and happiness (76%). Shame, surprise and embarrassment were endorsed by 40–50%. Least agreed basic emotions are guilt (37%), contempt (34%), love (32%), awe (31%), pain (28%), envy (28%), compassion (20%), pride (9%) and gratitude (6%).

Recent advances in the field of sentiment analysis and computational linguistics in general, allow us to accomplish more advanced tasks such as emotion detection in documents. To detect emotion, researchers use generally known algorithms created for sentiment analysis. There are three major approaches to detecting emotions in text:

- **Keyword-based methods**—the most intuitive approach. The main goal was to find out patterns similar to emotion keywords and match them. The first task is to find out the word which expresses the emotion in a sentence. This is usually done by tagging the words of a sentence with Parts-Of-Speech tagger and then extracting the Noun, Verb, Adjective and Adverb (NAVA) words—the most probable emotion carrying words. Then these words are matched against a list of words representing emotions according to a specific emotion model. Whichever emotion matches with the keyword is considered as the emotion of the specific sentence. Different approaches can be applied when the word matches with multiple emotions from the list. In some keyword-dictionaries, each word has a probability score for each emotion, and the emotion with the highest score is picked as the emotion of the word. In some other works, the first emotion

matched with the word is picked as the primary emotion of the word. The reference list of keywords or the keyword dictionary differs depending on the researcher.
- **Machine Learning methods**—both supervised and unsupervised methods are used for emotion classification. For supervised methods, an annotated emotions dataset is used from which one learns which features are most salient to distinguish between classes. The dataset is divided into training and testing sets. Naive Bayes classifier, Support Vector Machine, MaxEntropy and Decision Tree are the most used algorithms.
- **Hybrid methods**—combined methods defined to achieve the benefit of multiple methods and reach the maximum level of accuracy.

*2.3. Human–Robot Interaction*

Human–robot interaction (HRI) is a study of interaction dynamics between humans and robots, a multidisciplinary field that includes engineering (electrical, mechanical, industrial and design), computer science (human–computer interaction, artificial intelligence, robotics, natural language understanding, computer vision and speech recognition), social sciences (psychology, cognitive science, communications, anthropology and human factors) and humanities (ethics and philosophy) [20].

Robots are poised to fill a growing number of roles in today's society, from factory automation to service applications, medical care and entertainment. While robots were initially used for repetitive tasks where all human direction is given a priori, they are becoming involved in increasingly more complex and less structured tasks and activities, including interaction with the humans required to complete those tasks. The fundamental goal of HRI is to develop the principles and algorithms for robot systems that enable safe and effective interaction with humans [20].

The appearance and function of a robot affect the way that people perceive it, interact with it and build long-term relationships with it [21]. As every person is different, the success of robot acceptance lies in its capability to act as a social entity and its adaptability to differentiate behavior within appropriate response times and tasks.

Interaction, by definition, means "communication with each other or reacting to each other" (https://dictionary.cambridge.org/dictionary/english/interaction). There are several possibilities for robots to communicate with humans. The way of communication is largely influenced by whether the human and robot are in close proximity to each other or not. Therefore, the interaction can be categorized into remote and proximate interaction. Within these two general categories, we can differentiate applications that require mobility, physical manipulation and social interaction [22].

2.3.1. Socially Assistive Robotics

Social interaction includes social, emotive and cognitive aspects of interaction. It involves research areas of assistive robotics, social robotics and socially assistive robotics. Social Assistive Robotics (SAR) is defined as the intersection of assistive robotics and socially interactive robotics. It is a comparatively new field of robotics that focuses on developing robots capable of assisting users through social rather than physical interaction. Social robots have to be able to perceive, interpret and respond appropriately to verbal and nonverbal cues from the human. SAR compared with social robots, focuses on the challenges of providing motivation, education, therapy, coaching, training and rehabilitation through nonphysical interaction. An effective socially assistive robot must understand and interact with its environment, exhibit social behavior, focus its attention and communication on the user, sustain engagement with the user and achieve specific assistive goals. The robot must do all of this in a way that is safe, ethical and effective for the potentially vulnerable user. SAR has been shown to have promise as a therapeutic tool for children, the elderly, stroke patients and other special-needs populations requiring personalized care.

### 2.3.2. Long-Term Interaction

Many applications with social robots involve only short-term interactions. However, short-term interaction is not enough. Many real-world applications (e.g., education, therapy, companionship and elderly care) call for keeping people interested for longer. We have to maintain human engagement and build relationship and trust between human and robot through adaptation and personalization. An important aspect of long-term interaction is *memory*. As the robot memorizes information, he can better execute personalized behavior. Zheng [23] proposed four types of memory information (factual information: personal facts like names; an intention: knowledge of user's plans and future actions; interaction history: representation of past events; and meta-behavior: metadata of user's behaviors during interactions). Their preliminary results show that meta behavior elicits stronger positive feelings in comparison to the other three memory information. Richards and Bransky [24] performed an experiment about forgetting and recalling information (4 levels: complete recall; total loss of recall; partial recall; and incorrect recall). By exhibit forgetting, either explicitly stating forgetfulness or not mentioning it at all, the believability of the character was raised. The study also suggests that forgetting affects the level of trust the user feels.

Talking about long-term interaction, we have to take into account *novelty effect*. Novelty effect, in the context of HRI, can be explained in such a way that interaction with the robot can be initially highly triggering and engaging but after a couple of interactions, the newness wears off, and people can lose interest in interaction with the robot. To avoid such behavior, the challenge is to keep people engaged in the interaction and motivate them to interact longer (weeks, months or even years). This is not as simple as it may sound.

### 2.3.3. Personalization

Personalization is closely associated with long-term interaction mentioned above. It is another important research area in SAR. Personalization is an ability of the robot to adapt its behavior to a specific human, context, environment and task. There are numerous studies researching impact of personalization to HRI [25–29].

However, there are studies that contraindicate this claim. Kennedy et al. [30] implemented robot tutoring system. Their idea was to determine how social and adaptive behavior of the robot is desirable to support children in their learning. Task objective was to determine the prime numbers. Participants consisted of 45 children aged 7–8. Four scenarios were introduced—without a robot with a screen only, asocial robot and social personalized robot. Results show that learning with the robot in comparison to without robot (only screen) boosts learning gain, however, learning with the social personalized robot in comparison with a screen only robot does not improve further learning. Gao et al. [31] built a reinforcement learning framework for personalization that allows a robot to select supportive verbal behavior to maximize the user's task progress and positive reactions. Their conclusion was that people preferred robots that exhibited more varied behaviors in comparison to the robot whose behavior converged to the specific (personalized) one over time.

Nevertheless, we implemented personalized robot behavior in our user-case scenario described in Section 6.

### 2.3.4. Artificial Companionship

So far, robot companions lack many important social and emotional abilities (e.g., recognizing social, affective expressions and states, understanding intentions and accounting for the context of the situation, expressing appropriate social, affective behavior) to engage with humans in natural interaction.

An artificial companion should be capable of evaluating how humans feel about the interaction and how they interpret the agent's actions and use this information to adapt its behavior accordingly [32]. For instance, a robotic companion (Figure 2) should act empathically towards a user if it detects that she is sad or not willing to engage in an interaction, e.g., it would not disturb them trying to engage them in some activity if they do not approach it.

**Figure 2.** Robot companions. Humanoids in top row—from left to right (1) Zeno (Hanson Robotics), (2) NAO (Aldebaran Robotics), (3) Pepper (Aldebaran Robotics), (4) iCub (Italian Institute of Technology); Middle row—from left to right (1) Leonardo (MIT), (2) Kismet (MIT), (3) iCat (Philips), (4) Buddy (Blue Frog Robotics); Bottom row—from left to right (1) Paro (AIST), (2) TEGA (MIT), (3) New AIBO (Sony).

2.3.5. Affective Loop

Another challenging research task in SAR is endowing the robot with emotional intelligence. It is important that the interaction between human and robot would be affective; thus, it must have the ability to perceive, interpret, express and regulate emotions.

Understanding human emotions by robot and at the same time having the option to express emotion back to human was defined by Höök [33] as affective loop (AL). AL (see Figure 3) is the interactive process in which "the user [of the system] first expresses her emotions through some physical interaction involving her body, for example, through gestures or manipulations; and the system then responds by generating affective expression, using, for example, colours, animations, and haptics" which "in turn affects the user (mind and body) making the user response and step-by-step feel more and more involved with the system" [34].

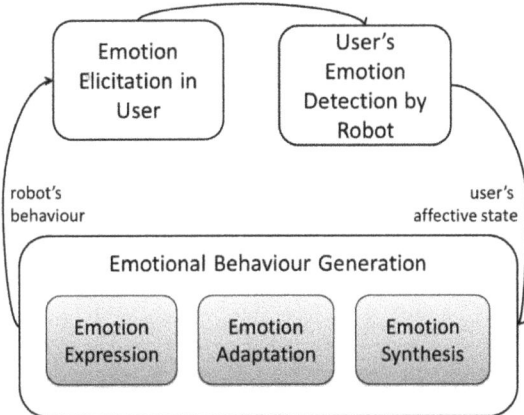

**Figure 3.** Affective loop adopted from Paiva et al. [34].

Emotion detection is part of the broader area of affective computing (AC) with aims to enable computers to recognize and express emotions [35]. AC defines emotion as playing an essential role in decision making and learning. Emotions influence the mechanisms of rational thinking. Picard [35] highlighted several results from neurological literature that indicate emotions play a necessary role in human creativity and intelligence, as well as rational human thinking and decision-making.

Computers that interact naturally and intelligently with humans need at least the ability to recognize and express affection. Affect plays a crucial role in understanding such phenomena as attention, memory and aesthetics. Emotion is necessary for creative behavior in humans. Neurological studies indicate that decision-making without emotion can be as impaired as that made with too much emotion. Picard [35] argues affective computers should not only provide better performance in assisting humans but also might enhance computers' abilities to make decisions.

Therefore, one of the main goals of AC is enabling computers to understand human emotional state and adjust its response accordingly. Human emotional state can be expressed either non-verbally, verbally or both. Pioneer researcher in body language [36] found that within the realm of interpreting the affect or emotional state of others, we perceive 55% non-verbally (facial expression), 45% verbally out of which 38% by speech (tone of voice, inflection and other sounds) and 7% by words.

Automatic affect recognition is a challenging task due to the various modalities emotions can be expressed with.

- **Facial expression**—the face is the most important component of human communication [37–40].
- **Body language**—bodily expressions (whole body static postures and whole body movement) and gestures provide strong and reliable cues to the emotional state of an observed individuals [41–44].
- **Speech**—pitch (level, range and variability), timing and loudness are considered the most influential parameters for expressing emotions through speech [45,46].

On the other hand, how and when, machines should exhibit emotions is also an important research question. Herewith with this is closely linked synthetic emotion. Synthetic emotion is an emotion produced by a robot. Integration of different modalities, when they are congruent and synchronous, leads to a significant increase in human emotion recognition accuracy [47]. However, when information is incongruent across different sensory modalities, integration may lead to a biased percept, and emotion recognition accuracy is impaired [47].

## 3. Related Work

There are numerous studies focusing on detecting emotion from text. Desmet and Hoste [48] used Support Vector Machines to differentiate between the 15 different emotions (abuse, anger, blame, fear, forgiveness, guilt, happiness, hopefulness, hopelessness, information, instructions, love, pride, sorrow, thankfulness), using lexical and semantic features (viz. Bags-of-Words of lemmas, Part-of-Speech tags and trigrams) and information from external resources that encode semantic relatedness and subjectivity. In Wicentowski and Sydes [49], they detected the same 15 emotions using maximum entropy classification. In Luyckx et al. [50], the authors presented experiments in fine-grained emotion detection using Support Vector Machine (SVM) into 15 categories. In Pak et al. [51], authors combined machine learning algorithm (SVM with features: n-grams, POS-tags, General Inquirer dictionary, Affective Norms of English Words lexicon, dependency graphs and lastly, heuristic features) with hand-written rules. Bandhakavi et al. [52] proposed a generative Unigram Mixture Model (UMM) to learn a word-emotion association lexicon from an input document. Alm et al. [53] uses Ekman's six basic emotions (fear, joy, sadness, disgust, anger, surprise +/−). Data were classified by linear classifier—a variation of the Winnow update rule—implemented in the Sparse Network of Winnows (SNoW) learning architecture [54] into two categories either emotional/non emotional or positive emotion/negative emotion.

Much attention these days centers on "reinventing" deep learning to solve varied tasks. Emotion detection is no exception, hence we see a burst of research papers in this area. Kratzwald et al. [55] authors proposed bi-directional LSTM networks (BiLSTMs). They proposed an extension of transfer learning called sent2affect—the network is first trained on the basis of sentiment analysis and, after exchanging the output layer, is then tuned to the task of emotion recognition. Khanpour and Caragea [56] detected six Ekman's emotion from Online Health Community messages. They proposed a computational model that combines the strengths of CNNs, LSTMs and lexicon-based approaches to capture the hidden semantics in messages. Kim and Klinger [57] used Plutchik's eight emotions and 'no emotion' as emotion categories. They applied several models: rule-based (as a feature dictionary), multi-layer perceptron (as a feature Bag-of-Words), conditional random fields (POS-tags, National Research Council (NRC) dictionary, English pronounce list), BiLSTM-CRF (as a feature FastText embeddings with dimension 300). Furthermore, it is worth mentioning that besides emotion, also experiences, causes and targets of the emotions were annotated. Gupta et al. [58], Chatterjee et al. [59] proposed deep learning approach called "Sentiment and Semantic LSTM (SS-LSTM)". Detection of emotions was viewed as a multi-classification problem into four classes—happy, sad, angry and others.

Table 2 shows emotion datasets widely used in the research community in emotion analysis. As our aim was to use text data in human–robot interaction (in comparison with works mentioned above), we could not use any of the presented corpuses. The text should be neither long nor very short and intriguing to keep the participants focused. Therefore, we chose fables as they are interesting short stories and compiled our own corpus which will be described in Section 4.1.

We see our problem as a multi-label classification task. Therefore, we decided to use Plutchik's eight emotions as emotional model together with 'no emotion' category. We applied lexicon-based approach (as we are using NRC emotional dictionary for features extraction) with supervised machine learning methods such as Naive Bayes and SVM. Whereas our dataset is small, we also decided to apply semi-supervised k-Means algorithm for expanding our training data.

**Table 2.** Overview of datasets used in emotion detection.

| Dataset | Content | Description |
|---|---|---|
| Fairy Tale's (Alm et al. [53]) | 185 children stories (1580 sentences) | Annotated with disgust, fear, joy, sadness, positive surprise and negative surprise |
| ISEAR [1] | 7666 sentences | Contains responses of questionnaires on seven emotions (joy, fear, anger, sadness, disgust, shame and guilt) from 37 countries from 5 continents |
| Affective set (Strapparava and Mihalcea [60]) | 1250 News Headlines | Annotated with anger, disgust, fear, joy, sadness, surprise and valence indication (positive/negative) |
| Hashtag Emotion Corpus (aka Twitter Emotion Corpus, or TEC) (Mohammad [61]) | 21,000 tweets | Annotated with anger, disgust, fear, joy, sadness, surprise |
| EmoBank (Buechel and Hahn [62], Buechel and Hahn [63]) | 10K sentences | Double annotation with valence, arousal and dominance were used from the perspectives of both writer and reader |
| Sentiment Analysis: Emotion in Text [2] | 40,000 Tweets | Annotated with anger, boredom, empty, enthusiasm, fun, happiness, hate, love, relief, sadness, surprise, worry, neutral |
| EmoInt2017 Data (Mohammad and Bravo-Marquez [64]) | 7097 tweets | Annotated with intensity of anger, fear, joy, sadness |
| REMAN (Kim and Klinger [57]) | 1720 sentence triples | Annotated with anger, fear, trust, disgust, joy, sadness, surprise, anticipation, other emotion |

[1] https://www.unige.ch/cisa/index.php/download_file/view/395/296/; [2] https://data.world/crowdflower/sentiment-analysis-in-text.

## 4. Methodology

We propose a learning algorithm based on lexicon methods and machine learning methods. The workflow of our approach is shown on Figure 4. Specifics of each box are explained in the following sections.

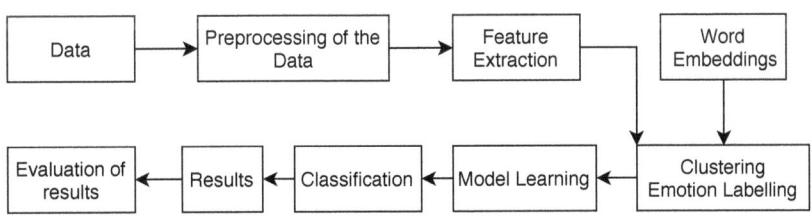

**Figure 4.** Emotion detection flow chart.

*4.1. Block: Data*

We build our own English corpus consisting of Aesop's fable. Fables were downloaded (http://www.aesopfables.com, http://read.gov/aesop/), cleaned and saved into .txt documents. Each document contained one fable. In total, we have 740 English fables.

We wanted stories to be read in the human–robot experiment scenario. To keep the audience interested and to stay focused, the text should be neither long nor very short and interesting. Therefore we chose fables as they are short stories with moral truth, using animals as the main characters.

Corpus of English fables consisted of 393 annotated sentences and 2999 unannotated sentences. Further, we will discuss only annotated sentences. Sentences were annotated into eight categories (Plutchik's eight emotions: joy, trust, sadness, fear, disgust, anger, anticipation, surprise). The number of emotions chosen for each sentence was arbitrary. In Figure 5, the count of each emotion across the dataset is depicted. Figure 6 displays the number of sentences with the number of emotions they contain. As we can see, sentences were mostly rated by one emotion, followed by neutral sentences. Having more than one emotion for a sentence means that we are dealing with a multi-label classification problem. There is no evidence of a positive/negative relationship between emotion's classes (Figure 7).

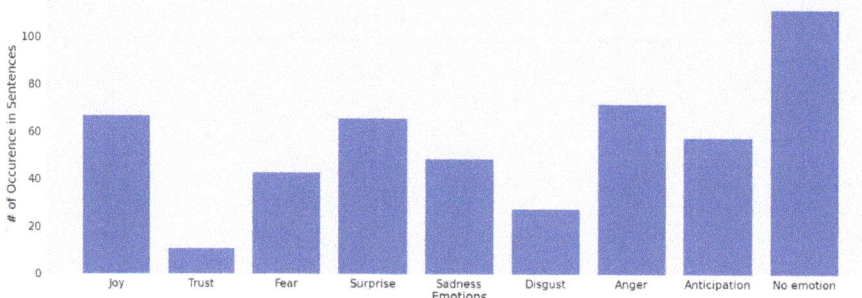

**Figure 5.** Number of emotions in annotated dataset.

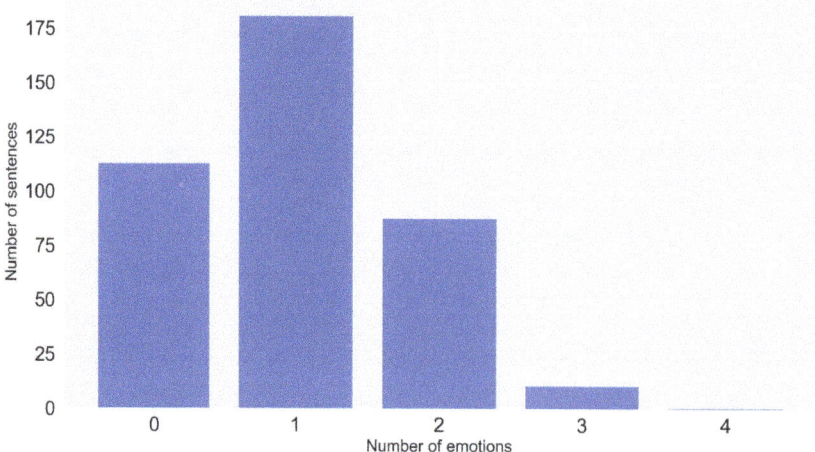

**Figure 6.** Number of sentences with multiple emotions.

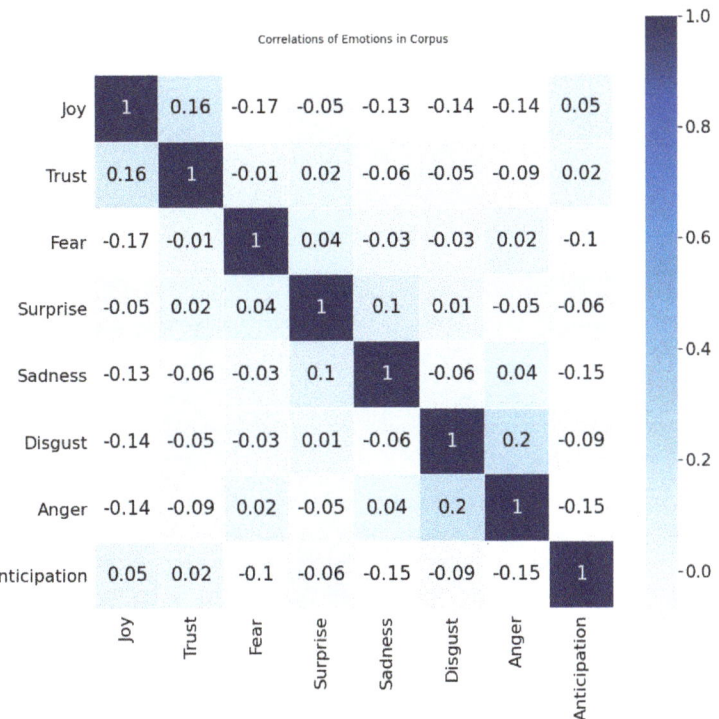

**Figure 7.** Correlation of emotion's classes in the dataset.

*4.2. Block: Processing of The Data*

The process of data preparation is shown in Figure 8. The first row in the picture represents the process with a sentence. Second-row displays wherein the process features are extracted (e.g., punctuation is gathered from raw sentences; matching emotional words from a dictionary and Part-of-Speech (POS) tagging is done after tokenization and removing high occurrence words). Fables were formatted as follows: one sentence = one row in a document. Firstly we unified every character to lower case; applied function for dividing shortened forms of words into two words (grammatical contractions—$we're \rightarrow we\ are$); and cleaned the text from interpunctuation (a sign of question mark, colon and an exclamation mark were used as features). Every sentence was tokenized into words. Afterwards, the POS tagger was applied. Next, we applied the National Research Council (NRC) dictionary to find out if any given word is a word from the vocabulary. In case the word was contained in the vocabulary, we assigned emotion to the word. Finally, we performed stopwords removal and lemmatization of the words (keeping words in their root form).

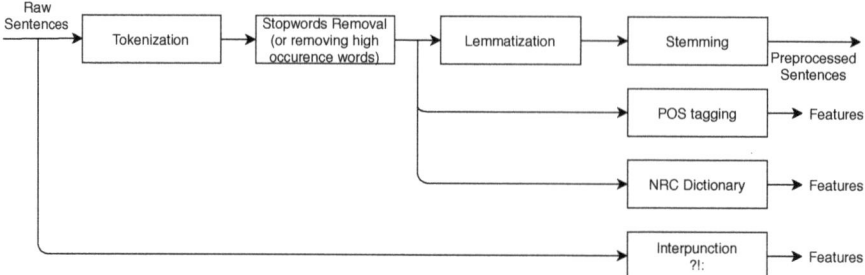

**Figure 8.** Process of cleaning and preparing data for vectorization.

*4.3. Block: Feature Extraction and Word Embeddings*

We used vector space representation of the text and very sentence was represented by a vector of features. Each sample in the dataset was described as follows:

- POS tagging (4 features): we used *pos_tag* function from *nltk* library. Every POS tag was represented as a number of occurrences in a given sentence. We chose 14 POS labels grouped into four categories:

    – noun: NN noun, singular, NNS noun, plural;
    – adjective: JJ adjective, JJR adjective, comparative, JJS adjective, superlative;
    – verb: VB verb, base form, VBD verb, past tense, VBG verb, gerund/present participle, VBN verb, past participle, VBP verb, sing. present, non-3d, VBZ verb, 3rd person sing. present;
    – adverb: RB adverb, RBR adverb, comparative, RBS adverb, superlative.

- emotion (8 features): we used the NRC dictionary to obtain counts of emotions occurring in each sentence—anger, fear, sadness, disgust, surprise, anticipation, trust and joy;
- punctuation (3 features): we extracted presence of colons ":", exclamation marks "!" and question marks "?";
- numerical feature vector: we extracted all words from pre-processed sentences (Figure 8) to create vocabulary:

    – Bag-of-Words (BoW) representation (number of features was dependent on thresholding occurrence of tokens in input): each sentence was represented as a number of occurrence of given words in the vocabulary. Vocabulary was generated from all tokens in sentences.
    – Term Frequency-Inverse Document Frequency (TF-IDF) (number of features was dependent on thresholding occurrence of tokens in input): similar to BoW, but instead of the number of occurrences, each token was represented as a proportion between the number of occurrence in given sentence and occurrence in the whole corpus.
    – sentence embeddings (300 features): every word (token) in a sentence is represented by its vector obtained from pretrained ConceptNet Numberbatch model. We used word embeddings to create sentence embeddings. Sentence embeddings are basically averaged sum of word embeddings vectors appertaining to the sentence.

*4.4. Block: Clustering*

Annotation of sentences is exhausting and time-consuming; therefore, we decided to utilize k-Means algorithm to annotate additional data. We have selected the k-Means, as it represent the reliable and fast clustering algorithm, frequently adopted in many real-world applications. In addition to the performance, another aspect was fast processing of new, unknown samples by the trained model, which was important factor during the run-time.

k-Means clustering algorithm is well-known algorithm that approximates the maximum-likelihood solution for determining the locations of the means of a mixture density of component densities.

$$E(em_1, ....em_K) = \frac{1}{S} \sum_{k=1}^{K} \sum_{w_n \in EM_k} ||w_n - em_k||^2 \qquad (1)$$

where:

- S—number of sentences in dataset,
- W—vector representation of sentences,
- K—number of emotion categories,
- $EM_k$—clusters of sentences,
- $em_k$—center of clusters.

The outcomes of the algorithm are clustered data annotated according to the centroid where they belong.

Our usage of k-Means can be described as follows: we randomly chose five representatives of each class (e.g., in-class joy—5 representatives for "0" category and five representatives for "1" category) and calculated centroid. Centroids were calculated as an average of the sum of vectors (from the vector representation of the data). We ended up with 18 centroids. Before every pair of centroid was fed into the k-Means algorithm, we calculated the distance of every sentence from given centroids and removed the furthest and closest one. After that, labels for every class were predicted. Acquired data gave us the option to expand the training dataset if needed.

*4.5. Block: Model Learning*

While working with multi-label classification problem we give a brief overview of three methods. In general, we focused on selection of the stable methods which are able to provide reliable results while also perform well from the run-time aspects. We can approach to multi-label classification problem in these ways:

- Problem transformation—transformation of the multi-label classification problem so that a binary classification algorithm can be applied. In this case, we applied one-vs.-rest approach, where each class was considered as a separate classification problem, so binary classifiers were trained to recognize each particular class.
- Multi-label algorithm—use of the algorithm which are directly adapted to the multi-label task without demanding transformation (Multi-Label k-NN, Decision Trees, etc.). In such a case, there was a possibility to directly use the model, which is suitable to perform the multi-label classification.
- Ensemble approach—model which combine the classification result from multiple models.

The following sections will describe the methods used and evaluated in our methodology.

4.5.1. Support Vector Machine Model

SVM is a classification model based on the idea of support vectors. The models separate the sample space into two or more classes with the widest margin possible. SVM is originally a linear classifier; however, it can relatively efficiently perform non-linear classification by using a kernel function [65]. Kernel is a method which maps features into higher dimensional space specified by the used kernel function. For the model building, we need training samples labeled −1 or 1 for each class. SVM then attempts to divide the classes with a parameterized (non)linear boundary in such a way to maximize the margin between given classes. A parameterized linear equation is defined as in formula (6). Values of $z(x)$ for each class are represented in the following way. If given a sample of class 1, values should be greater or equal to one, if given sample of class −1, values should be equal or smaller than −1, respectively:

$$wx_+ + b >= 1, wx_- + b <= -1 \quad (2)$$

Both of these conditions are ensuring that samples are on the correct side of the 'street'. Continuing to complete the solution, creating the widest margin between samples, it was observed that only two nearest points to the separating street determines its width. It can be expressed as a difference vector of these points multiplied by the vector of the street W and its magnitude $||W||$.

$$width = (x_+ - x_-) \frac{w}{||w||} \quad (3)$$

The objective is to maximize the width of the street, which is known as the primal problem of SVM. In our case, we used Radial Basis Function (RBF) as kernel.

### 4.5.2. Multi-Class Naive Bayes Model

Naive Bayes classifier is a probabilistic classifier based on Bayes' theorem and independence assumption between the features. Let us assume that event A and event B are independent and their conditional probability is defined according Bayes' theorem:

$$P(A|B) = \frac{P(A) * P(B|A)}{P(B)} \quad (4)$$

In practice, $P(B)$ can be an estimated constant calculated from the dataset. Replacing $P(B)$ with a constant $\beta^{-1}$, the previous formula is then expressed as:

$$P(A|B) = \beta * P(A) * P(B|A) \quad (5)$$

Let us assume that A represents class and B represents a feature relating to the class A. This equation then handles only one feature. Let us extend the rule with more features. Then the conditional probability of class A on features B, C is the following:

$$P(A|B,C) = \beta * P(A) * P(B,C|A) = \beta * P(A) * P(B|A) * P(C|A) \quad (6)$$

That assumes that features B and C are independent of each other. Then, simplifying the above expression is possible using the replacement of $P(B,C|A)$ with $P(B|A)P(C|A)$. For $n$ observations—features $x_1, \ldots, x_n$—the conditional probability for any class $y_j$ can be expressed as below:

$$P(y_j|x_1, \ldots, x_n) = \beta * P(y_j) \prod_{i=1}^{n} P(x_i, y_j) \quad (7)$$

This classification model is called Naive Bayes classifier. Naive Bayes is often applied as a baseline for text classification [66]. In this work, we used multi-class Naive Bayes classifier.

### 4.5.3. Feed-Forward Neural Network Model

Another popular models used in the text classification tasks are neural networks [67,68]. In our experiments, we used a feed-forward neural network model. It proved to be the most suitable neural network model for a given task, as the more advanced neural models (CNN, LSTM) require significantly more data to train them properly. Neural networks are flexible models composed of computational units—neurons, arranged in interconnected layers. Connections between neurons correspond to numerical parameters of the model—weights. The primary predictive model is feed-forward neural network [69], which consists of the following layers:

- input layer—input neurons correspond directly to the input attributes $x_1, x_2, \ldots, x_m$;
- one (or more) hidden layer—transform the input data in non-linear fashion;
- output layer—output neurons determine the prediction of the model; depending on the architecture, the network can provide multiple outputs $y_1, y_2, \ldots, y_k$.

The calculation for all neurons on the hidden and output layers is identical—the output value of each neuron (activation) is calculated as a weighted sum of inputs of the neurons transformed using the activation function. On the hidden layers, we used ReLU activation function [70]. The output of the ReLU function can be represented as:

$$f(x) = \max(0, x). \tag{8}$$

On the output layer, we used the sigmoid activation function [71], which transforms the output into a probability estimations:

$$f(x) = \frac{1}{1 + e^{-x}}. \tag{9}$$

We used Adaptive Moment Estimation (Adam) [72] as an optimization method during the training. RMSProp [73] and Momentum [74] methods are based on different approaches. Momentum accelerates the training in the direction of the minimum, while RMSProp reduces the oscillations by adaptive change of the learning rate. Adam algorithm combines both Momentum and RMSProp heuristics.

The loss function expresses the magnitude of the loss that the model will make in the prediction. By minimizing the loss function, we can obtain the weights for all network layers. In our work, we used Binary Cross-Entropy (BCE):

$$BCE = -(y \log(\hat{y}) + (1 - y) \log(1 - \hat{y})), \tag{10}$$

where $y$ is the actual value and $\hat{y}$ is the predicted value.

Based on the prediction and weights, we obtain an output loss which propagates back to the previous layers using the backpropagation algorithm [75]. The weights are then modified to minimize the output error.

In the experiments, we used a feed-forward neural network. The architecture of the network comprised of the input layer, four hidden fully connected layers with 32, 64, 128 and 256 neurons and the ReLU activation function. The output layer contained nine neurons, each representing a particular class and a sigmoid activating function. The model included 55,881 trainable parameters.

*4.6. Block: Classification*

Our approach to the classification lies in transforming our problem into 9 separate problems (8 emotion classes and one class without emotion). Based on the fact that emotions are not dependent on each other (Figure 7), we trained the classifiers for each emotion separately. When a new sample comes into the classification, all of the classifiers estimate the probability for each class. Each classifier has only one vote. The threshold is set to probability of 50% for accepting the label.

*4.7. Block: Evaluation of Results*

To evaluate results, we used statistical metrics usually used in text classification: precision, recall, F1 score, Matthews Correlation Coefficient and subset accuracy. The dataset was split into training and testing sets in a 70/30 ratio. We used stratified sampling for the multi-label classification implemented in scikit-multilearn (http://http://scikit.ml/stratification.html) library.

Firstly, we define the confusion matrix. The confusion matrix summarizes the classification performance of a classifier with respect to test data. It is a two-dimensional matrix, where one dimension represents the true class of a document and the second dimension represents class label predicted by the classifier. Table 3 presents an example of confusion matrix.

**Table 3.** Confusion matrix for two classes.

|                 | Predicted Positive  | Predicted Negative  |
|-----------------|---------------------|---------------------|
| Actual Positive | TP (True Positive)  | FP (False Positive) |
| Actual Negative | FP (False Negative) | TN (True Negative)  |

- **Precision**—defined as the fraction of the number of texts correctly labeled as belonging to the positive class among the total number of retrieved texts annotated as belonging to the positive class.

$$Precision = \frac{TP}{TP + FP} \tag{11}$$

- **Recall**—defined as the fraction of the number of texts correctly annotated as belonging to the positive class among the number of the retrieved text belonging to the positive class

$$Recall = \frac{TP}{TP + FN} \tag{12}$$

- **F1 score**—the weighted average of precision and recall. This score takes both false positives and false negatives into an account.

$$F1 = 2 \times \frac{Precision \times Recall}{Precision + Recall} \tag{13}$$

- **Matthews Correlation Coefficient** (MCC)—in comparison with F1 score, it is a more reliable statistical rate which produces a high score only if the prediction obtained good results in all of the four confusion matrix categories (true positives, false negatives, true negatives and false positives), proportionally both to the size of positive elements and the size of negative elements in the dataset [76]. It returns a value between $-1$ and $+1$. A coefficient of $+1$ represents a perfect prediction, $0$ no better than random prediction and $-1$ indicates total disagreement between prediction and actual class.

$$MCC = \frac{TP \times TN - FP \times FN}{\sqrt{(TP + FP)(TP + FN)(TN + FP)(TN + FN)}} \tag{14}$$

- **Subset Accuracy**—the percentage of samples that are classified correctly within the particular class.
- **Exact Accuracy**—the percentage of samples that are classified correctly across all labels (it ignores samples that are partially correct).

## 5. Experiments with Text Data

*5.1. Baseline*

Our baseline model consisted of NRC dictionary and 393 annotated sentences. We matched every word against the dictionary and assigned the number of appertaining occurrences to each emotion. Later we transformed the number of occurrences to binary representation ("0" if an emotion is not present, "1" if emotion has more than one occurrence). Table 4 shows that out of eight emotion, *Joy* is classified most accurately and *Disgust* with *Trust* the worst. The reason for it lies in our data. Looking back at Figure 5, we can see that trust and disgust are the least represented classes.

Table 4. Accuracy of emotion dictionary, lexicon approach.

|  | Precision | Recall | F1 Score | MCC | Subset Accuracy |
|---|---|---|---|---|---|
| Joy | 0.32 | 0.78 | 0.45 | 0.33 | 0.68 |
| Trust | 0.03 | 0.55 | 0.06 | 0.01 | 0.49 |
| Fear | 0.15 | 0.77 | 0.25 | 0.15 | 0.5 |
| Surprise | 0.20 | 0.38 | 0.27 | 0.07 | 0.65 |
| Sadness | 0.18 | 0.69 | 0.28 | 0.16 | 0.56 |
| Disgust | 0.08 | 0.54 | 0.14 | 0.04 | 0.53 |
| Anger | 0.22 | 0.65 | 0.33 | 0.11 | 0.52 |
| Anticipation | 0.2 | 0.69 | 0.31 | 0.15 | 0.55 |
| No emotion | 0.59 | 0.21 | 0.31 | 0.23 | 0.73 |
| $F_1$ micro | 0.18 | 0.55 | 0.27 | | |
| $F_1$ macro | 0.22 | 0.58 | 0.27 | | |
| Exact Accuracy | 0.22 | | | | |

## 5.2. Building of the Naive Bayes Model Using Bag-of-Words

We firstly begin by testing our data against the Bag-of-Words representation (Table 5). As we can see, the precision is rather low. Above-average results are obtained only in case of *No emotion* class. *Trust and Disgust* got 0, however looking at the subset accuracy we see that they achieve scores 97% and 91%, respectively. That means, even though we did not classify a positive case, we got a good estimate on the overall class. We experimented with several model's setups such as:

- changing threshold for minimal/maximal count of the word to be excluded from vocabulary when creating BoW representation;
- uni-grams, bi-grams;
- stopwords removing/not removing;
- changing the number of additional features for sentence representation (NRC, POS, punctuation);
- changing classifiers Multi-nomial Naive Bayes, Bernoulli Naive Bayes, Gaussian Naive Bayes, SVM;
- expanding training set for data annotated by k-Means.

Table 5. Accuracy of Bag-of-Words representation, Multi-nomial Naive Bayes classifier.

|  | Precision | Recall | F1 Score | MCC | Subset Accuracy |
|---|---|---|---|---|---|
| Joy | 0.36 | 0.25 | 0.29 | 0.18 | 0.79 |
| Trust | 0.00 | 0.00 | 0.00 | 0.00 | 0.97 |
| Fear | 0.10 | 0.08 | 0.09 | -0.01 | 0.82 |
| Surprise | 0.20 | 0.15 | 0.17 | 0.03 | 0.75 |
| Sadness | 0.25 | 0.07 | 0.11 | 0.07 | 0.85 |
| Disgust | 0.00 | 0.00 | 0.00 | -0.04 | 0.91 |
| Anger | 0.14 | 0.09 | 0.11 | -0.04 | 0.73 |
| Anticipation | 0.20 | 0.06 | 0.09 | 0.03 | 0.83 |
| No emotion | 0.67 | 0.29 | 0.41 | 0.32 | 0.75 |
| micro avg | 0.29 | 0.15 | 0.20 | | |
| macro avg | 0.21 | 0.11 | 0.14 | | |
| Exact Accuracy | 0.15 | | | | |

Fine-tuning with different pre-processing settings such as stopwords removing/not removing, uni-grams/bi-grams and the threshold for minimal/maximal count of a word to be excluded from vocabulary we improved *Joy* and *Anticipation* precision (Table 6).

**Table 6.** Accuracy of fine-tuned settings in Bag-of-Words representation, Multi-nominal Naive Bayes classifier.

|  | Precision | Recall | F1 Score | MCC | Subset Accuracy |
|---|---|---|---|---|---|
| Joy | 0.60 | 0.45 | 0.51 | 0.44 | 0.85 |
| Anticipation | 0.60 | 0.18 | 0.27 | 0.27 | 0.86 |

Then, we extended the features with emotions from NRC dictionary, POS tags, punctuation and continued tuning our model. We saw improvement on *No emotion* and *Anger* classes (Table 7.)

**Table 7.** Accuracy of fine-tuned setting in Bag-of-Words representation and added features, Multi-nomial Naive Bayes classifier.

|  | Precision | Recall | F1 Score | MCC | Subset Accuracy |
|---|---|---|---|---|---|
| Anger | 0.50 | 0.16 | 0.21 | 0.16 | 0.80 |
| No emotion | 0.71 | 0.12 | 0.20 | 0.0.19 | 0.73 |

We tried also every feature individually. We noticed increase in accuracy of *Fear* to 25%, *Surprise* to 50%, *Sadness* to 50% and *Disgust* to 25%. To increase the accuracy, we needed to use different setup for every class.

Adding k-Means annotated data to the training set we observe *Disgust* accuracy to rise to 67%. All other accuracy metrics remained at the same level.

*5.3. Building of the Naive Bayes Model Using TF-IDF*

Foundation of experiment 2 was the TF-IDF representation of sentences. Results from our experiment can be seen in Table 8. The highest score was obtained in the *Joy* class. The lowest were in *Trust* and *Disgust* classes.

**Table 8.** Accuracy of Term Frequency-Inverse Document Frequency (TF-IDF) representation, Multi-nomial Naive Bayes classifier.

|  | Precision | Recall | F1 Score | MCC | Subset Accuracy |
|---|---|---|---|---|---|
| Joy | 0.60 | 0.25 | 0.29 | 0.24 | 0.84 |
| Trust | 0.00 | 0.00 | 0.00 | 0.00 | 0.97 |
| Fear | 0.00 | 0.08 | 0.09 | -0.04 | 0.87 |
| Surprise | 0.25 | 0.15 | 0.17 | 0.05 | 0.79 |
| Sadness | 0.50 | 0.07 | 0.11 | 0.14 | 0.87 |
| Disgust | 0.00 | 0.00 | 0.00 | 0.00 | 0.93 |
| Anger | 0.50 | 0.09 | 0.11 | 0.10 | 0.81 |
| Anticipation | 0.00 | 0.06 | 0.09 | -0.05 | 0.83 |
| No emotion | 0.42 | 0.15 | 0.22 | 0.10 | 0.69 |
| micro avg | 0.36 | 0.08 | 0.13 |  |  |
| macro avg | 0.25 | 0.08 | 0.09 |  |  |
| Exact Accuracy | 0.15 |  |  |  |  |

After fine-tuning the parameters of our model, we trained the model and compared the results. Table 9 summarizes the results of the Multi-nomial Naive Bayes classifier with TF-IDF after fine-tuning, Table 10 summarizes the fine-tuning of the model trained using the extended set of features.

**Table 9.** Accuracy of fine-tuned settings in TF-IDF representation, Multi-nomial Naive Bayes classifier.

|  | Precision | Recall | F1 Score | MCC | Subset Accuracy |
|---|---|---|---|---|---|
| Joy | 0.67 | 0.20 | 0.31 | 0.31 | 0.85 |
| Trust | 0.50 | 0.45 | 0.51 | 0.44 | 0.85 |
| Fear | 0.33 | 0.08 | 0.12 | 0.11 | 0.88 |
| Anger | 0.67 | 0.45 | 0.51 | 0.44 | 0.85 |
| Anticipation | 0.50 | 0.18 | 0.26 | 0.23 | 0.85 |
| No emotion | 0.56 | 0.44 | 0.49 | 0.32 | 0.74 |

**Table 10.** Accuracy of fine-tuned setting in TF-IDF representation and added features, Multi-nomial Naive Bayes.

|  | Precision | Recall | F1 Score | MCC | Subset Accuracy |
|---|---|---|---|---|---|
| Joy | 0.83 | 0.25 | 0.38 | 0.41 | 0.86 |
| Surprise | 0.50 | 0.32 | 0.35 | 0.29 | 0.91 |
| Disgust | 0.50 | 0.25 | 0.33 | 0.32 | 0.93 |
| Anger | 0.80 | 0.18 | 0.30 | 0.33 | 0.84 |
| Anticipation | 0.67 | 0.12 | 0.20 | 0.24 | 0.86 |

Adding more semi-automatically labeled data further raised the accuracy of the *Sadness* class to 67%.

*5.4. ConceptNet Numberbatch Converted to Sentence Embeddings*

The base of this experiment was to use the sentence embeddings. On top of that, we added NRC emotional dictionary, punctuation and POS tags. Lastly, we used word embeddings—ConceptNet Numberbatch and converted them to the *sentence embeddings*. We can see from Table 11, that accuracy in classes is low but it covers all classes except one—*Trust*.

**Table 11.** ConceptNet Numberbatch—sentence embeddings.

|  | Precision | Recall | F1 Score | MCC | Subset Accuracy |
|---|---|---|---|---|---|
| Joy | 0.19 | 0.55 | 0.28 | 0.05 | 0.52 |
| Trust | 0.00 | 0.00 | 0.00 | −0.04 | 0.91 |
| Fear | 0.15 | 0.46 | 0.23 | 0.09 | 0.66 |
| Surprise | 0.24 | 0.65 | 0.35 | 0.17 | 0.59 |
| Sadness | 0.20 | 0.67 | 0.31 | 0.19 | 0.62 |
| Disgust | 0.14 | 0.38 | 0.20 | 0.12 | 0.79 |
| Anger | 0.23 | 0.23 | 0.23 | 0.04 | 0.71 |
| Anticipation | 0.19 | 0.53 | 0.28 | 0.10 | 0.6 |
| No emotion | 0.31 | 0.38 | 0.34 | 0.03 | 0.57 |
| micro avg | 0.20 | 0.46 | 0.28 |  |  |
| macro avg | 0.18 | 0.43 | 0.25 |  |  |
| Exact Accuracy | 0.20 |  |  |  |  |

Adding features to the model did not help to raise its accuracy significantly. Adding data labeled by k-Means helped to improve accuracy in the class *No emotion* to 68% by using SVM classifier. The average accuracy for the rest of the classes was 20%.

*5.5. Neural Network Classifier*

In this experiment, we trained feed-forward neural network classifier to compare the performance of the neural network approach with standard machine learning methods used in the previous experiments. The architecture of the network is described in Section 4.5.3. The performance of the model is summarized in Table 12. As we can see from the results, neural network classifier gained slightly better performance (when considering averaged metrics) to standard machine learning models.

However, the lack of the training data caused that the more advanced deep learning approaches (such as CNN or LSTM models) or more advanced popular language models (e.g., BERT) could not be properly trained to solve this task.

Table 12. Feed-forward neural network.

|  | Precision | Recall | F1 Score | MCC | Subset Accuracy |
|---|---|---|---|---|---|
| Joy | 0.42 | 0.40 | 0.41 | 0.29 | 0.80 |
| Trust | 0.00 | 0.00 | 0.00 | 0.00 | 0.97 |
| Fear | 0.22 | 0.15 | 0.18 | 0.10 | 0.85 |
| Surprise | 0.50 | 0.30 | 0.37 | 0.30 | 0.83 |
| Sadness | 0.22 | 0.13 | 0.17 | 0.08 | 0.83 |
| Disgust | 1.00 | 0.12 | 0.22 | 0.34 | 0.94 |
| Anger | 0.36 | 0.23 | 0.28 | 0.16 | 0.78 |
| Anticipation | 0.42 | 0.29 | 0.34 | 0.26 | 0.84 |
| No emotion | 0.43 | 0.35 | 0.39 | 0.17 | 0.68 |
| micro avg | 0.39 | 0.27 | 0.32 |  |  |
| macro avg | 0.40 | 0.22 | 0.26 |  |  |
| Exact Accuracy | 0.27 |  |  |  |  |

## 5.6. Ensemble Classifier

We combined the best-obtained models for each class and integrated them into the ensemble classifier, as shown in Table 13. We can see an increase in exact accuracy, which is the most strict metric and expresses how many completely correct rows (all labels are correct) we obtained from the classifier. We did not include the neural network model in the ensemble. The ensemble members were selected as a binary classifiers for each of the particular class, which in case of the neural network would require its re-training in one-vs-rest approach. Therefore, neural network was primarily used to compare the performance of the ensemble model.

Table 13. Ensemble of binary classifiers. NB: Multi-nominal Naive Bayes, SVM: Support Vector Machine, NRC: emotion dictionary, POS: Part-of-Speech tags, PUNC: punctuation, SW: stop words.

|  | Precision | Classifier | Representation | NRC | POS | PUNC | SW |
|---|---|---|---|---|---|---|---|
| Joy | 0.83 | NB | TF-IDF | - | + | - | - |
| Trust | 0.50 | SVM | TF-IDF | + | - | + | + |
| Fear | 0.33 | NB | TF-IDF | - | + | - | - |
| Surprise | 0.50 | SVM | TF-IDF | + | - | - | - |
| Sadness | 0.67 | NB | TF-IDF | + | - | - | - |
| Disgust | 0.90 | NB | BoW | - | + | - | - |
| Anger | 0.80 | NB | TF-IDF | + | + | + | - |
| Anticipation | 0.67 | NB | TF-IDF | - | + | + | - |
| No emotion | 0.71 | NB | TF-IDF | - | + | - | - |
| $F_1$ micro | 0.58 |  |  |  |  |  |  |
| $F_1$ macro | 0.66 |  |  |  |  |  |  |
| Exact Accuracy | 0.31 |  |  |  |  |  |  |

During the experiments, besides the initial base classifiers, we compared the ensemble model performance with some other machine learning algorithms. For the comparison purposes, we used the feed-forward neural network model described in Section 4.5.3. and also with the frequently used models from the popular Python machine learning library scikit-learn. In comparison, we included baseline classifiers (Logistic Regression, SVM, Decision Trees, k-NN) and also other ensemble models (e.g., Adaboost). As the proposed ensemble model combines different ensemble members, trained on different feature subsets, or expanded set of attributes, we compared the ensemble with other machine learning models trained on both, TF-IDF representation and on TF-IDF extended with expanded attributes. Following Table 14 summarizes the performance of the ensemble and other ML models. The results represent the averaged values of the 10-fold cross-validated models on the testing set. Inclusion of the extended set of features to TF-IDF representation brings a slight improvement to some of the models. In general, the performance of the base models is rather poor, in comparison to the ensemble model.

Table 14. Comparison of the ensemble model with other machine learning (ML) models.

| Classifier | F1 Micro | F1 Macro | Accuracy | F1 Micro | F1 Macro | Accuracy |
|---|---|---|---|---|---|---|
| | TF-IDF + Extra Features | | | TF-IDF Only | | |
| Decision Trees | 0.21 | 0.17 | 0.13 | 0.19 | 0.18 | 0.11 |
| k-NN (k = 3) | 0.19 | 0.13 | 0.14 | 0.22 | 0.17 | 0.12 |
| Extra Tree Classifier | 0.18 | 0.17 | 0.16 | 0.23 | 0.21 | 0.15 |
| ML Perceptron | 0.25 | 0.19 | 0.14 | 0.15 | 0.10 | 0.05 |
| FF NN | 0.39 | 0.40 | 0.27 | - | - | - |
| Logistic Regression | 0.30 | 0.17 | 0.27 | 0.27 | 0.24 | 0.29 |
| SGD | 0.22 | 0.13 | 0.07 | 0.23 | 0.11 | 0.26 |
| Linear SVC | 0.22 | 0.17 | 0.19 | 0.25 | 0.05 | 0.29 |
| Adaboost | 0.27 | 0.15 | 0.25 | 0.26 | 0.14 | 0.25 |
| Ensemble model | 0.58 | 0.66 | 0.31 | | | |

## 6. Experiments with Humanoid Robot NAO

We propose scenarios with humanoid robot NAO and humans (either kids, or adults). The controlled group was the same for each experiment. The group consisted of 8 participants (7 adults and 1 child). The age of the participants ranged from 3 to 50 years. In these experiments, we focused on the creation of the small, yet diverse group of subjects, represented by participants within different age groups. The participant was interacting with a robot alone; thus, it was one-on-one interaction. They were not accustomed with humanoid robot, thus it was their first interaction. All except one were educated people. The experimenter was behind the wall. During the experiments, we paid attention to two variables: length of the interaction, number of fables red.

Throughout the experiments, we used NAO robot v.5. NAO is a humanoid robot often utilized in HRI experiments. He can move with hands, walk, talk, listen. Taking into account its' very limited facial expression, he can make use of his eye's led lights to signal to blink, even changing color can suggest different emotional states (e.g., red led = anger). A pre-trained classifier was running on a server (standard desktop PC configuration) connected to the NAO robot. During the run-time, the classifier processed the sentences/fables. A computer was used to invoke the scripts for speech and moves to NAO.

### 6.1. Experiment 1A—Basic Setup

Setup of the first experiments is straightforward (Figure 9). NAO is presented as a "Narrator". He greets the participant of the experiment and asked him to sit down, facing him. Subsequently, he offers to tell a story. He starts narrating as soon as he hears "yes". Input to NAO is the fable without any emotional markup; thus, NAO is reading the fable without any expression (either movement or vocal). The recipient is facing NAO and listening to the story. After telling the whole story, NAO gives the option either to continue with another story or to finish. The number of stories is fully dependent on the participant. At the end of the experiment, we give every participant the questions shown in Table 15.

**Table 15.** Survey about robot performance in the first two scenarios.

| | Questions |
|---|---|
| Q1. | I like robot NAO narrating the story. |
| Q2. | I like to hear the story again. |
| Q3. | NAO was believable narrator. |
| Q4. | Experiment was not interesting. |
| Q5. | I was not lacking anything in the robot performance. |

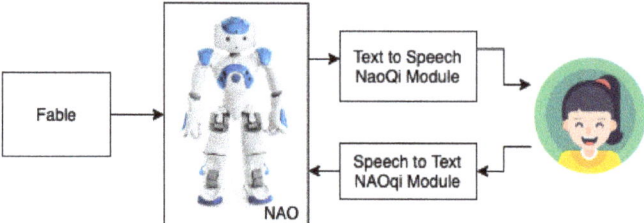

**Figure 9.** Setup for the experiment 1A.

We can break down our system to the following parts:

- Fable—NAO randomly picks one fable from a given set of 145 fables. Fables are preprocessed to the sentences.
- Text to Speech NAOqi Module—converts fable to speech. Input are sentences. Robot is not tracking human while telling a story.
- Speech to Text NAOqi Module—user can communicate short commands via this interface. It is used when NAO asks whether he can start telling the story or at the end of the story if the participant wants another story.
- Human—can request more stories.

### 6.2. Experiment 1B—Setup with Emotional Movements and Gestures

Setup for the second experiment (Figure 10) is the same as for the first experiment with three exceptions. Number one: The input to the NAO is Aesop's fable marked with emotion. Second is closely connected to the first: NAO is narrating the story with movements and changes in pitch. The third difference is in case the participant wants to hear another story. After requesting a second story, NAO is telling that he is tired and asks if the participator really wants to hear another story. If he gets a positive response, he continues, otherwise he thanks, and the experiment is finished. At the end of the experiment, the participant fills in the survey with the same question as before (Table 15).

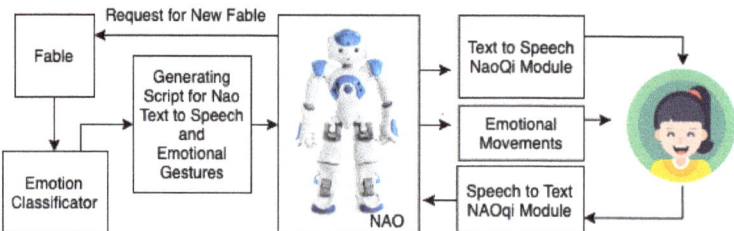

**Figure 10.** Setup for the experiment 1B.

We can break down our system to the parts similar to experiment 1. On top of the used block we added:

- Emotion classifier—used to automatically annotate sentences with their appertaining emotions.
- Generating script for NAO text-to-speech and emotional gestures—input to this block is fable annotated with emotions. The output of this block is a script for NAO to tell the story as well as add emotional cues to his behavior such as pitch change and gestures. Gestures are chosen randomly from a predefined set.

*6.3. Experiment 1C—Setup with Random Movements*

We took setup from experiment 2, removed classification block and modified block *Generating script for NAO text-to-speech and emotional gestures* to generate any gestures, incongruent to the emotions in written text (Figure 11).

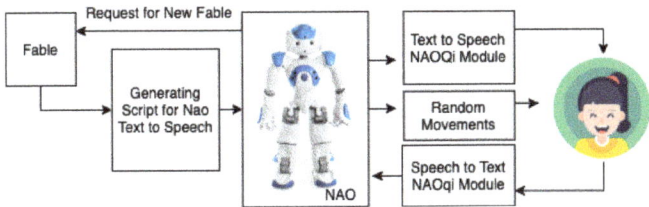

**Figure 11.** Setup for the experiment 1C.

*6.4. Results of the Experiment 1*

The results of the experiments are shown in Table 16. For responses we used a five-point Likert scale with options: 5—I agree extremely; 4—I agree very; 3—I agree moderately; 2—I agree slightly; 1—I do not agree. We took an average of scores for each question. The average length of the interaction was measured from the point where NAO robot greeted the person until he finished narrating his last fable rounded to the minutes. The average number of fables read indicates how many fables were read during one session.

**Table 16.** Results from the experiment 1.

|   | Questions | 1A | 1B | 1C |
|---|---|---|---|---|
| Q1. | I like robot NAO narrating the story. | 2.125 | 3.75 | 3 |
| Q2. | I like to hear the story again. | 2.5 | 3.5 | 3.125 |
| Q3. | NAO was believable narrator. | 1.625 | 3.875 | 3.25 |
| Q4. | Experiment was not interesting. | 3.25 | 1.875 | 1.625 |
| Q5. | I was not lacking anything in the robot performance. | 1.875 | 3.75 | 3 |
| a | **Average Length of the interaction** | 5 min | 8 min | 7 min |
| b | **Average number of fables read** | 1.25 | 1.75 | 1.5 |

From the results above, we can conclude that robot with emotional/random cues (experiments 1B, 1C) achieved better overall rating in comparison to the robot without emotional cues (experiment 1A). We demonstrate that there is a difference in perceiving text from robot to human by adding emotional/random manners to the robot. However, now the question is if it is really necessary to add emotional cues to the robot or any cues would be sufficient, i.e., randomly generated movements. Hence, we adjust the experiment 1B, where gesture generated by the robot were assigned randomly. Experiments 1B and 1C show that the difference between emotional movements and random gestures is not marginal; however, emotional movements are giving slightly better results. Only in (Q4) random gestures topped emotional. We assume, the reason for it was the randomness of generating movements. Participants were surprised by sudden movements and thus saw the robot as interesting.

## 6.5. Experiment 2—Robot Interaction to Human Spoken Words

Setup for the second experiment (Figure 12) is as follows: the participant is greeted by NAO and asked to sit down. After that, he tells the participant to tell him a story. The participant is given beforehand the story to read. While reading a story to the robot, Google Cloud Speech to Text Service is used to transcribe the text into a written format. Afterwards, our emotion classifier detects emotion in a given text. Text is processed into sentences; emotional gestures are automatically annotated to the text based on present emotion. NAO executes the script and makes emotional gestures. After reading the fable, the robot asks if you would like to read him another story. If he gets a negative response, he says thanks and says that he is looking forward to the next session. At the end of the experiment, participants fill in the survey (Table 17).

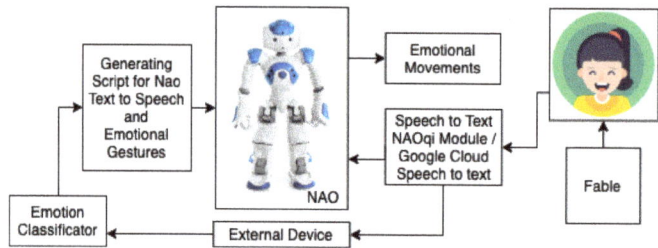

**Figure 12.** Setup for experiment 2.

## 6.6. Results of the Experiment 2

Results from Table 17 suggest that the robot reacting to the human spoken words had positive impact of robot perception (Q5). The robot even appeared as he was capable to understand what he was told (Q2). What surprised us was the low score of Q3, but it can be explained in two ways: either participant did not see the point in reading to the robot or they would like to tell the robot their text Q4. Despite this, in the current scenario, participants enjoyed reading to the robot. Q3 was also reflected in average numbers of read fables outcome and length of the interaction.

**Table 17.** Results from experiment 2.

| | Questions | |
|---|---|---|
| Q1. | I enjoyed reading to the robot. | 3.625 |
| Q2. | Robot appeared to understand me. | 3.125 |
| Q3. | I would like to read fable to the robot again. | 2.5 |
| Q4. | I want to chose my own text to read. | 3.25 |
| Q5. | Gesturing of the robot was adequate to read text. | 3.75 |
| a | **Average Length of the interaction** | 5 min |
| b | **Average number of fables read** | 1 |

## 7. Conclusions

The presented work connects two big areas of research namely sentiment analysis and human–robot interaction. We saw a gap in HRI years ago that SA could fulfill. Usually, there is no automation in HRI whatsoever while processing texts spoken by a robot. If a robot is able to speak, everything a robot says is scripted beforehand. Two problems arise from this. Firstly, script making is tedious work and you can not handle every possibility. Secondly, robot can not react adequately if surprised unexpectedly, thus it lowers its positive perception by humans. As a result that we are heading to the era of socially assistive robotics (such as artificial companions), we need to incorporate emotion detection from text in comparison to other modalities (face, voice, gestures) that get more attention from the scientific community.

To demonstrate our claim for emotion detection in text within HRI, we conducted experiments with humanoid robot NAO. We proposed quantitative research with surveys and trackable variables during the experiment (length of interaction and number of fables read) and qualitative research by asking our participants about the experiment to measure improved robot to human interaction. The results of the experiments show there is indeed positive feedback on the human side. From the questionnaire results, it is obvious adding gestures to robot increase positivity in interaction.

We used a lexicon approach and a machine learning approach for the emotion detection. Models for emotion classification were trained using various machine learning methods, as Naïve Bayes classifier, ConceptNet Numberbatch and feed-forward neural network using various data representations as Bag-of-Words, TF-IDF and sentence embeddings. Finally, the ensemble classifier, which consisted of the nine best models for each emotion, was used in scenarios with the humanoid robot NAO.

The results from emotion detection in text using machine learning approaches show an increase in precision and accuracy for each label. Adding additional features from emotional dictionary raised accuracy in some classes more, in some classes less. The biggest increase of accuracy can be seen in class *Disgust* = 90%, followed by *Joy* = 83%, *Anger* = 80%, *No emotion* = 71%, *Anticipation* = 67%, *Sadness* = 67%. The rest of the classes have accuracy equal to or lower than 50%. In comparison to baseline, it is negligible, but still present. Lastly, we observed a change in testing precision and accuracy when we added new data, annotated by K-means algorithm.

We see potential based on the obtained results in utilization of automatic emotion detection from text in human–robot interaction. As experiment 1C showed, the system did not have to be 100% accurate to arouse a positive response from the human. We can take a look from another angle as well: not showing happy gestures when the perceived emotion should be sad and vice-versa. That can transform into a classification as a problem where no occurrence of emotion should be observed.

**Author Contributions:** Conceptualization, M.S. (Martina Szabóová) and K.M.; methodology, M.S. (Martina Szabóová); software, M.S. (Martina Szabóová) and V.M.K.; validation, M.S. (Martina Szabóová) and V.M.K.; formal analysis, M.S. (Martina Szabóová) and M.S. (Martin Sarnovský); investigation, M.S. (Martina Szabóová), M.S. (Martin Sarnovský) and K.M.; resources, M.S. (Martina Szabóová) and M.S. (Martin Sarnovský); data curation, M.S. (Martina Szabóová); writing—original draft preparation, M.S. (Martina Szabóová), M.S. (Martin Sarnovský) and V.M.K.; writing—review and editing, M.S. (Martina Szabóová), K.M., M.S. (Martin Sarnovský) and V.M.K.; visualization, M.S. (Martina Szabóová); supervision, K.M.; project administration, K.M.; funding acquisition, K.M. All authors have read and agreed to the published version of the manuscript.

**Funding:** The work was supported by the Slovak Research and Development Agency under the contract No. APVV-16-0213 Knowledge-based approaches for intelligent analysis of big data and No. APVV-17-0267 Automated Recognition of Antisocial Behaviour in Online Communities.

**Conflicts of Interest:** The authors declare no conflict of interest.

### References

1. Chivarov, N.; Chikurtev, D.; Chivarov, S.; Pleva, M.; Ondas, S.; Juhar, J.; Yovchev, K. Case Study on Human-Robot Interaction of the Remote-Controlled Service Robot for Elderly and Disabled Care. *Comput. Inform.* **2020**, *38*, 1210–1236. [CrossRef]
2. Wada, K.; Shibata, T.; Saito, T.; Tanie, K. Analysis of factors that bring mental effects to elderly people in robot assisted activity. *IEEE Int. Conf. Intell. Robot. Syst.* **2002**, *2*, 1152–1157. [CrossRef]
3. Šabanovic, S.; Bennett, C.C.; Chang, W.L.; Huber, L. PARO robot affects diverse interaction modalities in group sensory therapy for older adults with dementia. *IEEE Int. Conf. Rehabil. Robot.* **2013**. [CrossRef]
4. Huang, T.; Huang, C. Elderly's acceptance of companion robots from the perspective of user factors. *Univers. Access Inf. Soc.* **2019**. [CrossRef]
5. De Albornoz, J.C.; Plaza, L.; Gervás, P. SentiSense: An easily scalable concept-based affective lexicon for sentiment analysis. In *Proceedings of the Eight International Conference on Language Resources and Evaluation (LREC'12)*; European Language Resources Association (ELRA): Istanbul, Turkey, 2012; pp. 23–25.
6. Taboada, M.; Brooke, J.; Tofiloski, M.; Voll, K.; Stede, M. Lexicon-Based Methods for Sentiment Analysis. *Comput. Linguist.* **2011**, *37*, 1–41. [CrossRef]

7. Szabo, P.; Machova, K. Various approaches to the opinion classification problems solving. In Proceedings of the 2012 IEEE 10th International Symposium on Applied Machine Intelligence and Informatics (SAMI), Herl'any, Slovakia, 26–28 January 2012, pp. 59–62. [CrossRef]
8. Mohammad, S.; Bravo-Marquez, F. WASSA-2017 Shared Task on Emotion Intensity. *arXiv* **2018**, arXiv:1708.03700. [CrossRef]
9. Gui, L.; Xu, R.; Lu, Q.; Wu, D.; Zhou, Y. Emotion cause extraction, a challenging task with corpus construction. In *Communications in Computer and Information Science*; Springer: Singapore, 2016; Volume 669, pp. 98–109. [CrossRef]
10. Ekman, P. Expression and the nature of emotion. *Approaches Emot.* **1984**, *3*, 344.
11. Amado-Boccara, I.; Donnet, D.; Olié, J.P. The concept of mood in psychology. *L'Encephale* **1993**, *19*, 117–122.
12. Grandjean, D.; Sander, D.; Scherer, K.R. Conscious emotional experience emerges as a function of multilevel, appraisal-driven response synchronization. *Conscious. Cogn.* **2008**, *17*, 484–495. [CrossRef]
13. Ortony, A.; Clore, G.L.; Collins, A. *The Cognitive Structure of Emotions*; Cambridge University Press: Cambridge, MA, USA 1988. [CrossRef]
14. Russell, J.A. A circumplex model of affect. *J. Personal. Soc. Psychol.* **1980**, *39*, 1161–1178. [CrossRef]
15. Lövheim, H. A new three-dimensional model for emotions and monoamine neurotransmitters. *Med. Hypotheses* **2012**, *78*, 341–348. [CrossRef]
16. Shuman, V.; Schlegel, K.; Scherer, K. *Geneva Emotion Wheel Rating Study PROPEREMO View Project A Developmental Perspective of Emotion Regulation View Project*; Technical Report; University of Geneva, Swiss Center for Affective Sciences: Geneva, Switzerland, 2016.
17. Ekman, P. What Scientists Who Study Emotion Agree About. *Perspect. Psychol. Sci.* **2016**, *11*, 31–34. [CrossRef]
18. Darwin, C. The Expression of the Emotions in Man and Animals. *J. Nerv. Ment. Dis.* **1956**, *123*, 90. [CrossRef]
19. Wundt, W. Grundriss der Psychologie. In *Grundriss der Psychologie, 13*; Leipzig, G., Ed.; Engelmann: Leipzig, Germany, 1896. [CrossRef]
20. Feil-seifer, D.; Mataric, M.J. Human-Robot Interaction. In *Encyclopedia of Complexity and Systems Science*; Springer: Berlin/Heidelberg, Germany 2009; pp. 4643–4659.
21. Fink, J. Anthropomorphism and human likeness in the design of robots and human-robot interaction. In *Lecture Notes in Computer Science (Including Subseries Lecture Notes in Artificial Intelligence and Lecture Notes in Bioinformatics)*; Springer: Berlin/Heidelberg, Germany 2012; Volume 7621 LNAI, pp. 199–208. [CrossRef]
22. Goodrich, M.A.; Schultz, A.C. Human-robot interaction: A survey. *Found. Trends Hum.* **2007**, *1*, 203–275. [CrossRef]
23. Zheng, X. Four memory categories to support socially-appropriate conversations in long-term HRI. In Proceedings of the Workshop on Personalization in Long-Term Human–Robot Interaction (14th Annual ACM/IEEE International Conference on Human–Robot Interaction), Daegu, Korea, 11–14 March 2019.
24. Richards, D.; Bransky, K. ForgetMeNot: What and how users expect intelligent virtual agents to recall and forget personal conversational content. *Int. J. Hum. Comput. Stud.* **2014**, *72*, 460–476. [CrossRef]
25. Lee, M.K.; Forlizzi, J.; Kiesler, S.; Rybski, P.; Antanitis, J.; Savetsila, S. Personalization in HRI: A longitudinal field experiment. In Proceedings of the 7th Annual ACM/IEEE International Conference on Human-Robot Interaction, Boston, MA, USA, 5–8 March 2012; pp. 319–326. [CrossRef]
26. Cao, H.L.; Van de Perre, G.; Kennedy, J.; Senft, E.; Esteban, P.G.; De Beir, A.; Simut, R.; Belpaeme, T.; Lefeber, D.; Vanderborght, B. A personalized and platform-independent behavior control system for social robots in therapy: development and applications. *IEEE Trans. Cogn. Dev. Syst.* **2018**. [CrossRef]
27. Churamani, N.; Anton, P.; Brügger, M.; Fliebwasser, E.; Hummel, T.; Mayer, J.; Mustafa, W.; Ng, H.G.; Nguyen, T.L.C.; Nguyen, Q.; et al The impact of personalisation on human-robot interaction in learning scenarios. In Proceedings of the 5th International Conference on Human Agent Interaction, Bielefeld, Germany, 17 October 2017; pp. 171–180. [CrossRef]
28. Iio, T.; Satake, S.; Kanda, T.; Hayashi, K.; Ferreri, F.; Hagita, N. Human-Like Guide Robot that Proactively Explains Exhibits. *Int. J. Soc. Robot.* **2019**. [CrossRef]
29. Kumagai, K.; Lin, D.; Mizuuchi, I.; Meng, L.; Blidaru, A.; Beesley, P.; Kulić, D. Towards Individualized Affective Human-Machine Interaction. In Proceedings of the 27th IEEE International Symposium on Robot and Human Interactive Communication, Nanjing, China, 27–31 August 2018; pp. 678–685. [CrossRef]

30. Kennedy, J.; Baxter, P.; Belpaeme, T. The Robot Who Tried Too Hard: Social Behaviour of a Robot Tutor Can Negatively Affect Child Learning. In Proceedings of the ACM/IEEE International Conference on Human-Robot Interaction, Portland, OR, USA, 2–5 March 2015; pp. 67–74. [CrossRef]
31. Gao, Y.; Barendregt, W.; Obaid, M.; Castellano, G. When Robot Personalisation Does Not Help: Insights from a Robot-Supported Learning Study. In Proceedings of the 27th IEEE International Symposium on Robot and Human Interactive Communication, Nanjing, China, 27–31 August 2018; pp. 705–712. [CrossRef]
32. Castellano, G.; Leite, I.; Pereira, A.; Martinho, C.; Paiva, A.; McOwan, P.W. Affect recognition for interactive companions: Challenges and design in real world scenarios. *J. Multimodal User Interfaces* **2010**, *3*, 89–98. [CrossRef]
33. Höök, K. Affective loop experiences: designing for interactional embodiment. *Philos. Trans. R. Soc. Biol. Sci.* **2009**, *364*, 3585–3595. [CrossRef]
34. Paiva, A.; Leite, I.; Ribeiro, T. Emotion Modelling for Social Robots. In *The Oxford Handbook of Affective Computing*; Oxford University Press: Oxford, UK, 2014. [CrossRef]
35. Picard, R.W. *Affective Computing*; MIT Press: Cambridge, MA, USA, 1997; Volume 73, p. 304. [CrossRef]
36. Mehrabian, A. *Nonverbal Communication*; Aldine Transaction: New Brunswick, NJ, USA, 1972.
37. Mehta, D.; Siddiqui, M.F.H.; Javaid, A.Y. Facial emotion recognition: A survey and real-world user experiences in mixed reality. *Sensors (Switzerland)* **2018**, *18*, 416. [CrossRef]
38. Sariyanidi, E.; Gunes, H.; Cavallaro, A. Automatic analysis of facial affect: A survey of registration, representation, and recognition. *IEEE Trans. Pattern Anal. Mach. Intell.* **2015**, *37*, 1113. [CrossRef]
39. Goulart, C.; Valadão, C.; Delisle-Rodriguez, D.; Funayama, D.; Favarato, A.; Baldo, G.; Binotte, V.; Caldeira, E.; Bastos-Filho, T. Visual and thermal image processing for facial specific landmark detection to infer emotions in a child-robot interaction. *Sensors (Switzerland)* **2019**, *19*, 2844. [CrossRef]
40. Liliana, D.Y.; Basaruddin, T.; Widyanto, M.R.; Oriza, I.I.D. Fuzzy emotion: a natural approach to automatic facial expression recognition from psychological perspective using fuzzy system. *Cogn. Process.* **2019**, *20*, 391–403. [CrossRef]
41. Kleinsmith, A.; Bianchi-Berthouze, N. Affective body expression perception and recognition: A survey. *IEEE Trans. Affect. Comput.* **2013**, *4*, 15–33. [CrossRef]
42. Dael, N.; Mortillaro, M.; Scherer, K.R. Emotion expression in body action and posture. *Emotion* **2012**, *12*, 1085–1101. [PubMed]
43. Witkower, Z.; Tracy, J.L. Bodily Communication of Emotion: Evidence for Extrafacial Behavioral Expressions and Available Coding Systems. *Emot. Rev.* **2018**. [CrossRef]
44. Bijlstra, G.; Holland, R.W.; Dotsch, R.; Wigboldus, D.H. Stereotypes and Prejudice Affect the Recognition of Emotional Body Postures. *Emotion* **2019**, *19*, 189–199. [CrossRef] [PubMed]
45. Vinciarelli, A.; Pantic, M.; Bourlard, H.; Pentland, A. Social signal processing: State-of-the-art and future perspectives of an emerging domain. In Proceedings of the 2008 ACM International Conference on Multimedia, with Co-Located Symposium and Workshops, Vancouver, BC, Canada, 12 October 2008; pp. 1061–1070. [CrossRef]
46. Swain, M.; Routray, A.; Kabisatpathy, P. Databases, features and classifiers for speech emotion recognition: A review. *Int. J. Speech Technol.* **2018**, *21*, 93–120. [CrossRef]
47. Mahani, M.A.N.; Sheybani, S.; Bausenhart, K.M.; Ulrich, R.; Ahmadabadi, M.N. Multisensory Perception of Contradictory Information in an Environment of Varying Reliability: Evidence for Conscious Perception and Optimal Causal Inference. *Sci. Rep.* **2017**, *7*. [CrossRef] [PubMed]
48. Desmet, B.; Hoste, V. Emotion Detection in Suicide Notes. *Expert Syst. Appl.* **2013**, *40*, 6351–6358. [CrossRef]
49. Wicentowski, R.; Sydes, M.R. Emotion Detection in Suicide Notes using Maximum Entropy Classification. *Biomed. Inform. Insights* **2012**, *5*, 51–60. [CrossRef] [PubMed]
50. Luyckx, K.; Vaassen, F.; Peersman, C.; Daelemans, W. Fine-grained emotion detection in suicide notes: A thresholding approach to multi-label classification. *Biomed. Inform. Insights* **2012**, *5*, 61–69. [PubMed]
51. Pak, A.; Bernhard, D.; Paroubek, P.; Grouin, C. A combined approach to emotion detection in suicide notes. *Biomed. Inform. Insights* **2012**, *5*, 105–114. [PubMed]
52. Bandhakavi, A.; Wiratunga, N.; Massie, S.; Padmanabhan, D. Lexicon Generation for Emotion Detection from Text. *IEEE Intell. Syst.* **2017**, *32*, 102–108. [CrossRef]

53. Alm, C.O.; Roth, D.; Sproat, R. *Emotions from Text*; Association for Computational Linguistics (ACL): Stroudsburg, PA, USA, 2005; pp. 579–586. [CrossRef]
54. Carlson, A.; Cumby, C.; Rosen, J.; Roth, D. *The SNoW Learning Architecture*; Technical Report UIUCDCS-R-99-2101; UIUC Computer Science Department: Champaign, IL, USA, 1999; p. 24.
55. Kratzwald, B.; Ilić, S.; Kraus, M.; Feuerriegel, S.; Prendinger, H. Deep learning for affective computing: Text-based emotion recognition in decision support. *Decis. Support Syst.* **2018**, *115*, 24–35. [CrossRef]
56. Khanpour, H.; Caragea, C. Fine-Grained Emotion Detection in Health-Related Online Posts. In *Proceedings of the 2018 Conference on Empirical Methods in Natural Language Processing*; Association for Computational Linguistics: Stroudsburg, PA, USA, 2019; pp. 1160–1166. [CrossRef]
57. Kim, E.; Klinger, R. Who Feels What and Why ? Annotation of a Literature Corpus with Semantic Roles of Emotions. In Proceedings of the 27th International Conference on Computational Linguistics, Santa Fe, NM, USA, 20–26 August 2018; pp. 1345–1359.
58. Gupta, U.; Chatterjee, A.; Srikanth, R.; Agrawal, P. A Sentiment-and-Semantics-Based Approach for Emotion Detection in Textual Conversations. *arXiv* **2017**, arXiv:1707.06996.
59. Chatterjee, A.; Gupta, U.; Chinnakotla, M.K.; Srikanth, R.; Galley, M.; Agrawal, P. Understanding Emotions in Text Using Deep Learning and Big Data. *Comput. Hum. Behav.* **2019**, *93*, 309–317. [CrossRef]
60. Strapparava, C.; Mihalcea, R. Learning to identify emotions in text. In Proceedings of the ACM Symposium on Applied Computing, Pau, France, 9–13 April 2008; pp. 1556–1560. [CrossRef]
61. Mohammad, S. #Emotional Tweets. In *SEM 2012: The First Joint Conference on Lexical and Computational Semantics – Volume 1: Proceedings of the main conference and the shared task, and Volume 2: Proceedings of the Sixth International Workshop on Semantic Evaluation (SemEval 2012)*; Association for Computational Linguistics: Montreal, QC, Canada, 2012; pp. 246–255.
62. Buechel, S.; Hahn, U. EmoBank: Studying the Impact of Annotation Perspective and Representation Format on Dimensional Emotion Analysis. In *Proceedings of the 15th Conference of the {E}uropean Chapter of the Association for Computational Linguistics: Volume 2, Short Papers*; Association for Computational Linguistics: Valencia, Spain, 2017; pp. 578–585.
63. Buechel, S.; Hahn, U. Readers vs. Writers vs. Texts: Coping with Different Perspectives of Text Understanding in Emotion Annotation. In Proceedings of the 11th Linguistic Annotation Workshop, Valencia, Spain, 3 April 2017; pp. 1–12. [CrossRef]
64. Mohammad, S.M.; Bravo-Marquez, F. Emotion intensities in tweets. In Proceedings of the SEM 2017—6th Joint Conference on Lexical and Computational Semantics, Proceedings, Vancouver, QC, Canada, 3–4 August 2017; pp. 65–77. [CrossRef]
65. Ben-Hur, A.; Weston, J. A user's guide to support vector machines. *Methods Mol. Biol.* **2010**. [CrossRef]
66. Ting, S.L.; Ip, W.H.; Tsang, A.H. Is Naïve bayes a good classifier for document classification? *Int. J. Softw. Eng. Appl.* **2011**, *5*, 37–46.
67. Sarnovský, M.; Butka, P.; Bednár, P.; Babič, F.; Paralič, J. Analytical platform based on Jbowl library providing text-mining services in distributed environment. In *Lecture Notes in Computer Science (Including Subseries Lecture Notes in Artificial Intelligence and Lecture Notes in Bioinformatics)*; Springer: Berlin/Heidelberg, Germany, 2015. [CrossRef]
68. Krešňáková, V.M.; Sarnovský, M.; Butka, P. Deep learning methods for Fake News detection. In Proceedings of the 2019 IEEE 19th International Symposium on Computational Intelligence and Informatics and 7th IEEE International Conference on Recent Achievements in Mechatronics, Automation, Computer Sciences and Robotics (CINTI-MACRo), Szeged, Hungary, 14–16 November 2019; pp. 000143–000148.
69. Goodfellow, I.; Bengio, Y.; Courville, A. *Deep Learning*; MIT Press: Cambridge, MA, USA, 2016.
70. Nair, V.; Hinton, G.E. Rectified linear units improve restricted boltzmann machines. In Proceedings of the 27th International Conference on International Conference on Machine Learning, Haifa, Israel, 21–24 June 2010; pp. 807–814.
71. Leshno, M.; Lin, V.Y.; Pinkus, A.; Schocken, S. Multilayer feedforward networks with a nonpolynomial activation function can approximate any function. *Neural Netw.* **1993**, *6*, 861–867. [CrossRef]
72. Kingma, D.P.; Ba, J. Adam: A method for stochastic optimization. *arXiv* **2014**, arXiv:1412.6980.
73. Hinton, G.E.; Srivastava, N.; Krizhevsky, A.; Sutskever, I.; Salakhutdinov, R.R. Improving neural networks by preventing co-adaptation of feature detectors. *arXiv* **2012**, arXiv:1207.0580.

74. Polyak, B.T. Some methods of speeding up the convergence of iteration methods. *USSR Comput. Math. Math. Phys.* **1964**, *4*, 1–17. [CrossRef]
75. Rumelhart, D.E.; Hinton, G.E.; Williams, R.J. Learning representations by back-propagating errors. *Nature* **1986**, *323*, 533–536. [CrossRef]
76. Chicco, D.; Jurman, G. The advantages of the Matthews correlation coefficient (MCC) over F1 score and accuracy in binary classification evaluation. *BMC Genom.* **2020**, *21*, 6. [CrossRef] [PubMed]

**Publisher's Note:** MDPI stays neutral with regard to jurisdictional claims in published maps and institutional affiliations.

© 2020 by the authors. Licensee MDPI, Basel, Switzerland. This article is an open access article distributed under the terms and conditions of the Creative Commons Attribution (CC BY) license (http://creativecommons.org/licenses/by/4.0/).

*Article*

# Research of HRV as a Measure of Mental Workload in Human and Dual-Arm Robot Interaction

**Shiliang Shao [1,2,*], Ting Wang [1,2], Yongliang Wang [1,2,3], Yun Su [1,2,3], Chunhe Song [1,2] and Chen Yao [1,2]**

1. State Key Laboratory of Robotics, Shenyang Institute of Automation, Chinese Academy of Sciences, Shenyang 110016, China; wangting@sia.cn (T.W.); wangyongliang@sia.cn (Y.W.); suyun@sia.cn (Y.S.); songchunhe@sia.cn (C.S.); cyao@sia.cn (C.Y.)
2. Institutes for Robotics and Intelligent Manufacturing, Chinese Academy of Sciences, Shenyang 110169, China
3. University of Chinese Academy of Sciences, Beijing 100049, China
* Correspondence: shaoshiliang@sia.cn

Received: 3 November 2020; Accepted: 13 December 2020; Published: 17 December 2020

**Abstract:** Robots instead of humans work in unstructured environments, expanding the scope of human work. The interactions between humans and robots are indirect through operating terminals. The mental workloads of human increase with the lack of direct perception to the real scenes. Thus, mental workload assessment is important, which could effectively avoid serious accidents caused by mental overloading. In this paper, the operating object is a dual-arm robot. The classification of operator's mental workload is studied by using the heart rate variability (HRV) signal. First, two kinds of electrocardiogram (ECG) signals are collected from six subjects who performed tasks or maintained a relaxed state. Then, HRV data is obtained from ECG signals and 20 kinds of HRV features are extracted. Last, six different classifications are used for mental workload classification. Using each subject's HRV signal to train the model, the subject's mental workload is classified. Average classification accuracy of 98.77% is obtained using the K-Nearest Neighbor (KNN) method. By using the HRV signal of five subjects for training and that of one subject for testing with the Gentle Boost (GB) method, the highest average classification accuracy (80.56%) is obtained. This study has implications for the analysis of HRV signals characteristic of mental workload in different subjects, which could improve operators' well-being and safety in the human-robot interaction process.

**Keywords:** human-robot interaction; mental workload; heart rate variability; machine learning

## 1. Introduction

In unstructured environments, robots replace humans to perform some complex tasks, which expends the scope of human work [1,2]. The dual-arm robot, a kind of typical robot, has been widely studied [3,4]. Dual-arm robots can simulate the movement of two arms of human, making an important step towards humanoid operation. Studies based on dual-arm robots have always moved towards the operation of humanization. In this paper, a dual-arm robot is studied as the operating object, which is controlled by a wearable exoskeleton controller in master-slave mode. The dual-arm robot's performance is not only limited by the performance of the system, but also related to the current state of the operator closely. Sometimes, a large mental workload can still lead to improper or wrong operation even when the system is stable and the operator has a good sense of presence. Therefore, it is crucial to monitor the mental workload of the operator. On this basis, the human-robot task assignment could be dynamically adjusted based on the mental workload. This kind of research improves human-robot system performance and safety and refine the subjective experience of operators. Therefore, it is of great theoretical significance and practical value to study the mental workload measurement of the operators of dual-arm robots.

In recent years, mental workload has gradually become a hot research topic. The concept was first proposed in the 1940s [5]; its purpose was to optimize the human–machine system. There are various definitions of mental workload; however, the primary content of the definitions is the relationship between 'requirement of resources for tasks' and 'ability of the operator to provide those resources' [6]. In reality, the traditional methods of evaluating mental workload are mainly subjective. However, the main defect of the subjective scale method is the lack of objectivity and continuity of measurement. Undeniably, the evaluation of mental workload by physiological signals, such as electroencephalogram (EEG) [7,8], respiration rate (RR) [9], blood pressure (BP) [10], skin temperature (ST) [11], galvanic skin response (GSR) [12], blink frequency (BF) [13], and heart rate variability (HRV) [14], has achieved some progress. Although more effective information can be obtained by using multi-sensors fusion to analyze mental workload, it causes great inconvenience to operators because they have to use a large number of electrodes, sensor units, and so on. HRV is the physiological phenomenon of fluctuation in the time interval between heartbeats. It is the most convenient and common physiological measurement method for mental workload. Thus, in this paper, HRV is studied as a measure of mental workload in human and dual-arm robot interaction.

The traditional mental workload measuring method using HRV is considered to be on the basis of time domain and frequency domain features. About the time domain features, the better performing ones are the standard deviation of the R-R interval (SDNN), the root mean square of the successive R-R interval difference (RMSSD), the proportion of the beats with a successive R-R interval difference exceeding 50 ms (PNN50), and the sum of all R-R intervals divided by the maximum density distribution (HRVTi) [15,16]. Moreover, in the frequency domain analysis method, the HRV signal is always decomposed into multi-frequency components. In fact, the power spectral of each frequency component and the sum of power spectral of all frequency bands are regarded as features for mental workload measurement. In detail, these features include power spectrum of very low frequency band (VLF: 0.003–0.040 Hz), low frequency band (LF: 0.04–0.15 Hz), high frequency band (HF: 0.15–0.4 Hz), and total power spectrum (TP: $\leq$ 0.4 Hz) [17,18]. However, the time domain indices cannot show the time-varying characteristics of HRV. Thus, it is limited for the response to the autonomic nervous system. Meanwhile, the frequency domain indices can only provide global frequency information, lacking in coupling information between local and different frequencies. A human body can be abstracted into a complex nonlinear system. Nevertheless, the time domain and frequency domain features of HRV signals are unable to express the nonlinear characteristics of HRV signals completely [19,20]. At present, relevant studies have used nonlinear analysis methods to analyze HRV signals for mental workload. Castaldo et al. [21] extracted the nonlinear features of HRV signals to achieve psychological load measurement analysis while playing games. Specifically, it includes Poincare plot, de-trending fluctuation analysis, recurrence plot, sample entropy, approximate entropy, and Shannon entropy, among others. Tiwari et al. [22] proposed an improved multi-scale permutation entropy analysis method to measure and analyze HRV signals. Finally, they accomplish the classification of mental workload in the process of MATB. Delliaux et al. [23] analyzed a variety of nonlinear features of HRV signals through statistical analysis.

However, there is no research on HRV as a measure of mental workload in human and dual-arm robot interaction. In this paper, HRV is studied as a measure of mental workload in human and dual-arm robot interaction. The main contributions of this work are summarized as follows: First, this paper extracts time domain features, frequency domain features, and nonlinear features of HRV signals, exploring the hidden layer of neural activity information deeply. Then, the mapping relationship between the HRV signal and mental workload is analyzed. In addition, models trained with the same subject data and across different subjects are researched, respectively.

The rest of the paper is structured as follows: In Section 2, the process of ECG data acquisition is described and the HRV signal extraction algorithm is presented. Additionally, the features extraction method is presented. Section 3 shows the experimental results, which reflect the statistical analysis of features and mental workload measures. The discussion of results are present in Section 4. In Section 5, the conclusion of this paper is presented.

## 2. Data and Methods

Firstly, the process of mental workload recognition in this paper is presented and shown in Figure 1. Then, the subjects that participated in the data acquisition are introduced, respectively. Subsequently, the data acquisition process is introduced and the features are extracted. Finally, the mental workload identification results based on the extraction features are presented.

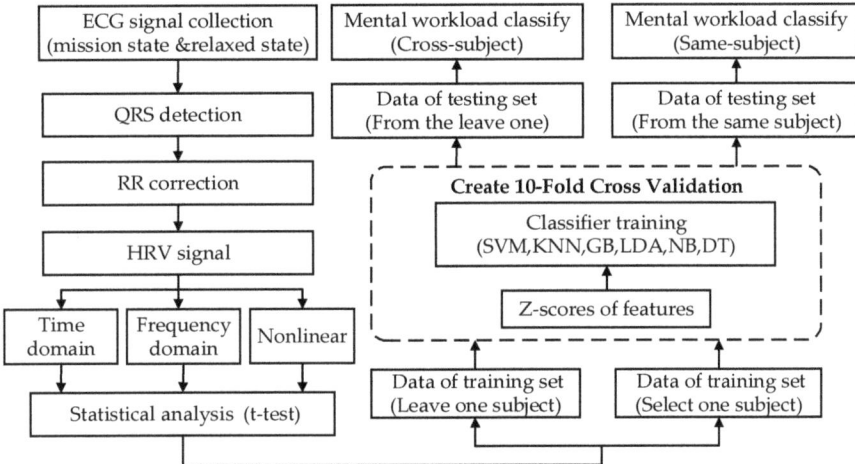

**Figure 1.** The processes of the mental workload classification based on HRV.

### 2.1. Participants

Subjects were, on average, 25.16 years old, and the study employed a total of six male participants, as shown in Table 1. They were selected from the Shenyang Institute of Automation, Chinese Academy of Sciences. They have normal or corrected vision, right-handedness, good health, and no heart, cerebrovascular, or nervous system problems. All participants were informed of the experiment, and participants were asked to wear loose and comfortable clothing.

**Table 1.** A description of the subjects.

|  | Gender | Stature (cm) | Weight (kg) | Age (year) | BMI |
| --- | --- | --- | --- | --- | --- |
| Subject1 | Male | 180 | 67.5 | 24 | 20.8 |
| Subject2 | Male | 175 | 78.5 | 24 | 25.6 |
| Subject3 | Male | 173 | 58 | 31 | 19.4 |
| Subject4 | Male | 180 | 55 | 23 | 17.0 |
| Subject5 | Male | 175 | 75 | 24 | 24.5 |
| Subject6 | Male | 178 | 72.5 | 25 | 22.9 |

### 2.2. Data Acquisition and Processing

The dual-arm robot utilized in this paper is shown in the Figure 2a. The robot has six independent driving wheels. Therefore, it can adapt to various complex topographic structures. Moreover, the robot is equipped with double arms, both with seven degrees of freedom, to imitate the number and structure of a human. The end of the arm is an open-close clamp, which can be used for precision operation. At the same time, the robot is equipped with a binocular camera, which can be used to enhance the operator's sense of presence. In order to facilitate operation, the manipulator of the dual-arm robot adopts a wearable controller, which is shown in Figure 2b. Obviously, the wearable controller has the same structure as arms of the dual-arm robot. Between the wearable controller and the dual-arm robot, the master-slave control mode is used, as shown in Figure 2c.

(**a**) Dual-arm robot.

(**b**) Wearable robot controller.

(**c**) Master-slave control mode.

**Figure 2.** Dual-arm robot and wearable controller.

The ECG signal acquisition sensor and software in this paper are shown in Figure 3a,b. The sensor is a portable chest strap that can be attached to the operator's chest. Additionally, The sensor is based on the BMD101 chip, which is the most widely used ECG signal acquisition sensor at present and can avoid interfering with the operator's normal operation. Then, the ECG data is transmitted via Bluetooth to a computer for collecting and displaying the ECG signals.

(**a**) ECG acquisition sensor

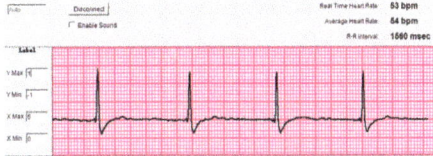

(**b**) ECG acquisition and display software

**Figure 3.** The operator's ECG signal acquisition system.

The flow chart of data acquisition is shown in Figure 4. Firstly, subjects read and sign the informed consent. Then, they are trained in operating the robot professionally. Only after passing the set assessment indicators can they participate in the experiment. Before the beginning of experiment, the ECG acquisition device needs to be placed on the subject's chest. Then the Karolinska Sleepiness Scale (KSS) is filled to determine the operator's sleepiness state. The KSS needs to be filled once the operator has completed their mission. After giving the operator a minute to concentrate, the experiment starts. ECG signals of each operator in two mental workload states are collected. The tasks performed under each level of mental workload are defined as follows: (1) The task of mental workload level 1: The operator does not perform any task and maintains a relaxed state. (2) The task of mental workload level 2: The operator operates the arms of robot to follow a specified trajectory. ECG signals of the operator are collected at each task for 10 min. At the end of the task, the data records are checked and the ECG acquisition equipment on the subject is removed. The experiment ends. A 3 min sliding window is used to process the data, which slides for 10 s each time. The sliding window segments the 10-min data of each state of each subject. Furthermore, the three-minute segments obtained are used for the identification and classification of the two mental workload states.

**Figure 4.** Flow chart of sample data collection.

The HRV is shown in Figure 5, which is obtained by ECG signal collected by sensor. In reality, the HRV signal is defined as the fluctuation in continuous RR intervals. Hence, for the sake of getting the HRV sequence from the ECG signal, a QRS wave group detection method is utilized to detect the Q wave, R wave, and S wave [24]. Nevertheless, the abnormal point maybe present in the HRV signal that is output by the QRS wave group detection method. In order to remove the exception value, a median filtering method is utilized [25].

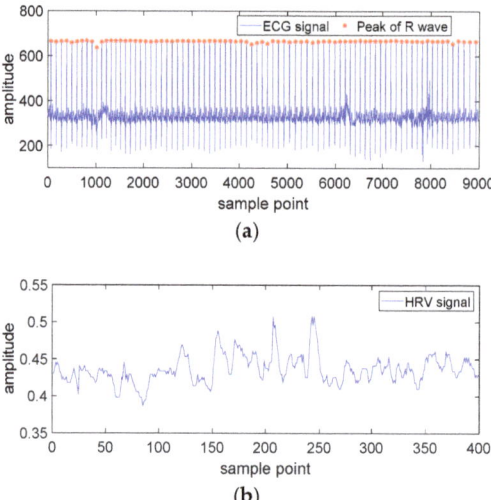

**Figure 5.** The ECG signal and HRV signal. (**a**) The obtained ECG signal. (**b**) The extracted HRV signal.

*2.3. Feature Extraction*

In this sub-section, extracting features from the HRV data obtained is presented. During the operation of the dual-arm robot operation tasks, the change of mental workload of operator is related to the volatility of sympathetic and parasympathetic nerve closely. In fact, the time domain features of the HRV signal reflect the overall volatility of the autonomic nervous system reaction. Additionally, frequency domain features of high frequency are related to the intensity of the modulation of parasympathetic nerve. Nevertheless, the low frequency band is influenced more by sympathetic nervous regulation. In addition, nonlinear features are expressed the chaotic and dynamic characteristics of HRV signal.

2.3.1. Linear Features

1. Time domain features

The main features used in time domain is shown in Table 2. They are SDNN, RMSSD, RMSSD, PNN50, and HRVTi. In addition, the mean and median of the HRV signal are also extracted as features.

**Table 2.** Statistical features in the time domain.

| Index | Unit | Definition and Description |
|---|---|---|
| SDNN | ms | The standard deviation of all successive R-R intervals. $$\text{SDNN} = \sqrt{\frac{1}{N}\sum_{i=1}^{N}\left(RRs_i - \frac{1}{N}\sum_{i=1}^{N}RRs_i\right)}$$ |
| RMSSD | ms | The root mean square of the successive R-R interval difference. $$\text{RMSSD} = \sqrt{\frac{1}{N-1}\sum_{i=1}^{N-1}(RRs_{i+1} - RRs_i)^2}$$ |
| PNN50 | % | The proportion of the beats with a successive R-R interval difference that exceed 50 ms. $$\text{PNN50} = \frac{num[(RRs_{i+1} - RRs_i) > 50]}{N-1}$$ |
| HRVTi | — | The sum of all R-R intervals divided by the maximum density distribution. |

2. Frequency domain features

The all frequency features used in this paper are based on the power spectra density. In this paper, a Lomb–Scamble periodic graph is used to calculate the power spectral density, which has a higher estimation accuracy than the FFT-based method [26]. The detailed description and definition are shown in Table 3.

Table 3. Statistical features in the frequency domain.

| Index | Unit | Definition and Description | Frequency |
|---|---|---|---|
| Total Power (aTotal) | $ms^2$ | The sum of the power spectra for all frequency ranges. | ≤0.4 Hz |
| aVLF | $ms^2$ | The sum of the power spectra for all frequency ranges. | 0.003–0.04 Hz |
| aLF | $ms^2$ | The sum of the power spectra for all frequency ranges. | 0.04–0.15 Hz |
| aHF | $ms^2$ | The sum of the power spectra for all frequency ranges. | 0.15–0.4 Hz |
| LF/HF | % | The ratio of LF $[ms^2]$ and HF $[ms^2]$ | / |
| pVLF | % | The ratio of aVLF $[ms^2]$ and TP $[ms^2]$ | / |
| pLF | % | The ratio of aLF $[ms^2]$ and TP $[ms^2]$ | / |
| pHF | % | The ratio of LF $[ms^2]$ and HF $[ms^2]$ | / |
| nLF | % | The ratio of aLF $[ms^2]$ and (aLF + aHF) $[ms^2]$ | / |
| nHF | % | The ratio of aHF $[ms^2]$ and (aLF + aHF) $[ms^2]$ | / |

2.3.2. Nonlinear Features

1. Sample Entropy (SaEn):

SaEn is a method that can be used for the measurement of physiological signal complexity. SaEn is a probability of two HRV signals matching at a length of $m + 1$ if they match at $m$. In addition, a tolerance parameter $r$ will determine the match result. In this paper, the value of $m$ is set to 2, and the value of $r$ is defined as $0.2 \times std$. The *std* in this paper represents the standard deviation of the input HRV data [27].

2. Detrended Fluctuation Analysis (DFA):

DFA can be used for the statistical self-affinity of physiological signal, which is used for removing the trend of a series of events. Especially, it can reflect the information about the long-term correlation in the HRV signal. Furthermore, it has been widely used in HRV signal analysis [28]. The fluctuations of the HRV signal can express as a function of time intervals: $F(n) = pn^{Alpha}$ where $p$ is a constant and *Alpha* is a scale factor. $F$ represents the fluctuations of HRV and $n$ is time intervals. The HRV signal fluctuations will be altered by changing the parameter $n$. Two parameters of *Alpha1* and *Alpha2* are defined as the slop of $F(n)$, which is a function of log$n$ in different time range.

3. Results

Using the time domain, frequency domain and nonlinear analysis method above, the HRV signals are analyzed when the subjects are in performing the task and relaxing state, respectively. Firstly, a t-test is used and the statistical significance of the extracted time domain, frequency domain, and nonlinear features are analyzed. Then, the features with statistical differences are selected for the classification of mental workload. Furthermore, for the sake of excluding the effects of classifier performance differences, six classifier algorithms are selected to identify and classify the mental workload, which are Support Vector Machine (SVM), Linear Discriminant Analysis (LDA), K-Nearest Neighbor (KNN), Decision Tree (DT), Gentle Boost (GB), and Naive Bayes (NB). The default parameters are selected as the parameters of the six classification algorithms in this paper. In addition, the HRV signals under different mental workload are divided into testing set and training set based on 10-fold cross-validation. Furthermore, the performance of mental workload levels are classified and evaluated by three indicators, which are defined as follows:

$$\text{Accuracy}: \text{Acc} = \frac{TP + TN}{TP + FP + TN + FN} \times 100\%;$$

$$\text{Sensitivity}: \text{Sen} = \frac{TP}{TP + FN} \times 100\%;$$

$$\text{Specificity}: \text{Spe} = \frac{TN}{FP + TN} \times 100\%.$$

where *TP* is defined as those samples in which the predicted and actual values are both positive. *FP* is defined as those samples that are classified as positive samples, but they are actually negative samples. *FN* is defined as those samples that are predicted to be negative samples, but their actual values are positive. Additionally, *TN* is defined as the actual values of samples that are positive but that are predicted to be negative. In this paper, the performing task state samples are defined as positive samples and the relaxing state samples are defined as negative samples.

*3.1. Statistical Analysis of Features*

3.1.1. Statistical Difference Analysis of Features from the Same Subject

Using the t-test, the statistical differences of time domain, frequency domain, and nonlinear features are analyzed in the same subject at different states (performing task state and relaxing state). Defining the sample set of subject1's performing task state as S1-M, sample set of subject1's relaxing state as S1-R. Meanwhile, the sample set of subject2's, subject3's, subject4's, subject5's, and subject6's different lengths of time is defined by this rule.

Table 4 shows the statistical differences among 6 subjects. Moreover, each subject has two different mental workload states (performing task state and relaxing state). In detail, Table 4 shows the statistical differences of time domain, frequency domain and nonlinear features. It can be seen that there are total 87 features that are most significant differences ($p < 0.001$) between two different mental workload states from Table 4.

Among them, subject1 has 20 features with most significant differences ($p < 0.001$), which consist of six time domain features, 10 frequency domain features, and four nonlinear features.

Subject2 has 13 features with most significant differences ($p < 0.001$), which consist of six time domain features, five frequency domain features, and two nonlinear features.

Subject3 has 15 features with most significant differences ($p < 0.001$), which consist of six time domain features, seven frequency domain features, and two nonlinear features.

Subject4 has 16 features with most significant differences ($p < 0.001$), which consist of five time domain features, seven frequency domain features, and four nonlinear features.

Subject5 has nine features with most significant differences ($p < 0.001$), which consist of five time domain features, and four frequency domain features.

Subject6 has 14 features with most significant differences ($p < 0.001$), which consist of five time domain features, five frequency domain features, and four nonlinear features.

Table 4. Statistical analysis results of HRV time domain, frequency domain, and nonlinear features.

|  |  | S1-M and S1-R | S2-M and S2-R | S3-M and S3-R | S4-M and S4-R | S5-M and S5-R | S6-M and S6-R |
|---|---|---|---|---|---|---|---|
| Time Domain | HRVTi | 0 *** | 0 *** | 0 *** | 0 *** | 0 *** | 0 *** |
|  | Mean | 0 *** | 0 *** | 0 *** | 0 *** | 0 *** | 0 *** |
|  | SDNN | 0 *** | 0 *** | 0 *** | 0 *** | 0 *** | 0 *** |
|  | Median | 0 *** | 0 *** | 0 *** | 0 *** | 0 *** | 0 *** |
|  | PNN50 | 0 *** | 0 *** | 0 *** | 0.28 | 0 *** | 0 *** |
|  | RMSSD | 0 *** | 0 *** | 0 *** | 0 *** | 0.15 | 0.16 |
|  | aHF | 0 *** | 0 *** | 0 *** | 0 *** | 0.06 | 0.61 |
|  | aLF | 0 *** | 0 *** | 0.02 * | 0 *** | 0.06 | 0.02 * |
|  | aTotal | 0 *** | 0 *** | 0 *** | 0 *** | 0.013 * | 0.19 |
|  | aVLF | 0 *** | 0 *** | 0.002 ** | 0 *** | 0 *** | 0 *** |
| Frequency Domain | LF/HF | 0 *** | 0.41 | 0 *** | 0.015 * | 0.004 ** | 0.05 |
|  | nHF | 0 *** | 0.08 | 0 *** | 0.24 | 0.56 | 0.07 |
|  | nLF | 0 *** | 0.08 | 0 *** | 0.24 | 0.56 | 0 *** |
|  | pHF | 0 *** | 0 *** | 0 *** | 0 *** | 0 *** | 0 *** |
|  | pLF | 0 *** | 0.02 * | 0 *** | 0 *** | 0 *** | 0 *** |
|  | pVLF | 0 *** | 0.008 ** | 0.13 | 0 *** | 0 *** | 0 *** |
| Nonlinear | SaEn | 0 *** | 0 *** | 0 *** | 0 *** | 0.16 | 0 *** |
|  | Alpha | 0 *** | 0.12 | 0.41 | 0 *** | 0.003 ** | 0 *** |
|  | Alpha1 | 0 *** | 0 *** | 0 *** | 0 *** | 0.27 | 0 *** |
|  | Alpha2 | 0 *** | 0.88 | 0.45 | 0 *** | 0.009 ** | 0 *** |

*, **, *** represent $p < 0.05$, $p < 0.01$, $p < 0.001$, respectively.

### 3.1.2. Statistical difference analysis of features cross the different subject

Using the t-test, the statistical differences of time domain, frequency domain, and nonlinear features are analyzed cross the different subject at different states (perform task state and relaxed state). The sample set of subject1's, subject2's, subject3's, subject4's, subject5's, and subject6's performing task state is defined as the CM group and the sample set of subject1's–subject6's in the relaxing state is defined as CR group.

Table 5 shows the statistical differences between two different mental workload state sample sets. Table 5 shows time domain and nonlinear features and Table 5 shows frequency domain features. It can be seen from Table 5 that there are 18 most significant difference ($p < 0.001$) features in the two groups of CM and CR.

Table 5. Statistical analysis results of HRV time domain, frequency domain, and nonlinear features.

|  |  | CM and CR |
|---|---|---|
| Time Domain | HRVTi | 0 *** |
|  | Mean | 0 *** |
|  | SDNN | 0 *** |
|  | Median | 0 *** |
|  | PNN50 | 0 *** |
|  | RMSSD | 0 *** |
|  | aHF | 0 *** |
|  | aLF | 0 *** |
|  | aTotal | 0 *** |
|  | aVLF | 0 *** |
| Frequency Domain | LF/HF | 0.054 |
|  | nHF | 0 *** |
|  | nLF | 0 *** |
|  | pHF | 0 *** |
|  | pLF | 0.60 |
|  | pVLF | 0 *** |
| Nonlinear | SaEn | 0 *** |
|  | Alpha | 0 *** |
|  | Alpha1 | 0 *** |
|  | Alpha2 | 0 *** |

*, **, *** represent $p < 0.05$, $p < 0.01$, $p < 0.001$, respectively.

## 3.2. Mental Workload Classification Based on the Same Subject

The classification and identification of mental workload are carried out on six subjects, respectively. Additionally, the features with statistical differences are selected for the classification of mental workload. The sample datasets for each experiment are divided into training set and testing set. In order to verify the classification performance of features, a total of six classification algorithms are used in this paper so each subject has trained six models. In this paper, there are six experimental subjects and 6 × 6 = 36 models are trained. The average value of 10-fold cross-validation is used as the final experimental result. In order to ensure the reliability of the experimental results, the 10-fold cross-validation is repeated 100 times.

Figure 6 and Table 6 are the classification results for each subject using different classifiers, as can be seen from Figure 6a and Table 6. SVM, KNN, and GB show better classification results for subject1. In addition, the KNN classification algorithm shows the highest Spe, Sen, and Acc: 99.26%, 98.86%, and 98.91%, respectively. It can be seen from Figure 6b and Table 6 that SVM, KNN GB, NB, and DT show better classification results for subject2. In addition, the KNN classification algorithm shows the highest Spe, Sen, and Acc: 99.99%, 98.94%, and 99.95%, respectively. It can be seen from Figure 6c and Table 6, for the subject3. LDA shows the worst classification effect and the KNN classification algorithm shows the highest Spe, Sen, and Acc: 99.15%, 99.07%, and 98.84%, respectively. As Figure 6d and Table 6 demonstrate, SVM, KNN, GB, and DT show better classification results for subject4. The SVM classification algorithm shows the highest Spe (98.43%) and KNN classification algorithm shows the highest Sen and Acc: 97.61% and 96.45%, respectively. As can be seen from Figure 6e and Table 6, for the subject5, all five classification algorithms, except LDA, show good performance of classification. The SVM classification algorithm shows the best Spe, Sen, and Acc: 99.97%, 99.99%, and 99.97%, respectively. It can be seen from Figure 6f and Table 6 that the KNN classification algorithm shows the highest Spe, Sen, and Acc: 98.61%, 99.34%, and 98.64%, respectively.

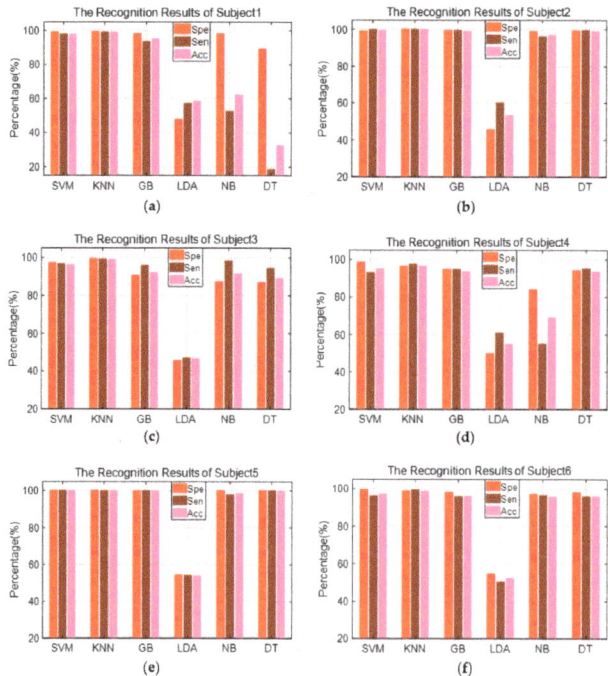

**Figure 6.** The classification results of each subject under different classifiers.

Table 6. The classification results of each subject under different classifiers.

| Subject | | S1 | S2 | S3 | S4 | S5 | S6 | Mean | std |
|---|---|---|---|---|---|---|---|---|---|
| SVM | Spe | 98.84 | 99.01 | 97.20 | 98.43 | 99.97 | 99.34 | 98.80 | 2.03 |
| | Sen | 97.81 | 99.86 | 96.72 | 92.95 | 99.99 | 95.96 | 97.22 | 0.39 |
| | Acc | 97.76 | 99.36 | 96.17 | 94.93 | 99.97 | 97.03 | 97.54 | 3.03 |
| KNN | Spe | 99.26 | 99.99 | 99.15 | 96.22 | 99.91 | 98.61 | 98.86 | 1.80 |
| | Sen | 98.86 | 99.94 | 99.07 | 97.61 | 99.78 | 99.34 | 99.10 | 0.11 |
| | Acc | 98.91 | 99.95 | 98.84 | 96.45 | 99.81 | 98.64 | 98.77 | 1.49 |
| GB | Spe | 98.20 | 99.25 | 90.61 | 94.71 | 99.75 | 97.90 | 96.74 | 2.03 |
| | Sen | 93.37 | 99.49 | 95.83 | 94.77 | 99.85 | 95.670 | 96.50 | 0.39 |
| | Acc | 94.95 | 99.10 | 92.09 | 93.65 | 99.70 | 95.90 | 95.90 | 3.03 |
| LDA | Spe | 47.67 | 45.58 | 45.46 | 49.78 | 54.3 | 54.47 | 49.54 | 24.83 |
| | Sen | 57.22 | 60.07 | 46.83 | 61.02 | 54.21 | 50.30 | 54.94 | 22.95 |
| | Acc | 52.53 | 53.31 | 46.69 | 54.94 | 53.92 | 52.23 | 52.27 | 22.70 |
| NB | Spe | 98.07 | 98.90 | 87.12 | 83.84 | 99.88 | 96.80 | 94.10 | 18.81 |
| | Sen | 18.43 | 96.08 | 98.31 | 54.93 | 97.65 | 96.28 | 76.95 | 22.58 |
| | Acc | 58.44 | 96.84 | 91.45 | 69.16 | 98.49 | 95.58 | 84.99 | 22.03 |
| DT | Spe | 89.05 | 99.21 | 86.73 | 94.13 | 99.91 | 97.75 | 94.46 | 24.83 |
| | Sen | 32.55 | 99.45 | 94.27 | 95.14 | 99.89 | 95.72 | 86.17 | 22.95 |
| | Acc | 62.04 | 99.03 | 89.10 | 93.64 | 99.84 | 95.78 | 89.91 | 22.70 |

Finally, the Spe, Sen, and Acc of the six subjects under different classification are presented in box plots (Figure 7). Box plots not only show the average values, but the distribution of the computed values can also be given. Additionally, the abnormal values are given by red points. As can be seen from the figure, while using the KNN classifier, all 6 subjects exhibit highest Spe, Sen, and Acc, with the least overall discreteness. However, in Spe and Acc, outliers appear. While using the SVM classifier, the six subjects perform higher Spe, Sen, and Acc, and the data are less discrete. Comparing with KNN and SVM classifiers, the GB classifier shows a large degree of discreteness but the classification results are stable. The performance of classification of the DT classifier is slightly worse than GB. The classification results of LDA and NB classifiers are the least satisfactory, with Spe, Sen, and Acc of LDA being lower, while the Spe, Sen, and Acc of NB classifier are the most discrete.

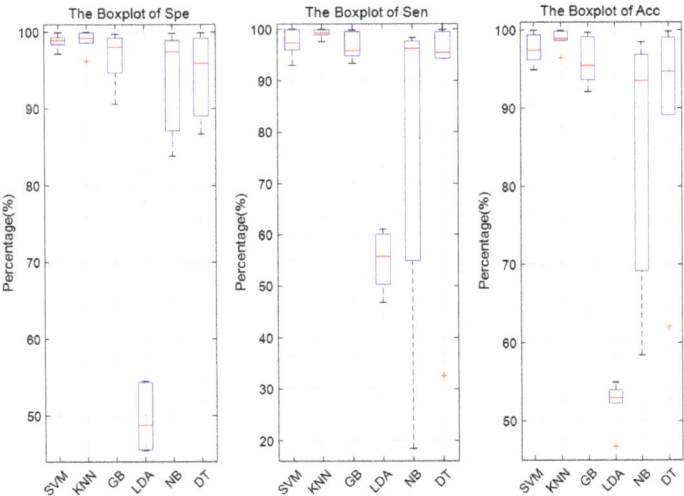

Figure 7. The box plots of Spe, Sen, Acc for six subjects.

## 3.3. Mental Workload Classification Cross Subject

In this sub-section, the performance differences of cross-subject mental workload classification are analyzed. The features with statistical differences are selected for the classification of mental workload. Samples of five subjects are used as a training set and samples of the leave-out subject who is not involved in the training are used as the testing set. Since there are six subjects, the validation process is performed six times.

Figure 8 and Table 7 are cross-subject classification results using different classifiers. As can be seen from Figure 8 and Table 7, for subject1, the KNN classification algorithm shows the highest Sen (100%), and the GB method shows the highest Spe (100%) and Acc (91.18%). For subject2, SVM and GB methods show the highest Spe (100%). At the same time, the GB method also shows the highest Spe (100%) and Acc (100%). For subject3, the LDA classification algorithm shows the best classification performance. The Spe, Sen, and Acc are 78.43%, 100.00%, and 89.22%, respectively. For subject4, SVM shows the highest Sen (98.43%). The KNN method shows the highest Acc (95.1%). Te NB method shows the highest Spe (100%). For subject5, SVM shows the highest Acc (81.76%). GB and DT show the highest Spe (100%) and the NB method shows the highest Spe (100%). For subject6, both SVM and KNN methods show the highest Spe (84.31%). SVM shows the best Acc (91.18%) and the NB method shows the highest Sen (100%).

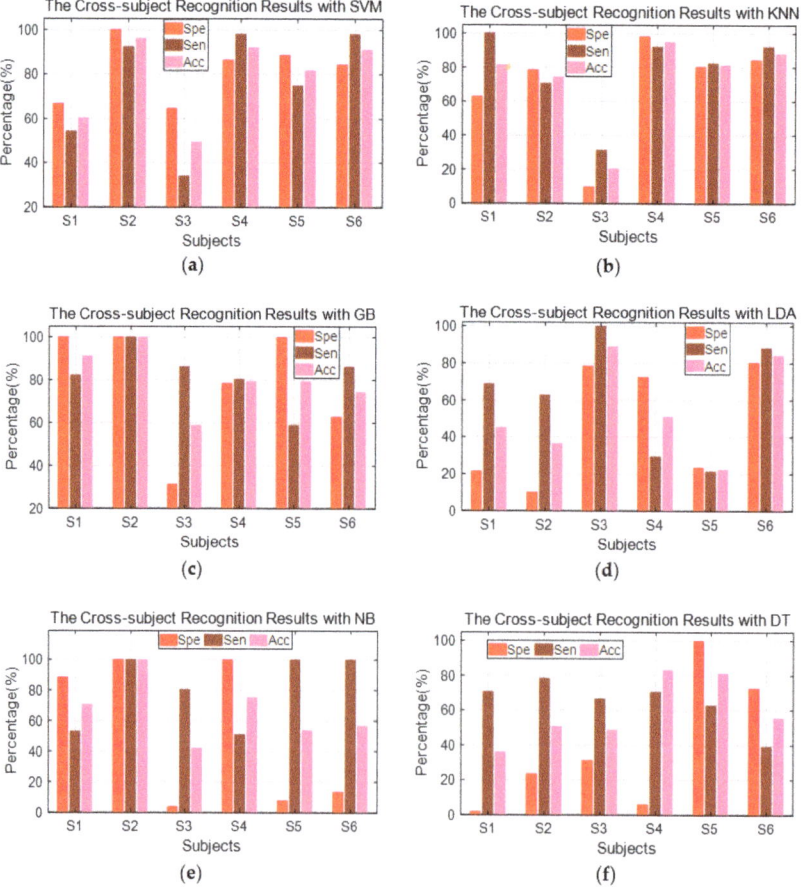

**Figure 8.** The cross-subject classification results under different classifiers.

**Table 7.** The classification results of cross-subject under different classifiers.

| Subject | | S1 | S2 | S3 | S4 | S5 | S6 | Mean | std |
|---|---|---|---|---|---|---|---|---|---|
| | Spe | 66.67 | 100 | 64.71 | 86.27 | 88.63 | 84.31 | 81.77 | 13.60 |
| SVM | Sen | 54.12 | 92.35 | 34.12 | 98.04 | 74.90 | 98.04 | 75.26 | 26.34 |
| | Acc | 60.39 | 96.18 | 49.41 | 92.16 | 81.76 | 91.18 | 78.51 | 19.21 |
| | Spe | 62.75 | 78.43 | 9.80 | 98.04 | 80.39 | 84.31 | 68.95 | 31.11 |
| KNN | Sen | 100 | 70.59 | 31.37 | 92.16 | 82.35 | 92.16 | 78.11 | 25.03 |
| | Acc | 81.37 | 74.51 | 20.59 | 95.10 | 81.37 | 88.24 | 73.53 | 26.86 |
| | Spe | 100 | 100 | 31.37 | 78.43 | 100 | 62.75 | 78.76 | 27.77 |
| GB | Sen | 82.35 | 100 | 86.27 | 80.39 | 58.82 | 86.27 | 82.35 | 13.41 |
| | Acc | 91.18 | 100 | 58.82 | 79.41 | 79.41 | 74.51 | 80.56 | 14.16 |
| | Spe | 21.57 | 10.05 | 78.43 | 72.55 | 23.53 | 80.39 | 46.08 | 35.09 |
| LDA | Sen | 68.63 | 62.75 | 100 | 29.41 | 21.57 | 88.24 | 61.77 | 31.25 |
| | Acc | 45.10 | 36.40 | 89.22 | 50.98 | 22.55 | 84.31 | 53.92 | 27.38 |
| | Spe | 88.24 | 100 | 3.92 | 100 | 7.84 | 13.73 | 52.29 | 48.26 |
| NB | Sen | 52.94 | 100 | 80.39 | 50.98 | 100 | 100 | 80.72 | 23.54 |
| | Acc | 70.59 | 100 | 42.16 | 75.49 | 53.92 | 56.86 | 66.50 | 20.31 |
| | Spe | 1.96 | 23.53 | 31.37 | 6.08 | 100 | 72.55 | 39.25 | 38.99 |
| DT | Sen | 70.59 | 78.43 | 66.67 | 70.59 | 62.75 | 39.22 | 64.71 | 13.53 |
| | Acc | 36.27 | 50.98 | 49.02 | 83.33 | 81.37 | 55.88 | 59.48 | 18.87 |

Finally, the results of cross-subject classification under different classifiers are presented in box plots (Figure 9). As can be seen from the figure, there are higher maximums of Spe, Sen, and Acc regardless of the classifier used. However, the figure also shows a more discrete distribution result and the red points represent abnormal values. The difference between the maximum and minimum values is large. In addition, for each subject, there is a classifier that achieves better classification results.

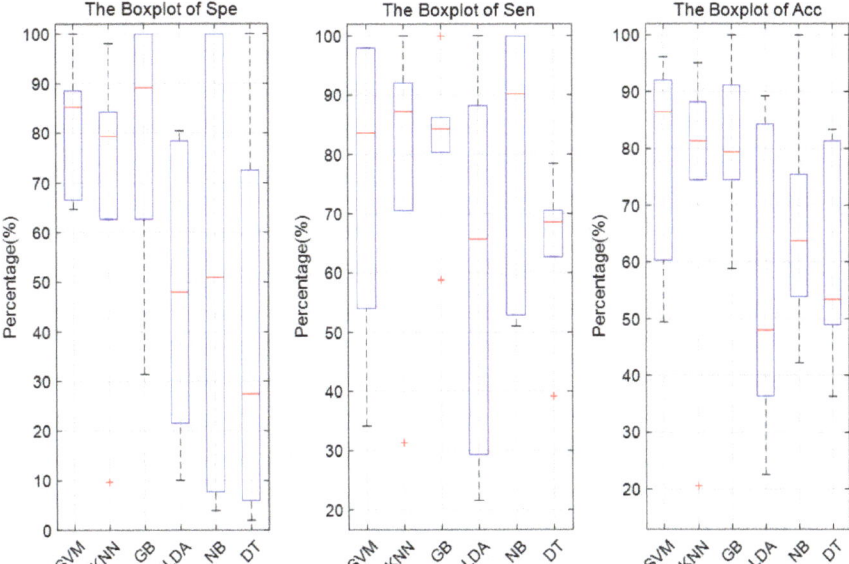

**Figure 9.** The box plots of Spe, Sen, and Acc for cross-subject classification.

## 4. Discussion

To the best of our knowledge, this is the first work to measure the operator's mental workload in human and dual-arm robot interaction process based on wearable exoskeleton controller. At present, many of the studies on mental workload are aimed at the n-back paradigm, simulated driving scenarios, and so on. In the process of interaction between human and dual-arm robot of this paper, the operator adopts the wearable controller. Additionally, the two arms of the dual-arm robot imitate the arms of human. This control mode of master-slave aims to reduce the operator's burden in the process of human and dual-arm robot interaction as much as possible. In addition, this control mode also excludes the operator's limb coordination ability differences, which significantly focuses the operator on the task. The study of mental workload in the process of human and dual-arm robot interaction has not been found. In addition, there is no corresponding public datasets. Thus, in this paper, the ECG signal data is collected. According to the ECG signals, the HRV for analysis is extracted.

Studies have shown that a stress response occurs [29] when the mental workload of the human increases. First, the sympathetic nervous system will be activated. Then the entire nervous system will respond to the increase of mental workload and improve human alertness. Furthermore, blood is transferred from the internal organs and skin to the skeletal muscles. Then the heart rate and heart contraction increase rapidly. These changes allow the body to accumulate large amounts of energy in a short period of time to prepare for external threats. Furthermore, the HRV signal contains information about the regulation of the cardiovascular system by body fluid factors, which can reflect fluctuations of the autonomic nervous system. Therefore, it is feasible to use the HRV signal for mental workload analysis.

More specifically, the existing studies show that the aTotal feature reflects the whole activity of the autonomic nervous system. LF-relative features are thought to be associated with sympathetic activity. HF-relative features are thought to have correlation between the parasympathetic activity. The physiological significance of the VLF-relative features have been identified with long-period rhythms. The relationship between LF components and HF components (LF/HF) is an important indicator of the sympathetic and parasympathetic balance in the body [30,31]. The SDNN index and HRVTi feature are believed to primarily measure autonomic influence on HRV [32]. Both RMSSD and PNN50 reflect parasympathetic (vagal) activity. Nonlinear features represent the fluctuation characteristics of the autonomic nervous system [33].

In this paper, the time domain features, frequency domain features, and nonlinear features between two mental workload states of the same subject or across different subjects, most features show statistical differences. Only individual features do not show statistical differences, which may be due to personalized differences between subjects. This does not affect the classification of the two mental workload states. Firstly, this paper analyzes the different mental workload states of the same subject. The results show that, for subject1–subject6, the highest Acc are 98.91% (KNN), 99.95% (KNN), 98.84% (KNN), 96.45% (KNN), 99.97% (SVM), and 98.64% (KNN), respectively. The KNN classifier has the highest average recognition accuracy (98.77%) when using the same classifier to identify six subjects separately. The SVM and GB classifiers also show good classification, with the Acc being 97.54% and 95.90%, respectively. None of the remaining three classifiers (LDA, NB, DT) have a classification accuracy rate of more than 90%. Therefore, the KNN algorithm is more suitable for the human and dual-arm robot interaction, using the sample data training model of the same subject and classifying the mental workload of the subject. Then, the different mental workload states cross-subject are classified. The results show that, for subject1–subject6, the highest Acc are 91.18% (GB), 100% (GB), 89.22% (LDA), 95.10% (KNN), 81.76% (SVM), and 91.18% (SVM). Thus, the average classification accuracy of the six subjects classifying using different classifiers is 91.41%. In the case of using the same classifier for the six subjects, the average accuracy of cross-subject identification is 80.56% (GB). Additionally, SVM and KNN also show good classification results, with classification accuracy of 78.51% and 73.53%, respectively. When identifying across subjects, each subject has a classifier that makes it better classified. Therefore, in the future, multiple classifiers should be considered for use and use the voting method to select the best classifier's classification results.

The analysis of mental workload is related to specific tasks and the study of mental workload in the process of master-to-slave interaction between a wearable controller and a dual-arm robot have not been reported. Therefore, this paper chooses to compare the studies related to mental workload or stress in other scenarios. In [34], a pilot study is conducted on whether machine learning can predict stress decrease after relaxation on the basis of a wearable sensor. The status before and after relaxation is classified using the ECG and GSR signals for 79.2% classification accuracy. In [35], detection of drivers' anxiety based on physiological signals is studied. The results show that classification on the basis of EEG alone shows the best accuracy, it is 77.01%. In [36], the cross-subject mental workload classification is studied on the basis of kernel spectral regression and transfer learning techniques. An average Acc of 72.66% is obtained for six subjects, the Acc of six subjects are 73.15%, 77.32%, 78.63%, 65.40%, 71.08%, and 70.36%, respectively. In [37], using wearable sensors, the mental workload of human and robot collaboration is analyzed. However, it is only the statistical analysis of HRV signals in different mental workload states. In addition, there is no study of classification and identification. In this paper, the data of two different mental workload states are collected and 20 kinds of HRV features are extracted. Then, the statistical significance of HRV signal features are analyzed in different states. The features with statistical differences ($p < 0.05$) are selected for the identification and analysis of mental workload. Models trained with the same subject data and models trained across different subjects all obtained higher Acc compared with [34–37].

In addition, in this paper, the heart beat data collection device is a custom one. Its functionality can be modified based on demand. Furthermore, it is cheap. However, with the rapid development of consumer electronics devices, most of the existing smart watches have heart beat monitoring capabilities. This will be more conducive to long-term detection. Thus, in the future, smart watches will be considered as the heart beat data collection device for research.

## 5. Conclusions

A human remote-controlled robot performs complex or dangerous tasks in unstructured environments, which expends the scope of human work. In the process of completing the tasks, the mental workload of the operator will change based on the different tasks of the robot. However, too much mental workload will not only affect the robot's working efficiency and safety, but also impact human physical and mental health. In order to assess the mental workload during human interaction with a dual-arm robot, in this paper, HRV is the measure that is studied. Firstly, the ECG signals of two kinds of mental workload states (performing task state and relaxing state) are collected. The ECG signals are collected from six subjects based on a custom device. Based on the ECG signal, the HRV signal is obtained. Then, 20 kinds of HRV features (time domain, frequency domain, and nonlinear features) are extracted. Finally, six different classifications are used to mental workload classification. The results are that, firstly, using each subject's HRV signal training model, the subject's mental workload is classified. The average classification accuracy of 98.77% is obtained using the KNN method. Then, using the HRV signal of five subjects for training, and the remaining one subject for testing, the GB method can obtain the highest average classification accuracy, with the average classification accuracy of six subjects being 80.56%. This study has demonstrated that the HRV can be used to measure the mental workload during human interaction with a dual-arm robot.

**Author Contributions:** Conceptualization: S.S. and T.W.; methodology: S.S., T.W., C.S. and C.Y.; software: S.S.; formal analysis: S.S. and C.S.; investigation: S.S., Y.W. and Y.S.; data curation: S.S., Y.W. and Y.S.; writing—original draft preparation: S.S. and C.S.; writing—review and editing: S.S. and C.S. All authors have read and agreed to the published version of the manuscript.

**Funding:** This research is funded by the National Natural Science Foundation of China (grant number U20A20201), the Doctoral Scientific Research Foundation of Liaoning Province (grant number 2020-BS-025), the LiaoNing Revitalization Talents Program (grant number XLYC1807018), and the National key research and development program of China (grant number 2016YFE0206200).

**Conflicts of Interest:** The authors declare no conflict of interest.

## References

1. Spiers, A.J.; Morgan, A.S.; Srinivasan, K.; Calli, B.; Dollar, A.M. Using a variable-friction robot hand to determine proprioceptive features for object classification during within-hand-manipulation. *IEEE Trans. Haptic.* **2020**, *13*, 600–610. [CrossRef]
2. Su, Y.; Wang, T.; Yao, C.; Shao, S.L.; Wang, Z.D. A target tracking method of UAV based on cooperative target. *Robot* **2019**, *4*, 425–432.
3. Zhao, T.; Deng, M.; Li, Z.; Hu, Y.B. Cooperative manipulation for a mobile dual-arm robot using sequences of dynamic movement primitives. *IEEE Trans. Cogn. Dev. Syst.* **2020**, *12*, 18–29. [CrossRef]
4. Li, Y.; Xu, D. Cooperative path planning of dual-arm robot based on attractive force self-adaptive step size RRT. *Robot* **2020**, *42*, 606–616.
5. Heard, J.; Harriott, C.E.; Adams, J.A. A survey of workload assessment algorithms. *IEEE Trans. Hum. Mach. Syst.* **2018**, *48*, 434–451. [CrossRef]
6. Young, M.S.; Brookhuis, K.A.; Wickens, C.D.; Hancock, P.A. State of science: Mental workload in ergonomics. *Ergonomics* **2015**, *58*, 1–17. [CrossRef] [PubMed]
7. Bajaj, N.; Carrionk, J.R.; Bellotti, F.; Berta, R.; de Gloria, A. Automatic and tunable algorithm for EEG artifact removal using wavelet decomposition with applications in predictive modeling during auditory tasks. *Biomed. Signal Process. Control.* **2020**, *55*, 101624. [CrossRef]
8. Aldridge, A.; Barnes, E.; Bethel, C.L.; Carruth, D.W.; Kocturova, M.; Pleva, M.; Juhar, J. Accessible electroencephalograms (EEGs): A comparative review with openbci's ultracortex mark IV headset. In Proceedings of the International Conference Radioelektronika, RADIOELEKTRONIKA-Microwave and Radio Electronics Week, Pardubice, Czech Republic, 16–18 April 2019.
9. Taishi, N.; Hiroshi, H. Workload induces changes in hemodynamics, respiratory rate and heart rate variability. In Proceedings of the IEEE International Conference on Bioinformatics and Bioengineering, Taichung, Taiwan, 31 October–2 November 2016.
10. Adams, C.E.; Leverland, M.B. Environmental and behavioral factors that can affect blood pressure. *Nurse Educ. Pract.* **1985**, *10*, 39–40. [CrossRef] [PubMed]
11. Mizuno, T.; Sakai, T.; Kawazura, S.; Asano, H. Measuring facial skin temperature changes caused by mental work-load with infrared thermography. *IEEE J. Trans. Electron. Inf. Syst.* **2016**, *136*, 1581–1585. [CrossRef]
12. Nourbakhsh, N.; Chen, F.; Wang, Y.; Calvo, R.A. Detecting users' cognitive load by galvanic skin response with affective interference. *ACM Trans. Interact. Intell. Syst.* **2017**, *7*, 1–19. [CrossRef]
13. Marquart, C.; Cabrall, C.; Winter, J.D. Review of eye-related measures of drivers' mental workload. *Procedia Manuf.* **2015**, *3*, 2854–2861. [CrossRef]
14. Sakai, R.; Yokoyama, K. Monitoring the work performance and HRV while mental work using surface pressure sensor. In Proceedings of the IEEE Global Conference on Consumer Electronics, Nara, Japan, 9–12 October 2018.
15. Keisuke, T.; Akihiro, C.; Kazuhiro, Y. Predicting changes in cognitive performance using heart rate variability. *IEICE Trans. Inf. Syst.* **2017**, *E100D*, 2411–2419.
16. Majid, F.; Majid, M.; Rashid, H. Effects of mental workload on physiological and subjective responses during traffic density monitoring: A field study. *Appl. Ergon.* **2016**, *52*, 95–103.
17. Sebastian, M.; Julio, L.; Angel, J.M. Simultaneous feature selection and heterogeneity control for SVM classification: An application to mental workload assessment. *Expert Sys. Appl.* **2020**, *143*, 112988.
18. Parent, M.; Peysakhovich, V.; Mandrick, K.; Tremblay, S.; Causse, M. The diagnosticity of psychophysiological signatures: Can we disentangle mental workload from acute stress with ECG and fNIRS. *Int. J. Psychophysiol.* **2020**, *146*, 139–147. [CrossRef]
19. Li, Y.; Pan, W.; Li, K.; Jiang, Q.; Liu, G. Sliding trend fuzzy approximate entropy as a novel descriptor of heart rate variability in obstructive sleep apnea. *IEEE J. Biomed. Health Informat.* **2019**, *23*, 175–183. [CrossRef]
20. Liu, D.Z.; Wang, J.; Li, J.; Li, Y.; Xu, W.M.; Zhao, X. Analysis on power spectrum and base-scale entropy for heart rate variability signals modulated by reversed sleep state. *Acta Phys. Sin.* **2014**, *63*, 426–432.

21. Castaldo, R.; Montesinos, L.; Wan, T.S.; Serban, A.; Massaro, S.; Pecchia, L. Heart rate variability analysis and performance during a repeated mental workload task. In *Proceedings of the European Medical and Biological Engineering Conference Nordic-Baltic Conference on Biomedical Engineering and Medical Physics, Tampere, Finland, 11–15 June 2017*; Springer: Tampere, Finland, 2017.
22. Tiwari, A.; Albuquerque, I.; Parent, M.; Gagnon, J.-F.; Lafond, D.; Tremblay, S.; Falk, T.H. Multi-scale heart beat entropy measures for mental workload assessment of ambulant users. *Entropy* **2019**, *21*, 783. [CrossRef]
23. Delliaux, S.; Delaforge, A.; Deharo, J.-C.; Chaumet, G. Mental workload alters heart rate variability, lowering non-linear dynamics. *Front. Physiol.* **2019**, *5*, 1–14. [CrossRef]
24. Pan, J.; Tompkins, W.J. A real-time QRS detection algorithm. *IEEE Trans. Biomed. Eng.* **1985**, *32*, 230–236. [CrossRef]
25. Chen, L.L.; Zhang, X.; Song, C.Y. An automatic screening approach for obstructive sleep apnea diagnosis based on single-lead electrocardiogram. *IEEE Trans. Autom. Sci. Eng.* **2015**, *12*, 106–115. [CrossRef]
26. Clifford, G.D.; Tarassenko, L. Quantifying errors in spectral estimates of HRV due to beat replacement and resampling. *IEEE Trans. Biomed. Eng.* **2005**, *52*, 630–638. [CrossRef] [PubMed]
27. Radhagayathri, K.U.; Chandan, K.; Marimuthu, P. Understanding irregularity characteristics of short-term HRV signals using sample entropy profile. *IEEE Trans. Biomed. Eng.* **2018**, *65*, 2569–2579.
28. Penzel, T.; Kantelhardt, J.W.; Grote, L.; Peter, J.H.; Bunde, A. Comparison of detrended fluctuation analysis and spectral analysis for heart rate variability in sleep and sleep apnea. *IEEE Trans. Biomed. Eng.* **2003**, *50*, 1143–1151. [CrossRef]
29. Alan, R.; James, A.B.; Jay, K. Impact of psychological factors on the pathogenesis of cardiovascular disease and implications for therapy. *Circulation* **1999**, *99*, 2192–2217.
30. Berntson, G.G.; Bigger, J.T.J.; Eckberg, D.L.; Grossman, P.; Kaufmann, P.G.; Malik, M.; Nagaraja, H.N.; Porges, S.W.; Saul, J.P.; Stone, P.H.; et al. Heart rate variability: Origins, methods, and interpretive caveats. *Psychophysiology* **1997**, *34*, 623–648. [CrossRef]
31. Clifford, G. *Signal Processing Methods for HRV*; University of Oxford: Oxford, UK, 2002.
32. Shaffer, F.; McCraty, R.; Zerr, C. A healthy heart is not a metronome: An integrative review of the heart's anatomy and heart rate variability. *Front. Psychol.* **2014**, *5*, 1040. [CrossRef]
33. Daniel, N.O.; Ricardo, V.S.; Joao, P.M.; Marcelo, D.M.; Hugo, P.S.; Claudia, Q.; Miguel, V.B.; Hugo, G.; Helena, L.A.V. Autonomic nervous system response to remote ischemic conditioning: Heart rate variability assessment. *BMC Cardiovasc. Disord.* **2019**, *19*, 211.
34. Alessandro, T.; Alessandro, D.; Andrea, D.; Lorenzo, B.; Francesco, S.; Raffffaele, C.; Lucia, B. Can machine learning predict stress reduction based on wearable sensors' data following relaxation at workplace? A Pilot Study. *Processes* **2020**, *8*, 448.
35. Seungji, L.; Taejun, L.; Taeyang, Y.; Changrak, Y.; Sung, P.K. Detection of drivers' anxiety invoked by driving situations using multimodal biosignals. *Processes* **2020**, *8*, 155.
36. Zhang, J.H.; Wang, Y.C.; Li, S.A. Cross-subject mental workload classification using kernel spectral regression and transfer learning techniques. *Cogn. Technol. Work* **2017**, *21*, 145–157. [CrossRef]
37. Villani, V.; Righi, M.; Sabattini, L.; Secchi, C. Wearable devices for the assessment of cognitive effort for human-robot interaction. *IEEE Sens. J.* **2020**, *20*, 13047–13056. [CrossRef]

**Publisher's Note:** MDPI stays neutral with regard to jurisdictional claims in published maps and institutional affiliations.

© 2020 by the authors. Licensee MDPI, Basel, Switzerland. This article is an open access article distributed under the terms and conditions of the Creative Commons Attribution (CC BY) license (http://creativecommons.org/licenses/by/4.0/).

*Article*

# Pediatric Speech Audiometry Web Application for Hearing Detection in the Home Environment

Stanislav Ondáš [1,*], Eva Kiktová [2], Matúš Pleva [1], Mária Oravcová [2], Lukáš Hudák [1], Jozef Juhár [1] and Július Zimmermann [2]

1. Department of Electronics and Multimedia Communications, Faculty of Electrical Engineering and Informatics, Technical University of Košice, Němcovej 32, 040 01 Košice, Slovakia; matus.pleva@tuke.sk (M.P.); lukas.hudak.4@student.tuke.sk (L.H.); jozef.juhar@tuke.sk (J.J.)
2. Language Information and Communication Laboratory, Faculty of Arts, Pavol Jozef Šafárik University in Košice, Šrobárova 2, 041 80 Košice, Slovakia; eva.kiktova@upjs.sk (E.K.); maria.oravcova@upjs.sk (M.O.); julius.zimmermann@upjs.sk (J.Z.)
* Correspondence: stanislav.ondas@tuke.sk

Received: 8 May 2020; Accepted: 11 June 2020; Published: 13 June 2020

**Abstract:** This paper describes the development of the speech audiometry application for pediatric patients in Slovak language and experiences obtained during testing with healthy children, hearing-impaired children, and elderly persons. The first motivation behind the presented work was to reduce the stress and fear of the children, who must undergo postoperative audiometry, but over time, we changed our direction to the simple game-like mobile application for the detection of possible hearing problems of children in the home environment. Conditioned play audiometry principles were adopted to create a speech audiometry application, where children help the virtual robot Thomas assign words to pictures; this can be described as a speech recognition test. Several game scenarios together with the setting condition issues were created, tested, and discussed. First experiences show a positive influence on the children's mood and motivation.

**Keywords:** pediatric speech audiometry; hearing tests; conditioned play audiometry; human–computer interaction

## 1. Introduction

Audiometry is generally aimed at measuring the perception of the audio signal by the human auditory system. Audiometric tests can be divided into two main categories: pure tone audiometry and speech audiometry. Speech audiometry is a standard part of the audiological test battery/collection. It is usually done after the pure tone audiometry and helps the audiologist to answer questions regarding a patient's ability to be involved in speech communication. In other words, speech audiometry enables to test the speech processing abilities at different levels within the auditory system [1].

Speech audiometry contains several types of speech tests which focus on different aspects of speech perception and processing. Tests can measure the patient's most comfortable and uncomfortable listening levels, their range of comfortable listening, and their ability to recognize and discriminate speech sounds. A typical setting for the speech audiometry is similar to the pure tone audiometry. Usually, a two-room setting is needed. A two-channel audiometer can be used to present the stimulus through a microphone (monitored live voice) or through an external device, in case of recorded speech. The patient's role in speech audiometry is to react to the provided stimuli. They can repeat proposed words, write down their response or point to the picture.

Speech audiometry tests can be divided into two main categories: threshold level testing and suprathreshold testing [2]. In the case of threshold level testing, audiologists try to find the lowest level of speech where patients can detect and recognize the speech stimulus. The speech detection threshold (SDT) can be seen as the basic parameter. SDT is the lowest level of speech that a patient is able to detect for at least 50% of the time. The next important measure focuses on the speech recognition threshold (SRT), which is the lowest level that a person recognizes and repeats speech back to the audiologist.

The next group of speech audiometry tests falls under suprathreshold tests. After finding the SDT and SRT, in suprathreshold testing the speech material is provided to the patient at a normal conversation level and we try to identify speech recognition and understand the ability of that person. There are several suprathreshold speech tests that can be done. One is the most comfortable loudness (MCL) test, which tries to identify the most comfortable speech level of the patient. Another important measure is the uncomfortable loudness level (UCL). The UCL imagines the maximum level in which you can perform word recognition testing, and together with the SDT enables you to determine the dynamic range for speech.

The next important speech audiometry tests are word recognition tests or speech recognition tests. Their purpose is to determine the person's ability to understand and repeat words presented at a conversation level. Speech recognition testing is performed with a specific set or list of words known as phonetically balanced words. These lists consist of commonly occurring words in their normal proportion in everyday speech. There exist a few standardized lists. The most known are the PB-50 (phonetically balanced 50 words), CID (Central Institute of Deaf) W-22 list or Northwestern University (NU-6) list. Words from these lists can be presented by a live voice, but the usage of a prerecorded voice is a better choice. Another advantage of pre-prepared sounds is that they allow identical measurements to be made repeatedly, thus they are preferred in audiometry. Typically, 25 or 50 words are presented to the patient and they are instructed to repeat them or point to the correct picture. Words are usually presented on a fixed level (sound pressure level (SPL)) at about 30 dB to 40 dB above the patient's SDT. The result is expressed in the percentage of words they get correct. The person without any hearing impairment should have a word recognition score (WRS) of 90–100%.

The current research in the pediatric audiometry domain is mainly focused on phonetically balanced sentence/word lists in different languages, such as Greek [2], German (German Oldenburg Sentence Test for Children [3] or Mainz speech test for children 3–7 years old [4]), Thai [5] or Chinese [6]. However, these word lists are not combined with pictures and audio samples to build an automated speech application for the home environment. On the other hand, a very interesting THear framework for mobile audiometry [6] is designed mainly for adults, where written text and Chinese traditional character pictures are used to choose the word heard. This is not suitable for pediatric patients.

When we tried to review the latest pediatric audiometry applications in Slavic languages, as there is no Slovak word list to our knowledge, we found the following: Polish hearing screening of school children is tone-based [7]; Serbian speech audiometry authors published a good speech audiometry word re-evaluation lately [8] but it is not oriented to the pediatric domain and has no picture set associated; Czech preschool children testing [9] was based on a whispered voice performed by pediatricians; Russian speech audiometry materials and SRT tests recorded high-quality audio samples [10] but are still not suitable for child audiometry as they do not have a picture set associated; Ukrainian phonetic tables [11] are not designed for speech audiometry and no word list for pediatric audiometry was found; for Bulgarian language, we found only newborn screening program results [12] with no Bulgarian phonetically-balanced word list available.

In the present paper we focus our attention on the pediatric speech audiometry, which has its own specifics. Children have a limited, specific vocabulary, which must be considered. A closed set of words instead of an open set are preferred. That means that the patient can select a correct result from a set of options. This can be done using picture cards, where a child can point to a picture related to what he or she heard. For children in the kindergarten age, phonetically-balanced kindergarten word lists exist (e.g., [13]).

During the audiometry testing of pediatric patients, we need to consider their abilities and limitations in the language area, which relates to their age. The above-mentioned audiometry tests need to be modified to adapt to pediatric patients. Pediatric audiometry is performed in case of hearing loss and the deafness of children in prelingual and post-lingual age, in range of postoperative, medication, and compensatory therapy. A high level of stress and distrust of a pediatric patient towards the therapist and the therapy is a commonly observed issue that arises during the application of the therapy, which results in a situation when checking the sound perception during an interview with the child becomes ineffective or even precluded. The level of stress in a child patient, low motivation, and involvement in therapy can be positively influenced using game-like approaches, smart technologies, or by involving robotic systems. Generally, studies indicate the positive effect of robots on therapy (see [14–17]).

Therapists often report problems with children concerning motivation and involvement during audiometry after implantation of a cochlear implant [18]; this thus became the motivation behind the current study. The initial idea lied in the use of a robot during the audiometry process, in order to positively influence the therapy by decreasing the stress and distrust of the pediatric patient towards the therapist/therapy. Our goal was to prepare a research platform that would enable us to study aspects of virtual robot-supported audiometry. After collecting first experiences we extended our focus to involve other smart devices, like smartphones and tablets, into speech audiometry. Our attention was focused on the development of a simple game-like mobile application for the detection of possible hearing loss problems in children at home conditions. Conditioned play audiometry (CPA) principles were adopted to create speech audiometry applications, where children help a virtual robot known as Thomas to assign words to pictures. We previously described a similar web-based audiology application [19] in which a telemetry application is presented with remote audiology measuring devices. The advantage of our proposed system is that it is not dependent on special devices and the purpose of home environment testing is different. We mainly propose a simple child-acceptable application that is easy to play with and can provide a short everyday testing of the current state of hearing with cochlear implants or Otitis media (middle ear inflammation).

Our initial aim to support child audiometry using robots was extended to use modern technologies for the above-mentioned purpose. One of the main reasons for addressing this problem was the experiences of therapists from post-operative therapy after cochlear implant implantation, where they described problems with fear and low motivation of children. Another reason was no commonly accepted pre-recorded speech stimuli for kindergarten children existed, nor any tool for diagnostics of children with hearing problems in the Slovak language, particularly in the home environment. Therefore, we started to develop the audiometry application, which can serve both therapists and parents and can be easily used in the home environment. Testing the application brought many ideas and findings, which were used to further improve the application.

Our work consists of several tasks. The first task was to select a child audiometry method, which is well suitable for pediatric speech audiometry and the desired application. The second task was to define the scenario of audiometry tests and prepare resources in the Slovak language. The next tasks were focused on the design and development of the research platform for robot-assisted child audiometry and speech audiometry application for smart devices.

The paper is organized as follows: Section 2 describes the design and development of the pediatric speech audiometry application including speech stimuli preparation. Section 3 presents details about the performed experiments, their results, and collected observations.

## 2. Development of Speech Audiometry Application for Pediatric Patients

### 2.1. Speech Stimuli

Speech stimuli are the most fundamental part of speech audiometry testing. To test speech perception and processing a therapist provides speech stimuli to the patient. Speech stimuli can be provided by a live voice or by a pre-recorded voice (recordings). Both live and pre-recorded voices have their own advantages and disadvantages. In the case of a live voice, the rapport between a patient and therapist can be reached easier. One the other hand, such measurement will be difficult to repeat at the same conditions. In the case of using a pre-recorded voice, the measurement can be easily repeated in the future.

Speech stimuli need to cover the phonetical set of the language, to be able to assess the speech understanding ability of the patient. Moreover, in the case of pediatric audiometry, they need to consider significant differences in speech and language ability in comparison to adult patients.

Speech audiometry can be performed with very young children (from approx. two and half years) and pediatric audiometry methods are substituted by adult audiometry in the case of ten- or twelve-year-old patients. Pediatric audiometry methods can also be used for adult patients with specific kinds of mental disabilities or for elderly patients. The child's mental processes up to two years depend on his or her experiences—what they see, what they hear, what they touch. This period is based on sensorimotor thinking and development of practical intelligence [20,21]. The vocabulary of a child of this age is very limited. A two-year-old child can actively use around 200–300 of words. Of course, his or her understanding capacity is larger [22].

Speech stimuli often form word lists, which contain words that are pronounced by the therapist or played through an audiometer or CD player. Several word lists exist, which were developed for other languages. The most well-known word list for children's speech audiometry is the Phonetically balanced Kindergarten List (PBK) defined by Haskins in 1949 [13]. It consists of 50 phonetically balanced word items, which were selected from the spoken vocabulary of normal-hearing kindergarten children [1]. There are also other lists, such as the Isophonemic Word Lists designed by Boothroyd in 1968 [23] or the Northwestern University Children's Perception of Speech (NU-CHIPS), which consists of 50 words with pictures [24].

To perform children's speech audiometry for Slovak children, Dr. Hapčo and Dr. Bargár designed a Slovak set of words, which contains 80 words; this set is well suitable for older children (school-age). Another set also exists, which is used by audiologists during behavioral audiometry, but it is not standardized or publicly available. Behavioral audiometry is usually performed with very young pediatric patients (from 6-months-old) and it is very interactive and subjective.

Due to the lack of an appropriate word list for Slovak kindergarten children with hearing disabilities, we decided to develop a new list, which will be well suited for children, two-years-old and older, although predominantly for kindergarten children. The newly designed unique Slovak kindergarten word list (SKWL) for child audiometry consists of 50-word items, related pictures, and audio files with recorded speech stimuli. The acquaintance criterion was the most important in the process of word selection. Words were separated into the following groups: transport/vehicles (5), colors (4), animals (10), toys/things (8), human body (5), food (5), and combinations (13). More information about the SKWL word list can be found elsewhere [25]. The group of animals is the biggest group (10) because animals are usually the first words in a child's vocabulary [26]. In early childhood, children imitate animal sounds, play with animal toys, and they are happy to watch them; thus, this category is representative. The category of the human body contains only one- and two-syllable words, so we consider it to be the least demanding for perception. Conversely, the food category contains one-, two-, three- and four-syllable words with Slovak phonemes č, dž, ĺ, ch, whose teaching is in the second part of the primer [27]. For these reasons, we consider this category to be the most challenging. A specific category is a combination of words and phrases. We graded the terms as two-word, three-word, and sentence, so that we can gradually distinguish what the patient hears and understands, and what is already too difficult for him/her, by the audiometric measurement.

There are several words in the database, which can serve as a distinctive element for stratifying the patient's audio capabilities [28], for example:

- the syllable length criterion (čokoládka, kravička, lietadielko);
- the occurrence of syllable phonemes [ḷ] and [ĺ] (žltá, jabĺčko);
- marginal phonemes in terms of frequency in Slovak [ŭo]-kôň, [ǯ]-džús;
- consonant groups (spí, strom).

A total of 23 words have their diminutive equivalent (e.g., *krava-kravička*; *pes-psík-havo*), so that we can get as close as possible to the child's speech in each household, where the same subject may be named differently.

Due to our focus on the conditioned play audiometry and behavioral audiometry, we decided to prepare a picture card for each word in the Slovak kindergarten word list. These pictures were carefully drawn by the artist for this research to be kind and suitable for pediatric patients. Five types of picture tests from our speech recognition test are depicted in Figures 1–5. Each of them focuses on a specific task connected with hearing capability.

**Figure 1.** Different category: Played sound: *červené auto* (red car), same color, different pictures.

**Figure 2.** Category: Played sound: *mačka* a *pes* (cat and dog), two words.

**Figure 3.** Phonic differentiation: Played sound—*vlak/vláčik* (train), similarly sounding words in Slovak (*vlak*, *vták*), different category.

**Figure 4.** Difficulty of phone: Played sound—*lietadlo/lietadielko* (airplane), 4 syllable sound, [ď]; -dl- same category.

**Figure 5.** Combinations: Played sound—*bábika spí* (doll is sleeping), three pictures, high similarity.

A picture identification speech recognition test is suitable for children up to 10-years-old. The pediatric patient correctly marks the appropriate image representation based on the heard sound stimuli. In this case, it is a closed set test.

### 2.2. Previous Experiences with HRI Audiometry

As mentioned in the abstract, the first motivation behind the presented work was to improve the user acceptance level and user experience and reduce stress and fear of children, who must undergo postoperative audiometry, which was induced by the experience of therapists. Our first idea was to involve real robots in the speech audiometry process, which is repeatedly performed after cochlear implant surgery. Previously, we started to design and develop a small application with a humanoid robot, where the robot prompts a child to help him to put together pictures on the table and sounds. This robot-assisted speech audiometry ran on VoMIS system (see [29]) and is described in detail elsewhere [25]. During the experiments with the robot in this role, we collected new ideas and experiences. One of the key findings was that healthy children liked to interact with the robot. The next experiments also brought several drawbacks:

- It was uncomfortable to use a magnetic table for the picture presented. A robot with a touchscreen could be more suitable. The used humanoid robot had no display.
- Using a humanoid robot enables one to perform only free field audiometry, which does not enable to measure the left ear and right ear separately and there was a high risk of cross hearing.
- Motors in the joints of the robot produce noise, during the gesticulation of the robot, which may be disturbing in such an audiometry scenario.
- Very young children may be afraid of humanoids (we performed tests with 4- to 6-year-old children only). Instead of a humanoid robot, it could be better to use some a family member, companion, or social robot (e.g., Asus Zenbo, currently not available for EU).
- Children speech audiometry with robot assistance cannot be easily used in home conditions.

In other words, the idea to use robots looks very nice, but obtained experiences showed that such a system was not usable or helpful for the therapy. Therefore, we turned to something more usable, simple, and helpful. We focused our attention to hearing detection in the home environment without any humanoids needed. We developed the idea to prepare a simple game-like mobile application, which can be easily used by parents, when they have some doubts about the speech and sound perception of their child. Due to the fact, that in home conditions, users will not be able to set the accurate acoustic conditions, the application focuses rather on suprathreshold speech tests instead of threshold levels testing. The designed application falls into the category of word recognition audiometry tests with the closed set.

### 2.3. Web-Based Application for Children Speech Audiometry

Conditioned play audiometry principles were adopted to create a speech audiometry application, where children help robot Thomas to assign words (sounds) to pictures, which can be marked as a kind of speech recognition. The selected test is a part of the behavioral audiometry.

The designed application was prepared as a web application, which enabled us to run it on each device with Internet connection and a web browser without any other requirements. The application can be used for free field speech audiometry and with a headset. The design is currently a simple HTML code with short task description and pictures to choose from, based on the heard voice command. The pictures were designed and completely sketched by one of the co-authors, and they are a unique and significant contribution to the Slovak audiology clinicians' community together with the SKWL word list and audio recordings.

The application is organized into levels. In each level five screens with a set of pictures are presented to the patient with randomly generated speech stimuli. After performing all levels, the word recognition score is computed. Speech stimuli are presented on the supposed most comfortable loudness level, which is around 50 dB. The application offers the introduction, which helps the therapist or parent to set required acoustic conditions (MCL). Cold running speech is used to set the MCL. Parent/therapist together with the patient can set the MCL by adjusting the volume while listening to a short story.

The first screens of the application contain the story description, basic setting page, and entry form. The story (Figure 6, screen 2) about robot Thomas was designed to motivate a child to undergo the audiometry. A child patient is invited to help robot Thomas to organize his collection of pictures and sounds, which is broken. We tried to engage emotions by placing on the screen gif-animation with the sad robot. The next screen offers the basic setting instructions, which help parents/therapists to set the MCL. The last initial screen is an entry form, where the user fills in his/her name (or nickname), gender, and age. He/she can also provide information about the sound level which was set for the experiment (in the case when audiometry is done on the most comfortable loudness level). Then, the application is ready to start the game.

**Figure 6.** Initial screens of the speech audiometry application.

The game is divided into several levels. In each level a set of pictures is provided with an appropriate randomly generated audio file with speech stimuli. On each screen with pictures, a word is played, which belongs to one of the pictures (see Figure 7). The task of the patient is to select the correct picture. After each level, the overall score is calculated, but it stays hidden from the patient. We decided to hide a partial score because initial testing showed that children stay demotivated in case of a bad score.

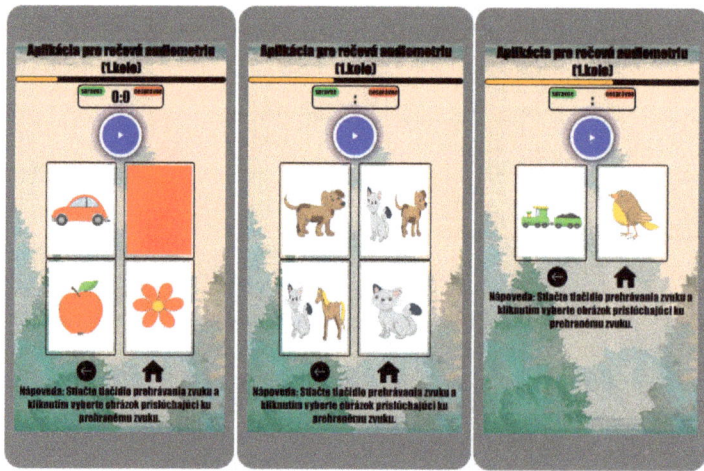

**Figure 7.** One level of the audiometry game.

Two versions of the game were developed: The first is for free field audiometry and the second one for testing each ear separately. Although free field audiometry is more comfortable and less stressful for pediatric patients, it brings less precise results. If it is possible, better results can be obtained using a headset, when each ear can be tested separately. A cross hearing problem may prevent proper diagnosis [30,31], therefore a special version of speech recordings was prepared for right and left ear testing. During testing of one ear, the masking noise is played into the second ear with the 10 dB distance to the speech stimuli.

## 3. Experiments and Results

Several game scenarios together with the setting condition issues were created, tested, and discussed. First experiences show a positive influence on the children's mood and motivation.

Eleven child participants were involved in the interaction with the audiometry application. Nine were healthy children mainly around kindergarten age. The two testing subjects were a 4 and 16 year old boy and girl with hearing impairment, respectively. The last participant was an elderly patient (72-year-old woman with a hearing aid in the right ear and hearing problems in both ears). The total number of test participants was 12.

All tests were performed in the home environment in a relatively quiet place. One of the parents played the role of a therapist. He set the sound pressure level (SPL) and read motivation stories and instructions to the child. Before testing, the child was not affected by any louder sound. Each test consists of three game levels. The role of the child is to pick up the correct picture from the provided set of pictures according to provided speech stimuli in the form of prerecorded words from the Slovak kindergarten word list. The audiometry application ran on mobile devices (Samsung Galaxy A70 and Xiaomi Redmi 4X) and tablets (Huawei MediaPad M5 lite). In the beginning, the application requires adjusting the SPL volume before playing the game.

The first version of our audiometry application used another mechanism to set the SPL and each level was played with a different SPL. To set the desired sound level, the therapist or parent needs to use the second device (smartphone) with a sound meter application to measure and set the correct SPL. Achieving stable acoustic conditions was very difficult. Additional problems were identified during the experiments:

- a movement or even the presence of other person causes a disturbance;
- variable position between the child and the sound source/smartphone (the child tends to be as close as possible to the sound source);
- impossible to test the left and right ear separately and occurrence of cross hearing;
- physical properties of sound emission (reflections, attenuation, etc.) had a significant impact on the resulting perceived level of acoustic information.

Therefore, in the second version of the application, we decided to perform testing on the most comfortable loudness level, which can be easily set at the beginning. According to analyzed literature around speech audiometry, we abandoned the strict adherence to acoustic conditions, because the appearance of some noises in the background can lead to more realistic results of audiometry, which closely reflects situations in the real environment.

Each game level has a different difficulty and allows us to test various aspects of the cognitive ability of patients. Tests can evaluate several distinctive levels of hearing and subsequent understanding (e.g., it includes phonetic similarity of words, the visual similarity of presented pictures, the same word base, different word length, etc.). All mentioned aspects focus on a specific task connected with the hearing capability and each of them can influence the perception results.

*3.1. Experiments with Healthy Children*

In these experiments, we considered as healthy children those who were not clinically diagnosed with any hearing problems before. From the testing of healthy children, two main observations were collected:

- For the children, it was very funny and exciting to play the audiometry game. They did not want to stop playing. They did not perceive that it was therapeutic testing.
- Testing showed that, in cases where the child marked an incorrect picture and the system displayed a picture of the sad robot, the child started to become demotivated, sad, and did not want to continue with the game.

When we decreased the SPL to approx. 30 dB, the word recognition score decreased to 65% for child #1 and #2, which is still higher than the threshold score for the healthy patients (WRS = 50%) [1].

According to the obtained observations we decided to remove the backchannel after each picture's set. Instead of a negative backchannel, the application provided in each situation a positive backchannel after each level.

The test routine in the second version of the application consisted of setting the MCL and SRT volume levels and selecting the test method (via the loudspeaker, so-called free field, or via headphones for the right and left ear). Both volume levels were adjusted by the parent in cooperation with the child subjectively. The precondition for such a setting is that the parent has no hearing impairment. MCL level is set correctly if the sound stimuli are well audible (not too loud or less loud). The child completes the test and based on the final score the parent obtains information about the child's hearing abilities; in cases where the parent performed the test too, he/she can compare the achieved results. The minimum audible level (SRT) was set again by the parent. He/she continuously increased the volume of the presented sounds from the zero level while observing the child's reactions and ability to repeat the proposed sound. This setting can be simplified by the fact that SRT is usually the lowest level that can be heard through the device used (computer, mobile phone, tablet). Similarly, if a parent completed the test, he/she could compare the obtained results with his/her child's results to get an idea of his/her hearing abilities.

## 3.2. Experiment with Hearing-Impaired Child

The third testing subject was a 4-year-old boy with hearing impairment. He interacted with the audiometry application several times both in the free field scenario and with headphones (see Figure 8). The first interactions were made on the MCL level interactively set in cooperation between the child and his parent. In these tests, all speech stimuli were recognized correctly and a WRS equal to 100% was achieved. Then we decided to change the sound pressure level in the range from 70 dB to the lowest possible level, which can be reached by the device (Samsung Galaxy A70). This level was around 35 dB. Recognition problems started to occur at such a low level and word recognition score declined below 50%. According to our observations, the incorrectly recognized words were those from the group of short words and phonetically similar words.

Since hearing problems were suspected, we decided to continue in the audiometry testing with headphones (Marshall Major III Bluetooth closed headphones). The same game scenario was performed. The tested subject was able to perform individual levels of the game without errors for SPL from 70 dB to 30 dB. All presented recordings were in mono mode, and although the sound was present on one side (for one ear), both ears participated in the process of perception of the sound stimulus via vibrations through the bone conduction.

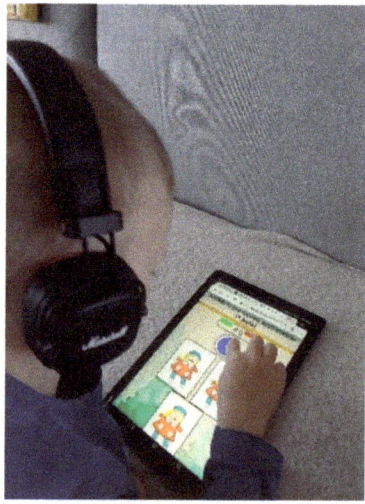

**Figure 8.** Hearing-impaired 4-year-old boy interacting with the audiometry application.

The last part of the experiment with the hearing-impaired boy was performed with in-ear headphones, which enabled us to partially reduce sound stimulation of the healthy ear via vibrations through the bone conduction. Speech stimuli in this scenario were provided only into the tested ear without precise masking of the untested ear.

The results for the left ear were very good. We obtained a WRS higher than 90%. A completely different situation occurred in the case of the right ear, where the word recognition score was very low, also for higher sound pressure level (higher than 50 dB was only 30%). When we decreased the sound pressure level below 50 dB, he became angry, demotivated, did not want to continue, and demanded to increase the volume.

For reliable evaluation of hearing in each ear separately it is necessary to mask the untested ear with noise. Therefore, later, we performed testing where the healthy ear was masked by cocktail-party noise. This noise pressure level was set to 10 dB below the speech stimuli provided into the tested ear.

During testing of the hearing-impaired child, we also focused our attention on observing the mood and motivation of the patient. The result was that during the audiometric game, the child was very motivated and really enjoyed the game. Some disappointment was observed when the child was unable to hear and correctly label multiple consecutive test sound items. The volume of the presented sound stimulus, when a child starts to become disappointed from failures in the game, is close to his or her speech detection threshold (SDT).

Table 1 contains results from all tested children who participated in our research. Most of the tested children managed both MCL and SRT levels very well in all tested scenarios. In child #3, the deterioration of hearing quality in the case of the right ear was confirmed. Child #7 (with cochlear implants (CI)) achieved very good results in the tests, which indicate the correct functioning of her cochlear implant.

**Table 1.** Results of the speech audiometry with the developed web-based audiometry application. CI * = cochlear implants; SPL = sound pressure level; MCL = most comfortable loudness; SRT = speech recognition threshold.

| Test Subject # | Age/Sex | Hearing Impairment | Free Field SPL = MCL | Headphones SPL = MCL | Free Field SPL = SRT | Headphones SPL = SRT |
|---|---|---|---|---|---|---|
| 1. | 6/F | no | 100% | Both: 100% | 65% | Left: 72% Right: 64% |
| 2. | 4/M | no | 90% | Both: 100% | 65% | Left: 100% Right: 100% |
| 3. | 4/M | yes | 100% | Left: 100% Right: 88% | 39% | Left: 100% Right: 30% |
| 4. | 11/M | no | 100% | Both: 96% | 92% | Left: 61% Right: 68% |
| 5. | 9/M | no | 100% | Both: 100% | 96% | Both: 91% |
| 6. | 6/M | no | 100% | Left: 100% Right: 96% | 100% | Left: 63% Right: 91% |
| 7. | 16/F | yes CI * | 100% | Both: 100% | 100% | Both: 100% |
| 8. | 5/F | no | 100% | Both: 100% | 100% | Left: 91% Right: 96% |
| 9. | 7/F | no | 100% | Both: 100% | 100% | Both: 100% |
| 10. | 5/M | no | 100% | Both: 100% | 100% | Both: 100% |
| 11. | 6/F | no | 100% | Both: 100% | 100% | Left: 91% Right: 91% |

### 3.3. Experiments with Hearing-Impaired Elderly Woman

The last participant of the audiometry tests was a 72-year-old hearing-impaired woman. She has detected 60% hearing loss and wears a hearing aid in her right ear. We decided to involve her in the experiment due to several facts. The first was that we did not have any other participant available currently with a hearing aid or cochlear implant. The second supporting idea was that we supposed that pediatric speech audiometry methods could be beneficial for testing elderly patients too. It was interesting to test a subject from this group and collect first observations.

Two main testing scenarios were conducted with this patient: with hearing aid and without hearing aid. We performed tests in a free field environment and with closed headphones. Results of all experiments are presented in Table 2.

**Table 2.** Results of the speech audiometry (word recognition score) tests of the elderly patient.

| Conditions | Free Field SPL = 70 dB | Free Field SPL = 35 dB | Headphones, SPL = MCL |
|---|---|---|---|
| with hearing aid | 75% | 50% | 89% |
| without hearing aid | <20% | 0% | - |

First tests were performed in the free field scenario by using a hearing aid. In the case of presentation of speech stimuli on MCL, we obtained word recognition score around 75% WRS. When we decreased the sound pressure level to 35 dB, the recognition score decreased to 50% WRS. It is necessary to note that she needed to listen to speech stimuli several times to be able to recognize the word. Phonetically similar words (e.g., "*vlak*" and "*vták*") were the most difficult for her to recognize. In the case of the words, where some part of them was the same, she anticipated the correct answer from the combination of pictures and listened to part of the word. This situation was observed and reported in the case of the words "*auto*" and "*autobus*", where "*auto*" is part of both.

When we tested without her hearing aid the situation was completely different. She was able to detect the sound only with a very loud stimuli around 70 dB and the word recognition score was very poor—under 20% WRS. Tests with closed headphones were performed too, but only with a hearing aid and with SPL equal to MCL. The result of this testing was 89% WRS.

These results show that the hearing aid works at an acceptable level when the lowest acceptable WRS equal to 50% is already reached near the SRT. The overall impression of using the designed audiometry application was interesting for us. Initially there was a reluctance to participate. After overcoming the initial rejection, she passed the whole testing without any problems, also for testing without her hearing aid. The overall length of the test was acceptable for her, but the provided pictures seemed to her too childish.

*3.4. Results Summary*

The evaluation was performed several times with healthy children, two children with hearing impairment, and one elderly (72 years) individual with a hearing aid. In these experiments, we considered as healthy children those who were not clinically diagnosed with any hearing problems before. The children's age was 4 and 16 year. In this study we instructed the parents to contact the clinician when the results of the test fell under 50%, as described elsewhere [1]. More accurate results can be obtained using headphones when each ear is measured separately, which eliminates the problem of cross-hearing.

Testing the app with an elderly person shows us that it can be easily used for speech audiometry testing in this group of patients. Both children and the elderly were able to easily interact with the application thanks to pointing gestures on the touchscreen. The large size of the pictures seems to be important too. The selection of words, which cover words known by children, is also suitable for testing elderly patients with reduced mental capabilities.

## 4. Conclusions

In this work the web-based pediatric speech audiometry application for hearing impairment detection was described and evaluated. The designed speech audiometry application is suitable for use in the home environment. It enabled us to measure the word recognition score (WRS) in a free field scenario and also to measure each ear separately using headphones. The application adopts conditioned play audiometry principles and can be classified as a speech recognition test. Recordings from the newly designed Slovak kindergarten word list (SKWL) were used as speech stimuli. SKWL meets all requirements for audiometric data and, together with the corresponding images and speech audio recordings, creates a unique novel database suitable especially for pediatric ontological patients during long-term therapy with high user acceptance level among pediatric and elderly patients.

The evaluation shows that the designed application can detect hearing problems at an early stage to support better intervention. The more accurate results can be obtained using headphones when each ear is measured separately, which eliminates the cross-hearing problem. Children accepted the application very well. They liked the application and did not want to stop playing it. Some portion of stress was observed when the child was not successful several times in a row or in situations when he or she perceived the presentation volume level as too low. In comparison with the classical speech audiometry methodology using live speech as a stimulus, the designed application removes the problem of lip reading. The application can be used to measure different levels and to evaluate the hearing loss or to verify the functionality of the hearing aid. Even though we initially intended to develop the application to support speech audiometry performed by therapists, experimentations with the application show us many other cases where the application can be used:

- by a therapist to increase motivation and reduce the fear of the pediatric patient during speech audiometry;
- by parents to verify hearing problems when they start to observe hearing problems in their child;
- for daily verification of correct functionality of a hearing aid or cochlear implant;
- for adults with specific disabilities and for audiometry testing of elderly patients, especially in situations when the patient is not able to answer by voice or writing;
- in the home environment;
- in each web browser without any special requirements.

In the future we plan to improve the application in several areas, by extending the number of levels, adding more phonetically similar word pairs, enabling parents to identify words which are unknown by their child. We also plan to add other types of tests, such as testing of speech detection and speech recognition threshold and to develop an application for the Ling 6-word test. We developed an Android-based application following the proposed web application and it will soon be available on Google play for free. The next idea is to use an automatic speech recognition system and natural language processing tools (see [32]) to enable the child to react using his/her voice or to prepare more sophisticated audiometric games. We plan to test the application with autistic pediatric patients and with a larger group of elderly patients. We already started a collaboration with the Bulgarian Academy of Sciences and EPU University for the Bulgarian version of this application for elderly people [33].

**Author Contributions:** Conceptualization, S.O. and J.Z.; data curation, E.K. and L.H.; formal analysis, E.K., M.O., and J.J.; funding acquisition, S.O., M.P., and J.Z.; investigation, M.P.; methodology, M.P. and M.O.; project administration, J.Z.; resources, E.K.; software, S.O. and L.H.; supervision, S.O.; visualization, L.H.; writing—original draft, S.O. and E.K.; writing—review and editing, M.P. and J.J. All authors have read and agreed to the published version of the manuscript.

**Funding:** This work was supported by the Slovak Research and Development Agency project numbers APVV-0077-11, APVV-15-0492, APVV-15-0731, the Cultural and Educational Grant Agency of the Slovak Republic project number KEGA 009TUKE-4-2019, and Scientific Grant Agency of the Ministry of Education, Science, Research and Sport of the Slovak Republic project number VEGA 1/0753/20.

**Conflicts of Interest:** The authors declare no conflicts of interest.

## References

1. Kabátová, Z.; Profant, M. *Audiológia. (en: Audiology)*; Vydala Grada: Bratislava, Slovakia, 2012; ISBN 978-80-247-7888-4.
2. Trimmis, N.; Papadeas, E.; Papadas, T.; Naxakis, S.; Papathanasopoulos, P.; Goumas, P. Speech audiometry: The development of modern Greek word lists for suprathreshold word recognition testing. *Mediterr. J. Otol.* **2006**, *3*, 117–126.
3. Neumann, K.; Baumeister, N.; Baumann, U.; Sick, U.; Euler, H.A.; Weißgerber, T. Speech audiometry in quiet with the Oldenburg Sentence Test for Children. *Int. J. Audiol.* **2012**, *51*, 157–163. [CrossRef] [PubMed]
4. Schirkonyer, V.; Keilmann, A.; Harmuth, C.; Wachtlin, B.; Rader, T.; Bohnert, A. The new Mainz speech test for children 3–7 years old (MATCH). *HNO* **2020**, *68*, 43–49. [CrossRef] [PubMed]
5. Munthuli, A.; Sirimujalin, P.; Tantibundhit, C.; Onsuwan, C.; Klangpornkun, N.; Kosawat, K. Constructing time phonetically balanced word recognition test in speech audiometry through large written corpora. In Proceedings of the 2014 17th Oriental Chapter of the International Committee for the Co-ordination and Standardization of Speech Databases and Assessment Techniques (COCOSDA), Phuket, Thailand, 10–12 September 2014; pp. 1–5.

6. Leung, W.K.; Jia, J.; Wu, Y.; Long, J.; Cai, L. THear: Development of a mobile multimodal audiometry application on a cross-platform framework. In Proceedings of the 2016 10th International Symposium on Chinese Spoken Language Processing (ISCSLP), Tianjin, China, 17–20 October 2016; pp. 1–5.
7. Śliwa, L.; Hatzopoulos, S.; Kochanek, K.; Piłka, A.; Senderski, A.; Skarżyński, P.H. A comparison of audiometric and objective methods in hearing screening of school children. A preliminary study. *Int. J. Pediatric Otorhinolaryngol.* **2011**, *75*, 483–488. [CrossRef] [PubMed]
8. Živanović, A.; Delić, V.; Suzić, S.; Sokolovac, I.; Marković, M. Re-evaluation of Words Used in Speech Audiometry. In *International Conference on Speech and Computer*; Springer: Cham, Germany, 2019; pp. 569–577.
9. Skoloudik, L.; Mejzlik, J.; Janouch, M.; Drsata, J.; Vodicka, J.; Chrobok, V. Hearing screenings for preschool children: A comparison between whispered voice and pure tone audiogram tests. *Int. J. Pediatric Otorhinolaryngol.* **2020**, *130*, 109798. [CrossRef] [PubMed]
10. Harris, R.W.; Nissen, S.L.; Pola, M.G.; McPherson, D.L.; Tavartkiladze, G.A.; Eggett, D.L. Psychometrically equivalent Russian speech audiometry materials by male and female talkers: Materiales de logoaudiometría en ruso psicométricamente equivalentes para hablantes masculinos y femeninos. *Int. J. Audiol.* **2002**, *46*, 47–66. [CrossRef] [PubMed]
11. Pedchenko, O.; Lunova, S. Analysis of Ukrainian diagnostic articulation tables. *Eureka Phys. Eng.* **2018**, *1*, 63–72. [CrossRef]
12. Rouev, P.; Mumdzhiev, H.; Spiridonova, J.; Dimov, P. Universal newborn hearing screening program in Bulgaria. *Int. J. Pediatric Otorhinolaryngol.* **2004**, *68*, 805–810. [CrossRef] [PubMed]
13. Haskins, H.A. A Phonetically Balanced Test of Speech Discrimination for Children. Ph.D Thesis, Northwestern University, Evanston, IL, USA, 1949.
14. Colton, M.B.; Ricks, D.J.; Goodrich, M.A.; Dariush, B.; Fujimura, K.; Fujiki, M. Toward therapist-in-the-loop assistive robotics for children with autism and specific language impairment. In Proceedings of the AISB 2009 Symposium on New Frontiers in Human-Robot Interaction, Edinburgh, UK, 8–9 April 2009; p. 5.
15. Krebs, H.I.; Ladenheim, B.; Hippolyte, C.; Monterroso, L.; Mast, J. Robot assisted task-specific training in cerebral palsy. *Dev. Med. Child Neurol.* **2009**, *51*, 140–145. [CrossRef] [PubMed]
16. Olze, H.; Gräbel, S.; Förster, U.; Zirke, N.; Huhnd, L.E.; Haupt, H.; Mazurek, B. Elderly patients benefit from cochlear implantation regarding auditory rehabilitation, quality of life, tinnitus, and stress. *Laryngoscope* **2012**, *122*, 196–203. [CrossRef] [PubMed]
17. Ondáš, S.; Juhár, J. Dialog manager based on the VoiceXML interpreter. In Proceedings of the 6th International Conference DSP-MCOM, Technical university of Košice, Letná, Košice, 13–14 September 2005; pp. 80–83.
18. Profant, M.; Šimková, Ľ. Kochleárna implantácia. (eng: Cochlear implantation). In *Audiológia*; Kabátová, Z., Profant, M., Eds.; Grada Publishing: Bratislava, Slovakia, 2012; pp. 288–305. ISBN 978-80-247-4173-4.
19. Yao, J.; Yao, D.; Givens, G. A browser-server-based tele-audiology system that supports multiple hearing test modalities. *Telemed. e-Health* **2015**, *21*, 697–704. [CrossRef] [PubMed]
20. Integrovaná stupnica vývoja: Počúvať, učiť sa a hovoriť. (eng: Integrated Development Scale: Listen Learn and Speak) guide from Cochlear company. 2015. p. 18. Available online: http://infosluch.sk/wp/wp-content/uploads/2018/09/Integrovana-stupnica-vyvoja-cochlear.pdf. (accessed on 12 June 2020).
21. Skrobek-Chmurska, K. Komunikácia—Jazyk—Myslienie detí s poruchou sluchu. (eng.: Communication—Language—Thinking of children with hearing impairment.). In *Od slova ku konverzácii: Využitie prvkov kultúry vo zvyšovaní jazykových zručností detí so stratou sluchu*; Bienkowska, K., Ed.; Stowarzyszenie Rodziców i Przyjaciół Dzieci z Wadą Słuchu: Krosno, Poland, 2013; pp. 19–26, ISBN 978-83-937353-7-2.
22. Langmeier, J.; Krejčířová, D. *Vývojová psychologie. (eng: Developmental psychology)*; Grada Publishing: Praha, Czech Republic, 1998; p. 344, ISBN 80-7169-1284-X.
23. Boothroyd, A. Statistical theory of the speech discrimination score. *J. Acoust. Soc. Am.* **1968**, *43*, 362–367. [CrossRef] [PubMed]
24. Elliott, L.L.; Katz, D.R. *Children's Perception of Speech: Technical Manual*; Northwestern University: St. Louis, MO, USA, 1980; p. 12.
25. Ondáš, S.; Hládek, D.; Pleva, M.; Juhár, J.; Kiktová, E.; Zimmermann, J.; Oravcová, M. Towards robot-assisted children speech audiometry. In Proceedings of the 2019 10th IEEE International Conference on Cognitive Infocommunications (CogInfoCom), Naples, Italy, 23–25 October 2019; IEEE: Piscataway, NJ, USA; pp. 119–124, ISBN 978-1-7281-4793-2.

26. Kapalková, S. *Hodnotenie komunikačných schopností detí v ranom veku. (eng.: Evaluation of communication skills of children at an early age)*; Slovenská asociácia: Bratislava, Slovakia, 2010; ISBN 978-80-89113-83-5.
27. Štefeková, K.; Culková, R. *Šlabikár pre prvý ročník základných škôl: 2. časť. (eng.: Syllabus for the first year of elementary schools, second part)*; Orbis Pictus Istropolitana: Bratislava, Slovakia, 2017; p. 64, ISBN 978-80-8120-495-1.
28. Slančová, D.; Sokolová, K.J. Vývin syntaxe v ranom veku. (eng.: Development of syntax at an early age). In *Desať štúdií o detskej reči. Lexika—Gramatika—Pragmatika*; Slančová, D., Ed.; Bratislava: VEDA, Slovakia, 2018; pp. 508–626, ISBN 978-80-224-1638-2.
29. Ondáš, S.; Juhár, J.; Pleva, M.; Ferčák, P.; Husovský, R. Multimodal dialogue system with NAO and VoiceXML dialogue manager. In Proceedings of the 2017 8th IEEE International Conference on Cognitive Infocommunications (CogInfoCom), Debrecen, Hungary, 11–14 September 2017; pp. 439–443, ISBN 978-1-5386-1264-4.
30. Chebenová, M. Starostlivosť o sluchovo postihnuté deti. (eng.: Care for hearing impaired children). In *Detská audiológia: 0—4 roky*; Jakubíková, J., Ed.; Slovak Academic Press: Bratislava, Slovakia, 2006; pp. 137–163. ISBN 80-89104-99-1.
31. Gerber, E. *Sandorf. The Handbook of Pediatric Audiology*; Aram, G., Ed.; Gallaudet University Press: Washington, DC, USA, 2001; p. 450. ISBN 9781563681097.
32. Hládek, D.; Ondáš, S.; Staš, J. Online natural language processing of the Slovak Language. In Proceedings of the 2014 5th IEEE Conference on Cognitive Infocommunications (CogInfoCom), Vietri sul Mare, Italy, 5–7 November 2014; pp. 315–316, ISBN 978-1-4799-7280-7.
33. Chivarov, N.; Marinov, M.; Lazarov, V.; Chikurtev, D.; Goranov, G. Wearable internet of things to trigger the actions of a tele-controlled service robot for increasing the quality of life of elderly and disabled-ROBCO 19. In Proceedings of the 2019 17th International Conference on Emerging eLearning Technologies and Applications (ICETA), Proceedings, Starý Smokovec, Slovakia, 21–22 November 2019; pp. 122–125.

© 2020 by the authors. Licensee MDPI, Basel, Switzerland. This article is an open access article distributed under the terms and conditions of the Creative Commons Attribution (CC BY) license (http://creativecommons.org/licenses/by/4.0/).

Article

# Lex-Pos Feature-Based Grammar Error Detection System for the English Language

Nancy Agarwal, Mudasir Ahmad Wani * and Patrick Bours

Department of Information Security and Communication Technology, Norwegian University of Science and Technology (NTNU), 2815 Gjøvik, Norway; nancy.agarwal@ntnu.no (N.A.); patrick.bours@ntnu.no (P.B.)
* Correspondence: mudasir.a.wani@ntnu.no

Received: 6 September 2020; Accepted: 1 October 2020; Published: 14 October 2020

**Abstract:** This work focuses on designing a grammar detection system that understands both structural and contextual information of sentences for validating whether the English sentences are grammatically correct. Most existing systems model a grammar detector by translating the sentences into sequences of either words appearing in the sentences or syntactic tags holding the grammar knowledge of the sentences. In this paper, we show that both these sequencing approaches have limitations. The former model is over specific, whereas the latter model is over generalized, which in turn affects the performance of the grammar classifier. Therefore, the paper proposes a new sequencing approach that contains both information, linguistic as well as syntactic, of a sentence. We call this sequence a Lex-Pos sequence. The main objective of the paper is to demonstrate that the proposed Lex-Pos sequence has the potential to imbibe the specific nature of the linguistic words (i.e., lexicals) and generic structural characteristics of a sentence via Part-Of-Speech (POS) tags, and so, can lead to a significant improvement in detecting grammar errors. Furthermore, the paper proposes a new vector representation technique, Word Embedding One-Hot Encoding ($W_E O_E$) to transform this Lex-Pos into mathematical values. The paper also introduces a new error induction technique to artificially generate the POS tag specific incorrect sentences for training. The classifier is trained using two corpora of incorrect sentences, one with general errors and another with POS tag specific errors. Long Short-Term Memory (LSTM) neural network architecture has been employed to build the grammar classifier. The study conducts nine experiments to validate the strength of the Lex-Pos sequences. The Lex-Pos -based models are observed as superior in two ways: (1) they give more accurate predictions; and (2) they are more stable as lesser accuracy drops have been recorded from training to testing. To further prove the potential of the proposed Lex-Pos -based model, we compare it with some well known existing studies.

**Keywords:** Natural Language Processing; deep learning; grammar error detection; word embedding

## 1. Introduction

With the advent and continuous advancement in Natural Language Processing (NLP) that aims to enable a machine to understand the human language, the problem of designing a grammar error detector for the natural language is also gaining much attention from researchers [1–4]. The non-native speakers of a language find a hard time in writing grammatically correct sentences. For example, there is a large section of English language learners who need a tool to check if their written content contains grammatical errors [3]. The primary task of a grammar classifier is to predict whether a sentence is grammatically valid or not. The automatic grammar detector can also be applied to grade the writing style of a person by counting the incorrect sentences in their content [1]. Furthermore, a grammar detector can be employed to evaluate the output of Machine Translation (MT) systems which are designed to produce grammatically correct sentences, by highlighting the translated sentences which contain errors [2].

The language error detection problem is mostly considered as a sequence labeling task where a supervised learning approach is adopted to predict whether the input sequence is grammatically correct or not. Most of the existing studies use one out of two approaches to convert an English sentence into a sequence for the classification task. In the first approach, the sentence is processed as a sequence of words as they appear in the text [1,5]. We refer to this sequence as a lexical sequence. For example, the sentence *"I am reading a book"* will be transformed into the sequence $<I>$ $<am>$ $<reading>$ $<a>$ $<book>$. In the second approach, a sentence is converted into the sequence of tokens which indicate its structural or syntactic information [6,7]. We call these types of sequences syntactic. For example, the syntactic sequence of the same sentence will be $<subject>$ $<helping-verb>$ $<verb>$ $<article>$ $<object>$. This is more like specifying the grammar-domain of words used in a sentence. Researchers use various tools such as dependency parser and Part-Of-Speech (POS) tagger to obtain the structural information of a sentence.

However, we observe that both types of sequences have their inherent limitations. The model trained on lexical sequences is highly specific to the domain of vocabulary of the sentences. Therefore, these models do not generalize well. This implies that, if the sentences in a training set are not enough to cover the large aspect of the English language, the words in test sequences would appear strange to the model. On the other hand, the model trained on syntactic sequences overcomes this limitation by providing the structural characteristics of the sentences, and hence, allow the model to generalize the rules. However, too much generalization is also not good for the model as it often provides insufficient knowledge about the grammar used in a sentence. For example, both words *"a"* and *"an"* are articles but they are used in a different context (e.g., *"an apple"*, *"a banana"*) which cannot be reflected by a syntactic sequence only.

We address this problem by proposing a novel sequence named as Lex-Pos sequence that attempts to capture the specific nature of the lexical sequence and generic nature of the syntactic sequence of a sentence. The structural organization of a sentence in the Lex-Pos format is represented using Part-Of-Speech tags. The required linguistic knowledge is added to the structural knowledge of the sentence to prevent the grammar error classifier from over-generalization.

Since the proposed Lex-Pos sequence contains both lexical tokens and POS-tag tokens, we introduce a new vector representation to represent this sequence in a machine-understandable format. We infused two vector representation techniques viz; word embedding and one-hot encoding to draw the vector of Lex-Pos sequences. We named this representation Word Embedding One-Hot Encoding ($W_E O_E$). In this $W_E O_E$ vector representation, the lexical tokens in a sequence are converted into embedding vectors, whereas syntactic tokens are converted into binary vectors.

In order to design the grammar error detector algorithm, a large corpus containing a satisfactory quantity of both correct and incorrect sentences is required. The correct sentences are acquired from the Lang-8 English learner corpus (https://sites.google.com/site/naistlang8corpora/). However, for designing a dataset of grammatically invalid sentences, an artificial error corpus is created by inducing the grammatical errors into the correct sentences of the Lang-8 dataset. Talking about the grammar error types, there are a variety of errors in English language and we distribute them in two categories, viz, syntactic errors and semantic errors. Syntactic errors are caused due to varied reasons for example, a word in a sentence does not spell right (misspelling error), a verb does not conform to the subject (subject-verb agreement error) or a preposition is incorrectly used (preposition error), etc. On the other hand, the sentences with semantic errors are structurally correct but does not make any sense in real life, for example, 'I am eating water', 'we are running a banana', etc. The proposed approach can detect all the syntactic errors in an English sentence and verifies the grammatical structure of a sentence but does not ensure if a sentence is semantically valid, (i.e., if the sentence is meaningful).

Since our target is to train the classifier to differentiate between a valid or invalid Lex-Pos sequence which contain two kinds of tokens, i.e., lexical and POS-tag, two sets of incorrect sentences are designed, one with general errors and another with POS-tag specific errors. The general errors are induced to make the model aware of lexical specific mistakes. The existing error introduction techniques such as *missing verb errors, repeated word errors, subject-verb agreement errors*, etc. [1] have been used to create different types of such ungrammatical sentences. However, for designing the second set of error corpus, a new error induction method has been implemented that induces POS-tags specific errors in the correct English sentences.

In this paper, the major focus is to show that the proposed Lex-Pos sequence which incorporates both linguistic and structural information of a sentence can markedly enhance the performance of the grammar error detection classifier. The source code for the proposed approach has been made available for the researchers (https://github.com/Machine-Learning-and-Data-Science/Lex-POS-Approach). The main contributions of the work are summarised as follows.

- A new sequence of the English sentence named Lex-Pos is proposed, which tends to infuse the specificity of linguistic and generalization of syntactic characteristics of a sentence;
- A novel vector representation for Lex-Pos sequence of sentences named as Word Embedding One-Hot Encoding ($W_E O_E$) has been presented by combining the word embedding and one-hot encoded sequences;
- The novel error induction methods have been proposed to create negative samples containing POS-tag errors for training;
- The grammar classifier is designed using LSTM deep learning architecture;
- Overall, nine experiments have been conducted on three designed datasets to reveal the potential of Lex-Pos sequences; and
- A comparative study is presented where two replicas of existing grammar-aware systems are designed and experiments are conducted to further demonstrate the strength of Lex-Pos sequences.

The remaining of the paper is structured as follows: Section 2 discusses the literature about grammar detection and correction systems. The proposed Lex-Pos sequence is explained in Section 3 and the datasets and pre-processing are presented in Section 4. In Section 5, different error induction methods are discussed including the newly introduced tag specific error induction. Section 6 presents a novel sequence representation technique that has been used for designing a grammar error detector in this study. The experimental setup and results are discussed in Section 7. Section 8 provides a comparison with existing studies. In Section 9, we have discussed a few limitations of our study, and finally, Section 10 concludes the overall work of Lex-Pos feature-based Grammar Error Detection system for the English Language.

## 2. Background Study

In the grammar detection problem, the sentences are mostly converted into some sequence to obtain a feature set for experiments. Prior works have majorly focused on either considering the sentence itself as a sequence of words or extracting the sequence of tokens which depicts the structure of a sentence. For example, [1] has combined the POS tags of the sentence and the output of the XLE parser (https://ling.sprachwiss.uni-konstanz.de/pages/xle/) to extract the feature set for identifying grammatically ill-formed sentences. The authors also proposed the design of an artificial error corpus for training the model by introducing four types of grammatical mistakes including missing word errors, extra word errors, spelling errors, and agreement errors. The work is further extended in [2], where probabilistic parsing features are incorporated with the POS $n$-grams and XLE-based features to improve the results. In [6], the authors propose a classifier to detect grammatical mistakes in the output produced by Statistical Machine Translation (SMT) systems. The structure of the sentences has been captured using multi-hot encoding where the word vector represents three types of information: *POS tag*, *morphology* and *dependency relation*.

A large section of researchers has focused on representing the sentences using word embedding vectors. The authors of [8] propose the Grammar Error Corrector (GEC) model using the convolutional encoder-decoder architecture which was trained on word embeddings of the sentences. Another work [3] proposes word embeddings that considers both the grammaticality of the target word and the error patterns. To create incorrect sentences in the corpus, the target word in the sentence has been replaced with a similar but different word that often confuses the learners. For example, replacing 'peace' with 'piece'. Authors in [9] have designed a translation model that assists in understanding the unseen word using its context. The encoder-decoder model which is capable of handling the Out Of Vocabulary (OOV) words has been employed. [10] also utilizes the Convolutional Neural Network (CNN) to build a GEC model. However, the problem is considered as a binary classification rather than a sequence-to-sequence problem. The task of the model is to predict the grammatical correctness of a word based on the context where it has been used in the sentence. The authors also implement word embeddings to represent the sequence of a sentence and substitution error induction method to artificially create the negative samples in the training set.

There are also several studies that attempt to integrate a different level of information of the sentence in the sequence. For example, in [11], word-based sequences represented using word embedding are applied to build a neural GEC model. They also infuse character-level information in the neural network where the word embedding representation of OOV words depends on their character sequences. Study [12] attempts to detect the prepositional mistakes in the sentences by extracting the contextual information of the prepositions. The authors in this study integrated the prepositional words (e.g., *into* or *at*) with the noun or verb phrases to predict the probability of their correct usage in the sentences. Similarly, [13] worked on identifying prepositional errors by combining POS-tagged and parsed information with English words. In our work, we convert the complete sentence into a sequence that contains both structural as well as contextual information. The structural tokens are represented using one-hot encoding and context tokens are represented using word embedding.

Other studies on grammatical error detection focus only on specific errors, such as article errors, adjective errors or preposition errors [7,14,15]. The authors of [7] proposed four error generation methods to introduce article mistakes statistically in English sentences to create negative samples that resemble grammar errors naturally occurring in second language learner texts. A model has been designed to detect and correct article errors. Similarly, the authors in [16] put their efforts into selectively correcting article errors in the sentences. Instead of using all the words in sentences, the model is trained on the sequence of words surrounding the articles only, i.e., $n$ words before and after the article. Article [14] focuses on the mistakes committed by the learner while using adjectives with nouns in sentences. In our study, an attempt is made to target all kinds of errors with special attention to POS-tag specific errors. Therefore, our work utilizes two corpora for negative samples, one with general errors and another with tag specific errors.

## 3. Lex-Pos Sequence

Earlier studies have mainly focused on either lexical knowledge of the sentences such as words appearing in the text or the syntax knowledge of the sentences such as POS tags, as features for training the grammar detection model. In a lexical-based approach, an English sentence can mostly be directly converted into a sequence of words by splitting it with space. Whereas, in a syntactic-based approach, the sentence is first converted into the grammatical structure using tools like dependency parser (http://www.nltk.org/howto/dependency.html) or tagger (https://www.nltk.org/book/ch05.html) and then a sequence is designed by extracting the relevant information.

However, lexical-based models highly depend on the vocabulary of sentences in the training set, therefore, these models are difficult to generalize. For example, a model trained on sentence $S_1$:

*"I have an umbrella"* might fail to understand the grammaticality of the sentence $S_2$: *"I have a cat"* during testing as the words *"a"* and *"cat"* appear new to the model. Therefore, the model trained on the words vocabulary of the sentences is highly vulnerable to categorizing unseen sentences as incorrect.

On the other hand, the learning structure of the sentences allows the model to generalize the rules. For example, the *NLTK pos-tagger* converts both of the above sentences ($S_1$ and $S_2$) into the same sequence of POS tags, i.e., $<PRP> <VBP> <DT> <NN>$ for denoting the *personal pronoun*, *present tense verb*, *determiner* and *noun* respectively. Therefore, the model trained on syntactic features of the sentence, *"I have an umbrella"* can easily predict the structure of the sentence, *"I have a cat"* as correct. However, too much generalization can also increase the false alarms. For example, the *pos-tagger* tool generates the same sequence for the two sentences *"I have a umbrella"* and *"I have an umbrella"*, i.e., $<PRP> <VBP> <DT> <NN>$. Here the articles *a* and *an* are both categorized under same tag $<DT>$.

Therefore, in this paper, we introduced a new sequence, viz, Lex-Pos by combining the specificity level of the lexical approach and generalization of structural characteristics of sentences. In this feature set, we embed the required linguistic knowledge in the POS-tag sequence of the sentence so that the model can learn to generalize the structure of sentence *"I have an umbrella"* to *"I have a cat"*, and at the same time, also distinguish it from the sentence *"I have a umbrella"*.

In order to construct the Lex-Pos sequence, we first need to identify the problematic POS tags which overgeneralize the structure of a sentence. For example, in the sentences, *"I have an umbrella"* and *"I have a umbrella"*, $<DT>$ is the tag which causes the problem. Once we identify these problematic POS tags, we embed additional linguistic knowledge to such tags. For example, the $<DT>$ tag is integrated with two tokens; first the article (i.e., a/an/the) itself, and second the pronouncing alphabet of the word that follows the article as shown in sentences 1, 2 and 3 in Table 1. The *pronouncing* (https://pypi.org/project/pronouncing/) library of python has been used to obtain the pronounced letter of the word.

In case of the *NLTK pos-tagger*, the other tags which were found problematic include $<PRP>$ representing personal pronoun (e.g., *he, she, I, we,* or *you*), $<VBP>$ representing verb such as *am, are,* or *have,* and $<IN>$ representing preposition/subordinating conjunction e.g., *in, at,* or *on*. All these tags in the syntactic sequence of a sentence are provided with extra linguistic information. Algorithm 1 illustrates the step-wise designing of the Lex-Pos sequence.

---

**Algorithm 1:** Lex-Pos Sequence.

**begin**
    Input: Sequence;
    Output: Lex_Pos_Seq;
    Calculate pos-tag sequence of Sentence (Pos_Seq);
    Initialize the list of problematic tags (Prob_Tags);
    Initialize empty Lex_Pos sequence (Lex_Pos_Seq);
    **foreach** *Pos_tag in Pos_Seq* **do**
        **if** *Pos_tag in Prob_Tags don* **then**
            Append (Pos_tag + Linguistic information) to Lex_Pos_Seq;
        **else**
            Append Pos_tag to Lex_Pos_Seq;
        **end**
    **end**
**end**

Table 1. Examples of Lex-Pos sequences.

| ID | Sentence | Lexical Sequence | POS-tag Sequence | Lex-Pos Sequence | Label |
|---|---|---|---|---|---|
| 1 | I have an umbrella | <i><have><an><umbrella> | <PRP><VBP><DT><NN> | <PRP><I><VBP><have><DT><an><A><NN> | correct |
| 2 | I have a cat | <i><have><a><cat> | <PRP><VBP><DT><NN> | <PRP><I><VBP><have><DT><a><K><NN> | correct |
| 3 | I have a umbrella | <i><have><a><umbrella> | <PRP><VBP><DT><NN> | <PRP><I><VBP><have><DT><a><A><NN> | incorrect |
| 4 | You are here | <you><are><here> | <PRP><VBP><RB> | <PRP><you><VBP><are><RB> | correct |
| 5 | I are here | <i><are><here> | <PRP><VBP><RB> | <PRP><I><VBP><are><RB> | incorrect |
| 6 | I am here | <i><am><here> | <PRP><VBP><RB> | <PRP><I><VBP><am><RB> | correct |
| 7 | I am sitting on the table | <i><am><sitting><on><the><table> | <PRP><VBP><VBG><IN><DT><NN> | <PRP><I><VBP><am><VBG><sitting><IN><on><table><DT><NN> | correct |

Table 1 shows a few instances of Lex-Pos sequences. It can be seen in Table 1 that the two tags $<PRP>$ and $<VBP>$ are appended with the information of personal pronoun and helping verb in sentences 4, 5 and 6. In the case of $<IN>$ tag, three lexical tokens, namely, preposition, word preceding the preposition and word following the preposition are appended. However, if the preceded or followed word comprises some $<DT>$ tag words such as *the*, or *some*, then these words are ignored and the next word in the sequence is appended as shown for the last sentence in Table 1.

## 4. Datasets and Pre-Processing

Training of grammar classifiers requires both correct and incorrect sentences in a dataset. We used the Lang-8 Corpus of the Learner English dataset as grammatically valid English sentences for our experiments. The dataset contains over 5 million sentences with the length of the sentences ranging from 1–80 words. We selected sentences with a length of less than 15 words in order to reduce the variation in the length of the sentences during the training of the model. Finally, we obtained around 1 million correct sentences. The incorrect sentences are obtained from the correct corpus by writing error induction programs which are explained in detail in Section 5.

Although the sentences in the Lang-8 corpus are already verified as grammatically correct, we performed a few pre-processing functions so as to design an efficient dataset for training. First, we converted the sentence into lower case. Then, we replaced the contracted form of auxiliaries in the sentences with their long-form (e.g., "I'm not" → "I am not"). Also, numbers in the sentences are replaced with the keyword *digit* to reduce variation (e.g., "I am 16 years old" → "I am digit years old"). However, we did not remove any punctuation marks from the sentences as they hold significant knowledge of the structure of the sentences. The python libraries, *nltk* (https://www.nltk.org/) and *re* (https://docs.python.org/3/library/re.html), were used to pre-process the sentences.

## 5. Error Induction Methods

In this section, we describe the procedure used to generate an artificial error corpus from the Lang-8 dataset which has been made available for the researchers (https://github.com/Machine-Learning-and-Data-Science/Lex-POS-Approach). Our target is to train the machine learning based model to differentiate the correct sequence of the sentence from the wrong ones. Various researchers have used the notion of breeding artificial error data for training the grammar detector model [1,2]. A sentence can be grammatically invalid due to varied reasons, for example, a word in a sentence does not spell right, a verb does not conform to the subject, or a preposition is incorrectly used. Training requires a large set of grammatically incorrect sentences containing enough samples for each kind of error, which is hard to collect in the sentences produced by native language speakers or writers. However, the dataset of grammatically incorrect sentences with a sufficient number of sentences can be created by performing certain transformations in the grammatically correct sentences (e.g., *inserting, replacing, repeating* or *deleting* words from the correct sentences). While inserting the errors, proper linguistic knowledge is required in order to ensure that the sentence produced by the script is grammatically unacceptable. For example, consider the sentence *"she bought two fresh apples"*, and only deleting the word *"fresh"* from the sentence does not make the sentence incorrect.

In this work, two types of error induction methods, namely General Error Induction and Tag-specific Error Induction, are employed. Sentences with general errors assist the detector in mainly learning the lexical mistakes and tag-based errors helps in making the model learn about POS-tag related mistakes. Both error induction methods are discussed in the following sub-sections.

### 5.1. General Error Induction Methods

General errors contain those methods which have been mostly adopted by the earlier studies for creating incorrect sentences. In our dataset, we introduce 5 types of errors, i.e., *misspelled error, repeated word error, subject-verb agreement error, word order error,* and *missing verb error*. Table 2 provides a brief description of the list of these general errors.

In order to ensure that the sentences created by the error induction procedure are grammatically invalid, a few things were taken into consideration. First, we ensure that we do not misspell the words which are proper nouns. Nouns are something for which a dictionary is unlimited, such as the name of a person. For example, *"Alice is having tea"*, *"Aliceee is having tea"*, and *"Ali is having tea"* are all correct sentences. Therefore, we avoid misspelling proper nouns while creating negative references.

Table 2. Examples of General Errors.

| Type | Error Induction Procedure | Correct Sentence | Negative Sample |
|---|---|---|---|
| Misspelled | Misspell an appropriate word in a sentence | Boys are playing outside. | Boys are playing **outsde**. |
| Repeated | Duplicate an appropriate word in a sentence | Boys are playing outside. | Boys are **are** playing outside. |
| Subject-Verb Agreement | Replace the verb with a verb disagreeing with the subject | Boys are playing outside. | Boys **is** playing outside. |
| Word Order | Swap the position of two appropriate words in a sentence | Boys are playing outside. | Boys playing are outside. |
| Missing Verb | Delete a verb from the sentence | Boys are playing outside. | Boys playing outside. |

For creating sentences with subject-verb agreement errors, we replace the singular verbs with the plural verbs or the other way round to create incorrect sentences. For example *are* is replaced with *is* or *"has"* is replaced with *"have"*.

While generating the repeated errors, we avoided repeating words like *very* or *so*, as a repetition of such words does not make a sentence grammatically incorrect. For example, both sentences *"I like you very much"* and *"I like you very, very much"* are treated as correct in grammar.

While creating word-order errors, we avoid swapping helping-verb with its subject if the sentence is interrogative as both sentences *"am I working"* and *"I am working"* are correct in the English language.

Table 3 provides the distribution of errors in the incorrect dataset. It can be noted from the table that the number of sub-verb agreement and missing verb errors are less when compared to other types of errors as these errors are limited to verbs in the sentences, whereas the domain of other types of errors is not limited to verbs only. It should be noticed that multiple errors can be introduced in a single sentence, i.e., a sentence can have more than one kind of error. Even though the total number of errors created is 85,092, the total number of negative samples produced by the general error method is only 62,899.

Table 3. Distribution of General Errors.

| Type of Error | #Negative Samples |
|---|---|
| Misspelled | 31,067 |
| Repeated | 24,648 |
| Subject-Verb Agreement | 5756 |
| Word Order | 16,158 |
| Missing Verb | 7463 |
| Total | 85,092 |

*5.2. Tag-Specific Error Induction Methods*

As discussed in the earlier sections, $<DT>$, $<PRP>$, $<VBP>$ and $<IN>$ are the tags which provide insufficient knowledge about the structure of a sentence, therefore, these tags must be provided with some additional linguistic knowledge for training a machine learning-based model to differentiate between grammatical correct and incorrect sentences. While creating the tag-specific errors, we introduce errors particularly for these problematic tags to obtain enough negative examples for assisting the model to learn such errors in the sequence structure. Table 4 provides examples of tag specific instances of the sentences.

The total number of negative samples produced by the tag-specific error method is 50,015, which is less than the total number of errors in Table 5 for the same reason as for the general errors. Table 5 provides the distribution of errors in the incorrect dataset.

Table 4. Examples of Tag-specific Errors.

| Type | Correct Sentence | Negative Sample |
|---|---|---|
| $<DT>$ error | I am eating **an** apple. | I am eating **a** apple. |
| $<PRP>$ error | **He** is coming tomorrow. | **You** is coming tomorrow. |
| $<VBP>$ error | I **am** reading a book. | I **are** reading a book. |
| $<IN>$ error | I am sitting **on** the table. | I am sitting **to** the table. |

Table 5. Distribution of Tag-specific Errors.

| Type of Error | #Negative Samples |
|---|---|
| $<DT>$ error | 18,169 |
| $<PRP>$ error | 15,008 |
| $<VBP>$ error | 20,295 |
| $<IN>$ error | 9872 |
| Total | 63,344 |

## 6. Feature Representation

In the proposed work, we convert every sentence (correct and incorrect) in the dataset to the Lex-Pos sequence as discussed in the earlier section. However, for training the machine learning-based model, the Lex-Pos sequence needs to be converted into some machine-understandable (mathematical) form. Researchers have employed a variety of ways to represent a linguistic sequence into useful features, e.g., Bag of Words (BoW), N-grams, TF-IDF, word embedding, and one-hot encoding [17], etc. The approaches such as Bag of Words (BoW), N-grams and TF-IDF rely on the set of tokens and their frequency in the dataset and are therefore insufficient to capture the exact structure of a sentence.

However, in one-hot encoding representation, each word in the vocabulary is assigned a unique binary vector. Therefore, in this encoding, all the distinct words receive distinct representation and the length of the one-hot vector is decided by the number of words in the vocabulary. Usually, the size of POS-tags vocabulary is limited, and hence employing one-hot encoding is a good choice to represent the POS-tag sequences. But the one-hot vector to represent an English word seems an inefficient approach as the length of the binary vector could be extremely long due to the large size of English vocabulary.

Word embedding is another feature representation technique in which every distinct word in the vocabulary is mapped to a numeric vector so that semantically similar words share similar representations in the vector space. One good advantage of using word embedding is that the words can be represented in a much lower dimension than the one-hot encoding. Therefore, word embedding seems an optimal choice to represent the English tokens.

Earlier studies have represented the sequences using either the one-hot vector or embedded-word vector. Since the proposed Lex-Pos sequence consists of both POS tags and English words, we present the feature representation that combines both techniques, named as $W_E O_E$. In this technique, we first maintain a list called *tag-list* which contains all the POS-tag tokens generated by *NLTK pos-tagger* along with their index values. The *tag-list* assists in identifying the tokens in the Lex-Pos sequence which need to be represented in one-hot encoded form. We also appended pronouncing alphabets of the words to the *tag-list* for adding the linguistic information to the <DT> tag as mentioned in Section 3. In order to obtain the word embedding vectors of the English tokens in the Lex-Pos sequence, Google's pre-trained *Word2Vec* model has been utilized. The model includes 300-dimensional word-vectors for around 3 million English words. The *Gensim* library (https://pypi.org/project/gensim/) of python has been used to extract the embeddings from the *Word2Vec* model.

The Algorithm 2 explains the procedure explains the procedure of changing the Lex-Pos sequence into the Word Embedding and one-hot Encoding ($W_E O_E$) representation. Three arguments are passed to the algorithm as input: (1) Lex-Pos sequence; (2) *tag-list*; and (3) *Word2Vec* model. The *sentVector* variable is initialized to store the vector representation of each token in the sequence. Also, every token of the Lex-Pos sequence is initialized with a fixed length ($n$) vector having all zero entries. In our case, the size of the *tag-list* is less than the size of the embedding vectors of the *Word2Vec* model. Therefore, the value of $n$ ranges from *min* to *max*, where the minimum value is the number of tokens in the *tag-list*, and the maximum value is the length of the embedded vector of the *Word2Vec* model.

---
**Algorithm 2:** $W_E O_E$ representation of a Lex-Pos Sequence.

   **begin**
      Input: Lex_Pos_Seq, POS_tag_list, word2vec;
      Output: Word Embedding and one-hot Encoding Vector $W_E O_E$_Sent_Vec;
      $W_E O_E$_Sent'_Vec = [];
      **foreach** *token in Lex_Pos_Seq* **do**
         Initialize a zero vector with n length ($W_E O_E$_token_Vec);
         **if** *token in POS_tag_list* **then**
            $W_E O_E$_token_Vec[POS_tag_list[token]] = 1;
         **else**
            **if** *token in word2vec_model* **then**
               $W_E O_E$_token_Vec = word2vec(token)[:n];
         **end**
         Append $W_E O_E$_token_Vec to $W_E O_E$_Sent_Vec;
      **end**
   **end**

---

In order to generate the $W_E O_E$ feature vector representation, every token of the Lex-Pos sequence is first passed through a filter to check if this token exists in *tag-list*. If found, the zero vector of the token is replaced with the respective binary vector, otherwise the token is searched in the *Word2Vec* model. If a token is found in the model, the zero vector is replaced with its embedded representation. The token is considered as unknown if it is not found in either of the lists. Finally, the vector values of a token are appended to the *sentVector*.

## 7. Experiments and Results

In Section 4, we discussed the corpus of grammatically correct sentences, and in Section 5, we presented two types of error induction methods for creating two different corpora of negative samples, i.e., one with incorrect sentences containing general errors and another with incorrect sentences having POS-tag specific errors. All three corpora are utilized to create three datasets in the following manner.

**Dataset 1:** Correct sentences + incorrect sentences with general errors;
**Dataset 2:** Correct sentences + incorrect sentences with tag-specific errors;
**Dataset 3:** Correct sentences + incorrect sentences with both general and tag-specific errors;

Earlier studies on grammar classifiers have employed either lexical sequences or POS-tag sequences of a sentence for grammar classification. This work presents a Lex-Pos sequence which tends to imbibe the specificity quality of lexical sequences and generalization trait of POS-tag sequences. Therefore, we compare the efficiency of a classifier trained on Lex-Pos sequences with the classifiers modeled using lexical and POS-tag sequences. We evaluate the performance of the proposed work on detecting grammatical errors using the 3 datasets described above. Sentences of each dataset are converted into the three types of sequences, lexical sequence, POS-tag sequence and Lex-Pos sequence as shown earlier in Table 1. There are a total of 3 datasets and 3 types of sequences to represent a sentence in each dataset, thus, in total, nine experiments are conducted for comparing the performances of the proposed grammar detector model.

In Section 6, we discussed the one-hot encoding and word embedding representations to denote a linguistic sequence in numeric form. In the experiments, we represent lexical sequences of sentences using a word embedding vector as it allows to represent a word in lower dimensions. The POS-tag sequences are represented using one-hot encoded vectors as the list of POS-tags is very limited. The Lex-Pos sequences are represented using the $W_E O_E$-feature vector. Before training the model, all three datasets were balanced by randomly removing the extra instances from the dataset where it was required. The final size of each dataset used in the experiments is shown in Table 6.

Table 6. Statistics of Corpuses.

| Dataset | #Positive Samples | #Negative Samples | #Total Samples |
|---|---|---|---|
| 1 | 60,000 | 60,000 (general errors) | 120,000 |
| 2 | 50,000 | 50,000 (specific errors) | 100,000 |
| 3 | 60,000 | 30,000 (general) + 30,000 (specific) | 120,000 |

The Long Short-Term Memory (LSTM) neural network architecture has been employed to build a classifier. An LSTM network is a variant of a Recurrent Neural Network (RNN) which is extensively used in solving NLP problems as they are capable of learning the structure of sequential data. All the datasets are split in the ratio of 80:20 for training and testing respectively. The *Keras* framework has been used for implementation. In all of the nine experiments, we have used *sparse-categorical-crossentropy* as a loss function and *adam* as an optimizer with a batch size of 2000. The outmost layer of the network is a *dense* layer with 2 nodes and a *softmax activation* function. Since we are using balanced datasets, the accuracy metric has been evaluated to assess the performance of the models.

The results shown in Tables 7 and 8 are for the grammar classifiers which were trained on lexical and POS-tag sequences of the sentences respectively. If we compare the vocabulary size (i.e., unique number of tokens in the training sets) of datasets of both sequences, it can be seen that the vocabulary size of pos-tag sequences (38 or 39) is much smaller than the lexical ones (15,796 to 20,725). This indicates the generalization capability of keeping the structure of the sentences in its syntactic form. The accuracy obtained on the testing sets of lexical sequences is 80%, 96% and 80% for dataset 1, 2 and 3 respectively. On the other hand, accuracy values obtained on the testing sets of POS-tag sequences are 79%, 75% and 73%, which are significantly lower than the accuracy recorded for the lexical-based classifier. This indicates that the classifier performs better with lexical sequences than the POS-tag sequences in all the datasets.

Table 7. Lexical Sequence—Word Embedding Representation.

| Dataset | Voc. Size | Training | | Testing | |
|---|---|---|---|---|---|
| | | Loss | Accuracy | Loss | Accuracy |
| 1 | 20,725 | 0.30 | 0.87 | 0.46 | 0.80 |
| 2 | 15,796 | 0.55 | 0.98 | 0.19 | 0.96 |
| 3 | 19,777 | 0.29 | 0.87 | 0.48 | 0.80 |

Table 8. POS-tag Sequence—One-hot Encoding Representation.

| Dataset | Voc. Size | Training | | Testing | |
|---|---|---|---|---|---|
| | | Loss | Accuracy | Loss | Accuracy |
| 1 | 39 | 0.38 | 0.83 | 0.44 | 0.79 |
| 2 | 38 | 0.41 | 0.79 | 0.49 | 0.75 |
| 3 | 39 | 0.45 | 0.77 | 0.52 | 0.73 |

Also, while creating the specific-tag errors, we mention that these are basically those errors for which the POS-tag classifier finds it difficult to discriminate. The statement is also reflected in the results of Table 8, where it can be seen that the pos-tag classifier achieves better accuracy in dataset 1, which contains general errors in negative samples (79%) than dataset 2, which contains specific errors in negative samples (75%).

However, it can also be noticed in the results shown in Tables 7 and 8 that the accuracy-drops from training to testing sets are higher for lexical sequences by significant margins. For example, the accuracy obtained in the training set for dataset 3 of lexical sequences (87%) is reduced to 80% in the testing set, i.e., a 7% decrement in the accuracy. The value of loss also increases from 0.29 (training) to 0.48 (testing), i.e., a 19% increase in the loss value. On the other hand, while evaluating the performances of the POS-tag based classifiers on the training and testing sets of dataset 3, there is 4% reduction in the accuracy value and 7% increment in the loss values. This indicates that although the POS-based model is not as accurate as the lexical-based model, it is more stable than the lexical-based model.

The objective of this paper is to combine the effectiveness and stability characteristics into one model by converting English sentences into the Lex-Pos sequences. Table 9 shows the results of the classifiers trained on the Lex-Pos sequences of the sentences with $W_E O_E$ feature representation. It can be seen that the vocabulary size of Lex-Pos sequences (1026 to 2122) in the training set lies between the vocabulary size of lexical (15,796 to 20,725) and POS-tag sequences (38 to 39). This indicates that the Lex-Pos sequences tend to maintain a balance between the generalization and specialization of the two sequence types. It is evident from the results that the Lex-Pos classifier outperforms both lexical and POS-tag based classifiers in all the three datasets. The accuracies obtained by the Lex-Pos models on datasets 1, 2 and 3 are 84%, 97% and 87% respectively.

The results also put the Lex-Pos sequences on top from the aspect of stability as they obtain lower values for both metrics, *increment in the loss* and *decrement in the accuracy* while deploying the classifiers from the training to the testing environment. For example, in dataset 3, the loss values of the Lex-Pos system for training and testing are 32% and 26% respectively (see Table 9), thereby, a total of 6% increment in the loss. The value is significantly lesser than the loss increment values for lexical (19%, see Table 7) and POS-tag systems (7%, see Table 8). A similar pattern is observed for the accuracy drop. In dataset 3, the value of accuracy decreases from 89% in training to 87% in testing in the case of Lex-Pos , a total of 2% drop in the accuracy. This accuracy drop of 2% is also markedly lower than the values obtained by lexical (7%) and POS-tag (4%) classifiers.

Table 9. Lex-Pos Sequence—$W_E O_E$ Representation.

| Dataset | Voc. Size | Training | | Testing | |
|---|---|---|---|---|---|
| | | Loss | Accuracy | Loss | Accuracy |
| 1 | 2122 | 0.29 | 0.88 | 0.39 | 0.84 |
| 2 | 1026 | 0.26 | 0.99 | 0.11 | 0.97 |
| 3 | 1918 | 0.26 | 0.89 | 0.32 | 0.87 |

## 8. Comparative Study

In this section, we compare the proposed work with two well known existing studies in order to further demonstrate the potential of Lex-Pos sequences. The experiment results show that the Lex-Pos sequences represented using $W_E O_E$-feature vectors have more potential to capture the grammatical structure of English sentences than the POS-tag sequences and lexical sequences, and so, are more suitable for designing the grammar aware systems. We compare our work with two other existing studies, [5,16]. In each comparison, we replicate the models proposed by the authors in their work and conduct two sets of experiments. In the first experimental setup, we feed the sequence mentioned by authors in [5,16] as input to the implemented model, and in the another setup, we feed the Lex-Pos sequence as input to the implemented model to see and compare the results.

In [5], the authors designed an essay scoring system to evaluate the writing skills. The objective of the system is to assign a rating (i.e., 0–5) to an English essay that reflects the quality of its content based on various parameters including grammatical correctness. The authors experimented with several deep learning models such as CNN, RNN, LSTM and LSTM+CNN and observed that the LSTM-based system outperformed the others. For comparison, we implemented a similar LSTM-based system which was claimed by the authors as the best. The values of the hyper-parameters are set same as by the authors. Table 10 lists the settings of these hyper-parameters used for training the model, referred to here as Essay model.

Table 10. Hyper-parameters settings for Author Model [5].

| Parameters | LSTM Nodes | Dropout | Epoch | Optimizer | Learning Rate |
|---|---|---|---|---|---|
| Values | 300 | 0.5 | 50 | RMSProp | 0.001 |

The authors evaluated the quality of English essays, including short ones, on a scale of 0 to 5. However, here, we evaluate the quality of English sentences based on its grammatical structure on the scale of 0 or 1 where 0 score refers to a correct and 1 score refers to an incorrect sentence. The three datasets discussed in Section 7 have been used for training and testing the Essay model. For comparison, two experimental setups have been established. In the first round of experiments, the Essay model takes the word embeddings of the lexical sequences of sentences (as mentioned by the authors in their work) as input. In the other round, we provided our proposed $W_E O_E$-feature vectors of Lex-Pos sequences as input features to the model.

The results obtained from the two rounds of experiments are shown in Tables 11 and 12 respectively. It can be seen that on the training set, the author methodology (lexical sequence and LSTM model) with the accuracies 0.89, 0.98 and 0.91 shows slightly better performance than the same model trained using Lex-Pos sequences on datasets 1, 2 and 3 respectively. However, while testing the Lex-Pos sequences-based trained model outperforms in all three datasets with accuracy values 0.84, 0.96 and 0.87 respectively. This confirms that models learn more efficiently on Lex-Pos sequences of sentences. Also, if we notice the accuracy drops from training to testing, we observe that it is less in the author model trained from Lex-Pos based features. The accuracy drops are 7%, 3% and 6% for the author model trained on lexical sequences of three datasets respectively, whereas the values, 4%, 1% and and 3% have been recorded for the author model trained on Lex-Pos sequences. These results further confirm that the Essay model trained on Lex-Pos sequences are more capable of generalization and so, are more stable and efficient.

Table 11. Performance of Model [5] on lexical sequences.

| Dataset | Training | | Testing | |
|---|---|---|---|---|
| | Loss | Accuracy | Loss | Accuracy |
| 1 | 0.08 | **0.89** | 0.13 | 0.82 |
| 2 | 0.02 | **0.98** | 0.04 | 0.95 |
| 3 | 0.07 | **0.91** | 0.11 | 0.85 |

**Table 12.** Performance of Model [5] on Lex-Pos sequences.

| Dataset | Training | | Testing | |
|---|---|---|---|---|
| | Loss | Accuracy | Loss | Accuracy |
| 1 | 0.09 | 0.88 | 0.12 | **0.84** |
| 2 | 0.02 | 0.97 | 0.03 | **0.96** |
| 3 | 0.08 | 0.90 | 0.10 | **0.87** |

For the second comparison, we carry out experiments on the work proposed by the authors of [16]. In that paper, the authors developed a deep learning model with convolution and pooling layers for detecting article errors in the English sentences. We refer here to this model as the Article model. The Article model takes a sequence of $k$ words before and after the article as input in order to learn the surrounding context of the articles. The sequence is translated into a mathematical vector using pre-trained word embeddings. In order to replicate the Article model, we also design a similar CNN model with the same parameters as mentioned in the paper. Table 13 provides the values of these hyper-parameters.

**Table 13.** Hyper-parameters settings for Author Model [16].

| Parameters | Context-Window Size (k) | Filter Windows | Dropout Rate | Regularizer | Classifier Layer |
|---|---|---|---|---|---|
| Values | 6 | 3, 4, 5 | 0.5 | $l_2$-constraint | softmax |

The output of the Article model is multiclass with labels *a*, *an*, *the* and $\epsilon$ where $\epsilon$ indicates no article. The three datasets that have been used so far for training cannot be applied in training this author-model as these datasets have labels 0 and 1 for denoting the correct and incorrect sentences respectively. Therefore, for this comparative study, we design a new dataset from the correct sentences that have been earlier used for training the models and assign three labels 0, 1, and 2 depending on whether the sentences contain *a*, *an* or no article respectively. We do not consider *"the"* article for prediction as the dataset contains instances of single sentences only which are not sufficient to provide enough knowledge of specific and non-specific nouns. Similar to the first comparison study, we conduct two rounds of experiments. In the first experiment, we extract the context words from the sentences with window size 6 as mentioned by the authors, and translate this sequence into numeric vectors using word embeddings. Afterward, these feature values are supplied to the CNN-based author-model for training and testing. In the second set up, we provide the Lex-Pos sequences of sentences transformed using $W_E O_E$-feature vectors as input to the Article model.

Table 14 displays the results of both experiments where it can be clearly noticed that the author model performed extremely well on the Lex-Pos sequences of the new dataset by obtaining 99% accuracy, significantly higher than the accuracy yielded by the context-based sequence model, i.e., 90%. The high performance of the Lex-Pos model could be the result of adding phonetic information of the word used immediately after the article into the syntactic sequence of a sentence.

**Table 14.** Performance of Context-based and Lex-Pos Sequence on Author Model [16].

| Sequence Type | Training | | Testing | |
|---|---|---|---|---|
| | Loss | Accuracy | Loss | Accuracy |
| Context-based Lexical Sequence | 0.27 | 0.92 | 0.33 | 0.90 |
| Lex-Pos Sequence | 0.01 | **0.99** | 0.02 | **0.99** |

In order to make sure that the proposed approach is statistically significant, we further conducted a number of experimental trials to determine if the Lex-Pos-based classifier can be trusted over the author model. In this regard, 15 pairs of training and testing subsets were constructed by randomly selecting 10,000 and 2000 instances for each pair from the main training and testing set respectively.

Afterward, on each pair, both Lex-Pos-based and author model [5] were trained and the respective accuracy values have been recorded. Figure 1 presents a plot drawn from these accuracy values where the x-axis and y-axis represent values obtained by author classifier [5] and Lex-Pos-based classifier respectively. The graph clearly shows that for every pair of subset, Lex-Pos based classifier has performed better by obtaining a higher accuracy score. We also applied paired Student's *t*-tests (https://www.ruf.rice.edu/~bioslabs/tools/stats/ttest.html) on the two sets of accuracy scores to know if the distribution difference is statistically significant. We recorded the *t*-value as 11.516 with a *p*-value less than 0.05 which implies that the accuracy distribution of the two models is statistically different. Therefore, there is sufficient evidence to consider that the Lex-Pos model is better than the author model [5]. It is to be noted that statistical significance test was not conducted for comparing Lex-Pos-based grammar detector with author model [16] as we observed a considerably large improvement in the results, i.e., 9% increment in accuracy.

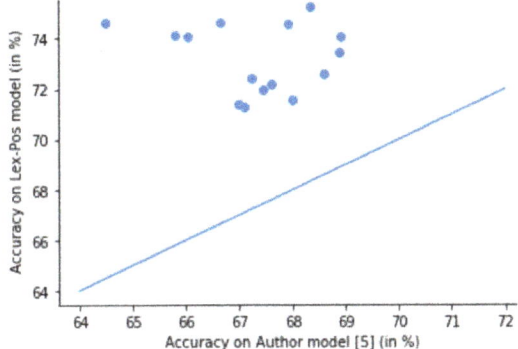

**Figure 1.** Accuracy values on 15 trials.

## 9. Discussion and Limitations

In this work, we have proposed the concept of converting an English sentence into a Lex-Pos sequence represented using a $W_E O_E$-feature vector in order to design a grammar detector that is capable of taking the advantage of both kinds of sequences, i.e., the specific nature of the lexical sequences and generic nature of syntactic sequences. We compare the performances of the Lex-Pos classifier with the models which are individually trained on lexical and POS-tag sequences of sentences. Lexical sequences were represented using word embedding vectors, while POS-tag sequences were represented using one-hot vector encoding. It is evident from the results that in terms of accuracy, the lexical-based models perform better than POS-tag-based models, whereas, in the context of stability, the POS-tag-based model proved to be more trustworthy. However, Lex-Pos sequence-based classifiers have proven to be the best systems in both aspects, accuracy and stability. This confirms the usefulness of providing additional linguistic knowledge to the POS-tag sequences of sentences and shows that the Lex-Pos sequences are more efficient in capturing the grammar structure of the English language.

In order to further demonstrate the potential of Lex-Pos , two grammar aware models of existing studies have been replicated. The first replica (LSTM-based Essay model) is designed to score the English sentence based on its correctness of grammar. And the second replica (CNN-based Article model) is modeled to classify the article errors in the sentence. The experiments show that both author models performed better on the Lex-Pos sequences than the sequences used in the respective papers. Furthermore, in these experiments also, Lex-Pos based trained author models are observed as more stable with lower accuracy-drops from training to testing.

Although the Lex-Pos models are found to be more efficient and trustworthy, there are also a few limitations associated with the present work. First, it does not ensure if a sentence is semantically valid, i.e., if the sentence is meaningful. The proposed model only verifies the grammatical structure of the sentence, and therefore, it will not be able to discriminate the two sentences, $S_1$: *"I am eating a banana"* and $S_2$: *"I am running a banana"*. Both sentences are valid on syntax grounds but the second sentence fails on semantic context since *"I am running a banana"* does not make any sense in real life. Secondly, the proposed model is limited to individual sentences only and does not consider dependency between sentences. For example, consider the two sentences, $S_3$: *"I talked to a boy"* and $S_4$: *"She is great"*. If these two sentences are considered independently, then both are correct. But if these two sentences are considered in combination where the second sentence follows the first one, then instead of *"She"* as a subject in the $S_4$, *"He"* should have been used. These limitations have been considered as the future scope in the proposed work's direction.

## 10. Conclusions and Future Scope

In this paper, our main aim was to demonstrate that the proposed sequence, namely, Lex-Pos which incorporates both linguistic and structural information of a sentence, can lead to a significant improvement in the performance of grammar error detection. Since the Lex-Pos sequences contain both lexical and POS-tag tokens, these sequences have been translated into numerical values by providing a new embedding technique, i.e., $W_E O_E$-encoding. Also, the two types of error corpora have been designed for making the model learn about the lexical and POS-tag specific mistakes respectively. A total of three types of datasets have been used for conducting the experiments where an LSTM architecture was employed to design the grammar detection system.

In the experiments, we found that classifiers trained on lexical sequences yield more accurate results than the classifiers trained on POS-tag sequences. On the contrary, POS-tag-based models are observed as more stable than the lexical- ones. However, Lex-Pos based classifiers outperform the others in both parameters, accuracy and stability. Lex-Pos sequences are also found to be more efficient and trustworthy on the replica systems designed on the basis of existing studies. The comparative study shows that the Lex-Pos sequences can be further employed to design other grammar aware systems other than error detection, e.g., essay scoring system and grammar error correction system. The future scope can be to extend these sequences by imbibing semantic information using methods like named entity recognition in order to make the model learn about semantically valid or invalid sentences.

**Author Contributions:** N.A. and M.A.W. conceived and designed the experiments; N.A. performed the experiments; N.A. and M.A.W. analyzed the data; N.A. prepared the first draft of the paper; M.A.W. edited the paper; P.B. proofread the paper and supervised the overall work. All authors have read and agreed to the published version of the manuscript.

**Funding:** This research received no external funding.

**Acknowledgments:** This work was carried out during the tenure of an ERCIM Alain Bensoussan Fellowship Program.

**Conflicts of Interest:** The authors declare no conflict of interest.

## References

1. Wagner, J.; Foster, J.; van Genabith, J. A comparative evaluation of deep and shallow approaches to the automatic detection of common grammatical errors. In Proceedings of the 2007 Joint Conference on Empirical Methods in Natural Language Processing and Computational Natural Language Learning (EMNLP-CoNLL), Prague, Czech Republic, 28–30 June 2007; pp. 112–121.
2. Wagner, J.; Foster, J.; van Genabith, J. Judging grammaticality: Experiments in sentence classification. *Calico J.* **2009**, *26*, 474–490. [CrossRef]
3. Kaneko, M.; Sakaizawa, Y.; Komachi, M. Grammatical error detection using error-and grammaticality-specific word embeddings. In Proceedings of the Eighth International Joint Conference on Natural Language Processing, Tapei, Taiwan, 27 November–1 December 2017; Volume 1: Long Papers, pp. 40–48.
4. Xiong, D.; Zhang, M.; Li, H. Error detection for statistical machine translation using linguistic features. In Proceedings of the 48th annual meeting of the Association for Computational Linguistics, Uppsala, Sweden, 11–16 July 2010; pp. 604–611.

5. Taghipour, K.; Ng, H.T. A neural approach to automated essay scoring. In Proceedings of the 2016 Conference On Empirical Methods in Natural Language Processing, Austin, TX, USA, 1–5 November 2016; pp. 1882–1891.
6. Tezcan, A.; Hoste, V.; Macken, L. A neural network architecture for detecting grammatical errors in statistical machine translation. *Prague Bull. Math. Linguist.* **2017**, *108*, 133–145. [CrossRef]
7. Rozovskaya, A.; Roth, D. Training paradigms for correcting errors in grammar and usage. In Proceedings of the Human Language Technologies: The 2010 Annual Conference of the North American Chapter of the Association for Computational Linguistics, Los Angeles, CA, USA, 2–4 June 2010; pp. 154–162.
8. Chollampatt, S.; Ng, H.T. A multilayer convolutional encoder-decoder neural network for grammatical error correction. *arXiv* **2018**, arXiv:1801.08831.
9. Yuan, Z.; Briscoe, T. Grammatical error correction using neural machine translation. In Proceedings of the 2016 Conference of the North American Chapter of the Association for Computational Linguistics: Human Language Technologies, San Diego, CA, USA, 12–17 June 2016; pp. 380–386.
10. Liu, Z.R.; Liu, Y. Exploiting unlabeled data for neural grammatical error detection. *J. Comput. Sci. Technol.* **2017**, *32*, 758–767. [CrossRef]
11. Ji, J.; Wang, Q.; Toutanova, K.; Gong, Y.; Truong, S.; Gao, J. A nested attention neural hybrid model for grammatical error correction. *arXiv* **2017**, arXiv:1707.02026.
12. Chodorow, M.; Tetreault, J.; Han, N.R. Detection of grammatical errors involving prepositions. In Proceedings of the Fourth ACL-SIGSEM Workshop on Prepositions, Prague, Czech Republic, 28 June 2007; pp. 25–30.
13. Tetreault, J.; Foster, J.; Chodorow, M. Using parse features for preposition selection and error detection. In Proceedings of the ACL 2010 Conference Short Papers. Association for Computational Linguistics, Uppsala, Sweden, 11–16 July 2010; pp. 353–358.
14. Kochmar, E.; Briscoe, E. Detecting learner errors in the choice of content words using compositional distributional semantics. In Proceedings of the Association for Computational Linguistics, Baltimore, MD, USA, 22–27 June 2014.
15. Tetreault, J.; Chodorow, M. The ups and downs of preposition error detection in ESL writing. In Proceedings of the 22nd International Conference on Computational Linguistics (Coling 2008), Manchester, UK, 18–22 August 2008; pp. 865–872.
16. Sun, C.; Jin, X.; Lin, L.; Zhao, Y.; Wang, X. Convolutional neural networks for correcting English article errors. In *Natural Language Processing and Chinese Computing*; Springer: Berlin/Heidelberg, Germany, 2015; pp. 102–110.
17. Yang, Z.; Yang, D.; Dyer, C.; He, X.; Smola, A.; Hovy, E. Hierarchical attention networks for document classification. In Proceedings of the 2016 Conference of The North American Chapter of the Association for Computational Linguistics: Human Language Technologies, San Diego, CA, USA, 12–17 June 2016; pp. 1480–1489.

**Publisher's Note:** MDPI stays neutral with regard to jurisdictional claims in published maps and institutional affiliations.

© 2020 by the authors. Licensee MDPI, Basel, Switzerland. This article is an open access article distributed under the terms and conditions of the Creative Commons Attribution (CC BY) license (http://creativecommons.org/licenses/by/4.0/).

Article

# Mapping Discrete Emotions in the Dimensional Space: An Acoustic Approach

Marián Trnka [1,*], Sakhia Darjaa [1], Marian Ritomský [1], Róbert Sabo [1], Milan Rusko [1,*], Meilin Schaper [2] and Tim H. Stelkens-Kobsch [2]

[1] Institute of Informatics of the Slovak Academy of Sciences, 845 07 Bratislava, Slovakia; utrrsach@savba.sk (S.D.); marian.ritomsky@savba.sk (M.R.); robert.sabo@savba.sk (R.S.)
[2] Institute of Flight Guidance, German Aerospace Center, 38108 Braunschweig, Germany; meilin.schaper@dlr.de (M.S.); Tim.Stelkens-Kobsch@dlr.de (T.H.S.-K.)
\* Correspondence: trnka@savba.sk (M.T.); milan.rusko@savba.sk (M.R.); Tel.: +421-25941-1101

**Citation:** Trnka, M.; Darjaa, S.; Ritomský, M.; Sabo, R.; Rusko, M.; Schaper, M.; Stelkens-Kobsch, T.H. Mapping Discrete Emotions in the Dimensional Space: An Acoustic Approach. *Electronics* **2021**, *10*, 2950. https://doi.org/10.3390/electronics10232950

Academic Editor: Chiman Kwan

Received: 30 September 2021
Accepted: 25 November 2021
Published: 27 November 2021

**Publisher's Note:** MDPI stays neutral with regard to jurisdictional claims in published maps and institutional affiliations.

**Copyright:** © 2021 by the authors. Licensee MDPI, Basel, Switzerland. This article is an open access article distributed under the terms and conditions of the Creative Commons Attribution (CC BY) license (https://creativecommons.org/licenses/by/4.0/).

**Abstract:** A frequently used procedure to examine the relationship between categorical and dimensional descriptions of emotions is to ask subjects to place verbal expressions representing emotions in a continuous multidimensional emotional space. This work chooses a different approach. It aims at creating a system predicting the values of Activation and Valence (AV) directly from the sound of emotional speech utterances without the use of its semantic content or any other additional information. The system uses X-vectors to represent sound characteristics of the utterance and Support Vector Regressor for the estimation the AV values. The system is trained on a pool of three publicly available databases with dimensional annotation of emotions. The quality of regression is evaluated on the test sets of the same databases. Mapping of categorical emotions to the dimensional space is tested on another pool of eight categorically annotated databases. The aim of the work was to test whether in each unseen database the predicted values of Valence and Activation will place emotion-tagged utterances in the AV space in accordance with expectations based on Russell's circumplex model of affective space. Due to the great variability of speech data, clusters of emotions create overlapping clouds. Their average location can be represented by centroids. A hypothesis on the position of these centroids is formulated and evaluated. The system's ability to separate the emotions is evaluated by measuring the distance of the centroids. It can be concluded that the system works as expected and the positions of the clusters follow the hypothesized rules. Although the variance in individual measurements is still very high and the overlap of emotion clusters is large, it can be stated that the AV coordinates predicted by the system lead to an observable separation of the emotions in accordance with the hypothesis. Knowledge from training databases can therefore be used to predict AV coordinates of unseen data of various origins. This could be used to detect high levels of stress or depression. With the appearance of more dimensionally annotated training data, the systems predicting emotional dimensions from speech sound will become more robust and usable in practical applications in call-centers, avatars, robots, information-providing systems, security applications, and the like.

**Keywords:** emotion recognition; dimensional to categorical emotion representation mapping; activation; arousal and valence regression; X-vectors; SVM

## 1. Introduction

According to Scherer's component process definition of emotion [1], vocal expression is one of the components of emotion fulfilling the function of communication of reaction and behavioral intention. It is therefore reasonable to assume that some information on the speaker's emotion can be extracted from the speech signal.

We dared to call our article "Mapping discrete emotions into the dimensional space: An acoustic approach", paraphrasing the title of the work [2], to draw attention to the fact that many authors attempt to identify the relationship between categorical and dimensional descriptions of emotions by trying to place a verbal term (label) expressing emotion, (i.e., the name of the category) in the dimensional space ([2,3], and others). This could be wrongly automatically taken for a typical position also for the vocal (acoustic) realizations of utterances of speech under the particular emotion. Evaluation of word terms designating emotions is a different task than evaluation of emotion contained in the sound of speech utterances; nevertheless, the correlation between the placement of emotion labels and the placement of the respective emotional utterances can intuitively be assumed. This work presents a system capable of predicting continuous values of Activation and Valence from the acoustic signal of an utterance and thus finding a position of the emotion presented vocally in the particular segment of speech in the AV space.

Affect, in psychology, refers to the underlying experience of feeling, emotion or mood [4]. AV space can be used to represent affective properties not only of emotional but also stressful, insisting, warning, or calming speech, vocal manifestations of a physical condition, such as pain, or a mental condition, such as depression. Coordinates in AV space can be used to map and compare different types of affective manifestations. For example, one can try to use emotional databases to train a speech stress indicator or an anxiety and depression detect. This work offers a system for predicting such coordinates from the sound of emotional utterance. However, it must always be kept in mind that representation in two-dimensional space greatly reduces affective (and acoustic) information, and the functionality of such indicative mapping must always be well verified with respect to the needs of the application.

## 2. Discrete (Categorical) versus Dimensional (Continuous) Characterization of Emotions

The properties of emotions are usually described either categorically, by assigning the emotion to one of the predefined categories or classes, or dimensionally, by defining the coordinates of the emotion in a continuum of multidimensional emotional space [5]. Affective states (i.e., emotion, mood, and feeling) are structured in two fundamental dimensions: Valence and Arousal [6]. Russell has proposed a circumplex model of affect ad has categorized verbal expressions in English language in the two-dimensional space of Arousal–Valence (AV) [3]. The degree-of-arousal dimension is also called activation–deactivation [7], or engagement–disengagement. In this work, we adopt this two-dimensional approach.

As all the three dimensionally annotated databases have the dimensions called Activation and Valence, from now on we use this terminology and difference between terms Arousal and Activation is neglected. The term Arousal will be used when referring to the Russell's work.

In many application scenarios, such as automatic information via voice, using avatars, customer services, etc., it would be useful to have an estimate available of the emotion or stress in the speaker's voice. The system could take the affective state of the customer into account and adapt the mode of communication.

### 2.1. Issues in Predicting Emotional Dimensions from the Sound of an Utterance

The possibilities of human's articulation system are physiologically limited. The acoustic cues of emotions are highly non-specific; the vocal realization of the utterance can be very similar in the presence of different emotions. Affective states form a continuum and dividing emotions into disjoint classes is an extreme oversimplification. The real emotions are complex; they almost never appear "in mixtures". The meaning of terms describing emotions is ambiguous and culturally and linguistically dependent. Projections of various utterances into the AV space cannot be expected to be well separable with respect to emotion category. However, certain trends in their placement can be expected.

As noted by Gunes and Schuller [5], Activation is known to be well accessible in particular by acoustic features and Valence or positivity is known to be well accessible by linguistic features. Estimating Valence from the sound itself can therefore be particularly challenging. Oflazoglu and Yildirim [8] even claim that the regression performance for the Valence dimension of their system is low and that "This result indicates that acoustic information alone is not enough to discriminate emotions in Valence dimension" ([8], page 9 of 11).

A special issue is that very little is known about the mutual dependency of the dimensions of the emotional space [9,10]. The authors of this research have noticed that it is very hard for the annotators to evaluate Valence independently of Activation when the semantic information is unavailable. The emotions with low activation are often assigned Valence values in the center of the range.

Activation and Dominance show even higher interdependencies. In the analysis of their Turkish emotional database, Oflazoglu and Yildrim [8] show in Figure 8 of their paper the distribution of Activation and Dominance, which appears as a narrow cloud lying on the diagonal, which indicates a strong dependence between the ratings of Activation and Dominance dimensions. Nevertheless, extending the representation of space to three-dimensional (Activation, Valence, Dominance) can help to differentiate emotions (for example, to distinguish Anger from Fear). In this work, Dominance is not addressed.

Ekman argued that emotion is fundamentally genetically determined so that facial expressions of discrete emotions are interpreted in the same way across most cultures or nations [11,12]. However, the inner image of emotion in a person's mind and the idea of how it is to be presented in speech depends to a large extent on his experience, education, and to a large extent on the culture in which he lives. Lim argues that culture constrains how emotions are felt and expressed and that cross-cultural differences in emotional arousal level have consistently been found. "Western culture is related to high-arousal emotions, whereas Eastern culture is related to low-arousal emotions" [12]. In this work, we examine the vocal manifestations of emotions in four Western languages (English, German, Italian, and Serbian) and in the first approximation we consider the task of automatic prediction of Activation and Valence from sound to be culture independent. One of the results of this work may be the information, whether the proposed approach works also on languages other than the one it was trained on.

The biggest problem is that there is no ground truth information available. One has to rely on the values estimated by annotators and consider them as ground truth. However, the number of annotators is often small and the reliability of the evaluation is debatable.

The available emotional speech databases were designed for various purposes, which also means they differ in methodology and annotation convention, instructions to annotators, choice of emotional categories, or even language. Moreover, the annotation of emotions was often done with a help of video, face and body gestures, text or semantic information. This information may be absent (not reflected) in the sound modality. The sound-based predictor then misses this information in the training process.

Other problem is the small volume and representativeness of the data available for emotional training. To achieve as large amount of data as possible for regressor training, to cover more variability, three publicly available databases with annotated Activation and Valence (AV) dimensions were combined in one pool.

Different emotional databases contain different choice of emotions. In this work, only the emotions that occur in the majority of the available emotional databases are addressed, namely, Angry, Happy, Neutral, and Sad.

The differences in definitions, methodology, and conditions of creation of individual databases have to be taken into account when evaluating the reliability and informative value of the obtained results.

*2.2. Hypothesis*

Emotional space is a multidimensional continuum. The cues of emotions in the voice are highly non-specific. Emotions are often present in mixtures, the meaning (inner representation) of the emotional terms in both speakers and raters are culture dependent. So, the areas into which the individual realizations of emotions are projected in the dimensional space largely overlap. Nevertheless, we assume that the centroids of the clusters of points to which the utterances are projected in the AV space, should meet certain basic expectations considering their emotion category.

In order to illustrate the expected distribution of emotions in the AV space, we present in Figure 1 the placement of the stimulus words Anger, Happy, and Sad in the space of pleasure–displeasure and degree of arousal according to Russell [3]. Neutral emotion was not addressed in his work. For simplicity, it can be assumed that Neutral emotion should be located at the origin of the coordinate system.

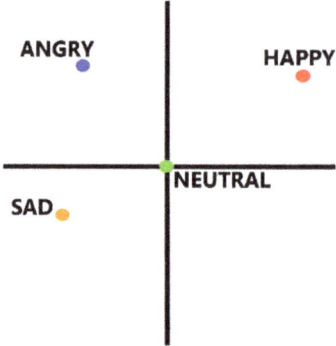

**Figure 1.** Placement of the stimulus words Anger, Happy, and Sad in the space of pleasure–displeasure (x-axis) and degree of arousal (y-axis) according to Russell [3].

Due to the various sources of uncertainty in dimension prediction and the early phase of research, the hypothesis can only be formulated very vaguely. Our working hypothesis is that when predicting the values of Activation and Valence, the centroid of Angry emotion utterances cluster should have a higher Activation value and a lower Valence value than the centroid of Neutral utterances. The centroid of Happy emotion utterances cluster should have a higher Activation value and a higher Valence value than the centroid of Neutral utterances. Sad emotion is less pronounced, and the centroid may lie close to the Neutral utterances; anyway, it should have observably overall lower Valence than Neutral and considerably lower Arousal than the Angry emotion.

### 3. The Data Used in the Experiments

#### 3.1. Training Databases

Three databases were available to the authors, in which values of Activation and Valence were annotated. Each of these three "training databases" was randomly divided into its training set (90% of data) and test set (remaining 10%). This ratio was chosen to preserve as much training data as possible.

IEMOCAP [13]. The Interactive Emotional Dyadic Motion Capture database is an acted, multimodal and multispeaker database in English (10 speakers, 10,000 utterances). It contains 12 h of audiovisual data. The actors perform improvisations or scripted scenarios. IEMOCAP database is annotated by multiple annotators into categorical labels, such as anger, happiness, sadness, neutrality, as well as dimensional labels: Valence, Activation, and Dominance.

MSP IMPROV [14]. MSP-IMPROV corpus is a multimodal emotional database in English (12 speakers, 8500 utterances). Pairs of actors improvised the emotion-specific situations. Categorical labels, such as anger, happiness, sadness, and neutrality, as well as dimensional labels—Valence, Activation, and Dominance—are provided.

VaM [15]. The database consists of 12 h of audio-visual recordings of the German TV talk show Vera am Mittag (47 speakers, 1000 utterances). This corpus contains spontaneous and emotional speech in German recorded from unscripted, authentic discussions. The emotion labels are given on a continuous valued scale for three emotion primitives: Valence, Activation, and Dominance.

Recognizing emotions from facial expressions is a common research topic nowadays (see e.g., [16,17]) and the categorical annotation is often based on facial expressions. A part of VaM database, the "VaM Faces", includes such a categorical annotation of emotion based on the facial expression, that can be linked to the corresponding speech utterance. However, this information is available only for very small number of utterances and the emotion information contained in the facial expression may not be present in the vocal presentation. Therefore, this categorical annotation of VaM was not used in this work.

The AV dimensions in all three databases were annotated using a five-point self-assessment manikins [18] scale. The final rating is the mean of the ratings of all raters. The values on the AV axes were mapped to the range from 1 to 5 in this work.

In addition to training on individual databases, we also trained on a mixture of all three databases, which we will refer to as MIX3, and on a mixture of two larger databases, IEMOCAP and MSP-IMPROV, which we will call MIX2.

### 3.2. Testing Databases

The ability of the regressor to differentiate between emotions resp. place the emotions in the AV space was tested on ten publicly available databases: EmoDB [19], EMOVO [20], RAVDESS [21], CREMA-D [22], SAVEE [23], VESUS [24], eNTERFACE [25], JL Corpus [26], TESS [27], and GEES [28]. These databases are categorically annotated and do not include information on AV values.

Their content used in this work is briefly listed in Table 1 (Abbreviations used in the table are: Ang—angry; bor—bored; anx—anxious; hap—happy; sad—sad; disg—disgusted; neu—neutral; fear—feared; surp—surprised; calm—calm; exc—excited; Au—audio; Vi—video)

Table 1. List of testing databases for cross-corpus experiments.

| Database | Modality | Language | Speakers/Total No. of Audio Files | Emotions |
|---|---|---|---|---|
| EmoDB | Au | German | 10/535 | ang, bor, anx, hap, sad, disg, neu. |
| EMOVO | Au | Italian | 6/588 | disg, fear, ang, joy, surp, sad, neu. |
| RAVDESS | AuVi | English | 24/1440 | calm, hap, sad, ang, fear, surp, disg. |
| CREMA-D | AuVi | English | 91/442 | hap, sad, ang, fear, disg, neu. |
| SAVEE | AuVi | English | 4/480 | ang, disg, fear, hap, sad, surp, neu. |
| VESUS | AuVi | English | 10/ | hap, sad, ang, fear, neu. |
| eNTERFACE | AuVi | English | 44/1293 | hap, sad, surp, ang, disg, fear, neutral is not included. |
| JL Corpus | Au | New Zealand English | 4/4840 | neu, hap, sad, ang, exc. |
| TESS | Au | Canadian English | 2/2800 | ang, disg, fear, hap, pleasant surp, sad, neu. |
| GEES | Au | Serbian | 6/2790 | neu, hap, ang, sad, fear. |

### 4. System Architecture

In the areas of applied machine learning, such as text or vision, embeddings extracted from discriminatively trained neural networks are the state-of-the-art. They are now also used in speaker recognition [29]. The approaches that have been successfully applied in speaker recognition are often adopted in emotion recognition (see e.g., [30–32]).

#### 4.1. X-Vector Approach to Signal Representation

The approach used in this work is based on neural network embeddings called X-vectors [29]. The X-vector extractor is based on Deep Neural Networks (DNN) and its training requires large amounts of training data. Ideally, training data should also include information describing emotions. However, to the knowledge of the authors of this work, any extra-large training database with emotions annotated that would be suitable for training emotion-focused extractor from scratch, is not available.

#### 4.1.1. X-Vector Extractor Training Phase

The X-vectors generated by extractor trained on speaker verification datasets provide primarily the information on speaker identity. However, it was shown they can also serve as a source of information on age, sex, language, and affective state of the speaker [33]. Therefore, the X-vector extractor was trained on the speaker-verification databases: VoxCeleb [34], having 1250 speakers and 150,000 utterances, and VoxCeleb2 [35] having 6000 speakers and 1.1 million utterances. The volume of training data was further augmented using reverberation and noising [36]. The feature extraction module transforms sound into representative features-30-dimensional Mel Frequency Cepstral Coefficients (MFCCs) with a frame-length of 25 ms, mean-normalized over a sliding window of up to 3 s [29]. The energy-based Voice Activity Detector (VAD) was used to filter out silence frames. The result of the training is DNN (X-vector extractor model). In the X-vector extraction process, an MFCC features matrix is fed to the input of this DNN, and an X-vector with a size of 512 is output.

#### 4.1.2. Regression Model Training Phase

The training and test sets for regression are organized in pairs of features representing particular utterances–an X-vector, and the corresponding value of the perceived Valence (for Valence regressor) or Activation (for Activation regressor). The Scikit-learn library was used for training of the Support Vector Regressor (SVR) [37]. Default settings were used for the SVR.

The regression models trained in this phase are able to predict the value of Valence resp. Activation from the input X-vector representing the incoming utterance.

Various types of regressors were tested: AdaBoost regressor, Random Forest regressor, Gradient Boosting regressor, Bagging regressor, Decision Tree regressor, K-neighbors regressor, and Multi-layer Perceptron regressor, but none of them gave consistently better results than Support Vector Regressor.

#### 4.1.3. Prediction Phase

In the prediction phase, the utterances from the pool of test-databases undergo the process of X-vector extraction and prediction values of Valence and Activation. The result is a pair of values indicating the coordinates in the AV space of each utterance.

### 4.2. Overall Architecture

The overall architecture of the system is shown in Figure 2.

As we have shown in Section 4.1, the whole process has three phases. In the first phase, we trained the X-vector extractor (or X-vector model) on large speaker verification databases. In the second phase, we trained regressors for Valence and Activation on dimensionally annotated databases. In the third phase, the prediction of AV dimension values for the addressed emotion categories in the categorically annotated test databases was performed. In real-world application operation, the test databases in the prediction phase will be replaced by a speech signal audio input.

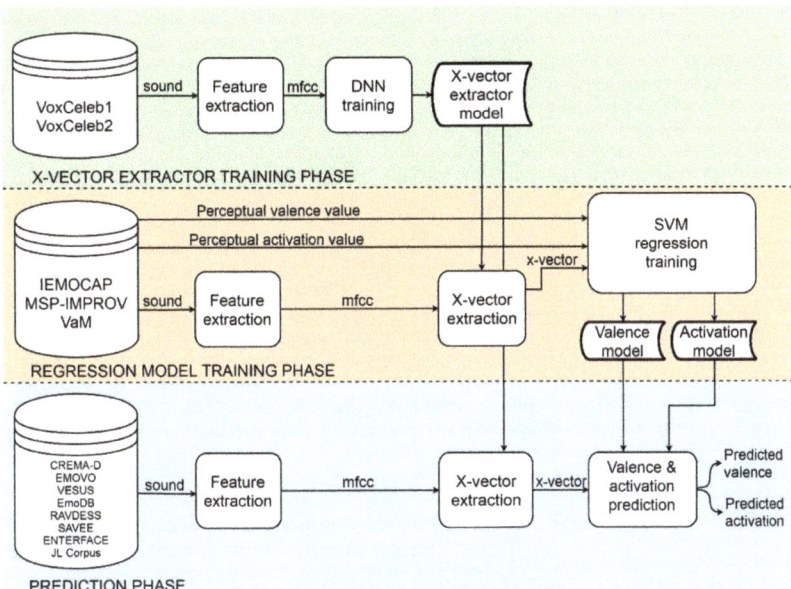

**Figure 2.** Schematic diagram of the system estimating the Activation and Valence values from speech utterances.

## 5. Results

*5.1. Visualization of Results*

The results are presented in the form of figures and tables. The figures show the position of utterances in the AV plane. Seaborn statistical data visualization library [38] was used for visualization. Due to variability the utterances belonging to one emotion in a certain database create clouds or clusters in the AV space. The center of gravity of each cluster is a centroid, marked with a small circle of the corresponding color. The clusters were depicted in a form of a cloud with contour lines representing iso-proportion levels. The graphs were plotted using the kdeplot function with the lowest iso-proportion level at which to draw the contour line set to 0.3 [39].

*5.2. Ground Truth—Original AV Values Indicated by Annotators*

The original AV values indicated by annotators (perceptual Activation and perceptual Valence values) are considered in our work as ground truth. Figure 3 presents the emotions, how they were rated in original annotations. As various corpora contain different sets of emotions, only four emotions were chosen for comparison, that were present in all databases—Angry, Happy, Neutral, and Sad.

The granularity of IEMOCAP data is caused by the fact that there were very few annotators. It can be seen that the layout of centroids of emotion clusters is similar for IEMOCAP and MSP-IMPROV. The graph for VaM original annotation is absent as VaM does not include annotation of emotion categories for vocal modality.

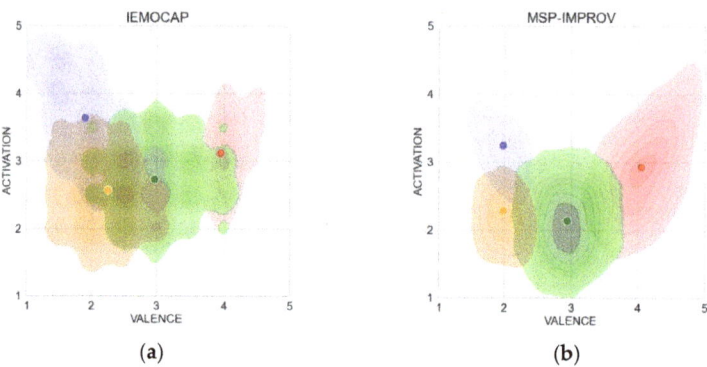

**Figure 3.** Clusters of emotions, as rated by annotators: (**a**) IEMOCAP-full (train + test); (**b**) MSP-IMPROV-full (train + test). Color code: blue—Angry; red—Happy; green—Neutral, orange—Sad.

*5.3. Regression Evaluation—AV Values Estimated on Combinations of the Test Sets*

Figure 4 presents clusters of emotions, estimated by regressor, trained on the mixture of the IEMOCAP-train and MSP-IMPROV-train (MIX2-train), and tested on of IEMOCAP-test and MSP-IMPROV-test sets.

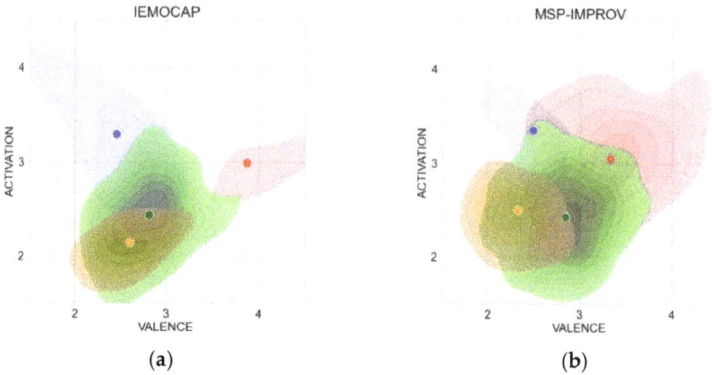

**Figure 4.** Clusters of emotions, estimated by regressor trained on the mix of the IEMOCAP-train and MSP-IMPROV-train sets, and tested on (**a**) IEMOCAP-test and (**b**) MSP-IMPROV-test sets. Color code identifying the emotion in the figure are as follows: blue—Angry; red—Happy; green—Neutral, orange—Sad.

Comparing the figures, it can be seen how the knowledge from the annotated values in the datasets (Figure 3) is reflected to the predicted values on the test set (Figure 4).

It can be seen that the distances of the centroids are considerably reduced. Either the scales are transformed, or the resolution resp. ability to separate the emotions was influenced by the regression. This can be caused by the fact that the training set does not include samples representing the whole AV plane; for some values, it has many realizations, for the others, they are completely missing—it is not representative, nor balanced.

As it is not sufficient to validate the regressor just from the figures, the Congruence Correlation Coefficient (*CCC*) and Mean Absolute Error (*MAE*) were used as regression quality measures to compare annotated and predicted values of Activation and Valence.

*CCC* is a correlation measure that was used for instance in the OMG-Emotion Challenge at the IEEE World Congress on Computational Intelligence in 2018 [39].

Let $N$ be the number of testing samples, $\{y_i\}_{i=1}^{N}$ be the true Valence (Arousal) levels, and $\{\hat{y}_i\}_{i=1}^{N}$ be the estimated Valence (Arousal) levels. Let $\mu$ and $\sigma$ be the mean and standard deviation of $\{y_i\}$, respectively; $\hat{\mu}$ and $\hat{\sigma}$ be the mean and standard deviation of $\{\hat{y}_i\}$, respectively; and $\rho$ be the Pearson correlation coefficient between $\{y_i\}$ and $\{\hat{y}_i\}$. Then, the CCC is computed as:

$$CCC = \frac{2\rho\sigma\hat{\sigma}}{\sigma^2 + \hat{\sigma}^2 + (\mu - \hat{\mu})^2} \quad (1)$$

CCC is still being used by many authors together with traditional error measure MAE.

$$MAE = \frac{\sum_{i=1}^{n}|y_i - \hat{y}_i|}{n} \quad (2)$$

where $y_i$ is true value; $\hat{y}_i$ is predicted value; and $n$ stands for total number of datapoints. The results of further experiments, evaluation of regression quality with various training and test sets by means of CCC and MAE are presented in Table 2.

**Table 2.** Evaluation of regression quality by means of CCC and MAE. (Dim stands for Dimension Val for Valence and Act for Activation. MIX2 is the mixture of IEMOCAP and MSP-IMPROV datasets and MIX3 is the mixture of IEMOCAP, MSP-IMPROV and VaM).

| Training Set | Dim | IEMOCAP Test Set | | MSP-IMPROV Test Set | | VaM Test Set | | MIX3 Test Set | | MIX2 Test Set | |
|---|---|---|---|---|---|---|---|---|---|---|---|
| | | CCC | MAE | CCC | MAE | CCC | MAE | CCC | MAE | CCC | MAE |
| IEMOCAP train | Val | 0.631 | 0.573 | 0.356 | 0.649 | 0.054 | 0.458 | 0.513 | 0.592 | 0.517 | 0.604 |
| | Act | 0.750 | 0.407 | 0.404 | 0.671 | 0.059 | 0.598 | 0.532 | 0.557 | 0.547 | 0.557 |
| MSP-IMPROV train | Val | 0.375 | 0.713 | 0.610 | 0.510 | −0.031 | 0.723 | 0.441 | 0.623 | 0.460 | 0.616 |
| | Act | 0.484 | 0.651 | 0.696 | 0.393 | 0.005 | 0.756 | 0.600 | 0.494 | 0.631 | 0.477 |
| VaM train | Val | −0.024 | 0.737 | −0.005 | 0.860 | 0.063 | 0.315 | −0.029 | 0.784 | −0.025 | 0.814 |
| | Act | 0.096 | 0.604 | 0.023 | 0.726 | 0.044 | 0.544 | 0.024 | 0.676 | 0.022 | 0.686 |
| MIX3 train | Val | 0.646 | 0.555 | 0.554 | 0.539 | 0.029 | 0.484 | 0.639 | 0.516 | 0.637 | 0.527 |
| | Act | 0.678 | 0.458 | 0.657 | 0.430 | −0.014 | 0.648 | 0.729 | 0.402 | 0.750 | 0.391 |
| MIX2 train | Val | 0.646 | 0.558 | 0.561 | 0.534 | 0.025 | 0.524 | 0.632 | 0.520 | 0.641 | 0.525 |
| | Act | 0.673 | 0.466 | 0.667 | 0.424 | −0.014 | 0.661 | 0.726 | 0.404 | 0.753 | 0.390 |

SVR trained on MIX2 give general slightly better results than with MIX3 trained on all the three datasets. This may indicate that vocal manifestation of emotions in VaM may be less pronounced and less prototypical; the data and the annotation may be more different from other two databases. Moreover, VaM is in German and IEMOCAP and MSP-IMPROV contain English speech.

The results also show that the model obtained by training on a mixture of databases is more universal and achieves better results on the mixed test set. In some cases, it also achieves better results for individual databases than a model trained on their own training set.

Both CCC and MAE show that the quality of prediction is better for Activation than for Valence, which is in line with the observation of Oflazoglu and Yildirim [8].

*5.4. Cross-Corpus Experiments, AV Values Estimated by Regression on "Unseen" Corpora*

In these experiments, the utterances from the categorically annotated emotional speech corpora are input to the AV predictor. The result is represented by predicted values of Activity and Valence for each utterance.

Cross-corpus emotion recognition has been addressed by many works, but most of them focus on a categorical approach or they try to identify to which quadrant of the AV space the utterance belongs (see e.g., [40]). Our approach tries to predict continuous values of the AV dimensions. Figure 5 presents clusters of emotions, estimated by the regressor trained on MIX2 and tested on different unseen emotional corpora. Experiments were also performed with MIX3, but the regressor using MIX2 performed better (Table 3).

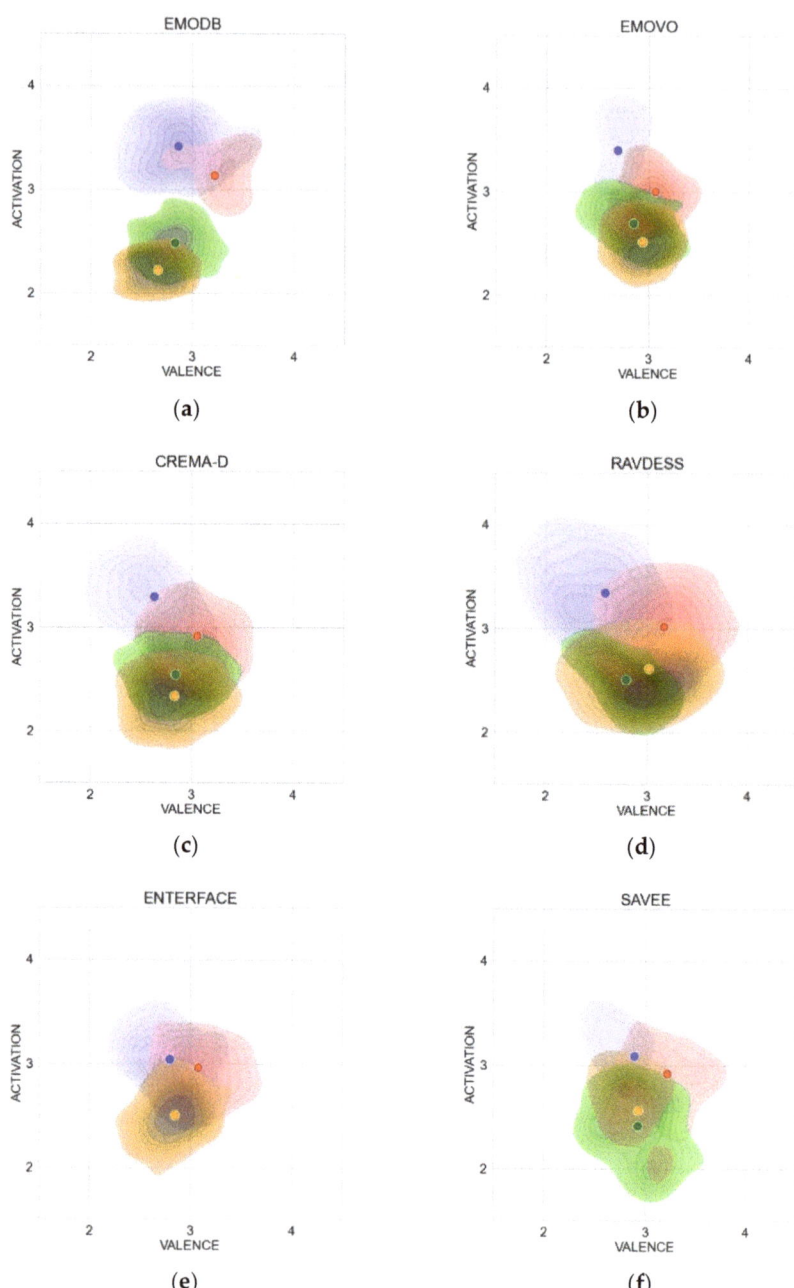

**Figure 5.** *Cont.*

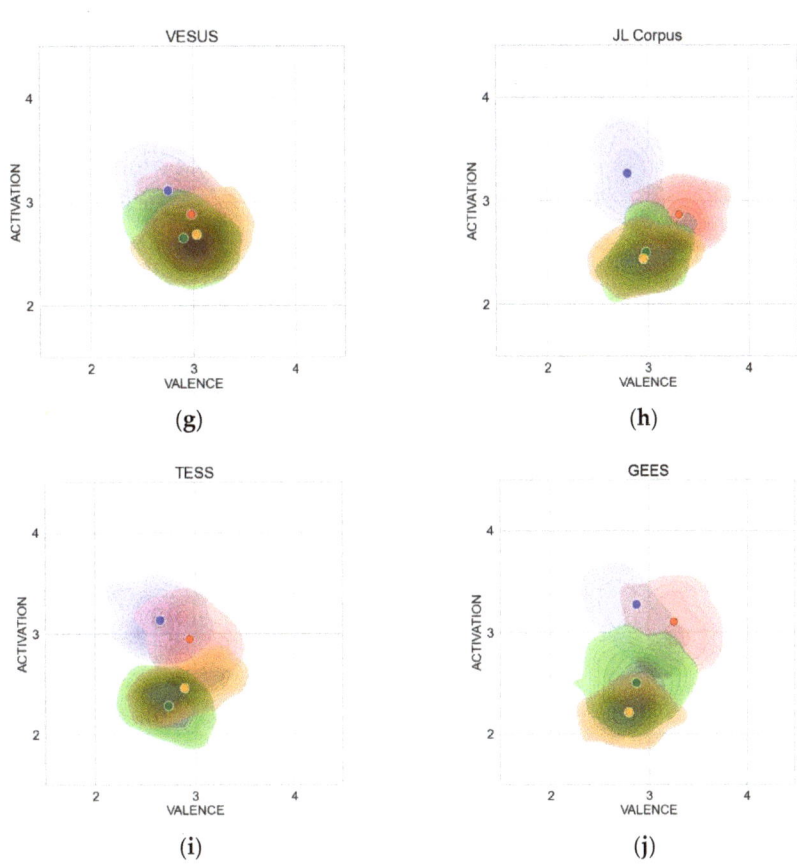

**Figure 5.** Clusters of emotions, estimated by regressor trained on MIX2 training set and tested on: (**a**) EmoDB; (**b**) EMOVO; (**c**) CREMA-D; (**d**) RAVDESS; (**e**) eNTERFACE; (**f**) SAVEE; (**g**) VESUS; (**h**) JL Corpus; (**i**) TESS and (**j**) GEES. Color code identifying the emotion in the figure are as follows: blue—Angry; red—Happy; green—Neutral, orange—Sad.

**Table 3.** Evaluation of the regression quality using distances between centroids.

| Tested Corpus | Dimension | Emotion Clusters | MIX3 Train Set | MIX2 Train Set |
|---|---|---|---|---|
| EMO DB | valence | angry-happy | 0.35 | 0.36 |
| | activation | angry-sad | 1.19 | 1.20 |
| CREMA-D | valence | angry-happy | 0.42 | 0.42 |
| | activation | angry-sad | 0.96 | 0.98 |
| RAVDESS | valence | angry-happy | 0.58 | 0.58 |
| | activation | angry-sad | 0.73 | 0.75 |
| eNTERFACE | valence | angry-happy | 0.28 | 0.28 |
| | activation | angry-sad | 0.54 | 0.55 |
| SAVEE | valence | angry-happy | 0.33 | 0.36 |
| | activation | angry-sad | 0.52 | 0.51 |
| VESUS | valence | angry-happy | 0.23 | 0.24 |
| | activation | angry-sad | 0.42 | 0.44 |
| EMOVO | valence | angry-happy | 0.37 | 0.35 |
| | activation | angry-sad | 0.88 | 0.90 |
| JL Corpus | valence | angry-happy | 0.48 | 0.52 |

Table 3. Cont.

| Tested Corpus | Dimension | Emotion Clusters | MIX3 Train Set | MIX2 Train Set |
|---|---|---|---|---|
| TESS | activation | angry-sad | 0.77 | 0.82 |
| | valence | angry-happy | 0.33 | 0.30 |
| GEES | activation | angry-sad | 0.62 | 0.67 |
| | valence | angry-happy | 0.38 | 0.39 |
| Mean distance | activation | angry-sad | 1.02 | 1.06 |
| Mean distance | valence | angry-happy | 0.375 | 0.380 |
| | activation | angry-sad | 0.765 | 0.788 |

Based on the figures, it is now possible to try to interpret the results obtained by the regressor on the corpora with annotated emotion categories:

The results of the EmoDB database confirm the observation that it contains strongly prototypical emotions [41]. The overlap of emotion clusters is smaller compared to other corpora. The clusters are significantly more differentiated, especially on the axis of Activation, which suggests that the actors performed full-blown emotions with a large range of arousal.

The results of the EMOVO database suggest a possible fact, which is also confirmed by observations in other databases, that Valence for Sad does not reach such low values as expected. The Sad cluster is located on the Valence axis even more towards higher values than the Neutral emotion cluster. According to the predicted AV values, the sound realization of Sad utterances seems to be hardly recognizable from that of Neutral ones in this database. It can be speculated that one of the possible sources of variance may be the inter-cultural difference, as the regressor was trained on English databases and EMOVO is Italian, but this possibility would need more extensive research.

The CREMA-D, RAVDESS, eNTERFACE, and JL Corpus databases give roughly the results as expected (see Section 2.2), although cluster differentiation is relatively small. The centroid of Sad in CREMA-D and JL Corpus have similar position on Valence axis as that of Neutral. The eNTERFACE database does not contain Neutral emotion, therefore the other three emotions cannot be compared to it.

Although the differentiation of clusters is not marked for the SAVEE database, it basically meets the expected trends. The exception is again the Sad emotion, which has higher mean value of Activation than one might expect and has approximately the same mean value of Valence as Neutral emotion.

The Canadian TESS database has the mutual placement of Angry, Happy, and Neutral emotions fully in line with the hypothesis. However, the centroid of the Sad cluster again achieves a higher value of Activation and Valence than expected.

GEES is a Serbian database meant for speech synthesis, which means that the prototypical emotions are presented very clearly and with high intensity. Therefore, the emotion centroids are placed on the expected positions. It is not any surprise that these positions are practically identical to other highly prototypical database, such as German EMO-DB.

*5.5. Centroid Distance as a Measure of Regression Quality*

In the following experiment, the distance of centroids of Angry and Happy emotion clusters on the Valence axis (for Valence regression) and the distance of centroids of Angry and Sad emotion clusters on the Activation axis (for Activation regression) were taken for an ad hoc objective measure of the ability of the regressor to differentiate between emotions. The evaluation of the regression quality using distances between centroids is presented in Table 3.

The two regressors have similar results, but in 15 of 20 cases the one trained on MIX2 (without VaM) has better resolution, and in two cases the results were the same. So, the conclusion could be that adding VaM data to the training set does not improve the universality of regression models and slightly degrades the performance of the regressors.

As was said in Section 3.1, due to the small amount of data in the corpora, we have only allocated 10% of the data for regression quality testing. To evaluate the possible impact of test data selection, we performed a 10-fold regression test on the "wining" mixture MIX2. The results of the individual folds showed only negligible differences with very low standard deviations both for Valence and Activation (see Table 4) and confirmed that 10% of the data is in this case a sufficiently representative sample for testing.

Table 4. Results the 10-fold regression on MIX2.

|  |  | CCC | MAE |
|---|---|---|---|
| Valence | mean | 0.637 | 0.519 |
|  | stdev | 0.015 | 0.009 |
| Activation | mean | 0.763 | 0.385 |
|  | stdev | 0.010 | 0.009 |

*5.6. Overall Picture of Emotion Positions in the AV Space*

We displayed emotion centroids for each database in one figure to assess whether the same emotion category from different databases has a similar location in the AV space, and whether that location corresponds to the hypothesized positions (Figure 6).

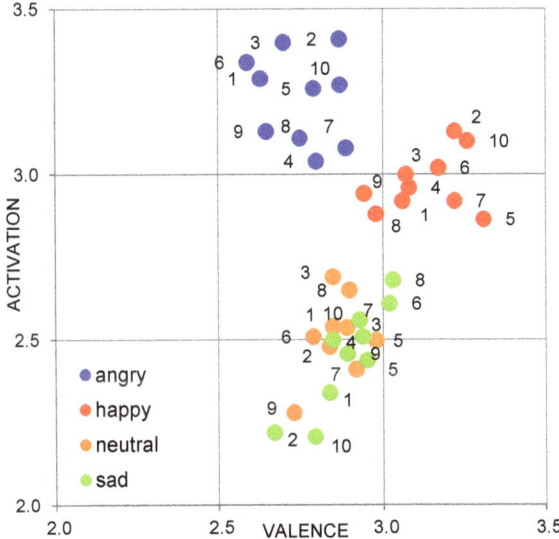

**Figure 6.** Centroids the emotions contained in the 10 testing databases, obtained by regression (each centroid belongs to the particular emotion in one database). Numeric code identifying the databases in the figure are as follows: 1 CREMA-D, 2 EMO-DB, 3 EMOVO, 4 eNTERFACE, 5 JL Corpus, 6 RAVDESS, 7 SAVEE, 8 VESUS, 9 TESS, 10 GEES.

Centroids of Angry, Happy, and Neutral emotion clusters form well-distinguishable groups located in the AV space in an expected manner. This fact confirms that the system can evaluate the position of the perceived emotion in the AV space from the sound of utterances.

However, the group of Sad emotion shows considerable variance and largely overlaps with the Neutral emotion. Sad utterances from some of the databases also achieve higher Valence values than expected.

## 6. Discussion and Conclusions

Due to the small volume and small number of training databases, the "ground truth" data is very sparse and unreliable. They cover only a small fraction of the variety of possible manifestations of emotions in speech. Moreover, the training data are not available for all the parts of the AV plane, and the frequencies of occurrence of training samples representing different points of the AV space are far from being balanced. A substantial part of the data belongs to the less intensely expressed emotions, and they hardly differ from neutral speech. Examples of intense emotions, with extremely low or high Valence and Activation values, are rare. This also leads to certain narrowing of the range of predicted AV values, which is well observable when comparing the positions of emotional category centroids from annotator ratings in Figure 3 with the positions of the respective centroids estimated by regressor in Figure 4.

It is not possible to make general statements about the absolute position of individual emotions in the AV space, but it is reasonable to evaluate their relative position.

From the results obtained by the proposed system, it can be seen that in general Anger has higher Activation and lower Valence, and Happy has higher Activation and higher Valence, than the Neutral emotion. Valence predicted by the proposed system for Sad utterances does not reach such low values as could be expected with respect to the values in original annotations (Figure 3) of the training databases and with respect to Russell's circumplex model. A valuable observation is that, despite the fact that the training data were in English, the emotions from the German, Serbian, and Italian databases were also placed in accordance with the hypothesis.

Due to the variety of sources of uncertainty in speech data and non-specificity of vocal cues of emotion, the clusters of emotions acquired by regression are close to each other and they overlap considerably. However, centroids of corresponding emotion clusters from various unseen databases form observable groups, which are well separable for Angry–Happy–Sad and Angry–Happy–Neutral triplets of emotions. The locations of these groups in the AV space correspond to hypothesized expectations for Angry, Happy, and Neutral emotions.

Some models (e.g., LSTM model as presented by Parry et al. [42] in Figure 2a of their paper) seem to be more successful in determining the affiliation of utterances to individual databases than in identifying emotions. This only confirms the fact that the utterances reflect various technical and methodological aspects of the design of databases, cultural and linguistic differences, and the like. It is therefore difficult to identify emotions from acoustic characteristics of voice. However, we have proven in our experiments that measurement of coordinates of speech utterances in emotional space is in principle feasible, but the resolution and the ability to differentiate various emotions is better for high-activity emotions (Angry–Happy), than for low-activity ones (Sad–Neutral). This may be caused by technical aspects of the solution, but also by the lack of reliable training data, inconsistencies in annotation, diversity of inner psychological interpretation of emotional categories, cultural and linguistic differences, and differences in methodology. At the same time, however, it is highly probable that the sound of speech expressing low-activity emotions contains much less marked distinctive features and is very similar to neutral speech.

In the meantime, the authors have obtained access to the additional dimensionally annotated database, OMG-Emotion Behavior Dataset [39], so one of the future steps will be an analysis, processing, and incorporating this dataset in the training database pool. The other areas of possible improvement are: finetuning of the X-vector extractor for the emotion recognition task, experimenting with combinations of different analysis timeframes, experimenting with various representative features, as well as experiments with new machine learning algorithms and architectures of regressors. Axes scales normalization and finding the position of the origin (center) of the AV space need to be implemented.

The research on the measurement of AV dimensions from speech sound is in its infancy, where the predicted values have high variance and the ranges and units of the dimension-axes are not well defined. However, with new databases, increasing volume of training data, more precise and representative annotation, and improved regression techniques, it will certainly be possible to achieve significantly higher accuracy and better applicability of AV dimensions estimation. Such a system could be used in practical applications in call-centers, avatars, robots, information-providing systems, security applications, and many more.

The designed regressor is currently utilized for a Valence prediction in stress detector from speech in the Air Traffic Management security tools developed in European project SATIE (Horizon 2020, No. 832969), and in a depression detection module developed in Slovak VEGA project No. 2/0165/21.

**Author Contributions:** Conceptualization, M.R. (Milan Rusko) and T.H.S.-K.; methodology, M.R. (Milan Rusko); software, M.T., M.R. (Marian Ritomský) and S.D.; validation, R.S. and M.S.; formal analysis, T.H.S.-K.; investigation, M.T., S.D. and M.R. (Milan Rusko); resources, R.S. and M.S.; data curation, R.S. and M.S.; writing—original draft preparation, M.R. (Milan Rusko); writing—review and editing, M.R. (Milan Rusko) and T.H.S.-K.; visualization, M.T., S.D., and M.R. (Marian Ritomský); supervision, M.R. (Milan Rusko); project administration, M.R. (Milan Rusko) and T.H.S.-K.; funding acquisition, T.H.S.-K. All authors have read and agreed to the published version of the manuscript.

**Funding:** This project has received funding from the European Union's Horizon 2020 research and innovation programme under grant agreement No. 832969. This output reflects the views only of the authors, and the European Union cannot be held responsible for any use which may be made of the information contained therein. For more information on the project, see: http://satie-h2020.eu/. The work was also funded by the Slovak Scientific Grant Agency VEGA, project No. 2/0165/21.

**Data Availability Statement:** Only publicly available databases VoxCeleb, Voxceleb2, IEMOCAP, MSP IMPROV, VaM, EmoDB, EMOVO, CREMA-D, RAVDESS, eNTERFACE, SAVEE, VESUS, JL Corpus, TESS, and GEES were used in this research.

**Conflicts of Interest:** The authors declare no conflict of interest.

# References

1. Scherer, K.R. What are emotions? And how can they be measured? *Soc. Sci. Inf.* **2005**, *44*, 695–729. [CrossRef]
2. Hoffmann, H.; Scheck, A.; Schuster, T.; Walter, S.; Limbrecht, K.; Traue, H.C.; Kessler, H. Mapping discrete emotions into the dimensional space: An empirical approach. In Proceedings of the 2012 IEEE International Conference on Systems, Man, and Cybernetics (SMC), Seoul, Korea, 14–17 October 2012; pp. 3316–3320.
3. Russell, J.A. A circumplex model of affect. *J. Personal. Soc. Psychol.* **1980**, *39*, 1161–1178. [CrossRef]
4. Hogg, M.A.; Abrams, D.; Martin, G.N. Social cognition and attitudes. In *Psychology*; Pearson Education: London, UK, 2010; pp. 646–677.
5. Gunes, H.; Schuller, B. Categorical and dimensional affect analysis in continuous input: Current trends and future directions. *Image Vis. Comput.* **2013**, *31*, 120–136. [CrossRef]
6. Watson, D.; Wiese, D.; Vaidya, J.; Tellegen, A. The two general activation systems of affect: Structural findings, evolutionary considerations, and psychobiological evidence. *J. Personal. Soc. Psychol.* **1999**, *76*, 820–838. [CrossRef]
7. Russell, J.A. Core affect and the psychological construction of emotion. *Psychol. Rev.* **2003**, *110*, 145–172. [CrossRef] [PubMed]
8. Oflazoglu, C.; Yildirim, S. Recognizing emotion from Turkish speech using acoustic features. *EURASIP J. Audio Speech Music Process.* **2013**, *2013*, 26. [CrossRef]
9. Teilegen, A. Structures of Mood and Personality and Their Relevance to Assessing Anxiety, with an Emphasis on Self-Report. In *Anxiety and the Anxiety Disorders*; Routledge: London, UK, 2019; pp. 681–706.
10. Bradley, M.M.; Lang, P.J. Affective reactions to acoustic stimuli. *Psychophysiology* **2000**, *37*, 204–215. [CrossRef] [PubMed]
11. Ekman, P. Universals and cultural differences in facial expressions of emotion. In *Nebraska Symposium on Motivation*; Cole, J., Ed.; University of Nebraska Press: Lincoln, NE, USA, 1972; Volume 19, pp. 207–282.
12. Lim, N. Cultural differences in emotion: Differences in emotional arousal level between the East and the West. *Integr. Med. Res.* **2016**, *5*, 105–109. [CrossRef] [PubMed]
13. Busso, C.; Bulut, M.; Lee, C.-C.; Kazemzadeh, A.; Mower, E.; Kim, S.; Chang, J.N.; Lee, S.; Narayanan, S.S. IEMOCAP: Interactive emotional dyadic motion capture database. *Lang. Resour. Eval.* **2008**, *42*, 335–359. [CrossRef]
14. Busso, C.; Parthasarathy, S.; Burmania, A.; Abdel-Wahab, M.; Sadoughi, N.; Provost, E. MSP-IMPROV: An Acted Corpus of Dyadic Interactions to Study Emotion Perception. *IEEE Trans. Affect. Comput.* **2017**, *8*, 67–80. [CrossRef]
15. Grimm, M.; Kroschel, K.; Narayanan, S. The Vera am Mittag German audio-visual emotional speech database. In Proceedings of the 2008 IEEE International Conference on Multimedia and Expo, Hannover, Germany, 23 June–26 April 2008; pp. 865–868.
16. Turabzadeh, S.; Meng, H.; Swash, R.M.; Pleva, M.; Juhar, J. Facial Expression Emotion Detection for Real-Time Embedded Systems. *Technologies* **2018**, *6*, 17. [CrossRef]

17. Albanie, S.; Nagrani, A.; Vedaldi, A.; Zisserman, A. Emotion Recognition in Speech using Cross-Modal Transfer in the Wild. In Proceedings of the 26th ACM International Conference on Multimedia, Seattle, WA, USA, 22–26 October 2018; pp. 292–301.
18. Bradley, M.M.; Lang, P.J. Measuring emotion: The self-assessment manikin and the semantic differential. *J. Behav. Ther. Exp. Psychiatry* **1994**, *25*, 49–59. [CrossRef]
19. Burkhardt, F.; Paeschke, A.; Rolfes, M.; Sendlmeier, W.F.; Weiss, B. A database of German emotional speech. In Proceedings of the Interspeech 2005, Lisbon, Portugal, 4–8 September 2005.
20. Costantini, G.; Iaderola, I.; Paoloni, A.; Todisco, M. EMOVO Corpus: An Italian Emotional Speech Database. In Proceedings of the International Conference on Language Resources and Evaluation (LREC), Reykjavik, Iceland, 26–31 May 2014.
21. Livingstone, S.R.; Russo, F.A. The Ryerson Audio-Visual Database of Emotional Speech and Song (RAVDESS): A dynamic, multimodal set of facial and vocal expressions in North American English. *PLoS ONE* **2018**, *13*, e0196391. [CrossRef] [PubMed]
22. Cao, H.; Cooper, D.G.; Keutmann, M.K.; Gur, R.C.; Nenkova, A.; Verma, R. CREMA-D: Crowd-sourced Emotional Multimodal Actors Dataset. *IEEE Trans. Affect. Comput.* **2014**, *5*, 377–390. [CrossRef] [PubMed]
23. University of Surrey. Surrey Audio-Visual Expressed Emotion (SAVEE) Database. Available online: http://kahlan.eps.surrey.ac.uk/savee/ (accessed on 12 October 2021).
24. Sager, J.; Shankar, R.; Reinhold, J.; Venkataraman, A. VESUS: A Crowd-Annotated Database to Study Emotion Production and Perception in Spoken English. In Proceedings of the Interspeech 2019, Graz, Austria, 15–19 September 2019.
25. Martin, O.; Kotsia, I.; Macq, B.; Pitas, I. The eNTERFACE'05 Audio-Visual Emotion Database. In Proceedings of the 22nd International Conference on Data Engineering Workshops (ICDEW'06), Atlanta, GA, USA, 3–7 April 2006; p. 8.
26. James, J.; Tian, L.; Watson, C.I. An Open Source Emotional Speech Corpus for Human Robot Interaction Applications. In Proceedings of the Interspeech 2018, Hyderabad, India, 2–6 September 2018.
27. Pichora-Fuller, M.K.; Dupuis, K. *Toronto Emotional Speech Set (TESS)*; University of Toronto: Toronto, ON, Canada, 2020.
28. Jovičić, T.S.; Kašić, Z.; Đorđević, M.; Rajković, M. Serbian emotional speech database: Design, processing and evaluation. In Proceedings of the SPECOM 2004: 9th Conference Speech and Computer, Saint-Peterburg, Russia, 20–22 September 2004.
29. Snyder, D.; Garcia-Romero, D.; Sell, G.; Povey, D.; Khudanpur, S. X-vectors: Robust DNN embeddings for speaker recognition. In Proceedings of the 2018 IEEE International Conference on Acoustic, Speech and Signal Processing (ICASSP), Calgary, AB, Canada, 15–20 April 2018; pp. 5329–5333.
30. Mackova, L.; Cizmar, A.; Juhar, J. Emotion recognition in i-vector space. In Proceedings of the 2016 26th International Conference Radioelektronika (RADIOELEKTRONIKA), Košice, Slovakia, 19–20 April 2016; pp. 372–375.
31. Abbaschian, B.; Sierra-Sosa, D.; Elmaghraby, A. Deep Learning Techniques for Speech Emotion Recognition, from Databases to Models. *Sensors* **2021**, *21*, 1249. [CrossRef] [PubMed]
32. Lieskovská, E.; Jakubec, M.; Jarina, R.; Chmulík, M. A Review on Speech Emotion Recognition Using Deep Learning and Attention Mechanism. *Electronics* **2021**, *10*, 1163. [CrossRef]
33. Raj, D.; Snyder, D.; Povey, D.; Khudanpur, S. Probing the Information Encoded in X-Vectors. 2019. Available online: https://arxiv.org/abs/1909.06351 (accessed on 12 October 2021).
34. Nagrani, A.; Chung, J.S.; Zisserman, A.V. VoxCeleb: A large-scale speaker identification dataset. In Proceedings of the Interspeech, Stockholm, Sweden, 20–24 August 2017; pp. 2616–2620.
35. Chung, J.S.; Nagrani, A.; Zisserman, A. VoxCeleb2: Deep Speaker Recognition. In Proceedings of the Interspeech 2018, Hyderabad, India, 2–6 September 2018.
36. Ko, T.; Peddinti, V.; Povey, D.; Khudanpur, S. Audio augmentation for speech recognition. In Proceedings of the Interspeech 2015, Dresden, Germany, 6–10 September 2015.
37. Scikit. Epsilon-Support Vector Regression. Available online: https://scikit-learn.org/stable/modules/generated/sklearn.svm.SVR.html (accessed on 12 October 2021).
38. Waskom, M.L. Seaborn: Statistical data visualization. *J. Open Source Softw.* **2021**, *6*, 3021. [CrossRef]
39. Barros, P.; Churamani, N.; Lakomkin, E.; Siqueira, H.; Sutherland, A.; Wermter, S. The OMG-Emotion Behavior Dataset. In Proceedings of the 2018 International Joint Conference on Neural Networks (IJCNN), Rio de Janeiro, Brazil, 8–13 July 2018.
40. Schuller, B.; Vlasenko, B.; Eyben, F.; Wollmer, M.; Stuhlsatz, A.; Wendemuth, A.; Rigoll, G. Cross-Corpus Acoustic Emotion Recognition: Variances and Strategies. *IEEE Trans. Affect. Comput.* **2010**, *1*, 119–131. [CrossRef]
41. Schuller, B.; Zhang, Z.; Weninger, F.; Rigoll, G. Selecting training data for cross-corpus speech emotion recognition: Prototypicality vs. generalization. In Proceedings of the Afeka-AVIOS Speech Processing Conference, Tel Aviv, Israel, 22 June 2011.
42. Parry, J.; Palaz, D.; Clarke, G.; Lecomte, P.; Mead, R.; Berger, M.; Hofer, G. Analysis of Deep Learning Architectures for Cross-Corpus Speech Emotion Recognition. In Proceedings of the Interspeech 2019, Graz, Austria, 15–19 September 2019.

Article

# Performance Evaluation of Offline Speech Recognition on Edge Devices

Santosh Gondi [1,*] and Vineel Pratap [2]

[1] Facebook Inc., Menlo Park, CA 94025, USA
[2] Facebook AI Research, Menlo Park, CA 94025, USA; vineelkpratap@fb.com
* Correspondence: sgondi@fb.com

**Abstract:** Deep learning–based speech recognition applications have made great strides in the past decade. Deep learning–based systems have evolved to achieve higher accuracy while using simpler end-to-end architectures, compared to their predecessor hybrid architectures. Most of these state-of-the-art systems run on backend servers with large amounts of memory and CPU/GPU resources. The major disadvantage of server-based speech recognition is the lack of privacy and security for user speech data. Additionally, because of network dependency, this server-based architecture cannot always be reliable, performant and available. Nevertheless, offline speech recognition on client devices overcomes these issues. However, resource constraints on smaller edge devices may pose challenges for achieving state-of-the-art speech recognition results. In this paper, we evaluate the performance and efficiency of transformer-based speech recognition systems on edge devices. We evaluate inference performance on two popular edge devices, Raspberry Pi and Nvidia Jetson Nano, running on CPU and GPU, respectively. We conclude that with PyTorch mobile optimization and quantization, the models can achieve real-time inference on the Raspberry Pi CPU with a small degradation to word error rate. On the Jetson Nano GPU, the inference latency is three to five times better, compared to Raspberry Pi. The word error rate on the edge is still higher, but it is not too far behind, compared to that on the server inference.

**Keywords:** ASR; speech-to-text; edge AI; Wav2Vec; transformers; PyTorch

**Citation:** Gondi, S.; Pratap, V. Performance Evaluation of Offline Speech Recognition on Edge Devices. *Electronics* **2021**, *10*, 2697. https://doi.org/10.3390/electronics10212697

Academic Editors: Matúš Pleva, Yuan-Fu Liao and Patrick Bours

Received: 23 September 2021
Accepted: 1 November 2021
Published: 4 November 2021

**Publisher's Note:** MDPI stays neutral with regard to jurisdictional claims in published maps and institutional affiliations.

**Copyright:** © 2021 by the authors. Licensee MDPI, Basel, Switzerland. This article is an open access article distributed under the terms and conditions of the Creative Commons Attribution (CC BY) license (https://creativecommons.org/licenses/by/4.0/).

## 1. Introduction

Automatic speech recognition (ASR) is a process of converting speech signals to text. It has a large number of real-world use cases, such as dictation, accessibility, voice assistants, AR/VR applications, captioning of videos, podcasts, searching audio recordings, and automated answering services, to name a few. On-device ASR makes more sense for many use cases where an internet connection is not available or cannot be used. Private and always-available on-device speech recognition can unblock many such applications in healthcare, automotive, legal and military fields, such as taking patient diagnosis notes, in-car voice command to initiate phone calls, real-time speech writing, etc.

Deep learning–based speech recognition has made great strides in the past decade [1]. It is a subfield of machine learning which essentially mimics the neural network structure of the human brain for pattern matching and classification. It typically consists of an input layer, an output layer and one or more hidden layers. The learning algorithm adjusts the weights between different layers, using gradient descent and backpropagation until the required accuracy is met [1,2]. The major reason for its popularity is that it does not need feature engineering. It autonomously extracts the features based on the patterns in the training dataset. The dramatic progress of deep learning in the past decade can be attributed to three main factors [3]: (1) large amounts of transcribed data sets; (2) rapid increase in GPU processing power; and (3) improvements in machine learning algorithms and architectures. Computer vision, object detection, speech recognition and other similar fields have advanced rapidly because of the progress of deep learning.

The majority of speech recognition systems run in backend servers. Since audio data need to be sent to the server for transcription, the privacy and security of the speech cannot be guaranteed. Additionally, because of the reliance on a network connection, the server-based ASR solution cannot always be reliable, fast and available.

On the other hand, on-device-based speech recognition inherently provides privacy and security for the user speech data. It is always available and improves the reliability and latency of the speech recognition by precluding the need for network connectivity [4]. Other non-obvious benefits of edge inference are energy and battery conservation for on-the-go products by avoiding Bluetooth/Wi-Fi/LTE connection establishments for data transfers.

Inferencing on edge can be achieved either by running computations on CPU or on hardware accelerators, such as GPU, DSP or using dedicated neural processing engines. The benefits and demand for on-device ML is driving modern phones to have dedicated neural engine or tensor processing units. For example, Apple iOS 15 will support on-device speech recognition for iPhones with Apple neural engine [5]. The Google Pixel 6 phone comes equipped with a tensor processing unit to handle on-device ML, including speech recognition [6]. Though dedicated neural hardwares might become a general trend in the future, at least in the short term, a large majority of IoT, mobile or wearable devices will not have these dedicated hardwares for on-device ML. Hence, training the models on backend and then pre-optimizing for CPU or general purpose GPU-based edge inferencing is a practical near term solution for on-edge inference [4].

In this paper, we evaluate the performance of ASR on Raspberry Pi and Nvidia Jetson Nano. Since the CPU, GPU and memory specification of these two devices are similar to those of typical edge devices, such as smart speakers, smart displays, etc., the evaluation outcomes in this paper should be similar to the results on a typical edge device. Related to our work, large vocabulary continuous speech recognition was previously evaluated on an embedded device, using CMU SPHINX-II [7]. In [8], the authors evaluated the on-device speech recognition performance with DeepSpeech [9], Kaldi [10] and Wav2Letter [11] models. Moreover, most on-the-edge evaluation papers focus on computer vision tasks, using CNN [12,13]. To the best of our knowledge, there have been no evaluations done for any type of transformer-based speech recognition models on low power edge devices, using both CPU- and GPU-based inferencing. The major contributions of this paper are as follows:

- We present the steps for preparing and inferencing the pre-trained PyTorch models for on edge CPU- and GPU-based inferencing.
- We measure and analyze the accuracy, latency and computational efficiency of ASR inference with transformer-based models on Raspberry Pi and Jetson Nano.
- We also provide a comparative analysis of inference between CPU- and GPU-based processing on edge.

The rest of the paper is organized as follows: In the background section, we discuss ASR and transformers. In the experimental setup, we go through the steps for preparing the models and setting up both the devices for inferencing. We highlight some of the challenges we faced while setting up the devices. We go over the accuracy, performance and efficiency metrics in the results section. Finally, we conclude with the summary and outlook.

## 2. Background

ASR is the process of converting audio signals to text. In simple terms, the audio signal is divided into frames and passed through fast Fourier transform to generate feature vectors. This goes through an acoustic model to output the probability distribution of phonemes. Then, a decoder model with a lexicon, vocabulary and language model is used to generate the word $n$-grams distributions. The hidden Markov model (HMM) [14] with a Gaussian mixture model (GMM) [15] was considered a mainstream ASR algorithm until a decade ago. Conventionally, the featurizer, acoustic modeling, pronunciation modeling, and decoding all were built separately and composed together to create an ASR system. Hybrid HMM–DNN approaches replaced GMM with deep neural networks with significant performance gains [16]. Further advances used CNN- [17,18] and RNN-based [19] models to replace some or all components in hybrid DNN [1,2] architecture. Over time, ASR model architectures have evolved to convert audio signals to text directly, called sequence-to-sequence models. These architectures have simplified the training and implementation of ASR models. The most successful end-to-end ASR are based on connectionist temporal classification (CTC) [20], recurrent neural network (RNN) transducer (RNN-T) [19], and attention-based encoder–decoder architecture [21].

Transformer is a sequence-to-sequence architecture originally proposed for machine translation [22]. When used for ASR, the input of transformer is audio frames instead of the text input, as in translation use case. Transformer uses multi head attention and positional embeddings. It learns sequential information through a self-attention mechanism instead of the recurrent connection used in RNN. Since their introduction, transformers are increasingly becoming the model of choice for NLP problems. The powerful natural language processing (NLP) models, such as GPT-3 [23], BERT [24], and AlphaFold 2 [25], which is the model that predicts the structures of proteins from their genetic sequences, are all based on transformer architecture. The major advantages of transformers over RNN/LSTM [26] is that they process the whole sequence at once, enabling parallel computation and hence, reducing the training time. They also do not suffer from long dependency issues; hence, they are more accurate. Since the transformer processes the whole sequence at once, they are not directly suitable for streaming-based applications, such as continuous dictation. In addition, their decoding complexity is quadratic over input sequence length because the attention is computed pairwise for each input. In this paper, we focus on the general viability and computational cost of transformer-based ASR on audio files. In future, we plan to explore streaming supported transformer architectures on edge.

*2.1. Wav2Vec 2.0 Model*

Wav2Vec 2.0 is a transformer-based speech recognition model trained using a self-supervised method with contrastive training [27]. The raw audio is encoded using a multilayer convolutional network, the output of which is fed to the transformer network to build latent speech representations. Some of the input representations are masked during training. The model is then fine tuned with a small set of labeled data, using the connectionist temporal classification (CTC) [20] loss function. The great advantage of Wav2Vec 2.0 is the ability to learn from unlabeled data, which is tremendously useful in training for speech recognition for languages with very limited labeled audio. For the remaining part of this paper, we refer to the Wav2Vec 2.0 model as Wav2Vec to reduce verbosity. In our evaluation, we use a pre-trained base Wav2Vec model, which was trained on 960 hr of unlabeled LibriSpeech audio. We evaluate a 100 hr and a 960 hr fine-tuned model.

Figure 1 shows the simplified flow of the ASR process with this model.

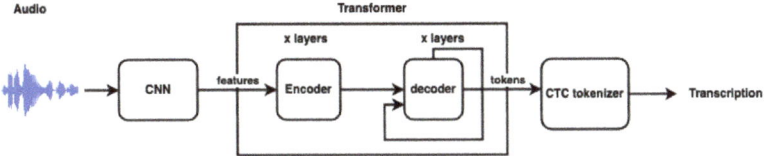

**Figure 1.** Wav2Vec2 inference.

*2.2. Speech2Text Model*

The Speech2Text model is a transformer-based speech recognition model trained using the supervised method [28]. The transformer architecture is based on [22]. In addition, it has an input subsampler. The purpose of the subsampler is to downsample the audio sequence to match the input dimensions of the transformer encoder. The model is trained with a LibriSpeech, 960 hr, labeled training data set. Unlike Wav2Vec, which takes raw audio samples as input, this model accepts 80-channel log Mel filter bank extracted features with a 25 ms window size and 10 ms shift. Additionally, utterance-level cepstral mean and variance normalization (CMVN) [29] is applied on the input frames before feeding to the subsampler. The decoder uses a 10,000 unigram vocabulary.

Figure 2 shows the simplified flow of the ASR process with this model.

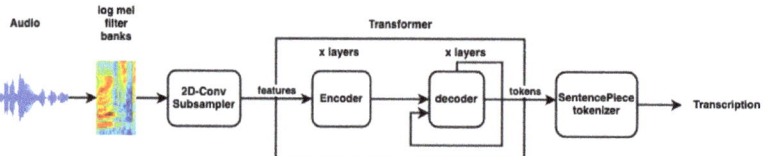

**Figure 2.** Speech2Text inference.

## 3. Experimental Setup

### 3.1. Model Preparation

We use PyTorch models for evaluation. PyTorch is an open-source machine learning framework based on the Torch library. Figure 3 shows the steps for preparing the models for inferencing on edge devices.

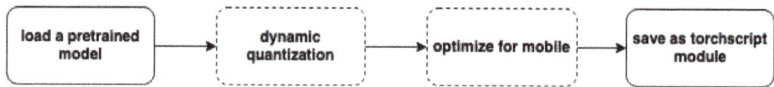

**Figure 3.** Model preparation steps.

We first go through a few of the PyTorch tools and APIs used in our evaluation.

#### 3.1.1. TorchScript

TorchScript is the means by which PyTorch models can be optimized, serialized and saved in intermediate representation (IR) format. *torch.jit* (https://pytorch.org/docs/stable/jit.html (accessed on 30 October 2021)) APIs are used for converting, saving and loading PyTorch models as ScriptModules. TorchScript itself is a subset of the Python language. As a result, sometimes, a model written in Python needs to be simplified to convert it into a script module. The TorchScript module can be created either using tracing or scripting methods. Tracing works by executing the model with sample inputs and capturing all computations, whereas scripting performs static inspection to go through the model recursively. The advantage of scripting over tracing is that it correctly handles the loops and control statements in the module. A saved script module can then be loaded either in a Python or C++ environment for inferencing purposes. For our evaluation, we generated ScriptModules for both Speech2Text and Wav2Vec models after applying any valid optimizations for specific devices.

#### 3.1.2. PyTorch Mobile Optimizations

PyTorch provides a set of APIs for optimizing the models for mobile platforms. It uses module fusing, operator fusing, and quantization among other things to optimize the models. We apply dynamic quantization for models used in this experiment. During this quantization, the scale factors are determined for activations dynamically based on the data range observed at runtime. By quantization, a neural network is converted to use a reduced precision integer representation for the weights and/or activations. This saves on model size and allows the use of higher throughput math operations on CPU or GPU.

#### 3.1.3. Models

We evaluated the Speech2Text and Wav2Vec transformer-based models on Raspberry Pi and Nvidia Jetson Nano. Inference on Raspberry Pi happens on CPU, while on Jetson Nano, it happens on GPU, using CUDA APIs. Given the limited RAM, CPU, and storage on these devices, we make use of Google Colab for importing, optimizing and saving the model as a TorchScript module. The saved modules are copied to Raspberry Pi and Jetson Nano for inferencing. On Raspberry Pi, which uses CPU-based inference, we evaluate both quantized and unquantized models. On Jetson Nano, we only evaluate unquantized models since CUDA only supports floating point operations.

Speech2Text Model

The Speech2Text pre-trained model is imported from *fairseq* (https://github.com/pytorch/fairseq/tree/master/examples/speech_to_text (accessed on 30 October 2021)). Fairseq is a sequence modeling toolkit that allows researchers and developers to train custom models for speech and text tasks. We needed to make minor syntactical changes, such as Python type hints, to export the generator model as a TorchScript module. We have used *s2t_transformer_s* small architecture for this evaluation. The decoding uses a beam search decoder with a beam size of 5 and a SentencePiece tokenizer.

Wav2Vec Model

Wav2Vec pre-trained models are imported from *huggingface* (https://huggingface.co/transformers/model_doc/wav2vec2.html (accessed on 30 October 2021)) using the *Wav2Vec2ForCTC* interface. We have used *Wav2Vec2CTCTokenizer* to decode the output indexes into transcribed text.

*3.2. Raspberry Pi Setup*

Raspberry Pi 4 B is used in this evaluation. The device specs are provided in Table 1. The default Raspberry Pi OS is 32 bit, which is not compatible with PyTorch. Hence, we installed a 64 bit OS.

**Table 1.** Raspberry Pi 4 B specs.

| Name | Spec |
| --- | --- |
| Chip | BCM2711 |
| CPU | Quad core Cortex-A72 (ARM v8) 64-bit SoC |
| Clock speed | 1.5GHz |
| RAM | 4 GB SDRAM |
| Caches | 32 KB data + 48 KB instruction L1 cache per core. 1 MB L2 cache |
| Storage | 32 GB micro SD card |
| OS | 64 bit Raspberry Pi OS |
| Python version | 3.7 |
| Power supply | 5 V DC via USB-C connector |

The main Python package required for inferencing is *PyTorch*. The default prebuilt wheel files of this package are mainly for Intel architecture, which depend on *Intel-MKL* (math kernel library) for math routines on CPU. The ARM-based architectures cannot use Intel MKL. They instead have to use *QNNPACK/XNNPACK* backend with other BLAS (basic linear algebra subprograms) libraries. QNNPACK (https://github.com/pytorch/QNNPACK (accessed on 30 October 2021)) (quantized neural networks package) is a mobile-optimized library for low-precision, high-performance neural network inference. Similarly, XNNPACK (https://github.com/google/XNNPACK (accessed on 30 October 2021)) is a mobile-optimized library for higher precision neural network inference. We built and installed the torch wheel file on Raspberry Pi from source with XNNPACK and QNNPACK cmake configs. We needed to set the device backend to QNNPACK during inference as *torch.backends.quantized.engine='qnnpack'*. Note that with the latest PyTorch release 1.9.0, the wheel files are available for ARM 64-bit architectures. Hence, there is no need to build *torch* from source anymore.

The lessons learnt during setup are as follows:

- Speech2Text transformer models expect Mel-frequency cepstral coefficients [30] as input features. However, we could not use *Torchaudio*, *PyKaldi*, *librosa* or *python_speech_features* libraries for this because of dependency issues. *Torchaudio* has dependency on Intel MKL. Building *PyKaldi* on device was not feasible because of memory limitations. The *librosa* and *python_speech_features* packages produced different outputs for MFCC, which were unsuitable for PyTorch models. Therefore, the MFCC features for the LibriSpeech data set were pre-generated, using *fairseq audio_utils* (https://github.com/pytorch/fairseq/blob/master/fairseq/data/audio/audio_utils.py (accessed on 30 October 2021)) on the server, and saved as NumPy files. These NumPy files were used as model input after applying CWVN transforms.

- Running *pip install* with or without *sudo* while installing packages, can cause silent dependency issues. This is especially true when the same package is installed multiple times with and without using *sudo*.
- To experiment with *huggingface* transformer models, the *datasets* package is required, which in turn has dependency on PyArrow (an Apache arrow library). Arrow library needs to be built and installed from source to use PyArrow.

### 3.3. Nvidia Jetson Nano Setup

We configured Jetson Nano using the instructions on the Nvidia website. The Nano flash file comes with JetPack pre-installed, which includes all the CUDA libraries required for inferencing on GPU. The full specs of the device are provided in Table 2.

**Table 2.** Jetson Nano specs.

| Name | Spec |
| --- | --- |
| GPU | 128-core Maxwell |
| CPU | Quad-core ARM A57 |
| Clock speed | 1.43 GHz |
| Memory | 4 GB 64-bit LPDDR4 |
| Caches | 262,144 bytes L2 cache |
| Storage | 32 GB micro SD card |
| OS | Ubuntu 18.04.5 LTS |
| Python version | 3.6 |
| CUDA | 10.2 |
| nvidia-jetpack | 4.5.1-b17 |
| Power supply | Barrel jack 5 V 4 A |

For Nano, we needed to build *torch* from source with CUDA cmake option. Further, an upgrade was needed to Clang and LLVM compiler toolchain to use Clang for compiling PyTorch.

The lessons learnt during setup are as follows:

- Need to use 5 V, 4 A barrel jack power supply for Jetson Nano. The USB C power supply does not provide sufficient power for continuous speech-to-text inferencing on CUDA.
- *cuDNN* benchmarking needs to be switched on for Nano to pick up the speed while executing. It takes a very long time for Nanto to execute the initial few samples. That is because the *cuDNN* tries to find the best algorithm for the configured input. After that, the RTF improves significantly and it executes very quickly.
- Jetson Nano froze on long duration audios while inferencing with the Wav2Vec model. Through trial and error, we figured out that by limiting the input audio duration to 8 s and batching the inputs to be of size 64 K (4 s audio) or less, we can allow the inference to continue without hiccups.

### 3.4. Evaluation Methodology

This section explains the methodologies used for collecting and presenting the metrics in this paper. The LibriSpeech [31] test and dev datasets were used to evaluate ASR performance on both Raspberry Pi and Jetson Nano. The test and dev datasets together contain 21 hr of audio. To save time, for these experiments we randomly sampled 300

(~10%) of the audio files in each of the four data sets for inference. The same set for each configuration was used so that the results would be comparable. Typically, ML practitioners only report the WER metric for server-based ASR. So, we did not have a server side reference for latency and efficiency metrics, such as memory, CPU or load times. Unlike backend servers, the edge devices are constrained in terms of memory, CPU, disk and energy. To achieve on-device ML, the inferencing needs to be efficient enough to fit within the device's resource budgets. Hence, we measured these efficiency metrics along with the accuracy to assess the plausibility of meeting these budgets on typical edge devices.

3.4.1. Accuracy

Accuracy is measured using word error rate (WER), a standard metric for speech-to-text tasks. It is defined as in Equation (1):

$$WER = (S + I + D)/N \qquad (1)$$

where $S$ is the number of substitutions, $D$ is the number of deletions, $I$ is the number of insertions and $N$ is the number of words in the reference.

WER for a dataset is computed as the total number of errors over the total number of reference words in the dataset. We compare the on-device WER on Raspberry Pi and Jetson Nano with the on-server-based WER as reported in Speech2Text [28] and Wav2Vec [27] papers. In both papers, the WER for all models was computed on LibriSpeech test and dev data sets with GPU in standalone mode. On server, the Speech2Text model used a beam size of 5 and vocabulary of 10,000 words for decoding, whereas the Wav2Vec model used a transformer-based language model for decoding. The pre-trained models used in this experiment have the same configuration as that of the server models.

3.4.2. Latency

The latency of ASR is measured using real time factor (RTF). It is defined in Equation (2). In simple terms, with a RTF of 0.5, two seconds of audio will be transcribed by the system in one second.

$$RTF = (read\ time + inference\ time + decoding\ time)/total\ uttterance\ duration \qquad (2)$$

We compute the avg, mean, pctl 75 and pctl 90 RTF over all the audio samples in each data set. We also used PyTorch profiler to visualize the CPU usage of various operators and functions inside the models.

3.4.3. Efficiency

We measure the CPU load and memory footprint during the entire data set evaluation, using the Linux *top* command. The top command is executed in the background every two minutes in order to avoid side effects on the main inference script.

The model load time is measured by collecting the *torch.jit.load* API latency to load the scripted model. We separately measured the load time by running 10 iterations and took an average. We ensured that the load time measurements were from a clean state, i.e., from the system boot, to discount any caching in the Linux OS layer for subsequent model loads.

## 4. Results

In this section, we present the accuracy, performance and efficiency metrics for Speech2Text and Wav2Vec model inference.

### 4.1. WER

Tables 3 and 4 show the WER on Raspberry Pi and Jetson Nano, respectively.

Table 3. WER on Raspberry Pi.

| Dataset | Model | Test Dataset | | Dataset | Model | Dev Dataset | |
|---|---|---|---|---|---|---|---|
| | | Edge WER | Server WER | | | Edge WER | Server WER |
| test-clean | S2T_q | 4.7% | | dev-clean | S2T_q | 4.3% | |
| | S2T | 4.4% | 4.4% | | S2T | 3.9% | 3.8% |
| | W2V100q | 7.3% | | | W2V100q | 7.9% | |
| | W2V100 | 6.9% | 2.6% | | W2V100 | 7.8% | 2.2% |
| | W2V960q | 4.1% | | | W2V960q | 4.3% | |
| | W2V960 | 4.1% | 2.1% | | W2V960 | 3.6% | 1.8% |
| test-other | S2T_q | 11.7% | | dev-other | S2T_q | 11.1% | |
| | S2T | 11.0% | 9.0% | | S2T | 10.6% | 8.9% |
| | W2V100q | 16.2% | | | W2V100q | 15.1% | |
| | W2V100 | 15.6% | 6.3% | | W2V100 | 14.9% | 6.3% |
| | W2V960q | 10.8% | | | W2V960q | 10.2% | |
| | W2V960 | 9.7% | 4.8% | | W2V960 | 9.8% | 4.7% |

The WER is slightly higher for the quantized models, compared to the unquantized ones by an avg of ∼0.5%. This is a small trade off in accuracy for better RTF and efficient inference. The *test-other* and *dev-other* data sets have a higher WER, compared to the *test-clean* and *dev-clean* data sets. This is expected because *other* datasets are noisier, compared to *clean* ones.

The WER on device for unquantized models is generally higher than what is reported on the server. We need to investigate further to understand this discrepancy. One plausible reason could be due to a smaller sampled dataset used in our evaluation, compared to the server WER, which is calculated over the entire dataset.

Table 4. WER on Jetson Nano.

| Dataset | Model | Test Dataset | | Dataset | Model | Dev Dataset | |
|---|---|---|---|---|---|---|---|
| | | Edge WER | Server WER | | | Edge WER | Server WER |
| test-clean | S2T | 4.4% | 4.4% | dev-clean | S2T | 3.3% | 3.8% |
| | W2V100 | 9.5% | 2.6% | | W2V100 | 10.2% | 2.2% |
| | W2V960 | 6.4% | 2.1% | | W2V960 | 6.2% | 1.8% |
| test-other | S2T | 8.6% | 9.0% | dev-other | S2T | 9.8% | 8.9% |
| | W2V100 | 20.5% | 6.3% | | W2V100 | 19.7% | 6.3% |
| | W2V960 | 13.1% | 4.8% | | W2V960 | 13.0% | 4.7% |

WER for the Wav2Vec case is higher because of batching of the input samples at the 64 K (4 s audio) boundary. If a sample duration is longer than 4 s, we divide it into two batches. See Section 3.3 for the reasoning. So, words at the boundary of 4 s can be misinterpreted. We plan to investigate this batching problem in future. We report the WER figures here for the purpose of completeness.

### 4.2. RTF

In our experiments, RTF is dominated by *model inference time* > 99% compared to other two factors in (2). Tables 5 and 6 show the RTF for Raspberry Pi and Jetson Nano, respectively. RTF does not vary between different data sets for the same models. Hence, we show the RTF (avg, mean, pctl 75 and pctl 90) per model instead of one per data set.

**Table 5.** RTF of Raspberry Pi.

| Model | Avg | Mean | P75 | P90 |
|---|---|---|---|---|
| Speech2Text | 0.33 | 0.33 | 0.38 | 0.45 |
| Speech2Text quantized | 0.29 | 0.29 | 0.34 | 0.39 |
| Wav2Vec 100 hr | 1.43 | 1.42 | 1.45 | 1.5 |
| Wav2Vec 100 hr quantized | 1.00 | 0.97 | 1.03 | 1.11 |
| Wav2Vec 960 hr | 1.49 | 1.48 | 1.54 | 1.58 |
| Wav2Vec 960 hr quantized | 1.03 | 1.00 | 1.07 | 1.18 |

RTF is improved by ∼10% for quantized models, compared to unquantized floating point models. This is because CPU has to load less memory and can run tensor computations more efficiently in int8 than in floating points. The inferencing of the Speech2Text model is three times faster than the Wav2Vec model. This can be explained by the fact that the Wav2Vec has three times more parameters than the Speech2Text model (refer to Table 7). There is no noticeable difference in RTF between 100 hr and 960 hr fine-tuned Wav2Vec models because the number of parameters do not change between 960 hr and 100 hr fine-tuned models.

**Table 6.** RTF on Jetson Nano.

| Model | Avg | Mean | P75 | P90 |
|---|---|---|---|---|
| Speech2Text | 0.13 | 0.13 | 0.15 | 0.17 |
| Wav2Vec 100 hr | 0.22 | 0.22 | 0.25 | 0.28 |
| Wav2Vec 960 hr | 0.23 | 0.22 | 0.26 | 0.29 |

**Table 7.** Model size.

| Model Name | Size | Parameters |
|---|---|---|
| Speech2Text quantized | 80 MB | 30 Million |
| Speech2Text | 125 MB | |
| Wav2Vec quantized | 207 MB | 93 Million |
| Wav2Vec | 377 MB | |

RTF on Jetson Nano is three times better for the Speech2Text model and five times better for the Wav2Vec model, compared to Raspberry Pi. Nano is able to make use of a large number of CUDA cores for tensor computations. We do not evaluate quantized models on Nano because CUDA only supports floating point computations.

Wav2Vec RTF on Raspberry Pi is close to real time, whereas in every other case, the RTF is far below 1. This implies that on-device ASR can be used for real-time dictation, accessibility, voice based app navigation, translation and other such tasks without much latency.

*4.3. Efficiency*

For both CPU and memory measurements over time, we use the Linux *top* command. The command is executed in loop every 2 min in order to not affect the main processing.

4.3.1. CPU Load

Figures 4 and 5 show the CPU load of all model inferences on Raspberry Pi and Jetson Nano, respectively. The CPU load in Nano for both the Speech2Text and Wav2Vec models is ∼85% in steady state. It mostly uses one of the four cores during operation. Most of the CPU processing on Nano is for copying the input to memory for GPU processing and also copying back the output. On Raspberry Pi, the CPU load is ∼380%. Since all the tensor computations happen on CPU, all CPU cores are utilized fully during model inference. On Nano, the initial few minutes are spent loading and benchmarking the model. That is why the CPU is not busy during the initial few minutes.

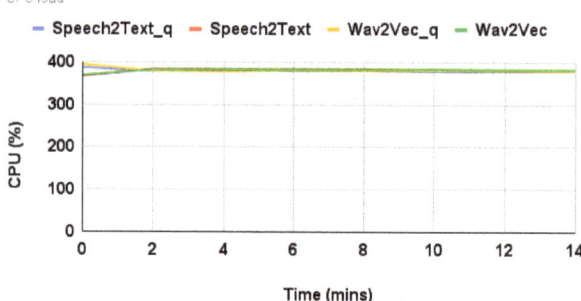

**Figure 4.** CPU load on Raspberry Pi.

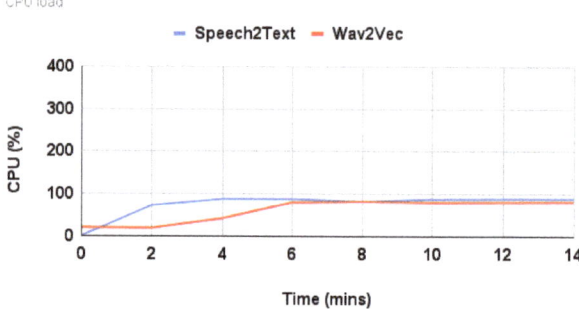

**Figure 5.** CPU load on Jetson Nano.

4.3.2. Memory Footprint

Figures 6 and 7 show the memory of all model inferences on Raspberry Pi and Jetson Nano, respectively. The memory values presented here are *RES (resident set size)* values from top command. On Raspberry Pi, the quantized Wav2Vec model consumes ~50% less memory (from 1 GB to 560 MB), compared to the unquantized model. Similarly, the Speech2Text model consumes ~40% less memory (from 480 MB to 320 MB), compared to the unquantized model. On Nano, memory consumption for the Speech2Text model is ~1 GB, and the Wav2Vec model is ~500 MB. On Nano, the same memory is shared between GPU and CPU.

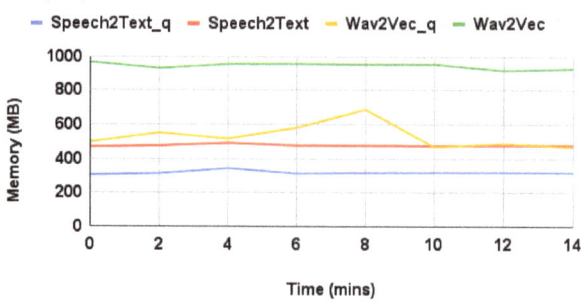

**Figure 6.** Memory footprint on Raspberry Pi.

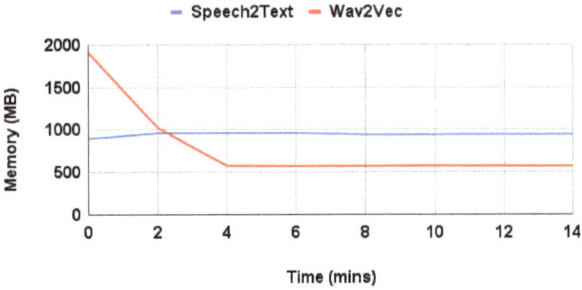

**Figure 7.** Memory footprint on Jetson Nano.

4.3.3. Model Load Time

Table 8 shows the model load times on Raspberry Pi and Jetson Nano. A load time of 1–2 s on Raspberry Pi seems reasonable for any practical application where the model is loaded once and the process inference requests multiple times. The load time on Nano is 15–20 times longer than on Raspberry Pi. Nano *cuDNN* has to allot some amount of cache for loading the model, which takes time.

**Table 8.** Model load times.

| Raspberry Pi | | Jetson Nano | |
|---|---|---|---|
| Model | Avg (sec) | Model | Avg (sec) |
| Speech2Text | 1.4 | Speech2Text | 24.2 |
| Speech2Text quantized | 1.07 | Wav2Vec | 33.5 |
| Wav2Vec | 1.9 | | |
| Wav2Vec quantized | 1.9 | | |

*4.4. PyTorch Profiler*

PyTorch profiler (https://pytorch.org/tutorials/recipes/recipes/profiler_recipe.html (accessed on 30 October 2021)) can be used to study the time and memory consumption of the model's operators. It is enabled through Context Manager in Python. The profiler is used to understand the distribution of CPU percentage over model operations. Some of the columns from the profiler are not shown in the table for simplicity.

4.4.1. Jetson Nano Profiles

Tables 9 and 10 show the profiles of Wav2Vec and Speech2Text models on Jetson Nano.

For Wav2Vec model, the majority of the CUDA time is spent in *aten::cudnn_convolution* for input convolutions followed by matrix multiplication (*aten::mm*). Additionally, the CPU and GPU spend a significant amount of time transferring data between each other, *aten::to*.

For the Speech2Text model, the majority of the CUDA time is spent in decoder *forward* followed by *aten::mm* for tensor multiplication operations.

4.4.2. Raspberry Pi profiles

Tables 11–14 show the profiles of Wav2Vec and Speech2Text models on Raspberry Pi.

**Table 9.** Jetson Nano profile for the Wav2Vec model.

| Name | Self CPU % | Self CUDA | Self CUDA % | # of Calls |
|---|---|---|---|---|
| forward | 0.70 | 5.373 ms | 0.51 | 1 |
| aten::conv1d | 0.14 | 576.000 us | 0.05 | 8 |
| aten::convolution | 0.10 | 228.000 us | 0.02 | 8 |
| aten::_convolution | 0.11 | 459.000 us | 0.04 | 8 |
| aten::cudnn_convolution | 0.32 | 527.416 ms | 50.32 | 8 |
| <foward op> | 0.63 | 1.054 ms | 0.10 | 61 |
| aten::matmul | 0.97 | 1.614 ms | 0.15 | 98 |
| aten::linear | 10.48 | 1.279 ms | 0.12 | 74 |
| aten::mm | 0.84 | 207.371 ms | 19.78 | 74 |
| aten::to | 38.43 | 185.175 ms | 17.67 | 3 |
| aten::bmm | 0.31 | 20.066 ms | 1.91 | 24 |
| aten::gelu | 0.27 | 20.261 ms | 1.93 | 20 |
| aten::group_norm | 0.03 | 4.000 us | 0.00 | 1 |
| aten::native_group_norm | 0.03 | 19.968 ms | 1.90 | 1 |
| aten::add_ | 0.8 | 16.373 ms | 1.56 | 75 |

**Table 10.** Jetson Nano profile for Speech2Text model.

| Name | Self CPU % | Self CUDA | Self CUDA % | # of Calls |
|---|---|---|---|---|
| forward | 6.21 | 307.304 ms | 14.28 | 1 |
| aten::linear | 3.12 | 86.356 ms | 4.01 | 672 |
| aten::matmul | 3.16 | 80.340 ms | 3.73 | 672 |
| aten::mm | 4.72 | 265.171 ms | 12.32 | 672 |
| aten::layer_norm | 1.01 | 20.434 ms | 0.95 | 253 |
| aten::transpose | 5.46 | 106.751 ms | 4.96 | 1398 |
| aten::native_layer_norm | 2.77 | 91.685 ms | 4.26 | 253 |
| aten::t | 2.93 | 57.888 ms | 2.69 | 710 |
| aten::view | 9.56 | 119.122 ms | 5.53 | 2724 |
| aten::empty | 8.34 | 102.937 ms | 4.78 | 2417 |
| aten::bmm | 2.26 | 83.940 ms | 3.90 | 312 |
| aten::as_strided | 6.86 | 77.660 ms | 3.61 | 2156 |
| aten::add_ | 4.07 | 67.874 ms | 3.15 | 675 |
| aten::softmax | 0.66 | 16.265 ms | 0.76 | 156 |
| aten::to | 2.38 | 41.231 ms | 1.92 | 433 |

**Table 11.** Raspberry Pi profile for Wav2Vec quantized on model.

| Name | Self CPU % | Self CPU | CPU Total | # of Calls |
|---|---|---|---|---|
| forward | 0.49 | 45.452 ms | 9.334 s | 1 |
| quantized::linear_dynamic | 30.77 | 2.872 s | 3.167 s | 74 |
| aten::conv1d | 0.00 | 347.000 us | 2.875 s | 8 |
| aten::convolution | 0.00 | 274.000 us | 2.875 s | 8 |
| aten::_convolution | 0.02 | 1.472 ms | 2.875 s | 8 |
| aten::_convolution_nogroup | 0.04 | 3.663 ms | 2.862 s | 23 |
| aten::thnn_conv2d | 0.30 | 28.075 ms | 2.858 s | 23 |
| aten::thnn_conv2d_forward | 5.46 | 509.250 ms | 2.830 s | 23 |
| aten::addmm_ | 24.79 | 2.314 s | 2.314 s | 23 |
| aten::matmul | 0.02 | 2.316 ms | 1.022 s | 24 |
| aten::bmm | 10.66 | 994.810 ms | 1.016 s | 24 |
| aten::gelu | 10.33 | 964.418 ms | 965.023 ms | 20 |
| aten::softmax | 0.01 | 597.000 us | 719.717 ms | 12 |
| aten::_softmax | 7.69 | 718.238 ms | 719.120 ms | 12 |
| aten::mul | 2.78 | 259.586 ms | 260.482 ms | 12 |

The CPU time is dominated by *linear_dynamic* for linear layer computations followed by *aten::addmm_* for tensor add multiplications.

**Table 12.** Raspberry Pi profile for Wav2Vec non-quantized model.

| Name | Self CPU % | Self CPU | CPU Total | # of Calls |
|---|---|---|---|---|
| forward | 0.41 | 58.280 ms | 14.227 s | 1 |
| prepacked::linear_clamp_run | 54.85 | 7.804 s | 7.994 s | 74 |
| aten::conv1d | 0.00 | 388.000 us | 2.865 s | 8 |
| aten::convolution | 0.00 | 266.000 us | 2.865 s | 8 |
| aten::_convolution | 0.01 | 1.790 ms | 2.865 s | 8 |
| aten::_convolution_nogroup | 0.01 | 813.000 us | 2.855 s | 23 |
| aten::thnn_conv2d | 0.20 | 28.328 ms | 2.854 s | 23 |
| aten::thnn_conv2d_forward | 3.18 | 452.048 ms | 2.826 s | 23 |
| aten::addmm_ | 16.63 | 2.366 s | 2.366 s | 23 |
| aten::matmul | 0.02 | 2.350 ms | 1.118 s | 24 |
| aten::bmm | 7.64 | 1.087 s | 1.113 s | 24 |
| aten::gelu | 6.54 | 930.477 ms | 931.136 ms | 20 |
| aten::softmax | 0.00 | 645.000 us | 637.379 ms | 12 |
| aten::_softmax | 4.47 | 635.864 ms | 636.734 ms | 12 |
| aten::mul | 2.43 | 345.998 ms | 346.924 ms | 12 |

Compared to the quantized model, the non-quantized model spends 5 s more time in linear computations, *prepacked::linear_clamp_run*.

**Table 13.** Raspberry Pi profile for Speech2Text quantized model.

| Name | Self CPU % | Self CPU | CPU Total | # of Calls |
|---|---|---|---|---|
| forward | 6.75 | 237.950 ms | 3.527 s | 1 |
| quantized::linear_dynamic | 29.46 | 1.039 s | 1.634 s | 1995 |
| aten::bmm | 14.56 | 513.414 ms | 654.848 ms | 960 |
| aten::min | 7.41 | 261.352 ms | 282.381 ms | 1995 |
| aten::max | 5.30 | 186.852 ms | 204.806 ms | 1996 |
| aten::select | 3.11 | 109.748 ms | 158.923 ms | 12,591 |
| aten::clamp_min | 2.18 | 76.946 ms | 150.032 ms | 492 |
| aten::layer_norm | 0.45 | 15.811 ms | 122.822 ms | 766 |
| aten::softmax | 0.18 | 6.385 ms | 114.797 ms | 480 |
| aten::_softmax | 2.95 | 104.130 ms | 108.412 ms | 480 |
| aten::native_layer_norm | 2.45 | 86.478 ms | 107.011 ms | 766 |
| aten::add | 3.01 | 106.317 ms | 106.365 ms | 924 |
| aten::relu | 0.11 | 3.752 ms | 82.349 ms | 246 |
| aten::copy_ | 2.17 | 76.565 ms | 76.565 ms | 1073 |
| aten::empty | 1.94 | 68.404 ms | 68.404 ms | 11,944 |

**Table 14.** Raspberry Pi profile for Speech2Text non-quantized model.

| Name | Self CPU % | Self CPU | CPU Total | # of Calls |
|---|---|---|---|---|
| forward | 7.93 | 287.466 ms | 3.623 s | 1 |
| prepacked::linear_clamp_run | 38.51 | 1.395 s | 1.683 s | 1995 |
| aten::bmm | 11.84 | 428.876 ms | 575.170 ms | 960 |
| aten::copy_ | 10.07 | 364.827 ms | 364.827 ms | 3068 |
| aten::select | 3.13 | 113.435 ms | 163.539 ms | 12591 |
| aten::clamp_min | 2.28 | 82.503 ms | 159.938 ms | 492 |
| aten::layer_norm | 0.49 | 17.881 ms | 150.078 ms | 766 |
| aten::native_layer_norm | 3.02 | 109.335 ms | 132.197 ms | 766 |
| aten::softmax | 0.18 | 6.389 ms | 130.655 ms | 480 |
| aten::_softmax | 3.32 | 120.186 ms | 124.266 ms | 480 |
| aten::add | 2.81 | 101.642 ms | 101.693 ms | 924 |
| aten::relu | 0.18 | 6.374 ms | 92.151 ms | 246 |
| aten::masked_fill | 0.02 | 640.000 us | 79.648 ms | 12 |
| aten::mul_ | 0.35 | 12.554 ms | 79.419 ms | 480 |
| aten::mul | 1.38 | 50.079 ms | 73.879 ms | 560 |

CPU percentages are dominated by forward function, linear layer computations and batched matrix multiplication in both quantized and unquantized models.

The unquantized linear layer processing is 40% higher than the quantized version.

## 5. Conclusions

We evaluated the ASR accuracy, performance and computational efficiency of transformer-based models on edge devices. By applying quantization and PyTorch mobile optimizations for CPU based inferencing, we gain $\sim$ 10% improvement in latency and $\sim$50% reduction in the memory footprint at the cost of $\sim$0.5% increase in WER, compared to the original model. Running the inference on Jetson Nano GPU improves the latency by a factor of 3 to 5. With 1–2 s load times, $\sim$300 MB of memory footprint and RTF < 1.0, the latest transformer models can be used on typical edge devices for private, secure, reliable and always-available ASR processing. For applications such as dictation, smart home control, accessibility, etc., a small trade off in WER for latency and efficiency gains is mostly acceptable since small ASR errors will not hamper the overall task completion rate for voice commands, such as turning off a lamp, opening an app on a device, etc. By offloading inference to a general purpose GPU, we can potentially gain 3–5$\times$ latency improvements.

In future, we are planning to explore other optimization techniques, such as pruning, sparsity, 4-bit quantization and different model architectures to further analyze the WER vs. performance trade offs. We also plan to measure the thermal and battery impact of various models in CPU and GPU platforms on mobile and wearable devices.

**Author Contributions:** Conceptualization—S.G. and V.P.; methodology—S.G. and V.P.; setup and experiments—S.G.; original draft preparation—S.G.; review and editing—S.G. and V.P. All authors have read and agreed to the published version of the manuscript.

**Funding:** This research received no external funding.

**Data Availability Statement:** Publicly available Librispeech datasets were used in this study. his data can be found here: https://www.openslr.org/12 (accessed on 30 October 2021).

**Conflicts of Interest:** The authors declare no conflict of interest.

## Abbreviations

The following abbreviations are used in this manuscript.

| | |
|---|---|
| DL | deep learning |
| CPU | central processing unit |
| GPU | graphics processing unit |
| ASR | automatic speech recognition |
| HMM | hidden Markov model |
| RNN | recurrent neural network |
| RNNT | recurrent neural network transducer |
| CNN | convolutional neural network |
| LSTM | long short-term memory |
| Speech2Text | speech to text transformer model from fairseq |
| Wav2Vec | Wav2Vec 2.0 model |
| GMM | Gaussian mixture model |
| DNN | deep neural network |
| CTC | connectionist temporal classification |
| CMVN | cepstral mean and variance normalization |
| MFCC | Mel-frequency cepstral coefficients |
| CUDA | a parallel computing platform and application programming interface by Nvidia |
| WER | word error rate |
| RTF | real time factor |
| NLP | natural language processing |

## References

1. Hinton, G.; Deng, L.; Yu, D.; Dahl, G.E.; Mohamed, A.R.; Jaitly, N.; Senior, A.; Vanhoucke, V.; Nguyen, P.; Sainath, T.N.; et al. Deep Neural Networks for Acoustic Modeling in Speech Recognition: The Shared Views of Four Research Groups. *IEEE Signal Process. Mag.* **2012**, *29*, 82–97. [CrossRef]
2. LeCun, Y.; Bengio, Y.; Hinton, G. Deep learning. *Nature* **2015**, *521*, 436–444. [CrossRef] [PubMed]
3. Hannun, A. The History of Speech Recognition to the Year 2030. *arXiv* **2021**, arXiv:2108.00084.
4. Wu, C.J.; Brooks, D.; Chen, K.; Chen, D.; Choudhury, S.; Dukhan, M.; Hazelwood, K.; Isaac, E.; Jia, Y.; Jia, B.; et al. Machine Learning at Facebook: Understanding Inference at the Edge. In Proceedings of the 2019 IEEE International Symposium on High Performance Computer Architecture (HPCA), Washington, DC, USA, 16–20 February 2019; pp. 331–344. [CrossRef]
5. Apple A12. Available online: https://en.wikipedia.org/wiki/Apple_A12 (accessed on 30 October 2021).
6. Pixel 6. Available online: https://en.wikipedia.org/wiki/Pixel_6 (accessed on 30 October 2021).
7. Huggins-Daines, D.; Kumar, M.; Chan, A.; Black, A.; Ravishankar, M.; Rudnicky, A.I. Pocketsphinx: A Free, Real-Time Continuous Speech Recognition System for Hand-Held Devices. In Proceedings of the 2006 IEEE International Conference on Acoustics Speech and Signal Processing Proceedings, Toulouse, France, 14–19 May 2006; Volume 1, p. I.
8. Peinl, R.; Rizk, B.; Szabad, R. Open Source Speech Recognition on Edge Devices. In Proceedings of the 2020 10th International Conference on Advanced Computer Information Technologies (ACIT), Deggendorf, Germany, 13–15 May 2020; pp. 441–445.
9. Hannun, A.; Case, C.; Casper, J.; Catanzaro, B.; Diamos, G.; Elsen, E.; Prenger, R.; Satheesh, S.; Sengupta, S.; Coates, A.; et al. Deep Speech: Scaling up end-to-end speech recognition. *arXiv* **2014**, arXiv:1412.5567.
10. Povey, D.; Ghoshal, A.; Boulianne, G.; Burget, L.; Glembek, O.; Goel, N.; Hannemann, M.; Motlicek, P.; Qian, Y.; Schwarz, P.; et al. The Kaldi Speech Recognition Toolkit. In Proceedings of the IEEE 2011 Workshop on Automatic Speech Recognition and Understanding, Waikoloa, HI, USA, 11–15 December 2011.
11. Pratap, V.; Hannun, A.; Xu, Q.; Cai, J.; Kahn, J.; Synnaeve, G.; Liptchinsky, V.; Collobert, R. Wav2Letter++: A Fast Open-source Speech Recognition System. In Proceedings of the ICASSP 2019—2019 IEEE International Conference on Acoustics, Speech and Signal Processing (ICASSP), Brighton, UK, 12–17 May 2019; pp. 6460–6464. [CrossRef]
12. Lee, J.; Chirkov, N.; Ignasheva, E.; Pisarchyk, Y.; Shieh, M.; Riccardi, F.; Sarokin, R.; Kulik, A.; Grundmann, M. On-Device Neural Net Inference with Mobile GPUs. *arXiv* **2019**, arXiv:1907.01989.
13. Hadidi, R.; Cao, J.; Xie, Y.; Asgari, B.; Krishna, T.; Kim, H. Characterizing the Deployment of Deep Neural Networks on Commercial Edge Devices. In Proceedings of the 2019 IEEE International Symposium on Workload Characterization (IISWC), Orlando, FL, USA, 3–5 November 2019; pp. 35–48.
14. Rabiner, L. A tutorial on hidden Markov models and selected applications in speech recognition. *Proc. IEEE* **1989**, *77*, 257–286. [CrossRef]
15. Juang, B.H.; Levinson, S.; Sondhi, M. Maximum likelihood estimation for multivariate mixture observations of markov chains (Corresp.). *IEEE Trans. Inf. Theory* **1986**, *32*, 307–309. [CrossRef]
16. Mohamed, A.R.; Sainath, T.N.; Dahl, G.; Ramabhadran, B.; Hinton, G.E.; Picheny, M.A. Deep Belief Networks using discriminative features for phone recognition. In Proceedings of the 2011 IEEE International Conference on Acoustics, Speech and Signal Processing (ICASSP), Prague, Czech Republic, 22–27 May 2011; pp. 5060–5063.
17. Gu, J.; Wang, Z.; Kuen, J.; Ma, L.; Shahroudy, A.; Shuai, B.; Liu, T.; Wang, X.; Wang, L.; Wang, G.; et al. Recent Advances in Convolutional Neural Networks. *Pattern Recognit.* **2017**, *77*, 354–377. [CrossRef]
18. Abdel-Hamid, O.; Mohamed, A.R.; Jiang, H.; Deng, L.; Penn, G.; Yu, D. Convolutional Neural Networks for Speech Recognition. *IEEE/ACM Trans. Audio Speech Lang. Process.* **2014**, *22*, 1533–1545. [CrossRef]
19. Graves, A. Sequence Transduction with Recurrent Neural Networks. *arXiv* **2012**, arXiv:1211.3711.
20. Graves, A.; Fernández, S.; Gomez, F.; Schmidhuber, J. Connectionist Temporal Classification: Labelling Unsegmented Sequence Data with Recurrent Neural Networks. In Proceedings of the 23rd International Conference on Machine Learning, ICML '06, Pittsburgh, PA, USA, 25–29 June 2006; Association for Computing Machinery: New York, NY, USA, 2006; pp. 369–376. [CrossRef]
21. Bahdanau, D.; Cho, K.; Bengio, Y. Neural Machine Translation by Jointly Learning to Align and Translate. *arXiv* **2016**, arXiv:1409.0473.
22. Vaswani, A.; Shazeer, N.; Parmar, N.; Uszkoreit, J.; Jones, L.; Gomez, A.N.; Kaiser, L.; Polosukhin, I. Attention Is All You Need. In Proceedings of the 31st Conference on Neural Information Processing Systems (NIPS 2017), Long Beach, CA, USA, 4–9 December 2017.
23. Brown, T.B.; Mann, B.; Ryder, N.; Subbiah, M.; Kaplan, J.; Dhariwal, P.; Neelakantan, A.; Shyam, P.; Sastry, G.; Askell, A.; et al. Language Models are Few-Shot Learners. *arXiv* **2020**, arXiv:2005.14165.
24. Devlin, J.; Chang, M.W.; Lee, K.; Toutanova, K. BERT: Pre-training of Deep Bidirectional Transformers for Language Understanding. *arXiv* **2018**, arXiv:1810.04805.
25. Senior, A.W.; Evans, R.; Jumper, J.; Kirkpatrick, J.; Sifre, L.; Green, T.; Qin, C.; Žídek, A.; Nelson, A.W.R.; Bridgland, A.; et al. Improved protein structure prediction using potentials from deep learning. *Nature* **2020**, *577*, 706–710. [CrossRef] [PubMed]
26. Greff, K.; Srivastava, R.K.; Koutnik, J.; Steunebrink, B.R.; Schmidhuber, J. LSTM: A Search Space Odyssey. *IEEE Trans. Neural Netw. Learn. Syst.* **2017**, *28*, 2222–2232. [CrossRef] [PubMed]
27. Baevski, A.; Zhou, H.; Mohamed, A.; Auli, M. wav2vec 2.0: A Framework for Self-Supervised Learning of Speech Representations. *arXiv* **2020**, arXiv:2006.11477.

28. Wang, C.; Tang, Y.; Ma, X.; Wu, A.; Okhonko, D.; Pino, J. fairseq S2T: Fast Speech-to-Text Modeling with fairseq. In Proceedings of the 2020 Conference of the Asian Chapter of the Association for Computational Linguistics (AACL), System Demonstrations, Suzhou, China, 4–7 December 2020.
29. Droppo, J.; Acero, A. 33. Environmental Robustness. Available online: http://ai.stanford.edu/~amaas/data/cmn_paper.pdf (accessed on 30 October 2021).
30. Muda, L.; Begam, M.; Elamvazuthi, I. Voice Recognition Algorithms using Mel Frequency Cepstral Coefficient (MFCC) and Dynamic Time Warping (DTW) Techniques. *arXiv* **2010**, arXiv:1003.4083.
31. Panayotov, V.; Chen, G.; Povey, D.; Khudanpur, S. Librispeech: An ASR corpus based on public domain audio books. In Proceedings of the 2015 IEEE International Conference on Acoustics, Speech and Signal Processing (ICASSP), South Brisbane, Australia, 19–24 April 2015; pp. 5206–5210.

Article

# Self-Attentive Multi-Layer Aggregation with Feature Recalibration and Deep Length Normalization for Text-Independent Speaker Verification System

Soonshin Seo and Ji-Hwan Kim *

Department of Computer Science and Engineering, Sogang University, Seoul 04107, Korea; ssseo@sogang.ac.kr
* Correspondence: kimjihwan@sogang.ac.kr; Tel.: +82-2-705-8924

Received: 19 August 2020; Accepted: 15 October 2020; Published: 17 October 2020

**Abstract:** One of the most important parts of a text-independent speaker verification system is speaker embedding generation. Previous studies demonstrated that shortcut connections-based multi-layer aggregation improves the representational power of a speaker embedding system. However, model parameters are relatively large in number, and unspecified variations increase in the multi-layer aggregation. Therefore, in this study, we propose a self-attentive multi-layer aggregation with feature recalibration and deep length normalization for a text-independent speaker verification system. To reduce the number of model parameters, we set the ResNet with the scaled channel width and layer depth as a baseline. To control the variability in the training, we apply a self-attention mechanism to perform multi-layer aggregation with dropout regularizations and batch normalizations. Subsequently, we apply a feature recalibration layer to the aggregated feature using fully-connected layers and nonlinear activation functions. Further, deep length normalization is used on a recalibrated feature in the training process. Experimental results using the VoxCeleb1 evaluation dataset showed that the performance of the proposed methods was comparable to that of state-of-the-art models (equal error rate of 4.95% and 2.86%, using the VoxCeleb1 and VoxCeleb2 training datasets, respectively).

**Keywords:** text-independent speaker verification system; self-attentive pooling; multi-layer aggregation; feature recalibration; deep length normalization; speaker embedding; shortcut connections; convolutional neural networks; ResNet

## 1. Introduction

Speaker recognition aims to analyze the speaker representation from input audio. A subfield of speaker recognition is speaker verification, which determines whether the utterance of the claimed speaker should be accepted or rejected by comparing it to the utterance of the registered speaker. Speaker verification is divided into text dependent and text independent. Text-dependent speaker verification aims to recognize only the specified utterances when verifying the speaker. Examples include Google's "OK Google" and Samsung's "Hi Bixby." Meanwhile, text-independent speaker verification is not limited to the type of utterances to be recognized. Therefore, the problems to be solved using text-independent speaker verification are more difficult. If the performance is guaranteed, text-independent speaker verification can be utilized in various biometric systems and e-learning platforms, such as biometric authentication for chatbots, voice ID, and virtual assistants.

Owing to advances in computational power and deep learning techniques, the performance of text-independent speaker verification has been improved. Text-independent speaker verification using deep neural networks (DNN) is divided into two streams. The first one is an end-to-end system [1]. The input of the DNN is a speech signal, and the output is the verification result. This is a single-pass operation in which all processes can be operated at once. However, the input speech of a variable length is difficult to handle. To address this problem, several studies have applied a pooling layer or temporal average layer to an end-to-end system [2,3]. The second is a speaker embedding-based system [4–14], which generates an input of variable length into a vector of fixed length using a DNN. The generated vector is used as an embedding to represent the speaker. The speaker embedding-based system can handle input speech of variable length and can generate speaker representations from various environments.

As shown in Figure 1, a DNN has been used as a speaker embedding extractor in a speaker embedding-based system. In general, a speaker embedding-based system executes the following processes [4–7]:

- The speaker classification model is trained.
- The speaker embedding is extracted by using the output value of the inner layer of the speaker classification model.
- The similarity between the embedding of the registered speaker and the claimed speaker is computed.
- The acceptance or rejection is determined by a previously decided threshold value.

In addition, back-end methods, for example, probabilistic linear discriminant analysis, can be used [8–10].

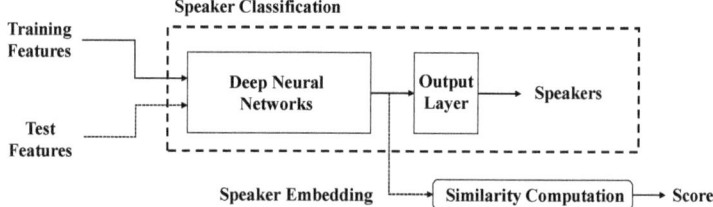

**Figure 1.** Overview of speaker embedding-based text-independent speaker verification system.

The most important part in the above system is the speaker embedding generation [13]. Speaker embedding is a high-dimensional feature vector that contains speaker information. An ideal speaker-embedding maximizes inter-class variations and minimizes intra-class variations [10,14,15]. The component that directly affects the speaker embedding generation is the encoding layer. The encoding layer takes a frame-level feature and converts it into a compact utterance-level feature. It also converts variable-length features to fixed-length features.

Most encoding layers are based on various pooling methods, for example, temporal average pooling (TAP) [10,14,16], global average pooling (GAP) [13,15], and statistical pooling (SP) [6,14,17,18]. In particular, self-attentive pooling (SAP) has improved performance by focusing on the frames for a more discriminative utterance-level feature [10,19,20], and pooling layers provide compressed speaker information by rescaling the input size. These are mainly used with convolutional neural networks (CNN) [10,13–17,20]. The speaker embedding is extracted using the output value of the last pooling layer in a CNN-based speaker model.

To improve the representational power of the speaker embedding, residual learning derived from ResNet [21] and squeeze-and-excitation (SE) blocks [22] were adapted for the speaker models [10,13–16,20,23]. Residual learning maintains input information through mappings between layers called "shortcut connections." A large-scale CNN using shortcut connections can avoid gradient degradation. The SE block consists of a squeeze operation (which condenses all of the information on the features) and an excitation operation (which scales the importance of each feature). Therefore, a channel-wise feature response can be adjusted without significantly increasing the model complexity in the training.

The main limitation of the previous encoding layers is that the model uses only the output feature of the last pooling layer as input. In other words, the model uses only one frame-level feature when performing speaker embedding. Therefore, similar to [14,24], a previous study presented a shortcut connection-based multi-layer aggregation to improve the speaker representations when calculating the weight at the encoding layer [13]. Specifically, the frame-level features are extracted from between each residual layer in ResNet. Then, these frame-level features are fed into the input of the encoding layer using shortcut connections. Consequently, a high-dimensional speaker embedding is generated.

However, the previous study [13] has limitations. First, the model parameter size is relatively large, and the model generates high-dimensional speaker embeddings (1024 dimensions, about 15 million model parameters). This leads to inefficient training and thus requires a sufficiently large amount of data for training. Second, the multi-layer aggregation approach increases not only the speaker's information but also the intrinsic and extrinsic variation factors, for example, emotion, noise, and reverberation. Some of these unspecified factors increase variability while generating speaker embedding.

Hence, we propose a self-attentive multi-layer aggregation with feature recalibration and deep length normalization for a text-independent speaker verification system, as shown in Figure 2. We present an improved version of the previous study, as described in the following steps:

- A ResNet with a scaled channel width and layer depth is used as a baseline. The scaled ResNet has fewer parameters than the standard ResNet [21].
- A self-attention mechanism is applied to perform multi-layer aggregation with dropout regularizations and batch normalizations [25]. It helps construct a more discriminative utterance-level feature while considering frame-level features of each layer.
- A feature recalibration layer is applied to the aggregated feature. Channel-wise dependencies are trained using fully-connected layers and nonlinear activation functions.
- Deep length normalization [11] is also used for a recalibrated feature in the training process.

The remainder of this paper is organized as follows. Section 2 describes a baseline system using shortcut connections-based multi-layer aggregation. Section 3 introduces the proposed self-attentive multi-layer aggregation method with feature recalibration and normalization. Section 4 discusses our experiments, and conclusions are drawn in Section 5.

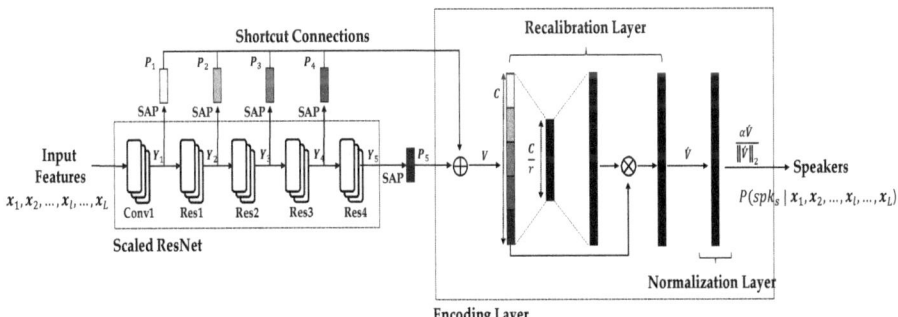

**Figure 2.** Overview of proposed network architecture: Self-attentive multi-layer aggregation with a feature recalibration layer and a deep length normalization layer (We extract a speaker embedding after the normalization layer on each utterance).

## 2. Baseline System: Shortcut Connections-Based Multi-Layer Aggregation

*2.1. Prior System*

In a previous study [13], a shortcut connections-based multi-layer aggregation with ResNet-18 was proposed. Its main difference from the standard ResNet-18 [21] is the manner that speaker embedding is aggregated. Multi-layer aggregation uses not only the output feature of the last residual layer but also the output features of all previous residual layers. These features are concatenated into one feature through shortcut connections. The concatenated feature is fed into several fully-connected layers to construct high-dimensional speaker embedding. The prior system improved the performance by a simple method.

However, it has large parameters because the system uses multi-layer aggregation, as presented in Table 1. The model parameters of standard ResNet-18 and standard ResNet-34 number are approximately 11.8 million and 21.9 million, respectively. Conversely, the model parameters of the prior system based on ResNet-18 and ResNet-34 are approximately 15.6 million and 25.7 million, respectively. In addition, the forward–backward training times of standard ResNet-18 and standard ResNet-34 are approximately 6.025 ms and 10.326 ms, respectively. However, the forward–backward training times of the prior system based on ResNet-18 and ResNet-34 are approximately 6.576 ms and 10.820 ms, respectively (when measuring the forward–backward training time, three units of GTX1080Ti and 96 mini-batch size were used).

**Table 1.** Comparison of model parameters and computational time in training between standard ResNet models and the prior system (MLA = multi-layer aggregation; Dim = speaker embedding dimension; Params = model parameters; FBTT = forward–backward training time (ms/batch)).

| Model | Use of MLA | Dim | Params | FBTT |
|---|---|---|---|---|
| Standard ResNet-18 | w/o | 512 | ≈11.8 M | ≈6.025 |
| Standard ResNet-34 | w/o | 512 | ≈21.9 M | ≈10.326 |
| (ResNet-18-based) prior system | w/ | 1024 | ≈15.6 M | ≈6.576 |
| (ResNet-34-based) prior system | w/ | 1024 | ≈25.7 M | ≈10.820 |

### 2.2. Modifications

As discussed in Section 2.1, the prior system improved the performance; however, the model parameters were too large. The prior system is modified considering scaling factors, such as layer depth, channel width, and input resolution, for efficient learning in the CNN [26]. First, we used high-dimensional log-Mel filter banks with data augmentation for the input resolution. We extracted an input feature map of size $D \times L$, where $D$ is the number of single-frame spectral features and $L$ is the number of frames. Here, Mel-filter banks determine dimension $D$ from zero to 8,000 Hz. Subsequently, the channel width is reduced, and the layer depth is expanded because ResNet can improve the performance without significantly increasing the parameters when the layer depth is increased.

Consequently, the scaled ResNet-34 was constructed, as shown in Table 2. The scaled ResNet-34 is composed of three, four, six, and three residual blocks. It has reduced the number of channels by half compared to the standard ResNet-34 [21]. In addition, shortcut connections-based multi-layer aggregation is added to the model using the GAP encoding method. The output features of each GAP are concatenated and fed into the output layer. Then, high-dimensional speaker embedding is generated from a penultimate layer in a network. Thus, the scaled ResNet-34 has only approximately 5.9 million model parameters compared to the prior system, as presented in Table 3. In addition, the forward–backward training time in milliseconds of the scaled ResNet-34 is faster than the prior system based on ResNet-34 (the forward–backward training time in milliseconds of the scaled ResNet-34 is approximately 5.658 ms).

**Table 2.** Architecture of scaled ResNet-34 using multi-layer aggregation as a baseline (D = input dimension; L = input length; N = number of speakers; GAP = global average pooling; SE = speaker embedding).

| Layer | Output Size | Channels | Blocks | Encoding |
|---|---|---|---|---|
| conv1 | $D \times L$ | 32 | - | - |
| pool1 | $1 \times 32$ | - | - | GAP |
| res1 | $D \times L$ | 32 | 3 | - |
| pool2 | $1 \times 32$ | - | - | GAP |
| res2 | $D/2 \times L/2$ | 64 | 4 | - |
| pool3 | $1 \times 64$ | - | - | GAP |
| res3 | $D/4 \times L/4$ | 128 | 6 | - |
| pool4 | $1 \times 128$ | - | - | GAP |
| res4 | $D/8 \times L/8$ | 256 | 3 | - |
| pool5 | $1 \times 256$ | - | - | GAP |
| concat | $1 \times 512$ | - | - | SE |
| output | $512 \times N$ | - | - | - |

**Table 3.** Comparison of model parameters and computational time in training between the prior system and the scaled ResNet model (MLA = multi-layer aggregation; Dim = speaker embedding dimension; Params = model parameters; FBTT = forward–backward training time (ms/batch)).

| Model | Use of MLA | Dim | Params | FBTT |
|---|---|---|---|---|
| (ResNet-34-based) prior system | w/ | 1024 | ≈25.7 M | ≈11.186 |
| Scaled ResNet-34 | w/ | 512 | ≈5.9 M | ≈5.658 |

## 3. Self-Attentive Multi-Layer Aggregation with Feature Recalibration and Normalization

As discussed in Section 1, the previous study has two problems. The model parameter problem is addressed by building a scaled ResNet-34. However, the problem of multi-layer aggregation remains. Multi-layer aggregation uses output features of multiple layers to develop the speaker embedding system. It is assumed that not only speaker information but also other unspecified factors exist in the output feature of the layer. The unspecified factor lowers the speaker verification performance. Therefore, we proposed three methods: self-attentive multi-layer aggregation, feature recalibration, and deep length normalization.

### 3.1. Model Architecture

As presented in Figure 2 and Table 4, the proposed network mainly consists of a scaled ResNet and an encoding layer. Frame-level features are trained in the scaled ResNet, and utterance-level features are trained in the encoding layer.

In the scaled ResNet, given an input feature $X = [x_1, x_2, \ldots, x_l, \ldots, x_L]$ of length $L$ ($x_l \in \mathbb{R}^d$), output features $P_i = [p_1, p_2, \ldots, p_c, \ldots, p_C]$ ($p_c \in \mathbb{R}$) from each residual layer of the scaled ResNet are generated using SAP. Here, the length $C_i$ is determined by the number of channels in the $i^{th}$ residual layer. Then, the generated output features are concatenated into one feature $V$ as in Equation (1) (where [+] indicates concatenation).

$$V = P_1 [+] P_2 [+] P_3 [+] P_4 [+] P_5 \tag{1}$$

The concatenated feature $V = [v_1, v_2, \ldots, v_c, \ldots, v_C]$ (length $C = C_1 + C_2 + C_3 + C_4 + C_5$, $v_c \in \mathbb{R}$) is a set of frame-level features and is used as the input of the encoding layer.

The encoding layer comprises a feature recalibration layer and a deep length normalization layer. In the feature recalibration layer, the concatenated feature $V$ is recalibrated by fully-connected layers and nonlinear activations. Consequently, a recalibrated feature $\acute{V} = [\acute{v}_1, \acute{v}_2, \ldots, \acute{v}_c, \ldots, \acute{v}_C]$ ($\acute{v}_c \in \mathbb{R}$) is generated. Then, the recalibrated feature is normalized according to the length of input $\acute{V}$ in the deep-length normalization layer. The normalized feature is used as a speaker embedding and is fed into the output layer. Further, a log probability for speaker classes $s$, $P(spk_s | x_1, x_2, \ldots, x_l, \ldots, x_L)$, is generated in the output layer.

Table 4. Architecture of proposed scaled ResNet-34 model using self-attentive multi-layer aggregation with feature recalibration and deep length normalization layers ($D$ = input dimension; $L$ = input length; $N$ = number of speakers; $P$ = output features of pooling layers; $V$ = output features of concatenation layer; $\acute{V}$ = output features of feature recalibration layer; FR = feature recalibration; DLN = deep length normalization; SAP = self-attentive pooling; SE = speaker embedding).

| Layer | Output Size | Channels | Blocks | Encoding |
|---|---|---|---|---|
| conv1 | D × L | 32 | - | - |
| pool1 | 1 × 32 | - | - | SAP ($P_1$) |
| res1 | D × L | 32 | 3 | - |
| pool2 | 1 × 32 | - | - | SAP ($P_2$) |
| res2 | D/2 × L/2 | 64 | 4 | - |
| pool3 | 1 × 64 | - | - | SAP ($P_3$) |
| res3 | D/4 × L/4 | 128 | 6 | - |
| pool4 | 1 × 128 | - | - | SAP ($P_4$) |
| res4 | D/8 × L/8 | 256 | 3 | - |
| pool5 | 1 × 256 | - | - | SAP ($P_5$) |
| concat | 1 × 512 | - | - | V |
| FR | 1 × 512 | - | - | $\acute{V}$ |
| DLN | 1 × 512 | - | - | SE |
| output | 512 × N | - | - | - |

*3.2. Self-Attentive Multi-Layer Aggregation*

As shown in Figures 2 and 3, SAP is applied to each residual layer using shortcut connections. For every input feature, given an output feature of the first convolution layer or the $i^{th}$ residual layers after conducting an average pooling, $Y_i = [y_1, y_2, \ldots, y_n, \ldots, y_N]$ of length $N$ ($y_n \in \mathbb{R}^c$) is obtained. The number of dimensions $c$ is determined by the number of channels.

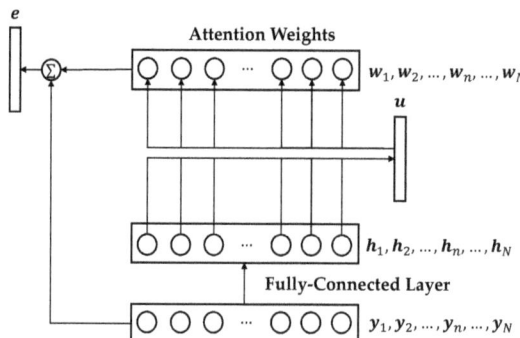

Figure 3. Overview of self-attentive pooling procedure.

Then, the average feature is fed into a fully-connected hidden layer to obtain $H_i = [h_1, h_2, \ldots, h_n, \ldots, h_N]$ using a hyperbolic tangent activation function. Given $h_n \in \mathbb{R}^c$ and a learnable context vector $u \in \mathbb{R}^c$, the attention weight $w_n$ is measured by training the similarity between $h_n$ and $u$ with a softmax normalization as in Equation (2).

$$w_n = \frac{exp(h_n^T u)}{\sum_{n=1}^{N} exp(h_n^T u)} \qquad (2)$$

Then, the embedding $e \in \mathbb{R}^c$ is generated using the weighted sum of the normalized attention weights $w_n$ and $y_n$ as in Equation (3).

$$e = \sum_{n=1}^{N} y_n w_n \qquad (3)$$

The embedding vector $e$ can be rewritten as $P_i = [p_1, p_2, \ldots, p_c, \ldots, p_C]$ ($p_c \in \mathbb{R}$) in the order of the dimensions. Consequently, the SAP output feature $P_i$ is generated. This process helps generate a more discriminative feature while focusing on the frame-level features of each layer. Moreover, dropout regularization and batch normalization are used in $P_i$. Then, the generated features are concatenated into one feature, $V$, as in Equation (1).

### 3.3. Feature Recalibration

After the self-attentive multi-layer aggregation, the concatenated feature $V$ is fed into the feature recalibration layer. The feature recalibration layer aims to train the correlations between each channel of the concatenated feature; this is inspired by [22].

Given an input feature $V = [v_1, v_2, \ldots, v_c, \ldots, v_C]$ ($v_c \in \mathbb{R}$, where $C$ is the sum of all channels), the feature channels are recalibrated using two fully-connected layers and nonlinear activations, as in Equation (4).

$$\acute{V} = f_{FR}(V, W) = \sigma(W_2 \delta(W_1 V)) \qquad (4)$$

Here, $\delta$ refers to the leaky rectified linear unit activation; $\sigma$ refers to the sigmoid activation; $W_1$ is the front fully-connected layer, $W_1 \in \mathbb{R}^{c \times \frac{c}{r}}$, and $W_2$ is the back fully-connected layer, $W_2 \in \mathbb{R}^{\frac{c}{r} \times c}$. According to the reduction ratio $r$, a dimensional transformation is performed between the two fully-connected layers, such as a bottleneck structure, while channel-wise multiplication is performed. The rescaled channels are then multiplied by the input feature $V$. Consequently, an output feature $\acute{V} = [\acute{v}_1, \acute{v}_2, \ldots, \acute{v}_c, \ldots, \acute{v}_C]$ ($\acute{v}_c \in \mathbb{R}$) is generated. This generated feature $\acute{V}$ is the result of recalibration according to the importance of the channels.

### 3.4. Deep Length Normalization

As in [11], deep length normalization was applied to the proposed model. The L2 constraint is applied to the length axis of the recalibrated feature $\acute{V}$ with a scale constant, $\alpha$, as in Equation (5).

$$f_{DLN}(\acute{V}) = \frac{\alpha \acute{V}}{\|\acute{V}\|_2} \qquad (5)$$

Then, the normalized $\acute{V}$ is fed into the output layer for speaker classification. This feature is used as a speaker embedding, as shown in Figure 4.

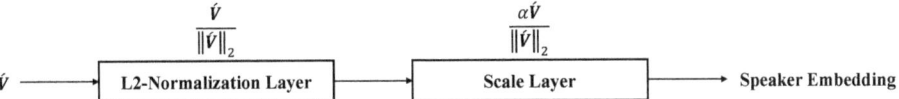

**Figure 4.** Overview of deep length normalization procedure.

## 4. Experiments and Discussions

### 4.1. Datasets

In our experiments, we used the VoxCeleb1 [27] and VoxCeleb2 [16] datasets presented in Table 5. These datasets comprise various utterances of celebrities collected in real environments from YouTube, including noise, laughter, cross talk, channel effects, music, and other sounds [27]. All utterances were encoded at a 16-kHz sampling rate with 2 bytes per sample. These are large-scale text-independent speaker verification datasets, comprising more than 100 thousand and 1 million utterances with 1251 and 6112 speakers, respectively.

Table 5. Dataset statistics for both VoxCeleb1 and VoxCeleb2. There are no duplicate utterances between VoxCeleb1 and VoxCeleb2 (POI = person of interest).

| Dataset | VoxCeleb1 | VoxCeleb2 |
|---|---|---|
| # of POIs (Total) | 1251 | 6112 |
| # of POIs (Training) | 1211 | 5994 |
| # of POIs (Evaluation) | 40 | 118 |
| # of utterances (Total) | 153,516 | 1,128,246 |
| # of utterances (Training) | 148,642 | 1,092,009 |
| # of utterances (Evaluation) | 4874 | 36,237 |
| # of hours | 352 | 2442 |
| Average # of utterances per POI | 116 | 185 |
| Average length of utterances (s) | 8.2 | 7.8 |

We used the VoxCeleb1 evaluation dataset, which includes 40 speakers and 37,220 pairs of official test protocols [27], as shown in Figure 5. The test protocols comprises eight pairs per utterance of the VoxCeleb1 evaluation set (four pairs of the same speaker and four pairs of different speakers). Among all possible 38,992 (4874 × 8) utterances, 37,720 pairs were determined. The pair decision is made in consideration of balance such as gender, utterance length, and the number of pairs per speaker. In addition, it is an open-set test that evaluates all speaker pairs that are unavailable for the training dataset.

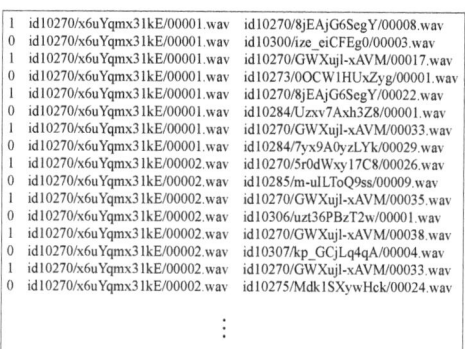

**Figure 5.** Example of official test protocol from VoxCeleb1 evaluation dataset (In the first column, 1 refers to the same speaker and 0 refers to different speakers. The second and third columns refer to the speakers to be compared).

*4.2. Experimental Setup*

During data preprocessing, we used 64-dimensional log Mel-filter-bank energies with a 25 ms frame length and 10 ms frame shift, which are the mean variance normalized over a sliding window of 3 s. For each training step, a 12 s interval was extracted from each utterance through cropping or padding. In addition, a preprocessing method was used to conduct time and frequency masking on the input features [28].

The model training specifications are as follows: we used a standard cross-entropy loss function, with a standard stochastic gradient descent optimizer, with a momentum of 0.9, a weight decay of 0.0001, and an initial learning rate of 0.1, reduced by a 0.1 scale factor on the plateau [29]. All experiments were trained for 200 epochs with a 96 mini-batch size. The scaling constant $\alpha$ was set to 10, and the reduction ratio $r$ was set to 8 [11,22]. As shown in Figure 6, we confirmed that the training loss converges for the baseline model, as described in Section 2.2, and the proposed model, as described in Section 3.1, was trained.

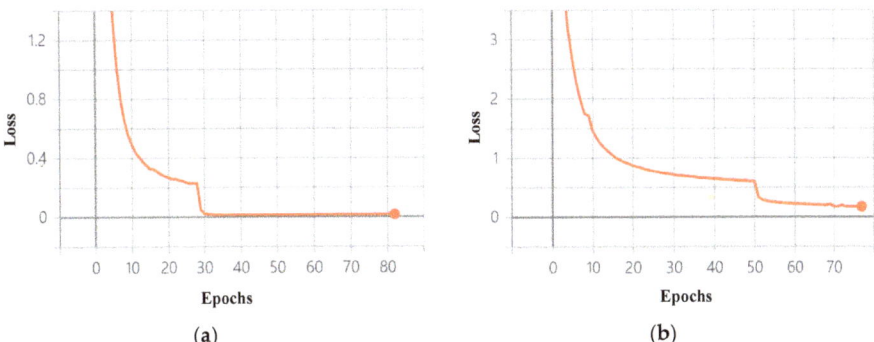

**Figure 6.** Training loss curve of (**a**) the baseline model and (**b**) the proposed model.

From the trained model, we generated a 512-dimensional speaker embedding for each utterance, as shown in Figure 7. The standard cosine similarity is computed for the speaker pair, and the equal error rate (EER, %) is calculated. The EER value is the crossing point of the two curves, the false rejection rate and the false acceptance rate, according to the decision threshold. This can also be expressed on the receiver operating characteristic (ROC) curve using the true-positive rate and false -positive rate. All of our proposed methods were implemented using the PyTorch toolkit [30].

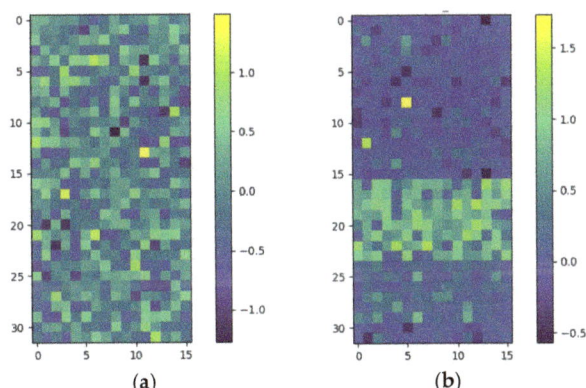

**Figure 7.** Examples of the 512-dimensional speaker embedding in one utterance of (**a**) baseline model and (**b**) proposed model (we converted the 512-dimension to 32 × 16).

### 4.3. Experimental Results

To evaluate the proposed methods, we first tested the baseline using different encoding methods and other networks and then we compared our proposed method with state-of-the-art encoding methods.

Table 6 presents the results of baseline modifications, as described in Section 2.2. It demonstrates the effectiveness of modifications to the encoding methods. We experimented with basic encoding layers, such as GAP and SAP. We then combined the proposed methods individually to the baseline, for example, self-attentive multi-layer aggregation, feature recalibration, and deep length normalization. Specifically, the scaled ResNet-34 with GAP and SAP achieved EER values of 6.85 % and 6.68%, respectively. Because multi-layer aggregation was not applied with these encoding methods, the number of dimensions of the speaker embedding was 256. In addition, the gap in performance between GAP and SAP was not large. We then applied the multi-layer aggregation for scaled ResNet-34 with GAP and SAP. In particular, the scaled ResNet-34 using multi-layer aggregation and GAP is our baseline system described in Section 2.2. Although speaker embedding dimensions and model parameters were larger in number than those of GAP and SAP, the EER value was reduced from 6.85% to 5.83% and from 6.68% to 5.42%, respectively. Additional applications to self-attentive multi-layer aggregation using feature recalibration and deep length normalization also achieved EER values of 5.07% and 4.95%, respectively. In addition, the ROC curve of the proposed model showed the EER point, as shown in Figure 8. Consequently, the experimental results showed that when all of the proposed methods were applied, the model parameters increased by approximately 0.5 M compared to the scaled ResNet-34 with GAP, whereas the EER value improved by 1.9%.

**Table 6.** Experimental results for modifying the baseline construction, using the VoxCeleb1 training and evaluation dataset (Dim = speaker embedding dimension; Params = model parameters; EER = equal error rate; GAP = global average pooling; SAP = self-attentive pooling; MLA = multi-layer aggregation; FR = feature recalibration; DLN = deep length normalization).

| Model | Encoding Method | Dim | Params | EER |
| --- | --- | --- | --- | --- |
| Scaled ResNet-34 | GAP | 256 | ≈5.6 M | 6.85 |
| | SAP | 256 | ≈5.7 M | 6.68 |
| | GAP-MLA | 512 | ≈5.9 M | 5.83 |
| | SAP-MLA | 512 | ≈6.0 M | 5.42 |
| | SAP-MLA-FR | 512 | ≈6.1 M | 5.07 |
| | SAP-MLA-FR-DLN | 512 | ≈6.1 M | 4.95 |

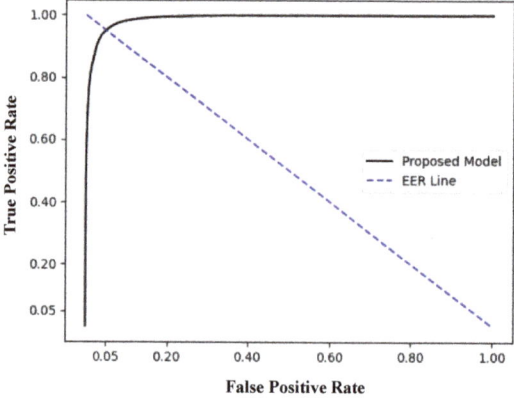

**Figure 8.** ROC curve of the proposed model (threshold value is 0.3362 and EER value is 4.95% using VoxCeleb1 training and evaluation dataset in Table 6).

Table 7 shows a comparison of our proposed methods with other networks. All experiments used the VoxCeleb1 training and evaluation datasets. First, the $i$-vector extractor was trained according to the implementation in [27]. After generating 400-dimensional $i$-vectors, PLDA was applied to reduce the number of dimensions of $i$-vectors to 200. The $i$-vector with the PLDA system achieved an EER value of 8.82%. In addition, an $x$-vector system was trained according to the implementation in [18]. The $x$-vector system is based on the use of time-delay neural networks (TDNN) using an SP method, which is commonly applied for text-independent speaker verification along with a ResNet-based system. The 1500-dimensional $x$-vector was extracted from the TDNN, which achieved an EER value of 8.19%. Our proposed methods based on the scaled ResNet-34 showed an improved performance, compared to the previous systems (i.e., EER value of 4.95%).

**Table 7.** Experimental results comparing our proposed methods with other networks using the VoxCeleb1 training and evaluation dataset (Dim = speaker embedding dimension; EER = equal error rate; SP = statistical pooling; GAP = global average pooling; SAP = self-attentive pooling; MLA = multi-layer aggregation; FR = feature recalibration; DLN = deep length normalization).

| Model | Encoding Method | Dim | EER |
|---|---|---|---|
| $i$-vector + PLDA | - | 200 | 8.82 |
| $x$-vector | SP | 1500 | 8.19 |
| Scaled ResNet-34 | SAP-MLA-FR-DLN | 512 | 4.95 |

Tables 8 and 9 show a comparison of our proposed methods with state-of-the-art encoding approaches. Here, we compared encoding methods using a ResNet-based model and the cross-entropy loss function. Various encoding methods were compared, including TAP [10,16], learnable dictionary encoding (LDE) [10], SAP [10], GAP [15], NetVLAD [7], and GhostVLAD [7].

**Table 8.** Experimental results comparing our proposed methods with state-of-the-art encoding methods using the VoxCeleb1 training and evaluation dataset (Dim = speaker embedding dimension; EER = equal error rate; TAP = temporal average pooling; LDE = learnable dictionary encoding; SAP = self-attentive pooling; GAP = global average pooling; MLA = multi-layer aggregation; FR = feature recalibration; DLN = deep length normalization).

| Model | Encoding Method | Dim | EER |
|---|---|---|---|
| ResNet-34 [10] | TAP | 128 | 5.48 |
| ResNet-34 [10] | LDE | 128 | 5.21 |
| ResNet-34 [10] | SAP | 128 | 5.51 |
| ResNet-34 [15] | GAP | 256 | 5.39 |
| Scaled ResNet-34 (proposed) | SAP-MLA-FR-DLN | 512 | 4.95 |

**Table 9.** Experimental results comparing our proposed methods with state-of-the-art encoding methods using the VoxCeleb2 training datasets and the VoxCeleb1 evaluation datasets (Dim = speaker embedding dimension; EER = equal error rate; TAP = temporal average pooling; SAP = self-attentive pooling; MLA = multi-layer aggregation; FR = feature recalibration; DLN = deep length normalization).

| Model | Encoding Method | Dim | EER |
|---|---|---|---|
| ResNet-34 [16] | TAP | 512 | 5.04 |
| ResNet-50 [16] | TAP | 512 | 4.19 |
| Thin-ResNet-34 [7] | NetVLAD | 512 | 3.57 |
| Thin-ResNet-34 [7] | GhostVLAD | 512 | 3.22 |
| Scaled ResNet-34 (proposed) | SAP-MLA-FR-DLN | 512 | 2.86 |

In Table 8, all experiments used the VoxCeleb1 training and evaluation datasets. ResNet-34 with TAP, LDE, SAP, or GAP achieved EER values of 5.48%, 5.21%, 5.51%, and 5.39%, respectively [10,15]. The speaker embedding dimensions of these systems were 128 or 256, which were smaller than those of the proposed methods. However, our proposed encoding methods based on the scaled ResNet-34 achieved an EER value of 4.95%. The performance was an improvement to that of other systems.

In Table 9, all experiments used the VoxCeleb2 training datasets and VoxCeleb1 evaluation datasets. As presented in Table 5, the VoxCeleb2 training datasets are seven times more than the VoxCeleb1 training datasets. Table 9 shows that increasing the amount of training dataset was effective for performance improvement. ResNet-34 and ResNet-50 with TAP achieved EER values of 5.04% and 4.95%, respectively [16]. In addition, a thin-ResNet-34 with NetVLAD and GhostVLAD achieved EER values of 3.57% and 3.22%, respectively [7]. The number of speaker embedding dimensions of these systems was 512, which is the same as that of our proposed methods. Our proposed encoding methods based on the scaled ResNet-34 achieved an EER value of 2.86%. Consequently, the experimental results showed that our proposed methods were superior to other state-of-the-art methods.

Furthermore, in the case of on-device speaker verification, the lower the speaker embedding dimension, the faster the system. Our proposed methods have limitations as a high-dimensional speaker embedding method, compared to other state-of-the-art encoding methods. Therefore, future research is required to address this dimension problem. In a future study, on-device speaker verification using low-dimensional speaker embedding will be conducted.

## 5. Conclusions

In previous multi-layer aggregation methods for text-independent speaker verification, the number of model parameters was relatively large, and unspecified variations increased during training. Therefore, we proposed a self-attentive multi-layer aggregation with feature recalibration and deep length normalization for a text-independent speaker verification system. First, we set the ResNet with the scaled channel width and layer depth as a baseline. Second, self-attentive multi-layer aggregation was applied when training the frame-level features of each residual layer in the scaled ResNet. Finally, the feature recalibration layer and deep length normalization were applied to train the utterance-level feature in the encoding layer. The experimental results using the VoxCeleb1 evaluation dataset showed that the proposed method achieved an EER value performance comparable to that of state-of-the-art models.

**Author Contributions:** Conceptualization, S.S.; methodology, S.S.; software, S.S.; validation, S.S.; formal analysis, S.S.; investigation, S.S.; resources, S.S.; data curation, S.S.; writing—original draft preparation, S.S.; writing—review and editing, S.S. and J.-H.K.; visualization, S.S.; supervision, J.-H.K.; project administration, J.-H.K. All authors have read and agreed to the published version of the manuscript.

**Funding:** This research received no external funding.

**Acknowledgments:** This work was supported by the National Research Foundation of Korea (NRF) grant funded by the Korea government (MSIT) (No.2020R1F1A1076562).

**Conflicts of Interest:** The authors declare no conflict of interest.

## Abbreviations

The following abbreviations are used in this manuscript:

| | |
|---|---|
| DNN | Deep Neural Networks |
| TAP | Temporal Average Pooling |
| GAP | Global Average Pooling |
| SP | Statistical Pooling |
| SAP | Self-Attentive Pooling |
| CNN | Convolutional Neural Networks |
| SE | Squeeze-and-Excitation |
| MLA | Multi-Layer Aggregation |
| FR | Feature Recalibration |
| DLN | Deep Length Normalization |
| ROC | Receiver Operating Characteristic |
| TDNN | Time delay Neural Networks |
| LDE | Learnable Dictionary Encoding |

## References

1. Heigold, G.; Moreno, I.; Bengio, S.; Shazeer, N. End-to-End Text-Dependent Speaker Verification. In Proceedings of the 2016 IEEE International Conference on Acoustics, Speech and Signal Processing (ICASSP), Shanghai, China, 20–25 March 2016; pp. 5115–5119.
2. Snyder, D.; Ghahremani, P.; Povey, D.; Garcia-Romero, D.; Carmiel, Y.; Khudanpur, S. Deep Neural Network-Based Speaker Embeddings for End-to-End Speaker Verification. In Proceedings of the 2016 IEEE Spoken Language Technology Workshop (SLT), San Diego, CA, USA, 13–16 December 2016; pp. 165–170.

3. Li, C.; Ma, X.; Jiang, B.; Li, X.; Zhang, X.; Liu, X.; Cao, Y.; Kannan, A.; Zhu, Z. Deep Speaker: An End-to-End Neural Speaker Embedding System. *arXiv* **2017**, arXiv:1705.02304.
4. Variani, E.; Lei, X.; McDermott, E.; Moreno, I.L.; González-Domínguez, J. Deep Neural Networks for Small Footprint Text-Dependent Speaker Verification. In Proceedings of the 2014 IEEE International Conference on Acoustics, Speech and Signal Processing (ICASSP), Florence, Italy, 4–9 May 2014; pp. 4052–4056.
5. Chen, Y.; Lopez-Moreno, I.; Sainath, T.N.; Visontai, M.; Alvarez, R.; Parada, C. Locally-Connected and Convolutional Neural Networks for Small Footprint Speaker Recognition. In Proceedings of the 16th Annual Conference of the International Speech Communication Association (INTERSPEECH), Dresden, Germany, 6–10 September 2015; pp. 1136–1140.
6. Snyder, D.; Garcia-Romero, D.; Povey, D.; Khudanpur, S. Deep Neural Network Embeddings for Text-Independent Speaker Verification. In Proceedings of the 18th Annual Conference of the International Speech Communication Association (INTERSPEECH), Stockholm, Sweden, 20–24 August 2017; pp. 999–1003.
7. Xie, W.; Nagrani, A.; Chung, J.S.; Zisserman, A. Utterance-level Aggregation for Speaker Recognition in the Wild. In Proceedings of the 44th IEEE International Conference on Acoustics, Speech and Signal Processing (ICASSP), Brighton, UK, 12–17 May 2019; pp. 5791–5795.
8. Garcia-Romero, D.; Espy-Wilson, C.Y. Analysis of I-Vector Length Normalization in Speaker Recognition Systems. In Proceedings of the 12th Annual Conference of the International Speech Communication Association (INTERSPEECH), Florence, Italy, 27–31 August 2011; pp. 249–252.
9. Bhattacharya, G.; Alam, J.; Kenny, P. Deep Speaker Embeddings for Short-Duration Speaker Verification. In Proceedings of the 18th Annual Conference of the International Speech Communication Association, Stockholm, Sweden, 20–24 August 2017; pp. 1517–1521.
10. Cai, W.; Chen, J.; Li, M. Exploring the Encoding Layer and Loss Function in End-to-End Speaker and Language Recognition System. In Proceedings of the 11th Speaker and Language Recognition Workshop (Odyssey), Les Sables d'Olonne, France, 26–29 June 2018; pp. 74–81.
11. Cai, W.; Chen, J.; Li, M. Analysis of Length Normalization in End-to-End Speaker Verification System. In Proceedings of the 19th Annual Conference of the International Speech Communication Association (INTERSPEECH), Hyderabad, India, 2–6 September 2018; pp. 3618–3622.
12. Jung, J.-W.; Heo, H.-S.; Kim, J.-H.; Shim, H.-J.; Yu, H.-J. RawNet: Advanced End-to-End Deep Neural Network Using Raw Waveforms for Text-Independent Speaker Verification. In Proceedings of the 20th Annual Conference of the International Speech Communication Association (INTERSPEECH), Graz, Austria, 15–19 September 2019; pp. 1268–1272.
13. Seo, S.; Rim, D.J.; Lim, M.; Lee, D.; Park, H.; Oh, J.; Kim, C.; Kim, J.-H. Shortcut Connections Based Deep Speaker Embeddings for End-to-End Speaker Verification System. In Proceedings of the 20th Annual Conference of the International Speech Communication Association (INTERSPEECH), Graz, Austria, 15–19 September 2019; pp. 2928–2932.
14. Gao, Z.; Song, Y.; McLoughlin, I.; Li, P.; Jiang, Y.; Dai, L.-R. Improving Aggregation and Loss Function for Better Embedding Learning in End-to-End Speaker Verification System. In Proceedings of the 20th Annual Conference of the International Speech Communication Association (INTERSPEECH), Graz, Austria, 15–19 September 2019; pp. 361–365.
15. Kim, I.; Kim, K.; Kim, J.; Choi, C. Deep Speaker Representation Using Orthogonal Decomposition and Recombination for Speaker Verification. In Proceedings of the 44th IEEE International Conference on Acoustics, Speech and Signal Processing (ICASSP); Brighton, UK, 12–17 May 2019; pp. 6126–6130.
16. Chung, J.S.; Nagrani, A.; Zisserman, A. VoxCeleb2: Deep Speaker Recognition. In Proceedings of the 19th Annual Conference of the International Speech Communication Association (INTERSPEECH), Hyderabad, India, 2–6 September 2018; pp. 1086–1090.
17. Gao, Z.; Song, Y.; McLoughlin, I.; Guo, W.; Dai, L. An Improved Deep Embedding Learning Method for Short Duration Speaker Verification. In Proceedings of the 19th Annual Conference of the International Speech Communication Association (INTERSPEECH), Hyderabad, India, 2–6 September 2018; pp. 3578–3582.
18. Snyder, D.; Garcia-Romero, D.; Sell, G.; Povey, D.; Khudanpur, S. X-Vectors: Robust DNN Embeddings for Speaker Recognition. In Proceedings of the 43rd IEEE International Conference on Acoustics, Speech and Signal Processing (ICASSP), Calgary, AB, Canada, 15–20 April 2018; pp. 5329–5333.

19. Zhu, Y.; Ko, T.; Snyder, D.; Mak, B.; Povey, D. Self-Attentive Speaker Embeddings for Text-Independent Speaker Verification. In Proceedings of the 19th Annual Conference of the International Speech Communication Association (INTERSPEECH), Hyderabad, India, 2–6 September 2018; pp. 3573–3577.
20. India, M.; Safari, P.; Hernando, J. Self Multi-Head Attention for Speaker Recognition. In Proceedings of the 20th Annual Conference of the International Speech Communication Association (INTERSPEECH), Graz, Austria, 15–19 September 2019; pp. 4305–4309.
21. He, K.; Zhang, X.; Ren, S.; Sun, J. Deep Residual Learning for Image Recognition. In Proceedings of the 29th IEEE/CVF Conference on Computer Vision and Pattern Recognition (CVPR), Las Vegas, NV, USA, 26 June–1 July 2016; pp. 770–778.
22. Hu, J.; Shen, L.; Sun, G. Squeeze-and-Excitation Networks. In Proceedings of the 31st IEEE/CVF Conference on Computer Vision and Pattern Recognition (CVPR), Salt Lake City, UT, USA, 18–22 June 2018; pp. 7132–7141.
23. Zhou, J.; Jiang, T.; Li, Z.; Li, L.; Hong, Q. Deep Speaker Embedding Extraction with Channel-Wise Feature Responses and Additive Supervision Softmax Loss Function. In Proceedings of the 20th Annual Conference of the International Speech Communication Association (INTERSPEECH), Graz, Austria, 15–19 September 2019; pp. 2883–2887.
24. Tang, Y.; Ding, G.; Huang, J.; He, X.; Zhou, B. Deep Speaker Embedding Learning with Multi-level Pooling for Text-independent Speaker Verification. In Proceedings of the 44th IEEE International Conference on Acoustics, Speech and Signal Processing (ICASSP), Brighton, UK, 12–17 May 2019; pp. 6116–6120.
25. Yan, Z.; Zhang, H.; Jia, Y.; Breuel, T.; Yu, Y. Combining the Best of Convolutional Layers and Recurrent Layers: A Hybrid Network for Semantic Segmentation 2016. *arXiv* **2016**, arXiv:1603.04871.
26. Tan, M.; Le, Q.V. EfficientNet: Rethinking Model Scaling for Convolutional Neural Networks 2019. *arXiv* **2019**, arXiv:1905.11946.
27. Nagrani, A.; Chung, J.S.; Zisserman, A. VoxCeleb: A Large-Scale Speaker Identification Dataset. In Proceedings of the 18th Annual Conference of the International Speech Communication Association (INTERSPEECH), Stockholm, Sweden, 20–24 August 2017; pp. 2616–2620.
28. Park, D.S.; Chan, W.; Zhang, Y.; Chiu, C.-C.; Zoph, B.; Cubuk, E.D.; Le, Q.V. SpecAugment: A Simple Data Augmentation Method for Automatic Speech Recognition. In Proceedings of the 20th Annual Conference of the International Speech Communication Association (INTERSPEECH), Graz, Austria, 15–19 September 2019; pp. 2613–2617.
29. Seo, S.; Kim, J.-H. MCSAE: Masked Cross Self-Attentive Encoding for Speaker Embedding. *arXiv* **2020**, arXiv:2001.10817.
30. Paszke, A.; Gross, S.; Massa, F.; Lerer, A.; Bradbury, J.; Chanan, G.; Killeen, T.; Lin, Z.; Gimelshein, N.; Antiga, L.; et al. PyTorch: An Imperative Style, High-Performance Deep Learning Library. In Proceedings of the 33rd Conference on Neural Information Processing Systems (NeurIPS), Vancouver, BC, Canada, 8–14 December 2019; pp. 8024–8035.

**Publisher's Note:** MDPI stays neutral with regard to jurisdictional claims in published maps and institutional affiliations.

© 2020 by the authors. Licensee MDPI, Basel, Switzerland. This article is an open access article distributed under the terms and conditions of the Creative Commons Attribution (CC BY) license (http://creativecommons.org/licenses/by/4.0/).

Article
# Domain Usability Evaluation

Michaela Bačíková *[image_ref id="..."], Jaroslav Porubän, Matúš Sulír, Sergej Chodarev, William Steingartner and Matej Madeja

Department of Computers and Informatics, Faculty of Electrical Engineering and Informatics, Technical University of Košice, Letná 9, 042 00 Košice, Slovakia; jaroslav.poruban@tuke.sk (J.P.); matus.sulir@tuke.sk (M.S.); sergej.chodarev@tuke.sk (S.C.); william.steingartner@tuke.sk (W.S.); info@madeja.sk (M.M.)
* Correspondence: michaela.bacikova@tuke.sk

**Abstract:** Contemporary software systems focus on usability and accessibility from the point of view of effectiveness and ergonomics. However, the correct usage of the domain dictionary and the description of domain relations and properties via their user interfaces are often neglected. We use the term *domain usability (DU)* to describe the aspects of the user interface related to the terminology and domain. Our experience showed that poor domain usability reduces the memorability and effectiveness of user interfaces. To address this problem, we describe a method called *ADUE (Automatic Domain Usability Evaluation)* for the automated evaluation of selected DU properties on existing user interfaces. As a prerequisite to the method, metrics for formal evaluation of domain usability, a form stereotype recognition algorithm, and general application terms filtering algorithm have been proposed. We executed ADUE on several real-world Java applications and report our findings. We also provide proposals to modify existing manual usability evaluation techniques for the purpose of domain usability evaluation.

**Keywords:** human–computer interaction; user experience; usability evaluation methods; domain usability; domain-specific languages; graphical user interfaces

**Citation:** Bačíková, M.; Porubän, J.; Sulír, M.; Chodarev, S.; Steingartner, W.; Madeja, M. Domain Usability Evaluation. *Electronics* **2021**, *10*, 1963. https://doi.org/10.3390/electronics10161963

Academic Editor: George A. Tsihrintzis

Received: 19 July 2021
Accepted: 10 August 2021
Published: 15 August 2021

**Publisher's Note:** MDPI stays neutral with regard to jurisdictional claims in published maps and institutional affiliations.

**Copyright:** © 2021 by the authors. Licensee MDPI, Basel, Switzerland. This article is an open access article distributed under the terms and conditions of the Creative Commons Attribution (CC BY) license (https://creativecommons.org/licenses/by/4.0/).

## 1. Introduction

User experience (UX) and usability is already ingrained in our everyday lives. Nielsen's concept of "usability engineering" [1] and Norman's [2] practical user interface (UI) design has become an inseparable part of design policies in many large companies, setting an example to the UX field throughout the world. Corporations such as Apple, Google, Amazon, and Facebook realized that when designing UIs, it is not only about how pretty the UI looks like, but from a long-time perspective, usability and UX bring economic benefits over competitors. Usability and UX are related to many aspects of the design, including consistency, efficiency, error rate, learnability, ease of use, utility, credibility, accessibility, desirability, and many more [1–5].

However, when analyzing common UIs of medium and small companies, we still find such UIs that are developed with respect to the practical usability and UX but not to the user's domain. From our experience, such cases are very common. The situation has slowly slowly become better with the introduction of UX courses into the curricula of universities and with the foundation of UX organizations spreading the word. The more specific the domain, the more evident is the problem of designs focused on usability that neglects the domain aspect. This fact has been identified by multiple researchers around the globe [6–9].

### 1.1. Domain Usability

We describe *Domain Usability (DU)* in terms of five UI aspects: domain content, consistency, world language, an adequate level of specificity, language barriers, and errors. For the purpose of clarity, we will present the full definition [10] of all five aspects here:

- *Domain content*: the interface terms, relations, and processes should match the ones from the domain for which the user interface is designed.
- *Consistency*: words used throughout the whole interface should not differ—if they describe the same functionality, the dictionary should be consistent.
- *The language used in the interface*: the language of the interface should be the language of the user, and the particular localization of the UI should be complete, i.e., there should be no foreign words.
- *Domain specificity*: the interface should not contain too general terms, even if they belong to the target domain. The used terms should be as specific as possible.
- *Language barriers and errors*: the interface should not create language barriers for the users, and it should not contain language errors.

Domain usability is not a separate aspect of each UI. On the contrary, it is a part of the general usability property. The *overall usability* is defined as a *combination* of ergonomic and domain usability. Successful completion of a task in a UI is affected by both ergonomic and domain factors:

- *Ergonomic aspect*: without the proper component placement, design, and ergonomic control, it is not possible to perform tasks effectively.
- *Domain aspect*: without the proper terminology, it is harder (or not possible at all) to identify the particular features needed to complete the chosen task. This results in total prevention of the task or at the very least, less effective user performance and lower memorability.

As we described in our previous works, all aspects of the overall usability (as defined by Nielsen [1]) are affected by DU. For more details on the definition of DU, we encourage the reader to see our earlier work [11].

*1.2. Problem and Motivation*

To summarize our knowledge, we identified the main issues in this area as follows:

(i) There are no clear *rules* to design the term structure of an application, so it would correspond with the domain.
(ii) There are no official *guidelines* explicitly describing UIs that should match the real world or map domain terms and processes. References can be found in the literature [12,13], but they are either too general or not focused on domain usability as a whole.
(iii) The variety of human thinking, *ambiguity, and diversity of natural language* represents an issue in evaluating the correctness of UI terminology.
(iv) No clear *manual methods* exist for the formal DU evaluation of existing UIs.
(v) There are no standardized *metrics* to evaluate domain usability.
(vi) No comprehensive *automated methods* exist for domain usability evaluation. Automated and semi-automated methods were devised only for the evaluation of usability in general (e.g., SYNOP [14], AIDE [15]; see the broader reviews [16–18] and the reviews about web usability evaluation [19,20]).

We have addressed issues (i) to (v) and also partially (vi) in our previous works:

- We introduced the concept of *DU* and examples to illustrate our definition [11,21]: (i), (ii).
- To address (iii), we performed a feasibility analysis of approaches for analyzing separate DU aspects [22].
- We proposed and experimentally verified multiple novel manual techniques for DU evaluation [10,23] (iv).
- We designed a domain usability metric consisting of five aspects [24] (v).
- We proposed a conceptual design and a proof-of-concept implementation of a method for automated evaluation of DU [22] and later presented its preliminary evaluation [25] (vi).

The *main contribution* of this paper is concerning issue (vi), in which we focus on automated evaluation. We would like to summarize and put into context our existing findings in this area and to describe the final design, implementation, and validation of this method. The novel additions and improvements include but are not limited to the General Application Terms Ontology (Section 4.2), the Form Stereotype Recognition algorithm (Section 4.3), the computation and display of the Domain Usability Score in the ADUE tool (in Section 6), and detailed presentation of the evaluation results on real-world applications (in Section 7). As a secondary contribution, we will propose modifications of existing general usability evaluation techniques to make them suitable for domain usability evaluation (Section 8).

*1.3. Paper Structure*

In Section 2, we introduce our DU metrics that can be used for formal DU evaluation. The metrics were used to calculate the DU score in our automated evaluation approach.

In Sections 3–5, we explain the design of our automated approach to DU evaluation. First, we explain the concept (Section 3), then describe the prerequisites needed for the approach to work (Section 4), and then we describe the method itself (Section 5). To verify the approach and show its viability, we implemented its prototype (Section 6) and used it to analyze multiple open-source applications (Section 7).

We summarize both manual and automated techniques of usability evaluation in Section 8, and for some of them, we comment on their potential to evaluate DU. Section 9 represents related work focused on DU and its references in the literature.

## 2. Domain Usability Metrics Design

As we have mentioned, DU is defined by five main aspects. In our previous research [24], we tried to determine whether all DU aspects impact the usability equally. Several preliminary experiments we performed in the domain of gospel music suggested the invalidity of this hypothesis [10,23]; e.g., consistency issues had a stronger impact on usability than language errors.

We decided to conduct two surveys [24] to evaluate the effect of five DU aspects on DU. Using the results of the surveys, we designed a metric for formal evaluation of DU. The metrics can be used in manual or automatized evaluation to represent *formal measurement of target UI's DU*. Next, we will explain the design of the DU metrics.

To formally measure the target UI's DU, we first determine the number of all user interface components containing textual data or icons. Next, we analyze the components to find out which of them have DU issues. Since we have the number of all terms $n$ and the number of DU issues, we can compute the percentage of the UI's correctness, where 100% represents the highest possible DU and 0% is the lowest one. Note that each component can have multiple issues at the same time (e.g., an incorrect term and a grammar error). If all UI components had multiple issues, the result would be lower than zero, so it is necessary to limit the minimum value. Given that each DU aspect has a different weight, we defined the formula to measure DU as follows:

$$du = \max\left(0,\ 100\left(1 - \frac{e}{n}\right)\right) \quad (1)$$

where $e$ is calculated as:

$$e = w_{dc}n_{dc} + w_{ds}n_{ds} + w_c n_c + w_{eb}n_{eb} + w_l n_l \quad (2)$$

Coefficients $w_x$ (where $x$ stands for $dc$, $ds$, $c$, $eb$ or $l$) are the weights of particular DU aspects as follows:

- $n_{dc}$—the number of domain content issues,
- $n_{ds}$—the count of domain specificity issues,
- $n_c$—the number of consistency issues,
- $n_{eb}$—the count of language errors and barriers,

- $n_l$—the number of world language issues.

The weights $w_x$ were determined by performing two surveys, first a general one with 73 respondents aged between 17 and 44 years and then a domain-specific one with 26 gospel singers and guitar players aged between 15 and 44 years. The general group consisted of general computer users, and the domain-specific group was selected from the participants of previous DU experimentation with manual DU evaluation techniques [10,23], as they experienced DU issues first-hand.

The questionnaires consisted of two parts. The first part contained five DU aspects represented by visual examples—screenshots from domain-specific UIs. To ensure that participants understood the issues, supplementary textual explanations were provided. The task of the participants was to study the provided examples and rate the importance of a particular DU aspect using a number from the Likert scale [26] with a range from 1 to 5 (1 being the least important).

In the second part, the task was to order the five aspects of DU from the least to the most important. The questionnaires given to the general and domain-specific group can be found at: http://hornad.fei.tuke.sk/~bacikova/domain-usability/surveys (accessed on 9 August 2021). Details about the surveys can be found in [24].

We merged the results of the first (rating) and second (ordering) part of the domain-specific questionnaire and computed the weight of each aspect. Therefore, we can substitute the weights $w_x$ (where $x \in \{dc, ds, c, eb, l\}$) in Equation (2):

$$e = 2.9\,n_{dc} + 2.6\,n_{ds} + 2.6\,n_c + 1.7\,n_{eb} + 1.54\,n_l \qquad (3)$$

Equation (1) then represents *the metric of DU considering its aspects*, with the result as a percentage. To interpret the results, evaluators can follow Table 1. The interpretation corresponds to the scale on which the participants rated the particular aspects in the surveys.

**Table 1.** Interpretation of the rating computed via the proposed DU metric.

| Rating | Interpretation |
| --- | --- |
| $100 \geq du \geq 90\%$ | Excellent |
| $90 > du \geq 80\%$ | Very good |
| $80 > du \geq 70\%$ | Good |
| $70 > du \geq 55\%$ | Satisfactory |
| less than 55% | Insufficient |

### 3. Automatic Evaluation of Domain Usability Aspects

In this section, we will analyze the boundaries of DU evaluation automation and the possibilities related to individual DU aspects. We explain the design of an automated approach to DU evaluation at a high level of abstraction.

*3.1. Domain Content and Specificity*

Domain content and specificity are the most difficult aspects to evaluate in a domain-specific application. Since a particular UI is usually designed for a domain expert, the domain content in the UI must be specific for the particular domain. Because of the ambiguity of natural language, the line determining whether a given word pertains to a particular domain or not may be very thin. We admit that evaluation performed by a domain expert should be considered the most appropriate in such cases. However, when no expert is available or when first UI prototypes are going to be evaluated, automated evaluation might be a helpful, fast, and cheap way to remove issues in the early stages. We will try to outline the situation in which such an automated evaluation would be utilized.

Imagine we have an existing user interface that has been used in some specific domain for ages. However, although this UI is usable, the used technology had become obsolete. The time has come to develop and deploy a new application version. The technologies will change, but for the domain users to accept the new UI, at least the terminology should be consistent with the previous version. However, testing the whole UI for domain-related content manually is a time-consuming, attention-demanding, and tiresome task. It would be helpful to have an automated way to compare both UIs. Suppose there is a way of extracting the terminology of both UIs into a formal form (e.g., an ontology). Then it would be possible to compare the results using a comparator tool. The result of the comparison would show the following:

- Any *new terms* are marked in the new UI ontology so that they can be checked by a domain expert.
- *Renamed* terms are marked for the same reason. We identify renamed items based on the representing component and its location in the component hierarchy.
- If the terms (UI components) were *moved*, then they are checked for consistency of their inclusion into the new group of terms (term hierarchy).
- *Removed terms* are marked in the old UI ontology because the domain experts, customers, or designers/developers should check whether their removal is reasonable.
- All terms (i.e., their representing components) that have undergone an *illogical change* are marked as a *usability issue*.

Illogical changes are the following: (i) from text input component (e.g., text boxes and text areas) to descriptional component (e.g., labels) and vice versa, (ii) from textual to functional (e.g., buttons and menu items) and vice versa, (iii) from functional to descriptional component and vice versa, and (iv) from grouping (containers, button groups, etc.) to other types of components and vice versa. For example, the term "Analyze results" which, in the old UI, was represented by a button, but in the new UI, it is a label—i.e., the representing component changed its type from functional to descriptional. When checking the mentioned type changes, we can confirm the term against its representing component in the old and new UI version.

The scenario described above is rather specific for situations in which there are two versions of the particular UI—whether it is an old UI and a new one, or two separate UIs from the same domain are developed by different vendors. However, when the UI is freshly designed specifically for the particular business area, there is usually only one UI available. In this case, some other source of ontological information is needed, which may be:

- a reference ontology modeling the specific domain and its language,
- generic ontological dictionaries or other sources of linguistic relations, such as web search.

In these cases, the feasibility of analysis strongly depends on the reference resources. The disadvantage of the first option is the necessity of the reference ontology, which would have to be created manually by the domain expert. On the other hand, such a manually created ontology would be of higher quality than an automatically generated one, presumably having defined all necessary domain objects, properties, and relations. Thus, it would be easier to check the correctness of the target UI than by applying the approach as with two UIs, since it is usually not possible to extract 100% of data from both UIs.

As for ontological dictionaries or web search, again, the analysis strongly depends on the resources. Current ontological dictionaries are quite good, but their size is limited and their ontologies are not very usable in any specific domain. It would be best to have a domain-specific ontological dictionary, but because we assume that in the future, domain-specific ontologies [27] would grow in both size and quality, and the approach proposed here will be applicable with greater value.

Current technologies and resources allow us only to use general ontologies to check *hierarchies of terms for linguistic relations using natural language processing*. Let us take an example of a *Person* form. The form has a list of check-box buttons for selecting a favorite color with values *red, yellow, blue,* and *green*. The task is to check whether the parent–child relation between the *Favorite color* term and individual color values is correct (Listing 1).

**Listing 1.** Hierarchy of terms for selecting favorite color in the domain dictionary of the Person form.

```
favoriteColor {children}: [
    red
    yellow
    blue
    green
]
```

From the linguistic point of view, *Favorite color* is a hypernym of the individual color values (or conversely, the latter are hyponyms of the *Favorite color*). Similar relations are *holonymy* and *meronymy* which represent a "part" or "member" relationship.

Suppose that we know and can automatically determine the hierarchy of terms in the UI (we know that components labeled by the color names are hierarchically child components of the container labeled by the term *Favorite color*), we can check if these linguistic relations exist between the parent term and its child terms.

Existing available ontological dictionaries (such as WordNet) usually provide a word-attribute relation of words including linguistic relations, such as hyponymy and holonymy. In the domain analysis process, all children and parents should be checked from the linguistic point of view, but mainly enumerations and button groups or menu items because they are designed with the "grouping" relation in mind. The same can be achieved by using web search instead of ontological dictionaries (more on using web search in Section 5.2).

As the last process of checking UI domain content, we propose to check the presence of *tooltips*. A tooltip is a small description of a graphical component, which explains its functionality or purpose. Tooltips are displayed after a short time when the mouse cursor position is over the component. Many times, tooltips are not necessary for general-purpose components, e.g., the OK, Cancel, Close, or Reset buttons. However, they can be extremely important for explaining the purpose of *domain-specific* functional components (components performing domain-specific operations) or when the description would take too much space when putting it on the component's label. Our experiment with open-source applications [25] showed that developers almost never use tooltips for functional components, even in cases when their label is not quite understandable even for domain-specific users. The common cases are acronyms and abbreviations used when the full name or description of the domain operation would take too much space on the display.

*3.2. Consistency*

All domain terminology should be checked for consistency and, thus, marked for checking. We can search for equal terms with case inconsistencies (Name-NAME-naMe) and/or similar terms (Cancel, Canceled) and their case inconsistencies.

*Note*: currently, it is not possible to automatically evaluate the so-called *feature consistency*, i.e., whether the same functionality is represented by the same term. The reason is the inability of current technologies to make this information available programmatically.

*3.3. Language Barriers and Errors*

Language errors and the completeness of language alternatives can be checked using standard spell-checking methods. For example, dictionaries (e.g., bundled with open-source text editors such as OpenOffice) may be leveraged to mark all incorrect and untranslated words similarly to spell checking in modern textual editors.

**4. Prerequisites**

In order to analyze the domain dictionary in any application, the means of extracting that dictionary into a formal form is necessary. For this extraction, we can use the DEAL (Domain Extraction ALgorithm) method described in [28,29].

In this section, we will describe the DEAL tool needed for extracting domain information from existing user interfaces. We also describe the design and implementation of supplementary algorithms that we implemented into DEAL to be able to focus on DU issues, namely:

(a) General Application Terms Ontology—serves for filtering out non-domain related terms from the user interface,
(b) Form Stereotype Recognizer—an algorithm making the analysis of forms more effective.

### 4.1. DEAL Method

DEAL (Domain Extraction ALgorithm) (https://git.kpi.fei.tuke.sk/michaela.bacikova/DEAL; accessed on 9 August 2021) is a method for extracting domain information from user interfaces of applications. Its implementation currently supports Java (Swing), HTML, and Windows applications (*.exe). The Windows application analyzer utilizes the output of Ranorex Spy (https://www.ranorex.com/help/latest/ranorex-studio-advanced/ranorex-spy/introduction/; accessed on 9 August 2021), which means it supports programs that are analyzable by Ranorex. The list of supported components is located at https://git.kpi.fei.tuke.sk/michaela.bacikova/DEAL/-/wikis/analyzing-windows-applications (accessed on 9 August 2021).

Except for the part of loading the input application, the whole process is fully automatized and takes place in two phases: *Extraction* and *Simplification*. The result of the *Extraction* phase is a domain model in the form of a graph. Nodes of the graph correspond to terms (concepts) of the analyzed user interface. Each such node contains information about:

- UI *component* that represents the term in the user interface;
- *name*—the label displayed on the component;
- *description*—the component's tooltip if it is present;
- *icon* (if present);
- *category of the component*—either functional, informative, textual, grouping (container), or custom;
- *type* of input data—in the case of input components, the type can be string, number, date, boolean, or enumeration;
- *relation* to other terms—mutual (non-)exclusivity;
- *parent* term (usually corresponds to lexical relation of hypernymy or holonymy);
- *child* terms (usually correspond to hyponyms or meronyms).

The extraction is followed by the *Simplification* phase, where structural components without domain information (e.g., panels and containers) are filtered out unless they are necessary to maintain the term hierarchy.

Properties of the terms and their hierarchy are used to check for the missing domain information in order to identify incorrect or missing data types and lexical relations between terms such as hyponymy, hypernymy, holonymy, and meronymy.

For example, let us have a form for entering the person's data such as name, surname, date of birth, marital status, or favorite color. The *Person* dialog contains the fields for entering the data. The resulting domain model can be seen in Listing 2. It contains the term *Person* with the child nodes corresponding to fields of the of form. The *status* term has the *enumeration* type with mutually exclusive values because in the UI it contains multiple options as radio buttons. The *favorite color*, on the other hand, uses check-box components, so the corresponding term contains *child terms* with all offered values, and they are not mutually exclusive. *Person* term also contains children corresponding to functional components, e.g., menu items or buttons (such as *OK* or *Close*). A similar graph of terms is created for every window in the user interface.

DEAL is able to export this hierarchy into the standard OWL ontological format.

**Listing 2.** The domain model of the Person form.

```
domain: 'Person' {children}: [
   'Name' {string}
   'Surname' {string}
   'Date of birth' {date}
   'Status' {mutually-exclusive}
      {enumeration}[
         'Single'
         'Married'
         'Divorced'
         'Widowed'
      ]
   'Favorite color' {mutually-not-exclusive}
      {children}: [
      'red'
      'yellow'
      'blue'
      'green'
   ]
   'OK'
   'Close'
   'Reset'
]
```

### 4.2. General Application Terms Ontology

In the Person form example in Listing 2, we have three terms (represented by three buttons) not related to the domain of Persons. If we are to analyze *domain* objects, properties, and relations, we need to filter out any terms potentially unrelated to the domain. To do so, we will use a new reference ontology that will list domain-independent general-purpose terms commonly used in applications, their alternatives, and their forms.

We built this ontology manually by analyzing 30 open-source Java applications from SourceForge, 4 operating systems and their applications (system applications, file managers, etc.), and 5 software systems from the domain of integrated development environments (IDEs). The specific domain of IDEs was selected to observe and compare the occurrence of domain-specific versus general application terms. We listed and counted the occurrence of all terms in all analyzed UIs. Then, we selected only those that had an occurrence rate over 50%.

The list of the most common terms can be seen in Table 2 (the *General Application Terms Ontology* can be found at https://bit.ly/2R6bm6p; accessed on 9 August 2021). According to this ontology, we implemented an additional module into DEAL, which is able to automatically filter out such terms from the domain model immediately after the domain model Extraction and Simplification phase and prior to the DU evaluation process.

The analysis of application terms in a specific domain showed that the domain-specific terminology is more common in a specific domain than general application terms.

### 4.3. Recognizing Form Stereotypes

Another drawback of the DEAL method is its insufficient form analysis. In more than 50 open-source applications we have analyzed, the most common problem were the missing references between the actual form data components (i.e., text fields) and their textual labels readable in the UI. Such a missing reference causes a component to be extracted without any label or description and, therefore, has no term to be represented by. As a result, it is filtered out in the DEAL's domain model Simplification phase as a component with no domain-specific content and is therefore excluded from the consecutive analyses.

Table 2. List of the most frequently occurring terms in UIs (the vertical bar character '|' denotes alternatives).

| Term | Occurrence | Most Common UI Element |
|---|---|---|
| About\|Credits | 90% | Menu item |
| Apply | 87% | Button |
| Cancel | 97% | Button |
| Close\|Exit\|Quit | 100% | Button\|Menu item |
| Copy | 70% | Menu item |
| Cut | 70% | Menu item |
| Edit | 70% | Menu |
| File | 90% | Menu |
| Help | 80% | Menu\|Menu item |
| New | 90% | Menu item |
| OK | 97% | Button |
| Open | 83% | Button\|Menu item |
| Paste | 70% | Menu item |
| Plug-ins\|Extensions | 40% | Menu\|Menu item |
| Preferences\|Settings | 60% | Menu\|Menu item |
| Redo | 83% | Menu item |
| Save | 83% | Button\|Menu item |
| Save as | 83% | Menu item |
| Tools | 53% | Menu |
| Undo | 83% | Menu item |
| View | 63% | Menu |
| Window | 70% | Menu |

However, such components are necessary to determine the data type of their input values, which is reflected in the domain model. For example, in Listing 2, *name* is of data type *string* and *dateOfBirth* is of data type *date*.

For the developers of component-based applications, it is usually possible to set a "labelFor" (Java) or "for" (HTML) attribute of the label component (from this point, we will refer to this attribute as to *labelFor*). However, since this attribute is not mandatory in most programming languages, the result is usually a large number of components with no label assigned.

To solve this issue, we designed a *Form Stereotype Recognition (FSR) algorithm* to recognize form stereotypes in target UIs and implemented it into the DEAL tool.

Prior to the implementation, we manually analyzed the source code of existing user interfaces for the most common *form stereotypes*. We selected web applications instead of desktop ones for better accessibility and higher occurrence of forms. Thirty web applications were analyzed, and we focused on registration forms, login forms, and their client applications. Based on the analyzed data we identified the five most common form stereotypes shown in Figure 1.

1. LEFT—most common, the text labels are located left to the form component.
2. ADDITIONAL RIGHT—similar to LEFT, but some form components have additional information added to the right of the component, e.g., validation messages.
3. ABOVE—labels are located above the form components.
4. ADDITIONAL BELOW—sometimes the cases with additional information occur under the particular form component. Usually, it is a text for showing another application window, in which the particular item is further explained, or it is a link with which the users are sent an email with new password activation in case of forgetting the old one.
5. PLACEHOLDER—labels are located inside the designated form component. In HTML, this property is called a *placeholder*. This stereotype is becoming more and more

common in modern web applications, although it is marked as less usable. In this case, there is rarely any other label around the form component.

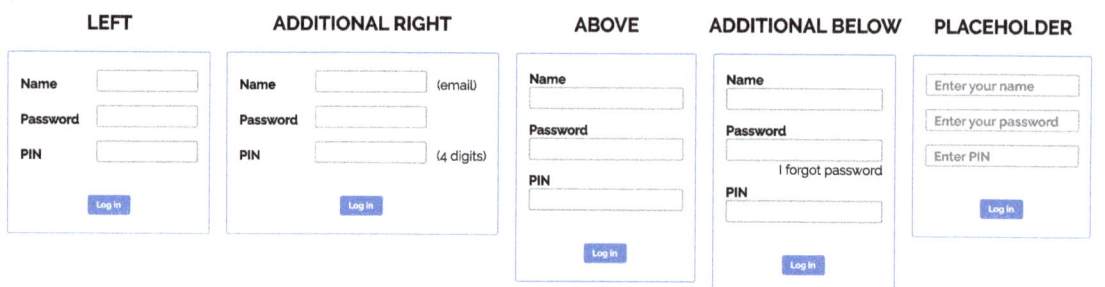

**Figure 1.** The most frequent form stereotypes.

The FSR algorithm analyzes these form stereotypes in the target UI, and based on the identified stereotype, it assigns a label to each form data component. In short, the main principle of the FSR algorithm is to find all form components around each particular label in a form container. Then for all labels (excluding the ones that have the *labelFor* attribute set), the FSR counts the number of components around them as displayed in the UI. The resulting form stereotype is the direction in which the largest number of form components is located relative to each label. If there is no explicit maximum (e.g., five components have labels on their left and five other components have labels on their right), then the form stereotype cannot be identified and is marked as MIXED.

The targets of the FSR algorithm are common form components, namely:

- a descriptional text component (label),
- textual components (input fields, text fields, text areas, password fields, etc.),
- switches (radio buttons, checkboxes),
- spinners,
- tables,
- lists and combo-boxes.

If the target container was identified as a form stereotype, FSR pairs the form components with their labels by defining their *labelFor* attribute. This step also enables us to mark all form components that have no automatically assignable label and represent them as *recommendations* for correction to the user. If there is any label that has no stereotype, then it is considered a *usability issue*, and a recommendation for assigning a label to the most probable component (closest according to one of the possible stereotypes) is displayed. An example of both issues can be seen in Figure 2 extracted from the OpenRocket (https://sourceforge.net/projects/openrocket/; accessed on 9 August 2021) user interface.

By using the FSR algorithm, we were able to successfully recognize the correct stereotypes of most of the tested form components.

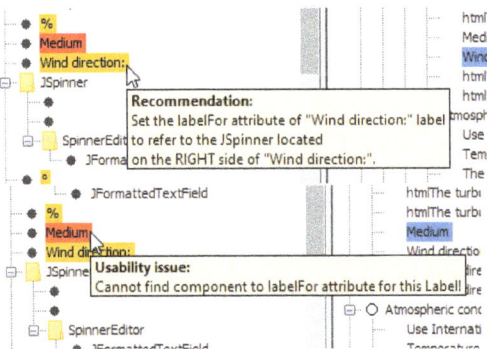

**Figure 2.** DEAL—Example of a recommendation indicating the successful recognition of a form stereotype and an issue because of a missing *labelFor* attribute. The domain model shown in this figure was extracted from OpenRocket.

## 5. ADUE Method

The ADUE method uses the techniques mentioned in Sections 3 and 4. To sum up, we propose the following approaches to the automatized analysis of DU:

- Ontological analysis with two ontologies (Section 5.1),
- Specificity evaluation by analyzing the term hierarchies using ontological dictionaries or a web search (Section 5.2),
- Grammar evaluation by searching for grammar errors and typos using an existing linguistic dictionary of the target language (Section 5.3),
- Analysis of form components and their labels based on the form stereotype recognition method (Section 4.3)
- Tooltip analysis (Section 5.4).

In the next subsections, we describe each of the methods in more detail (except the form analyzer that was already explained in Section 4.3). We use example applications to explain each approach and show the identification of usability issues and recommendations for fixing them.

*5.1. Ontological Analysis*

As mentioned in Section 3.1, the first option is to use two ontologies extracted from new and old application versions. In case there is only one ontology, only specificity (Section 5.2) and grammar evaluation (Section 5.3) are executed for this ontology. If there are two ontologies, both specificity and grammar evaluations are performed on the newer one along with ontological comparison. Now we will describe the ontological comparison approach.

The process is depicted in Figure 3. For technological reasons, DEAL is able to run only one application at a time; therefore the ontology extraction happens in two steps. First, we use the DEAL tool to extract domain information from the first application without any DU analysis, and export it into an ontological format (the top-left part of Figure 3). Then, we run DEAL again with the new application version (the top-right part), import the previously extracted ontology, and run the ADUE comparison and evaluation algorithm (the bottom part of Figure 3). The ontology evaluation results are then displayed to the user.

Each item in an extracted ontology represents one component of the UI, and it contains:

- The term's *text* representation. A term has such a text representation only if its representing component has a description in the form of a label or a tooltip.
- *ID* of the representing component. This is mainly because of the ontology format, where every item has to have an identifier. We used the text attribute as an identifier and added numbering to ensure uniqueness.
- The *class* of the component: a button, label, text field, check box, radio button, etc.

- The term's *parent* term.
- *Children*, i.e., the child terms.

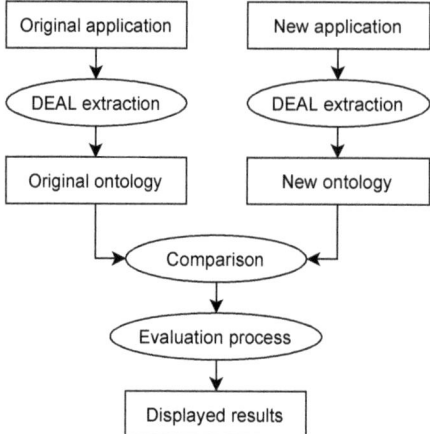

**Figure 3.** ADUE method—a high-level overview of the ontological evaluation process with two ontology versions. Processes are marked as ellipses, data as rectangles.

The algorithm compares the original ontology with the new one, searching for new, deleted, changed, and retained elements. We consider two elements equal if all their attributes (text, ID, class, parent, children) are equal. As a part of the evaluation, we consider the impact of the changes as follows:

- New elements—we do not consider newly added elements an issue. It is common that as user interfaces evolve in time, they get new and new features. However, the ADUE user should know about these changes to be able to check their correctness.
- Removed elements—these might or might not introduce an issue and feature depletion, depending on the evaluator whether the removal was justified.
- Changed elements—we consider *correctly* and *incorrectly* changed elements; incorrect changes are considered a usability issue. Incorrect changes include the illogical component type of changes described in Section 3.1.

The whole process is noted as the "Evaluation process" in Figure 3.

All results are stored in a list and then displayed to the evaluator in the UI. There, the user can see a list of all terms in the application. After selecting a specific term, details about the changes between the old and new ontology versions are shown, along with an error or a warning in case a potential issue was found.

After the comparison, *specificity evaluation* (Section 5.2) and *grammar evaluation* (Section 5.3) are performed on the new ontology version.

### 5.2. Specificity Evaluation

The goal of the *specificity evaluation* is to linguistically verify hierarchical relations found in the user interface. It uses ontological dictionaries and web search as a source of linguistic relations.

The algorithm traverses all grouping elements in the domain model graph. For each group, it selects the names of child terms and creates a *child word set*. From each child word set, we remove all forms of reflexive pronouns and auxiliary verbs (is, are, have, etc.) to get more precise results. The algorithm also uses natural language processing to recognize the word class of each word and keeps only nouns, verbs, and adjectives.

We use the *Ontological Dictionaries and Google Search evaluation algorithm (OD&GS)* to get a list of the *most probable parent terms* (hypernyms or holonyms) for each child word set.

The algorithm combines three sources: WordNet, Urban Dictionary, and Google web search. To optimize the results, it defines the following order in which the sources are utilized:
1. If any word from the input term set is a number, Google search is used first because it is optimal for numeric values.
2. In other cases, WordNet is used first since it is effective and available without restrictions.
3. If the probability of the result correctness using WordNet is lower than 80%, Urban Dictionary is tried as the next search engine.
4. Because of the restricted automated use, Google search is used as a last option in case the probability of the result correctness using Urban Dictionary is lower than 80%.

After that, the *OD&GS* algorithm returns the list of possible parent terms. The number of the results is limited to 9. This number was determined empirically based on the number of correct results in our experiments with the terminology of multiple existing UIs.

For each child term set, it is checked if the parent of the set is found in possible parent terms generated by *OD&GS* algorithm. If it is not the case, a warning is shown, and terms obtained by the *OD&GS* are suggested as alternatives.

The results of the *OD&GS* algorithm strongly depend on the quality of the used ontological dictionaries. In the next sections, we explain how each of the data sources is used.

5.2.1. WordNet

WordNet (https://wordnet.princeton.edu; accessed on 9 August 2021) is a dictionary and a lexical database. The dictionary provides direct and inherited hypernyms as a part of word definition for nouns, adjectives, and verbs. As a query result, WordNet returns so-called *synsets*, containing the information about words including the given word class. We filter out synsets with different word classes compared to the child word. To ensure higher accuracy of the results, we include only direct hypernyms. As a result, we construct a list of hypernyms for each child word set.

5.2.2. Urban Dictionary

Urban Dictionary (http://www.urbandictionary.com; accessed on 9 August 2021) is a crowdsourced dictionary. For each queried word it returns seven most popular definitions based on the votes of the Urban Dictionary users. For each query, we collect all meaningful words from the definitions. The words are sorted by the frequency of their occurrence. The result is a list of the words with the highest frequency that can be considered possible parent terms.

5.2.3. Google Web Search

While Google is not a linguistic tool, the current state of its multi-layered semantic network—*Knowledge Graph* [30,31]—enables gaining quite accurate results to confirm linguistic relations such as hyponymy, hypernymy, meronymy, and holonymy by using web search queries. The efficiency of data collection of Google's semantic network database enables it to grow its data into gigantic dimensions as opposed to any semantic network, including WordNet and UrbanDictionary, and for that reason, we see greater potential in web search than in current ontological dictionaries.

Based on our tests, Google search provides the most precise results compared to other sources we have used. On the other hand, it is not very suitable for automated requests. Because the Google web search approach provides results with high reliability, we present it in this paper despite the restrictions.

To search potential parent terms, we use two queries with the list of child words:

- `{words separated by commas} are common values for`
- `{words separated by commas} are`

For example: `"red, green, blue, brown are common values for"` or `"red, green, blue, brown are"`.

We parse the returned HTML documents and count the most common words. The probability of each word in the result is based on the frequency of its occurrence. Additionally, we ignore words of a different word class from the class of child words.

To verify the gained results we use the reverse queries for each child word: "`is {a possible parent term} value/kind of {word}`", for example, "`is color kind of blue`", "`is color kind of yellow`".

The number of occurrences of both words found in the resulting HTML page is used to determine the probability of the found words being the correct parent terms for the particular child word set. If there is low or no occurrence of a particular pair, this pair has the lowest probability in the result list.

*5.3. Grammar Evaluation*

There are two common grammatical issues occurring in user interfaces: an incorrectly written word (a typo), or a word that was not translated into the languages of the user interface. The second case is especially common in applications that are localized in multiple languages.

For this reason, usual spell checking is supplemented with the translation checking. If some word is not found in the dictionary for the current language, the algorithm checks the default language (usually English). If it is found, its translations are added to recommended replacements. Otherwise, the recommendations are based on similar words in the same way as it is done in modern text editors. In the end, a list of recommended corrections is provided to the evaluator.

*5.4. Tooltip Analysis*

The Tooltip analysis algorithm (TTA) selects all *functional* terms, i.e., terms extracted from functional components, from the domain model. Then for every such term, the presence of a tooltip is checked—either by inspecting the representing component or by checking the description property of the term node, where the component's tooltip text is usually stored. If no tooltip is found, this information is added to the list of warnings, and we advise the developer to add it.

Because general-purpose components (*OK, Open, Save, Exit, Cancel*, etc.) are common, frequently used, and generally understood, we presume that the importance of tooltips for such components is very small. Their purpose is clear from their description and/or icon. For this reason, we only analyze domain-specific components. General-purpose components are removed in the DEAL's *Extraction* phase using the general application terms ontology described in Section 4.2.

If no tooltip is found for some functional component, the result is displayed to the evaluator in one of two ways:

- *recommendation to add a tooltip*—if the component has at least one user-readable textual description (e.g., label),
- *usability issue*—if either the component is general-purpose and has *only* an icon, or it is a domain-specific one with *only* an icon or *only* a textual label, this is considered a *domain usability issue* and is displayed to the evaluator.

An example of the usability issue and its report to the user can be seen in the JSesh interface menu items (Figure 4) where there are two items with no visible textual information and/or tooltip.

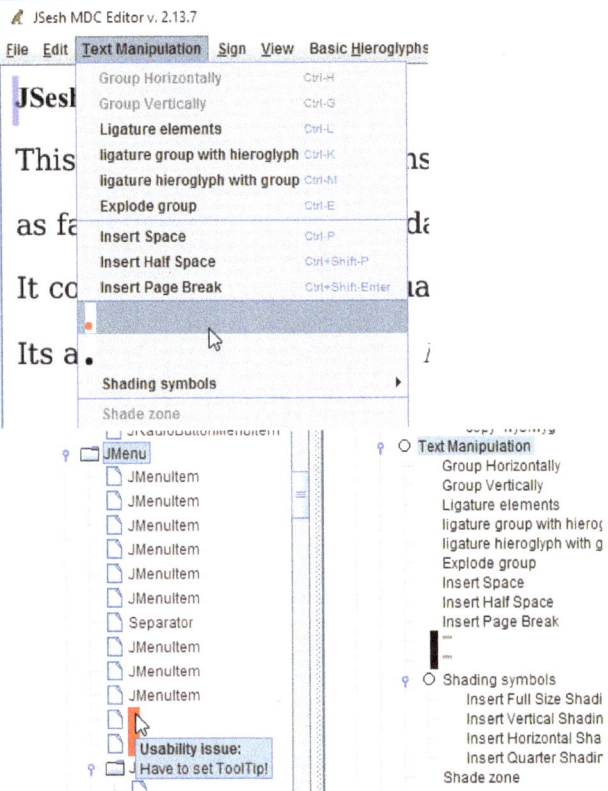

**Figure 4.** Example of JSesh menu items both without a tooltip and label (**top**) and a usability issue reported to the user (**bottom**).

## 6. Prototype

All processes mentioned in Section 5 were implemented and integrated into the DEAL tool. The results of tooltip and form stereotype analysis are displayed as tooltips in the DEAL's domain model as seen in Figures 2 and 4.

The process of domain usability evaluation can be activated using a menu item in DEAL. Results of the analysis are displayed as errors (highlighted with red color) and recommendations (highlighted with orange) in the DEAL's component tree. Recommendations for corrections are displayed in tooltips. DEAL enables us to look up any component in the application by clicking on it in the component tree. As a result, the component is highlighted by the yellow color directly in the analyzed application. This way the analyst can locate the component needing the recommended modification.

Ontological evaluation, grammar evaluation, and specificity evaluation are implemented in a tool called ADUE (Figure 5), which can be started directly from DEAL or as a standalone process. In the case of starting from DEAL, the newest ontology is automatically extracted from the application currently analyzed by the DEAL tool. In the latter case, both ontologies (old and new) have to be imported manually.

When running the process with only one ontology, then only grammar and specificity evaluation is performed, and results are displayed only in the right column.

When loading two ontologies, the former processes are performed on the newer ontology as an additional process, and both ontologies are compared. Results are similar to one ontology analysis, but in the left column, we can see the components (terms) in the older application.

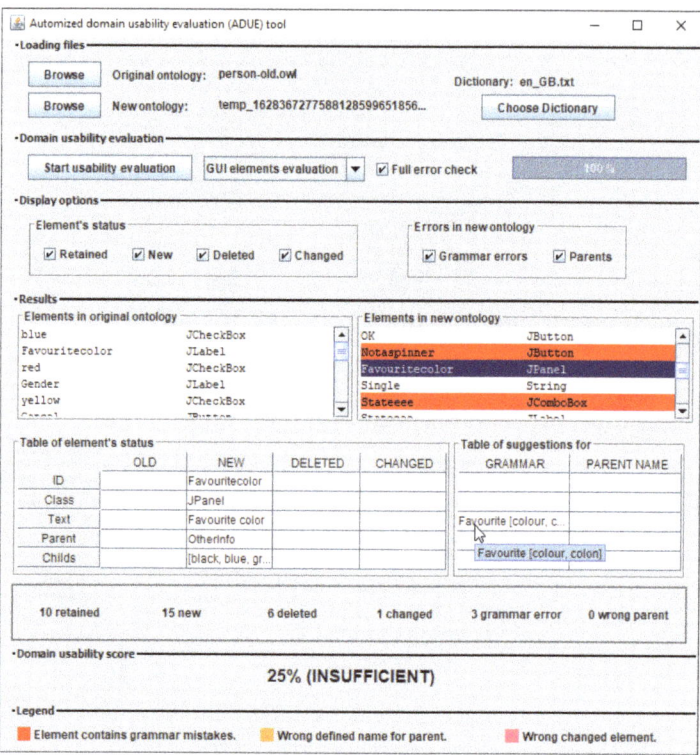

**Figure 5.** The ADUE evaluation tool displaying the results from comparing two sample applications.

Different types of errors are displayed using colors. Red is used for grammar errors. Orange means an incorrectly defined parent term (hypernym, holonym). Recommendations are displayed in a tooltip. The pink color is used for illogically changed components. The evaluator can also see all terms that were retained, added, deleted, or changed. In all cases, we display recommendations for change in the *Table of suggestions* (bottom right).

We used the metrics described in Section 2 to calculate the overall DU score of the evaluated user interface (the percentage in the bottom part of Figure 5). The errors are included in the DU as follows:

- the number of missing tooltips and incorrectly changed or deleted components is counted as domain content issues;
- the number of incorrectly defined parents is counted as domain specificity issues;
- the number of grammar errors is counted as language errors and barriers.

As explained in the paper, we were not able to analyze consistency issues, and world language issues are indistinguishable from grammar errors; therefore, the number of errors for these two aspects remains 0 and does not affect the DU score calculation.

*ADUE for Java Applications*

To be able to extract data from Java applications, DEAL uses Java *reflection* and *aspect-oriented programming* (AOP). AOP in load-time enables us to weave and also to analyze applications with custom class loaders, which would be problematic using a simple reflection. There are still limitations in some cases; e.g., AOP is not able to weave directly into Java packages such as *javax.swing*. Weaving directly into the JDK source code and thus creating our own version of Java to run the target application would solve the issue.

To extract, traverse, and compare ontologies, we used the *OWL API* library (https://github.com/owlcs/owlapi/wiki; accessed on 9 August 2021). As a dictionary in the grammar evaluation, we used the US English dictionary from the *OpenOffice* text editor (https://www.openoffice.org; accessed on 9 August 2021). We chose this dictionary because of the simple textual format with words separated by newline characters and because it can be freely edited and complemented by new words. In the same package, there are also multiple languages available, so they can be used for the evaluation of applications in other languages. To check the grammar, the *JAZZY* library (http://jazzy.sourceforge.net; accessed on 9 August 2021) was used. After identifying a typo in a text, *JAZZY* returns multiple replacement recommendations of the incorrect word. For natural language processing needed in the specificity evaluation, we used the *Apache OpenNLP* library (https://opennlp.apache.org; accessed on 9 August 2021), which can identify the word classes such as verbs, nouns, or adjectives. To query the WordNet dictionary, the *JAWS* library (https://github.com/jaytaylor/jaws; accessed on 9 August 2021) was used. Urban Dictionary does not provide a special API for machine usage. Therefore, we used standard HTTP GET requests to query the dictionary and then analyzed the source code of the response pages statically. To query the Google search engine, we used the publicly available API (https://developers.google.com/custom-search/v1/overview; accessed on 9 August 2021).

Ontologies were used because of good support for export and a comparison engine. However, in our approach, the main *limitation* of ontologies is considered the inability to use special characters and spaces in identifiers. In the case of comparing ontologies, it does not represent a problem. However, when analyzing grammar and specificity, this is usually the main issue.

## 7. Evaluation

In this section, we will assess the possibility of using ADUE on existing applications. Our main questions are whether ADUE is applicable to real-world programs and to what degree these programs contain domain usability errors.

*7.1. Method*

Since the implementation of ADUE for Java program analysis is the most mature one, we used several open-source Java GUI applications as study subjects. To obtain such applications, we utilized the SourceForge website (http://sourceforge.net; accessed on 9 August 2021). We selected programs from diverse domains and of various sizes to maximize generalizability. To simplify the interpretation of the results, we focused only on applications in the English language.

Specifically, the following applications were used to evaluate the ADUE prototype: Calculator, Sweet Home 3D, FreeMind (2014), FreePlane (2015), Finanx, JarsBrowser, JavaNotePad, TimeSlotTracker, Gait Monitoring+, Activity Prediction Tool, VOpR (a virtual optical rail), GDL Editor 0.9, and GDL Editor 0.95. The specific versions of the applications can be downloaded from https://git.kpi.fei.tuke.sk/michaela.bacikova/DEAL/-/tree/master/DEALexamples/examples (accessed on 9 August 2021).

We executed the complete analysis using our implemented ADUE tool and recorded the results. The form stereotype analysis, tooltip detection, grammar error evaluation, parent term evaluation, and the overall domain usability computation were executed on all applications. For some of the applications, we performed an ontology comparison between two different versions (GDL Editor 0.9 and 0.95) or editions (FreeMind and FreePlan). We also recorded the execution times of the analysis process. All results were written in a spreadsheet.

*7.2. Results*

We were able to successfully execute ADUE on all mentioned applications. Table 3 presents an overview of the obtained results. For each application, we can see the number of extracted terms and different kinds of errors and warnings detected by the ADUE prototype. The is also a weighted number of errors ($e$) calculated using Equation (3) and final domain usability index ($du$). The results of the two-ontology comparison are available in Table 4. The complete results can be viewed via Google Sheets using the following URL: http://bit.ly/3hZBImy (accessed on 9 August 2021).

**Table 3.** Results of the evaluation (applications where ontology comparison was used are marked with *).

| Application | Terms | Tooltip Errors | Tooltip Warnings | Grammar Errors | Incorrect Parents | $e$ | $du$ | Execution Time |
|---|---|---|---|---|---|---|---|---|
| Calculator | 40 | 0 | 0 | 1 | 0 | 1.7 | 96 | 0 s |
| Sweet Home 3D | 200 | 13 | 11 | 4 | 17 | 84.4 | 58 | 2 m 0 s |
| FreeMind 2014 | 273 | 1 | 94 | 14 | 17 | 68.3 | 75 | 1 m 50 s |
| FreePlane 2015 * | 873 | 13 | 323 | 128 | 33 | 833.5 | 5 | 5 m 6 s |
| Finanx | 74 | 39 | 9 | 4 | 8 | 140.7 | 90 | 36 s |
| JarsBrowser | 19 | 0 | 8 | 2 | 5 | 16.4 | 14 | 8 s |
| BaseFormApplication | 74 | 0 | 8 | 11 | 8 | 42.1 | 43 | 42 s |
| JavaNotePad | 19 | 0 | 17 | 0 | 5 | 13.0 | 32 | 32 s |
| TimeSlotTracker | 62 | 6 | 36 | 7 | 10 | 55.0 | 11 | 55 s |
| Gait Monitoring+ | 70 | 0 | 17 | 0 | 7 | 18.2 | 74 | 29 s |
| Activity Prediction Tool | 98 | 1 | 84 | 2 | 11 | 33.2 | 66 | 1 m 19 s |
| VOpR | 96 | 0 | 21 | 23 | 8 | 59.9 | 38 | 44 s |
| GDL Editor 0.9 | 73 | 4 | 8 | 4 | 11 | 45.3 | 38 | 58 s |
| GDL Editor 0.95 * | 75 | 4 | 8 | 4 | 11 | 61.5 | 18 | 15 s |

**Table 4.** Results of the ontology comparison.

| Application | Original Application | New Terms | Deleted Terms | Changed Terms | Incorrectly Changed Terms |
|---|---|---|---|---|---|
| FreePlane 2015 | FreeMind 2014 | 748 | 168 | 93 | 0 |
| GDL Editor 0.95 | GDL Editor 0.9 | 7 | 5 | 4 | 0 |

7.2.1. Tooltip Analysis

By using the tooltip verifier process, we extracted 136 components per application on average. From those, 52 function components per application on average had no tooltip defined (38%), from which 46 were a recommendation (34%) and 6 were an error (4%). We manually checked the components associated with the errors and confirmed that these issues were correctly identified.

The results show that DU issues concerning tooltips are very common in applications. Developers are probably not fully aware that tooltips are necessary for application usability.

7.2.2. Grammar and Specificity Evaluation

From each listed application, we extracted an ontology using the DEAL tool and performed the grammar evaluation on it. On average, we extracted 146 items per application from which 15 grammar errors and 11 incorrectly defined parents were identified.

Some of the detected issues represented acronyms, abbreviations, and proper nouns. It is questionable to what degree acronyms and abbreviations are comprehensible to the application users. A portion of the grammar errors was caused by the fact that we were using the US English dictionary, but some applications used British English (or possibly used a combination of US and British English, which is inconsistent).

7.2.3. Ontological Comparison

The two-ontology evaluation was applied only to the FreeMind/FreePlane and GDL Editor 0.9/0.95 applications since they are two versions of the same applications. As we can see in Table 4, numerous elements were added, deleted, or changed in the case of Free-Mind/FreePlane since this version change represents a major redesign of the application.

On the other hand, in GDL Editor, a smaller proportion of the terms was changed because this version update is minor.

Note that there were no incorrectly changed components detected in either application.

7.2.4. Overall Domain Usability

As we can see in Table 3, the computed domain usability ranged from 5% to 96%. The computed mean value is 47%. Therefore, the variability of the overall domain usability among the analyzed applications is relatively large.

Applications with low computed domain usability tend to have mainly a high number of detected grammar errors but also incorrectly defined parent terms and missing tooltips in places where they are necessary.

7.2.5. Execution Time

The execution process of DEAL and ADUE includes the traversal of GUI elements of the applications, querying Web services, and other time-consuming operations. For this reason, we would like to know whether the execution time of the domain usability evaluation process is not prohibitive with respect to its practical utilization.

According to our results, the execution time on the listed applications ranges from 0 s to 5 min and 6 s, with a mean of 1 min and 7 s. This means that automated domain usability evaluation could be potentially performed in a variety of contexts, including continuous integration (CI) builds.

*7.3. Examples of Issues*

To help the reader understand the nature of domain usability issues, we will now mention a few examples of specific issues found by ADUE.

OpenRocket is a model rocket simulator, containing buttons to zoom out and zoom in. Each of them contains an icon with a magnifying glass and a small sign "−" and "+", respectively. However, these buttons do not contain any textual label or a tooltip. ADUE suggests adding tooltips to these buttons.

OpenRocket also contains multiple sliders, e.g., to control the wind direction or various angles. Next to each slider, there is a numeric input field and a textual descriptive label. However, there is no programmatical connection between the label ("Wind direction:"), the numeric value ("0°"), and the graphical slider. ADUE reports the missing *labelFor* attributes.

An example of a questionable grammar error can be found in the financial calculator Finanx. It contains a list of languages that are translated to the corresponding language instead of English (e.g., Français instead of French). Technically, the word is incorrect, and it should be translated into the language of the application (English). On the other hand, in some contexts, e.g., UI language selection, it can practically help the user to find hist or her language in the list, particularly if the person does not speak English.

*7.4. Threats to Validity*

Regarding the internal validity, a portion of the detected issues might have been false positives. To mitigate this threat, for selected analysis types, we manually verified a subset of the results to check their correctness. To improve grammar error detection, in the future, we should implement an option to add a word to the dictionary in ADUE, similarly to traditional spell-checking applications.

The largest threat to the external validity is the selection of applications, which might not be representative of the whole set of Java GUI programs. However, we tried to select applications from multiple different domains and ranging from small one-window utilities to complex software systems.

*7.5. Evaluation Conclusion*

From the results, we can conclude that ADUE can be successfully used on existing real-world Java applications with graphical user interfaces. The tool discovered many domain usability errors, including tooltip errors and warnings, grammar errors, or incorrect parent terms. The overall domain usability of the analyzed applications has high variability (5–96%), which points to the fact that developers are often not aware of domain usability problems, and we need to raise awareness about domain usability issues among them.

## 8. Potential of Existing Methods for DU Evaluation

After describing the results of the evaluation of our prototype, in the next two sections, we will try to put our work into the context of existing approaches and propose their extensions if suitable.

The goals of usability evaluation methods are usually to specify the requirements for the UI design, evaluate design alternatives, identify specific usability issues, and improve UI performance [16]. In this section, we will summarize existing general techniques of usability evaluation, and for some of them, we will propose modifications that could make them suitable to evaluate domain usability.

*8.1. Universal Techniques*

Simple, universally usable techniques that include users, such as *thinking aloud* [32], *question-asking protocol* [33], *performance measurement*, or *log file analysis* [34,35], can be easily altered to focus on domain dictionary by just changing the questions or tasks included in the process to obtain the desired outcome. If there is a recording output, it can be analyzed with respect to DU. Informal or structured *interviews* and *focus groups* [36] might also be directed on the domain user dictionary by asking the participants (i) whether they understand such or such terminology in the UI, (ii) whether they use it in their everyday work life in their own domain, and (iii) if not, what would they use instead.

*8.2. User Testing Techniques*

There are multiple types of *user testing* [37] differentiated by automation, distance from the user (in the room, in the observation lab, remote testing), and recording outputs (sound or image recording of user and/or screen, user logs, notes, software usage records, eye tracking, brain waves, etc.). All of them are usually connected by a more or less functioning system or prototype and users performing pre-prepared scenarios.

Possible alterations to the user testing technique are the following:
- Before the testing begins, the user is instructed to focus on domain terminology issues when performing the test.
- In the types of testing where the usability expert is present during the test, questions about term understandability are asked by the usability expert during each task of the scenario.
- The subject user is prompted to express proposals for new terminology for any item in the system and to explain why (s)he thinks the new terminology is appropriate for the particular item (incorrect, inapposite, does not reflect the given concept, etc.). Proposals from all users are recorded and evaluated for the most common ones that should serve as future replacements in the UI.
- If alternative translations of the UI are being tested, the testing should take place with the users naturally speaking the language of the translation. The users are prompted to propose a different translation for any item in the system and explain why they think the new translation is more appropriate for the particular item (incorrect or erroneous translation, more suitable term). Proposals from all users are recorded and evaluated for the most common ones. They can also be evaluated in a second phase where participants see the replaced terminology directly in the UI and check for correctness.
- In A/B testing, multiple versions of UIs with different terminology alternatives are created and tested by the users.

## 8.3. Inspection Methods

In general usability inspection methods described by Boehm et al. [38] and Nielsen and Mack [39], the expert in usability usually performs the inspection of guidelines, heuristic rules, product consistency, or standards compliance of a prototype.

### 8.3.1. Specializations of General Methods

Narrowing to DU, we propose the following alternations to the general techniques:

- Guideline review, cognitive walkthrough, heuristic evaluation techniques, formal usability inspection, and standards inspection: an expert performs the check focusing on domain terminology, consistency, and errors.
- To achieve the best results on the aforementioned techniques, the expert needs to be a domain expert.
- Another option is a pluralistic walkthrough technique, where one evaluator is an expert on usability and UX and the other is a domain expert. They both cooperate to imagine how the user would work with the design and try to find potential DU issues.
- Consistency inspection: the expert performs consistency checks across multiple systems *and* across the same system. The focus should be on the terminology, including:
    - different terms naming the same functionality or concepts (e.g., *OK* on one place, *Confirm* on the other);
    - same terms naming different functionality or concepts;
    - uppercase and lowercase letters consistency (e.g., *File, file, FILE*);
    - consistency of term hierarchies, properties, and relations.

### 8.3.2. Cognitive Walkthrough

As for the *Cognitive Walkthrough (CW)*, we propose an alternation of the latest Wharton et al.'s method [40], marked by Mahatody et al. [41] as *CW3* (this notation will be used further in this subsection).

The evaluator in CW3 should imagine a specific scenario for each action that the target users must accomplish to achieve the completion of their task. To achieve the best results, again, the evaluator should be a domain expert. A scenario should also be credible according to Wharton et al. [40], which means that the user's background knowledge and the feedback from the interface should be justified when evaluating each action. When evaluating domain usability, we recommend focusing on the user's background and knowledge first.

We propose to answer the following supplements to CW3's questions [41] related to various user thoughts and actions (Note: Question Q1 remains unchanged, and our supplements are marked by italic font):

1. What is the user thinking at the beginning of the action? (Q1: Will the user try to achieve the right effect?)
2. Is the user able to locate the command? (Q2: Will the user notice that the correct action is available? *Is the action appropriately and consistently described by a domain-related term and/or understandable to the user?*)
3. Is the user able to identify the command? (Q3: Will the user associate the correct action with the effect that (s)he is trying to achieve? *Is there any other action with a similar label and/or graphics, which would lead the user astray?*)
4. Is the user able to interpret the feedback? (Q4: If the correct action is performed, will the user see that progress is being made toward the solution of the task? *Is the feedback reported to the user expressed in consistent terms and/or graphics understandable to the user?*).

Provided the fact that the target user is the best source of domain knowledge, it would be possible to use an alteration in the "CW with users" approach by Gonz et al. [42]. However, it is questionable whether "CW with users" is still a CW, since the essence of CW techniques is the evaluation by experts, excluding users. If available, we recommend using domain experts instead of target users.

*8.4. Inquiry*

Inquiry techniques are those that focus on user feedback. They include focus groups [43], interviews and surveys [44], questionnaires [45,46], and others. There are two categories of inquiry techniques we would like to focus on: in-system user feedback, and surveys and questionnaires.

8.4.1. In-System User Feedback

General techniques are based on the user sending feedback in a form of recorded events [47], captured screens, or submitted comments. We propose the following techniques for evaluating DU:

- For web UIs, it is possible to create a system or a browser plug-in enabling the user to mark any inappropriate terminology in the UI and/or change the label or tooltip of the particular element in the UI. Every change is logged and sent to a central server where the evaluator can review the logs recorded from multiple users. The priority of change is calculated automatically by the number of users proposing a particular terminology change. The proposed terms can be assessed as a percentage according to the number of users proposing the same term.
- For any UI, a separate form can be made where the user selects one of the pre-prepared lists of application features (labeled and with icons for better recognizability) and sends comments on how and why to change the description of the particular feature. However, it is best to comment directly in the target UI because of the context.
- For both possibilities, the users can assess the *appropriateness* of a particular term using the approach by Isohella and Nissila. [8].

8.4.2. Surveys and Questionnaires

Most of the common standard usability surveys and questionnaires [48] are defined too generally to be usable for DU evaluation. This was the primary reason for our proposal of a novel SDUS (System Domain Usability Scale) technique in 2018 [10]. SDUS is based on the common standardized System Usability Scale (SUS) [49,50], which is widely used in the user experience evaluation practice.

Similarly to SUS, our proposal also included a questionnaire with 10 statements targeted at all DU aspects. We designed SDUS similarly to SUS, which means that odd questions were positive and even questions were negative statements. The answers are in the standard five-point Likert scale (*1—Disagree, 5—Agree*). The overall DU metric is a sum of values for all answers. The calculation of the SDUS score is the same as the standard SUS [51].

*8.5. Analytical Modeling Techniques*

The goal of *GOMS (Goals, operations, methods, selection rules)* analysis [52,53] is to predict user execution and learning time. Learning time is partially determined by the appropriate terminology, but without a domain expert, it is not easy to evaluate it either automatically or manually. Calculating the overall *appropriateness* of terms [8] per system might provide a good view of the system improvement since the last prototype.

In *cognitive task analysis* [54], the evaluators try to predict usability problems. We claim that it is partially possible to semi-automatically evaluate existing UIs to find potential DU problems. We propose several techniques to support this claim in Section 3.

*Knowledge analysis* is aimed at system learnability prediction. It is only logical that the more appropriate the domain content of the UI is, the more learnable it is. This relates not only to the terminology but also to icons, which should be domain-centric, especially in cases when the particular feature or item is domain-related. Several techniques proposed in Section 3 address this issue.

*Design analysis* aims to assess the design complexity. From the point of view of DU, the complexity of textual content in web UIs can already be assessed by multiple online tools such as Readable (http://readable.com; accessed on 9 August 2021). Readability Score evaluates the given text or a URL and determines multiple reading complexity indices including Flesch–Kincaid [55,56], Keyword Density, and similar.

The goal of *Programmable User Models* [57] is to write a program that acts similarly to a user. Currently, our proposed tool is able to simulate users on existing UIs using a domain-specific language [58]. This automated approach was developed with the goal of testing user interfaces from the domain task-oriented point of view, and it is not related to the main goal of this paper.

*8.6. Simulation Techniques*

Simulation techniques, similarly to *Programmable User Model*, try to mimic user interaction. Many tools for end-to-end user testing exist, e.g., Protractor (Protractor end-to-end testing framework: https://www.protractortest.org; accessed on 9 August 2021) for Angular. However, similarly to *Programmable user Models*, simulation represents a general technique that is not specifically related to DU and therefore exceeds the focus of this paper.

*8.7. Automated Evaluation Methods*

To date, we have focused on manual or semi-automatized techniques. As for automated approaches, as mentioned in the introduction, we found only one by Mahajan and Shneiderman [59] that enables consistency checking of UI terminology. Their tool is quite obsolete and does not evaluate whether different terms are describing the same functionality. However, the methodical approach is applicable to all UIs. In Section 3, we introduced a novel approach to semi-automatic DU evaluation of existing UIs that includes consistency checking similar to Mahajan and Shneiderman's style, but extends the approach with multiple evaluation techniques.

## 9. Related Work

In this section, we selected the most important state-of-the-art works that refer to the aspects of DU, although they might have used different terminology compared to our definition. The number of works referring to matching the application's content to the real world indicates the importance of DU.

*9.1. Domain Content*

Most often, the existing literature refers to the *domain content* aspect of DU as to one of the following:

- *Textual content of UIs*—Jacob Nielsen refers to DU aspects only too generally and stresses the importance of "the system's addressing the user's knowledge of the domain" [1].
- *Domain dictionary, Ontology*—the importance of domain dictionary of UIs is stressed also by Artemieva [60], Kleshchev [61], and Gribova [62], who also presented a method of estimating usability of a UI based on its model. Her model is rather component-oriented than focused specifically on the domain, and she focuses primarily on general usability evaluation methods such as having too many menu items in a menu.
- *Domain structure*—by Billman et al. [63]. Their experiment with NASA users showed that there is a big difference in the performance of users with respect to the usability of the old application and that of the the new, as the new application was better in domain-specific terminology structure.
- *User interface semantics, Ambiguity*—Tilly and Porkoláb [64] propose using *semantic UIs* (SUI) to solve the problem of the ambiguity of UI terminology. The core of SUI is a general ontology that is a basis for creating all UIs in the specific domain. User interfaces can have a different appearance and arrangement but the domain dictionary must remain the same. Ontologies in general also deal with the semantics of UIs.

- *Complexity, reading complexity*—Becker [65], Kincaid et al. [55], and Mahajan and Shneiderman [66] stress that the complexity of the textual content should not be too high because that would make the application less usable. Kincaid et al. refer to the reading complexity indices (ARI, Kincaid). Complexity is closely related to the *domain content* DU aspect: the UI should have the reading complexity appropriate for the target users.
- *Matching with the real world or correspondence to the domain*—Many of the above-listed authors, along with Badashian et al. [12], also stress the importance of applications corresponding to the real world and address the user's domain knowledge. In fact, this is a more general description of our *domain content* DU aspect. Hilbert and Redmiles [47] stress the correspondence of event sequences with the real world as well as the domain dictionary.
- *Knowledge aspect of UI design*—One of the attributes of Eason's usability definition [67] refers to the *knowledge* aspect of UI design representing the knowledge that the user applies to the task, and it may be appropriate or inappropriate. In general, the *task match* attribute of Eason's definition also refers to processes mapping but does not explicitly target the mapping of specific domain tasks.
- *Appropriateness recognizability*—defined by ISO/IEC-25010 [68] as an aspect referring to the user understanding whether the software is appropriate for their needs and how it can be used for particular tasks and conditions of use. The term was redefined in 2011 from *Understandability*. However, again, the term appropriateness recognizability does not specifically refer to the target domain match,
- Other definitions such as ISO-9241-11 [5] or definitions by Nielsen [1], Shackel [69], and others [70] are too general but we do not exclude DU as a subset of them.

### 9.2. Consistency

Among other aspects, Badashian et al. [12] stress the importance of *consistency* in usable UIs. The survey by Ivory and Hearst [16] contains a wide list of automatic usability methods and tools. From over 100 works, only Mahajan and Shneiderman [59] deal with the domain content of applications, and their Sherlock tool is able to automatically check the consistency of UI terminology. Sherlock, however, does not evaluate whether different terms describe the same functionality or not.

### 9.3. World Language, Language Barriers, Errors

In addition to complexity, Becker [65] also deals with the *translation* of UIs, which corresponds to the *world language* DU aspect. In the area of web accessibility [13], the *understandability* of web documents is defined by W3C. Compared to our definition, however, it deals only with some of the attributes: *world language* of web UIs, *language barriers*, and *errors*. It focuses on web pages specifically, not on UIs in general.

### 9.4. All Domain Usability Aspects

Isohella and Nissila [8] evaluate the *appropriateness* of UI terminology based on the evaluation of users. In a broader sense, appropriateness is equivalent to our DU definition but Isohella and Nissila do not go deeper into the definition's aspects. According to the authors, appropriate terminology can increase the quality of information systems. The terminology should be selected, formed, evaluated, and used.

### 10. Conclusions

In this paper, we described the design and implementation of a method for automatized DU evaluation of existing user interfaces. The method not only evaluates the user interfaces for domain usability but also (probably even more importantly) provides recommendations for their improvement. The method was verified using the implemented prototype on several existing open-source Java applications with graphical user interfaces. Among other findings, we conclude that the variability of the computed domain usability of individual applications is high. Many components do not contain tooltips or have grammatical errors.

As a secondary contribution, we proposed several modifications of existing manual techniques of usability evaluation to utilize them specifically for domain usability evaluation.

Ontologies provide good tools for content comparison, but they have restrictions (such as ID uniqueness) that restrict our approach and the ontological format is rather extensive. Therefore, in the future, we plan to define a new domain-specific language (DSL) for formal domain model description [71] and a custom comparison engine for domain models exported in the DSL.

We believe that the ADUE method contributes to the field of UX and usability and hope that it improves the situation in DU of new user interfaces.

**Author Contributions:** Conceptualization, M.B. and J.P.; methodology, M.B., J.P., M.S., S.C., W.S. and M.M.; software, M.B.; formal analysis, M.B.; investigation, M.B.; data curation, M.B.; writing—original draft preparation, M.B.; writing—review and editing, M.B., J.P., M.S., S.C., W.S. and M.M.; visualization, M.B. and M.S.; funding acquisition, J.P. All authors have read and agreed to the published version of the manuscript.

**Funding:** This work was supported by Project VEGA No. 1/0762/19 Interactive pattern-driven language development.

**Data Availability Statement:** The evaluation results of ADUE can be found at http://bit.ly/3hZBImy (accessed on 9 August 2021). The General Application Terms Ontology can be found at https://bit.ly/2R6bm6p (accessed on 9 August 2021).

**Conflicts of Interest:** The authors declare no conflict of interest. The funders had no role in the design of the study, in the collection, analyses, or interpretation of data, in the writing of the manuscript, or in the decision to publish the results.

## References

1. Nielsen, J. *Usability Engineering*; Morgan Kaufmann Publishers, Inc.: San Francisco, CA, USA, 1993.
2. Norman, D. *The Design of Everyday Things: Revised and Expanded Edition*; Basic Books: New York, NY, USA, 2013.
3. Morville, P. User Experience Design. 2004. Available online: http://semanticstudios.com/user_experience_design (accessed on 9 August 2021).
4. Lewis, J.R. Usability: Lessons Learned ... and Yet to Be Learned. *Int. J. Hum. Comput. Interact.* **2014**, *30*, 663–684. [CrossRef]
5. ISO-9241-11. *Ergonomics of Human-System Interaction—Part 11: Usability: Definitions and Concepts*; ISO: Geneva, Switzerland, 2018.
6. Chilana, P.K.; Wobbrock, J.O.; Ko, A.J. Understanding Usability Practices in Complex Domains. In Proceedings of the SIGCHI Conference on Human Factors in Computing Systems (CHI '10), Atlanta, GA, USA, 10–15 April 2010; ACM: New York, NY, USA, 2010; pp. 2337–2346. [CrossRef]
7. Gulliksen, J. *Designing for Usability—Domain Specific Human-Computer Interfaces in Working Life*; Comprehensive Summaries of Uppsala Dissertations from the Faculty of Science & Technology; Acta Universitatis Upsaliensis: Uppsala, Switzerland, 1996; p. 28.
8. Isohella, S.; Nissila, N. Connecting usability with terminology: Achieving usability by using appropriate terms. In Proceedings of the 2015 IEEE International Professional Communication Conference (IPCC '15), Limerick, Ireland, 12–15 July 2015; pp. 1–5. [CrossRef]
9. Lanthaler, M.; Gütl, C. Model Your Application Domain, Not Your JSON Structures. In Proceedings of the 22nd International Conference on World Wide Web, Rio de Janeiro, Brazil, 13–17 May 2013; ACM: New York, NY, USA, 2013; pp. 1415–1420. [CrossRef]
10. Bačíková, M.; Galko, L. The design of manual domain usability evaluation techniques. *Open Comput. Sci.* **2018**, *8*, 51–67. [CrossRef]
11. Bačíková, M.; Porubän, J. Domain Usability, User's Perception. In *Human-Computer Systems Interaction: Backgrounds and Applications 3*; Springer International Publishing: Cham, Switzerland, 2014; pp. 15–26. [CrossRef]
12. Badashian, A.S.; Mahdavi, M.; Pourshirmohammadi, A.; Nejad, M.M. Fundamental Usability Guidelines for User Interface Design. In Proceedings of the 2008 International Conference on Computational Sciences and Its Applications (ICCSA '08), Perugia, Italy, 30 June–3 July 2008; IEEE Computer Society: Washington, DC, USA, 2008; pp. 106–113. [CrossRef]
13. W3C. Web Content Accessibility Guidelines (WCAG) 2.0, Part 3 about Understandability. 2008. Available online: https://www.w3.org/TR/WCAG20/#understandable (accessed on 9 August 2021).
14. Kolski, C.; Millot, P. A rule-based approach to the ergonomic "static" evaluation of man-machine graphic interface in industrial processes. *Int. J. Man Mach. Stud.* **1991**, *35*, 657–674. [CrossRef]

15. Sears, A. AIDE: A Step toward Metric-Based Interface Development Tools. In Proceedings of the 8th Annual ACM Symposium on User Interface and Software Technology (UIST '95), Pittsburgh, PA, USA, 15–17 November 1995; Association for Computing Machinery: New York, NY, USA, 1995; pp. 101–110. [CrossRef]
16. Ivory, M.Y.; Hearst, M.A. The state of the art in automating usability evaluation of user interfaces. *ACM Comput. Surv.* **2001**, *33*, 470–516. [CrossRef]
17. Tullis, T.S. The Formatting of Alphanumeric Displays: A Review and Analysis. *Hum. Factors* **1983**, *25*, 657–682. [CrossRef] [PubMed]
18. Paz, F.; Pow-Sang, J.A. Current Trends in Usability Evaluation Methods: A Systematic Review. In Proceedings of the 2014 7th International Conference on Advanced Software Engineering and Its Applications, Hainan, China, 20–23 December 2014; pp. 11–15. [CrossRef]
19. Bakaev, M.; Mamysheva, T.; Gaedke, M. Current trends in automating usability evaluation of websites: Can you manage what you ca not measure? In Proceedings of the 2016 11th International Forum on Strategic Technology (IFOST), Novosibirsk, Russia, 1–3 June 2016; pp. 510–514. [CrossRef]
20. Namoun, A.; Alrehaili, A.; Tufail, A. A Review of Automated Website Usability Evaluation Tools: Research Issues and Challenges. In *Design, User Experience, and Usability: UX Research and Design*; Springer: Cham, Switzerland, 2021; pp. 292–311. [CrossRef]
21. Bačíková, M.; Porubän, J. Ergonomic vs. domain usability of user interfaces. In Proceedings of the 2013 The 6th International Conference on Human System Interaction (HSI), Sopot, Poland, 6–8 June 2013; pp. 159–166. [CrossRef]
22. Bačíková, M.; Zbuška, M. Towards automated evaluation of domain usability. In Proceedings of the 2015 IEEE 13th International Scientific Conference on Informatics, Poprad, Slovakia, 18–20 November 2015; pp. 41–46. [CrossRef]
23. Bačíková, M.; Galko, L.; Hvizdová, E. Manual techniques for evaluating domain usability. In Proceedings of the 2017 IEEE 14th International Scientific Conference on Informatics, Poprad, Slovakia, 14–16 November 2017; pp. 24–30. [CrossRef]
24. Bačíková, M.; Galko, L.; Hvizdová, E. Experimental Design of Metrics for Domain Usability. In Proceedings of the International Conference on Computer-Human Interaction Research and Applications (CHIRA 2017), Funchal, Portugal, 31 October 2017; Volume 1, pp. 118–125. [CrossRef]
25. Galko, L.; Bačíková, M. Experiments with automated evaluation of domain usability. In Proceedings of the 2016 9th International Conference on Human System Interactions (HSI), Portsmouth, UK, 6–8 July 2016; pp. 252–258. [CrossRef]
26. Tomoko, N.; Beglar, D. Developing Likert-Scale Questionnaires. In *JALT Conference Proceedings*; Sonda, N., Krause, A., Eds.; JALT: Tokyo, Japan, 2014; pp. 1–8.
27. Varanda Pereira, M.J.; Fonseca, J.; Henriques, P.R. Ontological approach for DSL development. *Comput. Lang. Syst. Struct.* **2016**, *45*, 35–52. [CrossRef]
28. Bačíková, M. Domain Analysis of Graphical User Interfaces of Software Systems (extended dissertation abstract). In *Information Sciences and Technologies*; Bulletin of the ACM Slovakia; STU Press: Bratislava, Slovakia, 2014; Volume 6, pp. 17–23.
29. Bačíková, M.; Porubän, J.; Lakatoš, D. Defining Domain Language of Graphical User Interfaces. In Proceedings of the Symposium on Languages Applications and Technologies (SLATE), Porto, Portugal, 20–21 June 2013; pp. 187–202. [CrossRef]
30. Vrandečić, D.; Krötzsch, M. Wikidata: A Free Collaborative Knowledgebase. *Commun. ACM* **2014**, *57*, 78–85. [CrossRef]
31. Huynh, D.F.; Li, G.; Ding, C.; Huang, Y.; Chai, Y.; Hu, L.; Chen, J. Generating Insightful Connections between Graph Entitites. U.S. Patent 20140280044, 14 July 2020.
32. Lewis, C. *Using the "Thinking-Aloud" Method in Cognitive Interface Design*; Technical Report; IBM, T. J. Watson Research Center: New York, NY, USA, 1982.
33. Kato, T. What "question-asking protocols" can say about the user interface. *Int. J. Man Mach. Stud.* **1986**, *25*, 659–673. [CrossRef]
34. Lund, A.M. Expert Ratings of Usability Maxims. *Ergon. Des. Q. Hum. Factors Appl.* **1997**, *5*, 15–20. [CrossRef]
35. Marciniak, J. *Encyclopedia of Software Engineering*, 2nd ed.; Wiley: Chichester, UK, 2002.
36. Nielsen, J. The Use and Misuse of Focus Groups. 1997. Available online: http://www.nngroup.com/articles/focus-groups/ (accessed on 9 August 2021).
37. Stull, E. User Testing. In *UX Fundamentals for Non-UX Professionals*; Apress: New York, NY, USA, 2018; pp. 311–317. [CrossRef]
38. Boehm, B.W.; Brown, J.R.; Lipow, M. Quantitative Evaluation of Software Quality. In Proceedings of the 2nd International Conference on Software Engineering (ICSE '76), San Francisco, CA, USA, 13–15 October 1976; IEEE Computer Society Press: Washington, DC, USA, 1976; pp. 592–605.
39. Nielsen, J.; Mack, R.L. (Eds.) *Usability Inspection Methods*; John Wiley & Sons, Inc.: Hoboken, NJ, USA, 1994.
40. Wharton, C.; Rieman, J.; Lewis, C.; Polson, P. The Cognitive Walkthrough Method: A Practitioner's Guide. In *Usability Inspection Methods*; John Wiley & Sons, Inc.: Hoboken, NJ, USA, 1994; pp. 105–140.
41. Mahatody, T.; Sagar, M.; Kolski, C. State of the Art on the Cognitive Walkthrough Method, Its Variants and Evolutions. *Int. J. Hum.-Comput. Interact.* **2010**, *26*, 741–785. [CrossRef]
42. González, M.P.; Lorés, J.; Granollers, A. Assessing Usability Problems in Latin-American Academic Webpages with Cognitive Walkthroughs and Datamining Techniques. In *Usability and Internationalization. HCI and Culture*; Aykin, N., Ed.; Springer: Berlin/Heidelberg, Germany, 2007; pp. 306–316. [CrossRef]
43. Krueger, R.A.; Casey, M.A. *Focus Groups: A Practical Guide for Applied Research*, 5th ed.; SAGE Publications Inc.: Thousand Oaks, CA, USA, 2015.
44. Flanagan, J.C. The critical incident technique. *Psychol. Bull.* **1954**, *51*, 327–358. [CrossRef]

45. Harper, B.D.; Norman, K.L. Improving user satisfaction: The questionnaire for user interaction satisfaction version 5.5. In Proceedings of the 1st Annual Mid-Atlantic Human Factors Conference, Virginia Beach, VA, USA, 25–26 February 1993; pp. 224–228.
46. Tullis, T.S.; Stetson, J.N. A comparison of questionnaires for assessing website usability. In Proceedings of the Usability Professional Association Conference, Minneapolis, MN, USA, 7–11 June 2004; pp. 1–12.
47. Hilbert, D.M.; Redmiles, D.F. Extracting usability information from user interface events. *ACM Comput. Surv.* **2000**, *32*, 384–421. [CrossRef]
48. Assila, A.; de Oliveira, K.M.; Ezzedine, H. Standardized Usability Questionnaires: Features and Quality Focus. *Electron. J. Comput. Sci. Inf. Technol.* **2016**, *6*, 15–31.
49. Bangor, A.; Kortum, P.; Miller, J. Determining What Individual SUS Scores Mean: Adding an Adjective Rating Scale. *J. Usability Stud.* **2009**, *4*, 114–123.
50. McLellan, S.; Muddimer, A.; Peres, S.C. The Effect of Experience on System Usability Scale Ratings. *J. Usability Stud.* **2012**, *7*, 56–67.
51. Brooke, J. SUS: A Retrospective. *J. Usability Stud.* **2013**, *8*, 29–40.
52. John, B.E.; Kieras, D.E. The GOMS Family of User Interface Analysis Techniques: Comparison and Contrast. *ACM Trans. Comput. Hum. Interact.* **1996**, *3*, 320–351. [CrossRef]
53. Kieras, D. Chapter 31—A Guide to GOMS Model Usability Evaluation using NGOMSL. In *Handbook of Human-Computer Interaction*, 2nd ed.; North-Hollan: Amsterdam, The Netherlands, 1997; pp. 733–766. [CrossRef]
54. Clark, R.E.; Feldon, D.F.; van Merriënboer, J.J.G.; Kenneth, A.Y.; Early, S. Cognitive Task Analysis. In *Handbook of Research on Educational Communications and Technology*; Routledge: London, UK, 2007; Chapter 43. [CrossRef]
55. Kincaid, J.P.; Fishburne, R.P.; Rogers, R.L.; Chissom, B.S. *Derivation of New Readability Formulas (Automated Readability Index, Fog Count and Flesch Reading Ease Formula) for Navy Enlisted Personnel*; Technical Report; University of Central Florida: Orlando, FL, USA, 1975.
56. Kincaid, J.P.; McDaniel, W.C. *An Inexpensive Automated Way of Calculating Flesch Reading Ease Scores*; Patient Disclosure Document 031350; US Patient Office: Washington, DC, USA, 1974.
57. Young, R.M.; Green, T.R.G.; Simon, T. Programmable User Models for Predictive Evaluation of Interface Designs. *SIGCHI Bull.* **1989**, *20*, 15–19. [CrossRef]
58. Porubän, J.; Bačíková, M. *Definition of Computer Languages via User Interfaces*; Technical University of Košice: Košice, Slovakia, 2010; pp. 53–57.
59. Mahajan, R.; Shneiderman, B. Visual and Textual Consistency Checking Tools for Graphical User Interfaces. *IEEE Trans. Softw. Eng.* **1997**, *23*, 722–735. [CrossRef]
60. Artemieva, I.L. Ontology development for domains with complicated structures. In Proceedings of the First International Conference on Knowledge Processing and Data Analysis (KONT'07/KPP'07), Novosibirsk, Russia, 14–16 September 2011; Springer: Berlin/Heidelberg, Germany, 2011; pp. 184–202. [CrossRef]
61. Kleshchev, A.S. How can ontologies contribute to software development? In Proceedings of the First International Conference on Knowledge Processing and Data Analysis (KONT'07/KPP'07), Novosibirsk, Russia, 14–16 September 2011; Springer: Berlin/Heidelberg, Germany, 2011; pp. 121–135. [CrossRef]
62. Gribova, V. A Method of Estimating Usability of a User Interface Based on its Model. *Int. J. Inf. Theor. Appl.* **2007**, *14*, 43–47.
63. Billman, D.; Arsintescucu, L.; Feary, M.; Lee, J.; Smith, A.; Tiwary, R. Benefits of matching domain structure for planning software: The right stuff. In Proceedings of the 2011 Annual Conference on Human Factors in Computing Systems (CHI '11), Vancouver, BC, Canada, 7–12 May 2011; ACM: New York, NY, USA, 2011; pp. 2521–2530. [CrossRef]
64. Tilly, K.; Porkoláb, Z. Automatic classification of semantic user interface services. In Proceedings of the Ontology-Driven Software Engineering (ODiSE'10), Reno, NV, USA, 17–21 October 2010; ACM: New York, NY, USA, 2010; pp. 1–6. [CrossRef]
65. Becker, S.A. A study of web usability for older adults seeking online health resources. *ACM Trans. Comput. Hum. Interact.* **2004**, *11*, 387–406. [CrossRef]
66. Shneiderman, B. Response time and display rate in human performance with computers. *ACM Comput. Surv.* **1984**, *16*, 265–285. [CrossRef]
67. Eason, K.D. Towards the experimental study of usability. *Behav. Inform. Technol.* **1984**, *3*, 133–143. [CrossRef]
68. ISO/IEC-25010. *Systems and Software Engineering—Systems and Software, Quality Requirements and Evaluation (SQuaRE)—System and Software Quality Models*; ISO: Geneva, Switzerland, 2011.
69. Shackel, B. Usability—Context, framework, definition, design and evaluation. *Hum. Factors Inform. Usability* **1991**, *21*, 21–38. [CrossRef]

70. Madan, A.; Kumar, S. Usability evaluation methods: A literature review. *Int. J. Eng. Sci. Technol.* **2012**, *4*, 590–599.
71. Kordić, S.; Ristić, S.; Čeliković, M.; Dimitrieski, V.; Luković, I. Reverse Engineering of a Generic Relational Database Schema Into a Domain-Specific Data Model. In Proceedings of the Central European Conference on Information and Intelligent Systems, Varaždin, Croatia, 27–29 September 2017; pp. 19–28.

Article
# Posting Recommendations in Healthcare Q&A Forums

Yi-Ling Lin [1], Shih-Yi Chien [1,*] and Yi-Ju Chen [2]

1. Department of Management Information Systems, National Chengchi University, Taipei 11605, Taiwan; yl_lin@nccu.edu.tw
2. Department of Computer Science, The George Washington University, Washington, DC 20052, USA; sabrina11068@gmail.com
* Correspondence: sychien@nccu.edu.tw

**Abstract:** Online Q&A forums, unlike search engines, allow posting of various types of queries, thus attracting users to seek information and solve problems in specific domains. However, as insufficient knowledge leads to incomprehensible queries, unsuitable responses are common. We develop posting recommendation systems (RSs) to support users in composing reasonable posts and receiving effective answers. The posting RSs were evaluated by a user study containing 27 participants and three tasks to examine if users engaged more in the question generation process. Two medical experts were recruited to verify whether professionals can understand and answer posts supported by RSs. The results show that the proposed mechanism enables askers to produce posts with better understandability, which leads experts to devote more attention to answer their questions.

**Keywords:** question-answering forum; healthcare informatics; recommendation system; word embedding; user study

## 1. Introduction

Although search engines are the most popular channel for information retrieval, the retrieved results are often too general to find solutions that fulfill user needs. Information retrieved from search engines is usually selected and sorted using custom algorithms, which favor preselected hosts or Wikipedia results. When looking for information on an unfamiliar topic, users may lack the knowledge to formulate good search queries, resulting in improper or unexpected search results. The difficulty in composing concise queries for search engines has popularized online Q&A forums, which serve as alternatives by which to find detailed answers to questions. Online Q&A websites attract users because they can respond to detailed questions and query experts without time or geographical constraints [1]; however, for user questions that are incomplete or ambiguous, the resulting answers may not be what the user was looking for; finding professional and reliable answers can be difficult. This has led to many unsolved and unclear questions in online forums.

Generating effective questions on Q&A websites is not easy, particularly for highly specialized domains. In the healthcare field, for instance, people may possess little background on the questions and may not understand the relevant jargon, resulting in ambiguous questions. Most users can only think of simple terms to describe their disease and medical conditions: Phrases used in the queries often do not reflect standard medical terminology. Sometimes, even the asker is not sure how to describe his/her medical condition or to describe the encountered situation in various ways (e.g., different descriptions of the pain scale for the same illness) [2]. Lexical barriers such as partial misspellings and the use of abbreviations also makes questions hard to understand. For example, a typical general question is "Recently I have been suffering from back pain. What kind of lifestyle would help prevent back pain?" A more informative or knowledgeable post would be "I am staying at a healthy weight, but I recently began to suffer from severe back pain. I searched for information online and found that smoking ages the spine. I seldom smoke but my husband smokes a lot. Is it because of inhaling too much secondhand smoke?"

Since this difficulty in formulating effective posts on Q&A websites is rarely addressed, we propose a design that recommends more concepts (e.g., topics and terminology) to users to formulate their posts with more reasonable details, rather than presenting existing questions from the search pool (i.e., routing answers) or finding possible answerers as do most Q&A websites [3–5]. While most products provide recommendations to users at querying and browsing moments, only a few mechanisms (e.g., spellchecks) focus on helping users formulate posts, particularly for an online Q&A forum with a specific subject such as healthcare. Referring to the research thread [6–8], enhancing the quality of the input content not only increases the user's ability to get useful answers but also results in high-quality solutions faster. Recommendation systems (RSs) applied when composing posts could be enhanced by suggesting to users what content should be posted and how to describe the situations in the post, leading to a high input quality and better answers [8]. In this study, we seek to help participants who are unfamiliar with a domain to compose queries with a posting recommendation mechanism.

We propose two posting RSs: a word embedding-based and a semantic-based RS. Word embedding is a well-known tool for processing words into space vectors to improve the automatic understanding of human languages. Our word embedding-based posting RS (we use "the embedding model" in the following content), implemented by a Word2Vec model [9], is trained on 5319 questions and 500 abstracts of publication crawled from health-related websites. For the semantic-based posting RS, we adopt the WordNet (https://wordnet.princeton.edu/) model (we use "the semantic model" in the following content), a lexical database for English with several synonyms that are tagged artificially. It groups words from their meanings for computational linguistic and natural language processing (NLP). Both the embedding and semantic models are meant to recommend ideas and terminology that users may need in their current posts. These feature-based recommendations are expected to help users make more subject-specific posts.

We believe that using text analytics to participate more in the asking processes can be a good approach to support users formulating posts and enhance the clarity of the posts, which would encourage domain experts to reply to the posts and answer the questions. To verify whether reformulated queries yield better query wording and help users to find the desired answers more easily, we conducted a user study and a satisfaction questionnaire to understand user perspectives on our RSs. In addition, posts written by our study's participants were evaluated by experts with a health-related background to determine whether they could be easily solved. The research questions are posited as follows:

RQ1: Does the posting RS help users formulate questions in healthcare Q&A forums?
RQ2: Is it easier for experts to understand questions supported by the posting RS?

## 2. Related Work

Traditionally, healthcare professionals are the primary sources of health information; they provide and manage health information for their patients [10]. With the spread of the Internet, sources of health information have become more diverse and accessible to individuals and families. Despite this easy access to health information, its main use remains focused on supporting healthcare professionals, such as in hospital information systems [11]. Isern and Moreno [12] organize various agents in healthcare to inform decisions on cure plans and to alert patients when abnormal messages are detected. Although health information has been widely applied to support professionals, Frost et al. [13] state that health information is also beneficial for patients and people in need. Effective support in terms of health information can improve the doctor–patient relationship as well as the completeness and quality of diagnosis [13]. Thus, it is crucial to provide an effective communication channel between professionals and general users in the health information domain.

As the Internet provides a convenient way to access health information, people tend to seek health-related support online [10]. It is estimated that approximately 12.5 million of the 278 million daily Internet searches are health-related [14]. To find the most relevant answers on the Internet, RSs are essential for Q&A forums. Existing RSs generally focus on routing answers or finding answerers. Among various recommendation mechanisms, question routing and grouping are two main approaches to finding potential answers and answerers (people who have similar experiences in a specific area) in Q&A forums [3–5]. These methods consider underlying social network features (e.g., which query gets more hits), user activity (e.g., which category do experts tend to be active in and receive honor for the best answer), and public personal data on websites to improve system usability.

Most studies about RSs in online Q&A forums focus on general aspects rather than a specific subject such as healthcare. Budalakoti et al. [15] present a RS with three different methods for selecting the most appropriate responder given a question on Yahoo! Answer. One is calculating the cosine similarity between the words from an individual's (the author) historical Q&A data and his/her current question; another is grouping documents using K-means clustering; and the other is discovering the author-topic distributions as the general model and recommending the responders based on the marginalized probabilities. Yang and Amatriain [16] analyze the application of RSs at Quora and build a platform to experiment with different machine learning models for the developers. While most studies work on general Q&A forums, few studies focus on specific professional Q&A forums. Xin et al. [17] developed TagCombine, an automatic tag recommendation method to analyze objects in both Stack Overflow and Freecode websites to facilitate search and identify software objects. Pedro and Karatzoglou [18] presented a supervised Bayesian approach to model expertise with similar topics to support question recommendation and to avoid question starvation from the Stack Exchange (http://stats.stackexchange.com). Wang et al. [19] also provided an enhanced tag recommendation system, ENTAGREC++, for organizing questions and facilitating browsing questions on Stack Overflow. Singh and Simperl [20] implemented a system, Suman, which combines semantic keyword search with traditional text search to find answers for unanswered questions on Reddit and Stack Overflow. There are even fewer studies focus on healthcare Q&A domain. McCray et al. [21] developed a web-based terminology server which allows a diverse audience to easily access current health information by enforcing flexible query grammar, expanding synonyms and lexical variants for a term, and generating alternative spellings for unknown words. Cho et al. [22] helped users to receive satisfactory responses by improving the baseline retrieval model with semantic information to generate top 5 discussion threads that are potential responses for unresolved medical case-based queries. Although RSs have been widely employed in health areas, Jacobs et al. [10] state that the extant mechanisms for online health information search are insufficient.

Despite the popularity of Q&A forums, many questions lack answers due to ambiguous or misleading terms [20]. Baltadzhieva and Chrupała's study [8] on Stack Overflow (a programming Q&A forum) shows that the terms used, tags added, and the length of questions influence question quality. They conclude that questions that are too localized or that have incorrect tags or terms are considered to be of poor quality [8]. In the healthcare domain, Bochet et al. [23] demonstrated that most users are too inexperienced to formulate an effective search query on health information. Spink et al. [24] also showed that when posting medical and health queries, many users fail to retrieve information relevant to their condition due to an ignorance of specialized vocabulary or precise medical terms. Zhang [25] showed that queries posted about health support are usually simple and short and lack other aspects of individual information. For recommendation systems to facilitate the formulation of online questions that are more likely to be answered, it is essential to make posts more comprehensive.

Thus, in this study we focus on generating and improving questions to enhance the recommendation mechanisms in the healthcare domain. We develop posting RSs to suggest potential ideas, formulate user questions, and eliminate ambiguities that might decrease the likelihood of the question being answered or increase the time it takes for the question to be responded to.

## 3. Posting Recommender Systems (RSs)

*3.1. Interface Design*

After looking over Q&A online forums (e.g., Quora.com, Yahoo! Answer, Stack Overflow (https://stackoverflow.com/), and English Language & Usage (https://english.stackexchange.com/)), we included an input area and a recommendation area in the system layout (see Figure 1). The first column of the recommendation area (the table part) shows topics that askers may focus on and the rest of the columns show the top 10 terms related to the particular topic.

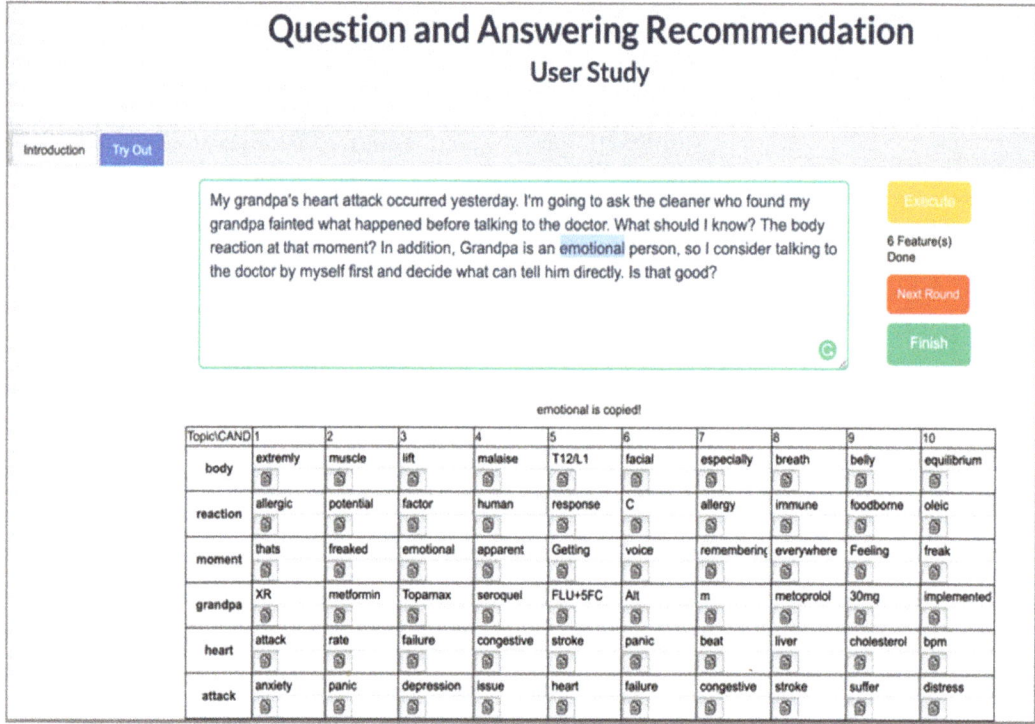

**Figure 1.** Interface of post RS.

Askers compose multi-sentence posts in the green input region (Figure 1). While users compose their posts, Grammarly (https://www.grammarly.com/), an auto-spellcheck extension from the Chrome web store, is activated to eliminate careless typos. If askers need ideas or assistance in generating the appropriate terms to pose their questions, they click on execute to receive system suggestions. In the recommendation table, askers click on the copy button to fetch the required terminology. The askers can click on execute at any time to receive new system recommendations. When askers are satisfied with the post, they click on finish to accomplish the question content. Figure 2 demonstrates how users interact with the proposed RSs.

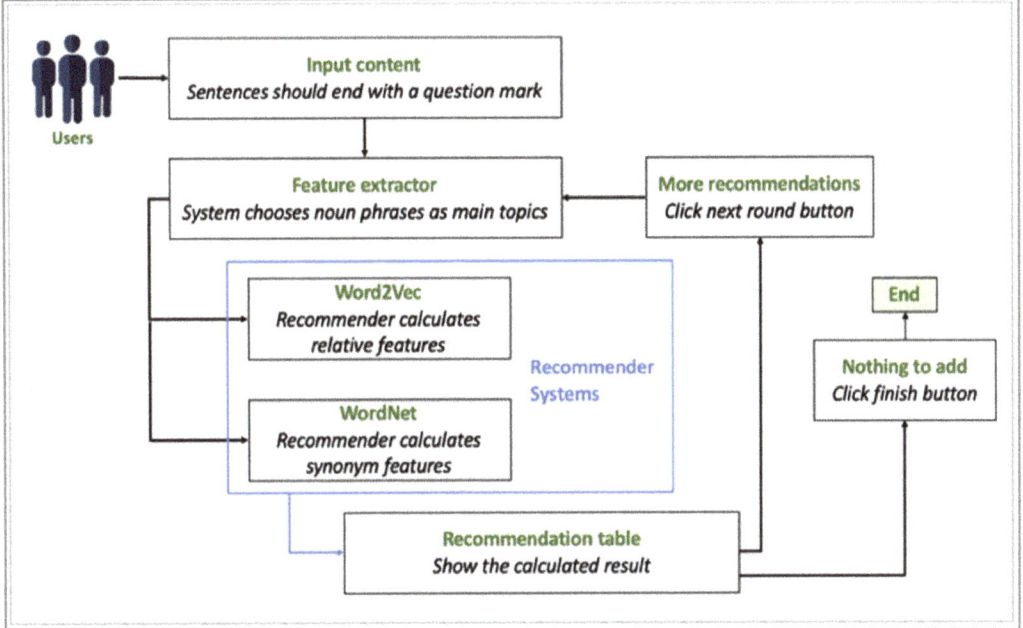

**Figure 2.** User perspective of interactive data flow.

The post recommendation mechanism is composed of three phases. First, the user inputs keywords, terms, or sentences to describe her questions. After receiving the user's queries, we attempt to understand what the user is asking or what concepts she is interested in. A post on Q&A forums is a kind of user-generated content (UGC) usually consisting of a question or a narrative. To identify user intentions from posts, we use a noun phrase extractor to extract the main topics from each post. Noun phrases are usually the core topics or objects in a sentence, whereas verb phrases describe actions between the objects in a sentence.

Second, we use embedding and semantic models to provide recommendations to help users construct their posts. In this study we use Word2Vec, a two-layer neural network model [9], as the embedding model. In addition, as the semantic model we use WordNet (https://wordnet.princeton.edu/), a well-processed English lexical database. We implemented the application using Python NLTK's WordNet package to generate recommendations. Both embedding-based and semantic-based recommendations are triggered by clicking on execute (more details about the recommendation models and dataset are provided in Sections 3.2 and 4.1).

Thirdly, the recommendation made by these models is prioritized and displayed with the top 10 recommended terminology, where the users can fetch the required content. They continue to modify the post (such as sentences and terms) until they are satisfied with the post, or until nothing new comes out from the recommendations.

### 3.2. Recommendation Models

Several state-of-art recommendation methods such as content-based [26–28], collaborative filtering-based [29] and hybrid methods [30] have been proposed to generate personalized recommendations based on the relationship between users and items. To provide recommendations to help users to construct their posts, we use embedding-based and semantic-based RSs that concentrate on interactive items (i.e., posts) without knowing the previous interactions of the user. To algorithmically understand the post and provide recommendations, text representation is important. Different from the traditional text representation such as continuous bag-of-words or Term Frequency-Inversed Document Frequency (TF-IDF) [31], WordNet and Word2Vec bring extra semantic features that help in identifying textual content. WordNet [32,33] is a human-curated ontological symbolic representation based on the similarity between words. It is often limited with its hierarchical representation. Word2Vec [9] is an unsupervised neural network method for determining words meaning by its surrounding context with a vector. The input words are transferred into an n-dimensional vector space, then similar words are identified by being near the input vector. It can perform effectively no matter how many words are included in the input vector, but is constrained by the corpus to the vector space. By incorporating the generalizable contexts into the model, Word2Vec has been proven to be more accurate than other models [9,34,35].

Pre-processing is essential for RS models. Data collected from websites and online forums often contain colloquial sayings and abbreviations (e.g., please → plz, pls). To eliminate meaningless words and punctuation (e.g., "?", ".", ";"), we tokenized sentences, removed stopwords, and regulated terms from the NLTK corpus before training. To reduce the number of inflectional forms, we lemmatized the words (e.g., am, are, is → be) using NLTK to get the general patterns of words. We then put all of the word packs of each sentence into a collection and used the gensim package (https://pypi.org/project/gensim/), a Python Library for scalable statistic semantics.

To give suitable ideas to help users compose their posts, we developed two models. We implemented the embedding model using Word2Vec, a shallow, two-layer neural network model that uses a large corpus of texts to perform unsupervised learning [36] and produces a vector space to reconstruct the linguistic contexts of words. In the new vector space, words sharing common contexts in the corpus are located in close proximity to each other. Vector relationships can be represented as "Kitten:Cat = Puppy:Dog". Thus, given expressions such as "Kitten:Cat = Dog: ?", we can infer what words should be inserted. In addition, there are two kinds of Word2Vec models: skip-gram (infers context words based on input words) and continuous bag of words (CBOW: infers input words based on context words). In this work, we followed the gensim tutorial (https://radimrehurek.com/gensim/tutorial.html) and used skip-grams to train Word2Vec on a corpus of medical terms and healthcare forum wording.

We also implemented another recommendation system using the WordNet semantic model. We did not change this much because its database is already well-organized. The recommendations are generated based on the English lexical database using the Python NLTK WordNet package given the input sentence.

We utilized selenium-web browser automatio (https://www.seleniumhq.org/) to support users to eliminate misspellings when formulating their posts. When a user types a period or clicks the execution button, the system considers the prior section to be a sentence, automatically normalizes their wordings and feeds them into two recommendation models. The embedding model would map the input words to its context word and offer recommendations. The semantic model would map the input words to the semantic graph of lexical items it pre-generated and then provide similar terms as recommended ideas.

## 4. Research Design

To assess whether the proposed posting RSs help users formulate queries that increase the probability of being answered, we conducted a user study to collect and analyze content written by users. We implemented two posting RSs: a word embedding model based on Word2Vec (suggesting ideas (terminology) related to the main topics of the input content), and a semantic WordNet-based model (suggesting synonyms (terminology) for the main topics of the input content), for comparison with the baseline model (no recommendation). We collected the participant behavior and posts using the three models for further analysis and expert evaluation.

## 4.1. Dataset

WebMD (https://www.webmd.com/) is one of the few healthcare Q&A forums in which medical specialists (called experts in the forum) offer suggestions to askers about their illness or concerns. The dataset was crawled from WebMD from March 2010 to September 2014 and contains 25,319 questions.

Apart from the daily conversations from WebMD, we also collected medical terminology and specialist wording from other professional healthcare-related websites (such as PubMed (https://www.ncbi.nlm.nih.gov/pubmed/)). Lai et al. (2016) suggest that for word embedding models, the domain of the corpus is more important than its size. Thus, we crawled the abstracts of biotechnology-related publications from PubMed to create the Word2Vec model.

## 4.2. Tasks and Experimental Materials

To generate posting ideas for the participants, the experiment provides a short introduction with a background story to simulate possible healthcare conditions. To complete the task, the participants were asked to compose a post associated with the background story.

To evaluate the experimental design, a pilot test was conducted in which three health tasks were examined: flu, asthma (https://www.webmd.com/a-to-z-guides/common-topics), and pregnancy. The results showed that it was difficult for participants to compose posts about asthma and pregnancy because they had little daily experience in these areas. Therefore, we changed the selection of health tasks to flu, allergy, and foodborne illness, which are more common among the public, and employed these in the official study (see Appendix A).

As a short introduction lacks sufficient information to formulate posts under a simulation condition, for each task we prepared supportive paragraphs from relevant medical websites. To cover various aspects of health situations, articles, news, and reports from healthcare agencies were collected as our materials. Finally, we selected supportive excerpts from a health agency's announcement with statistical data (the rate of an illness in a region) and sections gathered from news reports with common knowledge that the public can understand. Participants were to imagine the assigned task and write down their own or the character's experiences of specific illness after understanding the background information.

In addition, we prepared an example question in the try-out (Figure 3) to encourage participants to produce longer questions and not simply question sentences like "what are the symptoms of heart disease."

## 4.3. Participants and Procedure

Twenty-seven participants (14 females and 13 males, average age 27.7) were recruited from a social media website (i.e., Facebook). Fifteen out of the 27 participants' experience with Q&A forums was limited to browsing discussion threads, rather than composing or answering posts. Only five participants had experience using "professional" Q&A forums.

The within-subject design was used in the experiments. The three tasks were performed along with three algorithmic models (without RS, with Word2Vec RS, and with WordNet RS). Thus, each participant was asked to complete a total of six posts in three tasks. The Latin square design was applied to avoid the order effect [37]. The experiment used the following procedure (Figure 4):

(1) After signing the consent form, the participants took the pre-test questionnaire on their background and past experience using Q&A forums.
(2) A training task was then provided to ensure that participants fully understood the experimental systems and task requirements. An example of an expected post was given to encourage the participant to compose complete questions. Participants were allowed to ask any questions during this step.
(3) A brief description of the assigned model was also provided. The participant was given sufficient time to become familiar with the system.

(4) A description of the general context of the assigned task was provided to the participant, after which the participant began her posting.
(5) Another description of the complex context of the task was given to the participant. Then, the participant began her posting. Please note that as each participant completed all three tasks with the three models, she completed (3)–(5) three times.
(6) A post-questionnaire was issued to the participant to evaluate each user's experience with each model, including her perception of the system process, system speed, and the extent to which they would prefer using our RSs.

---

*[Task 1]*

**Background:**

Sandy's Grandfather has a family history of the heart attack. Unluckily, his illness occurred yesterday and was sent to the hospital. After receiving a phone call from Dad, Sandy tried to search for some information about the sickness. She will go to pick up Grandpa Johnson tomorrow on her way home but she has no ideas what she should know in advance. The following is the information she has now. If you are Sandy and want to get help on the health care online forum, what you will say?

**Supportive paragraphs of a daily scenario task:**

A guide to a heart attack

When blood can't get to your heart, your heart muscle doesn't get the oxygen it needs. Without oxygen, its cells can be damaged or die. Over time, cholesterol and a fatty material called plaque can build up on the walls inside blood vessels that take blood to your heart, called arteries. This makes it harder for blood to flow freely. Most heart attacks happen when a piece of this plaque breaks off. A blood clot forms around the broken-off plaque, and it blocks the artery.

The following is the call, from Sandy's dad:

"If Tracy (paid cleaner) wasn't there at that time, it may have been too late to rescue your grandpa. You know, Grandpa Johnson had a heart attack. He told me before that his chest was sometimes painful and that made it difficult for him to breath. And our hometown was pretty cold in the winter. I'm afraid that if Grandpa forgets to dress warm enough, the low temperature may stimulate another heart attack. Do you think I should find a personal physician for grandpa? Near his house? We are all working outside the county. When emergency happens, this protection may work."

**Example question from Sandy:**

My grandpa's heart attack occurred yesterday. I'm going to ask the cleaner who found my grandpa fainted what happened before talking to the doctor. What should I know? The body reaction at that moment? In addition, Grandpa is an emotional person, so I consider talking to the doctor by myself first and decide what can tell him directly. Is that good? By the way, the temperature here is pretty low. Does anyone know what things should be prepared for when grandpa goes back home?

---

**Figure 3.** Material read by participants before composing a post in the try-out.

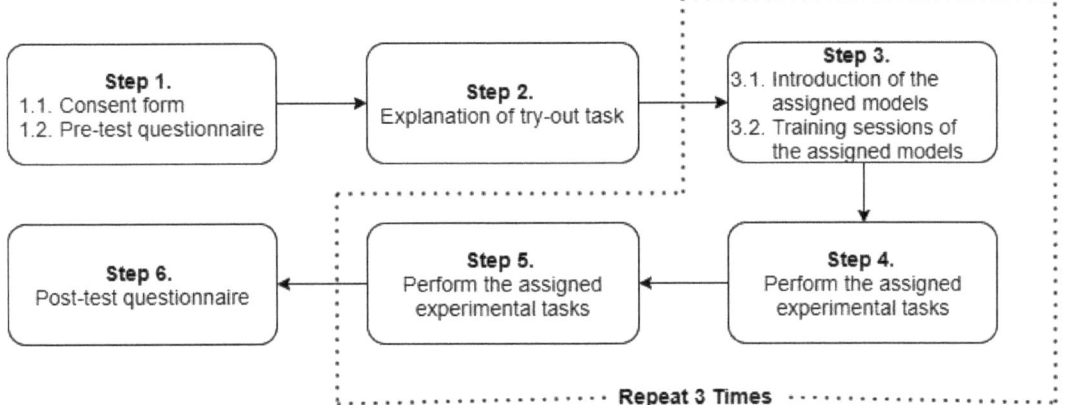

**Figure 4.** Experiment procedure.

*4.4. Analysis Method*

To answer the first research question, "Does the posting RS help users formulate questions in healthcare Q&A forums?", five measurements from the literature were used to evaluate outcomes: (1) input content length, (2) amount of medical terminology in input content [24], (3) presence of condition or self-description [25], (4) amount of recommended terminology adopted by user, and (5) total time to use to formulate post.

We used GEE [38] to analyze the data. Regardless of whether a variable data is continuous or nominal, GEE can estimate parameters. Even with missing data in a variable column, GEE can still calculate results from other columns containing data. GEE is suitable for repeatable experiments even if the input parameters are dependable or undependable and even if the population does not have a normal distribution. Lastly, the main effects and interaction terms of variables can be chosen under GEE manipulation.

To answer the second research question, "Is it easier for experts to understand questions supported by the posting RS?", we invited experts whose jobs were related to medical professions to rate the quality of posts composed by the participants. They noted that answering questions on a healthcare forum is similar to that of diagnosing patients in clinics. After patients describe the condition, professionals suggest possible solutions. The only risk is misunderstandings, as experts must judge illness given the posts alone, without face-to-face diagnosis.

Since an illness may present with different symptoms and complications in different people due to age, constitution, medical records, etc., it is difficult to draw conclusions when a replier sends ambiguous messages. To narrow down the range of possible solutions, it is necessary to obtain more details and transparent objectives (e.g., at least a query sentence and a self-description in a post). Therefore, when posting questions in the forum, the posting RS should assist users to adopt meaningful terminology and compose complete but concise posts. We requested professionals rate every post with one to five points (low to high quality) on three measurements: willingness, completeness, and clarity. Willingness evaluates whether the professionals were willing to answer c. Completeness and clarity concern the reason for their analysis. For example, informative contents (posts) were rated high in completeness, and contents (posts) with sufficient descriptions of what happened, as well as timing and location, were rated high in clarity.

## 5. Analysis of Results

The study was conducted with two posting RSs and one baseline model for three tasks. Each participant was requested to generate six posts in total. The system log was analyzed to objectively investigate user behavior given the various RSs and task conditions, and participant posts were used to investigate whether recommendation support helps experts to better understand the posts and encourages them to answer the posted questions. This section is organized into log analysis and opinion analysis based on the research questions.

*5.1. Log Analysis*

This section focuses on the perspective of effectiveness from the post length, the number of medical-related features, and the existence of detailed descriptions among three models, the number of adopted recommended features between two experimental recommender models, and the perspective of efficiency between with RS and without RS. Table 1 shows a basic descriptive statistic of the three models. We applied a linear function with GEE to evaluate the association between post length and three within-subject variables: model, task, and operating order. There is shown to be no significant effect on models, but there is a main effect on tasks $[\chi(2)^2 = 11.758, p < 0.003]$. Investigating pairwise comparisons with the least significant difference (LSD) reveals that a significant difference in post length exists between allergy (mean = 63.02, S.E. = 5.381) and foodborne illness (mean = 45.72, S.E. = 4.096) ($p < 0.001$), and between flu (mean = 58.64, S.E. = 2.725) and foodborne illness ($p < 0.004$), suggesting that foodborne illness has a significantly shorter post length than both allergy and flu. However, no significant differences were observed between allergy and flu.

**Table 1.** Descriptive statistics of three main measurements among models. (Note. "A" denotes word embedding model, "B" denotes semantic model, and "C" denotes baseline model.).

| Model | Post Length | | | | Med-Related Word Count | | | | Existence of Descriptions | | |
|---|---|---|---|---|---|---|---|---|---|---|---|
| | Mean | S.E. | Min. | Max. | Mean | S.E. | Min. | Max. | True | False | TTL. |
| A | 59.87 | 26.937 | 18 | 154 | 3.87 | 1.602 | 0 | 9 | 35 | 19 | 54 |
| B | 62.81 | 34.575 | 19 | 189 | 4.56 | 2.661 | 0 | 12 | 33 | 21 | 54 |
| C | 60.93 | 33.389 | 15 | 149 | 3.89 | 2.724 | 0 | 16 | 35 | 19 | 54 |

Using GEE, a linear function was applied to evaluate the association between medical-related terminology and three within-subject variables: model, task, and operating order. This reveals a main effect for model $[\chi(2)^2 = 23.941, p < 0.000]$, but no significant effects for task. A pairwise comparison with LSD reveals that participants composed posts using significantly more medical-related terminology ($p < 0.002$) with the semantic model (mean = 4.65, S.E. = 0.236) than with the word embedding model (mean = 3.21, S.E. = 0.560).

When a post includes more detailed context information, experts may better understand the user's questions and expectations. We asked the three curators to note whether posts contained descriptions about patient background and the timing of the illness outbreak. If the majority of the curators believed the post to be informative, it was labeled "T" (True); otherwise, it was labeled "F" (False). Using the GEE binary logistic function, we analyzed the association between the existence of descriptions and model, task, and operating order, revealing main effects of model $[\chi(2)^2 = 11.765, p < 0.003]$ and task $[\chi(2)^2 = 25.799, p < 0.000]$ on the existence of descriptions. In contrast to the baseline model (mean = 0.50, S.E. = 0.006), when using the word embedding model (mean = 0.48, S.E. = 0.006), participants were less likely to augment posts with descriptive information (OR = 0.910, $p < 0.002$). A pairwise model comparison demonstrated that participants were significantly less likely to add details when using the word embedding model than when using the semantic model ($p < 0.014$).

When comparing flu to the other two tasks, participants dealing with foodborne illness were more likely to add descriptions to their posts (OR = 1.107, $p < 0.004$). A pairwise task comparison indicated that (1) foodborne illness (mean = 0.51, S.E. = 0.006) and allergy (mean = 0.48, S.E. = 0.005) and (2) foodborne illness and flu (mean = 0.49, S.E. = 0.006) were significantly different. That is, participants were significantly more likely to include descriptions in a post about foodborne illness than about allergy ($p < 0.000$) or flu ($p < 0.004$). There was no significant difference between allergy and flu in terms of the existence of descriptions.

We also evaluated which RS better supported users to generate posts by examining the adoption of two experimental models (word embedding and semantic) and the usage of medical-related terms. To gauge the quality of the embedding and semantic models, we first counted the number of adoptions during the asking process. From the viewpoint of total acceptance of the recommended terminology, the embedding model (43 times) yielded more than the semantic model (31 times). However, no significant effect was observed in model or task on the number of adoptions. Different from observing effectiveness of RSs, we also examined the amount of used time between RS (i.e., the embedding model or the semantic model) and the baseline model that is without recommendations with the GEE method. No significant effect was found, which demonstrates that users did not spend more time when using RSs compared to the baseline model.

In summary, in terms of effectiveness, applying an RS (i.e., the embedding model and semantic model) does affect asker posting behavior and encourages them to use medical-related terminology and include more description in posts. There was no significant relation between post length and whether askers used an RS. Participants were less likely to describe situations in detail when using word embedding than the semantic system. When analyzing tasks, the result shows that longer posts were used for foodborne illness than for allergy and flu. Participants included more details for foodborne illness scenarios than for allergy and flu. In terms of efficiency, applying RSs will not cost users more time to formulate their posts when they provide more details in their questions.

*5.2. Opinion Analysis*

We recruited two experts—one a pharmacist and the other a physician—to go through three lists of posts categorized by different tasks. Before asking the experts for their opinions, we interviewed them to determine how they judge their willingness to answer questions. Both experts indicated that complete and clear descriptions of conditions provide better information to help users. We use "willingness" to indicate their willingness to provide answers, and "completeness" and "clarity" as two factors that affect their willingness. The experts were asked to rate the three factors of posts on a five-point Likert scale (ranging from strongly disagree "1" to strongly agree "5"). The descriptive results of the three factors from the two experts are provided in Table 2.

**Table 2.** Descriptive statistics of three factors.

|  | Factor | Word Embedding | Semantic | Baseline |
|---|---|---|---|---|
| Expert 1 (pharmacist) | Willingness | 3.59 ± 0.09 | 3.52 ± 0.09 | 3.57 ± 0.06 |
|  | Completeness | 3.93 ± 0.07 | 3.98 ± 0.08 | 3.94 ± 0.09 |
|  | Clarity | 4.22 ± 0.08 | 4.17 ± 0.08 | 4.15 ± 0.00 |
| Expert 2 (physician) | Willingness | 3.83 ± 0.09 | 3.70 ± 0.08 | 3.96 ± 0.09 |
|  | Completeness | 2.98 ± 0.11 | 2.85 ± 0.12 | 2.93 ± 0.07 |
|  | Clarity | 3.20 ± 0.10 | 3.19 ± 0.13 | 3.20 ± 0.14 |

Inter-rater reliability with Cohen's Kappa [39] was adopted to evaluate the rating agreement of the two experts, yielding low Kappa values for willingness, completeness, and clarity [40], which could be attributable to their different backgrounds (pharmacist vs. physician), leading to different opinions in communicating with their patients [41]. Since there was no significant difference among the models for each expert, a linear function with GEE was applied to evaluate the association between willingness, completeness, and clarity and the existence of description separately on the expert judgment. The judgment of both pharmacist and physician showed that willingness (pharmacist: $[\chi(1)^2 = 22.194, p < 0.000]$; physician: $[\chi(1)^2 = 9.693, p < 0.002]$) and completeness (pharmacist: $[\chi(1)^2 = 62.246, p < 0.000]$; physician: $[\chi(1)^2 = 87.103, p < 0.001]$) are highly related to the existence of description. The pairwise comparison of "False" and "True" label descriptions in the physician's willingness (False: mean = 3.61, S.E. = 0.42; True: mean = 3.78, S.E. = 0.40), the pharmacist's completeness (False: mean = 3.82, S.E. = 0.35; True: mean = 4.14, S.E. = 0.39), and the physician's completeness (False: mean = 2.32, S.E. = 0.73; True: mean=3.13, S.E. = 0.48) indicate that the "True" posts are more likely to get high points from experts. In terms of the effect of clarity on the existence of descriptions, a significant effect was found from the physician's judgment $[\chi(1)^2 = 36.817, p < 0.001]$. If askers did not include greater detail in posts, there was a 65.3% chance of getting less clarity points from the physician.

As we found that having a description contributes to higher points from experts, we directly investigated those posts with sufficient description between models to gain further insight. The judgment of both experts indicates that completeness is an important effect. The pairwise comparisons show that the semantic model is more likely to yield higher completeness points than word embedding and the baseline, whereas the word embedding model is more likely to get high completeness points from experts than baseline.

Clarity, the last measurement, was found to be significantly different between (1) word embedding and baseline ($p < 0.000$) and (2) semantic and baseline ($p < 0.002$). This suggests that using the posting RSs with sufficient post details is more likely to yield a high expert rating.

To examine the relationship between the quality of a user questions, the question's length (i.e., word count and med-related word count) and expert's opinions (including willingness, completeness and clarity) were investigated. As the recruited experts had diverse medical backgrounds and possessed non-identical perspectives, their opinions were therefore analyzed separately. The correlation results revealed that the experts' completeness and clarity were greatly affected by the word count and med-related word count (the results in Table 3 showed marginal differences in expert 1 and statistical differences in expert 2); however, experts' willingness was less likely to be influenced by the question length. In addition, the results indicated that the word count significantly impacted expert 2's opinions.

Table 3. Correlation results between word counts and expert opinions.

| | Factor | Word Count | Med-Related Word Count |
|---|---|---|---|
| Expert 1 (pharmacist) | Willingness | Nonsignificant | Nonsignificant |
| | Completeness | r = 0.136, p = 0.084 | Nonsignificant |
| | Clarity | r = 0.145, p = 0.066 | Nonsignificant |
| Expert 2 (physician) | Willingness | Nonsignificant | Nonsignificant |
| | Completeness | r = 0.468, p < 0.001 | r = 0.266, p = 0.001 |
| | Clarity | r = 0.192, p = 0.014 | r = 0.248, p = 0.001 |

## 6. Discussion

It is easy to find online Q&A forums with mechanisms to support finding existing relevant questions, but it is hard to find supportive systems that focus on post composition during the query process. This study demonstrates that the proposed posting RSs are more effective and efficient than the baseline (with no RS support).

The amount of medical-related terminology has a significant effect on models, showing that using an RS yields more medical-related terminology compared to when an RS is not used. However, the sematic model has a stronger influence than the embedding model, whereas the word embedding model usually yields more relevant topics based on common wordings than the semantic dictionary-based corpus. The semantic corpus, constructed by manipulating WordNet, performs well particularly when askers are able to query more professionally. The weaker performance of the embedding model might be due to the small training dataset, leading to imprecise or ambiguous recommendations. To improve the usefulness of the word embedding model, the future work must collect larger amounts of in-domain data and then re-train the model.

Detail in a post is an important element for experts to evaluate posts because they cannot diagnose a person via back-and-forth interaction: A single question is usually not enough for experts to solve the problem. Our data reveal the main effects between having descriptions on models and tasks. A deeper investigation indicates the embedding model is less likely to result in more details in a post, in contrast to the baseline. This indicates that people are still used to a posting procedure without interference. In addition, as it is merely a simulated scenario, most participants lacked a strong motivation to find a solution. They feel more comfortable writing posts in a stress-free situation without interruptions. In addition, as allergy and flu are common experiences, participants may assume that most readers are familiar with them and thus omit details when describing the malady. In contrast, when generating posts about foodborne illness, which is less familiar, participants provided more details when describing the conditions. Post length was not found to differ significantly between models but it did between tasks, which indicates that different illnesses do affect post length. The interviews revealed that most participants are not familiar with foodborne illness; this unfamiliarity caused participants to compose posts that were shorter than those for allergy and flu.

Suggestions from the embedding and semantic models were adopted 43 and 31 times, respectively. However, each model had 54 posts and adoption was unevenly distributed in each post: For many posts, none of the recommended terminology was selected. This indicates more resources would be needed in the future work to build a robust word embedding model. If a recommendation looks strange, even though the average score for "want to use this kind of topic RS someday" was 3.81/5.00 in the post-questionnaire, poor user experiences dictate that it would be difficult to attract attention.

To explain the connection between a post RS and higher scores from experts, we further conducted a pairwise evaluation between the interaction of models with descriptions labeled "True" and three measurements. According to the result of the first expert (the pharmacist), completeness is higher when using a posting RS with detailed descriptions. Completeness and clarity of the second expert (physician) are increased if an asker uses the RS and provides more details in a post. Although results vary between experts, we conclude it is possible to elicit a response from experts after using an RS and adding details. In addition, we found that willingness is not significantly affected by a post RS that adds details, because the professional ethic of medical experts is to answer patient questions; thus, they seldom refuse to answer such requests. Therefore, willingness may not be a good measurement.

As both physicians and pharmacists are highly specialized and regulated professions, through the rigorous medical training, we assume individual differences in attitude would inject little influence of the collected expert opinions. Therefore, in terms of expert opinions, since professionals from different disciplines have different norms in communicating with their patients, it is difficult to find common ground between physicians and pharmacists [41]. For physicians, the priority is to thoroughly understand the situation and any information that relates to the patient's symptoms [41,42], whereas as pharmacists tend to focus on medicinal instructions and materials; it is more important for them to gather all of the critical information than to understand the situation as a whole [41]. Despite the marked difference between the two experts' evaluations, both pharmacist and physician consider willingness and completeness to depend greatly on the existence of sufficient detail in the problem description. Posts labeled "False" are less likely to earn points from the expert. The physician's judgment also demonstrates that clarity is an important factor as well. According to the interviews with experts, getting a good score from the physician means the post is easily understood by experts. Easily comprehensible posts are more likely to be solved. Although some interesting results are observed, however, due to the small number of the experts used in this study, future work should address this issue and recruit more medical specialists to further validate our findings as well as exclude any potential issues that may arise from the sample size limitation.

## 7. Conclusions

In this work, we present a post RS that suggests relevant and useful ideas and terminology to support users who are composing posts to ask questions. Effectiveness and efficiency are evaluated in terms of the usability of the proposed post RSs (RQ1). Combining the result with RQ1, we evaluate the feasibility of the resultant posts to see if experts assign them higher scores (RQ2).

This research reveals that current Q&A forum RSs have reached a plateau because they only recommend relevant questions based on the words in the query and then send query requests to those who might be able to help the askers. These supportive methods may be infeasible when posts are difficult for the system to classify and users may decline to bother people who are reluctant to answer. In addition, most Q&A online forums do nothing about post actions in the asking process. Also, the existence of unanswered posts underlines the necessity of optimizing the posting process. After this user study, we found it is possible to change user posting behaviors by participating more in the asking process via a posting RS. Askers are also willing to be supported by the RS feature when formulating questions in unfamiliar domains. Whether the recommended terminology can be adopted directly or is relevant enough to modify posts conceptually, our RS suggests concrete and possible ideas to askers, which constitutes a new type of manipulation in the Q&A domain. We therefore anticipate that the posting RS will support users to better formulate posts and find solutions in a more efficient manner.

The proposed posting RS is also applicable to domains other than healthcare. Take e-commerce for example: when people are purchasing products that they are not familiar with, it is common for them to ask for details before and after the purchase. If there were a system that would help users compose better questions, the resultant posts would better match the FAQs. If solutions are still not found in the FAQs, websites present previous posts from other askers. An advanced posting RS could attempt to resolve questions before posting to the forum. The unanswered rate would decrease and the likelihood of getting a solution would increase. Any industry that fields many queries is suitable for more participation in the user's asking process.

For the future work, the number of participants should be increased, the illness selection should be reconsidered, and the data resources to make a RS should be expanded. The recommendation presentation should be made more user-friendly. Second, some participants felt the selected tasks to be so general that they did not need an RS to complete the post, whereas others considered the selected tasks too difficult to compose a post about, suggesting feedback varied widely among participants. In the future, a study with various tasks and more participants might be able to bring us more insights for designing the posting recommender systems. Also, the quality assessment of our posting RS is important. Collecting more data from healthcare forums is the most direct way to improve the performance of posting RSs. However, what kind of data resources should be selected to build the posting RS? If the quality of the input (existing posts on online forums) is low, there would be little chance of producing a high-quality RS. Therefore, training models on high quality posts is one way to enhance the usefulness of the RS.

Regardless of whether the RS data sources support high quality revisions, the quality of posting RSs should be evaluated in advance. One potential approach is to take the first sentence of good WebMD questions to see whether the proposed RS can suggest sufficient terminology to formulate the subsequent sentences. Sufficient terminology could be identified by mapping the recommendations to the rest of the sentences of good questions. Then we could observe if the relevant terminology suggested matches the terminology used in the subsequent sentences of every post. Further study with eye-tracking augmentation could be useful to learn more about interactions between the process of decision-making and types of posting RSs.

In addition, while posting recommendations can help to compose posts in a more detailed way to attract experts to answer, the more detailed content provided the more sensitive data releases online. This is always a dilemma between efficiency and privacy.

Practitioners might need to pay attention to the forum policy when providing a posting recommender system.

**Author Contributions:** Y.-L.L.: conceptualization, methodology, writing—original draft. S.-Y.C.: methodology, writing—review & editing. Y.-J.C.: software, validation, formal analysis, investigation, data curation. All authors have read and agreed to the published version of the manuscript.

**Funding:** This research was supported by the Ministry of Science and Technology, Taiwan, under Grant MOST 107-2410-H-004-098-MY3 and MOST 109-2410-H-004-067-MY2.

**Institutional Review Board Statement:** The study was conducted according to the guidelines of the Declaration of Helsinki, and approved by the Research Ethics Committee of National Chengchi University (protocol code: NCCU-REC-201709-I036; date of approval: 16 August 2019).

**Informed Consent Statement:** Informed consent was obtained from all subjects involved in the study.

**Data Availability Statement:** The data presented in this study are available on request from the corresponding author. The data are not publicly available due to privacy concerns.

**Acknowledgments:** The authors thank Tsung-Hua Shen, a research assistant in the College of Pharmacy at Taipei Medical University, and Po-Yu Liao, a Physician at Liao ENT Clinic, for their valuable assistance in reviewing and categorizing the participants' queries in the opinion analysis phase.

**Conflicts of Interest:** The authors declare no conflict of interest.

## Appendix A  Supportive Paragraphs for Participants

| | Foodborne Illness |
|---|---|
| [Task 1] | Lisa just got a call from her aunt who is a nurse in a nearby hospital. Many students were sent to the emergency room this afternoon because of a foodborne illness. It is said that the food vendor failed to check the expiration date for their meat and sent it to several chain restaurants. Unfortunately, Lisa's favorite restaurant gets meat from this vendor and she just went there for brunch. Just to be safe, Lisa looked up information on food contamination on Google. The following paragraph is what she found. Please write down the questions you would ask on the forum if you found yourself in a similar situation. You may post either as yourself or Lisa. |

Food poisoning symptoms vary with the source of contamination. Most types of food poisoning cause nausea, vomiting, watery or bloody diarrhea, abdominal pain, and cramps and fever. Signs and symptoms may start within hours after eating the contaminated food, or they may begin days or even weeks later. Sickness caused by food poisoning generally lasts from a few hours to several days. Sometimes, there are serious complications. Whether you become ill after eating contaminated food depends on the organism, the amount of exposure, your age and your health. High-risk groups include older adults, pregnant women, infants and young children, and people with chronic disease, who are highly affected by their immune system or changes in metabolism and circulation. Food poisoning is especially serious and potentially life-threatening for them. At home people can stay safe by taking preventions such as separating raw foods from ready-to-eat foods, washing hands before eating, and defrosting foods safely.

| | Foodborne Illness |
|---|---|
| [Task 2] | You are doing a term project related on foodborne illnesses. The professor has asked you to organize questions for a class discussion and to post them on the Online Discussion Board before next week's class. You may share your opinions in the post. You may also propose questions, for instance, concepts you didn't understand after reading the supportive paragraph, or alternatively, guess what questions corresponds to the concept. |

Food poisoning syndrome results from the ingestion of water and a wide variety of food contaminated with pathogenic organisms (bacteria, viruses, parasites, and fungi), their toxins and chemicals. Food poisoning must be suspected when an acute illness with gastrointestinal or neurological manifestations affects two or more persons or animals who have shared a meal during the previous 72 h. The term generally used encompasses both food-related infection and food-related intoxication. Some microbiologists consider microbial food poisoning to be different from foodborne infections. In microbial food poisoning, the microbes multiply readily in the food prior to consumption, whereas in foodborne infection, food is merely the vector for microbes that do not grow on their transient substrate. Other consider food poisoning as intoxication of food by chemicals or toxins from bacteria or fungi.

Foodborne illness (FBI), often called food poisoning, is caused by pathogens or certain chemicals present in ingested food bacteria, viruses, molds, and worms. Protozoa causing diseases are all pathogens, although there are also harmless and beneficial bacteria that are used to make yogurt and cheese. Some chemicals that cause foodborne illness are natural components of food, whereas others may be accidentally added during production and processing, either through carelessness or pollution. The two most common types of food borne illness are intoxication and infection. Intoxication occurs when toxins produced by the pathogens cause food poisoning, whereas infection is caused by the ingestion of food containing pathogens.

[Reference]

https://www.omicsonline.org/open-access/a-review-on-major-food-borne-bacterial-illnesses-2329-891X-1000176.pdf

https://www.mayoclinic.org/diseases-conditions/food-poisoning/symptoms-causes/syc-20356230

| | Allergy |
|---|---|
| [Task 1] | Steven has a nasal allergy. When the weather changes, his illness gets worse. Yesterday, his sneezing was so bad he went through a whole tissue box in 20 minutes! Interestingly, Steven recently discovered his 5-year-old son is allergic to seafood, especially crab and shrimp. If the food is not fresh enough, his son gets an itchy rash all over his body - symptoms totally different from his own. Although they have taken medicine for allergies, Steven wonders if they need to see a doctor. The paragraph below is an overview he found on Google. Please think of questions you would ask on the forum if you found yourself in a similar situation. You may post either as yourself or Steven. |

Some people suffer with seasonal allergies for years before learning about effective treatments. If allergy symptoms are not treated early, they can actually worsen over time. Here are five symptoms you should not ignore: runny or stuffy nose, sinus pressure, sneezing, itchy eyes, and postnasal drip. You may avoid your allergy triggers or ask doctors about other ways to get relief. Food allergies are an immune system reaction that occurs soon after eating a certain food. It is easy to confuse a food allergy with a much more common reaction known as food intolerance. While bothersome, food intolerance is a less serious condition that does not involve the immune system. Itching in the mouth, swelling of the lips, face, or other parts of the body, etc., are common signs of the food allergies. People who have similar symptoms should keep away from food triggers, for example, shellfish, peanuts, and fish.

---

[Task 2]

**Allergy**

You are doing a term project related to world allergy proportions. The professor has asked you to organize questions for a class discussion and to post them on the Online Discussion Board before next week's class. You may share your opinions in the post. You may also propose questions, for instance, concepts you didn't understand after reading the supportive paragraph, or alternatively, guess what questions corresponds to the concept.

---

Allergies involve almost every organ of the body in variable combinations with a broad spectrum of possible symptoms; thus, their manifestations cover a wide range of phenotypes. Studies in Europe have shown that up to 30% of the population suffer from allergic rhinoconjunctivitis, whereas up to 20% suffer from asthma and 15% from allergic skin conditions. These numbers match those reported for other parts of the world, such as the USA and Australia. Food allergies are becoming more frequent and severe; occupational allergies, drug allergies, and allergies to insect stings (occasionally fatal) further aggravate the burden of the allergy epidemic. Despite the popular belief that allergies are mild conditions, a considerable and increasing proportion of patients (15–20%) have severe, debilitating disease and are under constant fear of death from a possible asthma attack or anaphylactic shock. Within the EU, there are nevertheless wide geographical variations in the incidence of allergies with a south to north and east to west gradient. An alarming observation is that most allergic conditions start in childhood and peak during highly productive years of individuals, with allergic rhinitis affecting up to 45% of 20 to 40-year-old Europeans. The numbers may even be an underestimation, as many patients do not report their symptoms or are not properly diagnosed. Indeed, it is estimated that approximately 45% of patients have never received a diagnosis. Notwithstanding evidence suggesting a plateau in some areas, the European Academy of Allergy and Clinical Immunology (EAACI) warns that in less than 15 years more than half of the European population will suffer from some type of allergy!

[Reference]
https://www.ncbi.nlm.nih.gov/pmc/articles/PMC3539924/
https://www.webmd.com/allergies/features/allergy-symptoms#2
https://www.mayoclinic.org/diseases-conditions/food-allergy/symptoms-causes/syc-20355095

---

[Task 1]

**Flu**

In Tommy's school, one in four students has come down with the flu, so the junior high school committee has claimed it is necessary to close the school for disinfection. Tommy's mom is concerned about the symptoms of this flu because she forgot to have Tommy get the vaccination this year. Please think of questions you would ask on the forum if you were in a similar situation. You may post either as yourself or one of Tommy's parents. The following information seems useful to Tommy's mom. Feel free to refer to it if you need ideas about what to say.

---

I. Seasonal influenza (or "flu") is most often caused by type A or B influenza viruses. Symptoms include a sudden onset of fever, cough, headache, muscle and joint pain, sore throat, and a runny nose. The cough can be severe and can last 2 or more weeks. Most people recover from fever and other symptoms within a week without requiring medical attention. However, influenza can cause severe illness or death in high-risk groups.

II. Someone with the flu may have a high fever, for example, their temperature may be around 104 °F (40 °C). People with the flu often feel achy and extra tired. They may lose their appetites. The fever and aches usually disappear within a few days, but the sore throat, cough, stuffy nose, and tiredness may continue for a week or more. The flu also can cause vomiting, belly pain, and diarrhea. Most people who get the flu get better on their own after the virus runs its course. However, call your doctor if you have the flu and any of these things happen: (a) you are getting worse instead of better; (b) you have trouble breathing or develop other complications, such as a sinus infection; or (c) you have a medical condition (for example, diabetes, heart problems, asthma, or other lung problems). Most teens can take acetaminophen or ibuprofen to help with fever and aches.

| | Flu |
|---|---|
| [Task 2] | You are doing a term project on the flu. The professor has asked you to organize questions for a class discussion and to post them on the Online Discussion Board before next week's class. You may share your opinions in the post. You may also propose questions, for instance, concepts you didn't understand after reading the supportive paragraph, or alternatively, guess what questions will be provided by the human society to find information like the following paragraphs. |

What scientists dream of is a vaccine that can protect against any flu strain for years or even a lifetime. This so-called universal flu vaccine is still a long way off, if it is even possible. However, many labs are dusting off past projects on broad flu vaccines, spurred by new funding and fears that H5N1, the deadly avian influenza that has swept across half the world, could acquire the ability to be transmitted from human to human. Until now, "flu has never been before high enough on the radar screen" for companies in particular to follow through with a strong push for a universal vaccine, says Gary Nabel, director of the Vaccine Research Center at the U.S. National Institute of Allergy and Infectious Diseases (NIAID) in Bethesda, Maryland.

Doing so, however, means coming up with an alternative way to stimulate immunity to the virus. The tried-and-true technique for seasonal flu uses a killed virus vaccine that works mainly by triggering antibodies to hemagglutinin (HA), the glycoprotein on the virus's surface that it uses to bind to human cells. Hemagglutinin and neuraminidase (NA), another surface glycoprotein that helps newly made viruses exit cells, give strains their names (H5N1, for example). The sequences of HA and NA mutate easily, which is why each season's flu strain—although it may be the same in subtype, such as H3N2—"drifts" slightly from the previous year's, and the annual vaccine must be tailor-made.

To make a universal vaccine for influenza A, which includes the main seasonal flu strains and bird flu, as well as past pandemic strains, some scientists are hoping to use "conserved" flu proteins that do not mutate much year to year. (Influenza B, the other type, occurs only in humans and causes milder symptoms.) Some of the conserved protein vaccines in the works stimulate the production of antibodies as do conventional flu vaccines, whereas others rouse certain immune system cells to battle the virus.

[Reference]
http://science.sciencemag.org/content/312/5772/380
http://www.who.int/features/qa/seasonal-influenza/en/
https://kidshealth.org/en/teens/flu.html

## References

1. Tanis, M. Health-related on-line forums: What's the big attraction? *Health J. Commun.* **2008**, *13*, 698–714. [CrossRef]
2. Zeng, Q.; Kogan, S.; Ash, N.; Greenes, R.A.; Boxwala, A.A. Characteristics of consumer terminology for health information retrieval. *Methods Inf. Med.* **2002**, *41*, 289–298.
3. Riahi, F.; Zolaktaf, Z.; Shafiei, M.; Milios, E. Finding expert users in community question answering. In Proceedings of the 21st International Conference Companion on World Wide Web—WWW '12 Companion, Lyon, France, 16–20 April 2012; pp. 791–798.
4. Li, B.; King, I. Routing questions to appropriate answerers in community question answering services. In Proceedings of the 19th ACM International Conference on Information and Knowledge Management—CIKM '2010, Toronto, ON, Canada, 26–30 October 2010; Volume 10, pp. 1585–1588.
5. Neshati, M.; Fallahnejad, Z.; Beigy, H. On dynamicity of expert finding in community question answering. *Inf. Process. Manag.* **2017**, *53*, 1026–1042. [CrossRef]
6. Agichtein, E.; Castillo, C.; Donato, D.; Gionis, A.; Mishne, G. Finding high-quality content in social media. In Proceedings of the International Conference on Web Search and Web Data Mining—WSDM '08, Seattle, WA, USA, 8–12 February 2008; p. 183.
7. Li, B.; Jin, T.; Lyu, M.R.; King, I.; Mak, B. Analyzing and predicting question quality in community question answering services. In Proceedings of the 21st International Conference Companion on World Wide Web—WWW '12 Companion, Lyon, France, 16–20 April 2012; pp. 775–782.
8. Baltadzhieva. Question quality in community question answering forums: A survey. *ACM Sigkdd Explor. Newsl.* **2015**, *17*, 8–13. [CrossRef]
9. Mikolov, T.; Chen, K.; Corrado, G.; Dean, J. Distributed representations of words and phrases and their compositionality. In Proceedings of the 26th International Conference on Neural Information Processing Systems, Lake Tahoe, NV, USA, 5–8 December 2013; Volume 2, pp. 3111–3119.
10. Jacobs, W.; Amuta, A.O.; Jeon, K.C. Health information seeking in the digital age: An analysis of health information seeking behavior among US adults. *Cogent Soc. Sci.* **2017**, *3*, 1302785. [CrossRef]
11. Haux, R. Health information systems—Past, present, future. *Int. Med. J. Inform.* **2006**, *75*, 268–281. [CrossRef]
12. Isern, D.; Moreno, A. A systematic literature review of agents applied in healthcare. *J. Med. Syst.* **2016**, *40*, 43. [CrossRef]
13. Frost, J.H.; Massagli, M.P. Social uses of personal health information within PatientsLikeMe, an online patient community: What can happen when patients have access to one another's data. *Med. J. Internet Res.* **2008**, *10*, e15. [CrossRef]
14. Bakker, P.; Sádaba, C. The impact of the internet on users. In *The Internet and the Mass Media*; SAGE: London, UK, 2008; pp. 86–101.
15. Budalakoti, S.; Deangelis, D.; Barber, K.S. Expertise modeling and recommendation in online question and answer forums. In Proceedings of the 12th IEEE International Conference on Computational Science and Engineering CSE 2009, Vancouver, BC, Canada, 29–31 August 2009; Volume 4, pp. 481–488.
16. Yang, L.; Amatriain, X. Recommending the world's knowledge: Application of recommender systems at Quora. In Proceedings of the 10th ACM Conference on Recommender Systems, Boston, MA, USA, 15–19 September 2016; p. 389.
17. Xia, X.; Lo, D.; Wang, X.; Zhou, B. Tag recommendation in software information sites. In Proceedings of the 2013 10th Working Conference on Mining Software Repositories, San Francisco, CA USA, 18–19 May 2013; pp. 287–296.
18. Pedro, J.S.; Karatzoglou, A. Question recommendation for collaborative question answering systems with RankSLDA. In Proceedings of the 8th ACM Conference on Recommender Systems 2014, Foster City, CA, USA, 6–10 October 2014; pp. 193–200.
19. Wang, S.; Lo, D.; Vasilescu, B.; Serebrenik, A. EnTagRec++: An enhanced tag recommendation system for software information sites. *Empir. Softw. Eng.* **2018**, *23*, 800–832. [CrossRef]
20. Singh, Y.; Simperl, E. Using semantics to search answers for unanswered questions in Q&A forums. In Proceedings of the 25th International Conference Companion on World Wide Web, Montréal, QC, Canada, 11–15 May 2016; pp. 699–706.
21. Cray, A.T.; Dorfman, E.; Ripple, A.; Ide, N.C.; Jha, M.; Katz, D.G.; Loane, R.F.; Tse, T. Usability issues in developing a Web-based consumer health site. In Proceedings of the AMIA Symposium, Los Angeles, CA, USA, 4–8 November 2000; pp. 556–560.
22. Cho, D.J.H.; Sondhi, P.; Zhai, C.; Schatz, B. Resolving healthcare forum posts via similar thread retrieval. In Proceedings of the 5th ACM Conference on Bioinformatics, Computational Biology, and Health Informatics, Newport Beach, CA, USA, 20–23 September 2014; pp. 33–42.
23. Bochet, A.; Guisolan, S.C.; Munday, M.F.; Noury, O.M.; Polla, R.; Zhao, N.; Soulié, P.; Cosson, P. Cyberchondria. *Rev. Med. Suisse* **2014**, *10*, 4.
24. Spink, A.; Yang, Y.; Jansen, J.; Nykanen, P.; Lorence, D.P.; Ozmutlu, S.; Ozmutlu, H.C. A study of medical and health queries to web search engines. *Health Inform. Libr. J.* **2004**, *21*, 44–51. [CrossRef]
25. Zhang, Y. Contextualizing consumer health information searching: An analysis of questions in a social Q&A community. In Proceedings of the 1st ACM International Health Informatics Symposium 2010, Arlington, VA, USA, 11–12 November 2010; pp. 210–219.
26. Boratto, L.; Carta, S.; Fenu, G.; Saia, R. Semantics-aware content-based recommender systems: Design and architecture guidelines. *Neurocomputing* **2017**, *254*, 79–85. [CrossRef]
27. Ren, H.; Feng, W. Concert: A concept-centric web news recommendation system. In Proceedings of the International Conference on Web-Age Information Management, Beidaihe, China, 14–16 June 2013; pp. 796–798.
28. Hong, M.-D.; Oh, K.-J.; Ga, M.-H.; Jo, G.-S. Content-based recommendation based on social network for personalized news services. *Intell. J. Inf. Syst.* **2013**, *19*, 57–71.

29. Ortega, F.; Hernando, A.; Bobadilla, J.; Kang, J.H. Recommending items to group of users using matrix factorization based collaborative filtering. *Inf. Sci.* **2016**, *345*, 313–324. [CrossRef]
30. Rao, J.; Jia, A.; Feng, Y.; Zhao, D. Personalized news recommendation using ontologies harvested from the web. In Proceedings of the International Conference on Web-Age Information Management, Beidaihe, China, 14–16 June 2013; pp. 781–787.
31. Salton, G.; Buckley, C. Term-weighting approaches in automatic text retrieval. *Inf. Process. Manag.* **1988**, *24*, 513–523. [CrossRef]
32. Fellbaum. WordNet. In *The Encyclopedia of Applied Linguistics*; Wiley: Hoboken, NJ, USA, 2012.
33. Van Damme, C.; Hepp, M.; Siorpaes, K. FolksOntology: An integrated approach for turning folksonomies into ontologies. *Bridg. Gap Semant. Web Web* **2007**, *2*, 57–70.
34. Mikolov, T.; Yih, W.; Zweig, G. Linguistic regularities in continuous space word representations. In Proceedings of the 2013 Conference of the North American Chapter of the Association for Computational Linguistics: Human Language Technologies, Atlanta, GA, USA, 9–14 June 2013; pp. 746–751.
35. Esmeli, R.; Bader-El-Den, M.; Abdullahi, H. Using Word2Vec recommendation for improved purchase prediction. In Proceedings of the IEEE World Congress on Computational Intelligence (WCCI) 2020, Glasgow, UK, 19–24 July 2020.
36. Sapatinas, T. The elements of statistical learning. *Stat. J. R. Soc. Ser. A* **2004**, *167*, 192. [CrossRef]
37. Aigner, M.; Ziegler, G.M. Completing Latin squares. In *Proofs from THE BOOK*; Springer: Berlin/Heidelberg, Germany, 2001; pp. 161–166.
38. Liang, K.Y.; Zeger, S.L. Longitudinal data analysis using generalized linear models. *Biometrika* **1986**, *73*, 13–22. [CrossRef]
39. McHugh, M.L. Interrater reliability: The kappa statistic. *Biochem. Med.* **2012**, *22*, 276–282. [CrossRef]
40. Viera, J.; Garrett, J.M. Understanding interobserver agreement: The kappa statistic. *Fam. Med.* **2005**, *37*, 360–363.
41. Schwartzberg, J.G.; Cowett, A.; VanGeest, J.; Wolf, M.S. Communication techniques for patients with low health literacy: A survey of physicians, nurses, and pharmacists. *Am. Health J. Behav.* **2007**, *1*, 96–104. [CrossRef]
42. Zeng, Q.; Cimino, J.J. Providing multiple views to meet physician information needs. In Proceedings of the Hawaii International Conference on System Sciences, Maui, HI, USA, 7 January 2000; p. 111.

Article

# Sentiment Level Evaluation of 3D Handicraft Products Application for Smartphones Usage

Natinai Jinsakul [1,2], Cheng-Fa Tsai [2,*] and Paohsi Wang [3]

1. Department of Tropical Agriculture and International Cooperation, National Pingtung University of Science and Technology, Pingtung 912, Taiwan; natinai.jin@sru.ac.th
2. Department of Management Information Systems, National Pingtung University of Science and Technology, Pingtung 912, Taiwan
3. Department of Food and Beverage Management, Cheng Shiu University, Kaohsiung 833, Taiwan; 0627@gcloud.csu.edu.tw
* Correspondence: cftsai@mail.npust.edu.tw; Tel.: +886-08-7703201 (ext. 7906)

**Abstract:** Three-dimensional (3D) technology has attracted users' attention because it creates objects that can interact with a given product in a system. Nowadays, Thailand's government encourages sustainability projects through advertising, trade shows and information systems for small rural entrepreneurship. However, the government's systems do not include virtual products with a 3D display. The objective of this study was four-fold: (1) develop a prototype of 3D handicraft product application for smartphones; (2) create an online questionnaire to collect user usage assessment data in terms of five sentiment levels—strongly negative, negative, neutral, positive and strongly positive—in response to the usage of the proposed 3D application; (3) evaluate users' sentiment level in 3D handicraft product application usage; and (4) investigate attracting users' attention to handicraft products after using the proposed 3D handicraft product application. The results indicate that 78.87% of participants' sentiment was positive and strongly positive under accept using 3D handicraft product application, and evaluations in terms of assessing attention paid by participants to the handicraft products revealed that positive and strongly positive sentiment was described by 79.61% of participants. The participants' evaluation results in this study prove that our proposed 3D handicraft product application affected users by attracting their attention towards handicraft products.

**Keywords:** sentiment level evaluation; handicraft product; 3D handicraft products; smartphone applications; user interaction; user's attracting attention

## 1. Introduction

Various advanced and interactive technologies have displayed their efficiency in the processing, promotion and demonstration of products by displaying three-dimensional (3D) products [1,2] of high quality on a screen. Users can access these via their own digital devices such as smartphones [3,4]. The capability and advantages of mobile technology have resulted in the incremental influence and utilization of smartphones, which have also led to the BYOD (Bring Your Own Device) policy. Using a smartphone for e-commerce has led to a gradual increase in online shopping [5]. Increased interest in online shopping [6] has resulted in various studies on 3D technology [1,2,7,8]. This is because 3D technology can show how objects interact with products. Consequently, this affects the shopping motivation of consumers, attracting their interest in the products.

Regarding the context of Thailand, in 2019, the Thai economy was projected to grow moderately by 2.7% in 2020, and it continues to experience growth due to foreign demand [9]. The agricultural sector grew by 1.5% in Quarter 3 of 2019 in accordance with the government's policy [9]. In addition, Thailand's digital economy has gained importance since establishing a new ministry called the Ministry for Digital Economic and Society in 2016 [10]. This was because the utilization of the Internet, accessed by smartphones, became more widespread in Thai society; by 2020, Thai people had superior Internet usage compared to the global average with 59% [11] of Thailand's population (65.9 million) having access [10]. This has influenced the generation of new business forms; the Thai government has announced significant projects related to the digital economy's growth, such as Digital Thailand, Thailand 4.0, Digital Park and University 4.0. The digital strategy of Thailand is described as follows [10]:

- Analyze the main schemes that provide opportunities for the development of a digital economy.
- Create flexibility to help decrease the strictness of government organizations.
- Quick wins and high performance are significant.
- Utilize universal innovation and professionalism for establishing a better digital economy.

Thai handicraft products can provide people in rural areas with supplementary income through products from their local resources. Various previous studies have recognized the importance of handicraft products [7,12–15]. Areas of community development expertise have been developed, with the One Tambon (subdistrict) One Product (OTOP) project supporting the sustainability of products from rural areas [16–18]. This scheme is modeled on One Village One Product (OVOP) in Japan [19]. OTOP is a small rural entrepreneurship that produces several kinds of products from raw natural resources, using inherited abilities that rely on the local area's ancient wisdom. Products such as textiles, wooden products, baskets and food include Thai handicraft products sold to tourists [16–18].

Thailand's government encouraged OTOP marketing through advertising, established trade show exhibitions and generated an information system for trading between manufacturers and consumers [16–18]. Our study refers to the government-provided information system, which does not support 3D product displays. Such displays could better attract consumers' attention to products than the current system can and could be one channel through which to support local handicraft producers and small rural entrepreneurship. This work investigates customers' sentiment level evaluation regarding the proposed 3D handicraft product application prototype we developed, and for which the study seeks to determine the users' feelings when using the application by collecting sentiment data utilizing an online questionnaire.

In this study, inspired by the idea of sentiment level evaluation, we used data that came from participants' questionnaire answers. The concept diagram of this work is shown in Figure 1. In the first step, a participant, using our 3D handicraft product application on their smartphone, completed an online questionnaire, with the answers collected in cloud storage.

In the second step, data preprocessing downloaded participants' answer data from cloud drive, imported to data to statistical software and removed useless attributes. These are appropriate steps for using in the final process of sentiment level evaluation by applying statistical software with average function for a 3D handicraft product application usage and five levels: strongly negative, negative, neutral, positive and strongly positive.

The purpose of this study was to examine how users feel when using a 3D handicraft product application on a smartphone, using questionnaire data of participants' answer, which offers the advantage of representing the user sentiment level after application usage. Consequently, this study was divided into four objectives: (1) develop a 3D handicraft product application for smartphones; (2) create an online questionnaire to collect user usage assessment data; (3) evaluate users' sentiment level in 3D handicraft product application usage; and (4) investigate attracting users' attention to handicraft products after using the proposed 3D handicraft product application.

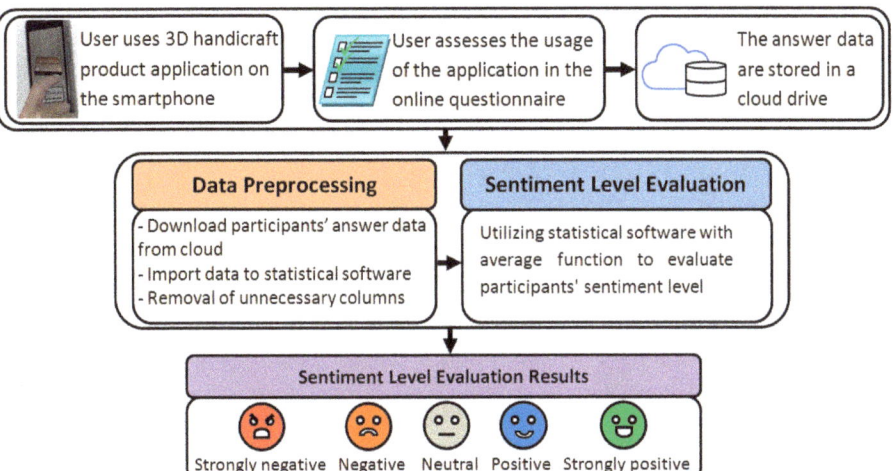

**Figure 1.** The concept of sentiment level evaluation approach employs data from an online questionnaire.

This paper is structured as follows. Section 1 provides the rationale and objective of the research. Section 2 includes related works and strengths for comparing with our work. Section 3 includes the 3D handicraft product application, the literature review for generating the online questionnaire and the data collection method. Section 4 gives the experimental results of sentiment level evaluation and attracting users' attention. Section 5 provides a discussion of the research findings and suggests directions for future study. Finally, Section 6 presents our conclusions.

## 2. Related Works

There are several related works regarding sentiment analysis applied for tracking human behavior. For example, the authors of [20] utilized data from online social media posts for training with the proposed machine learning techniques to generate a dynamic dictionary system for separating people's opinions, reaching good accuracy results of 90.21%. The authors of [21] produced machine learning models to identify people's activity in social networking by the activity providing the emotional sentiment by the proposed models, which obtained the positive rate of 87.50% and a negative rate of 95.90%. The authors of [22] generated machine learning for sentiment prediction based on people's ranking in online social media by combining behavior with social data with word polarity classes, and the proposed method obtained an accuracy of 85%.

Because sentiment analysis using natural language processing can be adopted in the area of linguistics, the authors of [23] created the experiment to compare machine learning approaches for the human language in the text data for sentiment classification by defining the verb, adjective and adverbs for the classes, gaining the accuracy of 88.74%. The authors of [24] used a sentiment dataset to train a machine learning method for extracting the meaning from each vocabulary item to the sentences in the micro-blog by the proposed machine learning method, achieving the precision of 92.87%. Furthermore, the authors of [25] also proposed machine learning for sentiment analysis by using text and message data in English and Chinese from micro-blogs to match in sentiment classes and then provided an indication represented by an emoticon—the performance obtained the accuracy of 88.30%. The authors of [26] considered that the conversation in social networking has several topics for which the researchers established multi-sentiment classification using the proposed machine learning method trained with a domain sentiment media dataset. The proposed model gained an overall sentiment classification accuracy of 71.79%.

Sentiment analysis is also applied in the field of education. For example, the authors of [27] investigated student satisfaction with massive open online courses (MOOCs) by employing supervised machine learning models to identify the course features, where the capability evaluation indicated an F-score of 88.32% for student satisfaction for learning via video instruction. In comparison, the authors of [28] focused on using sentiment classification to enhance higher education standards by adopting machine learning as the classifier to isolate students' comments, achieving an accuracy of 83% for classification performance.

Several works in the literature cover e-commerce and online shopping by conducting the sentiment analysis concentrating on customer comments on products and services. The authors of [29] developed a voting classification technique with machine learning by using data from customer reviews for customers' decisions. The results show that the proposed approach increases classification ability by producing an accuracy of 86.13%. The authors of [30] analyzed posts and discussions regarding multi-sentiment class across several topics in employing products and services with machine learning algorithms. The proposed method obtained an accuracy of 60.2% for seven categories and two classes produced an accuracy of 81.3%. The authors of [31] implemented machine learning techniques with customer experiences in reviews of products and service quality in e-commerce, where the information can be represented in emotions and opinions by the results in terms of precision at 80.10%. The authors of [32] generated a machine learning technique for multi-domains for e-commerce goods reviews and sentiment classification by gaining the average classification accuracy for cross-domain sentiment classification of 77.52% and average accuracy for domain-specific classification of 85.58%. The authors of [33] applied machine learning algorithms for identifying sentiment by big consumer review data for the experience in using e-commerce and real-time shopping. The ability of the system is effective, achieving accuracy close to 98%.

Machine learning for sentiment analysis has been applied in the case of hotel and tourism services. For example, the authors of [34] utilized the contextual data in the text comments of hotel service training with ensemble learning by achieving an accuracy of 96.03%. The authors of [35] developed machine learning methods for sentiment analysis of online tourist comments to provide good comments and suggestions for other interested tourists, with the classification results obtaining an accuracy of 81.87%.

The entertainment area can also utilize sentiment analysis. For example, the authors of [36] conducted the extraction of machine learning models, with the results showing a suitable machine learning algorithm that obtained a classification accuracy of 82.50%. The authors of [37] studied the machine learning technique for sentiment analysis by creating a sentiment dictionary for users to message online while watching shows in a real-time video on the screen, for which the proposed technique obtained a classification accuracy of 88.20% and extracted emotional data from the video by using words consisting of several emotions.

In cases of disaster and security, the authors of [38] applied an approach driven by big data for disaster response via sentiment classification, with the data of the disaster gathered from social networks and classified information following the affected people's requirements, categorized with the machine learning algorithm for analyzing the people's sentiment by extracting features of parts of speech and lexicon, indicating good results and achieving high classification precision up to 95%. The authors of [39] investigated sentiment analysis in terms of authentication, availability, integrity and confidentiality to estimate that reviews are trustworthy, by using the machine learning categorization. The outcome showed that 23% of applications have reliability over 0.5. In comparison, 77% of other remaining applications had reliability lower than 0.5. The appropriate application related to topical reliability contained poor security.

The above related works apply machine learning techniques for sentiment analysis in several areas, which differ from this study. We provide the summarized strengths and key differences between these related works and our work in Table 1.

Table 1. Related works and strengths for comparing with our work.

| Related Works | Strengths and Key Differences |
|---|---|
| Tracking human behavior [20–22] | - These related works applied micro-blog datasets for developing the model for sentiment analysis.<br>- The system can analyze sentiment from online posts and classifies opinions in real-time.<br>- The model can identify the online behavioral characteristics of users and generate emotion ratings.<br>- The machine learning model can analyze text polarity and assist in indicating the people's sentiments from comments. |
| Linguistic [23–26] | - These related studies utilized datasets from micro-blogs.<br>- The developed a new technique suitable for sentiment analysis.<br>- The approach can represent the emotional tendencies from the sentiment of Chinese sentences.<br>- The model can enhance the capability of micro-blog sentiment identification, especially for Chinese. |
| Education [27,28] | - These collected datasets came from student comments after registering for the course.<br>- They generated the suitable framework of machine learning for student sentiment analysis to the course.<br>- Machine learning is able to determine the importance of identifying student satisfaction for the course. |
| E-commerce and online shopping [29–33] | - These related works employed micro-blog datasets in e-commerce and online shopping to develop the model for sentiment analysis.<br>- Machine learning in multiple classifiers can improve the sentiment classification ability for the goods and services reviews.<br>- The model can indicate different feelings and present the methodology to understand the product review's sentiment relationships.<br>- The proposed technique can conduct sentiment multi-classification based on the directed weighted ability to identify the product review with good results.<br>- They created a fine-tuned method with the ability to adapt to different topics in terms of product reviews. |
| Hotel and tourism [34,35] | - These works collected datasets from tourist reviews and comments.<br>- The ensemble model's ability in sentiment prediction by integrating many sub-models learned on various sub-datasets.<br>- They generated the framework by integrating multiple machine learning techniques to identify cost, services, transportation and hotels that benefit tourists. |
| Entertainment [36,37] | - These studies obtained datasets from movie reviews and television shows.<br>- The machine learning model can improve multi-sentiment classes for entertainment in the movie review dataset.<br>- The model can handle the emotional direction of the television shows and can identify popularity. |
| Disaster and security [38,39] | - These studies obtained datasets from micro-blogs and application reviews.<br>- The method can visualize and classify the sentiments on several basic infrastructures when affected by the disaster.<br>- The technique can score solutions to notify developers' concerns in confidentiality, integrity, availability and authentication for coding enhancement. |
| Proposed study | - The proposed approach of this study is different from related works in user interface evaluation.<br>- Our work employs datasets collected from simple questionnaires that classified user sentiments level.<br>- Statistical software with average function is applied to evaluate users' sentiment level of 3D handicraft production application for smartphone usage.<br>- The proposed 3D handicraft production application for the smartphone of this study can attract users' attention to handicraft products. |

## 3. Materials and Methods

To prepare for this study, we created the proposed 3D handicraft product application and user interaction. We also reviewed the literature to generate a questionnaire, the data collection methods, the evaluation of sentiment level of proposed application usage and sentiment in terms of attracting participants' attention to handicraft product.

*3.1. 3D Handicraft Product Application*

Each 3D handicraft model was created in open-source software named Blender (version 2.80, Blender Foundation, Amsterdam, The Netherlands) [40] and used to develop an application for a smartphone. The 3D handicraft product application was developed using game engine software Unity (version 2019.4.9, Unity Technologies, San Francisco, CA, USA) [41] and an installed Android SDK to generate an application that would be compatible with an Android system in a smartphone. The application is in both Thai and English; users can change between languages and use the buttons to select and view the 3D handicraft products (Figure 2).

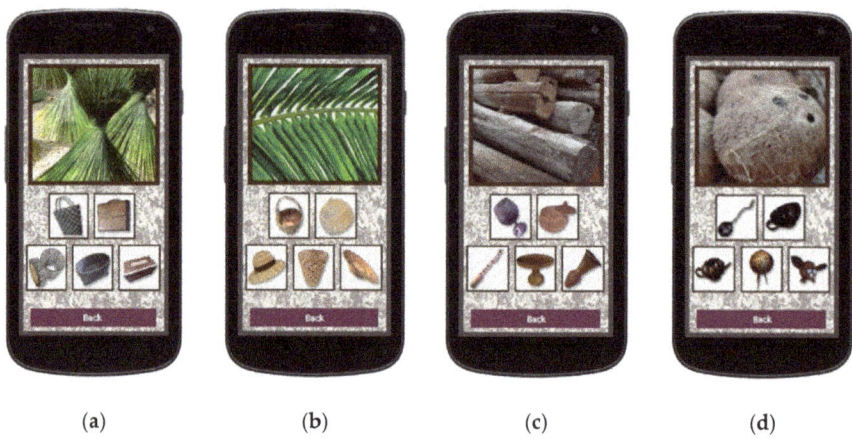

(a)        (b)        (c)        (d)

**Figure 2.** Menu options of several handicraft products created from various rural natural materials: (**a**) sedge; (**b**) mangrove palm leaves; (**c**) timber; and (**d**) coconut shell.

The Thai handicraft products in the application focused on products from rural resources in four categories: sedge, mangrove palm leaves, timber, and coconut shell (Figure 3). A participant can use the application on a smartphone to get a 360-degree look at the product (Figure 4); in addition, the 3D product system displayed text with details on each 3D product, including the product's name, size, price, and usability.

*3.2. Questionnaire Creation*

The literature review investigated several related works in the field of technology assessment, as presented in Table 2, including the perceived ease of use, perceived usefulness, user attitudes, behavioral intention, user interaction, 3D product display and ability to attract attention.

*3.3. Data Collection and Demographic Information*

In total, 2500 participants, who were alumni and students from universities in several locations (thus explaining why the study had many participants), were sent online questionnaires constructed via Google Forms and distributed to their email addresses. Participants were recruited from six regions of Thailand (north, northeast, east, west, central and south). The email included a hyperlink for downloading the 3D handicraft product application for use with the participant's smartphone. Furthermore, participants had to provide primary data and smartphone use habits as smartphone application interaction information. Both the questionnaire and 3D handicraft product application were in the Thai language; the participants' data, including full name and identifying details, were not shown in the collected data. The preliminary participants' information appears, with the total and demographics as percentages, in Table 3; the total and percentage of participants' use smartphone answer are shown in Table 4. The online questionnaire answers were developed on a five-point scale (strongly negative = 1, negative = 2, neutral = 3, positive = 4 and strongly positive = 5) to evaluate sentiment in questions assessing perceived ease of use (PEOU), perceived usefulness (PU), attitude toward (AT), behavioral intention (BT), 3D user interaction (3DUI), 3D product display (3DPD) and attracting attention (AA). After sending the online questionnaire to the 2500 participants' email addresses, 1775 questionnaires were received by the scheduled deadline, for a response rate of 71% (questionnaire sending began 1 June 2019; we waited for responses until 31 December 2019).

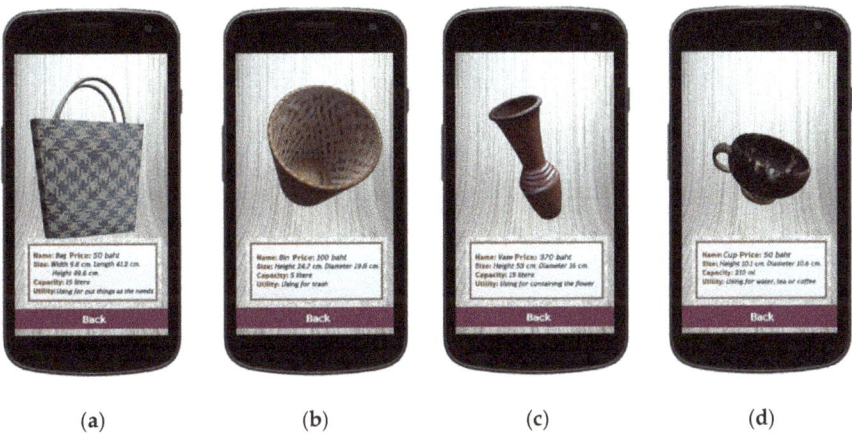

**Figure 3.** 3D handicraft products and details in the smartphone application: (**a**) bag created from sedge, (**b**) bin crafted from mangrove palm leaves, (**c**) vase produced from timber, and (**d**) cup made from coconut shell.

**Figure 4.** User interaction with a 3D handicraft product.

Table 2. Several related works in the field of technology assessment for generating the questionnaire.

| Questionnaire Item | Literature |
| --- | --- |
| 1. Perceived Ease of Use (PEOU)<br>1.1 How easy is it to learn how to use a 3D handicraft product application on a smartphone?<br>1.2 How convenient is it to use a 3D handicraft product application on a smartphone?<br>1.3 How flexible is the 3D handicraft product application on a smartphone? | Users' feelings toward an application are easy to assess. The perceived ease of use indicates the type of user who is expected to employ the application without any difficulty [2,42]. Perceived ease of use (PEOU) was mentioned in the technology acceptance model (TAM) [43]. The TAM in terms of PEOU was tested in an earlier study to describe users' acceptance of the system and related applications, namely mobile entertainment [44], virtual worlds [45] and the social virtual world market [46]. This indicated that the application system's performance was appropriate, and the user would feel at ease. Thus, the expected probability could be applied to the system [47]. |
| 2. Perceived Usefulness (PU)<br>2.1 Does the 3D handicraft product application help you to see the details of the handicraft products?<br>2.2 Does the 3D handicraft product application demonstrate the handicraft products?<br>2.3 Does the 3D handicraft product application help you to decide whether to buy the handicraft products? | The factors of user acceptance and behavioral intentions affect other aspects of the TAM that have perceived usefulness (PU) [43]. This term indicates that user intention could affect the utilization of that technology [42]. PU has been applied in various studies to indicate user acceptance and intention, as well as related applications such as 3D virtual worlds [48], virtual reality [2] and 3D architectural visualization [49]. PU means a user can believe that the application system will be adaptable to their own preferences [49]. |
| 3. User Attitudes toward the Application (AT)<br>3.1 Is the use of a 3D handicraft product application on a smartphone a good idea?<br>3.2 Does a 3D handicraft product application on a smartphone accurately represent handicraft products?<br>3.3 Do you have a positive feeling about handicraft products thanks to the 3D handicraft product application on a smartphone? | The attitude measures section appears in both the theory of planned behavior (TPB) [50] and TAM [43]. It has been applied to investigate consumers' perceptions [51] and user behavior, as well as in TAM to detail and forecast the adoption of the technology system. Attitude toward (AT) would, directly and indirectly, affect the PEOU and PU [2,47]. |
| 4. Behavioral Intention (BI)<br>4.1 If there were a 3D handicraft product application available on a smartphone, would you have a serious intention to use it?<br>4.2 Would you use a 3D handicraft product application on a smartphone to select other types of products? | Behavioral intention (BI) can apply to information systems and explain the acceptance of the system's use [52]. BI is forecast by the user's assessment of themselves and compares the user's intention to use the system in the future or not [53]. BI generally agrees with AT [47]. |
| 5. Three-Dimensional (3D) User Interaction (3DUI)<br>5.1 Does the 3D handicraft product application on a smartphone demonstrate the 3D interaction?<br>5.2 Is the pattern of 3D interaction in the 3D handicraft product application on a smartphone clear?<br>5.3 Can you operate the 3D interaction in a 3D handicraft product application on a smartphone effectively? | This section refers to Human–Computer Interaction (HCI), a computer science field [54]. Computer systems' design for effectiveness and simplicity will make users more likely to use the system [55]. The development of 3D user interactions (3DUI) and the display started in the 1960s [56]. More recently, there have been several studies and experiments on 3D interaction [57–59]. Because human users use the application system, the 3D interaction will allude to human psychology and factors resulting in the significance of HCI as part of the interactive design. For this reason, the evaluation of user interfaces is important [56]. |
| 6. Three-Dimensional (3D) Product Display (3DPD)<br>6.1 Does the 3D handicraft product application on a smartphone include a clear display of details and information?<br>6.2 Does the 3D handicraft product application on a smartphone assist you with viewing the said products? | Human–television interactions are correlated with 3D products (3DPD). The majority of the studies focused on the display [60]. Several research studies investigated the 3D display to indicate whether a 3D display was better than a 2D display [61–63]. A 3D display offers a new virtual system with factors that should attract increased attention [64,65]. For this study, a 3D product has the same meaning when applied to 3D handicraft products. |
| 7. Attracting Attention (AA)<br>7.1 Doe the 3D handicraft product application on a smartphone aid to increase attention of the handicraft products?<br>7.2 Can the 3D handicraft product application on a smartphone attract the attention in the handicraft products? | This part is correlated with advertising and marketing because advertising is how consumers get to know about products and services [66] and can affect consumer attention [66]. The most powerful new multimedia device and technologies, such as the Internet, tablets, smartphones and social networks, can connect users [66]. Several studies have focused on attracting attention (AA) with the new technologies [49,67–69]. In this study, the 3D handicraft product application was developed to attract users' attention to the handicraft products of Thailand. |

Table 3. Total and percentage of participants' demographics.

| Demographic Attributes | Sub-Attributes | Total (n = 1775) | Percentage |
|---|---|---|---|
| Gender | Male | 789 | 44.45% |
| | Female | 986 | 55.55% |
| Age | Under 25 | 401 | 22.59% |
| | 25–30 | 546 | 30.76% |
| | 31–40 | 486 | 27.38% |
| | 41–50 | 191 | 10.76% |
| | Over 50 | 151 | 8.51% |
| Location | Northern | 309 | 17.49% |
| | Northeastern | 330 | 18.68% |
| | Eastern | 298 | 16.86% |
| | Western | 257 | 14.54% |
| | Central | 297 | 16.81% |
| | Southern | 284 | 16.07% |
| Occupation | Student | 343 | 19.41% |
| | Employee | 351 | 19.86% |
| | Self-employed | 367 | 20.77% |
| | Civil service | 337 | 19.07% |
| | Agriculturist | 224 | 12.68% |
| | No career | 153 | 8.66% |
| Income per month | Less than 5000 Baht | 314 | 17.77% |
| | 5001–10,000 Baht | 291 | 16.47% |
| | 10,001–15,000 Baht | 439 | 24.84% |
| | 15,001–20,000 Baht | 405 | 22.92% |
| | 20,001–25,000 Baht | 175 | 9.90% |
| | More than 25,000 Baht | 151 | 8.55% |

Table 4. Total and percentage of participants' smartphone use information for evaluation.

| Question Attributes | Answers | Total (n = 1775) | Percentage |
|---|---|---|---|
| The main purpose for using a smartphone application in a day. | News | 371 | 20.90% |
| | Playing games | 320 | 18.03% |
| | Social media | 403 | 22.70% |
| | Watching video clips | 355 | 20.00% |
| | Online shopping | 326 | 18.37% |
| The number of participants who have ever and never used a 3D application on a smartphone. | Ever | 1189 | 66.99% |
| | Never | 586 | 33.01% |
| The number of participants who have ever/never used a 3D product on a smartphone. | Ever | 705 | 39.72% |
| | Never | 1070 | 60.28% |

Demographic information indicates that, of 1775 total participants, 986 were female, accounting for 55.55% (versus 789 male participants for a percentage of 44.45%), and most were in the age range of 25–30 years old (546, or 30.76%; the smallest group was of participants older than 50, who numbered 151, or 8.51%). The most participants (330) were from the northeast (18.86%); the fewest were from the west (257; 14.54%). In terms of occupation, the most participants (367) were self-employed (20.77%), with the smallest group being the unemployed (153; 8.66%) and the average income per month for most participants (291) was 10,001–15,000 baht (24.84%). The smallest group, with 151 participants (8.55%), was for those who earn more than 25,000 baht.

The most frequent answer to the main purpose of using a smartphone application in a day was using social media (403; 33.70%); the least popular answer was using smartphones to play games (371; 18.03%). A question regarding using 3D applications on a smartphone revealed that 1189 participants, or 66.99%, had used them, while 586 participants (33.01%) had never used them. A question about using 3D products on a smartphone revealed that

705 (39.72%) had ever used this function, while 1070, accounting for 60.28%, had never used it.

### 3.4. Data Preparation and Sentiment Level Evaluation Method

The questionnaire data were divided into two parts: the part used for users' sentiment level evaluation is the second part of the questionnaire refers to application usage. The first part is the participants' demography—we used only the participants' preliminary information, which does not contain any identifiable information. Thus, we decided not to apply the first part, which is unnecessary for sentiment level evaluation. After obtaining data from the questionnaire, we applied statistical software to prepare our data and evaluate participants' sentiment level by calculating the average in every seven main attributes (PEOU, PU, AT, BI, 3DUI, 3DVP and AA) from its sub-attributes. After that, we computed the average value of all seven main attributes, abd then created the new attribute for the average total, which employs the average value from all seven main attributes to the total average outcome by using an average function provided by statistical software (see Figure 5 for a more in-depth explanation). Once the average total value was obtained, we used this attribute to determine sentiment level by condition (see Table 5).

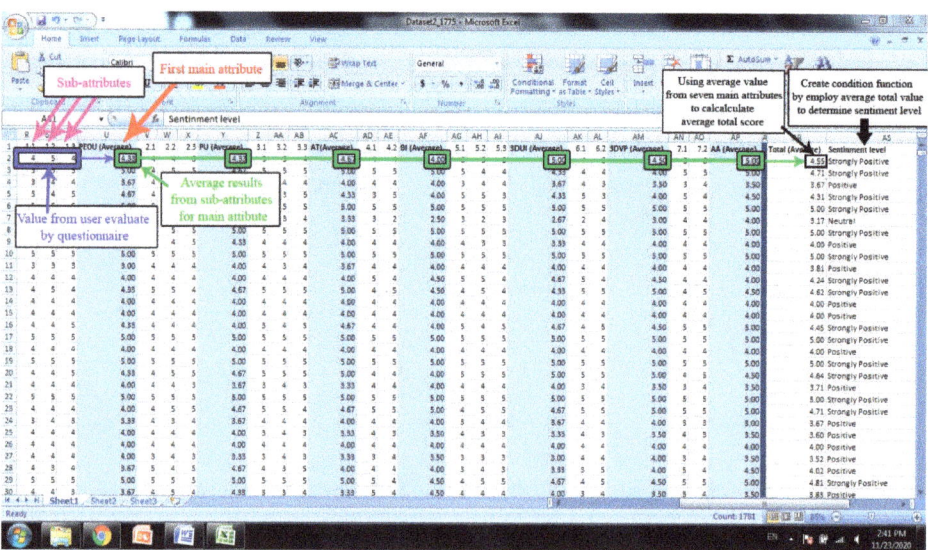

**Figure 5.** Average results of seven main attributes, average total results and the calculation of sentiment level.

**Table 5.** The condition to gain sentiment level result.

| Conditions | Sentiment Level |
|---|---|
| 0–1.80 | Strongly negative |
| 1.81–2.60 | Negative |
| 2.61–3.40 | Neutral |
| 3.41–4.20 | Positive |
| 4.21–5 | Strongly positive |

## 4. Results

This study's contribution is that our proposed 3D handicraft product application is appropriate for usage and can attract users' or customers' attention to handicraft products after using the proposed application. The results for the assessment of attention paid by participants and the utilization of the statistical software for sentiment level evaluation after using the proposed 3D product application are described in this section.

### 4.1. Results of Participants' Sentiment Level Evaluation of Proposed 3D Product Application Usage

As mentioned, data preparation employed statistical software to evaluated participants' sentiment level and users' attention by calculating the average in seven main attributes from its sub-attributes and then created the new attribute for the average total to determine sentiment level by the condition. For the sentiment level evaluation results of a 3D handicraft product application usage, we investigated the general statistics regarding the number and percentage by an average function of each sentiment level of the 1775 participants indicated in Table 6. Participants whose sentiment was strongly negative, negative or neutral were combined under the heading of "reject" using 3D handicraft products, which totaled 375 participants accounting for 21.13%, while participants who showed positive and strongly positive sentiment totaled 1400 (78.87%). This demonstrates that participants accept the 3D handicraft product application and generally have positive feelings.

Table 6. Total number and percentage of sentiment levels evaluation.

| Sentiments | Number | Negative and Neutral Score | Positive Score |
|---|---|---|---|
| Strongly negative | 123 (6.93%) | | - |
| Negative | 126 (7.10%) | 375 (21.13%) | |
| Neutral | 126 (7.10%) | | |
| Positive | 775 (43.66%) | - | 1400 (78.87%) |
| Strongly positive | 625 (35.21%) | | |

### 4.2. Results for the Sentiment of Attracting Attention to Handicraft Products

By collecting data from participants' usage evaluations, we can analyze the results for the attention paid by participants by applying only the attracting attention attribute or AA to calculate the percentage represented in Table 7. The participants' evaluations in terms of sentiment after using the proposed application, assessing attention paid by participants to the handicraft products, revealed that a positive sentiment was described by 688 participants, accounting for 38.76%, while a strongly positive sentiment was described by 725 participants, or 40.85%. Thus, the total positive score of 1413 participants accounted for 79.61%. In comparison with the total of the negative and neutral scores of 362 participants, accounting for 20.39%, participants expressing positive sentiments in relation to their attention being drawn towards handicraft products were found in much greater numbers, and the participants' evaluation results of this survey prove that our proposed 3D handicraft product application affected users by attracting their attention towards handicraft products.

Table 7. Total number and percentages of types of attention paid by participants.

| Sentiments of Attracting Attention | Participants' Number | Negative and Neutral Score | Positive Score |
|---|---|---|---|
| Strongly negative | 130 (7.32%) | | - |
| Negative | 135 (7.61%) | 362 (20.39%) | |
| Neutral | 97 (5.46%) | | |
| Positive | 688 (38.76%) | - | 1413 (79.61%) |
| Strongly positive | 725 (40.85%) | | |

## 5. Discussion

The return of 1775 participants' questionnaires answer from the sending of 2500 emails in Thailand represents a response rate of 71%. The interesting data from participants' demography represent that females returned more the questionnaires than male, and most were in the age range of 25–30 years old. In terms of occupation, the largest share of participants were self-employed, the average income per month for most participants being 10,001–15,000 baht.

According to the evaluation results of 1775 participants' sentiment level in using the proposed 3D handicraft product application, we found that participants' sentiment level was positive and strongly positive sentiment with a total score of 1400 (78.87%). This demonstrates that participants accept the 3D handicraft product application and generally have positive feelings. For the results of attracting users' attention to handicraft products after using the proposed 3D handicraft product application, the participants were evaluated in terms of sentiment after using the proposed application. The attention paid by participants to the handicraft products had a total positive score of 1413 participants, accounting for 79.61%. The participants expressing positive sentiments in relation to the attention paid to handicraft products were found in much greater numbers than negative sentiments. The participants' evaluation results in this survey prove that our proposed 3D handicraft product application affected users by attracting their attention towards handicraft products.

Further studies should consider collecting more types of handicraft products to add to the 3D product applications. In the case of sentiment level categories, this study specifically defined only five scales; future research could have scales of 1–7 or 1–3, and we could compare the sentiment level outcome. The proposed questionnaire of this study only contained the answer as a number for an estimate of the sentiment level, while the next study could use the interview method to obtain the users' comments and suggestions and use machine learning for text classification. This study only sampled participants living in different parts of Thailand. In a future study, we could select the sample to include expatriates or international tourists, who may be more likely to pay attention to Thai handicraft products.

## 6. Conclusions

This research developed a 3D handicraft product application for smartphones. 3D technology can promote the sustainability of small rural entrepreneurship by advertising a product and attracting consumers' attention. User reactions to the proposed 3D application must be investigated to improve the application and provide greater usage capability. The purpose of this study was to examine how users feel about and how attention can be drawn towards handicraft products by using a 3D handicraft product application on a smartphone, developed a 3D handicraft product application for smartphones, using an online questionnaire to collect user usage assessment data.

The proposed questionnaire of this work was divided into two parts. The demographic information part illustrated that, of 1775 total participants, the most frequent answer to the main purpose of a smartphone application usage in a day was using social media. A question regarding using 3D applications on a smartphone revealed that 66.99% of participants had used them, while 33.01% of participants had never used them. A question about using 3D products on a smartphone revealed that 39.72% had ever used this function, while 60.28% had never used it.

In the second part of questionnaire, the answers were measured on a five-point scale (strongly negative, negative, neutral, positive and strongly positive). The attributes assessed included perceived ease of use, perceived usefulness, attitude toward, behavioral intention, user interaction, 3D product display and attracting attention. Participants whose sentiment was under reject using 3D handicraft products totaled 21.13%, while participants who showed positive and strongly positive sentiment totaled 1400, accounting for 78.87%. This demonstrates that participants accept the 3D handicraft product application and generally have positive feelings. The participants were evaluated in terms of sentiment after using the proposed application, assessing the attention paid by participants to the handicraft products. It revealed that a positive sentiment was described by 38.76%, while a strongly positive sentiment was described by 40.85%. Thus, the total positive score of 1413 participants accounted for 79.61%. The attention paid by participants to handicraft products after using the proposed 3D handicraft product application and participants expressing positive sentiments related to attracting attention were found in much greater numbers than negative sentiments, while the participants' evaluation results in this study prove that our proposed 3D handicraft product application affected users by attracting their attention towards handicraft products.

**Author Contributions:** Conceptualization, N.J. and C.-F.T.; Data curation, P.W.; Formal analysis, N.J.; Funding acquisition, C.-F.T.; Investigation, N.J. and C.-F.T.; Methodology, N.J. and C.-F.T.; Project administration, C.-F.T.; Resources, N.J.; Software, N.J.; Supervision, C.-F.T.; Validation, P.W.; Visualization, N.J.; Writing—original draft, N.J.; and Writing—review and editing, C.-F.T. and N.J. All authors have read and agreed to the published version of the manuscript.

**Funding:** This research was funded by the Ministry of Science and Technology, Republic of China, Taiwan, grant numbers MOST-108-2637-E-020-003 and MOST-108-2321-B-020-003.

**Data Availability Statement:** Publicly available datasets were analyzed in this study. This data can be found here: https://zenodo.org/record/4442207.

**Acknowledgments:** The authors would like to express their sincere gratitude to the anonymous reviewers for their useful comments and suggestions for improving the quality of this paper, as well as the Department of Tropical Agriculture and International Cooperation, Department of Management Information Systems, National Pingtung University of Science and Technology, Taiwan, Ministry of Science and Technology, Republic of China, Taiwan and Suratthani Rajabhat University, Suratthani, Thailand for supporting this research.

**Conflicts of Interest:** The authors declare no conflict of interest.

# References

1. Hu, K.; Hua, H.; Zhang, Y. Research on 3D Interactive Model Selection and Customization of Ceramic Products Based on Big Data Cloud Service Platform. In Proceedings of the 5th IEEE International Conference on Big Data Security on Cloud (BigDataSecurity), IEEE International Conference on High Performance and Smart Computing, (HPSC) and IEEE International Conference on Intelligent Data and Security (IDS), Washington, DC, USA, 27–29 May 2019; pp. 144–148.
2. Altarteer, S.; Charissis, V. Technology Acceptance Model for 3D Virtual Reality System in Luxury Brands Online Stores. *IEEE Access* **2019**, *7*, 64053–64062. [CrossRef]
3. Pantano, E. Engaging consumer through the storefront: Evidences from integrating interactive technologies. *J. Retail. Consum. Serv.* **2016**, *28*, 149–154. [CrossRef]
4. Yim, M.Y.C.; Chu, S.C.; Sauer, P.L. Is Augmented Reality Technology an Effective Tool for E-commerce? An Interactivity and Vividness Perspective. *J. Interact. Mark.* **2017**, *39*, 89–103. [CrossRef]
5. Burtăverde, V.; Vlăsceanu, S.; Avram, E. Exploring the relationship between personality structure and smartphone usage. *Curr. Psychol.* **2019**, 1–13. [CrossRef]
6. Sebald, A.K.; Jacob, F. Help welcome or not: Understanding consumer shopping motivation in curated fashion retailing. *J. Retail. Consum. Serv.* **2018**, *40*, 188–203. [CrossRef]
7. Gang, Z.; Jun, L.; Shan, L.; Zhuoran, L.; Tao, H.; Hui, Z. Research on Tujia nationality's brocade three-dimensional character modeling and animation integration. In Proceedings of the 6th International Conference on Industrial Technology and Management (ICITM), Cambridge, UK, 7–10 March 2017; pp. 205–209.
8. Saal, C.; Lipp, C.; Lohse, O.; Krause, S. 3D Model-Based Product Definition and Production—A Mind Change with Technical Hurdles. In Proceedings of the 3rd International Symposium on Small-Scale Intelligent Manufacturing Systems (SIMS), Gjøvik, Norway, 10–12 June 2020; pp. 1–4.
9. World Bank. Thailand Economic Monitor 2020 Productivity for Prosperity. 2020. Available online: http://documents1.worldbank.org/curated/en/394501579357102381/pdf/Thailand-Economic-Monitor-Productivity-for-Prosperity.pdf (accessed on 13 November 2020).
10. World Bank. Thailand Economic Monitor 2017 Digital Transformation. 2017. Available online: http://pubdocs.worldbank.org/en/823661503543356520/Thailand-Economic-Monitor-August-2017.pdf (accessed on 28 August 2020).
11. United Nations Development Programme. about Thailand. 2020. Available online: https://www.th.undp.org/content/thailand/en/home/ (accessed on 8 September 2020).

12. Nayak, J.K.; Bhalla, N. Factors motivating visitors for attending handicraft exhibitions: Special reference to Uttarakhand, India. *Tour. Manag. Perspect.* **2016**, *20*, 238–245. [CrossRef]
13. Zhang, Y.; Han, M.; Chen, W. The strategy of digital scenic area planning from the perspective of intangible cultural heritage protection. *J. Image. Video Proc.* **2018**, *2018*, 130. [CrossRef]
14. Masoud, H.; Mortazavi, M.; Farsani, N.T. A study on tourists' tendency towards intangible cultural heritage as an attraction (case study: Isfahan, Iran). *City Cult. Soc.* **2019**, *17*, 54–60. [CrossRef]
15. Covarrubia, P. Geographical Indications of Traditional Handicrafts: A Cultural Element in a Predominantly Economic Activity. *IIC-Int. Rev. Intellect. Prop. Compet. Law* **2019**, *50*, 441–466. [CrossRef]
16. United Nations Development Programme. Thailand's Best Practices and Lessons Learned in Development Volume 1. 2012. Available online: https://www.undp.org/content/dam/thailand/docs/TICAUNDPbpVol1.pdf (accessed on 2 September 2020).
17. Snodin, N.S.; Higgins, J.; Yoovathaworn, S. How Thai businesses utilize English in their product names. *Kasetsart J. Soc. Sci.* **2017**, *38*, 123–128. [CrossRef]
18. Luangpaiboon, P. Strategic design for dynamic multi-zone truckload shipments: A study of OTOP agricultural products in Thailand. *Comput. Electron. Agr.* **2017**, *135*, 11–22. [CrossRef]
19. Natsuda, K.; Igusa, K.; Wiboonpongse, A.; Thoburn, J. One Village One Product—Rural Development Strategy in Asia: The Case of OTOP in Thailand. *Can. J. Dev. Stud.* **2012**, *33*, 369–385. [CrossRef]
20. Alaoui, I.E.; Gahi, Y.; Messoussi, R.; Chaabi, Y.; Todoskoff, A.; Kobi, A. A novel adaptable approach for sentiment analysis on big social data. *J. Big Data* **2018**, *5*, 12. [CrossRef]
21. Sharma, P.; Sharma, A.K. Experimental investigation of automated system for twitter sentiment analysis to predict the public emotions using machine learning algorithms. *Mater. Today Proc.* **2020**. [CrossRef]
22. Madbouly, M.M.; Darwish, S.M.; Essameldin, R. Modified fuzzy sentiment analysis approach based on user ranking suitable for online social networks. *IET Softw.* **2020**, *14*, 300–307. [CrossRef]
23. Zhang, X.; Zheng, X. Comparison of Text Sentiment Analysis Based on Machine Learning. In Proceedings of the 15th International Symposium on Parallel and Distributed Computing (ISPDC), Fuzhou, China, 8–10 July 2016; pp. 230–233.
24. Liang, Y.; Liu, H.; Zhang, S. Micro-blog sentiment classification using Doc2vec + SVM model with data purification. *J. Eng.* **2020**, *7*, 407–410. [CrossRef]
25. Wang, Y. Iteration-based naive Bayes sentiment classification of microblog multimedia posts considering emoticon attributes. *Multimed. Tools Appl.* **2020**, *79*, 19151–19166. [CrossRef]
26. Alzamzami, F.; Hoda, M.; Saddik, A.E. Light Gradient Boosting Machine for General Sentiment Classification on Short Texts: A Comparative Evaluation. *IEEE Access* **2020**, *8*, 101840–101858. [CrossRef]
27. Hew, K.F.; Hu, X.; Qiao, C.; Tang, Y. What predicts student satisfaction with MOOCs: A gradient boosting trees supervised machine learning and sentiment analysis approach. *Comput. Educ.* **2020**, *145*, 103724. [CrossRef]
28. Mostafa, L. Student Sentiment Analysis Using Gamification for Education Context. In *Advances in Intelligent Systems and Computing, Proceedings of the International Conference on Advanced Intelligent Systems and Informatics, Cairo, Egypt, 26–28 October 2019*; Hassanien, A., Shaalan, K., Tolba, M., Eds.; Springer International Publishing: Cham, Switzerland; New York City, NY, USA, 2020.
29. Catal, C.; Nangir, M. A sentiment classification model based on multiple classifiers. *Appl. Soft Comput.* **2017**, *50*, 135–141. [CrossRef]
30. Bouazizi, M.; Ohtsuki, T. Multi-class sentiment analysis on twitter: Classification performance and challenges. *Big Data Min. Anal.* **2019**, *2*, 181–194. [CrossRef]
31. Zhang, S.; Zhang, D.; Zhong, H.; Wang, G. A Multiclassification Model of Sentiment for E-Commerce Reviews. *IEEE Access* **2020**, *8*, 189513–189526. [CrossRef]
32. Xu, F.; Pan, Z.; Xia, R. E-commerce product review sentiment classification based on a naïve Bayes continuous learning framework. *Inform. Process. Manag.* **2020**, *57*, 102221. [CrossRef]
33. Yi, S.; Liu, X. Machine learning based customer sentiment analysis for recommending shoppers, shops based on customers' review. *Complex Intell. Syst.* **2020**, *6*, 621–634. [CrossRef]
34. Tran, T.K.; Phan, T.T. Capturing Contextual Factors in Sentiment Classification: An Ensemble Approach. *IEEE Access* **2020**, *8*, 116856–116865. [CrossRef]
35. Luo, Y.; He, J.; Mou, Y.; Wang, J.; Liu, T. Exploring China's 5A global geoparks through online tourism reviews: A mining model based on machine learning approach. *Tour. Manag. Perspec.* **2021**, *37*, 100769.
36. Liu, Y.; Bi, J.; Fan, Z. Multi-class sentiment classification: The experimental comparisons of feature selection and machine learning algorithms. *Expert Syst. Appl.* **2017**, *80*, 323–339. [CrossRef]
37. Li, Z.; Li, R.; Jin, G. Sentiment Analysis of Danmaku Videos Based on Naïve Bayes and Sentiment Dictionary. *IEEE Access* **2020**, *8*, 75073–75084. [CrossRef]
38. Ragini, J.R.; Anand, P.M.R.; Bhaskar, V. Big data analytics for disaster response and recovery through sentiment analysis. *Int. J. Inf. Manag.* **2018**, *42*, 13–24. [CrossRef]
39. Tchakounté, F.; Pagor, A.E.Y.; Kamgang, J.C.; Atemkeng, M. CIAA-RepDroid: A Fine-Grained and Probabilistic Reputation Scheme for Android Apps Based on Sentiment Analysis of Reviews. *Future Internet* **2020**, *12*, 145. [CrossRef]
40. Community, B.O. *Blender—A 3D Modelling and Rendering Package*; Stichting Blender Foundation: Amsterdam, The Netherlands, 2018. Available online: http://www.blender.org (accessed on 12 September 2020).

41. Haas, J.K. A History of the Unity Game Engine. 2014. Available online: https://web.wpi.edu/Pubs/E-project/Available/E-project-030614-143124/unrestricted/Haas_IQP_Final.pdf (accessed on 12 September 2020).
42. Mostafa, M.M.; El-Masry, A.A. Citizens as consumers: Profiling e-government services' users in Egypt via data mining techniques. *Int. J. Inf. Manag.* **2013**, *33*, 627–641. [CrossRef]
43. Davis, F.D. Perceived Usefulness, Perceived Ease of Use, and User Acceptance of Information Technology. *MIS Q.* **1989**, *13*, 319–340. [CrossRef]
44. Alalwan, A.A.; Baabdullah, A.M.; Rana, N.P.; Tamilmani, K.; Dwivedi, Y.K. Examining adoption of mobile internet in Saudi Arabia: Extending TAM with perceived enjoyment, innovativeness and trust. *Technol. Soc.* **2018**, *55*, 100–110. [CrossRef]
45. White, B.E.; Hubona, G.S.; Srite, M. Does "Being There" Matter? The Impact of Web-Based and Virtual World's Shopping Experiences on Consumer Purchase Attitudes. *Inform. Manag.* **2019**, *56*, 103153. [CrossRef]
46. Zhang, X.; de Pablos, P.O.; Wang, X.; Wang, W.; Sun, Y.; She, J. Understanding the users' continuous adoption of 3D social virtual world in China: A comparative case study. *Comput. Hum. Behav.* **2014**, *35*, 578–585. [CrossRef]
47. Nikou, S.A.; Economides, A.A. Mobile-Based Assessment: Integrating acceptance and motivational factors into a combined model of Self-Determination Theory and Technology Acceptance. *Comput. Hum. Behav.* **2017**, *68*, 83–95. [CrossRef]
48. Huang, Y.C.; Backman, S.J.; Backman, K.F.; Moore, D. Exploring user acceptance of 3D virtual worlds in travel and tourism marketing. *Tour. Manag.* **2013**, *36*, 490–501. [CrossRef]
49. Fonseca, D.; Redondo, E.; Valls, F.; Villagrasa, S. Technological adaptation of the student to the educational density of the course. A case study: 3D architectural visualization. *Comput. Hum. Behav.* **2017**, *72*, 599–611. [CrossRef]
50. Ajzen, I. The theory of planned behavior. *Organ. Behav. Hum. Dec.* **1991**, *50*, 179–211. [CrossRef]
51. Li, R.; Chung, T.; Fiore, A.M. Factors affecting current users' attitude towards e-auctions in China: An extended TAM study. *J. Retail. Consum. Serv.* **2017**, *34*, 19–29. [CrossRef]
52. Andre, H.; Sihombing, P.P.; Sfenrianto, S.; Wang, G. Measuring Consumer Trust in Online Booking Application. In Proceedings of the 4th International Conference on Information Technology, Information Systems and Electrical Engineering (ICITISEE), Yogyakarta, Indonesia, 20–21 November 2019; pp. 446–451.
53. Triberti, S.; Villani, D.; Riva, G. Unconscious goal pursuit primes attitudes towards technology usage: A virtual reality experiment. *Comput. Hum. Behav.* **2016**, *64*, 163–172. [CrossRef]
54. Pargman, D.S.; Eriksson, E.; Bates, O.; Kirman, B.; Comber, R.; Hedman, A.; van den Broeck, M. The future of computing and wisdom: Insights from Human–Computer Interaction. *Futures* **2019**, *113*, 102434. [CrossRef]
55. Dix, A.; Finlay, J.; Abowd, G.D.; Beale, R. *Human-Computer Interaction*, 3rd ed.; Pearson Prentice Hall: Upper Saddle River, NJ, USA, 2004.
56. Bowman, D.A.; Kruijff, E.; LaViola, J.J.; Poupyrev, I. *3D User Interfaces: Theory and Practice*; Addison Wesley Longman Publishing Co., Inc.: Redwood City, CA, USA, 2004.
57. Deng, S.; Jiang, N.; Chang, J.; Guo, S.; Zhang, J.J. Understanding the impact of multimodal interaction using gaze informed mid-air gesture control in 3D virtual objects manipulation. *Int. J. Hum-Comput. Stud.* **2017**, *105*, 68–80. [CrossRef]
58. Dong, L.; Feng, R.; Bi, J.; Shen, S.; Lu, H.; Zhang, J. Insight into the interaction mechanism of human SGLT2 with its inhibitors: 3D-QSAR studies, homology modeling, and molecular docking and molecular dynamics simulations. *J. Mol. Model* **2018**, *24*, 86. [CrossRef] [PubMed]
59. Wang, L.; Wong, L.; Xu, Y.; Zhou, X.; Qiu, S.; Meng, X.; Yang, C. The design and empirical evaluations of 3D positioning techniques for pressure-based touch control on mobile devices. *Pers. Ubiquit. Comput.* **2018**, *22*, 525–533. [CrossRef]
60. Cho, E.J.; Lee, K.M. Effects of 3D displays: A comparison between shuttered and polarized displays. *Displays* **2013**, *34*, 353–358. [CrossRef]
61. Visinescu, L.L.; Sidorova, A.; Jones, M.C.; Prybutok, V.R. The influence of website dimensionality on customer experiences, perceptions and behavioral intentions: An exploration of 2D vs. 3D web design. *Inform. Manag.* **2015**, *52*, 1–17. [CrossRef]
62. Currò, G.; La Malfa, G.; Caizzone, A.; Rampulla, V.; Navarra, G. Three-Dimensional (3D) Versus Two-Dimensional (2D) Laparoscopic Bariatric Surgery: A Single-Surgeon Prospective Randomized Comparative Study. *Obes. Surg.* **2015**, *25*, 2120–2124. [CrossRef]
63. Cho, T.H.; Chen, C.Y.; Wu, P.J.; Chen, K.S.; Yin, L.T. The comparison of accommodative response and ocular movements in viewing 3D and 2D displays. *Displays* **2017**, *49*, 59–64. [CrossRef]
64. Su, C.C.; Moorthy, A.K.; Bovik, A.C. Visual Quality Assessment of Stereoscopic Image and Video: Challenges, Advances, and Future Trends. In *Visual Signal Quality Assessment: Quality of Experience (QoE)*; Deng, C., Ma, L., Lin, W., Ngan, K.N., Eds.; Springer International Publishing: Cham, Switzerland; New York City, NY, USA, 2015.
65. Xu, H.; Jiang, G.; Yu, M.; Luo, T.; Peng, Z.; Shao, F.; Jiang, H. 3D visual discomfort predictor based on subjective perceived-constraint sparse representation in 3D display system. *Future Gener. Comput. Syst.* **2018**, *83*, 85–94. [CrossRef]
66. Terkan, R. Importance of Creative Advertising and Marketing According to University Students Perspective. *Int. Rev. Manag. Mark.* **2014**, *4*, 239–246.
67. Teixeira, T.S. The Rising Cost of Consumer Attention Why You Should Care, and What You Can Do about It. *Harv. Bus. Sch. Work. Pap.* **2014**, *1*, 14-055.

68. Sun, B.; Wang, H. Research on the Influencing Factors of Leading Technology Diffusion Based on Technology Acceptance Model. In Proceedings of the IEEE International Symposium on Innovation and Entrepreneurship (TEMS-ISIE), Hangzhou, China, 24–26 October 2019; pp. 1–8.
69. Van Wermeskerken, M.; Ravensbergen, S.; van Gog, T. Effects of instructor presence in video modeling examples on attention and learning. *Comput. Hum. Behav.* **2017**, *89*, 430–438. [CrossRef]

MDPI
St. Alban-Anlage 66
4052 Basel
Switzerland
Tel. +41 61 683 77 34
Fax +41 61 302 89 18
www.mdpi.com

*Electronics* Editorial Office
E-mail: electronics@mdpi.com
www.mdpi.com/journal/electronics

www.ingramcontent.com/pod-product-compliance
Lightning Source LLC
LaVergne TN
LVHW070051120526
838202LV00102B/2048

*9 7 8 3 0 3 6 5 6 5 7 7 4*